Toward a
Structural Theory of Action

Network Models of
Social Structure, Perception, and Action

QUANTITATIVE STUDIES IN SOCIAL RELATIONS

Consulting Editor: Peter H. Rossi

UNIVERSITY OF MASSACHUSETTS
AMHERST, MASSACHUSETTS

The list of titles in this series continues on the last page of this volume

Toward a
Structural Theory of Action

Network Models of
Social Structure, Perception, and Action

RONALD S. BURT

Department of Sociology and Center for the Social Sciences
Columbia University
New York, New York

1982

ACADEMIC PRESS
A Subsidiary of Harcourt Brace Jovanovich, Publishers
New York   London
Paris   San Diego   San Francisco   São Paulo   Sydney   Tokyo   Toronto

ACADEMIC PRESS, INC.
111 Fifth Avenue, New York, New York 10003

United Kingdom Edition published by
ACADEMIC PRESS, INC. (LONDON) LTD.
24/28 Oval Road, London NW1 7DX

Library of Congress Cataloging in Publication Data

Burt, Ronald S.
  Toward a structural theory of action.

  (Quantitative studies in social relations)
  Bibliography: p.
  Includes index.
  1. Social action. 2. Social structure.
3. Structuralism. 4. Social perception. 5. Network
analysis (Planning) I. Title. II. Series.
HM51.B96   302   82-6790
ISBN 0-12-147150-0   AACR2

82 83 84 85   9 8 7 6 5 4 3 2 1

Contents

3 Stratification in Elite Sociological Methodology   95

4 Stratification in American Manufacturing   131

SECOND COMPONENT: ACTOR INTEREST

5 Interest: The Perception of Utility   173

Preface

My experiences with people lead me to hold two beliefs as a fruitful foundation for constructing systematic social theory. First, people as individual or group actors are purposive, in the sense of using their resources to realize their interests. Second, these purposive actors pursue their interests in the context of social structure generated by the division of labor in society. The intersection of these two beliefs provides my premise for a structural theory of action: Actors are purposive under social structural constraint. Steps toward action theory based on this premise are reported here.

This book is about social structure, perceptions, and action. It is about these items as concepts. It is about strategies through which these items guide empirical research. I propose a model of status/role-sets as patterns of relationships defining positions in the stratification space—the social topology—of a system of actors. Processes are proposed by which positions in this space generate actor interests as perceptual norms and feelings of relative deprivation or advantage. Processes are proposed by which the pattern of relationships defining a position creates constraint on the freedom with which actors occupying the position can realize their interests. These processes, captured in mathematical models, are used to describe two strategically important systems of actors: large American corporations involved in manufacturing in 1967 and elite experts in sociological methodology as of 1975. A detailed overview of the book can be obtained quickly. Chapter 1 introduces the goals and organization of the book. The final section of each subsequent chapter summarizes the chapter's content leading to the concluding chapter, Chapter 9, in which I contrast alternative approaches to action theory with the structural perspective represented here.

I am writing to sociologists pursuing basic as well as applied interests. I review alternative models of the substantive phenomena addressed here and discuss methodological issues invoked by their application in empirical research. Numerical illustration is provided for the models proposed. These illustrations have been a convenient basis for out-of-class assignments when I have covered this material in seminars on mathematical sociology and structural sociology. Although I explicitly address myself to sociologists, the proposals are not discipline-specific. I hope that anthropologists, economists, political scientists, and psychologists will find something of value, since I have freely drawn upon their research and theories.

Acknowledgments

The work reported here has been mainly supported by the National Science Foundation and carried out in facilities provided by the University of Chicago, the University of California at Berkeley, and the State University of New York at Albany. My support at the University of Chicago was provided by a National Science Foundation grant to James S. Coleman, who generously supported my research activities at the National Opinion Research Center; a National Institute of Mental Health Trainee Fellowship; and a small grant from the Director's Fund, then administered by James A. Davis for the National Opinion Research Center. The bulk of the work reported here has been carried out at the University of California at Berkeley. It has been supported by two grants from the National Science Foundation (SOC77-22938, SOC79-25728) administered through the Survey Research Center, and it has received modest support for computer programming assistance from the Committee on Research. The Survey Research Center's facilities have been invaluable to me in pursuing my research interests. I owe a special debt to its directors, Merrill Shanks and his successor Percy Tannenbaum, for facilitating my access to the Center's resources. Finally, Nan Lin and Ronald A. Farrell made it possible for me to spend a highly productive leave of absence at the State University of New York at Albany, from 1978 to 1979. The special conditions provided there allowed me to complete a first draft of the book.

This book grows out of my doctoral dissertation submitted in 1977 to the Department of Sociology, University of Chicago. Three persons have been especially generous with their time and comments across the many topics addressed here: Terry N. Clark, James S. Coleman, and Edward O. Laumann. These three scholars graciously criticized long manuscripts that developed a perspective with which no one of them could feel comfortable, since my methodology was a composite of their diversity. In analyzing their often conflicting opinions about statements I had made, I came to a more subtle understanding of the issues being addressed than otherwise would have been possible.

I owe an unanticipated debt to the students in my seminars on mathematical sociology and structural sociology. Their stimulating questions encouraged me to present my ideas from a variety of perspectives, and these perspectives found their way into the text. The detailed reading to which participants subjected the manuscript helped me to locate weak points in the text. In particular, Rumi Price and William Glick provided detailed commentary on the first draft. Scott Pimley, then an undergraduate student brought to the Survey Research Center, helped in preparing the manuscript by painstakingly checking quoted material against the original. Davida Weinberg provided a careful second reading of the page proofs, minimizing the number of typographical errors that survive in the final book.

A great many colleagues have affected the presentation, of course, but their contributions have been specific to one or another substantive or methodological issue addressed. An exception is Peter V. Marsden, at the University of North Carolina, who gave me the benefit of his detailed comments on the whole manuscript during my final revisions. I am grateful to Harold L. Wilensky for his incisive comments on the introductory portions of the draft manuscript, comments resulting in a complete rewriting of the material. My intellectual debts to colleagues whose comments affected my discussion of specialized substantive or methodological topics are recorded in published papers on those topics. I draw on these papers in the forthcoming discussion; they are cited where relevant. I appreciate permission to use this material granted by the publishers of the *Administrative Science Quarterly*, the *American Journal of Sociology*, the *American Sociological Review*, the *Annual Review of Sociology*, *Social Forces*, *Social Networks*, *Social Science Research*, *Sociological Inquiry*, and *Sociological Methods & Research*.

In addition, I am grateful to the following for permission to reproduce extracts from the indicated copyright material:

Addison-Wesley Publishing, for the quote on page 24 from page 510 of "Measurement of Social Choice and Interpersonal Attractiveness" by Gardner Lindzey and Donn Byrne in volume 2 of *The Handbook of Social*

Psychology, Gardner Lindzey and Elliot Aronson, editors (Copyright © 1968 by Addison-Wesley Publishing Company).

American Philosophical Society, for the quote on page 217 from page 11 of *Induction and Intuition in Scientific Thought* by Peter B. Medawar (Copyright © 1969 by The American Philosophical Society).

Beacon Press, for the quotes on pages 343, 344 from pages 178, 265 of *The Elementary Structures of Kinship* by Claude Levi-Strauss, trans. by James Harle Bell, John Richard von Sturmer and Rodney Needham, editor (Copyright © 1969 by Beacon Press).

Bobbs-Merrill Company, for the quotes on pages 199, 201, 219 from pages 32, 118, 119 of *Medical Innovation* by James S. Coleman, Elihu Katz and Herbert Menzel (Copyright © 1966 by The Bobbs-Merrill Company).

Cambridge University Press, for the quotes on pages 216, 217, 223 from pages 79, 119 of *Public Knowledge* by John Ziman (Copyright © 1968 by Cambridge University Press).

Doubleday and Company and Edward T. Hall, for the quote on page 7 from page 27 of *The Silent Language* by Edward T. Hall (Copyright © 1959 by Edward T. Hall).

E. P. Dutton and Company, for the quotes on pages 325, 326, 342 from pages 83, 510, 511 of *Argonauts of the Western Pacific* by Bronislaw Malinowski (U. S. Publication 1961 by E. P. Dutton & Co., Inc.).

Harcourt, Brace Jovanovich, for the quotes on page 340 from pages 232, 248 of *Social Behavior: Its Elementary Forms* by George C. Homans (Copyright © 1961 by Harcourt, Brace & World, Inc.).

Harvard University Graduate School of Business Administration, Division of Research, for the quotes on pages 140, 141, 142 from pages 13, 146, 200 of *Directors: Myth and Reality* by Myles L. Mace (Copyright © 1971 by the President and Fellows of Harvard College).

Harvard University Press, for the quote on page 46 from page 24 of *Toward a General Theory of Action*, Talcott Parsons and Edward A. Shils (Copyright © 1951 by the President and Fellows of Harvard College).

Houghton Mifflin Company, for the quote on page 312 from page 126 of *Economics and the Public Purpose* by John Kenneth Galbraith (Copyright © 1973 by John Kenneth Galbraith).

John Wiley and Sons, for the quote on page 340 from page 2 of *Exchange and Power in Social Life* by Peter M. Blau (Copyright © 1964 by John Wiley & Sons, Inc.).

Jossey-Bass, for the quote on page 349 from pages 93, 94 of "The Allocation of Time Among Individuals" by Christopher Winship in *Sociological Methodology 1978*, Karl F. Schuessler, editor (Copyright © 1977 by Jossey-Bass, Inc., Publishers).

Macmillan Publishing for quotes on: (1) page 3 from pages 44, 45 of *The Structure of Social Action* by Talcott Parsons (Copyright 1937 by The Free

Press, renewed 1965 by Talcott Parsons); (2) pages 22, 269 from pages 40, 41, 121 of *The Sociology of Georg Simmel,* trans. by Kurt H. Wolff (Copyright © 1950, renewed 1978 by The Free Press, a Division of Macmillan Publishing Co., Inc.); (3) page 191 from page 288 of *Social Theory and Social Structure* 1968 Enlarged Edition by Robert K. Merton (Copyright © 1968, 1976 by Robert K. Merton); (4) pages 268, 269, 334, 335, 336 from pages 131, 237, 257, 260, 262, 266, 267, 278 of *The Division of Labor in Society* by Emile Durkheim, trans. by George Simpson (Copyright 1933 by Macmillan Publishing Co., Inc.); (5) page 269 from pages 140, 141 of *Conflict and the Web of Group Affiliations* by Georg Simmel, trans. by Kurt H. Wolff and Reinhardt Bendix (Copyright 1955 by The Free Press); (6) page 269 from page 72 of *Sociology and Philosophy* by Emile Durkheim, trans. by D. F. Pocock (issued by The Free Press in 1953, reissued in 1974); (7) pages 340, 341 from page 454 of "Social Exchange" by Peter M. Blau in volume 7 of the *International Encyclopedia of the Social Sciences,* David L. Sills, editor (Copyright © 1968 by Crowell Coller and Macmillan, Inc.).

Oxford University Press, for the quote on page 339 from page 15 of *Input-Output Analysis* by Wassily Leontief (published in 1966 by Oxford University Press).

Prentice-Hall, for quotes on pages 41, 352, 353 from pages 114, 257, 258 of *The Study of Man: An Introduction* by Ralph Linton (Copyright © 1936, copyright renewed 1964, Prentice-Hall, Inc., Englewood Cliffs, NJ).

Princeton University Press, for quotes on pages 195, 196 from pages 250, 263, 264 of *The American Soldier: Adjustment During Army Life* by Samuel A. Stouffer, E. A. Suchman, L. C. DeVinney, S. A. Star and R. M. Williams (Copyright 1949, copyright © renewed by Princeton University Press).

Routledge and Kegan Paul, for quotes on: (1) page 343 from page 3 of *The Gift* by Marcel Mauss, trans. by Ian Cunnison (published in 1967 by W. W. Norton by arrangement with Routledge & Kegan Paul Ltd.); (2) pages 345, 346 from pages 12, 106, 108, 150 of *The Theory of Social Structure* by S. F. Nadel (published in 1957 by Cohen & West Ltd.).

Royal Anthropological Institute of Great Britain and Ireland, for quotes on page 339 from pages 190, 191, 192 of "On Social Structure" by A. R. Radcliffe-Brown in volume 70 of the *Journal of the Royal Anthropological Society of Great Britain and Ireland,* 1940.

The Scandinavian Journal of Economics and Gary S. Becker, for the quote on pages 347, 348 from page 133 of "On the New Theory of Consumer Behavior" by Robert T. Michael and Gary S. Becker in *The Economic Approach to Human Behavior,* Gary S. Becker, editor (published in 1976 by University of Chicago Press).

Stanford University Press, for quotes on pages 37, 187, 188, 219 from pages 91, 168, 169, 175 of *Social Pressures in Informal Groups* by Leon Festinger, Stanley Schachter and Kurt Back (Copyright 1950 by Leon Festinger, Stanley Schachter and Kurt Back, reissued in 1963 by Stanford University Press).

University of Chicago Press, for the quotes on pages 189, 190 from pages 154, 155 of *Mind, Self, and Society* by George H. Mead (Copyright 1934 by The University of Chicago), and (with the simultaneous permission of the Wenner-Gren Foundation) the quotes on page 344 from pages 525, 541, 542 of "Social Structure" by Claude Levi-Strauss in *Anthropology Today*, A. L. Kroeber et al., editors (Copyright © 1953 by The University of Chicago).

1

Introduction*

Human action is commonly believed to be purposive. It is assumed to have a rationale, a goal. This idea is more a social norm than an explanation. We expect action to be purposive. If I do not have a purpose for something I have done, I am likely to construct one when asked to explain the action. The omnipresence of the belief that action is purposive makes a postulate of purposive action an attractive basis for action theory. A further consideration makes it much more attractive. It offers a commonsense and familiar baseline of psychological motivation so as to cast into stronger relief those features to be captured by a social theory of action.[1]

Such a postulate is established as an intellectual tradition by the work of

---

*Portions of this chapter are drawn from an article reprinted with the permission of *Sociological Inquiry* (Burt 1980b).

[1] This strategy of making reasonable assumptions concerning the psychological features of action in order to discern more clearly social features is an application of Mill's (1881:221–223) discussion of a method of residues and is found in Merton's (1949:74–104) emphasis on the impropriety of merging motivations for action with objective consequences of action and Coleman's (1964:Chap. 15) discussion of the method of residues. It is by pursuing such a methodology that economics, usually assuming what will be termed "atomistic action," has been able to develop the most powerful (deductively, if not empirically) social theory of all the social sciences.

Hobbes,[2] Locke,[3] and Smith[4] (e.g., see Parsons 1937, Macpherson 1962). Responding to the social conditions of their time, these philosophers argued for the right of a person to control his property in the pursuit of his own interests. In this tradition, I take a postulate of purposive action to mean that a person has the right to the product of his private property and is motivated to use that

[2]Hobbes (1651:Chap. 13) makes his views on the natural equality of men clear:

> Nature hath made men so equall, in the faculties of body and mind; as that though there bee found one man sometimes manifestly stronger in body, or of quicker mind than another; yet when all is reckoned together, the difference between man, and man, is not so considerable, as that one man can thereupon claim to himselfe any benefit, to which another may not pretend, as well as he. . . . From this equality of ability, ariseth equality of hope in attaining of our Ends.

His views on the rights of individuals to own property and dispose of it according to their own wishes are not as clear. However, Macpherson (1962:61–68) draws on both the range of Hobbes's work and the existing conditions in England to demonstrate that he probably did believe in those rights.

[3]In his discussion of the natural state of men, Locke (1689:Chap. 2) begins, "We must consider what state all men are naturally in, and that is a state of perfect freedom to order their actions and dispose of their possessions and persons as they think fit, within the bounds of the law of nature, without asking leave, or depending upon the will of any other man."

[4]Smith exhibits this postulate not so much in clear statements after the manner of Locke (perhaps owing to the obviousness of the postulate by then) but rather in his manifest distain for government policies that violate the postulate. For example, there is his discussion of the English poor laws:

> The very unequal price of labor which we frequently find in England in places at no great distance from one another, is probably owing to the obstruction which the law of settlements gives to a poor man who would carry his industry from one parish to another without a certificate. . . . To remove a man who has committed no misdemeanour from the parish where he chuses to reside, is an evident violation of natural liberty and justice [pp. 140–141].

Similarly, he comments on the regulated corn trade:

> The law which prohibited the manufacturer from exercising the trade of a shopkeeper, endeavoured to force this division in the employment of stock to go on faster than it might otherwise have done. The law which obliged the farmer to exercise the trade of a corn merchant, endeavoured to hinder it from going on so fast. Both laws were evident violations of natural liberty, and therefore unjust; and they were both too as impolitic as they were unjust. It is in the interest of every society that things of this kind should never either be forced or obstructed [p. 497].

Smith describes the condition, similar to the postulate of purposive action, that he thinks would result if government policy were restricted to the minimum level necessary to preserve the natural rights of individuals.

> All systems either of preference or of restraint, therefore being thus completely taken away, the obvious and simple system of natural liberty establishes itself of its ow.. accord. Every man, as long as he does not violate the laws of justice, is left perfectly free to pursue his own interest his own way, and to bring both his industry and capital into competition with those of any other man, or order of men. The sovereign is completely discharged from a duty, in the attempting to perform which he must always be exposed to innumerable delusions, and for the proper performance of which no human wisdom or knowledge could ever be sufficient, the duty of superintending the industry of private people, and of directing it towards the employments most suitable to the interest of the society [p. 651].

property in ways that he perceives to be rewarding. More specifically, the postulate defines four elements of action:

1. There exist persons or groups of persons as *actors* capable of acting without regard to other actors.
2. The private property of an actor in the form of goods and labor is solely controlled by the actor. To the extent that property is valued by other actors, it is a *resource.*
3. Each actor is *motivated* to engage in action that he perceives as improving his personal well-being, or, as is more commonly stated in political economy, his utility.
4. Finally, the postulate states that each actor *evaluates the utility of alternative actions* and performs those he perceives as yielding the greatest reward.[5]

These four elements define diverse conceptions of action that remove problematic actor-specific features of action by specifying an ideal type of actor. The first element defines the source of action—persons or groups of persons

[5]Parsons (1937) specifies related elements in a unit act:

An 'act' involves logically the following: (1) It implies an agent, an 'actor.' (2) For purposes of definition the act must have an 'end,' a future state of affairs toward which the process of action is oriented. (3) It must be initiated in a 'situation' of which the trends of development differ in one or more important respects from the state of affairs to which the action is oriented, the end. This situation is in turn analyzable into two elements: those over which the actor has no control, . . . and those over which he has such control. The former may be termed the 'conditions' of action, the latter the 'means.' Finally (4) . . . in the choice of alternative means to the end, in so far as the situation allows alternatives, there is a 'normative orientation' of action. Within the area of control of the actor, the means employed cannot, in general, be conceived either as chosen at random or as dependent exclusively on the conditions of action, but must in some sense be subject to the influence of an independent, determinate selective factor, a knowledge of which is necessary to the understanding of the concrete course of action [pp. 44–45].

The first elements of Parsons' specification and that given here clearly correspond. Actors are the sources of action. Parsons's second element corresponds to the third element given here; however, "ends" in general are given here as any increase in an actor's well-being that the actor perceives to be promised by an action. Parson's third element corresponds to the second element given here; however, means and conditions are merged in a statement of the natural rights of individuals to exercise sole control of their private property. Conditions for action here do not include other actors' property or norms within the postulate of purposive action. These situational features are external to the individual actor. Although they are situational features as discussed by Parsons, I want to distinguish clearly the actor-specific features of action from the features emergent in a system of actors. Parson's fourth element corresponds to the fourth element given here. However, I have focused on this evaluative element as the basis for distinguishing, and subsequently bridging, alternative theories of action. Parsons, in contrast, uses both situational features and evaluative features of action to distinguish concepts of action. By defining the first three elements of action in a manner consistent with current usage in political economy and leaving the evaluative element as an unknown, I believe that differences between the atomistic and normative perspectives are both clearly distinguished and explicitly bridged in a structural perspective. By assuming different types of evaluative processes in actors, the postulate of purposive action can cover the full range of action theories that Parsons distinguishes. This will be accomplished by distinguishing the extent to which actors consider other actors' property in an evaluation.

capable of action. The second element defines conditions for action—legitimate control of private property constituting resources. The third element defines the reason for action—self-interest. The fourth element defines the probability of alternative actions being performed. That action perceived by an individual as promising the greatest reward will be the action he performs. These third and fourth elements are brought together in terms of an actor's interests (Coleman 1966, 1972, 1973). An actor is interested in controlling a specific resource to the extent that it is consequential for his utility. He is interested in controlling what Coleman more generally terms an event to the extent that alternative outcomes or consequences of the event yield widely different levels of utility. Actor interests, in other words, are determined by the actor's evaluation of the utility in alternative actions.

Note the absence in these elements of any specification of the manner in which actors perceive utility in an action. Experiments in psychophysics over the last 200 years demonstrate that subjective evaluations of objective stimuli are relativistic, not absolute, judgments (e.g., Stevens 1968). To the extent that actor evaluations follow the laws of psychophysics, a "postulate of marginal evaluation" is suggested. Actors evaluate the increase in utility offered by alternative actions in reference to some criterion, that is to say, in terms of the marginal increase in utility provided by alternative actions in reference to the criterion. I defer a formal treatment of this idea to Chapter 5, but as a simple illustration consider a person's evaluation of weight. Imagine that you have asked someone to stretch out an arm while holding a palm out flat. You begin placing fishing sinkers on his hand and ask him to guess how much each sinker weighs. At first he might do well in guessing the weights. As the absolute amount of weight on his hand increases, however, he will be decreasingly sensitive to additional weights. While he might be able to guess the weight of a 1-oz sinker when it is first placed on his hand, the increase in weight of a 1-oz sinker when he already holds 2 lb of sinkers is negligible. In this example, the current weight of sinkers is the criterion against which subsequent weights are evaluated. Different theories of action can be distinguished by the criterion that is assumed in each to underlie marginal evaluations.

1.1 A FUNDAMENTAL SCHISM IN ACTION THEORY

There are two classic assumptions regarding the criterion that actors use to evaluate the marginal utility of alternative actions. These assumptions are answers to the following question, How is one actor's perception of utility in an action affected by other actors?

As an individual, or social atom, an actor exists today in reference to his previous conditions and evaluates alternative future actions in reference to his current conditions. An "atomistic" perspective assumes that alternative actions are evaluated independently by separate actors so that evaluations are made without reference to other actors. For the purposes here, the atomistic perspective is defined by separate actors having exogenously formed interests, one actor's interests, or preferences, being analytically independent of another's (cf. Parsons 1937:59–60 on the randomness of "ends"). Such a perspective lays the foundation for twentieth-century liberal democratic theory as it is based on the property concept that Macpherson terms "possessive individualism" (assuming that political institutions are only formed to ensure the ownership of private property and its orderly exchange among actors [Macpherson 1962, especially pp. 263–264]). This is the perspective that Smith develops in *The Wealth of Nations* to elaborate market mechanisms in terms of supply and demand.[6] Assuming further that such evaluations are made in terms of decreasing marginal utility (a unit increase in control over a resource having decreasing utility as one's current control increases, e.g., the sinker example above[7]) lays the foundation for twentieth-century utility theory (e.g., Stigler 1950) and accordingly for work building on utility theory to describe social exchange (Thibaut & Kelley 1959; Homans 1961; Blau 1964; Coleman 1973; see review by Ekeh 1974) and political processes (e.g., Downs 1957; Buchanon & Tullock 1962; Olson 1965; see reviews by Barry 1970; Riker & Ordeshook 1973).

But actors do not exist as social atoms. As a member of society, an actor exists within a system of actors and evaluates alternative actions within that context. A "normative" perspective assumes that actions are evaluated interdependently by separate actors as a function of socializing processes that integrate them within a system of actors. For the purposes of this discussion, the normative perspective is defined by separate actors within a system having interdependent interests as social norms generated by actors socializing one another. This normative perspective has a long history reflected in Aristotle's *De Anima*, Berkeley's essays on perception (Turbayne 1963), and twentieth-century social psychology emphasizing a social definition of a situation (see Thomas & Znaniecki 1918, the basic tenets of symbolic interactionism in Mead 1934, and those of ethnomethodology in Garfinkel 1967, cf. review by Denzin 1969). Using broad concepts, Parsons (1937) gives a synthesis of early twentieth-century social theory that seeks to introduce normative themes into

---

[6]That Smith gave political institutions minimal rights to meddle in the private affairs of individuals is clear from the closing quotation in footnote 4. He is careful to distinguish, however, between ostensible violations of natural rights and actual violations in terms of the interests of individuals within the overall society (e.g., p. 308) and distinguishes three duties of the sovereign (p. 651): protecting the society from other independent societies, protecting each member of society from other members, and maintaining those public works and institutions which would not be supported by private interests owing to the insufficient profit support would yield.

[7]Formally, decreasing marginal utility means that the exponent in Steven's law of perception is less than one and greater than zero (see Eq. 5.1).

theory otherwise based on an atomistic perspective.[8] More subtle distinctions within these broad concepts are subsequently used to outline a general conceptual framework for the study of action (Parsons 1951; Parsons & Shils 1951). Barry (1970: Chaps. 3, 4) reviews social theory concerning political processes assuming a normative perspective, and Ekeh (1974: Chaps. 3, 4), largely building on Levi-Strauss (1949), reviews social theory concerning exchange processes assuming a normative perspective.

Empirical evidence supports a normative perspective over an atomistic one. Perceptions and evaluations are significantly affected by the social context in which they are made. This evidence spans a wide range of types of data ranging from experiments[9] to surveys within a system of actors[10] to ethnographic studies

[8]I wish to separate clearly Parson's (1937:77–82) distinction between three approaches to action (positivistic, voluntaristic, and idealistic) from the three approaches distinguished here. There is a rough correspondence. Although the atomistic-positivistic, structural-voluntaristic, and normative-idealistic trichotomy is similar in regard to the extent to which evaluations of actions are interdependent among separate actors, and I perceive a similarity in spirit between the two classifications, Parsons uses many more parameters in his classification than I am able, or need, to consider here (e.g., he considers the extent to which evaluations must be scientific, the specification of particular means and ends). I am here distinguishing three action theories solely in terms of differences in the assumed interdependency of separate actors' evaluations. The terms I have used make clear these different levels of interdependency.

[9]For example, establishing the experimental approach to normative judgments as reflected in errors of evaluating ambiguous stimuli presented in a social context, Sherif (1935) sought to understand "differential responses determined by social factors when individuals face the same stimulus situation [p. 52]." Sherif took advantage of the "autokinetic effect." When placed in a dark room so that there is no objective basis for comparison, a single, stationary, small light will appear to an individual to move and can move in any direction. Subjects (students at Columbia University) were asked to indicate the range of movement when presented with the stimulus. When alone in the room, "subjects subjectively establish a range and a point within the range (of movement in inches) which is peculiar to the individual [Sherif 1935: 25; parentheses added]." These individual ranges and points within the range were presented by the individual as "norms" of evaluation in subsequent experiments when the individual was alone in the room. Differences in the median perceived distance travelled by the light were significantly different between pairs of subjects. When groups of three subjects were asked to evaluate the same stimulus simultaneously (not a group decision), however, the significant interpersonal differences disappeared within each group. Moreover, "once an individual faces a stimulus situation in the group situation for the first time and reacts to it with the norm of the group, there is a tendency to continue to react to the same situation with the same norm established in the group, even when the subject is no longer in the group situation [Sherif 1935:31, 34]." In other words, the group situation suppresses individual evaluations in favor of a group norm, and the dominance of that group norm continues for evaluations made by one of the group when he is alone. About 75% of the subjects, however, claimed that they were not influenced by the judgments of other persons in the experiment (Sherif 1935:42)! The same normative evaluation effects can be demonstrated with unambiguous stimuli. Asch (1951) presented subjects with a line flashed on a screen and subsequently asked them to indicate which of three lines then presented to them was the same length as the original line flashed on the screen. The three lines were of very different lengths, so evaluation was not difficult. Unfortunately for the subject, all but one of the persons in the room were experimenter confederates and were instructed to unanimously select the wrong line as most similar to the original line. When faced with this situation, the actual subject had a statistically significant tendency to choose the wrong line, the line unanimously chosen by the confederates. By refining this experiment, Deutsch and Gerard (1955) demonstrated that the normative evaluations made by subjects (again, students from a single university, this time New York University) in the above experiments were indeed due to normative influence and not just a result of information transfer between individuals.

[10]Two classic examples are discussed in Chapter 5, the Festinger, Schacter & Back (1950) study

across systems.[11] Reviews and codifications of this evidence are readily available (e.g., Merton & Rossi 1950; Merton 1957b; McGuire 1969; and especially Tajfel 1969). As an empirical generalization, social context affects an individual's evaluations of alternative actions (and thus his interests) in the sense that evaluations are based on the characteristics of each actor in the system as a function of the social similarity the individual perceives between himself and each other actor.[12]

Unfortunately, what is clear empirically is not clear conceptually. There is a fundamental schism between what can be characterized as atomistic action theory and normative action theory. Taking an atomistic perspective facilitates rigorous deductive reasoning in a manner that is completely impossible if a normative perspective is adopted in its traditional form. Usually taking an atomistic perspective, economists have outstripped other social scientists in developing sophisticated deductive theory. A notable example is Becker's (1976) general treatment of human behavior (a contribution to which I return in Chapter 9 in which alternative action theories are compared). Indeed, the situation with respect to action theory suggests that a normative perspective is assumed for descriptive work while an atomistic perspective is assumed for deductive work (cf. Barry 1970:3–7, 165–168).

---

of group pressure on attitudes expressed by group members, using data on married college students, and the Stouffer, Suchman, DeVinney, Star, and Williams (1949) study of American soldiers in World War II that demonstrated the widely different evaluations of their military life that soldiers made depending on their standards of comparison.

[11]Ethnographic studies of different cultural groups have long demonstrated the normative basis of evaluation (Sherif 1935:5–11 reviews early studies); however, the significance of normative evaluation emerges most clearly when persons using different normative standards of evaluation are put into interaction with one another. Consider the American attaché of the embassy in a Latin American country who, upon scheduling an appointment with his counterpart in the country, generated the following observation described by Hall (1959:27):

> Arriving a little before the hour (the American respect pattern), he waited. The hour came and passed; five minutes—ten minutes—fifteen minutes. At this point he suggested to the secretary that perhaps the minister did not know he was waiting in the outer office. This gave him the feeling he had done something concrete and also helped to overcome the great anxiety that was stirring inside him. Twenty minutes—twenty-five minutes—thirty minutes—forty-five minutes (the insult period)! He jumped up and told the secretary that he had been 'cooling his heels' in an outer office for forty-five minutes and he was 'damned sick and tired' of this type of treatment. This message was relayed to the minister, who said, in effect, 'Let him cool his heels.' The attaché's stay in the country was not a happy one. The principal source of misunderstanding lay in the fact that in the country in question five-minute delay interval was not significant. Forty-five minutes, on the other hand, instead of being at the tail end of the waiting scale, was just barely at the beginning. To suggest to an American's secretary that perhaps her boss didn't know you were there after waiting sixty seconds would seem absurd, as would raising a storm about 'cooling your heels' for five minutes. Yet this is precisely the way the minister registered the protestations of the American in his outer office! He felt, as usual, that Americans were totally unreasonable.

[12]This need not preclude the use of negative reference groups in evaluations, as should be clear from the discussion in Section 5.3 and Chapter 9.

Social theorists, attempting a synthesis of the atomistic and normative perspectives within a single postulate of purposive action after the spirit of Parson's (1937) concept of "voluntaristic action," have failed to go beyond what Dumont and Wilson (1967) term a "theory sketch" in their elaboration of the "explanation sketch" idea proposed by Hempel (1942) as "a more or less vague indication of the laws and initial conditions considered as relevant (to a phenomenon) [p. 238, parentheses added]." Further, the prospects for such development seem dim within existing modes of thought. After conducting extensive reviews of basic features of theory within the atomistic versus the normative perspectives, Barry (1970) cautions against simplistic efforts to squeeze the two perspectives into one: "More speculative is the prospect for further attempts to stir the contents of the two packages together. The spirit of compromise is out of place here. There is no intrinsic advantage in mixing up opposed ideas, and the result can easily be a muddle [p. 183]." Similarly, Ekeh (1974:5) warns that the two perspectives "exist in nonmarriageable terms—only joined by the virulence of the polemics against each other's tradition of thought."

1.2 A STRUCTURAL THEORY OF ACTION: ANALYTICAL STRATEGY AND OVERVIEW

The virulence of their polemics notwithstanding, my purpose in this book is to develop a perspective that circumvents the schism between atomistic and normative action. My argument is less a synthesis of the existing two perspectives on action than it is a third view intellectually bridging the two views. The principal difference between the structural perspective to be developed here and those of atomistic and normative action lies in the criterion for the postulate of marginal evaluation. The criterion assumed by the proposed structural perspective is an actor's status/role-set as generated by the division of labor. An actor evaluates the utility of alternative actions partly in regard to his personal conditions and partly in regard to the conditions of others. The exact mixture of these criteria in his evaluation depends on the status he occupies. Naturally, the structural perspective borrows extensively from the already well-developed atomistic and normative perspectives. As I discuss in Chapter 9, it is a logical extension of the former and an empirically accurate restriction of the latter. Still, the structural perspective seems preferable to the two alternative perspectives. This point too is developed in Chapter 9. The structural perspective is deductively superior to normative action since its use of network models provides a rigorous algebraic representation of system stratification from which hypotheses can be derived. It is descriptively superior to atomistic action since it explicitly takes into account the social context within which actors make evaluations.

Let me explain my analytical strategy before I jump into the substance of my argument. This explanation provides an overview of the forthcoming discussion in answers to the following three questions.

How Can the Task of Mathematically Capturing a Structural Theory of Action Be Addressed with a Realistic Hope of Success?

I judge the mathematical representation to be successful here to the extent that it does justice to the scope of substantive issues spanned by a structural theory of action while preserving sufficient precision to be vulnerable to falsification by empirical data. The key terms here are scope and precision.

As discussed above, the premise underlying a structural theory of action, namely, actors are purposive under social structural constraints, implies a very general scope of substantive issues within a causal cycle. Actors find themselves in a social structure. That social structure defines their social similarities, which in turn pattern their perceptions of the advantages to be had by taking each of several alternative actions. At the same time, social structure differentially constrains actors in their ability to take actions. Actions eventually taken are therefore a joint function of actors pursuing their interests to the limit of their ability where both interests and ability are patterned by social structure. Finally, actions taken under social structural constraint can modify social structure itself and these modifications have the potential to create new constraints to be faced by actors within the structure. Figure 1.1 distinguishes three components within this causal cycle: social structure as the context of action, actor interests, and action itself. The causal relations among these

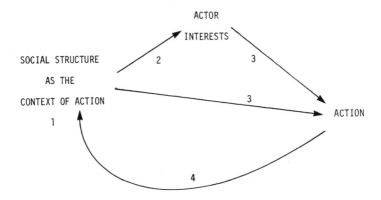

Figure 1.1. Components in a structural theory of action (numbers indicate sequential problems addressed here).

components indicate four tasks to be addressed in constructing a structural theory of action:

1. Capturing an actor's position in a stratified system as the social context of evaluation
2. Describing the manner in which actor interests are patterned by social structure so captured
3. Describing the manner in which actions, determined by interests, are constrained by the relational pattern defining a position in social structure
4. Describing the manner in which actors pursuing their interests in the proposed manner could be responsible for the patterns of relations first observed as social structure

While it seems an impossible task to construct one model that encompasses all of Figure 1.1 with an acceptable level of precision, a small number of separate models can be constructed so as to collectively achieve the desired scope and precision. Each model to be proposed here is analytically compatible with, and in part builds from, the others. However, each model alone only purports to capture a single component in Figure 1.1. This means that each model can be stated with precision sufficient to allow its implications to be tested with empirical data. In short, I have made the task of constructing a structural theory of action tractable by disaggregating the task into more narrowly defined, complementary tasks.

How Should Empirical Data be Used in Developing the Component Models?

The construction of models as components in a structural theory of action must be a logical more than an empirical venture. Unlike explanations proposed for an unambiguous population (in a statistical sense), such as Blau and Duncan's (1967) model describing father to son occupational mobility within the United States, a structural theory purports to explain systems of actors more generally, for example, families, neighborhoods, bureaucracies, communities, nations, or world systems. The theory does not refer to a single population in terms of which a statistically "best fitting" model can be specified. There is a temptation in such circumstances to treat data on a large collection of systems as if they were representative of a population, the number of observations replacing representativeness in an erroneously routine statistical inference. However, the fact that a model is adequate in describing an arbitrary collection of data sets permits no inference beyond the model's usefulness for those data. In other words, structural models offered as empirical generalizations from data on one or more systems are doomed to appear ad hoc.

Yet it seems even less useful to propose models completely uninformed by the corrective feedback of observations on diverse systems. A model specified as optimally describing a single system is unacceptably narrow in scope, but at least it offers some substantive description.

I have chosen a deductive approach to theory construction combined with the strategic use of empirical data. I alternate conceptual and applied chapters. In the former, three items are presented:

1. Initial ideas are introduced as aspects of a component in Figure 1.1 to be captured.
2. These ideas are formalized as a mathematical model.
3. Some of the model's empirical implications are then derived as hypotheses, and the model, together with its implications, is illustrated with heuristically hypothetical data.

This abstract discussion is then given empirical meaning in an application chapter by the use of the model to describe a particularly relevant system of actors. I rely on two systems: large corporations involved in American manufacturing during the late 1960s and elite academicians in sociological methodology during the mid 1970s. These two systems are particularly relevant to a proposed model in one or more of three ways: (*a*) Uniqueness. While the models to be proposed pertain to all systems of actors, not all systems are equally suitable for testing their implications. Specifically, the data on corporations are nicely suited for assessing hypotheses regarding autonomy and cooptation (Chapter 8), and those on expert perceptions of journal significance are nicely suited for assessing hypotheses regarding the social basis for group norms (Chapter 6). (*b*) Substance. The systems described represent substantive areas that are inherently concerned with relational patterns so that fruitful applications of the proposed models have the potential to inform ongoing substantive research. As will be clear from the literature discussed in each application chapter, the sociology of science and organizational behavior are areas that have historically offered analytically sophisticated descriptions of relations among actors. To the extent that the proposed models are adequate in describing the two systems considered here, they are more than empirically illustrated or verified: they are interesting in their own right as developments in substantive research traditions. (*c*) Familiarity. Finally, these two systems are not far removed from the reader's day-to-day experience. Since the purpose of applying the proposed models is to give them empirical meaning, it is important that the reader be able to draw from his own experience in interpreting the applications. Virtually everyone is exposed to the actions of large corporate bureaucracies. Most of us work within them. Even if the reader has no familiarity with research on interorganizational relations, the discussion of large manufacturing firms here is likely to strike a familiar chord. Those readers at all affiliated with academia will quickly recognize the issues raised in the discussion of academic stratification and the perception of significance in journals among the elite experts in sociological methodology. In particular, sociologists will quickly recognize the principal characters, core journals, and subgroups within the system.

In short, I am making strategic use of empirical data. Particularly relevant data are used to empirically inform each proposed model as well as to demonstrate some way in which the model informs ongoing substantive research. However, the data are in no sense used to justify proposed models as empirical generalizations.

How Are Models Coordinated in the Book so as to Cumulate in a Structural Theory of Action?

The three components of a structural theory of action as presented in Figure 1.1 are captured here in three models: a model of status/role-sets interconnected as social structure, a model of actor interests, and a model of actor autonomy to act without constraint.[13] These models are introduced in a cumulative fashion reflecting the causal processes indicated in Figure 1.1 among the three components. Arranging conceptual chapters vertically and their respective application chapters on a horizontal axis, the logical order of the forthcoming chapters is given as

$$
\begin{array}{ll}
\text{introduction} & 1 \\
& \downarrow \\
\text{social structure} & 2 \rightarrow 3,4 \\
& \downarrow \\
\text{actor interests} & 5 \rightarrow 6 \\
& \downarrow \\
\text{action} & 7 \rightarrow 8 \\
& \downarrow \\
\text{conclusion} & 9
\end{array}
$$

[13]Obviously, there is more to action than is covered by the concept of structural autonomy. In particular, there is the concept of power. In contrast to structural autonomy as an ability to realize interests *without* constraint, I have elsewhere discussed concepts of power as an ability to realize interests *despite* constraint (Burt 1977a, 1979b). Central in this discussion is the replacement of possessing valued resources with occupying network positions in which control over such resources is concentrated. With the division of labor, the argument goes, control over different kinds of valued resources is concentrated in the hands of actors occupying different statuses as network positions. With a shared understanding regarding status-appropriate behavior, these resources are used to the joint benefit of actors occupying the status, so that merely occupying the status becomes a resource in its own right. Processes by which position occupancy becomes a resource to be possessed and exchanged are discussed in the above articles; however, there is no model of structural power developed on a par with the models of status/role-sets, structural interests, or structural autonomy. Nor have the power models been assessed in substantive research on a par with the models discussed in this book. Reflecting the current state of development, I have focused on status/role-sets, interests, and autonomy as cornerstones for a structural theory of action. Readers interested in power as an additional, and eventually necessary, component in such a theory are referred to the above two articles, to recent developments specifying processes by which social networks might constrain exchange processes underlying collective action (Marsden & Laumann 1977; Marsden 1981a, 1982a), and to recent laboratory experiments describing some ways in which an individual's power over the process of exchange is determined by the pattern of exchange relations defining the individual's network position (Cook & Emerson 1978; Cook 1982).

Given the cumulative nature of the discussion, I have not attempted to summarize it here. For the reader interested in obtaining a quick overview, I have written the concluding section of each chapter so that when these sections are read in the above logical order, they summarize the discussion cumulating to Chapter 9. The conceptual developments cumulating to Chapter 9 can be quickly reviewed by reading the concluding sections of Chapters 2, 5, and 7. The substantive results presented can be similarly obtained from the conclusions to Chapters 3, 4, 6, and 8. Some brief comments on the chapters would be helpful at this point in order to fill in the above logical order.

Social structure is captured by network models built from the social topology of a multiple network system. Chapter 2 provides an analytical synopsis of available network models of social differentiation. That class of models best suited to capturing actors and subgroups in the context of overall system stratification is based on the system's social topology. Within this class of models, the complete set of relations in which an actor is involved defines his network position within a system and the extent to which he occupies the status/role-sets in terms of which the system is stratified. These models are then used in Chapters 3 and 4 to describe actual stratification. Chapter 3 contains a description of the status/role-sets in terms of which the invisible college of elite experts in sociological methodology was stratified as of 1975. This chapter provides me with an opportunity to discuss the application of the positional models in detail. Three groups of leaders are distinguished among the elites: a social statistics elite, methodological leaders in social psychology, and a mathematical sociology elite. The relative prominence of these groups is associated with the extent to which they had been successful in merging their methodological talents with a substantive problem. This is discussed in terms of the coordination of their substantive and methodological advising relations with one another. The social statistics elite occupied the most prominent status in the system, turned to one another for substantive advice, principally on questions of stratification and mobility, and had developed an entire satellite status occupied by a mobility elite who relied on them for methodological advice. The divergence of substantive relations among the methodology leaders in social psychology, some pursuing questions on affect in triadic groups while others pursued more general social psychological issues, resulted in their occupying two separate statuses, neither of which was as prominent as that occupied by the social statistics elite. Finally, the lack of similar substantive relations among the mathematical sociology elite resulted in their prominent position within a network of methodological advice relations splitting into many nonequivalent positions within the system as a whole. Failure to coordinate their substantive efforts was associated with these elite experts being invisible as a group in sociological methodology, even though many were prominent as individuals. These relative tendencies for experts in the three groups of leaders to have coordinated their substantive interests is somewhat tied to their common graduate training, which is argued as evidence of the stability of stratification within the speciality of sociological methodology. The theme of coordinating different types of relations is raised again in Chapter 4, but in a very different context. Relational patterns are described among organizations rather than people. Relational data is obtained on a very small sample of actors in the system rather than the more typical case of having data on most actors in the system. Network models centered on individual actors as egos are used to guide the analysis of relational patterns within the system containing them. Chapter 4 is a description of the manner in which manufacturing establishments were connected in 1967 through corporate boards of directors to diverse sectors of the American economy. Such ties are argued to have the cooptive potential of creating a nonmarket context for the transaction of essential buying and selling among establishments. Directorate ties were extensive between sectors of the economy, and types of ties were coordinated in connecting the same sectors. Economic sectors represented on a corporate board by ownership tended to be represented there by direct interlocking as well as indirect interlocking through financial institutions, two firms being interlocked when one or more of the directors in one firm were directors in the other. Beyond the observed structure of directorate ties typical at the time, there were significant differences in the extent to which different types of firms were responsible for directorate ties. The firms most responsible for creating coordinated directorate ties among establishments were the firms most likely to benefit from cooptive relations: large firms controlled by dispersed interest groups. Since these firms were typically found operating within the prominent core industries of the American economy, their greater responsibility for coordinated directorate ties had the result that core industries tended to have such ties to diverse sectors of the economy. In short, the economy was stratified in terms of coordinated ties through the directorates of differentially prominent firms operating within differentially prominent industries.

Moving to the manner in which network structure as a social context might affect perceptions, Chapter 5 provides a model in which actor interests are captured by bringing together Stevens's work in psychophysics on subjective perceptions of objective stimuli with the status/role-set models discussed in Chapter 2. The result is a model of structural interest in which an actor's perception of the utility offered by an action is determined by his network position vis-à-vis the positions of others. The proposed model defines conditions under which a set of actors can be expected to share the same subjective evaluation as a social norm, and it defines a functional form for feelings of relative deprivation. These results are used to generate hypotheses in a traditional area of application for network models, innovation adoption. The most problematic of the model's empirical implications is its prediction that occupants of a status will share a status norm even if they have no direct relations with one another. This implication contradicts the relational tradition in sociometry, the traditional argument being that social norms are shared by people tied by strong socializing relations to one another. In Chapter 6, I assess the empirical adequacy of these two predictions by describing the manner in which the elite experts perceived specific journals to be significant outlets for their work in sociological methodology. It is argued that, given the empirical ambiguity of evaluations of significance, such evaluations are determined by the social context in which they are made, which in turn determines the interest of individuals in specific journals as significant outlets for their work. The traditional relational model is argued to state that an expert should have expressed interests similar to those expressed by persons from whom he acknowledged influential comments on his work. This homophily of interests is expected as a result of interpersonal communication—actual communication. The proposed positional model predicts interest homophily among experts jointly occupying the same network position; experts who are structurally equivalent. This homophily is expected as a result of each expert symbolically role-playing the position of his structural peers in the college when he evaluates the significance of a journal article. Freed of the requirement that expert interests be affected only by actual communication between experts, the proposed model predicts interest homophily among structurally equivalent experts. The analysis supports the positional model in preference to the relational. Not only does the positional model do as well as the relational in describing the interests of experts tied to one another by advice relations, it goes on to describe much better the interests of followers—experts who had no direct advice relations with one another but whose unreciprocated relations to the same other experts made them structurally equivalent to one another. The analysis of conformity and deviance with respect to normative interest in journals also augments the analysis of stratification given in Chapter 3. As a further indicator of the stability of stratification in sociological methodology, the differential prominence of leading groups of experts is reproduced by their relative consensus on specific journals as significant outlets for their work; prominence increasing with consensus.

Finally, Chapter 7 provides a network model of constraint. The occupants of a status have high structural autonomy to the extent that they are able to realize interests without constraint from others. The concept of oligopoly is brought together with the concept of conflicting group affiliations to define the extent to which a status provides its occupants with structural autonomy. The occupants of a status enjoy high structural autonomy to the extent that their relational patterns ensure low competition with one another while simultaneously ensuring high competition among the nonoccupant actors with whom they interact. Beyond defining the relative level of structural autonomy that occupants of different status could be expected to have within a system, the model indicates the extent to which occupants of any one status are constrained by occupants of each other status. In Chapter 8 I return to American manufacturing industries in order to assess the empirical adequacy of the proposed model. The model correctly predicts the relative profit margins typically obtained in different industries; an industry's typical profit margin being high to the extent that the industry's typical sales and purchase transactions with economic sectors generally ensure the industry high structural autonomy. The model is then used to estimate the extent to which each sector of the economy constrained the structural autonomy of an industry and thereby the typical industry profit margin. As expected, cooptive relations tended to connect establishments in each industry with those sectors posing the most severe market constraint for industry profits. Coordinated directorate ties tended to occur with sectors which were the source of severe market constraint. In fact, the intensity of the market constraint a sector posed for an industry's typical profit margin predicts the frequency of ownership ties, direct interlock ties, and indirect financial interlock ties connecting establishments in the industry to those in the sector. The analysis of market constraint and directorate ties in Chapter 8 significantly augments the analysis of stratification given in Chapter 4. In the descriptive analysis in Chapter 4 I conclude that the pattern of directorate ties involving manufacturing establishments in the 1967 American economy looked as if such ties were being used to coopt sources of market constraint. The analysis in Chapter 8, guided by a network theory of constraint, documents that coordinated directorate ties were quite strongly patterned by market constraints from competitors, suppliers, and consumers, even the frequency of ties being predictable from the intensity of constraint.

In conclusion, I discuss the proposed status/role-set, structural interest, and structural autonomy models as a start toward a structural theory of action in light of its alternatives—atomistic action versus normative action. Needless to say, my description in Chapter 9 of the future for such a theory is optimistic.

FIRST COMPONENT: SOCIAL STRUCTURE

2

Network Structure: The Social Context*

At once a connection between micro- and macrolevel social theory as well as an epistemic link between abstract concepts and empirical research, network models offer a powerful framework for describing social differentiation in terms of relational patterns among actors in a system. I shall rely upon such models in subsequent chapters in order to algebraically capture the social context for action. My purpose here is to present an analytical synopsis of network models representing social context.

This purpose places several constraints on the discussion. Given my focus on describing social differentiation, its causes and consequences are topics set aside for other chapters. Moreover, I have no intention of covering the many substantive applications to which network models have been put, the complete range of network models that have been proposed, nor the various problems of using alternative algorithms to apply network models. References to other reviews are given where appropriate.

Neither can I pretend that network analysis is a single corpus of knowledge cumulating with each passing year. Anyone reading through what purports to be a "network" literature will readily perceive the wisdom of Barnes' (1972)

---

*Portions of this chapter are drawn from articles reprinted with the permission of: *Social Forces, Sociological Methods & Research,* and the *Annual Review of Sociology* (Burt 1976b, 1977b, 1978b, 1980c).

analogy between that literature and "a terminological jungle in which any newcomer may plant a tree." There is currently a loose federation of approaches referenced as network analysis. In a very real sense, network analysis is progressing on many fronts as a result of the efforts of many persons. My efforts here to discuss these separate fronts without forcing them into a single perspective does not condone past parochialisms. By making distinctions among separate approaches, I hope to highlight their conceptual complementarity so as to make more apparent their relative strengths for my purpose of developing a structural theory of action.

Before introducing any models, I briefly discuss the data that network models purport to describe. This aside is useful in two senses: (a) It makes explicit the scope and primitive concepts of network models. (b) It provides a setting for distinguishing models that generate data from models of network structure per se. Section 2.2 provides an overview of the models to be discussed in the subsequent six sections. Section 2.9 describes various methods of testing network models as hypotheses, and Section 2.10 closes with conclusions on the optimality of alternative models in capturing the social context of action.

2.1 THE DATA DESCRIBED BY MODELS OF NETWORK STRUCTURE

Network models describe the structure of one or more networks of relations within a system of actors. Specific models can focus on specific aspects of structure in these multiple networks, but at a maximum, the data described are elements in K $(1 \leq K)$ matrices; $Z_1, Z_2, \ldots, Z_K$, of order (N, N) in a system of N actors where the relation from actor j to actor i within network k is z_{jik}, element (j, i) in Z_K. When models describe a single network of relations, I refer to z_{jik} without the third subscript. Further, the availability of multiple networks removes the need for relations to be negative, so there is no loss in assuming all relations are to be nonnegative ($z_{jik} \leq 0$). The models to be discussed take as exogenous "networks of relations" in a "system of actors."

Systems of Actors

There is no micro- or macrolevel of analysis inherent in network data; however, such data are typically gathered on small systems of actors. The N actors can be persons, informal groups, or formal corporate groups, but popular research designs for gathering network data are intended to obtain information on all relations among the N actors. Putting to one side systems with clear boundaries (e.g., students in a classroom), systems are often defined empirically by combined positional and snowball sampling. A "core" set of actors is located by their prominent positions in the system to be studied. Each actor in this positional sample is then asked to indicate other actors who are significant in the system. By means of successive interviews, the original sample "snowballs" into a final sample. Coleman (1958) and Erickson (1978) review these and other chain methods (cf. Killworth & Bernard 1978 on small world data and for applications of chain methods; Travers and Milgram 1969; Erickson & Kringas 1975; Klovdahl, Dhofier, Oddy, O'Hara, Stoutjesdajk, and Whish 1977; Lin, Dayton, and Greenwald 1978). Actors here can be defined at a micro- or macrolevel (cf. Chapters 3, 4): employees in a bureaucracy (Lincoln & Miller 1979), elites in a community (Hunter 1953; Freeman 1968; Laumann & Pappi 1976; Laumann, Marsden, and Galaskiewicz 1977; Breiger 1979), elites in an invisible college (Crane 1972; Breiger 1976; Mullins, Hargens, Hecht, and Kick 1977), large corporations in a community (Perrucci & Pilisuk 1970; Galaskiewicz & Marsden 1978; Laumann, Galaskiewicz, and Marsden 1978; Galaskiewicz 1979), or nations in a world system (Snyder & Kick 1979). Although systems usually consist of fewer than 100 distinct actors, some involving up to 1000 actors have been described despite the expense involved in analyzing such systems (Kadushin 1974; Mariolis 1975; Sonquist & Koenig 1975; Alba & Moore 1978). Laumann, Marsden, and Prensky (1982) provide a useful discussion of issues in defining boundaries for a system of actors.

There have been efforts to estimate population network parameters using statistics computed from data on a random sample of actors. Goodman (1961) combines an initial random sample of actors with snowball sampling to estimate the number of persons who will be named in the snowball sampling and the number of reciprocated relations in the population. Procter (1967) and Frank (1978, 1979) use data on a random sample to estimate the extent to which actors in a population are involved in relations. Building on Frank's work, Granovetter (1976) offers an estimator of population network density, the average relation between any two actors in the population. Alternatively, traditional survey research designs have been used to describe the prevalence of different types of relations in a large population and the attributes of persons involved in each type of relation (Laumann 1973, Fischer, Jackson, Stueve, Gerson, Jones, and Baldassare 1977; Verbrugge 1977, 1979; McCallister & Fischer 1978; Wellman 1979). Combining the data collection strategy of Fischer with Blau's (1974) treatment of attributes as structural parameters, Burt (1981a) presents one method of using survey interviews with a random sample to determine and estimate relations among status groups in a large population. If status groups can be given prior to sampling, however, then actors can be sampled as occupants of status groups rather than as individuals. With the usual advantages of stratified sampling, relations within and between status groups can be estimated from data on actors within each group. Beniger (1976) describes a method for estimating relations between groups in a large population from a random sample of persons in each group. By aggregating actors into status groups, network data have been obtained on large populations (see Chapter 4, 8; for different examples see Laumann 1966; Laumann & Pappi

1976; Burt 1975, 1981b; Burt & Lin 1977; Burt, Leiben, and Fischer 1980).

Although recent developments in network sampling are promising, they are preliminary. The network concepts that can be estimated in large systems are quite rudimentary and/or have not been used extensively in substantive research (see the exchange between Granovetter 1976 and Morgan & Rytina 1977). For the purposes here, I sidestep the question of network sampling. I assume that, by one method or another, it is feasible to obtain network data on all N actors in a system.

Networks of Relations

The relation from actor j to actor i within network k, z_{jik}, has a form and a content.[1] The form of z_{jik} is a measure of the strength of the relation from j to i that it represents. Its content is the type of relation that it represents. Network k consists of all relations with the content of z_{jik}. For example, z_{jik} would be found in a network of social relations if it referred to j's tendency to initiate informal social interactions with i. The K networks in a system refer to the relational contents in terms of which the system is stratified: social relations, economic relations, kinship relations, and so on. Distinctions among relational contents are not well understood at a general level. Once network data are gathered on K networks, however, there are models for describing the extent to which relations in two or more networks are redundant with one another (e.g., the discussion of Figure 2.3 in Section 2.9).

Within a network, the form of z_{ji} has been measured in two ways: the strength of the link from j to i and their level of joint involvement in the same activities. As a notational convenience here, I use the symbol z_{ji} to refer to a relation from j to i. In other words, z_{ji} in one equation need not quantitatively measure the same thing as z_{ji} in another equation, but all measures of z_{ji} as a relational form

---

[1]In his widely cited introduction to network analysis, Mitchell (1969:12) distinguishes form and content respectively as morphological and interactional characteristics of a network (cf. Mitchell 1974:288). Simmel (1917) provides an early source for the form versus content distinction in interaction:

> Everything present in the individual . . . in the form of drive, interest, purpose, inclination, psychic state, movement—everything that is present in them in such a way as to engender or mediate effects upon others or to receive such effects, I designate as the content, as the material, as it were, of sociation. . . . They are factors in sociation only when they transform the mere aggregation of isolated individuals into specific forms of being with and for one another—forms that are subsumed under the general concept of interaction [pp. 40–41].

Of course, there is no necessary separation between concepts of relational content and concepts of relational form. Network models of form can be quite useful in describing qualities of relational content. This point is pursued in detail elsewhere (e.g., Burt 1982a), but is secondary to my purpose here.

reflect an intensity of connection between two actors as a dyad apart from the other N-2 actors in their system.[2]

Given N actors and M activities, relations among the actors as well as among the activities are implied by an (N,M) matrix A where element a_{ij} equals 1 if actor i is involved in activity j and 0 otherwise. An (N,N) matrix representing relations among actors is given as

$$\mathbf{Z} = \mathbf{A}\mathbf{A}', \qquad\qquad (2.1)$$

where element z_{ji} is the number of activities in which actors i and j are simultaneously involved. An (M,M) interactivity network is given as

$$\mathbf{Z} = \mathbf{A}'\mathbf{A}, \qquad\qquad (2.2)$$

where element z_{ji} is the number of actors simultaneously involved in activities i and j. Breiger (1974) provides a cogent discussion of the dual networks implied by the matrix $\mathbf{A}$. Networks of joint activities have been used for some time in diverse substantive areas. The most common use of A is in network studies of interorganizational relations created by corporate directors and officers interlocking separate organizations (e.g., Perrucci & Pilisuk 1970; Levine 1972; Allen 1974). Where the N actors are individuals and the M activities are corporate boards of directors, z_{ij} in Eq. (1) is the number of corporations for which persons i and j are simultaneously directors, and z_{ij} in Eq. (2) is the number of persons simultaneously sitting on the boards of corporations i and j. Among other relations as joint involvement are joint memberships in professional associations (Coleman, Katz, and Menzel 1966; Laumann et al. 1974), joint prominence in newspaper articles or community issues (Burt & Lin 1977; Burt et al. 1980), joint membership in informal social groups (Coleman 1961; Bonacich 1972b; Alba & Kadushin 1976), as well as joint involvement in the determination of events (Coleman 1972, 1973; Marsden & Laumann 1977; Marsden 1981a). Asymmetric Z matrices are discussed by Coleman, Marsden, and Burt and Lin.

More often than not, the strength of the link from j to i is derived from binary sociometric choices.[3] Taking their name from Moreno's (1934, 1960) develop-

---

[2]Equations (2.3) and (2.4) are partial exceptions to this statement. However, even these measures of relational form only consider as many other actors as are necessary to complete a chain of steps from one actor to another. Even when z_{ji} is generated by a nonmetric algorithm for reducing the order of Z to a specified number of dimensions lower than N (e.g., Laumann & Pappi 1976; Laumann, Verbrugge, and Pappi 1974; Laumann et al. 1977), the reliance by these algorithms on the criterion of monotonicity (a criterion only concerned with the connection between pairs of actors) means that connections among the other N-2 actors are at best indirectly considered. Coleman (1970) discusses the inability of methods of analysis based on the monotonicity criterion to consider indirect linkages.

[3]It is not impossible, however, to find network models describing relations observed directly (e.g., Bernard & Killworth 1977) or coded from archival records such as published articles (e.g., Mullins et al. 1977), corporate sales and purchase records (e.g., Lustgarten 1975), migration rates between geographic areas (e.g., Jedlicka 1979), trade probabilities between geographic areas (e.g., Pitts 1979), and so on. The analysis in Chapter 3 combines archival records with interview data, and the analysis in Chapters 4 and 8 relies entirely on archival records.

ment of sociometry, sociometric questions are asked of each of the N actors in a system: Who are your best friends? From whom do you most often seek advice? With whom do you most often discuss personal problems? Answers to these questions can prescribe a fixed number of choices, allow any number of choices, or ask for a rank order of choices. Arguments for specific question styles are available (e.g., Holland & Leinhardt 1973; Hallinan 1974a: 24–30; Killworth & Bernard 1974; Bernard & Killworth 1977); however, the chapter by Lindzey and Byrne (1968) remains the most general review of sociometric measurement. Paraphrasing Lindzey and Byrne's discussion (pp. 445–456) of Moreno's original prescriptions for sociometric questions provides five useful guidelines for gathering choice data:[4]

1. System boundaries should be made clear to respondents.
2. "Under many circumstances it is preferable to specify the number of choices to be made."
3. Respondents should be asked to indicate the individuals they choose or reject in terms of specific criteria, that is, relational content.
4. Citations should be made privately so that other respondents are not able to identify the citations.
5. The sociometric questions should be gauged to the level of understanding of the respondents.

Sociometric choices obtained under these guidelines are assembled in an (N,N) adjacency matrix A for each question; a_{ji} is zero unless actor j cited actor i in

---

[4]These choice data have been more extensively tested in research than have alternative rating, ranking, or comparison data. Lindzey and Byrne (1968) conclude their review by noting that

The use of sociometric measures has been accompanied by a reasonable incidence of studies that are intended to contribute to better understanding of the measurement properties of these instruments. On the other hand, the ratings of interpersonal attraction that have been employed have typically been ad hoc in nature, and there has been little systematic attempt to explore the consequences of the many variations in procedure that are unsystematically or casually introduced by different investigators, or even by the same investigator on different occasions [p. 510].

The Hallinan, Holland and Leinhardt and Bernard and Killworth papers cited previously are recent exceptions to this comment; however, there are still no systematic studies of differences in basic network findings across different measures of relational form. Random errors can be tolerated to the extent that statistical inference is used in testing network models. Systematic errors are another matter. Consider an invisible college in which scientist j is asked to name those other scientists in the college who most influence his work. If the criterion for making this citation is set very low (for example at a level asking j to name experts whose work is familiar to him), then most scientists would have a citation to most other scientists, since persons within an invisible college tend to be aware of one another. On the other hand, if the criterion is set very high (for example at a level asking who directly supervised j's dissertation), then very few scientists would be connected by citations. Somewhere between such extreme criteria for coding binary choices in particular and sociometric data in general is an appropriate criterion. Consequential as this criterion is for the interpretation and testing of network models, little is known about it.

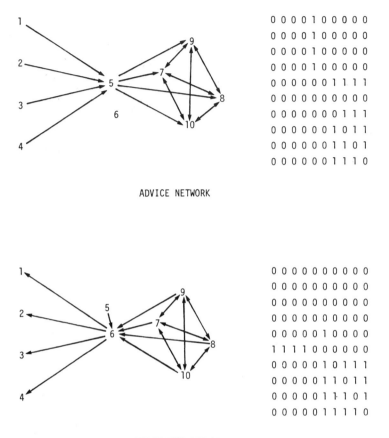

```
0 0 0 0 1 0 0 0 0 0
0 0 0 0 1 0 0 0 0 0
0 0 0 0 1 0 0 0 0 0
0 0 0 0 1 0 0 0 0 0
0 0 0 0 0 0 1 1 1 1
0 0 0 0 0 0 0 0 0 0
0 0 0 0 0 0 0 1 1 1
0 0 0 0 0 0 1 0 1 1
0 0 0 0 0 0 1 1 0 1
0 0 0 0 0 0 1 1 1 0
```

ADVICE NETWORK

```
0 0 0 0 0 0 0 0 0 0
0 0 0 0 0 0 0 0 0 0
0 0 0 0 0 0 0 0 0 0
0 0 0 0 0 0 0 0 0 0
0 0 0 0 0 1 0 0 0 0
1 1 1 1 0 0 0 0 0 0
0 0 0 0 0 1 0 1 1 1
0 0 0 0 0 1 1 0 1 1
0 0 0 0 0 1 1 1 0 1
0 0 0 0 0 1 1 1 1 0
```

FRIENDSHIP NETWORK

Figure 2.1. Sociograms and adjacency matrices for a two network system of ten actors.

response to the question. For example, Figure 2.1 presents sociometric choices among a hypothetical system of ten actors. Choices indicate to whom each actor goes for advice and whom he claims as friends. Choices are presented as a sociogram (e.g., actor 1 goes to actor 5 for advice; $1 \rightarrow 5$) and as an adjacency matrix ($a_{151} = 1$). These data will be useful in illustrating network models throughout the chapter, but this section only considers the advice network.

At times, the adjacency matrix A has been treated as a matrix of relations Z to be described by a network model. A compelling reason for treating A as Z is the simplicity of interpreting and analyzing binary relations; z_{ji} is present or absent. Simultaneously, this is its major weakness. Although binary relations are tractable, they raise to crucial significance the criterion used to distinguish present from absent relations, even though such criteria are usually ad hoc (see footnote 4.) Indirect relations are only implicit in binary sociometric choices.

For example, actor 1 has no direct advice connection to actor 9 in Figure 2.1, but through actor 5 he has a 2-step connection to 9 ($1 \rightarrow 5 \rightarrow 9$). In contrast, actor 6 has no direct or indirect connection to actor 9.

Following the initial work by Festinger (1949) and Luce and Perry (1949), adjacency matrices are often used to measure relations in terms of indirect connections by raising A to successive powers. The (j, i)th element in A^n equals the number of n-step connections leading from actor j to actor i. For example, squaring and cubing the advice adjacency matrix in Figure 2.1 yields the number of 2-step and 3-step connections leading from each actor to each other actor:

$$
\begin{array}{l}
0\ 0\ 0\ 0\ 0\ 0\ 1\ 1\ 1\ 1 \\
0\ 0\ 0\ 0\ 0\ 0\ 1\ 1\ 1\ 1 \\
0\ 0\ 0\ 0\ 0\ 0\ 1\ 1\ 1\ 1 \\
0\ 0\ 0\ 0\ 0\ 0\ 1\ 1\ 1\ 1 \\
0\ 0\ 0\ 0\ 0\ 0\ 3\ 3\ 3\ 3 \\
0\ 0\ 0\ 0\ 0\ 0\ 0\ 0\ 0\ 0 \\
0\ 0\ 0\ 0\ 0\ 0\ 3\ 2\ 2\ 2 \\
0\ 0\ 0\ 0\ 0\ 0\ 2\ 3\ 2\ 2 \\
0\ 0\ 0\ 0\ 0\ 0\ 2\ 2\ 3\ 2 \\
0\ 0\ 0\ 0\ 0\ 0\ 2\ 2\ 2\ 3
\end{array}
= A^2
\qquad
A^3 =
\begin{array}{l}
0\ 0\ 0\ 0\ 0\ 0\ 3\ 3\ 3\ 3 \\
0\ 0\ 0\ 0\ 0\ 0\ 3\ 3\ 3\ 3 \\
0\ 0\ 0\ 0\ 0\ 0\ 3\ 3\ 3\ 3 \\
0\ 0\ 0\ 0\ 0\ 0\ 3\ 3\ 3\ 3 \\
0\ 0\ 0\ 0\ 0\ 0\ 9\ 9\ 9\ 9 \\
0\ 0\ 0\ 0\ 0\ 0\ 0\ 0\ 0\ 0 \\
0\ 0\ 0\ 0\ 0\ 0\ 6\ 7\ 7\ 7 \\
0\ 0\ 0\ 0\ 0\ 0\ 7\ 6\ 7\ 7 \\
0\ 0\ 0\ 0\ 0\ 0\ 7\ 7\ 6\ 7 \\
0\ 0\ 0\ 0\ 0\ 0\ 7\ 7\ 7\ 6
\end{array}
$$

This shows, among other things, that the first four actors all have one 2-step connection to actor 9 (the first four elements in column nine of A^2 are 1's referring to $1 \rightarrow 5 \rightarrow 9$, $2 \rightarrow 5 \rightarrow 9$, $3 \rightarrow 5 \rightarrow 9$ and $4 \rightarrow 5 \rightarrow 9$) that actor 5 has three 2-step connections to actor 9 (element 5,9 of A^2 equals 3 referring to $5 \rightarrow 7 \rightarrow 9$, $5 \rightarrow 8 \rightarrow 9$ and $5 \rightarrow 10 \rightarrow 9$), that actor 1 has three 3-step connections to actor 9 (element 1,9 of A^3 equals 3 referring to $1 \rightarrow 5 \rightarrow 7 \rightarrow 9$, $1 \rightarrow 5 \rightarrow 8 \rightarrow 9$, and $1 \rightarrow 5 \rightarrow 10 \rightarrow 9$), and that actor 6 has no 2-step or 3-step connections to any actors (row six of A^2 and A^3 is all 0's). The total number of connections involving N or fewer steps between each pair of actors is given as the sum of adjacency matrices raised to successive powers:

$$
Z = A + A^2 + A^3 + \cdots + A^N,
\tag{2.3}
$$

and the connection involving the minimum number of steps between each pair of actors is given as

$$
Z = A + A^{*2} A^{*3} + \cdots + A^{*N},
\tag{2.4}
$$

where A^{*n} equals A^n with all nonzero elements set equal to n except those elements (j,i) set equal to 0 because element (j,i) is nonzero in A raised to a power less than n and the diagonal elements (j,j) set equal to 0. Equation (2.4) is often preferred to Eq. (2.3) as an operationalization of relational form since it excludes redundant connections. In Figure 2.1, for example, the 2-step advice connection $1 \rightarrow 5 \rightarrow 9$ is contained within the 5-step advice connection $1 \rightarrow 5$

$\to$ 9 $\to$ 8 $\to$ 7 $\to$ 9. Discussed in terms of reachability and connectivity, z_{ji} in Eq. (2.4) is termed the "path distance" from j to i in graph theory. A nonzero path distance from j to some actor i means that i is "reachable" from j. For example, the matrix of path distances for the advice network in Figure 2.1 is given as

$$
\begin{matrix}
0 & 0 & 0 & 0 & 1 & 0 & 2 & 2 & 2 & 2 \\
0 & 0 & 0 & 0 & 1 & 0 & 2 & 2 & 2 & 2 \\
0 & 0 & 0 & 0 & 1 & 0 & 2 & 2 & 2 & 2 \\
0 & 0 & 0 & 0 & 1 & 0 & 2 & 2 & 2 & 2 \\
0 & 0 & 0 & 0 & 0 & 0 & 1 & 1 & 1 & 1 \\
0 & 0 & 0 & 0 & 0 & 0 & 0 & 0 & 0 & 0 \\
0 & 0 & 0 & 0 & 0 & 0 & 0 & 1 & 1 & 1 \\
0 & 0 & 0 & 0 & 0 & 0 & 1 & 0 & 1 & 1 \\
0 & 0 & 0 & 0 & 0 & 0 & 1 & 1 & 0 & 1 \\
0 & 0 & 0 & 0 & 0 & 0 & 1 & 1 & 1 & 0 \\
\end{matrix}
$$

which shows, among other things, that actors 1 through 4 cannot be reached in any number of steps by any actors. Harary, Norman, and Cartwright (1965:110–158) discuss matrix manipulations of the adjacency matrix. In keeping with the popularity of these measures of relational form, however, there are several discussions building more directly on the original network concerns in the Festinger and Luce and Perry articles (e.g., Coleman 1964:444–455; Barnes 1969; Mitchell 1969; Peay 1974, 1976; Doreian 1974).

Various methods have been used to normalize the connections generated by Eqs. (2.3) and (2.4). These normalizations are usually intended to improve the substantive meaning of operationalized relational form.

Katz (1953) and Hubbell (1965) normalize relations generated by Eq. (2.3). Katz proposed that the 1's in the adjacency matrix be replaced with a fraction so that the elements in A raised to successive powers would be decreasing. In this manner, relations composed of many steps would be smaller than those composed of few steps. Eliminating the arbitrary fraction, Hubbell proposed that the adjacency matrix be normalized so that each actor's choices summed to a total of 1 (e.g., $0 \leq a_{ji} \leq 1$, $\Sigma_i a_{ji} = 1$).[5] Again, successive powers of A will have elements with decreasing magnitudes. However, there is no need now to raise A to successive powers since the sum in Eq. (2.3), when continued past A^N to A^∞ and added to an (N,N) identity matrix, converges to the following solution: $(I - A)^{-1} = Z$. There are special conditions required in A before this convergence is guaranteed (see footnote 5). Since the sum here includes an identity matrix, z_{jj} will not be 0. The element z_{ji} will vary from 0 to 1 as the total

---

[5]This normalization, however, includes an additional column beyond the N actors in a system. That final column, labeled E for exogenous system inputs, is deleted here since such inputs are not typically considered in network models. The exogenous inputs are a consideration in computing the inverse matrix $(I - A)^{-1}$ as the limit of summed powers (Hubbell 1965:384–385).

direct and indirect connection from actor j to actor i. Hubbell's measure of total relation remains the most elegant, although rarely used, measure of relational form.

Given the redundant connections in Eq. (2.3), the cost of raising A to all powers less than N, or problems in meeting the conditions under which such a sum of powers converges on Hubbell's analytical solution, relations are often normalized path distances (Eq. [2.4]). For example, Laumann and his colleagues usually subject path distances to a smallest space analysis in order to more directly capture the essential features of the strength of relations (Laumann & Pappi 1976; Laumann et al. 1974; Laumann et al. 1977). In the resulting space, actor j is close to actor i to the extent that he requires fewer steps to reach i than is required to connect other actors. Alba and Kadushin (1976) use path distances to measure relational strength in terms of overlapping social circles. Actor j is close to actor i to the extent that they both can reach the same persons in chains of less than a specified number of steps. Both of these normalizations are based on symmetric, binary choices. An alternative is to normalize path distances by the number of actors j can reach at each number of steps.

I have found one such normalization to be informative. The relation z_{ji} is a monotonic, nonlinear function of the path distance from actor j to actor i; the relation's intensity decreases with increasing path distance. An actor's connection to himself is a maximum strength relation. Let z_{jj} equal 1. His connection to actors separated from him by infinite path distances is a minimum strength relation. Let z_{ji} equal 0 for all actors i that j cannot reach in any number of steps. Given these anchors for the maximum and minimum values of z_{ji}, the rate of change in z_{ji} with increasing choice links separating i from j can be drawn from research on human perception. That research demonstrates the limited ability of persons to retain information past a boundary level of stimulation and an inverse ability to discriminate differences in levels of stimulation as the absolute level of stimulation approaches the boundary level (e.g., Haber 1968; Simon 1974). The total set of actors to whom actor j has nonzero path distances can be discussed as his social circle. Let the proportion of actors in this social circle receiving interaction from j be a level of stimulation for actor j. Assume that j interacts with others as a function of his path distances to them in the sense that he is most likely to interact with those to whom he has a direct connection, most likely next to interact with those to whom he has a 2-step connection, and so on. Given interaction as an energy-consuming stimulation for actor j, the probability of his initiating interaction with a new person decreases to the extent that he is already interacting with the bulk of the people in his social circle. The strength of his relation to actor i could be expected to decrease in proportion to the number of persons closer to him than i. Let the N path distances from j be rank ordered from lowest to highest so that f_{ji} is the number of actors that actor j can reach in fewer or equal to the number of steps he requires to reach i. The strength of the relation from j to i can now be given as 1 minus the ratio of the number of actors with whom j would interact if he interacts with i (f_{ji}) over the number of actors with whom j might interact (the number of actors he can reach including himself, n_j):

$$z_{ji} = \begin{cases} 1, & \text{if } j = i \\ 1 - (f_{ji}/n_j), & \text{if } j \text{ can reach } i \\ 0, & \text{if } j \text{ cannot reach } i. \end{cases} \qquad (2.5)$$

The strength of the relation from j to i will be close to 1 to the extent that j can reach i in fewer steps than he requires to reach other actors. For example, actor 2 is connected to five others in the advice network in Figure 2.1 while actor 9 is connected to three others; $n_2 = 6$ and $n_9 = 4$. Since there are three actors that actor 9 can reach in the number of steps he requires to reach actor 7, the relation from him to 7 is .25 ($z_{97} = 1 - \frac{3}{4}$). There is only one actor that actor 2 can reach in one step, so his relation to actor 5 is .83 ($z_{25} = 1 - \frac{1}{6}$). Since he can reach five actors in the number of steps (or fewer) that he requires to reach actor 9, his relation to 9 is .17 ($z_{29} = 1 - \frac{5}{6}$). These relations reflect the fact that actor 5 is much closer to actor 2 than are other actors in actor 2's social circle: The relation from 2 to 5 is stronger than the relation from 9 to one of his peers, actor 7 ($z_{25} = .83 > .25 = z_{97}$), even though both relations are based on direct connections ($a_{51} = 1 = a_{97}$). In other words, the important characteristic of relational form here is not the absolute number of steps j requires in order to reach i, but rather the location of i in actor j's social circle. The decision to interact with a specific actor can be viewed as a marginal decision in the following sense: From an initial path distance for which $z_{ji} = .5$, increases in the number of steps j requires to reach i will result in smaller and smaller decreases in z_{ji} as it approaches its minimum of 0.0. From the same point, decreases in the number of steps j requires to reach i will result in smaller and smaller increases z_{ji} as it approaches its maximum of 1.0. As the path distance from j to actor i approaches its limits either at the center or the boundary of his social circle, there is decreasing change in the strength of his relation to i Since it captures indirect connections implied by intitial choice data and normalizes connections in terms of each actor's social circle so that path distances can be compared to a known minimum/maximum of 0/1 across actors, Eq. (2.5) will be used to measure relational form in subsequent chapters when relations are to be derived from sociometric choice data.

2.2 MODELS IN SIX MODES OF NETWORK ANALYSIS

As a device for organizing the many models purporting to describe relations in one or more Z matrices, I have found it useful to refer to a sixfold typology defined by two axes—the aggregation of actors in a unit of analysis versus the

TABLE 2.1
Concepts of Network Structure within Each of Six Modes of Network Analysis

Analytical approaches	Actor aggregation in a unit of analysis		
	Actor	Multiple actors as a network subgroup	Multiple actors/ subgroups as a structured system
Relational	Ego network as extensive, dense and/or multiplex (Section 2.3)	Primary group as a network clique: a set of actors connected by cohesive relations (Section 2.5)	System structure as dense and/or transitive (Section 2.7)
Positional	Occupant of a network position as central and/or prestigious (Section 2.4)	Status/role-set as a network position: a set of structurally equivalent actors (Section 2.6)	System structure as a stratification of status/role-sets (Section 2.8)

frame of reference within which actors are analyzed. As an overview of network models, Table 2.1 presents types of models in each of the six analytical modes.

Three levels of aggregation are distinguished across Table 2.1. At the highest level, some network models treat relations among all actors in a system as a single unit of analysis. Other models describe the relations in which one actor is involved so that the individual is the unit of analysis. Between these extremes there are models that aggregate actors into network subgroups so that subgroups within a system can be compared as units of analysis.

At each level of aggregation, Table 2.1 distinguishes two analytical approaches within which network models have been proposed. Without going into the details that are the substance of this chapter, I shall note that these two approaches differ in the frame of reference within which an actor is analyzed. In a "relational" approach, network models describe the intensity of relationship between pairs of actors. Network models within a "positional" approach describe the pattern of relations defining an actor's position in a system of actors. The relational approach fosters models in which an actor's involvement in one or a few relations can be described without attending to his many other relations. The positional approach fosters models in which an actor is one of many in a system of interconnected actors in the sense that all defined relations in which he is involved must be considered.

Models in both the relational and positional approaches purport to describe networks of relations, but they do so from the perspective of very different intellectual traditions. By focusing on aspects of social differentiation emphasized in these different traditions, the relational approach generates network models that are quite distinct from those generated by the positional approach. At the individual level of aggregation (first column in Table 2.1), the relations to be described are those in which actor j is involved, the $2NK$ elements in rows and columns j of the K networks $Z_1, Z_2, \ldots, Z_K$. There is a long history of network models that generate a score for actor j describing some aspect of these relations. Models of ego-networks have been developed from the relational perspective (Section 2.3) while the positional approach has offered models of network positions (Section 2.4). From the one or more networks in a system, an (N, N) symmetric matrix of criterion links between actors can be generated such that a subset of actors can be identified as a network subgroup. Where these aggregated actors are socially homophilous in the sense of having similar perceptions, attitudes, beliefs, and so on, the specific criterion used to aggregate actors will depend on how relations are assumed to generate homophily. Perhaps for this reason, the different conceptual foundations of the relational versus positional approaches are most apparent in their aggregation of actors into network subgroups. The relational approach offers models of the primary group as a network clique (Section 2.5). The positional approach offers models of the status/role-set duality as a jointly occupied network position (Section 2.6). Finally, there are network models that describe the structure of relations among all actors in a system. Building within a relational approach, there are models of system density and transitivity (Section 2.7). Relations among actors in dyads and triads are described by these models without reference to the overall relational patterns in which actors are involved. Building within a positional approach, there are stratification models of system social structure as interlocking status/role-sets (Section 2.8).

2.3 THE EGO-NETWORK

The network for which actor j is ego consists of all persons with whom j has a direct relation and the relations among these persons. Since relations in a system are only considered when they are present for a specific actor as ego, models of these relations describe an ego-network anchored on a single actor (Mitchell 1969:12–15). Such network models are also discussed as primary stars, primary zones, first-order zones, and personal networks.[6] They can be anchored on any aggregation of persons as an actor, for example, families (e.g., Bott 1957) or corporations (e.g., see Chapter 4). To some extent, Moreno (1934) adumbrates subsequent work with his network analysis of the social atom centered around a specific person. Models of ego-networks have been most extensively developed, however, by anthropologists extending sociometry in order to conduct empirical research on large populations (see reviews by Barnes 1969, 1972; Mitchell 1969, 1974; Wolfe 1970; Boissevain & Mitchell 1973; Boissevain 1974; Whitten & Wolfe 1973). Since the actor on whom an

---

[6]The most popular of these alternative labels is "personal' network. I have avoided this label in order to avoid the connotation that ego-networks must be anchored on persons as actors.

ego-network is anchored can be treated as a randomly selected survey respondent, models of ego-networks have become popular in sociology, especially for
describing the social psychology of urban life (Laumann 1973; Fischer *et al.*
1977; Verbrugge 1977, 1979; Wellman 1979).

Among the many aspects of ego-networks that the above reviews discuss,
three are widely used—range, density, and multiplexity. More often than not,
models capturing these aspects are used to measure the extent to which ego can
rely on his network for social support. An ego-network has range to the extent
that it includes a diversity of actors as ego's contacts. This diversity can be
captured as the social heterogeneity and/or number of actors in the network
(e.g., Mitchell 1969:19–20; Burt 1982b). An ego-network is dense to the extent
that all actors in it are connected by intense relations. Where the network
contains n actors, its density in regard to the kth type of relation is the mean
such relation between separate actors in the network:

$$(\sum_i \sum_j z_{jik})/n(n-1), \qquad (2.6)$$

for all N actors $i \neq j$ in a network where z_{ji} increases with the strength of j's
proportion of possible relations that are observed (cf. Kephart 1950; Barnes
1969:63–64). For example, advice relations in the ego-network of actor 2 in
Figure 2.1 have a density of .17 since the network is composed of three actors
(2, 5, and 6) among whom there is one of a possible six relations (2 cites 5 but
he does not cite 6 and although 6 claims 2 as a friend, neither 5 nor 6 cite 2 as a
source of advice). Since the five actors with whom 9 is directly connected tend
to have direct connections with one another, 9's ego-network has a higher
density of advice relations ($16/30 = .53$). Moving to the overlap of relations, an
actor's network is multiplex to the extent that he has multiple types of relations
to each actor in the network. For example, the connection from j to i would be
multiplex if i is j's friend, is a source of advice, is a blood relative, and so on.
The connection would be uniplex if only one of the ties existed. Actor j's
network has high multiplexity to the extent that he is connected to a high portion
of actors in the network by multiple types of relations:

$$(\sum_i z_{ji(m)})/(n-1), \qquad (2.7)$$

for all actors i in j's network where $z_{ji(m)}$ is 0 unless j has more than one type of
relation to i, whereupon it equals 1 (cf. Kapferer 1969:226 on star multiplexity).
For example, actor 2 in Figure 2.1 has no multiplexity in his network while
actor 9 has high multiplexity ($3/5 = .6$); three of his friends are also sources of
advice.

2.4 THE NETWORK POSITION

Actor j's network position consists of all his relations with the N actors in a
system. It differs from his ego-network principally because the relations he does

not have to others in a system are as important as the relations he has, the latter defining his ego-network. Within a single network operationalized as Z, actor j's ego-network consists of the nonnegligible elements in row and column j. His network position is defined by all $2N$ elements in the row and column. This involves a change in frame of reference from j's immediate contacts to some larger system of actors. Since the concept of network position depends on clearly defined system boundaries, it is not surprising to find that models of the relations defining a network position have been developed from Moreno's proposed area of sociometry by social psychologists analyzing small systems with clearly defined boundaries such as classrooms or laboratory groups (see reviews by Moreno 1960; Glanzer & Glaser 1959, 1961; Bonacich 1972a; Leik & Meeker 1975:84–91; Freeman 1979).[7]

For the most part, models describing the relations that define a network position have been used as measures of social integration. An actor is "isolated" on the periphery of a system if he has no relations with others in the system. Two models have been used extensively to describe socially "integrated" actors—centrality and prestige. Although occasionally used interchangeably in empirical research (cf. Coleman et al. 1966; Becker 1970), these two terms usually refer to distinct network models.[8]

Models of position centrality in a network stem from the analysis of communication networks by Bavelas (1948, 1950) and Leavitt (1951). An actor's position is central to the extent that all relations in the network involve him. One measure of this is the proportion of the sum of relations in a network that involve actor j:

$$\sum_i (z_{ji} + z_{ij}) / (\sum_i \sum_j z_{ji}), \qquad (2.8)$$

for all N actors $i \neq j$ in a network where z_{ji} increases with the strength of j's relation to i. For binary relations, this equation is the proportion of all relations

---

[7]Similarly, when anthropologists working with ego-networks analyze systems sufficiently small to allow relations among all actors in a system to be described in a matrix Z, the whole system is often taken as a frame of reference. For example, Kapferer (1969:222) analyzes ego-network span as z_e/z_t; the proportion of all relations among actors in a system (z_t) that appear in the ego-network (z_e). More generally, Barnes (1969, 1972) distinguishes "zones" (the first order zone corresponding to an ego network), "partial networks" (corresponding to a single Z matrix), and the "total network" (corresponding to all system Z matrices).

[8]There are, of course, other types of network positions. Section 2.6 offers further discussion of types of positions; however, a particularly well-known position for which there is no model other than a definition is the broker. An actor occupies a position as a network broker to the extent that he is the only connection between two subgroups (cf. Freeman's 1977 discussion of centrality as betweenness). Discussed as a bridge in graph theory (Harary et al. 1965:194–223), the broker has substantive importance as a communication link between groups within which information might flow but between which it would not flow without him (see Granovetter 1973; Boissevain 1974:147–169 for substantive discussion). In Figure 2.1, for example, actors 1 through 4 have no advice connection with actors 7 through 10 except through actor 5. Actor 5 could act as a broker between the two groups.

in a network that involve actor j.[9] For example, actor 5 is most central and actor 6 is least central in the advice network of Figure 2.1. Of the twenty relations in the network, eight involve actor 5 (for a centrality score of 8/20 or .40) while actor 6 is involved in no relations. The majority of centrality models, however, operationalize relations in terms of path distances where z_{ji} is the minimum number of binary links required by j to reach i [Eq. (2.4)]. As the basis for Eq. (2.8), Bavelas' (1950) widely used centrality model is the ratio of the sum of all path distances among actors in a network divided by the sum of path distances from j to each actor i.[10] Similarly describing symmetric path distances, Freeman (1977, 1979) proposes what is perhaps the most conceptually satisfying model of the original Bavelas centrality concept. An actor's position is central to the extent that he is "between" any two actors who wish to contact one another. Betweenness is captured by geodesics where a geodesic from j to i is any chain of links equal to the path distance from j to i. Although there is only one path distance from j to i, there can be many indirect connections as geodesics. Deleting the direct advice link from actor 5 to actor 9 in Figure 2.1, for example, would result in three geodesics from 5 to 9 equal to the path distance of two (5 $\rightarrow$ 7 $\rightarrow$ 9, 5 $\rightarrow$ 8 $\rightarrow$ 9 and 5 $\rightarrow$ 10 $\rightarrow$ 9). An actor j is between two others i and t to the extent that all geodesics from i to t involve j: $\Sigma_i \Sigma_j (2g_{itj}/g_{it})/(N^2 - 3N + 2)$, for all actors $i < t, i \neq j \neq t$ in the network of N actors where g_{it} is the number of geodesics from actor i to actor t and g_{itj} is the number of those connections that involve actor j. This model has the advantages of a meaningful metric (varying from 0 as no centrality to 1 as maximum centrality) and applicability in networks where some actors cannot be reached by others.[11] It has the disadvantages of being restricted to binary, symmetric choice data and treating as equally peripheral an actor who is an isolate and an actor who is a peer in a completely connected network (see footnote 12).

There are other models of centrality in which an actor's position is central to the extent that he has strong relations with others. In some, an actor is central to the extent that he is reachable as in Eq. (2.3) (e.g., Nieminin 1974; Freeman 1979). In others, an actor is central to the extent that he has low path distances to others as in Eq. (2.4) (e.g., Beauchamp 1965; Nieminin 1973; Moxley &

[9] Extending the numerator in Eq. (2.8) to include relations between the actors connected to j, anthropologists have discussed this concept as network span (cf. Kapferer 1969:222, 1972).

[10] Also describing symmetric path distances in a network, Laumann & Pappi (1976) analyze an actor's integrative centrality as the extent to which he occupies the centroid in a smallest space analysis of the path distances. The centroid is the geometric center of the space and is occupied by an actor whose distances to others in a network are, on average, lower than any other actor's path distances. In this sense, the Laumann and Pappi concept of integrative centrality is quite similar to the classic Bavelas centrality concept.

[11] As a substantive advantage, Freeman's centrality model offers a monotonic association between centrality and work satisfaction where that association is nonmonotonic, using the original Bavelas model (see Freeman 1977:40). Moreover, his betweenness model has a much stronger association with recognition of central leaders and work satisfaction than does the original model in a replication of the original experiment (Freeman, Roeder, and Mulholland 1980).

Moxley 1974; Freeman 1979). These models should be interpreted with caution since they do not discriminate between an actor who is central in a network as discussed previously and an actor who is a peer in a completely connected network.[12]

Models of position prestige in a network stem from Moreno's analysis of popularity as the extent to which an actor is the object of strong relations.[13] More precisely, an actor's position has prestige to the extent that he is the object of strong relations from other actors who themselves have prestige. A measure of actor j's prestige in this sense is the sum of each actor i's prestige (p_i) weighted by the strength of his relation to j (z_{ij}):

$$p_j = \sum_i p_i z_{ij} \qquad (2.9)$$

In matrix form, Eq. (2.9) is given as $P' = P'Z$ so that

$$0 = P'(Z + I), \qquad (2.10)$$

where P is a vector of N prestige scores and Z is an (N,N) matrix of relations where z_{ji} increases with the strength of relation from actor j to actor i. Let the relations in Z be normalized in some manner so that the matrix is row stochastic $(0 \le z_{ji} \le 1, \Sigma_i z_{ji} = 1)$. Equation (2.10) is then the well-known characteristic equation for Z, and the vector of prestige scores can be computed as the left-hand eigenvector corresponding to the maximum eigenvalue of Z (which is 1 since Z is row stochastic). If Z cannot be normalized easily into a row stochastic form, prestige scores can still be obtained by introducing a variable

[12]Flament (1963:51) raises the question of how to describe centrality in a completely connected network. He criticizes Bavelas' model describing network centrality (as opposed to position centrality) since it does not discriminate between a completely connected network and a circle network. As illustration, consider a five-actor network of symmetric, binary relations among persons 1, 2, 3, 4, and j. If j has no relations, he will not be described as central under any of the available models; he can reach no other actors in the network and he is not involved in any of the network relations. At the other extreme, if the only relations in the network are those linking j to each other person (a star network), then j is maximally central under most models; he can reach all other actors in a minimal number of steps and he is involved in all of the network's relations so that Eq. (2.8) and Freeman's model equal 1. A problem rises when all five persons are directly connected. In this case, Eq. (2.8) gives actor j a centrality score of .4, showing that he is not an isolate, but neither is he central. Under Freeman's model, actor j is a centrality of 0 as if he were isolated. There are direct connections between actors so no one is required to go through j in order to reach any other actor. As in the star network, however, actor j is able to reach all other actors in a minimum number of steps. Under reachability or closeness models of centrality, therefore, an actor who is involved in all relations can have the same centrality as an actor who is involved in a small fraction of all relations.

[13]What I am discussing as the prestige of a network position is often discussed as the status of a person following Moreno's social psychological concern with the social deference given a person. In order to facilitate the discussion of a diversity of network models, I reserve the label "status" for a significant position in social structure (Section 2.6) and discuss the deference given to occupants of the position as prestige.

eigenvalue into Eq. (2.10) so that it is given as (cf. Bonacich 1972a): $0 = P'(Z - \lambda I)$.

There are two well-known models in which Z is analyzed as the row stochastic matrix in (2.10)—one for sociometric choice data and one for joint involvement data. Hubbell (1965) provides the most elegant discussion in regard to choice data. Begin with a normalized adjacency matrix ($0 \leq a_{ji} \leq 1$, Σ_i $a_{ji} = 1$). Drawing on Leontief's input–output model, Hubbell (1965:382) states prestige to be a function of exogenous inputs to the system (a vector of N inputs, E) and the weighted sum of choices with prestige ($A'P$) so that $P = E + A'P$.[14] This equation can be rewritten as $P' = E' + P'A$ so that $-E' = P'(A - I)$. Since exogenous inputs to a system of actors are almost never given, E is usually a null vector ($e_i = 0$), which makes Hubbell's expression identical to Eq. (2.10) given A as an operationalization of Z. The prestige of actor j will be high to the extent that he is the object of direct relations from many actors who are themselves the object of direct relations from many actors. Coleman (1966, 1972, 1973) provides the most elegant discussion in regard to actor's joint involvement in events. Given a system of N actors and a set of events over which the actors have partial control and in which they have partial interest, z_{ji} is the extent to which actor j is interested in events controlled by actor i. The Z matrix composed of the z_{ji} is row stochastic where elements in row j show the proportion of actor j's interests that is controlled by each other actor in the system (cf. Eq. [2.1] with Coleman 1973:73). Coleman considers an actor powerful (in the sense of having extensive resources) to the extent that he controls events of interest to each actor i (z_{ij}), who is in turn powerful (r_i) in the system (Coleman 1966: 627, 1972:148, 1973:78–79); $r_j = \Sigma_i r_i z_{ij}$. When the symbol for resources, r, is replaced with the symbol for prestige, p, this expression is identical to Eq. (2.9). In other words, Coleman's model of power can be viewed as a network model of prestige. So viewed, an actor has prestige to the extent that he controls events of interest to prestigious actors. Although stated for actors involved in events, this model extends in a natural manner to describe sociometric data as well (e.g., Burt 1979b; Taylor & Coleman 1979).

There are some models in which prestige is the extent to which an actor is merely the object of strong relations from others. Although less elegant than Eq. (2.10), these models are more easily used in research. Again, Hubbell provides a convenient model. His prestige model, $P = E + A'P$, can be rewritten as $P'(I - A) = E'$, so that prestige is given as $P' = E'(I - A)^{-1}$. As discussed in

---

[14]Following Moreno, Hubbell discusses prestige as status, so his vector S corresponds to P. Another difference in notation between Hubbell's discussion and that given here is his treatment of an adjacency matrix as column stochastic rather than row stochastic where w_{ij} is the normalized choice from j to i (i.e., his matrix W is A'). As a more significant difference, the adjacency matrix is forced to be row stochastic here in the absence of exogenous inputs (see footnote 5). Without this constraint, the presence of isolates in the network would not be acceptable.

Section 2.1, this inverted matrix is one operationalization of Z. Specifically the (i, j)th element of $(I - A)^{-1}$ is the sum of direct and indirect connections from actor i to actor j. If exogenous system inputs are assumed equal for each actor, E can be replaced with a unit vector ($e_i = 1$) so that actor j's prestige is the sum of direct and indirect relations in which he is the object (cf. Hubbell 1965:383); $p_j = \Sigma_i z_{ij}$. Variations on this model include choice status as the ratio of total relations for which actor j is the object over the total possible (e.g., Moreno 1934:98–103; Arney 1973) and reachability as the extent to which all actors in the network have direct, or very short indirect, ties to actor j (e.g., Katz 1953; Taylor 1969; Lin 1976:340–349). A further variation is discussed below in which multiple dimensions of prestige are distinguished in terms of the asymmetry of relations defining a status and the extent to which the status' role set is similar to an actor's relational pattern (Section 2.6).

2.5 THE NETWORK CLIQUE

Operationalizing the classic concept of a primary group, the clique is a set of actors in a network who are connected to one another by strong relations. As introduced in Cooley's (1909) discussion of families, play-groups, and communities, the primary group is "characterized by intimate face-to-face association and cooperation. . . . The result of intimate association, psychologically, is a certain fusion of individualities in a common whole, so that one's very self, for many purposes at least, is the common life and purpose of the group [pp. 23ff]." Current network models of cliques capture primary groups as described by Festinger et al. (1950) and Homans (1950). Analyzing friendship networks, Festinger et al. (1950) state: "The more cohesive the group, that is, the more friendship ties there are within the group, and the more active the process of communication which goes on within the group, the greater will be the effect of the process of communication in producing uniformity of attitudes, opinions, and behavior [p. 175]." Analyzing friendships and antagonisms, Homans (1950) states a similar conclusion in terms of his now well known proposition: "the more frequently persons interact with one another, the stronger their sentiments of friendship for one another are apt to be [pp. 133–136]." Subsequent models follow these two substantively successful works. As representatively stated by Cartwright and Zander (1968), "a group is a collection of individuals who have relations to one another that make them interdependent to some significant degree [p. 46]" (cf. reviews by Lott & Lott 1965; Collins & Raven 1968:119–126; Homans 1968). Although models of cliques have utility in macrolevel studies of elites (e.g., Domhoff 1970) and have been discussed in reference to actors outside the clique (e.g., Stein 1976) and have been described as cohesive to the extent that clique members prefer intraclique to interclique relations (e.g., Cartwright 1968, Alba 1973), the models themselves are stated in terms of the strength of relations among clique members without reference to the strength of ties outside the clique.[15]

The criterion for aggregating actors together as a clique is typically based on sociometric choice data (or other relations transformed to binary form) interpreted in terms of graph theory. As defined in graph theory (e.g., Harary 1969), a clique is a "maximal complete subgraph [p. 207]." Actors a, b, and c define a clique if they are connected by mutual, maximum strength relations where no further actor can be added to the clique without loosing this property of strong mutual ties (cf. Luce & Perry 1949; Festinger et al. 1950:144). In other words, actors i and j can be aggregated together in a clique if z_{ji} and z_{ij} are both maximum strength:

$$z_{ij} = \text{maximum}, \qquad z_{ji} = \text{maximum}. \tag{2.11}$$

For binary data, this means that every member of a clique cites every other member. The advice network in Figure 2.1 contains only one clique under Eq. (2.11), actors 7, 8, 9, and 10. Actor 5 cannot be included in it since none of its members reciprocate his citations. Although clear and corresponding to a commonsense understanding of a face-to-face group, restricting cliques to maximal complete subgraphs is too limited for empirical research (for more detailed discussion, see Alba & Moore 1978).

Rather than require maximum strength relations between all clique members, the majority of clique models require that the minimum relation between any two members of a clique be stronger than some criterion α.[16] Cliques are still maximal in the sense that they include all actors in a system who can be

---

[15]Most clique models are not concerned with interclique relations (see review by Arabie 1977), although there are some efforts to minimize positive ties between cliques (e.g., Spilerman 1966; Davis 1967) and some efforts to use occasional interclique relations to create a hierarchy of cliques (see footnote 38). An obvious exception is the factor analytic clique model in which clique members have similar relations with actors outside the clique. Such subgroups are actually an ersatz status as discussed below in reference to Eqs. (2.13) and (2.15). Nevertheless, it is possible for an actor to be a member of multiple cliques. Interclique relations have been discussed in terms of overlapping subgroups (e.g., Alba & Kadushin 1976; Alba & Moore 1978); however, such models require some subgroup model before they can describe subgroup overlap, and the subgroup model typically focuses on intragroup relations.

[16]Rather than weakening the strength of relations within a clique directly, Seidman and Foster (1978) relax the complete subgraph model by weakening the number of clique members that must be connected by maximum strength relations. A k-plex clique is one in which each member has maximum strength relations with all but k members of the clique. Since it allows less variability in the relations among clique members, the k-plex model generates cliques with more predictable internal structure. Seidman and Foster's k-plex model is in accord with the operationalization used to capture Kadushin's (1966, 1968) concept of a social circle. A social circle is a set of actors with similar interests having direct or minimally indirect relations with one another. Social circles have been operationalized, however, in terms of overlapping strong components (Alba & Kadushin 1976; Alba & Moore 1978). Although each actor in the social circle model need not have a maximum strength relation with each other actor in the circle, he is required to have such relations with a large proportion of the actors (Alba & Moore 1978:174).

aggregated together without some pair having a relation lower than the criterion. In other words, actors i and j can be aggregated together into a clique if z_{ij} or z_{ji}, whichever is smaller, is stronger than some criterion:

$$\text{minimum } (z_{ij}, z_{ji}) > \alpha. \qquad (2.12)$$

Relaxing the graph theoretic clique concept, for example, Doreian (1969) suggests that continuous relations in a network be dichotomized so that z_{ij} is 0 unless it is greater than some criterion level, whereupon it is one. He then uses Eq. (2.11) to define cliques. In this case, cliques conform to Eq. (2.12) since z_{ij} and z_{ji} will both equal 1 (maximum strength) only if the smaller of the two is greater than the criterion level. This treatment of (2.12) is discussed as a complete-link or diameter aggregation of actors since the weakest relation between any pair of actors in the clique (i.e., the diameter of the clique) is greater than α (e.g., Johnson 1967; Peay 1974; Baker & Hubert 1976; Arabie 1977). Graph theory can offer a multitude of plausible definitions for the criterion (e.g., Hubert 1974). A particularly well-known criterion is used by Luce (1950) to define the n-clique. A set of actors is an n-clique if relations between each pair of actors are measured as 1 over path distances and conform to Eq. (2.12) where $\alpha = 1/(n + 1)$ and no additional actor can be added to the clique without violating (2.12). In other words, all members of an n-clique can reach one another in n or fewer binary links. Since it is possible for a pair of actors in an n-clique to be connected by a geodesic of n or fewer links that goes through actors outside the clique (a point noted by Luce [1950] and Spilerman [1966]), Alba (1973) further restricts the clique to be an n-clique where every pair of members is connected by a geodesic composed solely of other clique members.[17]

Each of the above cliques are special cases of the general subgroup termed a "maximal strong component" in graph theory. A set of actors falls within this subgroup if every actor is reachable from every other actor in the set and no additional actor can be included in the set without destroying the intraclique mutual reachability (e.g., Harary et al. 1965:53–55). For example, a three-person group is a strong component if $1 \rightarrow 2$, $2 \rightarrow 3$ and $3 \rightarrow 1$, but it is not a strong component if $1 \rightarrow 2$, $1 \rightarrow 3$ and $2 \rightarrow 3$ since person 1 cannot be reached by 2 or 3. Where relations are measured as path distances, in other words, actors i and j can be aggregated together in a clique as a strong component if Eq. (2.12) is true for them where $\alpha = 0$. Although the strong component model allows extensive variation in the internal structure of cliques, it is the basis for

[17]Alba (1973) defines his restriction of the n-clique model as "a maximal subgraph of diameter n [p.120]." This is the largest group of actors that can be aggregated as a network subgroup without any pair of them being separated by a path distance greater than n. Mokken (1979) discusses such a group as an n-club and shows that it is not equivalent to Alba's restriction of the n-clique, which he discusses as an n-clan. By ignoring the requirement that subgroups be maximal, Boyle (1969:105) defines a third type of clique contained in the class described by Alba. Boyle defines a clique simply to include all persons on the geodesic(s) between j and i when j and i are both in the clique.

Hubbell's (1965) theoretically elegant clique model and has been fruitfully employed in substantive research (Laumann & Pappi 1976:104ff; Laumann & Marsden 1979).[18]

2.6 THE JOINTLY OCCUPIED NETWORK POSITION

Operationalizing the classic status/role-set duality, the jointly occupied network position is a set of structurally equivalent actors. The actors are structurally equivalent in the sense of having similar relations with the occupants of each status in the system. Since I shall use models of the status/role-set duality to capture the social context of action in subsequent chapters (for reasons that will accumulate throughout the chapter and will be summarized in the conclusion), I discuss it here in some detail.

Status and Role-Set as Dual Aspects of Position

As introduced in Linton's (1936:113ff) discussion of social differentiation, status and role are a duality between a pattern of behaviors and relations with other actors (role) and the rights and duties defined by the pattern (status). The multiple role relations (role-set) defining a status emphasize not only the fact that an actor has multiple relations in a system, but also that these relations are often varied and potentially conflicting (Merton 1957a).[19] All statuses are

[18]A still more sweeping class of subgroups is defined by the maximal weak component model. A set of actors is a maximal weak component if each pair of actors is at least asymmetrically reachable (z_{kj} or z_{ji} is greater than 0 when measured as path distances) and no additional actor can be included in the subgroup without destroying the intraclique asymmetric reachability (e.g., Harary et al. 1965:53–55). In Figure 2.1, for example, all actors except 6 are members of a single advice clique as a maximal weak component. Of course, all strong components are also weak components. Although useful in describing sparse networks, the weak component model allows so much variation in the internal structure of cliques that it is rarely offered as a network model per se (see Killworth & Bernard 1976 on "snowballs" as an interesting exception). Describing cliques in terms of multidimensional scaling is similarly ambiguous. In a smallest space representation of relations, for example, a set of actors will be close in the space to the extent that their relations with one another are higher than their relations with actors outside the set (e.g., Levine 1972; Laumann & Pappi 1976; Burt 1976b; Laumann et al. 1977). Since the strength of relations among actors aggregated into a clique under the maximal weak component model or multidimensional scaling model is enormously variable, analyses that rely on these models to describe social differentiation should be interpreted with caution (cf. Levine 1972:25–26).

[19]By linking the concept of role-set to a single status, Merton distinguishes his conception from Linton's (1936) idea of the multiple roles fulfilled by an individual: "Every individual has a series of rôles deriving from the various patterns in which he participates and at the same time a rôle, general, which represents the sum total of these rôles and determines what he does for his society and what he can expect from it [p.114]." In other words, Linton acknowledges the multiple, potentially conflicting, roles in which a person can be involved as a result of the different statuses he occupies. Merton goes one step further by emphasizing the possibly conflicting role relations that define a single status.

network positions in the sense of being defined by patterns of relations linking status occupants with other actors in a system. As stated by Linton (1936), "a status, in the abstract, is a position in a particular pattern [p. 113]." As repeated in his review many years later, Sarbin (1954) notes that "whatever agreement has been attained in the use of the term role centers around the organized actions of a person coordinate with a given status or position [p. 225]" (cf. Catton 1964; Sarbin & Allen 1968). However, not all relational patterns defining positions in turn define statuses. A position only constitutes a status when its constituent relations define rights and duties uniquely significant within a system. When a position is a status, then its relational pattern can be discussed as a role-set. In short, status and role-set are different features of a particularly significant position; the status is the rights and duties involved in the performance of the relational pattern (role-set) defining the position. There is a symbiotic tie between status and role-set as a duality, one being given in terms of the other. As emphasized in Linton's (1936) original discussion:

> A rôle represents the dynamic aspect of a status. The individual is socially assigned to a status and occupies it with relation to other statuses. When he puts the rights and duties which constitute the status into effect, he is performing a rôle. Rôle and status are quite inseparable, and the distinction between them is of only academic interest. There are no rôles without statuses or statuses without rôles [p. 114].

Specialization and Aggregation of Relational Patterns

A division of labor within a system distinguishes the relational patterns involving individuals as significant in two processes of social differentiation. The division of labor itself adds to the postulate of purposive action given in Chapter 1 by focusing on a particular type of action—interaction. It implies that what was once whole is now divided so that systems of interdependent actors exist—the performance of increasing types of interdependent activities by a single actor not in itself constituting a division of labor.[20] Beyond a mere increase in the density of relations, this division of labor ensures that patterns of particularly significant relations develop so as to socially differentiate actors. Particular relations acquire a special significance through specialization and aggregation. The division of labor ensures that the production of a given commodity requires particular input commodities so that stable relations occur between suppliers and consumers in specialized chains of production. For example, a member of a small tribe who finds that he can support himself by producing bows and arrows does not have identical relations with all members of the tribe in the pursuit of his occupation. He might require arrowheads from one individual, timber from another, and consumption of his goods by hunters in the

---

[20]In *The Wealth of Nations*, for example, Smith (1776:4–5) discusses the absence of a division of labor in the manufacture of pins when a single individual performs all tasks in the production process.

tribe. The relational pattern linking him to other tribe members can be viewed in either of two ways. It defines his network position as a member of the tribe. However, it also defines the position of "maker of bows and arrows" within the tribe. The individual has, in the sense meaning, ceased to be just any member of the tribe. He is a type of member, a forerunner of the modern armaments manufacturer who depends on steel and chemical manufacturers for the commodities he uses as inputs and on government bureaucracies for consumption of his product. However, merely occupying a position defined by a specialized relational pattern need not make the pattern a status defining role-set. Although manifest in the relational patterns among individuals, status defining role-sets are not in general reducible to relations between individual actors (cf. Levi-Strauss 1953:525, 541–542).[21] Rather, they are composed of relations that occur repeatedly in a system so as to constrain and give unique opportunities to the actors involved in them (cf. Radcliffe-Brown 1940:191–192). The repeated occurrence of a specialized relational pattern entails an aggregation of actors into types. For example, instead of the single armaments manufacturer given above, the repeated occurrence of his relational pattern means that there are multiple actors involved in the same pattern. In this sense of being involved in the same relational pattern, the armaments manufacturers are structurally equivalent with one another. They occupy a single network position defined by their common relational pattern. In short, the specialization of relational patterns in a division of labor combined with a resulting aggregation of actors in a single position defined by the pattern gives the position a special significance.[22] Accordingly, a network position jointly occupied by multiple structurally equivalent actors constitutes a status and the actors's relational patterns indicate the status's role-set.

Structurally Equivalent Relational Patterns

Specialization and aggregation ensure social differentiation within a system of actors; each actor's relational pattern will be differentially similar to each other actor's pattern. Borrowing the topological concept of equivalence (e.g., Kelley 1955:9–10); Lorrain and White (1971, especially p. 63) discuss two actors as structurally equivalent if they have identical relations with all actors in a system. This is a strong criterion of equivalence. Two actors i and j are structurally

----

[21] As suggested by Nadel (1957) in his theory of social structure, these role relations "operate in that strategic area where individual behavior becomes social conduct [p. 20]."

[22] These processes of specialization and aggregation are clearly emphasized in indices of a division of labor proposed by Gibbs and his colleagues (e.g., Gibbs & Martin 1962; Gibbs & Poston 1975). They give attention both to the separation of positions in social structure as well as the number of persons occupying each position, respectively, as "structural" versus "distributive" differentiation.

equivalent under this criterion when the Euclidean distance between their respective network positions is 0:

$$d_{ij} = 0, \tag{2.13}$$

where distance is symmetric and equal to the square root of the sum of squared differences in corresponding relations defining the two actors' respective positions:

$$d_{ij} = d_{ji} = \left\{ \sum_{k=1}^{K} \sum_{q=1}^{N} \left[(z_{iqk} - z_{jqk})^2 + (z_{qik} - z_{qjk})^2 \right] \right\}^{\frac{1}{2}}, \tag{2.14}$$

given the relation from actor j to actor q in network k as z_{jqk}. Equation (2.14) defines an (N, N) matrix D in which actors structurally equivalent under a strong criterion are separated by zero distance.[23]

A jointly occupied network position can now be defined as a maximal set of structurally equivalent actors. A network position jointly occupied by three or more actors can be discussed as a status S. The arbitrary criterion of three actors is taken from a similar convention in clique models. The occupants of a status jointly occupy a single network position in the sense that each of them is involved in the same relational pattern. The role-set defining a status is then the typical pattern of relations linking its occupants with one another and the occupants of other statuses.

Figure 2.1 provides useful illustration here. Let relations be operationalized in terms of direct and indirect relations involving no more than one intermediary. As given in Section 2.1, the number of 1- and 2-step connections leading from actor j to actor i is the (j, i)th element in $Z = A + A^2$. Advice and

---

[23]Equation (2.14) makes several assumptions about the manner in which relations involving actors i and j contribute to the distance between them (see Burt 1976b, 1977b). Perhaps the most glaring assumption is that each actor is given equal weight in determining distance. This assumption can be eliminated without greatly complicating Eq. (2.14). Let Z_j be the $2NK$ column vector composed of all relations in which actor j is involved, the NK relations to him (i.e., the z_{qjk}) and the NK relations he directs toward others (i.e., the z_{jqk}). Equation (2.14) can be given in terms of Z_j and the corresponding vector for actor i, Z_i, as

$$d_{ij} = d_{ji} = [(Z_j - Z_i)' (Z_j - Z_i)]^{1/2},$$

or more generally as

$$d_{ij} = d_{ji} = [(Z_j - Z_i)' W(Z_j - Z_i)]^{1/2},$$

where the $(2NK, 2NK)$ matrix W is an identity matrix. By changing the elements in W, differential importance can be given to different actors in determining distances. For example, it seems reasonable to say that relations involving prestigious actors are more important than relations involving peripheral actors. The distance between actors i and j may be greater if they have different relations with prestigious actors than if they have different relations with peripheral actors. Such a weighted distance can be generated from the above equation by replacing the diagonal elements of W with prestige scores; $p_q = w_{qq} = w_{(q+N,q+N)}$, where p_q is a prestige score for actor q. There are many alternative conditions in terms of which weights in W can be stated (e.g., Cronbach & Gleser 1953: 467–471); however, I have used the less sophisticated distance in Eq. (2.14) because it corresponds directly to the meaning of structural equivalence under a strong criterion, and I do not have a critical substantive reason for complicating the equation.

TABLE 2.2
Example Relations for the Two-Network System in Figure 2.1 and the Distances They Generate

Actor	Advice relations (z_{ji1})	Friendship relations (z_{ji2})	Distances (d_{ji})
1	0 0 0 0 1 0 1 1 1 1	0 0 0 0 0 0 0 0 0 0	0.0
2	0 0 0 0 1 0 1 1 1 1	0 0 0 0 0 0 0 0 0 0	0.0 0.0
3	0 0 0 0 1 0 1 1 1 1	0 0 0 0 0 0 0 0 0 0	0.0 0.0 0.0
4	0 0 0 0 1 0 1 1 1 1	0 0 0 0 0 0 0 0 0 0	0.0 0.0 0.0 0.0
5	0 0 0 0 0 0 4 4 4 4	1 1 1 1 0 1 0 0 0 0	7.2 7.2 7.2 7.2 0.0
6	0 0 0 0 0 0 0 0 0 0	1 1 1 1 0 0 0 0 0 0	6.8 6.8 6.8 6.8 11.6 0.0
7	0 0 0 0 0 0 3 3 3 3	1 1 1 1 0 4 3 3 3 3	12.1 12.1 12.1 12.1 11.7 12.2 0.0
8	0 0 0 0 0 0 3 3 3 3	1 1 1 1 0 4 3 3 3 3	12.1 12.1 12.1 12.1 11.7 12.2 0.0 0.0
9	0 0 0 0 0 0 3 3 3 3	1 1 1 1 0 4 3 3 3 3	12.1 12.1 12.1 12.1 11.7 12.2 0.0 0.0 0.0
10	0 0 0 0 0 0 3 3 3 3	1 1 1 1 0 4 3 3 3 3	12.1 12.1 12.1 12.1 11.7 12.2 0.0 0.0 0.0 0.0

[a]Relations are the number of direct and 2-step connections from one actor to another ($Z_1 = A_1 + A_1^2$ and $Z_2 = A_2 + A_2^2$). Distances are computed from the relations according to Eq. (2.14).

friendship relations, respectively, for Figure 2.1 are given in Table 2.2. Also given there are distances between the ten relational patterns defined across both networks of relations (Eq. [2.14]).

The zero distances in Table 2.2 show that there are two statuses in the system, S_1 jointly occupied by actors 1 through 4 and S_2 jointly occupied by actors 7 through 10. The role-set defining each status is therefore composed of six typical relations among actors within each of the two networks: relations from occupants of the other status, relations among status occupants, and relations to occupants of the other status. Consider the role-set defining status S_2. Within the advice network it involves the typical relation from the occupants of S_1 (all these relations are 1), the typical relation among occupants of S_2 (all these relations are 3), and the typical relation to the occupants of S_1 (all these relations are 0). Within the friendship network it involves the same three typical relations respectively observed as 0, 3, and 1. Across the two networks then, the role-set defining status S_2 is given as the vector $(1 \ 3 \ 0 \ 0 \ 3 \ 1)$ representing the vector of role relations $(z_{121} \ z_{221} \ z_{211} \ z_{122} \ z_{222} \ z_{122})$ where z_{ijk} is the typical relation from occupants of status S_i to occupants of S_j within network k. The order of elements here is arbitrary as long as it is consistent across role-sets (see Section 2.8 on role-sets in density tables and blockmodels).

Note the absence of relations among the occupants of status S_1. Actors 1 through 4 are neither connected by advice nor friendship relations. In contrast to cliques as subgroups composed of actors connected by strong relations, network positions can be jointly occupied by actors who may (e.g., S_2 is a maximal complete subgraph in both networks) or may not (e.g., S_1) have strong relations with one another. If, as has been argued by some (e.g., MacRae 1960; Boyle 1969), actors in a cohesive clique can be expected to have similar relations with actors outside the clique, then a clique is merely a special type of jointly occupied position. Such a view of cliques is reexamined in the concluding section. This is an important extension of the clique model since it explicitly brings into network models nonclique statuses, statuses occupied by actors whose similarity is defined by their common relations to actors external to the status rather than their intrastatus relations. Such statuses have been discussed under various labels as quasi-groups (Ginsberg 1934:40), latent groups (Olson 1965:50), leveling coalitions (Thoden van Velzen 1973:241–242), and latent corporate actors (Burt 1975) and are discussed below as secondary statuses in the treatment of prestige.

Equation (2.13) is an incomplete model of the status/role-set duality. There are good reasons for expecting two occupants of a single status not to be structurally equivalent under a strong criterion. Obviously, random errors and arbitrary decisions in measuring relations could result in the ostensible nonequivalence of status occupants. More importantly, statuses should not be defined too strictly in terms of relations among individual actors. Given two actors occupying the same status, there is no reason to expect them both to perform their role relations in an identical manner. As discussed at length by Firth

(1951) and Nadel (1957, especially pp. 136–141), the different ways in which different people perform the same role relation will guarantee variability in observed relations reflecting a single role. This variability is not random error in observing the role so much as it is legitimate variability necessary to ensure continued role behaviors. An interdisciplinary group of colleagues at Harvard put the matter quite succinctly (Parsons & Shils 1951):

> An important feature of a large proportion of social roles is that the actions which make them up are not minutely prescribed and that a certain range of variability is regarded as legitimate. Sanctions are not invoked against deviance within certain limits. This range of freedom makes it possible for actors with different personalities to fulfill within considerable limits the expectations associated with roughly the same roles without undue strain [p. 24].

With these empirical and theoretical considerations in mind, it is not surprising to find that network models of the status/role-set duality have relied on a weak criterion of structural equivalence. Actors i and j are structurally equivalent under a weak criterion when the distance between their respective network positions is negligible:

$$d_{ij} \leq \alpha, \tag{2.15}$$

where alpha is an arbitrary criterion of negligible distance, usually selected on the basis of some hierarchical clustering algorithm (e.g., see Chapter 3).

Clearly, the weakness of the criterion under which a status is jointly occupied increases the ambiguity of its occupants's structural equivalence. If alpha is set at 12.2 in Table 2.2, for example, then all ten actors are structurally equivalent under Eq. (2.15), even though there is considerable social differentiation in the system. In order to avoid aggregating significantly nonequivalent actors together under a weak criterion, their structural equivalence can be assessed as a statistical hypothesis (see Section 2.9).

In addition, the relations among individual actors need not equal relations between status jointly occupied under Eq. (2.15). However, interstatus densities offer an obvious correction for this. Where n_a and n_b, respectively, are the number of actors occupying statuses $\mathbf{S}_a$ and $\mathbf{S}_b$, the typical relation in network k from occupants of $\mathbf{S}_a$ to occupants of $\mathbf{S}_b$ can be described as the mean relation, or density of relations, from one status to the other;

$$z_{abk} = \sum_{j=1}^{n_a} \sum_{q=1}^{n_b} z_{jqk}/(n_a n_b), \tag{2.16a}$$

and the intrastatus relations among occupants of $\mathbf{S}_a$ can be described as (cf. Eq. [2.6])

$$z_{aak} = \sum_{j=1}^{n_a} \sum_{i=1}^{n_a} z_{jik}/n_a(n_a - 1), \qquad j \neq i \tag{2.16b}$$

where summation is over all actors i, j occuying status $\mathbf{S}_a$ and actors q occupying status $\mathbf{S}_b$. Since these aggregate relations refer to (n_a by n_b) and (n_a by n_a) blocks of relations, White et al. (1976) propose that they be discussed as "block" relations (not to be confused with blocks in graph theory, Harary 1969:26ff). Network models composed of such relations are discussed in Section 2.8.

There are other models of structural equivalence under a weak criterion. These models rely on an eigenvalue decomposition of proximities into sub-groups.[24] MacRae (1960) and Wright and Evitts (1961) propose a direct decomposition of relational patterns. Although occasionally discussed as clique models (e.g., Lankford 1974), their direct factor analysis model was anticipated and proposed as a position model (e.g., Glanzer & Glaser 1959:326; Wright & Evitts 1961:85–86). They are cliques only if clique members are required to be structurally equivalent, that is to say, have similar relations with actors outside the clique (MacRae 1960:361; 'cf. Boyle 1969:102). Each subgroup corresponds to an eigenvalue, and members of the subgroup have high positive entries in the eigenvector corresponding to their subgroup's eigenvalue. For a given subgroup, some actors are members because they are similarly the object of relations from others as given by high positive elements in an eigenvector V in the characteristic equation $0 = (Z'Z - \lambda I)V$, and some actors are members because they have similar relations to others as given by high positive elements in an eigenvector U in the equation $0 = (ZZ' - \lambda I)U$. In these equations, actors i and j will be "chooser" members of a subgroup to the extent that the (i,j)th element of ZZ', which is $\Sigma_q z_{iq} z_{jq}$, is high, and they will be "chosen" members of the subgroup to the extent that the same element of ZZ', which is $\Sigma_q z_{qi} z_{qj}$, is high. Note that the product term $z_{iq} z_{jq}$ or $z_{qi} z_{qj}$ is 0 when actor q has a relation with i or j but not with both actors. In other words, the extent to which actors i and j have relations with different actors is obliterated by the cross-products matrices analyzed by MacRae and Wright and Evitts. The (i,j)th element of these matrices is 0 if i and j are isolates or if they have relations with completely different actors. This problem is eliminated by using correlations rather than

---

[24]Yet another approach involves relaxing the definition of strong equivalence. This approach has not been used in substantive work and provides no statistical model for testing structural equivalence as discussed in Section 2.9; however, it deserves notice since it more directly captures the status/role-set duality. Several alternatives are discussed by White (1982). For example, Sailer (1978) iteratively computes distances so as to capture the extent to which actors are similarly related to structurally equivalent actors. The asymmetric coefficient b_{ij} is the extent to which actor j is "structurally related" to i in the sense that the structurally equivalent actors who have relations with i similarly have relations with j. In a different and more general perspective, Mandel and Winship (1979) explicitly redefine equivalence in a theoretically important manner: Two actors who have different relational patterns but occupy similar types of positions can be treated as equivalent. For example, two persons who are leaders in separate cliques have different relational patterns yet they occupy equivalent types of positions as leaders. The symmetric distance coefficient $P(R_i, R_j)$ is low to the extent that for each of actor i's direct and indirect relations to actor k there are relations from j that are similarly direct and involve similar patterns of indirect ties. White (1982) discusses this approach to structural equivalence in detail.

cross-products. Katz (1947) and Bock and Husain (1950) use the correlations between elements in rows i and j of Z to measure the extent to which actors i and j have similar relations to others in the network. Alternatively, elements of columns i and j could be correlated to measure the similarity in relations to i and j (e.g., Breiger, Boorman, and Arabie 1975; White, Boorman, and Breiger 1976; Arabie, Boorman, and Levitt 1978). It is an obvious extension to correlate the elements in rows and columns i, j so that r_{ji} measures the extent to which actors i and j are involved in the same relations. Given correlations between actor positions, the (N,N) correlation matrix could be decomposed where actors i and j are structurally equivalent to the extent that they have high positive elements in the same eigenvector W; $(R - \lambda I)W = 0$. Like the direct factor model, however, this model is biased toward overstating equivalence. The widely cited article by Cronbach and Gleser (1953) provides detailed discussion of why Euclidean distances are preferred measures of pattern similarity. Figure 2.1 can provide illustration. Where relations are operationalized as $Z = A + A^2$, consider the patterns of advice relations to actors 6, 7, 8 ($z_{i6} z_{i7} z_{i8}$) for three actors i, 2, 5, and 9. As given in Table 2.2, the relational patterns for actors 2, 5, and 9, respectively, are (0 1 1), (0 4 4), and (0 3 3). All three actors have no connections to the isolate (actor 6) but different numbers of connections to the clique members; actor 2 has only one connection to 7 and 8, while actor 5 has four connections. When covariances are used to compare relational patterns, means are held constant and the three patterns are compared as ($-.7$ .3 .3), (-2.7 1.3 1.3), and (-2 1 1). The previously nonoverlapping patterns are now overlapping; all three actors have an above average number of connections to the clique members and a below average number to the isolate. When correlations are used to compare relational patterns, means and variances are held constant so that the above patterns appear as (-1.2 .6 .6), (-1.2 .6 .6), and (-1.2 .6 .6). All three patterns appear to be identical. In other words, the differences in the relational patterns linking 2, 5, and 9 to actors 6 through 8 have been destroyed by removing what Cronbach and Gleser term the "level" and the "dispersion" in the patterns.

To summarize these alternative models then, they are biased in the sense of ignoring aspects of relational pattern. This bias varies across different measures of relations but results in an overestimation of structural equivalence to the extent that it exists. Accordingly, extreme caution is required in interpreting the role sets generated by the above models—especially if they are presented without tests of the structural equivalence of status occupants.

Differences in capturing distance notwithstanding, all of the above models have in common their treatment of distance as a quality of dissimilarity in two relational patterns defining network positions. This concept is analytically distinct from the concept of social distance, usually attributed to Bogardus (e.g., 1925), in which persons occupying separate positions (e.g., occupational statuses) are separated by social distance to the extent that they do not have, or wish to have, intimate relations with one another (see reviews by Laumann

1966; McFarland & Brown 1973; Laumann & Senter 1976). Although some network models do discuss the strength of relations between two actors as social distance (e.g., Wright & Evitts 1961; Foster & Horvath 1971; Bernard & Killworth 1973), this practice is not recommended since it introduces unnecessary ambiguity into a general discussion of network models (e.g., McFarland and Brown [1973] juggle two concepts of distance). Rather, the Bogardus concept of social distance and the graph theoretic concept of path distance can be treated as measures of relational strength. This frees the concept of distance to refer unambiguously to the dissimilarity of two position defining relational patterns.[25]

Prestige: Primary versus Secondary Relational Forms

More than ensuring social differentiation through the specialization and aggregation of relational patterns, a division of labor ensures social differentiation through the concentration of control over valued commodities as resources. Occupying each of the statuses created in a division of labor are actors controlling status-specific types of commodities as their property. For example, the armaments manufacturer used as an illustration previously would control those commodities necessary to the production of armaments from his typical input commodities. In regard to individuals, Blau (1974:627) points to the "bifurcation of skills" as a parameter in social differentiation. If the activities defining a status rely on extensive skills, a person occupying the status is likely to possess those skills. Skills in this sense are a type of commodity concentrated in the status. Interview a reputable surgeon and you are likely to find that he has had years of medical training. Interview a university professor and you are likely to find that she has had several years of post-graduate training. The property typically associated with occupants of a status varies across statuses in two important ways—value and coordination.

To the extent that some commodity concentrated among occupants of status **S** is highly valued within a network (e.g., medical expertise in a network of advice seeking relations among physicians), the relational pattern of its occupants within the network has a predictable asymmetry. Occupants of the status can go to one another for exchange relations, but actors not occupying the status would be expected to have unreciprocated exchange relations directed at the occupants. I shall discuss this asymmetric pattern as primary since it indicates that occupants of a position control some commodity that they do not require from others but that others require from them. While control is concentrated in the hands of actors occupying status **S**, there typically will be other actors not occupying the status who do not control the commodity but rely on its control by

---

[25]I focus on two relational forms of central importance to describing stratification; however, there are a great many interesting forms to consider. Marsden (1982b) describes a general method for characterizing role-set form.

occupants of **S** and in some cases help in exercising control, for example, secretaries, graduate students, law clerks, fans of an entertainment star, social hangers-on, domestic servants, mistresses, clients, the protagonist's side-kick, and so on. Examples of such positions are discussed by Coser (1974) and in several articles reprinted in Schmidt, Scott, Landé, and Guasti (1977). These actors are unlikely to be the object of exchange relations seeking the commodity since its control is concentrated in the hands of actors occupying **S**. Additionality, these actors will typically direct unreciprocated relations toward the occupants of **S** since they rely on those actors for the status's commodity. I shall discuss such a relational pattern as secondary since it indicates that occupants of a position require some commodity from occupants of other status(es) and are not themselves the object of relations seeking the commodity.

When the commodities valued in one network are controlled by the same actors as the commodities valued in other networks, then the control of valued commodities can be treated as coordinated across different types of relations. The relational pattern of status occupants within one network need not have the same form that it does in other networks. A commodity valued within one network need not be highly valued in another. However, when the role-set defining a status has a primary form, then its occupants represent a coordination of valued commodities across the networks in a system.

Such a status is prestigious within its system. Its occupants represent an oligopoly of control over commodities highly valued in the system's multiple networks. This oligopoly has reached a point where the occupants only seek out one another in relationships but are themselves the object of strong relations they do not reciprocate from many actors occupying other statuses. The role-set defining a status is given by the relational patterns in which its occupants are involved so that a status is prestigious to the extent that actors involved in relational patterns with primary form have low distance from the status. Conversely, an actor involved in a relational pattern similar to the role-set defining a prestigious status has prestige of the type conferred by occupying the status. This ostensible circularity, statuses deriving prestige from actors and conferring prestige on actors, requires a more explicit statement of primary and secondary relational forms.

Primary form differs from secondary form in two key aspects of relational pattern, prominence and structural equivalence. Actors involved in a relational pattern with primary form are prominent (in the sense of being the object of relations from many other actors) but only initiate relations with actors structurally equivalent to themselves. Actors involved in a relational pattern with secondary form are not prominent (in the sense that no actors direct relations at them) and initiate relations with actors structurally nonequivalent to themselves (since their relations are directed at actors who are the object of extensive relations within a system).

Within network k, let these two key aspects for actor j's relational pattern be referenced $prom_{jk}$ and $self_{jk}$, respectively. The extent to which actor j is prominent within the network is given by the extent to which he is the object of strong relations as discussed previously under prestige models. The index

$$\text{prom}_{jk} = \sum_i z_{ijk}/N$$

varies from 0 to 1 as the extent to which actor j is the object of strong relations from all actors in network k where z_{ijk} is a measure of relational form ranging from 0 to 1 [e.g., sociometric citations or some normalization of chain relations such as Eq. (2.5)]. Actor j only initiates interaction within the network with actors structurally equivalent to himself to the extent that the z_{jik} are directed at actors i who are separated from him by zero distance within the network. The index

$$\text{self}_{jk} = \sum_i (1 - z_{jik})d_{ijk}/(\sum_i d_{ijk})$$

varies from 0 to 1 as the extent to which actor j only has nonzero relations to actors structurally equivalent to himself within the network (i.e., actors i for whom the product $d_{ijk}z_{jik}$ is 0). Intranetwork distances are given by Eq. (2.14) where there is no summation across networks (i.e., $K = 1$). A relational pattern has primary form to the extent that both of these equations equals 1 so that the product

$$(\text{prom}_{jk}) \, (\text{self}_{jk}), \qquad (2.17)$$

equals 1 when actor j's relational pattern within network k conforms perfectly to the idealized primary form. Similarly, a relational pattern has secondary form to the extent that both of the above indices equal 0 so that the product

$$(1 - \text{prom}_{jk}) \, (1 - \text{self}_{jk}), \qquad (2.18)$$

equals 1 when actor j's relational pattern within network k conforms perfectly to the idealized secondary form.

To the extent that status $\mathbf{S}$ is jointly occupied by actors having relational patterns with primary form in each of K networks, its role-set has primary form and the status is prestigious. An index of the status's prestige is then given as the expected value of Eq. (2.17) across the K networks in a system and the n actors occupying the status:[26]

$$p_s = \sum_j^n [p_j/n] = \sum_j [\sum_k (\text{prom}_{jk}) \, (\text{self}_{jk})/Kn], \qquad (2.19)$$

where p_j is the primary form in actor j's relational pattern defined across all K networks. Equation (2.19) varies from 0 to 1 as the extent to which the role-set

[26]In practice, actors jointly occupy a status under a weak criterion of equivalence so occupants j in Eqs. (2.19) and (2.20) should be weighted by the extent to which their relational patterns define their status's role-set. Coefficients for this are discussed under hypothesis testing.

defining status **S** conforms perfectly to the idealized primary form. A similar index measuring the extent to which the status's role-set conforms perfectly to the idealized secondary form is given as the expected value of Eq. (2.18) across networks and status occupants:

$$s_s = \sum_j^n [s_j/n] = \sum_j [\sum_k (1 - \text{prom}_{jk}) \, (1 - \text{self}_{jk})/Kn]. \qquad (2.20)$$

In terms of these indices, status **S** is prestigious to the extent that its role-set has high primary form (p_s close to 1) and low secondary form (s_s close to 0). If the status is jointly occupied under a strong criterion of structural equivalence, then actor j's distance to the status, d_{js} is equal to his distance from any of its occupants. This point is developed for statuses jointly occupied under a weak criterion in Section 2.9 below. To the extent that actor j has low distance from status **S** and the status is prestigious, the relational pattern in which he is involved has a primary form similar to that found in the role-set defining the status. In other words, distance from a prestigious status is negatively correlated with being involved in a relational pattern of the prestige represented by the role-set defining the status. Assuming this negative correlation to be perfect (selecting the simplest representation given no information suggesting an alternative), actor j's prestige in reference to prestigious status **S** is given as his lack of distance from the status:

$$p_{js} = -d_{js} \qquad (2.21)$$

where his distance from the status is derived from his distances to its occupants given by Eq. (2.14). Equation (2.21) is not intended as a direct measure of the primary form to be found in an actor's relational pattern. Such a measure of prestige is given directly by p_j in Eq. (2.19). While p_j expresses the extent to which actor j's relational pattern has the abstract property of primary form, Eq. (2.21) captures the extent to which his relational pattern is similar to the role-set defining a prestigious status in his system. Since it is in reference to such statuses that prestige is conferred within a system (as opposed to being conferred in reference to my conception of primary relational form), it is in reference to such statuses that actor prestige should be expressed. Not incidently, Eq. (2.21) provides a structural conception of multiple dimensions of prestige within a system; actor j can have prestige in regard to two or more prestigious statuses. Numerical illustration helps communicate this point.

First, Table 2.3 illustrates the use of Eqs. (2.19) and (2.20) in detecting prestigious statuses. Values of the primary and secondary form in the role-sets defining the two statuses stratifying Figure 2.1 are presented. Intranetwork distances have been computed from the relations in Table 2.2, and the z_{jik} in prom_{jk} and self_{jk} are the relations in Table 2.2 normalized by their maximum for each actor in each network (e.g., the maximum strength friendship relation from

TABLE 2.3
Primary and Secondary Form in the Role-Sets Defining S_1 and S_2 in the Two-Network System in Figure 2.1[a]

	Statuses	
	S_1	S_2
Primary form		
p_s	.15	.55
$r_{d_{js}p_j}$	.84	−.99
Secondary Form		
s_s	.48	.11
$r_{d_{js}s_j}$	−.91	.85

[a]Measures of role-set form are given in Eqs. (2.19) and (2.20).

actor 7 is 4 so that his normalized relations in the network are given as $z_{7i2}/4$).[27] Table 2.3 shows that the role-set defining status S_2 has a primary form while that defining S_1 has a secondary form. However, neither role-set conforms perfectly to an idealized relational form. For status S_1, p_{s_1} is low (.15) while s_{s_1} is high (.48). Status S_2 is prestigious in the sense that p_{s_2} is high (.55) while s_{s_2} is low (.11). The correlations between relational form and distance to S_2 offer a more compelling justification for labeling the status as prestigious. Those actors involved in relational patterns with high primary form have low distance to S_2 ($r_{d_{js_2}p_j} = -.99$), while those whose relational patterns have high secondary form are distant from the status ($r_{d_{js_2}s_j} = .85$). The reason that the role-set of this status does not have a perfect primary form is clear from the relations in Table 2.2. Within the advice network, occupants of status S_2 are the object of strong relations from others and only have relations with one another. There is high primary form in their advice relations (p_s based on advice relations is .90). However, in the friendship network, they are only the object of relations from one another and direct relations to actors not occupying their status as well as to one another (p_s based on friendship relations is .20). Since there is only one prestigious status in the system, actor prestige can be given in terms of primary form in his relational pattern [p_j in Eq. (2.19)] or in terms of his lack of distance from the prestigious status [p_{js_2} in Eq. (2.21)]. The two measures will be highly correlated. For this example the correlation between p_j and p_{js_2} is .99.

Table 2.4 illustrates the structural basis for multiple dimensions of prestige. Table 2.4 presents two patterns of typical relations among occupants of four

---

[27]The intranetwork distances themselves are given in Table 2.7 in the discussion of hypothesis testing.

TABLE 2.4
Illustration of One and Two Prestige Dimensions

Prestige as low distance from status S_1

	S_1	S_2	S_3	S_4
S_1	1	0	0	0
S_2	1	1	0	0
S_3	1	1	1	0
S_4	1	1	1	1

Prestige as low distance to statuses S_1 and/or S_2

	S_1	S_2	S_3	S_4
S_1	1	0	0	0
S_2	0	1	0	0
S_3	1	1	1	0
S_4	1	1	1	1

[a]Cell (i,j) is zero if there are no nonzero relations from the occupants of status S_i to the occupants of status S_j.

statuses in two systems. The upper table presents a system with one dimension of prestige. Status S_1 is most prestigious since its occupants are the object of relations from all other statuses, but these relations are not reciprocated beyond occupants of the status. The remaining three statuses form a perfect hierarchy in the sense that occupants of S_2 are the object of relations from S_3 and S_4 but themselves only cite one another and the occupants of S_1, and the occupants of statuses S_3 and S_4 similarly cite one another or occupants of statuses having higher prestige. The distances of each status from S_1 are given by Eq. (2.14) as 0, 1.4, 2.0, and 2.5, respectively, for S_1, S_2, S_3, and S_4. The four statuses therefore have the following prestige order under Eq. (2.21): $p_1 > p_2 > p_3 > p_4$. The lower part of the table presents a system with two dimensions of prestige. The occupants of S_2 no longer direct relations at occupants of status S_1. In this system, statuses S_1 and S_2 are defined by role-sets with equivalently high primary form. Using S_1 as a reference status, distances from it yield one prestige ordering under Eq. (2.21), $p_1 > p_3 > p_2 > p_4$. Distances from status S_2, however, yield a different prestige ordering, $p_2 > p_3 > p_1 > p_4$. There are no grounds for choosing one ordering over the other; making such a choice or somehow averaging the prestige levels would misrepresent the distribution of prestige. What the two orderings demonstrate is that two dimensions of prestige exist in the system. Occupying status S_1 involves high prestige as does occupying S_2. But the respective prestige of actors occupying the two statuses is qualitatively different. In the same manner that the occupational status of doctor is prestigious in a sense different from that in which the status of astronaut is prestigious (both having high prestige), actors occupying S_1 at the bottom of

Table 2.4 are prestigious in a sense other than the sense in which those occupying S_2 are prestigious. In general, there are as many dimensions of prestige in a system as there are statuses defined by role-sets with high primary form. Like the prestige models discussed in Section 2.4, prestige here is defined only up to a limit of proportionality; actor j's lack of distance to a prestigious status has meaning only in comparison to some other actor's distance from the status.[28] In contrast to the usual models, prestige here is conceptualized as a potentially multidimensional phenomenon refering to oligopolistic control of commodities valued across multiple networks of relations in a system.

2.7 NETWORK DENSITY AND TRANSITIVITY

Leaving network subgroups to proceed to the higher level of aggregation in which all relations among actors in a system are described simultaneously, the relational approach offers models of network density and transitivity. Density is a simple, yet theoretically important, aspect of system structure. To what extent are actors in a system connected, on average, to one another? The concept can be deceptively simple. De Sola Pool and Kochen (1978) explore a variety of network models describing the nature of expected contacts among actors in systems of different sizes and structures (cf. Mahew & Levinger 1976 on the connection between system size and density). For small systems, the mean relation from any one actor to any other actor is the density in Eq. (2.6) when n is replaced by N. Where relations can be transformed into an adjacency matrix, however, two advantages can be obtained by describing network structure in terms of relations among all possible triads of actors:

1. Several substantively interesting aspects of the network's structure can be summarized as combinations of all triads in the network.
2. Hypotheses stated in terms of triad combinations can be subjected to statistical test.

Let the (N,N) matrix of relations in a network be transformed into an adjacency matrix A in which all diagonal elements are 0 and a_{ji} is 0 unless z_{ji} is sufficiently strong to warrant a_{ji} equalling 1. There are $\binom{N}{3}$, or $(N^3 - 3N^2 + 2N)/6$, possible triads of actors. For example, there are 120 possible combinations of three actors in Figure 2.1. However, there are only 16 unique triad structures in any size system (e.g., Harary et al. 1965:18–22). Consider the advice network in Figure 2.1. Although composed of different actors, the triads composed of actors 1, 7, 8 versus 2, 9, 10 have the same triad structure—two

---

[28]This is not true of p_j in Eq. (2.19) since it has a fixed upper and lower bound, both with unambiguous interpretations.

mutual null relations and one mutual strong relation. This is an example of triad three in Table 2.5. The other 15 types of triad structures are listed in Table 2.5 in the order used by Holland and Leinhardt (1975, 1978). The first three columns after the triad structures contain the three numbers Holland and Leinhardt (1970) and Davis and Leinhardt (1972) proposed to "catalogue" triads; the number of mutual strong relations in the triad, the number of asymmetric relations, and the number of mutual null relations. For example, the second triad is the 0–1–2 triad. It contains one asymmetric and two mutual null relations. The frequency with which each of the possible triad structures occurs in a network is referenced by the triad census of the network, a $(16,1)$ vector T in which the ith element t_i is the frequency of the ith type of triad (Holland & Leinhardt 1975). Various combinations of the elements in a network's triad census describe specific

TABLE 2.5
Weights for Network Models of Structures in the Triad Census

		m_i a_i n_i	Balance	Cluster	Ranked cluster	Transitivity
1		0 0 3	N (1)	Y (0)	Y (0)	Y (0,0)
2		0 1 2	− (0)	− (0)	N (1)	Y (0,0)
3		1 0 2	Y (0)	Y (0)	Y (0)	Y (0,0)
4		0 2 1	− (0)	− (0)	Y (0)	Y (0,0)
5		0 2 1	− (0)	− (0)	Y (0)	Y (0,0)
6		0 2 1	− (0)	− (0)	N (1)	N (0,1)
7		1 1 1	− (0)	− (0)	N (1)	N (0,1)
8		1 1 1	− (0)	− (0)	N (1)	N (0,1)
9		0 3 0	− (0)	− (0)	Y (0)	Y (1,0)
10		0 3 0	− (0)	− (0)	N (1)	N (0,3)
11		2 0 1	N (1)	N (1)	N (1)	N (0,2)
12		1 2 0	− (0)	− (0)	Y (0)	Y (2,0)
13		1 2 0	− (0)	− (0)	Y (0)	Y (2,0)
14		1 2 0	− (0)	− (0)	N (1)	N (1,2)
15		2 1 0	− (0)	− (0)	N (1)	N (3,1)
16		3 0 0	Y (0)	Y (0)	Y (0)	Y (6,0)

features of relations in the network. Let U be a $(16,1)$ unit vector of 1's and let W be a $(16,1)$ vector of weights. The sum of the elements of the triad census $(U'T = \Sigma_i t_i)$ equals the number of different combinations of actors possible as triads $\binom{N}{3}$. Let the terms m_i, a_i, and c_i, respectively, refer to the number of mutual strong relations in the ith type of triad, the number of asymmetric relations, and the total number of relations $(c_i = 2m_i + a_i)$. For example, $m_7 = 1$, $a_7 = 1$, and $c_7 = 3$ in Table 2.5. Since each pair of actors occurs in $N - 2$ different triads, the sum $\Sigma_i m_i t_i$ equals $N - 2$ times the number of mutual strong relations in the network, the sum $\Sigma_i a_i t_i$ equals $N - 2$ times the number of asymmetric relations, and the sum $\Sigma_i c_i t_i$ is $N - 2$ times the total number of relations (Holland & Leinhardt 1975). Since there are $N(N - 1)/2$ possible mutual or asymmetric relations in the network and $N(N - 1)$ possible relations, the density of these relations is given as

$$W' T = \sum_i w_i t_i, \tag{2.22}$$

where the ratio of observed to possible mutual strong relations is obtained when $w_i = 2m_i/N(N - 1)(N - 2)$; the ratio of observed to possible asymmetric relations is obtained when $w_i = 2a_i/N(N - 1)(N - 2)$; and the ratio of observed to possible relations generally is obtained when $w_i = c_i/N(N - 1)(N - 2)$.

This information on relational density extending Eq. (2.6) is merely a bonus to the more interesting information the triad census contains regarding four triad models of local structure—the balance model, the cluster model, the ranked cluster model, and the transitivity model. An exegesis of these models and their development is provided by Leik and Meeker (1975:54–73). Drawing on their discussion, Table 2.5 presents the types of triad structures acceptable under each model (Y), structures not acceptable (N), and structures ignored ($-$). As a final item, the table presents a weight vector W that uses the triad census to describe the extent to which a network's structure contradicts each model.

Note that each triad rejected by the transitivity model is rejected or ignored by the other three models. The transitivity model is the most general of the four models and provides the most adequate description of relational data.[29] Nevertheless, it is best understood in terms of its predecessors. All four models are described in terms of the cycles they predict. Within a triad composed of actors 1, 2, and 3, a cycle is a product of three relations in a chain beginning and ending with one actor. For each actor there are two cycles, one moving

---

[29]There are more general triad models available; however, these alternatives have not yet been used as widely to describe observed relations. For example, Cartwright and Harary (1977) discuss quasitransitivity in which partially ordered clusters of actors are allowed. Flament (1963:93–124) discusses the degree of unbalance in a network as the minimum number of relations in the network that must be changed in order to make it balanced. Hallinan and McFarland (1975) and Holland and Leinhardt (1976) give the conditions under which change in a relation will increase the transitivity of a network. Winship (1977a) discusses a model of network balance that describes continuous, rather than binary, z_{ji}. A triad is d-balanced if z_{jq} is less than or equal to the combination of z_{ji} and z_{iq} where relations are combined in alternative manners (e.g., Winship 1977a: 25–26) and the model can be seen as equivalent to the transitivity model (Winship 1977a:35).

clockwise and the other moving counterclockwise around the triad. The two cycles for actor 1 would be $a_{12}a_{23}a_{31}$ and $a_{13}a_{32}a_{21}$. Where null and asymmetric relations can be treated as negative ones when desired (e.g., Davis 1967; Davis & Leinhardt 1972), these cycles will be either positive or negative. As a network model describing the extent to which symmetric, binary relations conform to balance theory (Heider 1958), Cartwright and Harary (1956:278) quote from Heider that there will be no negative cycles in triads within a balanced network. They (1956:286) show that a network is balanced if and only if actors can be separated into two subgroups where all positive relations connect members of the same subgroup and all negative relations connect members of separate subgroups. In this case, all my friends are one another's friends and all the people I dislike are one another's friends and are disliked by my friends. Of the four triad structures composed of symmetric relations (triads 1, 3, 11, and 16 in Table 2.5), the 0–0–3 and 2–0–1 triads are composed entirely of negative cycles where mutual null relations are defined as negative. Since these two triads should not occur in a balanced network, an observed network is unbalanced to the extent that these two structures constitute a high proportion of the total number of triads observed in the network. In terms of the triad census, this ratio is given as[30]

$$W'T/U'T = (t_1 + t_{11})/(\sum_i t_i), \tag{2.23}$$

where the weight vector W contains only two nonzero elements corresponding to the two unbalanced triads (cf. Table 2.5). Davis (1967) extends the balance model to a cluster model. The cluster model too does not allow unbalanced positive relations; however, it does allow unbalanced negative relations. The people I like should like one another, but the people I dislike could dislike one another. This means that multiple clusters of actors can occur as cliques where intracluster relations are positive and intercluster relations are negative. Davis (1967:181–183) shows that a network conforms to the cluster model if and only if there are no triads with a single negative relation. The balance model is extended in the sense that the 0–0–3 triad is now possible as the structure of relations among members of three separate cliques. The only triad rejected by the cluster model is the 2–0–1 triad in which two people who dislike each other both like the same third actor. Lack of fit to the cluster model is then given by

---

[30]I should stress that indices such as (2.23) are rarely used to describe networks. Rather statistical tests are applied directly. In keeping with the other models discussed here, however, I have reserved hypothesis testing for a separate section. There have been nonstatistical efforts to measure aspects of triad structure, however. Equation (2.23) is similar to the measure of network balance proposed by Cartwright and Harary (1956:288) as the ratio of all positive cycles over all cycles. Flament (1963:99) proposes one minus their measure as network imbalance. I have measured imbalance rather than balance because subsequent models allow some triads to occur without expressly predicting that they should occur (they are "vacuously" acceptable), so a test of these models requires assessing the extent to which they are rejected, as opposed to accepted, by observed relations. In keeping with subsequent work, Eq. (2.23) only considers triad cycles rather than cycles of all lengths. Finally, for the balance and cluster models, I have ignored asymmetric relations as ambiguous in the sense that they are neither positive nor negative.

Eq. (2.23) where the weight vector is given in Table 2.5 as containing a single nonzero element ($w_{11} = 1$). Davis and Leinhardt (1972) extend the cluster model to allow asymmetric relations between clusters of different prestige ranks. Among persons of the same prestige rank, the cluster model is assumed to hold. Prestige ranks are ordered if and only if asymmetric relations connect persons on different prestige ranks, the lower directing the relation to the higher, and no mutual relations occur between persons on different prestige ranks. Davis and Leinhardt (1972:225–226) show that the eight triads marked with an "N" in Table 2.5 are rejected by their ranked cluster model. For example, the model predicts that the people I respect as having higher prestige than myself should not respect a peer of mine whom I dislike so that triad 6 is rejected. Using the weight vector W given in Table 2.5 for the ranked cluster model, Eq. (2.23) is the proportion of triads observed in a network that do not conform to the model. Finally, Holland and Leinhardt (1971) generalize the ranked cluster model in terms of the more elegant transitivity model. An adjacency matrix is transitive if and only if $a_{jq} = 1$ whenever $a_{ji} = a_{iq} = 1$ for all actors j, i, and q (e.g., Harary et al. 1965:7). Drawing on some of Heider's remarks concerning the transitivity of balanced relations, Holland and Leinhardt (1971:108–109) suggest that transitivity is an important aspect of network structure. If I like a person and she likes a third person, I too shall like the third person. Whenever a cycle in a triad does not meet the "if" condition of transitivity ($a_{ji} = a_{iq} = 1$ above), then the cycle does not contradict the model and it can be treated as "vacuously" transitive. The transitivity model extends the ranked cluster model because it allows the second triad in Table 2.5 to occur as vacuously transitive. As illustration, consider the tenth triad in Table 2.5—the 0–3–0 triad composed of actors 1, 2, 3 among whom the only positive relations are a_{12}, a_{23}, and a_{31}. Since a_{12} and a_{23} are positive, a_{13} should be positive. The absence of a_{13} means that this cycle is intransitive. The other cycle for actor 1 is vacuously transitive since a_{13} and a_{23} are not both positive. Each actor in the tenth triad is involved in a vacuously transitive and an intransitive cycle so that three of the six cycles in the the triad contradict the transitivity model. Two of the triad types contain cycles that support and reject the transitivity model (triads 14 and 15 in Table 2.5). Even though the fifteenth triad, the 2–1–0 triad, contains an intransitive cycle, it also contains three times as many transitive cycles. This results in three different weight vectors for the transitivity model in terms of cycles. As given elsewhere (Holland & Leinhardt 1971:123, 1975:13; Hallinan 1974a:60, 1974b:371), Table 2.5 presents two numbers for each triad under the transitivity model; (tr_i, in_i) where tr_i and in_i, respectively, are the number of transitive and intransitive cycles in the ith triad (e.g., $\text{tr}_{15} = 3$, $\text{in}_{15} = 1$). If a weight vector W is constructed in which $w_i = \text{tr}_i/6$, Eq. (2.23) will equal the proportion of cycles in a network that are transitive. If $w_i = \text{in}_i/6$, then Eq. (2.23) will equal the proportion of cycles that are intransitive. Arguing that tendencies toward transitivity counteract intransitivities, Hallinan (1974a,b) proposes a weighted transitivity model in which w_i is the extent to which there are more transitive than intransitive cycles in the ith triad. Where $w_i = (\text{tr}_i -$ $\text{in}_i)/6$, Eq. (2.23) will vary between -1 and $+1$ as the proportion of observed cycles by which transitive cycles exceed intransitive cycles. In one sense, this weighted transitivity model extends the transitivity model. The fifteenth triad (2–1–0), rejected by the transitivity model, is acceptable under a weighted model since the number of transitive cycles it contains exceeds its one intransitive cycle.

The density and transitivity models presented here by no means exhaust the network models contained in the triad census (e.g., Holland & Leinhardt 1975:32–37, 1978). However, none of the network models stated in terms of the triad census purport to reduce overall network structure down to triadic structure (e.g., Holland & Leinhardt 1976:317–318, 1978:253–254). Rather, these triad models describe typical relations in which individuals are involved. While describing the extent to which observed relations are consistent with a specific model, they do not describe the extent to which the model is required to describe the data. Given a network known to be perfectly transitive, for example, there are an infinite variety of ranked and unranked structures of subgroups that could be responsible for the transitivity. Consider a network composed of four maximal complete subgraphs as cliques, A, B, C, and D. This network will be perfectly transitive if it has any of the following four structures: (*a*) disconnected (no interclique relations); (*b*) centralized (members of cliques B, C, and D all direct unreciprocated relations to members of clique A); (*c*) factionalized (members of clique B direct unreciprocated relations to members of clique A while clique D is similarly tied to clique C); (*d*) competitive (members of cliques B and D both direct unreciprocated relations to the competing leaders in cliques A and C). These are substantively very different social structures. There are many others equally undistinguished by the transitivity model. This inability to describe more than the typical relations in which individuals are involved is an identification problem. The number of and patterns of relations among subgroups in a network described by the transitivity model are unidentified.[31]

[31]This is not to say that inferences about overall network structure cannot be made from the triad census. For example, a network is disconnected to the extent that its triad census is described by the balance model. Perhaps the most likely inferences to be made about overall network structure from triads concern the positions of individual actors. For example, actors who are brokers or bridges (see footnote 8) are likely to have simultaneously high node transitivity and node intransitivity. Cartwright and Harary (1956:289) define local balance as an actor who is only contained in positive cycles. Killworth (1974:5ff) discusses node transitivity and node intransitivity as the number of transitive and intransitive triads, respectively, for which an actor is a node. Actor i is the node in the definition of transitivity; if $a_{ji} = a_{iq} = 1$, then a_{jq} should be 1. Killworth finds that actors with high node transitivity also have high node intransitivity. He argues that an actor on the edge of a clique in the sense of being a member of the clique but having one or more relations to actors outside the clique is likely to be a node in many 3–0–0 triads (number sixteen in Table 2.5) and therefore have high node transitivity. Because his relations extend outside the clique, however, such an actor is also likely to be a node in many 2–0–1 triads (number eleven in Table 2.5) and therefore have high node intransitivity. As the actors who have relations with members of separate subgroups, brokers correspond to Killworth's idea of actors on the edge of cliques and would be expected to have simultaneously high node transitivity and intransitivity (cf. Granovetter's 1973:1363ff discussion of the 2–0–1 triad as forbidden in the context of bridges between cliques).

2.8 THE SOCIAL STRUCTURE OF NETWORK STRATIFICATION

There are models that explicitly describe the overall structure of networks.
These models build from a positional perspective in the sense that they not only
attend to the intensity of relations between actors, they also attend to the overall
patterns of relations linking actors within and across subgroups. Descriptions of
relational patterns linking the occupants of network positions, these are models
of social structure in the traditional sense (e.g., Sorokin 1927; Linton 1936;
Radcliffe-Brown 1940; Parsons 1951; Levi-Strauss 1953; Nadel 1957, as will
be discussed in Chapter 9). There are models of the extent to which a system is
stratified and models of the status/role-sets in terms of which actors are
stratified.

Inequality Models of the Extent of Stratification

Extent of stratification is captured by network models of hierarchy and
centralization. A system is centralized to the extent that all relations in it
involve a single actor. It has a hierarchical structure to the extent that a single
actor is the direct or indirect object of all relations in it. Hierarchy refers to the
prestige of positions. A system is hierarchical to the extent that a single actor
has high prestige. Although both these models describe the extent to which a
dominant elite is defined by networks, they are not identical. A centralized
structure of symmetric relations is not a hierarchy.

Nevertheless, centrality and hierarchy both describe inequality in the extent
to which actors are involved in relations. Concluding a review of centrality
models, Freeman (1979) proposes a general form for such models as the ratio of
summed differences between all actors and the most central actor over the
maximum possible sum.[32] Where the centrality of actor j, c_j, is given by Eq.
(2.8) and c_{max} is the highest centrality observed in the system, a model of the
form suggested by Freeman would be $\Sigma_j (c_{max} - c_j)/(N - 2)$.[33] This equation
equals 1 when a system is completely centralized and equals 0 when actors are
equally involved in relations. Similarly, a system has a hierarchical structure to
the extent that there are differences in the prestige of positions actors occupy.
For example, Coleman (1964:434–444) proposes two models of network
hierarchy. A network is hierarchical to the extent that the distribution of p_j
across all actors j is nonrandom or unequal where p_j is the proportion of all

---

[32]Bavelas (1950) proposed the well-known idea of summing centrality scores across actors to
describe network centrality. Problems with this index (Flament 1963:50–52; Freeman 1979)
suggest that centrality models are better stated in terms of differences in actor centrality.

[33]The quantity $(N - 2)$ is the maximum value of the numerator in this expression only if diagonal
elements of the Z matrices are 0. For nonzero diagonals, the appropriate numerator is $N - 2 - \Sigma_k$
$2z_{jjk}/(\Sigma_i\Sigma_j\Sigma_k z_{jik})$, where z_{jjk} is the relation of the most central actor to himself. Freeman
(1979) provides alternative denominators for the special case of symmetric, binary relations in one
network and alternative centrality models.

relations (sociometric choices) in the network that are directed at actor j. A diversity of network models are used to describe centrality and hierarchy, but there are good reasons for treating such models as applications of more general inequality models. Such a treatment would bring these network models directly into the mainstream of macrolevel descriptions of social structure (e.g., Blau 1977). Moreover, such a view would enable centrality and hierarchy to be stated in terms of models with well-known properties (Allison 1978).

As a fortunate coincidence, Coleman's (1964:441–444) hierarchy model based on the information theoretic concept of disorder is equivalent to Theil's (1967:91–95) well studied inequality model if the latter is normalized by its maximum value. In terms of this model, a system is stratified to the extent that there is no disorder in its relations.[34] Relations are disordered to the extent that all actors are equally involved in them. Where y_j is the extent to which actor j is involved in relations (ignoring for the moment how he is involved), a system is stratified to the extent that there is a maximum inequality in the y_j:

$$[\sum_j (y_j/\bar{y}) \ln(y_j/\bar{y})]/N \ln(N), \qquad (2.24)$$

where ln refers to the natural logarithm for which $\ln(0)$ is assumed to be 0 and $\bar{y}$ is the mean of all y_j. Equation (2.24) varies from 0 to a maximum of 1. When the y_j are proportions summing to 1 (e.g., choice status as $p_j = \Sigma_i \Sigma_k z_{jik} / \Sigma_i \Sigma_j \Sigma_k z_{jik} = y_j/N\bar{y}$), then (2.24) simplifies to equal Coleman's disorder model of hierarchy, $\Sigma_j p_j \ln(N p_j)/\ln(N)$.

Equation (2.24) is a general model describing the extent to which a system is stratified. Where y_j is given by Equation (2.8) as the centrality of actor j's position, Eq. (2.24) will describe the extent to which all relations involve a single actor. Where y_j is given by Eq. (2.9) as the prestige of j's position, Eq. (2.24) will describe the extent to which a single actor is the direct or indirect object of all relations. Other models of position centrality and prestige would result in different models of centralization and hierarchy. For example, using choice status as y_j would result in Eq. (2.24)'s describing the extent to which a single actor is the direct object of all relations.

Drawing from Allison (1978), Eq. (2.24) has several desirable properties (not the least of which is the fact that the properties are known):[35]

---

[34]The concept of disorder in information has also been used to describe the extent to which occupants of positions are stratified in terms of attributes (McFarland 1969; Horan 1975).

[35]Two minor points deserve notice. (a) Equation (2.24) need not have an upper limit of one for all models of position centrality or prestige. Its upper limit is reached when one and only one actor in a system has nonzero centrality/prestige. If such a condition is impossible (e.g., Eq. 2.8), then the upper limit of (2.24) will be a determinable amount less than 1. (b) Since equal involvement in relations represents complete disorder, a set of actors is unstratified if they have no relations with one another or maximum relations with one another. For analyses in which stratification is used to capture collusion or coordination of actors, Eq. (2.24) might be replaced with the maximum centrality or prestige of any position in the network (e.g., see Chapters 7 and 8).

(1) It is scale invarient in the sense that multiplying all relations by a constant (either as a result of arbitrary relational measures or summation across an arbitrary number of separate, but similarly structured, networks) will not alter the extent of stratification.

(2) It implies marginally decreasing effects of changes in centrality/prestige in the sense that a unit change in the centrality/prestige of an actor in a highly stratified system will have less effect on Eq. (2.24) than the same amount of change in an unstratified system.

(3) It can be disaggregated across nonoverlapping, jointly occupied statuses so as to describe the extent to which each status contributes to overall system stratification.

(4) It is similar in interpretation to the well-known Gini index, but is more easily computed and is theoretically grounded in information theory.

Status/Role-Sets Interlocked in the Social Topology of a System

Describing system stratification in more detail, there are network models that describe the status/role-sets in terms of which actors are stratified. These statuses and role-sets are manifest as relations between actors. All aspects of relational patterns in a system are combined to define the distances in Eq. (2.14). In other words, system social structure is contained in the $2NK$ dimensional stratification space wherein actors are close together to the extent that they are structurally equivalent (Eqs. [2.13, 2.15]). This space is a topology of the system (e.g., Kelley 1955:37ff), and since the topological concepts of equivalence, isomorphism, and homomorphism are integral to network models of the status/role-sets defined by this space, I shall discuss the stratification space of a system as its social topology.[36] As a representation of social structure and basis for network models, the social topology of a system has three desirable properties.

(1) All levels of abstraction are contained in a social topology. Equation (2.14) defines the distances between any actor and any empirical or abstract relational pattern translated into relations between actors. For example, the concept of prestige is treated as a lack of distance between an actor's observed relational pattern and that constituting a role-set in his system (Eq. 2.21). That role-set is treated as prestigious to the extent that it has an abstract relational form (Eq. 2.19). The homomorphisms abstracted from observed relational

[36]In contrast to Lewin's (1936) discussion of a psychological topology as interrelated sets of perceptions, a social topology refers to relational patterns in a system. An argument can be made for synthesizing the two by means of symbolic interaction and ethnomethodology since perceptions are intimately connected to relational patterns (Chapter 5); however, it is difficult to match psychological with social topologies, since the latter are stated with considerably more rigor than the former.

structure below imply specific relational patterns among actors and as such are linked to those patterns by the distance given in Eq. (2.14). The link between abstract and observed relational patterns means that all abstract models of social structure purporting to represent observed relations in a system are quantitatively linked to observed relations in the social topology of the system. Such models are at all times subject to empirical test as descriptions of observed relational patterns.

(2)   These empirical tests are easily carried out since the analysis of relational and covariance structures merge in a natural and useful manner within a system's social topology. Actors jointly occupying a status provide inter-changeable representations of the role-set defining the status and accordingly provide interchangeable indicators of distance to the status. The actor-status epistemic linkage is thus logically isomorphic with the indicator-concept epistemic correlation. As a result, the well-developed statistics of multiple indicator structural equation models can be used to test hypotheses regarding the status/role-set duality. This point is developed below in Section 2.9 and applied in Chapter 3.

(3)   The social topology of a system defines homomorphisms of networks observed in the system. Let M equal the number of statuses in a system. Each of these statuses is jointly occupied by actors separated by little or no distance so as to correspond to a single dense point in the system's social topology (a point developed below in Section 2.9). This grouping of actors into statuses within a social topology is a homomorphism of observed relations in the sense that relations observed between any actor j and two structurally equivalent actors i,q are given by the relations between j and the status jointly occupied by i, q (e.g., Kelley 1955:12–13; Bonacich 1977 on homomorphisms). A model of observed networks can be taken from the social topology as K different (M,M) tables in which element (j,i) of table K is the density of relations from occupants of status S_j to the occupants of status S_i within network K (Eq. [2.16]). If each actor occupies a system status (i.e., $N = \Sigma_i \, n_i$), then such a model is a homomor-phism of all observed relations. It is often the case that some actors do not occupy a status (as a result of arbitrary system boundaries, persons observed in the process of moving from one status to another, or some other reason), so that the K tables are only a homomorphism of relations among N^* status occupants $(N > N^* = \Sigma_i n_i)$. It is useful in this case to create a residual category of actors in which no more than two actors are structurally equivalent. For example, two statuses were described for the system in Figure 2.1 when relations were measured as the number of direct and 2-step connections between actors (Table 2.2). Actors 5 and 6 are residual, or structurally unique, in the system since they are neither structurally equivalent with one another nor with occupants of either status.[37] As described in the preceding then, a model of the system in Figure 2.1

consists of two $(K = 2)$, three by three $(M = 2$ and there is one residual category) density tables:

	S_1	S_2	R		S_1	S_2	R
S_1	0.0	1.0	0.5	S_1	0.0	0.0	0.0
S_2	0.0	3.0	0.0	S_2	1.0	3.0	2.0
R	0.0	2.0	0.0	R	1.0	0.0	0.5

for the advice and friendship networks respectively. Note that the $2MK$ elements in the first M elements of row/column j contain the role-set defining status S_j as discussed in Section 2.6. Ignoring the issue of residual actors, these models describing observed relations in terms of typical relations among network positions jointly occupied by structurally equivalent actors were proposed in substantive analyses by Burt (1975, 1976b, 1977a, 1977b, 1977c, 1978a) and White, Boorman, and Breiger (White & Breiger 1975; Breiger 1976; White, Boorman, and Breiger 1976).

Social structure can be abstracted still further by idealizing relations between status occupants as binary bonds.[38] If z_{abk}, the density of relations from occupants of status S_a to ocupants of status S_b within network k, is coded as a 1 if it is nonzero, then the above two density tables can be represented as image matrices of advice and friendship bonds:

$$\begin{bmatrix} 0 & 1 \\ 0 & 1 \end{bmatrix} \begin{bmatrix} 0 & 0 \\ 1 & 1 \end{bmatrix}$$

and together constitute a blockmodel of relations among the eight actors jointly occupying statuses. An alternative to coding all nonzero densities as 1's is to select a cutoff density [usually the overall mean, Eq. (2.6) when n is replaced with N] and code densities over the cutoff as 1, those equal to or under it as 0. Whatever the cutoff, the coded binary elements are "bonds," the K matrices containing them are "images matrices," and the K image matrices for a system constitute a "blockmodel" of the system (e.g., White *et al.* 1976:739; Boorman & White 1976:1387; Arbie, Boorman, and Levitt 1978:32, 56). A block-model is a homomorphism of observed relations if the cutoff density is 0.

---

[37]It would be dangerous to dismiss actors in the residual category as random error just because they do not mirror one of the role-sets in a system. Brokers between status groups (e.g., actor 5 in Figure 2.1) are typically unique within their systems and will be found in the residual category.

[38]There are homomorphisms specifically concerned with hierarchy. Friedell (1967), Boyle (1969), Doreian (1970:95–104), and Bonacich (1977) present models of subgroups in a hierarchy. Boyle (1969:115) discusses cliques as subgroups similar to Friedell's (1967:50–51) concept of an office. Actors are combined into a clique/office as a function of the similarity in their relations to persons of higher prestige/authority. The advice network in Figure 2.1, for example, could be viewed as a two-office structure in which actors 1 through 5 constitute an office (actor 5 is included as the lowest common supervisor) subordinate to actors 7 through 10 as an executive office. Actor 6 is deleted as a residual (cf. Friedell 1967:52; Boyle 1969:114).

In this case every nonzero z_{jik} between status occupants is represented by a bond in an image matrix. Note that a blockmodel need not be an accurate description of observed relations. All actors in a system need not occupy one of the system statuses, and relations between actors can certainly exist in finer gradations than present versus absent.

Although arguably implausible descriptions of observed relations, block-models represent those relations in a form nicely suited to comparisons across networks. Viewing an image matrix as an adjacency matrix in which diagonal elements can be nonzero, the same matrix multiplication methods used to find indirect connections among actors in Section 2.1 can be used to trace patterns of role relations among statuses. Separate systems have the same social structure to the extent that they contain the same patterns of role relations among statuses. Discussed for general network structures by Boorman & White (1976), this idea is the central component of Levi-Strauss' (1949) generalized exchange concept regarding kinship systems and the comparative models of kinship networks by Weil (1949), White (1963), Boyd (1969, 1980), and Boyd, Haehl, and Sailer (1972) (for reviews of basic concepts, see Fararo 1973:525–569; Leik & Meeker 1975:76–85; White 1982).

Consider the blockmodel given above. Let A be the image matrix of advice bonds

$$\begin{bmatrix} 0 & 1 \\ 0 & 1 \end{bmatrix}$$

and let F be the image matrix of friendship bonds

$$\begin{bmatrix} 0 & 0 \\ 1 & 1 \end{bmatrix}$$

Boorman and White (1976:1392) define a compound image matrix as any Boolean product of image matrices. In other words, all nonzero elements in a routine matrix product of two matrices are recoded as 1's. The concern here is with the presence and absence of connections rather than the number of connections. The product AF is a compound matrix composed of 1's

$$\begin{bmatrix} 1 & 1 \\ 1 & 1 \end{bmatrix}$$

This shows that every status occupant can reach every other occupant of a status by a 2-step connection composed of an initial advice bond and a subsequent friendship bond. The reverse does not hold. Multiplying F times A yields a compound matrix FA predominantly composed of 0's

$$\begin{bmatrix} 0 & 0 \\ 0 & 1 \end{bmatrix}$$

This compound image shows that 2-step connections composed of an initial friendship bond and a subsequent advice bond only connect the occupants of $\mathbf{S}_2$.

Any product of images can be generated as a compound image matrix, but whenever two matrices have identical elements in the sense that each element (i,j) in one matrix equals element (i,j) in the other, then they refer to a single structure of role relations. This is the Axiom of Extent in set theory (e.g., Kelley 1955:252), but is renamed by Boorman & White (1976:1393) as the Axiom of Quality in order to distinguish its application to blockmodels. With this axiom, a multiplication table can be constructed in which cell (1,2) contains the product of the first image matrix times the second and all possible compound image matrices are represented by a row and column in the table. Such a table for the above blockmodel is

	A	F	AF	FA
A	A	AF	AF	A
F	FA	F	F	FA
AF	A	AF	AF	A
FA	FA	F	F	FA

which shows, for example, that the product AFA equals A (cells 1,4 and 3,1) and that there are only four possible image matrices generated from the blockmodel. Boorman and White (1976:1395) refer to the multiplication table generated from a blockmodel as the role structure of a system.

Two strategies have been described for comparing such role structures across systems. The strategy providing a more accurate description of images within each system locates the role structure "common" to all systems by describing the intersection of congruence classes of image matrices in each role structure (Bonacich 1980; Bonacich & McConaghy 1979; McConaghy 1981). A second strategy describes the "joint" role structure of separate systems in terms of a homomorphic representation appropriate to each role structure (Boorman & White 1976; Breiger & Pattison 1978; Boorman & Arabie 1980; Pattison 1981).

Bonacich (1980) describes the role structure common to multiple role structures as the nonempty intersections of their congruence classes. The number of congruence classes in a role structure equals the number of rows/columns in its multiplication table. The above table defines four congruence classes: $A = A^2 = AFA = AFFA$, $F = F^2 = FAF = FAAF$, $AF = AAF = AFF = AFAF$ and $FA = FFA = FAA = FAFA$. Image matrices within each congruence class are equivalent in the sense of containing identical corresponding elements as labeled by the Axiom of Quality. There are many more compounds within each class (e.g., $A = A^2 = A^3 = \cdots = A^\infty$); however, the compounds in the multiplication table are all that need be considered in order to specify congruence classes. These classes define equivalent role patterns. In the above table, for example, patterns of 3-step connections composed of an initial advice bond, a subsequent friendship bond, and a final advice bond connect the same statuses as the initial advice bonds themselves $(AFA = A)$. In other words, the source of advice for a friend of a person to whom an actor goes for advice is also a source of advice for the actor. A natural extension here for comparing separate role structures is to locate images congruent across the role structures. For example, suppose some other system is observed in which advice and friendship relations are identical so that there is only one congruence class in the system, $A = F = A^2 = F^2 = AF = FA$. Across this system and the one given previously, A is congruent with A^2 and F is congruent with F^2. The four matrices A, F^2, A^2, and F cannot appear in a single congruence class across the two systems, however, since they are not all congruent within each system. The task for comparative analysis of role structures within this approach is to find the complete set of nonempty intersections between congruence classes in multiple role structures. The one such set is then the set of congruence classes common to all of the role structures.

Boorman and White (1976) propose a more abstract representation as the "joint" role structure of multiple systems. They discuss homomorphic representations of role structures. A homomorphic model of a role structure contains a set of groups $(G_1, G_2, \dots)$ each consisting of one or more images such that all products of elements from two groups are contained in a single group. In other words, given A_i, A_j as image matrices in group G_a, and A_k, A_m as image matrices in group G_b, then the products A_iA_k, A_iA_m, A_jA_k, and A_jA_m are all within a single group G where G can be any group in the homomorphism. There are many alternative homomorphisms of a role structure. For example, the above role structure can be collapsed into a single group or maintained as four separate groups. As a more useful homomorphism, each initial image matrix in the blockmodel could be placed in a separate group, and compound matrices could be added to each group where possible. Such a homomorphism of the above role structure could combine A with FA in a group G_a containing the image matrix of the advice bonds and combine F with AF in a group G_f containing the image matrix of friendship bonds. The resulting homomorphism is

$$
\begin{array}{ccc}
      & G_a & G_f \\
G_a & G_a & G_f \\
G_f & G_a & G_f
\end{array}
$$

which shows, for example, that the product of any image matrix in the advice group times any image in the friendship group yields a matrix in the friendship group. In other words, the role structure among status occupants in Figure 1 falls into a class in which any matrix of bonds multiplied times a matrix in an advice group results in an image within the advice group. Any matrix multiplied times a matrix in the friendship group results in an image within the friendship group. The task for comparative analysis of role structures within this approach is to find the largest set of image groups that define a homomorphism of all the role structures compared (cf. Boorman & White 1976:1406–1407).

Of course, comparative analyses of network structures observed among different actors or at different points in time do not require blockmodels.

Routine statistical methods can be used to distinguish types of structures (e.g., Burt 1975, 1981b) and Markoff models provide a useful framework for describing relational change over time (Sørenson & Hallinan 1976; Holland & Leinhardt 1977; Hallinan 1978; Wasserman 1978; Galaskiewicz & Wasserman 1979). In keeping with basic rules in comparative analysis, the systems compared are composed of similar actors in similar boundaries. Wolfe (1970), Swanson (1971), and Zelditch (1971) discuss issues in making structural comparisons.

However, blockmodels offer three advantages for comparative analyses of role structures:

1. They explicitly describe connections between role-sets in multiple networks.

2. They allow entirely different types of systems to be rigorously compared as long as they are defined by the same initial relational contents (e.g., Boorman and White (1976) compare students in a fraternity with monks in a monastery).

3. They provide a model in which wholly different systems, systems containing different numbers of statuses and different patterns of role-sets, can be shown to have similar patterns of role connections so as to be treated as equivalent in terms of their fundamental role structure (e.g., Boorman & White 1976:1401–1403).

In contrast, the blockmodel of a single system is not particularly useful. It is too abstract to accurately describe the typical relations in role-sets defining system statuses. Except in the special cases discussed previously, a blockmodel of social structure is a description decidedly inferior to the original density tables from which it was abstracted.

2.9 HYPOTHESIS TESTING

Once a network model is used to describe the structure of one or more observed networks, the proposed description can be tested as a hypothesis. The test hypothesis is that the proposed description adequately describes the observed network(s) of relations given the possibility of random errors in observing the relations. Table 2.6 reproduces Table 2.1 except that in place of the network models given in Table 2.1 for each of six analytical modes, Table 2.6 presents statistical tests for assessing applications of those models as hypotheses.

Models Without Tests

Three cells of Table 2.6 are labeled "none" to indicate that network models in these modes of analysis are not tested as hypotheses. These cells refer to

TABLE 2.6
Testing Network Models as Statistical Hypotheses within Each of the Six Modes of Network Analysis

	Actor aggregation in a unit of analysis		
Analytical approaches	Actor	Multiple actors as a network subgroup	Multiple actors/subgroups as a stratified system
Relational	None	None	τ-tests
Positional	None	Confirmatory covariance tests	Confirmatory covariance tests

models of ego-networks, models of the relational pattern defining an actor's network position, and clique models.

At the actor level of aggregation, network models are not tested as hypotheses per se. Rather, they are used as variables. They do describe aspects of the relations in which an actor is involved. However, they do not test the extent to which any one aspect characterizes an actor so much as they measure the extent to which that aspect is present for the actor.

Nevertheless, it is at this level that network models have been most fruitful in substantive research. If for no other reason than this one, such models deserve serious attention. Once scores are generated from models such as Eqs. (2.6) to (2.9), they can be correlated or cross-tabulated with scores on other variables. For example, having an extensive range of weak (as opposed to strong) relations in one's ego-network is correlated with having access to diverse types of information (see Lee 1969 on locating illegal abortionists, Katz 1958 and Granovetter 1974 on locating job information, and Granovetter 1973 for a general discussion). Segregation of conjugal roles (the husband performing stereotypically male activities such as economic support while the wife performs stereotypically female activities such as housekeeping) is correlated with the extent to which the husband's ego-network is dense and nonoverlapping with the dense ego-network of his wife (see Bott 1957, 1971 for an initial formulation and Kapferer 1973 for discussion of ambiguities). Multiplexity has been useful in explaining conflict mobilization. Given two actors in conflict, a third actor is likely to support and unlikely to oppose a combatant to whom he has a multiplex (rather than uniplex) relation. As succinctly stated by Mitchell (1974): "if people are tied to one another by a variety of different links, then they will find it difficult to sever social relationships and therefore be obliged to carry out the expectations and obligations entailed in those relationships [p. 283]." Thus, an actor can more easily mobilize an "action-set" from his ego-network if he has multiplex (termed "multipronged" by Mayer [1966]) relations to actors in the network. As might be expected, central and prestigious network positions are occupied by leaders in a system. Position centrality is correlated with work satisfaction in communication networks (e.g., Collins & Raven 1968). The centrality/prestige of an actor's position is correlated with adoption and early awareness of innovations (see review in Section 5.5). In studies of community elites (e.g., Laumann & Pappi 1976; Burt 1977a,c) and academic elites (e.g., Cole & Cole 1973:90–122; Burt 1978a), position prestige is associated with control over valued resources.

Similarly, extensions of position centrality/prestige intended to describe the extent to which a system is stratified are not tested as hypotheses. Models of system centralization and hierarchy are typically used descriptively to compare systems. Nevertheless, these models have been substantively rewarding. Among a diversity of applications, for example, strong positive correlations have been found between the centralization of community elites and the enactment of community-wide policies (e.g., Clark 1975) as well as the centrality of laboratory task groups and the adequacy with which they perform their task (e.g., Collins & Raven 1968).

At the subgroup level of aggregation, there are no statistical tests of the hypothesis that a set of actors constitute a network clique. Clique models are definitions. Given a clique model, an observed set of actors either is or is not a clique under the model. This is a considerable weakness. In the absence of agreement on what constitutes a clique as a cohesive group in all networks (a weak component in a sparse network being perhaps as much a clique as a strong component in some other network), it seems legitimate to question the utility of exploring one mathematical clique model in preference to another. For the purposes of basic and applied research, what is needed is a network model of "cliqueness" under which a set of actors hypothesized to be a clique in a specific network can be subjected to statistical test. There are measures of clique members' preference for one another's company as discussed in Section 2.4, and these measures (rather than clique definitions themselves) have been fruitful in substantive research (e.g., the classic Festinger *et al.* 1950 analysis relies on the density of within group relations to explain social norms rather than whether or not the group constitutes a clique, see Section 5.3). However, these arbitrary measures do not define cliques as statistical hypotheses. Multidimensional scaling can be used to define cliques, but the cliques generated are defined too ambiguously (see footnote 18). This ambiguity might be removed in future work with the availability of maximum-likelihood methods (Ramsay 1978), but it pervades the work available at this time. Fortunately, the structural equivalence of a set of actors can be tested statistically as discussed below. Where cliques are defined as structurally equivalent actors tied to one another by strong relations, cliques are a special type of jointly occupied position and they too can be subjected to statistical test.

τ-tests

One of the attractive features of triad models is their capacity to be tested as hypotheses using the triad census. As discussed in Section 2.7, a weight vector

W uses the frequency with which each of sixteen types of triads occurs in a network to describe some aspect of the typical relations in which actors are involved. The fit of a hypothesized weight vector to observed relations can be tested with the τ statistic proposed by Holland and Leinhardt (1975:35) as a development of earlier work (Davis & Leinhardt 1972; Holland & Leinhardt 1970):

$$\tau = W' \ (T - \mu)/(W'\Sigma W)^{1/2}, \qquad\qquad (2.25)$$

where T is the triad census, μ is the triad census expected for a specific random adjacency matrix ($\mu = E(T)$), and Σ is the (16,16) covariance matrix in which element (i,j) is the tendency for triad structures i and j to occur simultaneously in the random adjacency matrix. Holland and Leinhardt (1975:23–31) present equations defining μ and Σ in terms of the number of mutual, asymmetric, and null relations observed in a network. For all random adjacency matrices with the number of mutual, asymmetric, and null relations observed in T, Eq. (2.25) has an approximate normal distribution with mean of 0. Large negative values of τ reject the hypothesis expressed as W. Under different hypotheses expressed as different weight vectors, different values of the test statistic can result. For a given T, μ, and Σ, however, Holland and Leinhardt (1978:238) define the one weight vector W_{max} that maximizes Eq. (2.25). If the test statistic generated by W_{max} is not statistically significant (see Holland & Heinhardt 1978:242), then triad structure is random given the observed number of mutual, asymmetric, and null relations. Moreover, if the squared ratio of τ for a given weight vector W over τ for W_{max} is close to 1, then the hypothesis expressed as W captures most of the triad structure in the network.

Test statistics such as Eq. (2.25) have had little use in substantive research other than to demonstrate that affective relations tend to be transitive (Davis 1970; Davis & Leinhardt 1972; Holland & Leinhardt 1970; Hallinan 1974a,b; Hallinan & Felmlee 1975).[39] Leinhardt (1972) extends this work to link transitivity with age. The average age of elementary school classes is negatively correlated with the tendency for affect relations to show nonrandom intransitivity. Wasserman (1977) discusses aspects of an adjacency matrix on which μ and Σ can be conditioned as alternatives to the number of mutual, asymmetric,

---

[39]Another approach offering statistical tests of models describing the typical relations in which actors are involved, an approach that has been even less used in substantive research than has Eq. (2.25), is the biased nets approach encouraged by Rapoport and his colleagues (e.g., Rapoport 1957; Rapoport & Hovarth 1961; Foster & Hovarth 1971). The basic idea in this approach is to specify a probability model capturing types of biases that describe deviations from randomness in relations. Using sociometric friendship choices in a junior high school, for example, Rapoport and Hovarth (1961) show that the number of choices received by different persons cannot be explained as random under a Poisson model. They introduce a popularity bias into the model that states a linearly increasing tendency for a person to receive a choice conditional on the number he has already received. This biased popularity model predicts a negative binomial distribution for choice data and describes their observed data quite well using a chi-square test. However, as noted by Leinhardt (1977:xxviii), the mathematics are formidable in this approach. Explanation of how models are derived and tested is elegantly sparce.

and null relations it contains. In his one example, the transitivity model can be rejected as well as accepted for the same data set depending on the aspects of relations on which μ and Σ are conditioned. Sørenson and Hallinan (1976) avoid this ambiguity. Using data on a class observed four times during a six-month interval, they show that intransitive triads are more likely to change over time than transitive triads and when changes do occur, the resulting triad is not likely to be intransitive. Using regression equations to control for sex, class-room, and change in the relation from some "other," Hallinan and Hutchins (1979) show that changes in best-friend citations to the other during a school year occur so as to decrease intransitivity. Unfortunately, these over-time descriptions do not offer statistical tests of transitivity comparable to Eq. (2.25).

Confirmatory Covariance Tests

One of the three attractive features of network models based on the social topology of a system is the isomorphism the topology creates between relational and covariance structures. The isomorphism allows hypotheses concerning the status/role-sets in a system to be statistically tested in terms of confirmatory covariance models.

TESTING THE STRUCTURAL EQUIVALENCE OF STATUS OCCUPANTS

A set of T actors jointly occupy status S under a strong criterion of equivalence to the extent that they are separated by zero distance. Separated by zero distance, they occupy a single point in the social topology defined by the distances in Eq. (2.14). In other words, the distance between any actor j and status S, d_{js}, is equal to j's distance from each of the status' occupants. For each actor t occupying status S, d_{js} equals d_{jt}. For example, the distance between actor 6 and each occupant of status S_1 in Table 2.2 is a constant: $d_{6s_1} = 6.8 = d_{16} = d_{26} = d_{36} = d_{46}$. If relations are measured with random error, however, then the computed distance between actor j and status occupant t will contain a random error component η_{jt}. Further, this random error can affect the occupants of status S differently so that a coefficient is required to express the extent to which the pattern of relations in which status occupant t is involved is an accurate indicator of the role-set defining status S, δ_t^*. In sum, the distance between any actor j and status occupant t is equal to j's distance to status S weighted by t's accuracy as an indicator of the status role-set ($\delta_t^* d_{js}$) plus a random error (η_{jt}) for each actor t occupying the status

$$d_{jt} = \delta_t^* d_{js} + \eta_{jt}. \tag{2.26}$$

Equation (2.26) defines a single-dimension factor analytic model. The expected distance to actor t is given as $E(d_{jt}) = \bar{d}_t = \delta_t^* \bar{d}_s = \delta_t^* E(d_{js})$, so that the mean distance to t divided by the adequacy with which t's relational pattern reflects the status role-set is a constant for all occupants; $\bar{d}_s = \bar{d}_t/\delta_t^*$. Without δ_t^*, this is a hollow statement about structural equivalence. When a status is jointly occupied by three or more actors, however, the relative magnitudes of the δ_t^* are implied by Eq. (2.26). Given actor q also an occupant of the status, the expected product of actor j's distances to t and q corrected for their means is the covariance of distances to t and q; $\sigma_{tq} = E[(d_{jt} - \bar{d}_t)(d_{jq} - \bar{d}_q)]$ $= \delta_t^* E[(d_{js} - \bar{d}_s)]\delta_q^* = \delta_t^*\phi\delta_q^*$, where ϕ is the variation in the distances to status **S**. Since variation in distance to the status is not included in the hypothesis of structural equivalence, it can be absorbed into the indicator coefficients. The covariance of distances to two occupants t and q of a status is then equal to the product of their standardized coefficients indicating the extent to which their relational patterns reflect the status' role-set:

$$\sigma_{tq} = (\delta_t^*\phi^{1/2})(\phi^{1/2}\delta_q^*) = \delta_t\delta_q.$$

The expected variance in distances to t can similarly be obtained from Eq. (2.26) as

$$\sigma_{tt} = E(d_{jt} - \bar{d}_t)^2 = \delta_t^*\phi\delta_t^* + \theta_t^2 = \delta_t\delta_t + \theta_t^2$$

where θ_t^2 is the expected variance of random errors in distances to actor t. In matrix form, the covariance matrix for distances to actors t and q is given as

$$\Delta\Delta' + \Theta^2 = \begin{bmatrix} \delta_t \\ \delta_q \end{bmatrix} [\delta_t \ \ \delta_q] + \begin{bmatrix} \theta_t^2 & 0 \\ 0 & \theta_t^2 \end{bmatrix} = \begin{bmatrix} \delta_t\delta_t + \theta_t^2 & \delta_t\delta_q \\ \delta_q\delta_t & \delta_q\delta_q + \theta_q^2 \end{bmatrix}$$

The analogous statement for all T actors jointly occupying status **S** is then a single-dimension factor analysis model:[40]

$$S \simeq \Sigma = \Delta\Delta' + \Theta^2, \qquad (2.27)$$

where Δ is a vector containing the T indicator coefficients (δ_t), Θ is a (T,T) diagonal matrix of the θ_t, and Σ is the (T, T) expected covariance matrix estimated as the moment matrix S. Given maximum likelihood estimates of the parameters in Eq. (2.27) which combine in an estimate of the expected moment matrix $\hat{\Sigma}$, the likelihood ratio test for rejecting the hypothesis that the T actors occupying status **S** are structurally equivalent under a strong criterion allowing for random errors is given as (e.g., Jöreskog 1969; Lawley & Maxwell 1971:35; Morrison 1976:314–315)

---

[40]It might seem inconsistent to argue against factor analytic models of network subgroups and then use such models for hypothesis testing. Factor analytic models per se are not in question. It is their use that is questioned. When used to describe relations or correlations between relational patterns, factor analytic models can overestimate structural equivalence. Euclidean distances from any one actor to structurally equivalent actors, on the other hand, will be linearly correlated so that the statistical theory developed to test factor analytic models is ideally suited to testing structural equivalence by means of Eq. (2.27).

$$\chi^2 = N*[\ln (|\hat{\Sigma}| / |S|) + \text{trace} (S\hat{\Sigma}^1) - T], \qquad (2.28)$$

where $|\ |$ represents the determinant of a matrix and ln refers to the natural logarithm. If the hypothesis is true, then the test statistic has an approximate chi-square distribution with $(T^2 + 3T)/2$ degrees of freedom. Large values of the test statistic invalidate the hypothesis. Identical values of Eq. (2.28) will result from estimating Eq. (2.27) from S as a correlation matrix or covariance matrix. $N*$ is a scalar indicating the number of independent observations used to compute S. Since S is computed from Euclidean distances, $N*$ is less than the usual $N - 1$ appropriate when S has been computed from N independent observations. But there is no theory available defining exactly how many independent observations are used in computing S from N Euclidean distances, so I shall treat each actor in the system as a separate observation, that is, I shall adopt routine computational procedures. This means that $N*$ is larger than it should be, so that chi-square statistics will be conservative, overstating the extent to which a set of T actors hypothesized to be structurally equivalent are not equivalent. Even so, it seems reasonable to adopt a small sample correction given the typically small number of actors considered in a network analysis. Using the correction proposed by Box (as discussed in Lawley & Maxwell 1971:34–36, 92–93), $N*$ in Eq. (2.28) would have the following value: $N - 1 - (2T+5)/6$. Under the convention that a status is jointly occupied by three or more actors, Eq. (2.27) is identified and maximum likelihood estimates of the indicator coefficients (δ_t) and error variances (θ_t^2) are readily available (e.g., Jöreskog & Sörbom 1979:235).[41] Mean distances to each occupant of the status when divided by the indicator coefficient will be a constant to the extent that the hypothesized structural equivalence is true (i.e., $\bar{d}_t/\delta_t = \bar{d}_q/\delta_q = \ldots$).

Equation (2.27) assumes that the hypothesized status **S** is "true" social structure and the relational patterns in which its occupants are involved are merely fallible manifestations of the status role-set. Under this assumption, the true distance to a status is latent in distance to its occupants as given by Eq. (2.26). Alternatively, one could assume that the relational patterns in which a set of actors are involved are "true" social structure, and the status/role-set abstracted from those patterns is merely an analytically useful summary of that structure.[42] If the latter assumption is made, the observed distance to an occupant of status **S** is not given by Eq. (2.26), and the covariance model in Eq. (2.27) is inappropriate. That is, if a status/role-set is merely an aggregation of accurately observed relational patterns, then distance to the status is a weighted

[41]Information output on the test statistic in Eq. (2.28) by such a canned program should be corrected in two ways. First, the test statistic, typically computed with $N* = N - 1$, should be multiplied by the ratio $N*/(N-1)$, thereby adjusting it downward for the lower value of $N*$. Second, the variance in distance to the status is not part of the hypothesis being assessed, so it should not be counted as an estimated parameter. When it is, the reported degrees of freedom is 1 less than the correct number.

[42]These two perspectives underlie the well-known difference of opinion between Radcliffe-Brown and Levi-Strauss regarding the proper analytical focus for studying social structure (see Chapter 9).

A. Status/Role-Set Is "True" Social Structure (Eqs. 2.26, 2.27)

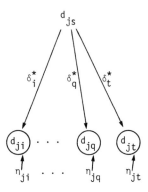

B. Observed Relational Patterns Are "True" Social Structure (Eq. 2.29)

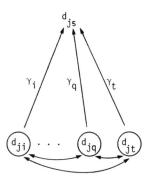

Figure 2.2. Covariance models for testing the hypothesis that the occupants of status **S** are structurally equivalent under a strong criterion.

sum of distance to the actors proposed as jointly occupying the status:[43]

$$d_{js} = \gamma_1 d_{jl} + \gamma_2 d_{j2} + \cdots + \gamma_q d_{jq} + \gamma_t d_{jt}, \qquad (2.29)$$

where γ_q is an indicator coefficient measuring the extent to which an actor j's distance to actor q, a proposed occupant of the status, determines j's distance to the status itself. Figure 2.2 presents path diagrams of Eqs. (2.26) and (2.29)

[43]Note that distance to the status in this equation is not an estimate of d_{js} in Eq. (2.26). The distance in Eq. (2.26) can be estimated as a factor score once the indicator coefficients in Δ have been obtained. For example, a popular procedure is to use least squares estimates: $S^{-1}\Delta = \Gamma^*$, where the regression weights for Eq. (2.29) are given in Γ^* (e.g., Lawley & Maxwell 1971:106–108). Since distances to actors are measured with random error in the factor analysis model, however, the factor scores generated by these γ^* are to be interpreted with caution (e.g., Mulaik 1972:327–331).

that make more apparent their different conceptions of true social structure. Observed variables are circled. By convention, curved double-headed arrows represent symmetric covariation and straight arrows represent asymmetric "causal" determination of the variable at the end of the arrow by the variable at the beginning of the arrow. Duncan (1975:1–24) provides a succinct introduction to path diagrams of covariance structures. The factor analysis model in Figure 2.2a determines distance to an actor by distance to his status, and the covariation in distances to two occupants of a status is the product of the coefficients indicating the extent to which their relational patterns reflect the status role-set (e.g., $\sigma_{tq} = \delta_t\delta_q$). Equation (2.29) is diagrammed in Figure 2.2b. In this model, the distances to a set of actors determines distance to a hypothesized status, and the covariation in distances to two occupants of the status is estimated directly from observed distances.

Where S is the covariance matrix among distances to the T actors proposed as jointly occupying a status, those values of the indicator coefficients in Eq. (2.29) that generate a composite distance to the status representing a maximum amount of variance in distances to the actors are given by the eigenvector corresponding to the maximum eigenvalue extracted from S:

$$(S - \lambda I)\Gamma = 0, \tag{2.30}$$

where Γ consists of the T indicator coefficients γ_t, and λ is the maximum eigenvalue extracted from S. The γ_t are unique up to a limit of proportionality and define distance to the status $\mathbf{S}$ as the first principal component of distances to its proposed occupants (e.g., Lawley & Maxwell 1971:15–23; Morrison 1976:267–274). Without loss of generality, the indicator coefficients can be normalized so that their sum of squares is 1 (i.e., $1 = \Sigma_{q=1}^T \gamma_q^2$). So normalized, the eigenvalue λ is the variance of distance to the status $\mathbf{S}$. In the forthcoming chapters, I make extensive use of Eq. (2.30) in combination with the statistical model in Eq. (2.27) because:

1. It requires no assumptions about system size or the distribution of distances in generating Γ and γ.

2. It provides an unambiguous measure of distance to a jointly occupied position (see footnote 43).

3. It provides an intuitive measure of the extent to which a set of actors are structurally equivalent under a strong criterion. The ratio of the maximum eigenvalue over the trace of S is often discussed as the proportion of observed variance described by the first principal component:

$$\lambda / \sum_{q=1}^T s_q^2, \tag{2.31}$$

where s_q^2 is the observed variance in distance to actor q. This index is less than 1 to the extent that the T actors proposed as jointly occupying a single position in fact occupy significantly different positions.

4. A final but not inconsiderable feature of the principal component model is

its availability. Most computer centers have several packages for extracting eigenvalues and eigenvectors, so Eqs. (2.29)–(2.31) are readily available.[44]

However structural equivalence is assessed, whether by the factor analysis model in Figure 2.2a or the principal component model in Figure 2.2b, tests are based on a useful property of a system's social topology: To the extent that T actors jointly occupy a status under a strong criterion of structural equivalence, they occupy a single point in their system's social topology, and this means that the moment matrix among distances to them has a rank of 1. A single dimension of distance to their jointly occupied status can adequately represent distance to each of them. There is a single principal component to be extracted from S (i.e., Eq. 2.31 equals 1), and S is identical to the estimate of the moment matrix ($\hat{\Sigma}$) expected under a single-dimension factor analytic model (i.e., Eq. 2.28 equals 0).

Of course, status occupants need not conform to these stringent conditions. If a status is jointly occupied under a weak criterion of equivalence not because of random errors in measuring relations but rather because of genuine variation in the performance of role relations (as argued by Firth and Nadel and discussed in Section 2.6), then the status does not correspond to a single point in a social topology so much as it corresponds to a densely occupied field surrounding such a point. The matrix S need not have a rank of 1 in this case; however, the first principal component extracted from it should describe the preponderance of variation in distances to its occupants. As a necessary but not sufficient condition, there should not be a second significant dimension or principal component of distance to the status occupants. If there are two uncorrelated dimensions of distance to the status occupants, then some of the occupants are in fact structurally nonequivalent to some others. Whether a status is jointly occupied under a weak criterion of equivalence for substantive or methodological reasons, the actors whose relational patterns are most similar to the status role-set are those actors having the highest values of the indicator coefficients for the status (δ_t and γ_t). Throughout the monograph, I will focus on such "indicator actors" as best typifying the occupants of their system status.

DISAGGREGATING THE CONTENT OF A STATUS/ROLE-SET

The distance between two actors whose relational patterns are defined across multiple networks does not indicate the extent to which structure in each network is responsible for distance. Equation (2.14) can be stated as the square root of the sum of squared Euclidean distances between actors i and j within each of K networks:

$$d_{ij} = \{ \sum_{K=1}^{K} d_{ijk}^2 \}^{1/2},$$

---

[44]Some packages only extract principal components from the correlation matrix. These packages should be used with caution since the relative values of the indicator coefficients computed from a correlation matrix need not be a simple rescaling of those extracted from the original covariance matrix (e.g., Morrison 1976:268).

TABLE 2.7
Network Specific Distances for a Hypothetical System

Network	Actors	Actors									
		1	2	3	4	5	6	7	8	9	10
Advice	1	0.0									
	2	0.0	0.0								
	3	0.0	0.0	0.0							
	4	0.0	0.0	0.0	0.0						
	5	6.4	6.4	6.4	6.4	0.0					
	6	2.2	2.2	2.2	2.2	8.3	0.0				
	7	8.5	8.5	8.5	8.5	7.5	9.6	0.0			
	8	8.5	8.5	8.5	8.5	7.5	9.6	0.0	0.0		
	9	8.5	8.5	8.5	8.5	7.5	9.6	0.0	0.0	0.0	
	10	8.5	8.5	8.5	8.5	7.5	9.6	0.0	0.0	0.0	0.0
Friendship	1	0.0									
	2	0.0	0.0								
	3	0.0	0.0	0.0							
	4	0.0	0.0	0.0	0.0						
	5	3.3	3.3	3.3	3.3	0.0					
	6	6.4	6.4	6.4	6.4	8.1	0.0				
	7	8.6	8.6	8.6	8.6	9.0	7.6	0.0			
	8	8.6	8.6	8.6	8.6	9.0	7.6	0.0	0.0		
	9	8.6	8.6	8.6	8.6	9.0	7.6	0.0	0.0	0.0	
	10	8.6	8.6	8.6	8.6	9.0	7.6	0.0	0.0	0.0	0.0
Intimacy	1	0.0									
	2	0.0	0.0								
	3	0.0	0.0	0.0							
	4	0.0	0.0	0.0	0.0						
	5	6.0	6.0	6.0	6.0	0.0					
	6	6.0	6.0	6.0	6.0	0.0	0.0				
	7	0.0	0.0	0.0	0.0	6.0	6.0	0.0			
	8	0.0	0.0	0.0	0.0	6.0	6.0	0.0	0.0		
	9	0.0	0.0	0.0	0.0	6.0	6.0	0.0	0.0	0.0	
	10	0.0	0.0	0.0	0.0	6.0	6.0	0.0	0.0	0.0	0.0

where d_{ijk} is the Euclidean distance between respective elements of actor i's and actor j's relational patterns within network k. Although distance within each network is given equal weight here, this does not mean that structure in each network contributes equally to overall system structure. Fortunately, the isomorphism between covariance and relational structures provided by a system's social topology permits a test of whether or not a status role-set is equally determined by structure in each network as well as the extent to which it is determined by structure in each network.

In order to clarify what I mean by a status/role-set's being differentially determined by structure in each of a system's networks, consider Table 2.7. The first two matrices in the table are intranetwork distances among the ten actors in the system presented in Figure 2.1, using the number of direct and 2-step connections between actors as relations. Distances are computed from Eq. (2.14) without summing across networks. Using the above equation, these intranetwork distances can be combined to yield the across-network distances in Table 2.2. For example, the distance between actors 4 and 6 in the advice network (d_{641}) is 2.2 and the distance between them in the friendship network (d_{642}) is 6.4, so the distance between them across both networks is given as 6.8 in Table 2.2 ($6.8 = [d_{641}^2 + d_{642}^2]^{1/2}$). In addition to these two networks, Table 2.7 presents intranetwork distances for a third network not presented elsewhere. In this third network, each actor has named actors 5 and 6 as persons with whom they discuss intimate problems. The third set of distances in Table 2.7 is computed from intimacy relations similar to the advice and friendship relations, $Z_3 = A_3 + A_3^2$, where A_3 is all 0's except that columns 5 and 6 are all 1's excluding the diagonal elements. Table 2.8 presents the distances among actors that are obtained from Eq. (2.14) when all three networks are considered. For example, the distance between actors 4 and 6 is slightly higher than it was in Table 2.3; $9.0 = [d_{641}^2 + d_{642}^2 + d_{643}^2]^{1/2}$. Slight increases notwithstanding, the same system structure is implied by distances in Table 2.8 that was implied by distances in Table 2.2. In both tables actors 1 through 4 are separated by zero distance as jointly occupying status S_1; actors 7 through 10 are separated by zero distance as jointly occupying status S_2; and actors 5 and 6 are nonequivalent to one another as well as the two statuses so that they fall into a residual category. In other words, the introduction of the intimacy network has had no effect on the specification of statuses and their occupants. Of course, the role sets defining the two statuses would be extended to include intimacy relations as well as advice and friendship relations. But finding no change in overall system structure as a result of considering intimacy relations does not mean that intimacy relations have the same patterns of social differentiation characterizing the overall system. Advice and friendship relations do reflect overall system structure. In both networks, actors 1–4 jointly occupy a position nonequivalent to that jointly occupied by actors 7–10 while actors 5 and 6 are nonequivalent to one another as well as both jointly occupied positions. In the intimacy network, however, the distances in Table 2.7 show that occupants of both statuses are structurally equivalent to one another and nonequivalent to actors 5 and 6, who are equivalent to one another. This condition of the constituent networks in a system patterned by structural equivalence in varying degrees of conformity to the patterning in the overall system is what I shall test as rejecting the hypothesis that system structure is equally reflected in each of multiple networks.[45] For this hypothetical system, internetwork differences are easily

---

[45]The model outlined here for testing the hypothesis has greater intuitive meaning than the one given elsewhere as a variation on the canonical correlation model (Burt 1977c). Neither model exhausts the range of possible models that could be designed to test the hypothesis given the logical merger of covariance and relational structures in a system's social topology.

detected. The task is quite formidable in larger systems with complex patterns of social differentiation.

For the same reasons that distances from any actor j to two structurally equivalent actors are equal in the overall system social topology, they are equal within a network-specific social topology. Actors structurally equivalent within a network occupy a single point in the network's social topology so that distances to any two of them from a single other actor must be equivalent. Consider the distances among actors in Table 2.7. Every element in the first four columns of any row is the same. These are distances to the structurally equivalent occupants of status S_1. For example, the distance between actor 6 and each occupant of status S_1 within the advice network is a constant; $d_{6s_11} = 2.2 = d_{611} = d_{621} = d_{631} = d_{641}$, where d_{jtk} is the distance between actors j and t within network k. Given the equality of distances from some actor j to all occupants of a single position within a network and the equality of distances from that actor to all occupants of a status defined across networks, the product of the distance to an occupant of the position multiplied times the distance to an occupant of the status must be a constant. This is illustrated in Tables 2.7 and 2.8. Again consider actor 6 within the advice network. The product of his intranetwork distance and across-network distance to any occupant of status S_1, for example, is a constant; e.g., $d_{6s_1}d_{6s_1k} = 19.8 = d_{61}d_{611} = d_{62}d_{621} = d_{63}d_{631} = d_{64}d_{641}$. This constant product means that there is a single covariance between intranetwork distances to occupants of a status and across-network distances to them. Not only should distance to each actor occupying a status be a good indicator of distance to the status itself (as argued in testing structural equivalence), it should in addition have a single correlation with distance to any other jointly occupied position.[46] Of course, these results assume structural equivalence under a strong criterion. Given the possibility of random errors differentially affecting the adequacy with which an actor's relational pattern reflects his status' role-set, distance between any actor j and some status occupant i is given by Eq. (2.26). The same equation describing distances within network k would be given as

$$d_{jtk} = \delta_{tk}^* d_{jsk} + \eta_{jtk}, \tag{2.32}$$

where d_{jsk} is the unobserved distance from actor j to occupants of status S within network k, δ_{tk}^* is a coefficient expressing the adequacy with which actor t indicates status occupants within network k, and η_{jtk} is an intranetwork error component in the measurement of distance between actors t and j. Ignoring mean distances, since they are treated in regard to Eq. (2.26), the expected product for any actor j of deviations from mean distances to status S within

---

[46]In keeping with the isomorphism between actor-status and concept-variable epistemic links, note that this is precisely Lazarsfeld's (1959:60–67) point in discussing the interchangeability of indices: two indices of the same concept should not only be highly correlated with one another, but they should in addition be similarly correlated with other concepts. This is the premise on which unobserved variables in structural equation models are based (see Burt 1976a for elaboration).

TABLE 2.8
Distances Defined Across the Three Networks in Table 2.5

	Actors									
Actors	1	2	3	4	5	6	7	8	9	10
1	0.0									
2	0.0	0.0								
3	0.0	0.0	0.0							
4	0.0	0.0	0.0	0.0						
5	9.4	9.4	9.4	9.4	0.0					
6	9.0	9.0	9.0	9.0	11.6	0.0				
7	12.1	12.1	12.1	12.1	13.2	13.6	0.0			
8	12.1	12.1	12.1	12.1	13.2	13.6	0.0	0.0		
9	12.1	12.1	12.1	12.1	13.2	13.6	0.0	0.0	0.0	
10	12.1	12.1	12.1	12.1	13.2	13.6	0.0	0.0	0.0	0.0

network k and across all networks is the covariance in distances to the status within the network and across all networks:

$$\phi_{ks}^* = E[(d_{js} - \bar{d}_s)(d_{jsk} - \bar{d}_{sk})].$$

This covariance underlies each covariation between distances within the network and across all networks for occupants of the status. For example, the expected covariance between distance to actor t and distance within network k to actor q where t and q both occupy status **S** is given by Eqs. (2.26) and (2.32) as

$$\sigma_{tqk} = E[(d_{jt} - \bar{d}_t)(d_{jqt} - \bar{d}_{qk})],$$
$$= \delta_t^* E[(d_{js} - \bar{d}_s)(d_{jsk} - \bar{d}_{sk})]\delta_{qk}^*,$$
$$= \delta_t^* \phi_{ks}^* \delta_{qk}^*,$$
$$= \delta_t \phi_{ks} \delta_{qk},$$

where δ_t and δ_{qk} are indicator coefficients standardized so that variance in distances to jointly occupied positions is 1, and ϕ_{ks} is the correlation between distance to status **S** within network k and distance to the status across all networks. In matrix form, the expected covariance matrix among $(K+1)$ distances to each of the T occupants of status **S** is given as an extension of Eq. (2.27) to a multidimensional factor analysis model:

$$S \simeq \Sigma = \Delta\Phi\Delta' + \Theta^2, \tag{2.33}$$

where S and Σ contain $T(K+1)$ rows/columns, Θ^2 is a diagonal matrix of the same order where diagonal elements contain error variances, Δ is a $[T(K+1), K+1]$ matrix containing the indicator coefficients, and Φ is a $(K+1, K+1)$ correlation matrix among distances to status **S** within each of K networks and distance to the status across all networks. For example, suppose actors t and q jointly occupy a status **S** defined in a two-network system of actors. Then Φ and Δ could be given as (cf. Figure 3.2)

$$
\Phi = \begin{bmatrix} 1.0 & \phi_{12} & \sigma_{1s} \\ & 1.0 & \phi_{2s} \\ & & 1.0 \end{bmatrix} \quad \text{and} \quad \Delta' = \begin{bmatrix} \delta_{t1} & \delta_{q1} & 0 & 0 & 0 & 0 \\ 0 & 0 & \delta_{t2} & \delta_{q2} & 0 & 0 \\ 0 & 0 & 0 & 0 & \delta_{t} & \delta_{q} \end{bmatrix}.
$$

Since there are two networks, there are three factors in the model $(K+1)$ representing distance to the status within the first network, within the second network, and across all networks. Since there are two status occupants t and q, there are six observed variables $[T(K+1)]$ representing distance to each occupant within the first network, within the second network, and across all networks. Figure 2.3 presents a path diagram of the covariance model in Eq. (2.33) when stated for the general case of T actors occupying status **S** in a K network system. Since most of the elements of Δ are a priori forced to equal 0, Eq. (2.33) is a highly restricted confirmatory factor analytic model. Under the convention that a status is jointly occupied by three or more actors, the model is identified, and maximum likelihood estimates of the indicator coefficients, error variances, and internetwork correlations between distances to the status occupants are readily available (e.g., Jöreskog & Sörbom 1976).

The correlations in Φ show the extent to which the pattern of structural equivalence defining a status in the overall system is repeated in each network. To the extent that the overall pattern is identical to that observed in network k, ϕ_{ks} will equal 1, i.e., every actor has the same relative distance to occupants of status **S** within network k that they have across all networks. Thus, the hypothesis that actors jointly occupy status **S** in the same manner that they are structurally equivalent within each of K networks is the same as assessing the restriction that all correlations between distance to the status and distance to the actors within each network equal 1:[47]

$$
1 = \phi_{1s} = \phi_{2s} = \cdots = \phi_{ks}. \tag{2.34}
$$

But if this restriction is imposed, it means that all elements of Φ must equal 1 since two variables perfectly correlated with a third are themselves perfectly

---

[47]This is a stringent test. An alternative not requiring perfect correlations would be an equality restriction that does not force the equality to have a specific value. In other words, Eq. (2.34) could be replaced with the constraint

$$
\phi_{1s} = \phi_{2s} = \cdots = \phi_{ks}.
$$

This hypothesis is also tested with the chi-square approximation in Eq. (2.35) where reestimation is done under the above constraint. The test statistic is distributed with K-1 degrees of freedom. It does not state that actors jointly occupy status **S** in the same manner that they are structurally equivalent within each of K networks. It states that they jointly occupy **S** in a manner equally well repeated by their structural equivalence in each of K networks. As an extreme example of the difference between the two hypotheses, actors could jointly occupy **S** in a manner completely, but equally, dissimilar to their structural equivalence in each of the K networks if all the correlations in the constraint were 0.

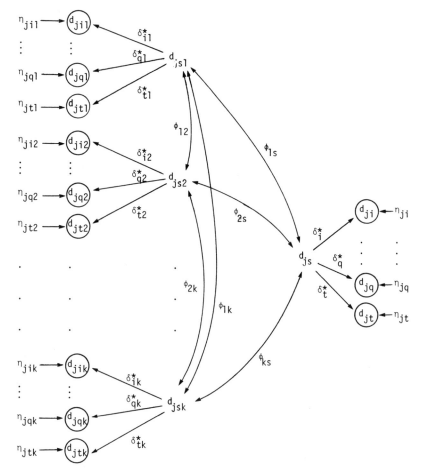

Figure 2.3. Covariance model for testing the hypothesis that the actors jointly occupying status **S** under a strong criterion are similarly structurally equivalent in each of K networks (Eqs. 2.32, 2.33).

correlated. If all elements of Φ equal 1, then the $K+1$ unobserved distance measures in the covariance model in fact measure a single dimension of distance. In other words, the constraint in Eq. (2.34) is identical to the rank constraint in Eq. (2.27) when applied to a different covariance matrix S. The hypothesis that a status is jointly occupied similarly in each of multiple networks is identical to the hypothesis that there is a single dimension of distance to the status occupants across and within each network (allowing for differences in variances captured by the elements of Θ^2). To the extent that this hypothesis is true, the following test statistic will have an approximate chi-square distribution with $(K^2 + K)/2$ degrees of freedom:

$$\chi^2 = N^*[\ln |\hat{\Sigma}_0| - \ln|\hat{\Sigma}| + \text{trace}(S\hat{\Sigma}_0^{-1}) - \text{trace}(S\hat{\Sigma}^{-1})], \quad (2.35)$$

where $|\ |$ represents the determinant of a matrix, ln refers to the natural logarithm, $\hat{\Sigma}$ is the expected covariance matrix in Eq. (2.33) given maximum likelihood estimates of the unknown parameters, and $\hat{\Sigma}_0$ is the same matrix when parameters are reestimated under the constraint that all elements of Φ equal one. In other words, Σ_0 is the expected matrix when the covariance model in Eq. (2.27) is fit to the observed S matrix in Eq. (2.33). This test statistic is the difference in two chi-squares—the chi-square obtained under the hypothesized restrictions minus that obtained in the absence of the restrictions. The former is given by Eq. (2.28) when the model in Eq. (2.27) is fit to the observed matrix in Eq. (2.33), and the latter is given by Eq. (2.28) when the covariance model in Eq. (2.33) is estimated as given. Large values of (2.35) invalidate the hypothesis. The statistic is a large sample approximation, so even the small sample correction for N^* does not justify using the statistic for the ten-actor system in Table 2.7. Lawley and Maxwell (1971:36) suggest that the statistic has a reasonable approximation to the chi-square distribution when N minus the number of observed variables (here equal to $TK + T$) is about 50 or more.

While not offering the same sophistication in hypothesis testing, the principal component model can be put to practical descriptive advantage here. First, since the hypothesis in Eq. (2.34) implies a rank of 1 in the $(TK + T, TK + T)$ moment matrix S in Eq. (2.33), the principal component model can be used to describe the extent to which a single dimension of distance can recreate the observed moments in S. This would involve decomposing S into its eigenvalues and eigenvectors by Eq. (2.30) and computing the ratio in Eq. (2.31) where summation would be over all $TK + T$ diagonal elements in S. The ratio will equal 1 to the extent that the hypothesized constraint in Eq. (2.34) is true. Second, the principal component model can be used to construct distance measures to the status occupants in each network so as to compute ordinary Pearson correlations in lieu of the elements of Φ in Eq. (2.33). Actor j's distance within network k to the occupants of status $\mathbf{S}$, d_{jsk}, is given by the sum of his distances to each of the T occupants weighted by the extent to which each indicates the status in the network:[48]

$$d_{jsk} = \gamma_{1k}d_{j1k} + \gamma_{2k}d_{j2k} + \cdots + \gamma_{tk}d_{jtk}, \quad (2.36)$$

where the indicator coefficients are given in the $(T,1)$ vector Γ_k in the characteristic equation $0 = (S_k - \lambda I)\Gamma_k$, and S_k is the (T,T) covariance matrix among distances to the status occupants within network k. Where the indicator coefficients are normalized so that $1 = \Sigma_q^T \gamma_{qk}^2$, the eigenvalue λ is the variance of distance to the occupants of $\mathbf{S}$ within network k. With distances to the status

---

[48]Here again, I should point out that distance to the status occupants within network k given by this equation is not an estimate of d_{jsk} in Eq. (2.32). See footnote 43.

available from Eq. (2.29) and intranetwork distances given by Eq. (2.36), the elements of Φ can be computed as ordinary Pearson correlations.

Or, by focusing on indicator actors, the elements of Φ can be computed as ordinary Pearson correlations without using the principal component model. For example, consider the four occupants of status S_1 in Tables 2.7 and 2.8. Since these actors are structurally equivalent under a strong criterion, the distance from some actor j to any one of the occupants is no advantage in computing his distance to any other occupant. In this case there is no purpose to examining a linear composite of distances to the occupants. Distances to any one actor are perfectly representative of distances to his status. In other cases, such as the invisible college described in Chapter 3, statuses are jointly occupied under a weak criterion of equivalence so that hypotheses concern the persons at the center of each status rather than all status occupants per se. Take actor 1 as an indicator of status S_1. Intranetwork distances to him are given in the first column of Table 2.7, and distances to him across all three networks are given in column one of Table 2.8. Using these distances as distances to status S_1 yields the following estimates of elements in Φ as Pearson correlations:

$$
\begin{array}{ccccl}
1.00 & .91 & .01 & .95 & \text{advice} \\
 & 1.00 & .06 & .97 & \text{friendship} \\
 & & 1.00 & .23 & \text{intimacy} \\
 & & & 1.00 & \text{across all networks}
\end{array}
$$

which shows that the pattern of structural equivalence defining the status in the overall system is repeated in the networks of advice and friendship relations, but not in the intimacy network. The correlations between distance to the status in the overall system and distance to its occupants in the advice and friendship networks are almost perfect ($\hat{\phi}_{14} = .95$ and $\hat{\phi}_{24} = .97$). However, the same correlation is quite low for the intimacy network ($\hat{\phi}_{34}$ is .23). This corroborates the conclusion reached in a direct examination of the distances in Table 2.7 and leads one to suspect that the constraint in Eq. (2.34) would be rejected if the system was larger so that the test statistic in Eq. (2.35) could be applied.

TESTING THE STRUCTURAL EQUIVALENCE OF
INTERLOCKED STATUSES

The above covariance models are concerned with occupants of a single status vis-à-vis their system as a whole. Since there are usually multiple, interlocked statuses in a system, it would be convenient to conduct a simultaneous test of the structural equivalence of occupants of all M statuses in a system. Unfortunately, this is not a simple extension of the above tests.

In the same manner that the multiple factor model in Eq. (2.33) was derived from the social topology of a system, the same model can be derived regarding multiple statuses in the system. Where distances to status occupants are given by Eq. (2.26), the covariance matrix S among distances within the overall system to the M^* actors occupying M statuses in the system is given as Eq. (2.33) where Θ^2 is an (M^*, M^*) diagonal matrix of error variances, Δ is an (M^*, M) matrix of indicator coefficients where element (q,m) is the extent to which distance to actor q indicates distance to status S_m, and Φ is an (M,M) correlation matrix among distances to the M statuses. To the extent that two statuses, S_1 and S_2, are defined by similar role-sets, they will be separated by low distance in the system social topology and ϕ_{12} will be positive. To the extent that their role-sets are maximally different within the system, they will be on opposite ends of the social topology and ϕ_{12} will be negative. Here again, Eq. (2.33) is a highly restricted confirmatory factor analysis since most elements of Δ should be 0.[49] Nonzero δ_{tm} occur when actor t occupies status S_m. Under the convention that three or more actors occupy a status, elements of Δ, Φ, and Θ should always be identified and maximum likelihood estimates of unknown parameters are easily available (e.g., Jöreskog & Sörbom 1979). Given maximum likelihood estimates yielding an estimate of the expected covariance matrix in Eq. (2.33), the statistic

$$\chi^2 = N^*[\ln(|\hat{\Sigma}|/|S|) + \text{trace}(S\hat{\Sigma}^{-1}) - M^*] \qquad (2.37)$$

has an approximate chi-square distribution under the hypothesis that there are M statuses in the system jointly occupied by the M^* actors where actor t occupies status S_m to the extent that δ_{tm} is greater than 0 (e.g., Jöreskog 1969; Lawley & Maxwell 1971:92–93). Here again, a small sample value of N^* is appropriate; $N - 2 - (2M^* + 5)/6$. Since variances in Φ are forced to equal 1 because they are not intrinsic to structural equivalence as a hypothesis, there are $M(M-1)/2$ correlations to be estimated in Φ. Where distance to each actor is measured with error and indicates distance to a single status, there are $2M^*$ parameters to be estimated in Δ and Θ. In this fairly typical case, Eq. (2.37) would be distributed with $M^*(M^* + 1)/2 - M(M - 1)/2 - 2M^*$ degrees of freedom.[50]

Unfortunately, Eq. (2.37) cannot be used to test the fit of a hypothesized network model to all actors. It is stated for M^* actors, and in order for the test

[49]Here again, I caution against directly describing relations with the factor analytic model. Bonacich (1972b) builds on MacRae (1960) and Wright and Evitts (1961) to propose a model of the form $Z = \Delta\Phi\Delta'$, where Z is an (N,N) symmetric matrix of ties between actors, Δ is an (N,M) coefficient matrix, and Φ is a diagonal matrix of eigenvalues. Element ϕ_{ii} is large to the extent that group S_i is prominent in the sense of being occupied by many actors where those actors have strong ties with one another and most other actors in the network. As discussed in Section 2.6, the groups detected by such models are ersatz statuses.

[50]As a representation of overlapping network subgroups, Arabie (1977) presents a model identical in form to Eq. (2.33) except that Φ is forced to be diagonal and Δ is forced to be binary. Reanalyzing a three-network system of biomedical researchers, Arabie (1977:121–126) describes the overlap between sets of actors structurally equivalent under a weak criterion. Such a description could be statistically tested as a hypothesis under Eq. (2.37) when off-diagonal elements of Φ are forced to equal 0 and the only δ_{ta} not equal to 0 are forced to equal 1 for actor t occupying status S_a.

statistic to be a reasonable approximation to a chi-square statistic, Lawley and
Maxwell (1971:36) suggest that $N - M^*$ should be about 50 or more. For
systems composed of fewer than sixty or seventy actors, therefore, structural
equivalence must be tested for statuses separately and/or for a small number of
statuses simultaneously.

An ostensible exception to this generalization is provided by Hubert and
Baker (1978). Building on Katz and Powell's (1953) correlation between two
types of sociometric choices, Hubert and Baker propose a test for the
conformity of two networks. Given relations in two networks as (N,N) matrices
Z_a and Z_b, the mean relation between actors (i.e., ignoring the diagonal
elements) is given for each network k as $\bar{z}_k = (\Sigma_i \Sigma_j z_{ijk})/N(N-1)$, where $i \neq j$.
The covariance between relations in the two networks is given as $s_{ab} = \Sigma_i \Sigma_j (z_{ija} - \bar{z}_a)(z_{ijb} - \bar{z}_b)/N(N - 1, j \neq i$, so that the correlation between
relations in the two networks is given as

$$\gamma = s_{ab}/(s_{aa}s_{bb})^{1/2}. \qquad (2.38)$$

This is precisely the measure Laumann et al. (1974) use to describe the
similarity of relations in different networks among elites in a community.
Standard significance tests are inappropriate here since $N(N-1)$ relations have
been correlated, but only N independent observations have been made. Hubert
and Baker (1978:39–40) provide an approximation to the variance of Eq.
(2.38), s_γ^2, so that they can suggest a measure of the significance with which the
hypothesis of no similarity between Z_a and Z_b can be rejected: $s_\gamma^2/(\gamma^2 + s_\gamma^2)$.
This is only an approximation, but it is biased against accepting Z_a and Z_b as
similar. The similarity of an observed network and a density table abstracted
from it is a direct extension. Let Z_b refer to the relations in network Z_a as such
relations would be reconstructed from a density table. In other words, let z_{jib}
equal $z_{s_1 s_2 a}$ where actor j occupies status S_1, actor i occupies status S_2, and $z_{s_1 s_2 a}$
is the density of relations from the occupants of S_1 to the occupants of S_2. So
coded, Eq. (2.38) is the correlation between the observed and abstracted
relations in network Z_a. Small values of the test statistic would reject the
hypothesis of no similarity between the observed and abstracted relations. Note
that Eq. (2.38) does not extend to a comparison of observed relations with
bonds in a blockmodel. Bonds in an image matrix are not descriptive of relations
among actors but rather they capture the presence versus absence of ties
between statuses. As discussed in Section 2.8, an image matrix need not
accurately describe observed relations in order to be a useful homomorphism in
comparative analyses of role structures. Arabie et al. (1978:48) discuss this
point in regard to Eq. (2.38) as the impropriety of testing a blockmodel as if it
were a "fat fit."[51]

---

[51]Carrington and Heil (1979) suggest an extension of Eq. (2.38) specifically for blockmodels.
Although the extension provides no statistical inference, it varies from −1 to +1 as the extent to
which observed relations between structurally equivalent actors are homogeneous. In other words,
an adequate blockmodel is one in which a bond between two statuses in an image matrix is perfectly

Although useful as a measure of the similarity between an observed network and the status defining role-sets abstracted from it, Eq. (2.38) is not a test of the adequacy of those role-sets. The density table of relations among status occupants has been abstracted from observed relations. Surely it should be able to describe more than a random amount of variation in those relations. To the extent that it is adequate, it should be able to describe *all* but the random variation. Unfortunately, there is no test for the hypothesis that $\gamma = 1$.[52]

2.10 CONCLUSIONS

My purpose in this chapter has been to provide an analytical synopsis of network models as a powerful framework for describing social differentiation among actors in a system. The discussion has been organized in terms of modes of analysis in Table 2.1. Network models are grouped in the table by their analytical features—their assumed frame of reference for describing relations (pairs of actors in the relational approach versus systems of actors in the positional approach) and their aggregation of actors in a unit of analysis (individuals, subgroups, and whole systems). My discussion has been slanted in the sense of providing more detail on those models to be used in subsequent chapters; however, the basic features of models in all six modes of network analysis have been reviewed. Throughout the review, I have separated those models which seem most adequate within each mode from less adequate alternatives. Conclusions regarding these alternatives have been argued in the review. I see no purpose in repeating those conclusions here. Instead, I wish to consider the relative merits of models in different modes of analysis. Given a system of actors in which social differentiation is to be described, what does the preceding discussion suggest as an appropriate network model? An answer to this question depends entirely on one's purpose in describing social differentiation.

If the purpose is to describe differentiation in terms of the typical relations in which actors are involved, then the relational approach offers optimal models of ego-networks and the triad census.

1. Ego-networks offer unique advantages in capturing empirical structure.

---

reflected in a relation between each pair of actors occupying the two statuses. A direct extension of Eq. (2.38) focusing on blocking in this sense would involve one-way analysis of variance. The variance of relations within a block (i.e., all observed relations referenced by a single bond in an image matrix) should be much lower than the variance in relations across blocks. As with Eq. (2.38), however, the null hypothesis being rejected is trivial. Not only should the variance of relations across blocks be greater than the variance of relations within blocks, the variance across blocks should consist of all but random error in the variance of relations generally.

[52]A start in this direction is offered by White (1977). Taking as a given a blockmodel hypothesized prior to observing adjacency matrices for a system, White offers upper and lower bounds on the probability that there is at least one partition of the observed matrices that corresponds to the hypothesized blockmodel given a cutoff density of 0.

Since they are anchored on specific actors, ego-networks allow standard survey research designs to be employed in gathering network data. This means that inferences can be made about the typical relations in large populations based on interviews with a random sample of actors. The resulting relational demographics on a large population include items such as the number of friendships, co-worker relations, or intimate relations in which persons are typically involved, the typical frequency with which these relations occur, the typical manner in which they occur as multiplex relations, and a host of other summary statements. In contrast, and with few exceptions, models in the positional approach require data on all actors in the population so they cannot be used with a traditional survey research design.

2. The triad census provides an elegant summary of typical relations in which actors are involved. More important than merely summarizing those relations, it provides a sophisticated basis for statistically testing the appropriateness of alternative hypotheses regarding local structure such as transitivity. There is no comparable machinery in the positional approach.

3. Ego-network multiplexity provides a concept for analyzing the coordination of relations with different contents. Knowing the typical extent to which relations with different contents occur together as multiplex relations offers two advantages: It helps address the problem of distinguishing genuinely separate contents, an issue poorly understood at present, and it also indicates the extent to which a multiple network system is differentiated in a consistent manner across different relational bases, which is an important issue in assessing the extent to which existing differentiation is crystalized so as to be immutable as a reliable basis for mobilizing social support. The similar structure of separate networks is a concern in status/role-set models; however, nowhere in the positional approach is there a model as simply suited to the task as ego-network multiplexity.

On the other hand, if one's purpose is to describe actors or subgroups in the context of overall social differentiation, then the positional approach offers optimal models based on the social topology of a system.

1. An actor's position in the stratification space defined by distances between actors, that is, his position in the social topology of a system, considers all aspects of relations linking him with statuses in terms of which his system is stratified—the relations in which he is involved as well as those in which he is not involved. Ignoring portions of this relational pattern, models in the relational approach are unable to capture actors in the context of overall social structure. Triad models completely decompose relational patterns into discrete triads. Ego-networks attend to the relations in which an actor is involved, missing the potential importance of his lack of relations with significant status occupants. In this sense, an actor's ego-network focuses on a subset of the relations defining his network position (e.g., Eq. [2.7] defines the multiplexity of an actor's network position as well as his ego-network). When used to organize network

data on large populations in a traditional survey research design, moreover, ego-networks only report ego's relations to others, missing the potential asymmetry of unreciprocated relations.

2. The isomorphism created in a social topology between the actor-status epistemic link and the indicator-concept epistemic correlation provides an explicit statistical basis for rejecting proposed network subgroups. In contrast, there is no strategy for statistically rejecting the hypothesis that a set of actors constitute a clique, the subgroup modeled in the relational approach. Any formal clique model can be justified for some context, but few (if any) are justified for all contexts. As is argued in the preceding review, it seems advisable to follow the lead of some clique models by specifying cliques as a special type of jointly occupied network position. A set of structurally equivalent actors, within which relations meet the definition of a specific clique model, constitutes a clique under that model. This course of action retains a hypothesis testing capability regarding all network subgroups and extends the scope of network subgroups to include those composed of actors with no relations among themselves (e.g., status S_1 in Table 2.2, the secondary relational form). Further, this natural merger of relational and covariance structures within the social topology allows hypotheses concerning the form, content, and concomitant attributes of status/role-sets to be statistically tested on a status-by-status basis rather than testing hypotheses for the system as a whole.

3. Finally, the density tables defined by a system's social topology (and the role structure generated by blockmodels created by recoding density tables) are analytically convenient homomorphisms of observed relations. The density table for a system summarizes the unique, significant features of relational patterns in the system as interlocked status/role-sets. There are no models in the relational approach with a corresponding ability to describe the subgroups in terms of which actors are differentiated. Assumptions about hierarchically differentiated cliques are used to derive models of triadic structure. However, the transitivity model leaves the number of, and patterns of relations among, network subgroups unidentified.

I conclude that network models built from the social topology of a system are optimal for the purposes here. Such models are optimal for describing actors in the context of overall system structure, and my purpose in this monograph is to algebraically capture the manner in which actions are contingent on the social structural context in which actors find themselves. In other words, the social context in which I assume an actor evaluates and takes actions is given by his relational pattern within a system stratified by M status/role-sets. This context is depicted in Figure 2.4. Actor j occupies status S_j with other actors similarly involved in relations so as to be structurally equivalent with j and one another. The status exists as a densely occupied point in the social topology of their system, actors j and i being separated in the social topology by distance (d_{ji} in Eq. 2.14), to the extent that they have different relations with different actors.

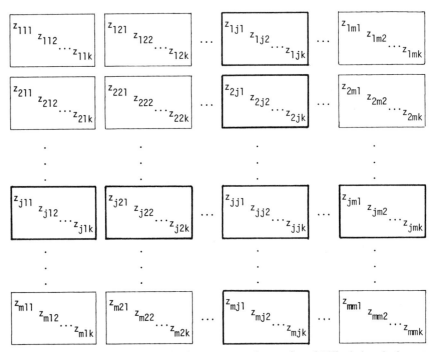

Figure 2.4. The social context for action by occupants of status $\mathbf{S}_j$ as $2MK$ relations in the status role-set (elements in row and column j).

The role-set defining status $\mathbf{S}_j$ is a relational pattern containing K typical relations within each of the elements of row and column j in Figure 2.4—a typical relation to the occupants of status $\mathbf{S}_1$ within network K (z_{j1K}), a typical relation to the occupants of status $\mathbf{S}_2$ within network 1 (z_{j21}), a typical relation from the occupants of status $\mathbf{S}_m$ within network 2 (z_{mj2}), and so on. These typical relations are average relations, or densities, between status occupants and have been explained at length (Eq. [2.16] and pp. 65ff).

I wish to stress that network models describing social differentiation in terms of a system's social topology are not theoretical. A structural model is a theory to the extent that it implies one or more hypotheses that can be falsified by empirical data. With the exception of the triad models, none of the network models reviewed here are theoretical in this sense. Rather, they are methods of describing relations among actors in the same manner that a regression model is a method of describing relations among variables. Given network data on a system, the models in Table 2.1 offer parameters in terms of which the data can be described. For example, a blockmodel is a representation abstracted from network data. It can be statistically tested for its adequacy as a description of the data. But it is not a hypothesis about the data any more than an exploratory factor analysis is a hypothesis about the correlation matrix from which it is abstracted or the correlation matrix itself is a hypothesis about the set of variables from which it is computed. At best, the network model is a useful representation of the data from which it is abstracted.

Network models describing social differentiation in terms of a system's social topology are useful here because they capture social differentiation in a manner that is at once consistent with classic concepts of social structure (the status/role-set), statistically testable for its adequacy (the isomorphism between actor-status versus concept-variable), and optimally suited to the task of constructing a structural theory of action (capturing purposive actors in the context of overall social structure). In short, an actor's network position in a social topology is the descriptive base on which subsequent chapters are built. In Chapter 5, two actors are described as having perceptions in the same social context to the extent that they occupy the same network position, i.e., are similarly involved in relations with the same actors. In Chapter 7, I focus on the form of those relations, structural autonomy being determined by the absence of strong relations with oligopolistic statuses. Before moving on to these conceptual issues, however, I wish to give the idea of an actor's network position greater substantive meaning by describing the manner in which two actual systems were stratified in terms of network structure.

3

Stratification in
Elite Sociological Methodology*

There is a rich and growing literature in which the social structure of science is described in terms of networks within invisible colleges, an invisible college being a system of scientists tied to one another less by their common institutional affiliation than by their interpersonal relations of advice and collaboration. My purpose in this chapter is to describe stratification within the invisible college of elite experts in sociological methodology. This system of actors is probably already somewhat familiar to the reader, if not in the terms to be used here. By describing the topology of this relatively familiar system, I hope to make more apparent the substantive meaning of a jointly occupied position as a social context for perceptions and action. I begin by describing the experts as a system and the extent to which they were stratified in 1975. I then describe the form and content of the status/role-sets in terms of which they were stratified.

3.1 ELITE EXPERTS IN SOCIOLOGICAL METHODOLOGY

In the spring of 1975, the area of sociological methodology consisted of work in methodology, applied statistics, and applied mathematics. The content of the annual volume, *Sociological Methodology*, sponsored by the American Socio-

*Portions of this chapter are drawn from an article reprinted with the permission of *Social Networks* (Burt 1978a).

logical Association, represented the balance of work being done in the area—some discussion of qualitative methodology, some discussion of mathematical models, but an overwhelming emphasis on statistical models of covariance structures. At that time, sociological methodology as a collection of specialities was quite prominent in the discipline. Indeed, the presidential address that year closed with the admonition that "preoccupation with method largely has led to neglect of significance and substance [Coser 1975:698]." In fairness, one must acknowledge that sociological methodology covers an enormous area ranging from bias and efficiency in estimating population parameters to abstract conceptual schemes. The single characteristic that makes the area methodological rather than theoretical is its falsifiability. Theories can be rejected by observations. Methods merely help in making and interpreting observations. At the time, the bulk of sociological work seemed to fall into the latter category. However, it was certainly true that applied statistics had achieved a seemingly dominent position in the area. I think it fair to say that methodology for many sociologists at the time referred to the process of making empirical "findings" and demonstrating their significant difference from "no finding."

The then dominant mood notwithstanding, I planned on working within sociological methodology myself. I had paid some attention to the social organization of its best recognized practitioners and had had the good fortune to see at close quarters how some of them attacked an intellectual problem. My intention in the spring of 1975 was to gain a much clearer picture of that social organization.

Locating Elite Experts

Elite experts were located in a combined positional and snowball sampling procedure. The positional sampling located those persons likely to be experts, and the snowball sampling refined the sample to consist of recognized experts. Fifty-nine persons were located as a positional sample. Each person had three attributes: (a) He listed mathematical sociology and/or methods and statistics as an area of special competence in the 1973 American Sociological Association (ASA) *Directory of Members*. (b) He was an editor or reader during 1973–1974 for at least one of the principal journals publishing significant work in sociological methodology as of 1975.[1] (c) He received a high number of citations to his work according to the *Social Science Citation Index* for 1973–1974. The first two criteria yielded a list of 138 persons. Of these, the 59 receiving the highest number of citations received 93% of all citations given to the 138 persons. Each member of this positional sample was sent a questionnaire asking about his involvement with journals publishing significant work in his expressed areas of special competence and the names of persons with whom

[1]Nine journals were considered: the eight core journals discussed in Chapter 6 and *Sociometry* (renamed the *Social Psychology Quarterly* in 1979).

he had personal communication whose comments had the highest influence on his work in these areas. The number of persons cited for each area ranged from 0 to 5. Persons cited more than once as influencing methodological work were also sent a questionnaire if they were not in the positional sample.[2] In this manner the positional sample was snowballed into a sample of 75 persons. The added experts were persons who did not list mathematical sociology or methods and statistics as a speciality because they were interested in two substantive areas or because they were not sociologists. Also added by the snowball sampling were persons who did not publish a great deal but whose competence made them a source of influential comments in the area. Moreover, it refined the positional sample. Sixteen persons in the positional sample were not cited by anyone as sources of influence nor did they claim that anyone in the positional or snowball sample influenced their own work. They were deleted from the system under the assumption that they were not recognized experts in sociological methodology. In other words, the snowball sampling located those persons who were erroneously specified as experts in the positional sample and located those persons exercising influence in the area without occupying a prominent position in it. Questionnaires from 52 of the final 59 recognized experts provided complete information on the variables discussed here (88% completion rate).

The final system of 59 recognized experts is an elite group in more than one sense. Of all persons claiming expertise in methods and/or mathematical sociology in the 1975 ASA *Directory of Members*, only 3% are recognized elites. The graduate school and 1975 attributes of these elite experts are given in Table 3.1 and 3.2, respectively. Most received their highest degree in sociology (68%). Of the other disciplines, statistics was the most common source of graduates (12%) with a sprinkling from economics, psychology, and mathematics. Most of the experts had received the Ph.D., although they varied considerably in the length of time separating the B.A. from the Ph.D. degree. In terms of cohorts, about a third of the system received the doctorate during the 1950s and another third received it during the 1960s. No elite expert received it after 1972. There was a tendency for the experts to have graduated from elite institutions. Forty-eight percent of the system received the Ph.D. from institutions of the highest prestige. To be more specific, Columbia University and the University of Chicago produced the largest number of experts, nine each. The three remaining institutions, the University of Michigan, Harvard University, and the University of California at Berkeley produced five, four, and one,

---

[2]One unanticipated problem was a negative reaction to the methodologist label on the part of some respondents. An expert widely known for his qualitative methodology wrote back: "There has never been even so much as a single table in anything that I have ever published. I do not intend to unbalance your sample but there was clearly some error in choosing me in the first place." While this expert was reacting to the then dominant quantitative aspect of methodology, reaction to the methodologist label was not confined to experts in qualitative work. One expert widely known for his quantitative work responded in part: "When anyone calls me a methodologist, it makes me mad." Fortunately, there were few reactions of this type.

TABLE 3.1

Graduate School Characteristics of the Elite Experts (Frequencies for Missing Experts Are Given in Parentheses)[a]

Characteristics	Frequencies	Percentages ($N = 59$)
Discipline granting highest degree		
Sociology	40(6)	68
Economics	1	2
Psychology	2	3
Mathematics	3	5
Statistics	6(1)	12
Year in which Ph.D. was obtained		
No Ph.D. or unknown	2(1)	5
Before 1950	5(1)	10
1950–1959	17(3)	34
1960–1969	21(1)	37
1970–1972	7(1)	14
Years between B.A. and Ph.D.		
No Ph.D. or unknown	4(2)	10
Less than 5	7(1)	14
5	11(1)	20
6	3	5
7	7(1)	14
8	4	7
More than 8	16(2)	31
Prestige of Ph.D. granting institution		
Average (includes no. Ph.D.)	8(1)	15
Above average	2	3
High	6(4)	17
Very high	9(1)	17
Highest	27(1)	48
Ph.D. granting institutions		
University of Chicago	8(1)	15
Columbia University	9	15
University of Michigan	5	9
Harvard University	4	7
Princeton University	2(2)	7
University of Wisconsin, Madison	3(1)	7
Johns Hopkins University	3	5
University of North Carolina	3	5
Thirteen institutions granting one or two degrees	15(3)	30

[a]Data have been taken from the 1975–1976 *Directors of Members* of the American Sociological Association and, where necessary, from *American Men and Women of Science, Social and Behavioral Sciences* (New York: R. R. Bowker). Institutions have been coded according to the aggregated Clemente and Sturgis (1974:Table 2) classification of graduate programs over the 1950–1969 time interval.

TABLE 3.2

1975 Characteristics of the Elite Experts (Frequencies for Missing Experts Are Given in Parentheses)[a]

Characteristics	Frequencies	Percentage ($N = 59$)
Sex		
Male	49(6)	93
Female	3(1)	7
Current employment status		
Research Associate	8	14
Assistant Professor	4(1)	8
Associate Professor	10	17
Professor	30(6)	61
Prestige of current institutional affiliation		
Unrated (includes research firms)	12(1)	22
Adequate	5	9
Good	2	3
Strong	16(5)	36
Top 5	17(1)	31
Institutional affiliations		
University of Chicago	5	9
University of Wisconsin, Madison	5	9
Harvard University	3(1)	7
University of California, Berkeley	3	5
Columbia University	3	5
University of Michigan	3	5
University of Pittsburgh	3	5
University of Washington	2(1)	5
Twenty-four institutions employing one or two elite experts	25(5)	50
Areas of expressed competence		
Methodology	36(3)	66
Mathematics	15(2)	29
Methodology and mathematics	12(1)	22
Demography/ecology	5(1)	10
Macrosociology (social change, comparative sociology, theory, social organization, political sociology)	5(1)	10
Social psychology (socialization, education, marriage and family)	14	24
Stratification and mobility	7(2)	15

[a]Data sources are given in the note to Table 3.1, but institutions here have been coded according to the 1970 prestige ratings of American graduate programs as reported by Abbott (1973:Table 3).

respectively. Table 3.2 presents the characteristics of the experts in 1975. Most were male and had achieved the rank of full professor. The University of Chicago and the University of Wisconsin at Madison employed the largest number of experts, five each. Harvard University was next with four experts. Several institutions employed three experts. Although the "top five" institutions employed almost a third of the recognized experts, this was considerably below the percentage who received the Ph.D. from those institutions. However, there was no systematic flow of experts from the top five institutions into less prestigious institutions. There was upward and downward mobility among the experts to the extent that there was no significant association of the prestige of the institution that granted an expert the Ph.D with his or her current affiliation (Burt 1978a:110). Not surprisingly, most of the experts claimed competence in either methodology or mathematics (73% of the system). Of the substantive specialities claimed, social psychology was most common (24% of the system). Stratification and mobility was next (15% of the system) with noticeable clusters in demography/ecology and macrosociology (10% of the system claiming one or the other).

Relations Among Elite Experts

I have distinguished two types of relations among the experts, relations concerned with methodological issues and relations concerned with substantive issues. Both relations are based on binary sociometric citations. The adjacency matrix of methodology citations is composed of elements a_{ji1} equal to 0 unless expert j cited expert i as a colleague with whom he had personal communication whose comments had the highest influence on his work in methodological/ mathematical sociology. For statisticians the criterion was listed as work in statistics rather than sociology. The adjacency matrix of substantive citations is composed of elements a_{ji2} equal to 0 unless (a) the expert j cited expert i as a colleague with whom he had personal communication whose comments had the highest influence on his work within the substantive area of expertise he listed in the 1973 ASA *Directory of Members,*[3] or (b) expert j cited expert i in an acknowledgment footnote as a source of helpful comments on a substantive article published in one of the eight core journals between 1969 and 1976, or (c) expert j coauthored such an article with expert i in one of the eight core journals between 1969 and 1976. The eight core journals in sociological methodology are discussed in Chapter 5.[4] An article in one of these journals was taken to be substantive if it did more with a set of observations than run them through a statistical or mathematical model in order to illustrate the model. Even though

---

[3]Statisticians and those sociologists claiming mathematical sociology and methodology as areas of expertise were unable to claim a substantive area of expertise. In order to obtain information on their substantive influence relations, to the extent that such relations existed, the acknowledgment citations and coauthorship citations were included as substantive citations.

[4]Consideration of all 23 journals in Table 6.1 between 1974 and 1976 only generated one additional linkage between experts, so core journals are retained here as capturing the bulk of substantive citations between 1969 and 1976.

the well-known article by Hauser and Goldberger (1971) describes two samples of observations, for example, it was treated as nonsubstantive since the data are only used to illustrate the statistical models they discuss. These two adjacency matrices were raised to successive powers in order to locate the minimum number of steps required to each expert to reach each other expert within each network (path distances in Eq. [2.4]). The resulting connections were then normalized as given in Eq. (2.5) so that z_{jik} ranges from 0 to 1 as the extent to which expert j can reach expert i within network k in fewer steps than he requires to reach other experts.[5] Within the network of methodology relations, for example, z_{ji1} equals 0 if there was no direct or indirect chain of citations by which comments from expert i could influence the work of expert j. It approaches 1 to the extent that i had a direct influence on j's methodological work.

An Elite Invisible College

The system of elite experts in sociological methodology met the usual criteria for defining an invisible college (cf. Crane 1972:Chap. 3; Gaston 1973:Chap. 7). First, there was high intrasystem influence on methodological work. About three quarters of all methodology citations made (76%) were made to other elite experts. Second, experts had been sampled so that they had direct personal communication with at least one other expert. This means that each expert was connected with every other expert in the system by a chain of citations. In graph theoretic terms, the system was a weak component. However, most of these connections were indirect. The density of direct connections (Eq. [2.6] where $n = 52$) was low (3.8% in the network of methodology relations and 2.9% in the network of substantive relations), and experts were not equally involved as intermediaries in these indirect connections. Table 3.3 shows that a great many experts received no citations—37% in the methodology network and 42% in the substantive network. A small proportion of the experts received a majority of the citations made. In the methodology network, 29% of the experts received three or more citations, but their combined citations were 74% of the total number made. In the substantive network, 19% of the experts received three or more citations, but their combined citations were 61% of the total number made. While the elite experts were connected to one another indirectly by means of a small number of leaders as intermediaries, the college was far from a perfect hierarchy. The inequality with which they were the object of citations is low, .173 and .194 for methodology and substance, respectively (according to the inequality model in Eq. [2.24]). This could mean either that there was a single, loosely connected group of leaders at the center of the college or that there were multiple groups of leaders loosely connected across groups.

[5]The actual choice matrix raised to successive powers in computing relations was (61,61) in size. Rows/columns 53 through 59 referred to the seven missing experts and two persons named by experts as influencing their substantive (but not methodological) work. The last nine rows of both choice matrices contained only 0's. These nonrespondents were included in the computation of relations and distances so as to represent similarities in the relational patterns of respondents citing them. After distances were computed, the nonrespondents were deleted from the analysis.

TABLE 3.3
Distribution of Sociometric Citations among Elite Experts

Number received	Frequency of methodology citations	Frequency of substantive citations
9	0	1
8	2	0
7	2	0
6	0	1
5	4	2
4	4	3
3	3	3
2	8	10
1	10	10
0	19	22

3.2 THE FORM OF STRATIFICATION

The number and organization of groups of leaders in the college concerns the form of stratification in the college. Perhaps the most basic feature of the social context in Figure 2.4 is its structural form. How many statuses are there and how are they interlocked by role relations? The formal answer to this question is given by a density table of relations among structurally equivalent actors. Abstracting this formal structure one step further, role-sets can be characterized in terms of their relational form. Which statuses are defined by role-sets with primary form, with secondary form, by neither type of form? In short, a description of the structural form of Figure 2.4 as a social context shows the strength of role relations connecting occupants of status S_j to each other status and the relative standing of those statuses within the system.

Locating Jointly Occupied Statuses

The immediate task is to locate structurally equivalent experts jointly occupying statuses. This is a two-step process. First, distances between experts are subjected to a nonmetric cluster analysis to locate potential statuses corresponding to clusters of experts separated by negligible distance. A second step consists of statistically testing the structural equivalence of each set of status occupants.

The first step is presented in Figure 3.1 as a hierarchical cluster analysis of distances between experts considering both networks simultaneously.[6] The columns in Figure 3.1 refer to individual experts, for example, column one

[6]The analysis here has been carried out using the network analysis computer package STRUCTURE (Project 1981). Binary citations are input. Path distances, normalized relations, sociometric indices, distances, two hierarchical cluster analyses, and density tables are output. As

(*Continued*)

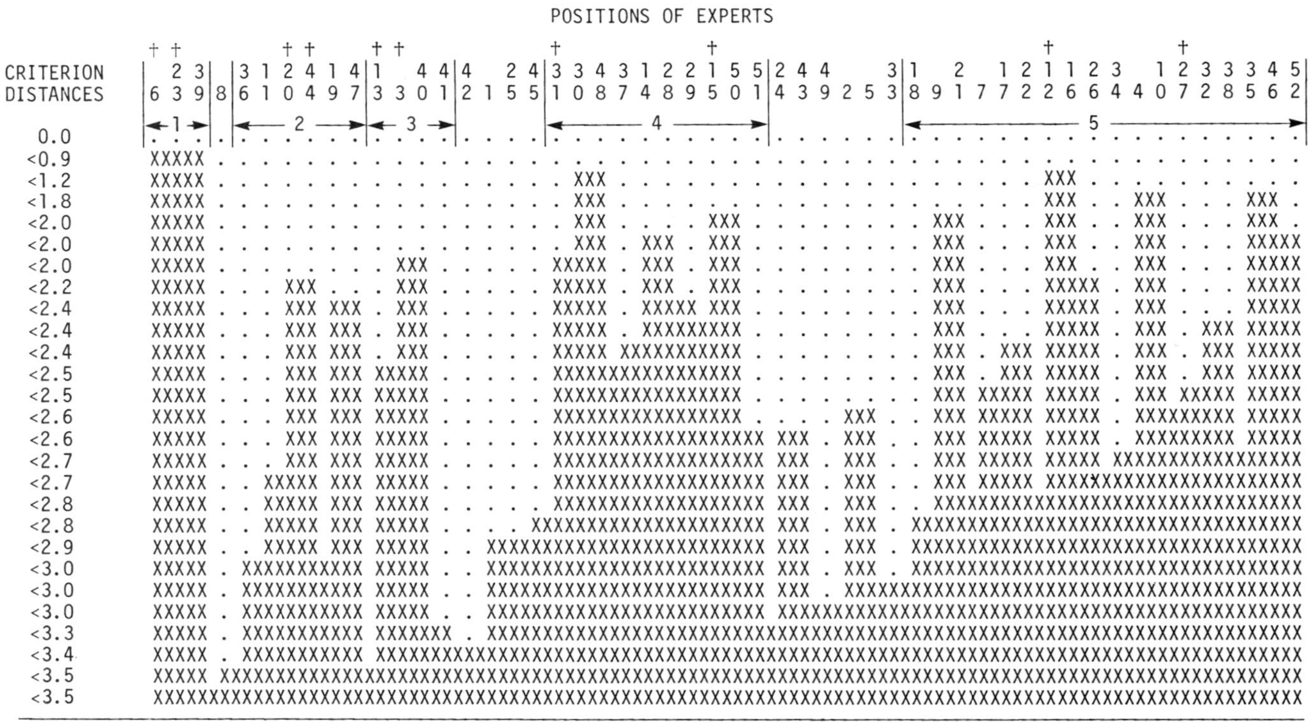

Figure 3.1. Hierarchical cluster analysis suggesting jointly occupied statuses (a dagger marks the position of an indicator expert and the clustering algorithm is described in footnote 7).

refers to expert 6, column two refers to expert 23, and so on. The rows indicate partitions of experts into structurally equivalent clusters. When two experts are clustered together as structurally equivalent, their respective columns are connected by X's in a row. For example, under a criterion distance of 0.9 (second row from the top of Figure 3.1), experts 6, 23, and 39 are clustered together as structurally equivalent. The clustering is based on Johnson's (1967) connectedness algorithm.[7] If every expert had equal distance from every other expert, Figure 3.1 would appear as a hill of X's beginning at the upper right-hand corner and descending to the lower left-hand corner. The mounds of X's in the figure, however, show that the experts are stratified across multiple statuses.

None of the experts jointly occupied a status under a strong criterion of equivalence. The first row of Figure 3.1 corresponds to a criterion distance of 0. No experts are clustered together in row one.

Five groups of experts jointly occupied statuses under a weak criterion of equivalence. Although not separated by zero distance, status occupants were separated by negligible distances (Eq. [2.15]). Those experts not classified in Figure 3.1 as jointly occupying a status constitute a residual group.

The most ideal-typical illustration of a cluster of structurally equivalent experts is provided by status S_1. The experts specified as occupying S_1 are clustered together in the initial rows of the cluster analysis (top of Figure 3.1) when the criterion distance is low. They are not clustered with experts occupying other statuses until the criterion distance has nearly reached its maximum value at the end of the cluster analysis (bottom of Figure 3.1). The

---

(Continued from p. 102)

stated in footnote 5, relations and distances are computed from available data on 61 social scientists, 9 more than the 52 actually completed questionnaires. Distances were computed from Eq. (2.14) with the minor modification of deleting two redundant differences involving the arbitrarily constant self relations in each network, the z_{jjk} (cf. Burt 1976b:95,115). The (52,52) matrix of distances was then used as input to STRUCTURE to generate Figure 3.1.

[7]Johnson's connectedness algorithm (also termed the "minimum method") produces the N-1 partitions output by STRUCTURE in four steps: (a) Partition C_0, the first row of the hierarchical analysis, groups together those experts separated by zero distance (if there are any). (b) Given partition C_{j-1}, which groups together experts under criterion distance α_{j-1} and given distances between experts and clusters of experts in this partition, let d_j equal the minimum nonzero distance between any two experts or cluster of experts in the partition C_{j-1}. Merge the pair of experts separated by d_j to create a new cluster partition C_j that is defined under the criterion distance $\alpha_j = d_j$. (c) New distances between the pair of experts clustered to form C_j and the other experts or clusters of experts are formed as follows: if x and y are the experts clustered together in C_j and not in C_{j-1}, define the distance from the cluster xy and any third expert or cluster of experts z as $d_{xy,z} = $ minimum (d_{xz}, d_{yz}), where minimum means to select whichever of the two distances is smaller. If x and y are experts in C_{j-1} not clustered together in C_j, then d_{xy} remains unchanged. (d) Repeat steps (b) and (c) until all experts have been clustered together in the last partition. In order to save space, Figure 3.1 presents every other partition, i.e., each partition in Figure 3.1 clusters together two columns unclustered in the previous partitions. This connectedness algorithm is useful in the first, exploratory, phase of locating statuses since it allows occasional outlier distances among occupants of a status by focusing on the minimum distances in which structurally equivalent actors are involved. The consequence of this is a conservative distinction among statuses. The algorithm can understate the distances among actors. Since the second phase of locating statuses involves the statistical tests of structural equivalence, however, this conservative bias is quite useful. It limits the number of separate statuses to be considered, but can be corrected by means of statistical tests if the bias is misleading.

other sets of experts specified as jointly occupying statuses are similarly clustered together before they are clustered with experts occupying other statuses.

The specification of jointly occupied statuses in Figure 3.1 is not solely based on the cluster analysis. Statistical tests have been used as an aid in some cases. Table 3.4 presents aspects of assessing the hypothesis that experts occupying each status are structurally equivalent under a strong criterion—allowing random errors in distances. As a general indication of adequacy, the second row of the table presents the ratio of observed to predicted variance in distances to experts jointly occupying a status. Predicted variance is given by the first principal component, and the ratio (given in Eq. [2.31]) should be close to 1. The next row of the table presents estimates of the indicator coefficients in Eq. (2.27). If the relational pattern in which expert j is involved corresponds perfectly to the role-set defining his status, the coefficient δ_j equals 1. The two experts with the highest coefficients have a posteriori been specified as optimal indicators of their status.[8] These indicator experts are marked with daggers in Figure 3.1 and Table 3.4. Presented at the bottom of Table 3.4 are chi-square statistics for the hypothesis that each status is jointly occupied under a strong criterion of equivalence (Eq. [2.28]). The chi-square tests show that status S_3 was the only one jointly occupied under a strong criterion of equivalence assuming intrastatus distances are based on random error ($\chi^2 = 2.12$ with 4 degrees of freedom). This is surprising since expert 41 is not clustered into the status until the criterion distance is close to its maximum value (see the row in Figure 3.1 with a criterion distance <3.3). He is specified as an occupant for two reasons: (a) he is structurally equivalent with the other occupants of the status in both networks when each network is analyzed separately and (b) his

---

[8] Unobserved variables of distances to statuses are defined in Table 3.1 for the maximum likelihood factor analysis as they will be used in the forthcoming analyses, i.e., in terms of distance to indicator experts. The application of a posteriori restrictions to force a particular meaning on an unobserved variable is discussed elsewhere (Burt 1976a). Indicator experts were selected as the two status occupants with the highest loadings on the first principal component representing their status (the gammas in Eq. [2.29]). Distance to status S is then defined by the distance to its two indicator experts i and j as follows. Specify the variance of S to equal unity and the variance of errors of observation of the distance to the experts i and j to be equal (the latter under the assumption that both experts have equal susceptibility to errors of observation regarding status S). These restrictions are sufficient to identify unknown parameters in three estimation equations: $\sigma_i^2 = \delta_i^2 + \theta^2$, $\sigma_j^2 = \delta_j^2 + \theta^2$, and $\sigma_{ij} = \delta_j \delta_i$, where σ_i^2 and σ_j^2 are the variances of the distance to experts i and j, respectively, and σ_{ij} is the covariance between distances to the two experts' empirical positions. The first two equations yield $\theta^2 = \delta_j^2 - \sigma_j^2 = \delta_i^2 - \sigma_i^2$, which yields $\delta_j^2 - \delta_i^2 = \sigma_j^2 - \sigma_i^2$, and substituting δ_i from the third equation yields $\delta_j^2 - (\sigma_{ij}/\delta_j)^2 = \sigma_j^2 - \sigma_i^2$, which can be rearranged as $0 = (\delta_j^2)^2 - \delta_j^2(\sigma_j^2 - \sigma_i^2) - \sigma_{ij}^2$. In this quadratic form, the epistemic covariances are now given as

$$\{(s_j^2 - s_i^2) \geq [(s_j^2 - s_i^2)^2 + 4s_{ij}]\}^{1/2}/2$$

where δ_j is given by the positive root and δ_i by the negative root, s_j, s_i, and s_{ij} are the respective estimates of σ_j, σ_i, and σ_{ij}, and θ^2 is now estimated from the last of the three estimation equations above. Having estimated the three unknown parameters, these three parameters can be specified as constant, thereby holding the interpretation of distance S constant during the estimation of remaining epistemic covariances and error variances for nonindicator experts occupying status S.

TABLE 3.4

Assessing the Hypothesis That Experts Jointly Occupied Statuses under a Strong Criterion of Equivalence while Allowing for Errors of Observation[a]

	Status				
	S_1	S_2	S_3	S_4	S_5
Number of experts occupying status	3	6	4	10	18
Variation described by first principal component	97%	70%	93%	89%	62%
Standardized values of the δ_j as expert indicator coefficients [expert ID# given in in brackets]	0.99[6]† 0.99[23]† 0.94[39]	0.74[36] 0.78[11] 0.94[20]† 0.94[44]† 0.60[19] 0.64[47]	0.90[13]† 0.92[3]† 0.99[40] 0.71[41]	0.95[31]† 0.94[30] 0.94[48] 0.92[37] 0.94[14] 0.94[28] 0.95[29] 0.95[15]† 0.94[50] 0.89[51]	0.78[18] 0.25[9] 0.33[21] 0.73[7] 0.83[17] 0.90[22] 0.91[12]† 0.87[16] 0.88[26] 0.89[34] 0.91[4] 0.89[10] 0.88[27]† 0.91[32] 0.87[38] 0.24[35] 0.04[46] 0.50[52]
Probability that the status is jointly occupied under a strong criterion of equivalence	<.001	<.001	>.50	<.001	<.001
χ^2	55.27	57.95	2.12	120.60	585.08
Degrees of freedom	2	11	4	37	137

[a]The ratio of predicted over observed variance is given in Eq. (2.31). The indicator coefficients are taken from a factor analysis model as specified in Eq. (2.27) for which the chi-square statistic is given in Eq. (2.38), see footnote 8. The reported degrees of freedom are lower limits since parameters for indicator experts (marked with a dagger, cf. Figure 3.1) have been estimated a priori to other unknowns as described in footnote 8. The identification number for each expert is given in brackets (cf. Figure 3.1).

inclusion in the status does not reject the hypothesis that the status is jointly occupied under a strong criterion. Even after allowing for random errors in distances, however, the hypothesis of structural equivalence under a strong criterion can be rejected at beyond the .001 level of confidence for the remaining four statuses.

This is particularly disconcerting in regard to status S_1 since it is an ideal-typical cluster in Figure 3.1. Moreover, 97% of the variance in distances to its three occupants is described by a single principal component. Further, distance to each occupant has a high correlation with distance to the unobserved variable of distance to the status. The indicator coefficients for experts 6, 23, and 39 are .99, .99, and .94, respectively. Despite the fact that the status can be rejected as jointly occupied under a strong criterion, it has been retained as descriptively adequate given the high indicator coefficients and the high ratio of predicted to observed variance.

Statuses S_2 and S_3 are similar to S_1, although not as clear cut. Both are discernible in the cluster analysis as jointly occupied positions. The first principal component for each status describes a substantial amount of variance in distances to occupants of each status (70% and 89%, respectively). in addition, the high indicator coefficients for experts occupying each status show that distance to each status is captured extensively, if not exhaustively, by distance to indicator experts occupying the center of each status.

Status S_5 is the most problematic of the five. Only 62% of the variance in distance to its occupants is described by the first principal component. Four of the indicator coefficients are quite low (.25, .33, .24, and .03 for experts 9, 21, 35, and 46, respectively). Nevertheless, the remaining fourteen coefficients are high (average δ_j of .84). Perhaps more important, there is no clear indication of how the status might be specified more adequately in terms of substatuses within it. Alternative covariance models allowing multiple centers in the status as multiple unobserved variables of distance to occupants of S_5 do not reduce the chi-square statistic to insignificance.[9] Therefore, the status has been specified as jointly occupied by the experts indicated in Figure 3.1 under a very weak criterion of equivalence. A more accurate picture of the structure of relations within this status is obtained when the content of stratification is addressed below.

Characterizing Role-Set Form

In the same manner that Table 2.3 characterized the form of hypothetical relational patterns, Table 3.5 presents information characterizing the form of the five role-sets observed in 1975 among the elite experts. The first row

[9]Alternative models were considered in which unobserved variables were specified for the ostensible centers within the status. These centers are indicated in Figure 3.1 as dyads and triads of experts clustered together under a strong criterion before being clustered together as status S_5 when the criterion allows structurally equivalent experts to be separated by distances less than 2.7 and 2.8. A detailed example of disaggregating a jointly occupied position into component positions is given in footnote 12.

TABLE 3.5
Role-Set Forms[a]

	Statuses				
	S_1	S_2	S_3	S_4	S_5
Primary form					
p_s	.11	.08	.29	.03	.06
$r_{d_{js}p_j}$	−.16	.11	−.87*	.78*	.80*
Secondary form					
s_s	.15	.15	.04	.02	.10
$r_{d_{js}s_j}$	−.38	−.63*	.11	.42*	−.09

[a]Measures of role-set form are given in Eqs. (2.19) and (2.20), and correlations are between p_j, s_j, and the average distance of expert j to the two experts indicating each status (cf. Table 2.3). An asterisk marks a correlation significantly different from zero beyond the .01 level of confidence.

concerns the extent to which a role-set had a primary form (Eq. [2.19]), and the second row concerns the extent to which it had a secondary form (Eq. [2.20]). These coefficients equal 1 when a role-set perfectly conforms to either abstract relational form.[10]

Four points summarize Table 3.5. The most obvious feature of the table is the fact that no role-set even came close to perfectly reflecting a primary or secondary form. Most of the values of p_s and s_s are closer to 0 than to 1. In comparison to one another, however, the role-sets differed significantly in the extent to which they reflected either form. Looking across the first row, that concerned with primary form, status S_3 strongly resembled a primary form in comparison to the other statuses ($p_3 = .29$ while the mean score for the others is .07). Only the correlation between distance to status S_3 and primary form is significantly negative. In other words, the experts whose relational patterns most closely resemble a primary form had little distance from S_3, and those whose patterns least resemble a primary form were distant from the status. In short, status S_3 was the only prestigious status in the college, and an expert's distance from the status was an indicator of his relative prestige in the system (Eq. [2.19]). Looking across the second row of Table 3.5, that concerned with secondary form, statuses S_1 and S_2 equally reflected a secondary form ($s_s = .15$). However, the correlations show that it is the role set defining S_2 that most closely resembled a secondary form. Only the correlation between distance to S_2 and secondary form is significantly negative. Unlike status S_2, status S_1 was defined by a role-set with some aspects of primary and secondary form (note the two negative correlations for this status). Unlike the first three statuses, the last two statuses were defined by role-sets that reflect neither a primary nor a secondary form. This means that their occupants neither directed relations

[10]However, the coefficients in Table 3.5 have a bias. Nine extra persons are included in the sociometric data beyond the 52 elite experts completing a questionnaire (see footnote 5). Since the bottom nine rows of the choice matrix are forced to be 0, none of the 52 respondents could have been the object of relations from all 61 persons in the networks used to compute prominence ($prom_{jk}$ in Eq. [2.17]). Each respondent's prominence should be 61/52, or 1.17, times as large as it is. This means that the p_s is underestimated in Table 3.5 and s_s is overestimated.

toward experts structurally nonequivalent to themselves nor were they themselves the object of extensive relations from others. The fourth feature of Table 3.5 is the suggestion that these statuses, S_4 and S_5, were isolated within elite sociological methodology.

The points summarizing Table 3.5 can be illustrated by considering the overall density of relations among the status occupants. Densities are given in Table 3.6; the upper part is based on the normalized relations used to compute distances (the z_{jik}) and the lower part is based on sociometric citations (the a_{jik}). Densities in the upper part of the table give the typical maximum direct or indirect relation from one status to another while those in the lower part give the typical direct connection. The densities have been computed as the average of Eq. (2.16) across the two networks. For example, there were three experts occupying status S_1 and four occupying S_3. There were 12 possible citations from S_1 to S_3 within each network, or 24 citations across both networks. Only 1 citation was made, so the sociometric density from S_1 to S_3 was 1/24, or .042, yielding the 4% in the lower part of the table. Recalling the discussion in Chapter 2, the role-set defining status S_j is given by the densities in row/column j of the table.

Status S_3 was clearly prestigious within the college. A high proportion of the elite experts directed relations to occupants of this status. Every density in the third column of Table 3.6 is nonzero. In other words, at least one expert (usually several experts) in every status of the college directed relation(s) to experts occupying S_3. At the same time, the occupants of S_3 tended to direct

TABLE 3.6
Overall Densities Involving Status Occupants

Densities based on normalized relations (z_{jik})

	S_1	S_2	S_3	S_4	S_5	Residual
S_1	88	14	59	N	10	38
S_2	10	30	68	N	7	28
S_3	N	17	44	N	3	11
S_4	N	N	9	3	N	3
S_5	19	N	27	1	8	22
R	9	9	34	1	6	21

Densities based on sociometric choices (a_{jik})

	S_1	S_2	S_3	S_4	S_5	Residual
S_1	92	N	4	N	1	3
S_2	N	18	42	N	1	5
S_3	N	6	67	N	N	5
S_4	N	N	3	3	N	3
S_5	2	N	1	1	4	4
R	2	2	14	0	1	9

[a]Densities are computed as the average of Eq. (2.16) across the two networks multiplied by 100. Experts occupying each status are given in Figure 3.1, and the residual category is composed of experts not occupying a status. An "N" in a cell means that there are no non-zero relations from the row to the column categories involved.

relations only to one another. The highest density in row three of Table 3.6 is in column three, the density of relations among the occupants of S_3. Further, occupants of the status directed no relations to the occupants of statuses S_1, S_4, or S_5. They did acknowledge some influence from the occupants of status S_2 ($a_{32} = .063$).

Despite this acknowledgment from the only prestigious status in the college, status S_2 was defined by a role-set with secondary form. Occupants of this status tended not to be the object of relations in the college, even from one another. With the exception of three citations from the occupants of status S_3, occupants of no other status cited the occupants of S_2 as a source of methodological or substantive influence. At the same time, the experts occupying S_2 directed the bulk of their relations to the occupants of S_3. The density of cell (2,3) is far and away the strongest in row two of either part of Table 3.6. Since little of this interaction was reciprocated by the occupants of S_3, status S_2 appears to have been a satellite of status S_3.

As might be expected from Table 3.5, statuses S_4 and S_5 were relatively isolated within the college. Their occupants did have personal contact with experts occupying other statuses; however, those contacts were sparse. The occupants of status S_4 in particular were the object of almost no citations from other experts, even from one another (column four of Table 3.6). The role-set defining status S_5 was similar, but to a lesser extent; its occupants did have relations with the occupants of status S_1. In contrast to statuses S_4 and S_5, status S_1 was jointly occupied by experts who had very strong relations with one another. This accounts for the primary and secondary form of its role-set; its occupants did not seek out experts in other statuses, but neither were they sought out themselves as a source of influential comments.

The densities in Table 3.6 correspond to cells in Figure 2.4 as a social context. They indicate the number of statuses in the college and the strength of their connections. The densities can be abstracted still further in an image matrix generated by coding bonds as 0 unless the density of sociometric citations from one status to another is no less than the density of citations in the college as a whole (3.4%). The image matrix corresponding to this criterion density is[11]

$$\begin{bmatrix} 1 & 0 & 1 & 0 & 0 \\ 0 & 1 & 1 & 0 & 0 \\ 0 & 1 & 1 & 0 & 0 \\ 0 & 0 & 0 & 0 & 0 \\ 0 & 0 & 0 & 0 & 1 \end{bmatrix}$$

This image matrix is not a perfect homomorphism of the observed choice data since it ignores citations in low density cells of Table 3.6 and ignores residual

[11]This recoding of densities into bonds in an image matrix is discussed in Section 2.8 as the creation of a blockmodel. Since networks have been combined here, however, the image matrix does not correspond to the usual sense of a blockmodel in which an image matrix is generated for each network separately.

experts. It presents above average densities as bonds among status occupants. It, like Table 3.6, provides a representation of Figure 2.4 as a social context. It too summarizes stratification form in the college as of 1975: There were five jointly occupied statuses varying in the form of their role-sets. The only prestigious status was S_3 to which a secondary status, S_2, was attached as a satellite. One status had an ambiguous form (S_1; part primary, part secondary) while the two remaining statuses, S_4 and S_5, were comparatively isolated within the college.

But this is merely the overall skeleton of stratification in the college. What was the nature of role relations between the statuses? How did these relations integrate status occupants within an invisible college?

3.3 THE CONTENT OF STRATIFICATION

The substance of role relations among the elite experts concerns the content of stratification in their college. Given the above form of stratification, the most immediate question concerns the consistency with which experts were stratified within each network. Would the distribution of experts across jointly occupied positions in Figure 3.1 result from an analysis of each network separately? If not, then how were the two types of relations combined in defining the five role-sets?

Role-Set Multiplexity

Table 3.7 presents the intranetwork sociometric choice densities that were averaged as overall choice densities in Table 3.6. To the extent that a role-set was equally composed of both methodology and substantive relations, the upper and lower densities in each cell of the table should be equal. This is clearly not the case. In fact, there are several uniplex role relations. For example, the occupants of statuses S_4 and S_5 both acknowledged the occupants of S_3 as sources of methodological influence but never acknowledged them as sources of substantive influence (cells 4,3 and 5,3 are 5% and 0% versus 3% and 0%, respectively). The lack of multiplexity in role relations within the college is succinctly summarized in two image matrices constructed by coding the densities in Table 3.7 as 0 unless they are not less than the overall system choice density of 3.4%:

$$
\begin{bmatrix} 1 & 0 & 0 & 0 & 0 \\ 0 & 0 & 1 & 0 & 0 \\ 0 & 0 & 1 & 0 & 0 \\ 0 & 0 & 1 & 1 & 0 \\ 1 & 0 & 0 & 0 & 1 \end{bmatrix}
\begin{bmatrix} 1 & 0 & 1 & 0 & 0 \\ 0 & 1 & 1 & 0 & 0 \\ 0 & 1 & 1 & 0 & 0 \\ 0 & 0 & 0 & 0 & 0 \\ 0 & 0 & 0 & 0 & 0 \end{bmatrix}
$$

TABLE 3.7
Intranetwork Choice Densities Involving Status Occupants[a]

	S_1	S_2	S_3	S_4	S_5	Residual
S_1	83	N	N	N	2	3
	100	N	8	N	N	3
S_2	N	3	33	N	1	8
	N	33	50	N	2	3
S_3	N	N	75	N	N	N
	N	13	58	N	N	9
S_4	N	N	5	4	N	6
	N	N	N	1	N	N
S_5	4	N	3	1	6	7
	N	N	N	N	3	1
Residual	3	N	18	1	2	12
	N	5	9	N	1	6

[a] Upper density is based on methodology citations and lower density is based on substantive citations. Averages of these densities are given in the lower part of Table 3.6.

where the image matrix on the left refers to methodology bonds and that on the right refers to substantive bonds. As a condensation of Table 3.7, this blockmodel shows some basic mixtures of relational contents. First, there are only three multiplex bonds in the model: a_{11}, a_{23}, and a_{33}. The occupants of statuses S_1 and S_3 relied on other occupants of their respective statuses for both substantive and methodological comments. The occupants of status S_2 had an asymmetric reliance on S_3 for both types of comments. Remaining bonds in the model are uniplex. The occupants of S_2 used one another predominantly as sources of substantive comments (a_{22}), and the occupants of statuses S_4, S_5 used other occupants of their respective statuses predominantly as sources of methodological comments (a_{44}, a_{55}). Statuses S_4 and S_5 were similarly isolated in terms of substantive bonds, but their occupants had different sources of methodological comments; occupants of S_4 went to one another and status S_3 (a_{43}), occupants of S_5 went to one another and status S_1 (a_{51}). The remaining uniplex bonds concern the relations between occupants of the prestigious and secondary statuses in the college, S_3 and S_2, respectively. Experts occupying these two statuses relied on one another for substantive comments but only acknowledged influential methodological comments from the occupants of the prestigious status S_3. It is in the network of methodological relations that the secondary form of S_2 is most apparent; its occupants were not sought out as sources of influential comments from any status and they themselves relied on the occupants of S_3 for such comments.

Table 3.8 offers statistical results that substantiate the lack of multiplexity in the college while modifying its importance for overall stratification in the

TABLE 3.8
Role-Set Consistency[a]

	S_1	S_2	S_3	S_4	S_5
Correlations					
ϕ_{ms}	$.70_{(.69)}$	$.14_{(.14)}$	$.64_{(.55)}$	$.53_{(.51)}$	$.52_{(.47)}$
ϕ_m	$.94_{(.92)}$	$.79_{(.75)}$	$1.00_{(.93)}$	$.95_{(.90)}$	$1.00_{(.87)}$
ϕ_s	$.93_{(.92)}$	$.79_{(.75)}$	$.96_{(.82)}$	$.87_{(.84)}$	$.90_{(.84)}$
Probability that the status is perfectly consistent across both networks	<.001	<.001	<.001	<.001	<.001
χ^2	295.35	242.07	193.87	255.68	226.42
Variation described by first principal component	.89	.68	.78	.80	.75

[a]Correlations are maximum likelihood estimates of the parameters in the restricted covariance model in Figure 3.2. Corresponding Pearson correlations are given in parentheses and were computed by averaging the distances to each pair of experts indicating an unobserved variable in Figure 3.2. The chi-square test is given in Eq. (2.35) and has three degrees of freedom. The principal component analog is the ratio of variance in all six observed variables in Figure 3.2 that is described by a single principal component. The principal component results are based on correlations rather than covariances.

college. Recall from Section 2.9 that if the occupants of a status are similarly structurally equivalent within multiple networks, then distance to them within each network will be perfectly correlated with distance to them across all networks (Eq. [2.34]). Figure 3.2 presents the covariance model used to assess this hypothesis for the elite experts (cf. Figure 2.3 and Eq. [2.33]). Distance to the two experts indicating status S_j is correlated with distance to them within the network of methodology relations (ϕ_m) and the network of substantive relations (ϕ_s). Random error in observing distance is anticipated, but restricted to be equal for both experts within each network since they are structurally equivalent indicators of the same status. Under the hypothesis of consistent structure within each network, the two correlations ϕ_m and ϕ_s both equal 1 (Eq. [2.34]). Table 3.8 presents the chi-square test of this hypothesis, its principal component analog, maximum likelihood estimates of the correlations ϕ_m, ϕ_s, ϕ_{ms}, and corresponding Pearson correlations computed by averaging distance to indicator experts (e.g., the distance between expert j and status S_1 across both networks would be the sum of his or her distances to indicator experts 6 and 23 divided by two).

No role-sets were consistent across methodology and substantive relations. The correlations between intranetwork distances to each status are far from perfect ($\hat{\phi}_{ms} = .70, .14, .64, .53,$ and $.52$, respectively for the five statuses), and the chi-square test rejects the hypothesis of perfect consistency in each role-set at well beyond the .001 level of confidence.

Nevertheless, the two networks are not independently structured. A single

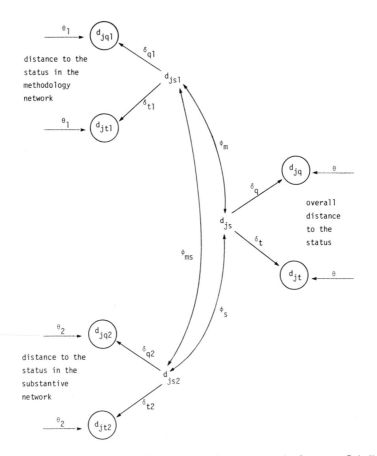

Figure 3.2. Assessing role-set consistency across the two networks for status **S** indicated by experts q and t (cf. Figure 2.3).

principal component can describe a high proportion of variance in both intranetwork and internetwork distances. Moreover, intranetwork distances to each status are highly correlated with overall distance to it. While methodology relations are a slightly better reflection of overall stratification than substantive relations ($\hat{\phi}_m \geq \hat{\phi}_s$ for each status), neither correlation is particularly low for any status. Both reach their minimum of .79 for the secondary status S_2. These high correlations are perhaps most consequential with regard to status S_3. Status S_3 was the one prestigious status in the college, so each expert's overall distance to S_3 indicated his overall prestige within the college. This prestige ordering of experts in terms of their overall distance to status S_3 is by and large replicated in both networks. Allowing for random error in observed distances, it is almost perfectly replicated by distances within the methodology network ($\hat{\phi}_m = .995$)

and quite strongly replicated by distances within the substantive network ($\hat{\phi}_s = .960$).

In summary, there were some multiplex role relations among the elite experts and some consistency in their stratification within each network. However, uniplex role relations were more typical of the college, and the hypothesis of perfect consistency across the two networks is rejected at well beyond the .001 level of confidence. In other words, there is every indication that a full understanding of stratification in the college requires an understanding of intranetwork stratification.

Intranetwork Stratification

Figures 3.3 and 3.4 bear out this suspicion. Figure 3.3 presents a hierarchical cluster analysis similar to that given in Figure 3.1 except that distances in Figure 3.3 are based only on the z_{jik} derived from methodology citations. Figure 3.4 is a similar summary of the relations derived from substantive citations. Jointly occupied intranetwork positions have been located in the same way that statuses were located. Positions are suggested by the cluster analysis and then subjected to statistical test. Perhaps most problematic are three positions in the methodology network: the third, fourth, and seventh. The first two are distinguished, although they appear as similar as two subgroups within the seventh position according to the cluster analysis. This specification rests on the statistical tests.[12] Distances to experts occupying the third and fourth positions generate two poorly correlated unobserved distance variables. This indicates that there are two sets of structurally equivalent experts present. Distances to experts occupying the seventh position generate two highly correlated unob-

[12]If experts occupying the third and fourth positions were to be treated as jointly occupying a single position, expert 18 would be joined to the group consisting of eleven experts (reading columns in Figure 3.3 from left to right: 18, 22, 17, 7, 36, 21, 9, 6, 23, 39, and 42). Within this group, experts 21, 9, 6, 23, 39, and 42 appear to define one position, and 22, 17, 7, and 36 appear to define another. A two factor covariance model such as Eq. (2.33) was fit to the (11,11) covariance matrix among distances to these eleven experts within the network where distance to expert 18 was allowed to load on both factors, distances to experts specified in Figure 3.3 as occupying the third position were allowed to load on the first factor, distances to experts specified in the figure as occupying the fourth position were allowed to load on the second factor, and the two factors were allowed to be correlated. All other factor loadings were forced to equal 0. The estimated correlation between the two factors was .28, a low correlation, so the two factors were treated as two nonequivalent points in the stratification space, and the two positions were distinguished as specified in Figure 3.3. Similarly, a two factor covariance model was fit to the (9,9) covariance matrix among distances to the nine experts jointly occupying the seventh position. Distances to experts 5, 2, 24, 33, 43, and 49 were allowed to load on the first factor, distances to experts 35, 36, and 52 were allowed to load on the second factor, and the two factors were allowed to be correlated. This partition of the position into two groups is based on the deep cleavage in X's among the experts in Figure 3.3. The estimated correlation between the two factors was high, .76, so the two factors were treated as measuring distance to the same area in the stratification space, and all nine experts were specified as jointly occupying position seven.

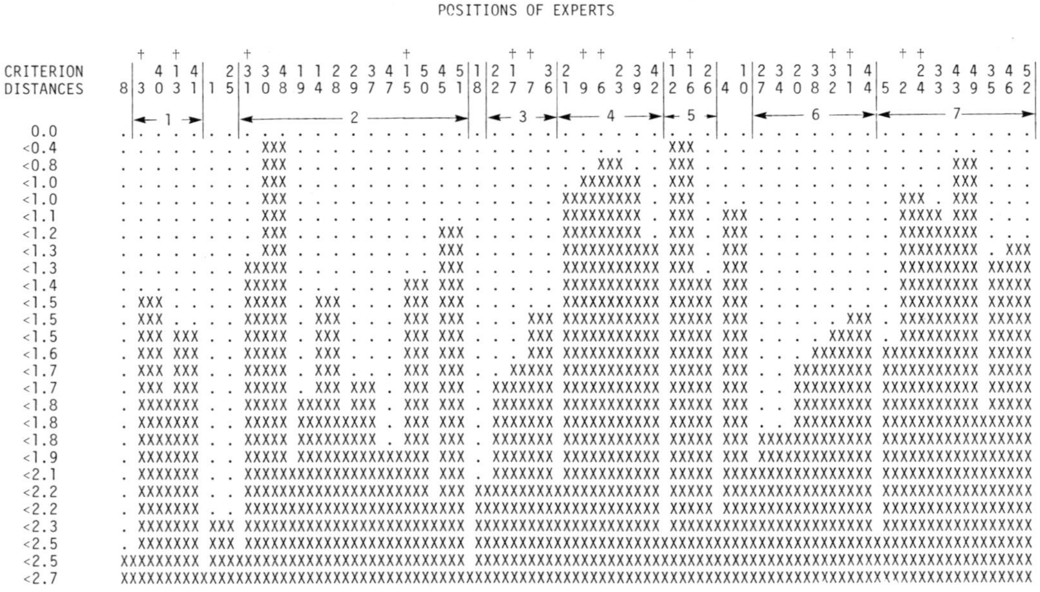

POSITIONS OF EXPERTS
CRITERION DISTANCES
0.0
<0.4
<0.8
<1.0
<1.0
<1.1
<1.2
<1.3
<1.3
<1.4
<1.5
<1.5
<1.5
<1.6
<1.7
<1.7
<1.8
<1.8
<1.8
<1.9
<2.1
<2.2
<2.2
<2.3
<2.5
<2.5
<2.7
1
2
3
4
5
6
7

33	N	N	N	N	N	N
19	7	N	N	N	N	N
67	N	N	70	N	N	26
63	N	N	72	N	N	30
36	12	N	19	63	N	57
67	1	N	22	N	N	63
59	N	N	26	N	N	62

Figure 3.3. Hierarchical cluster analysis suggesting jointly occupied positions in the network of methodology relations and the density of relations (z_{ji1} multiplied by 100) among their occupants.

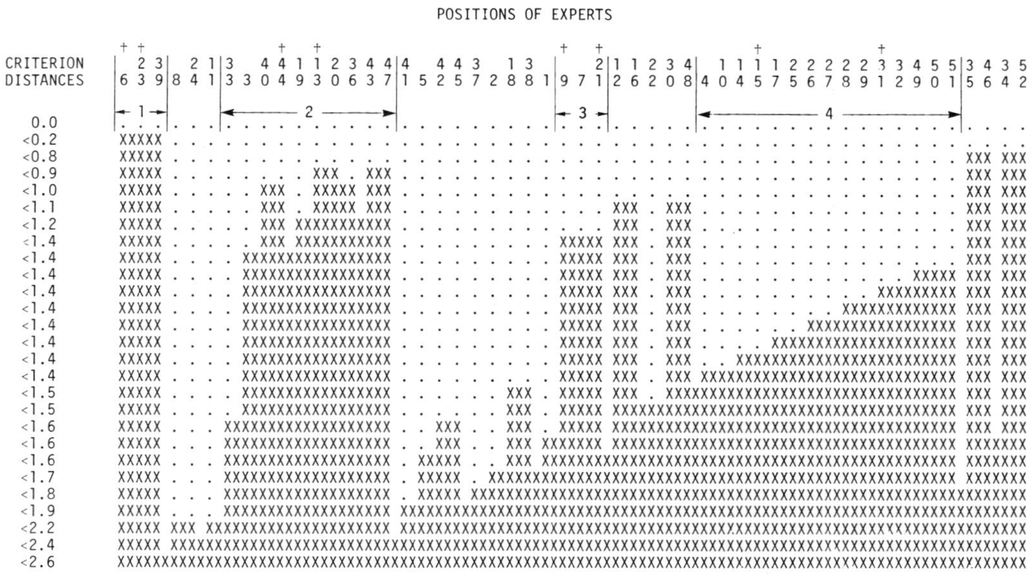

91	37	15	N
N	58	10	N
N	N	16	N
N	N	N	N

Figure 3.4. Hierarchical cluster analysis suggesting jointly occupied positions in the network of substantive relations and the density of relations (z_{ji2} multiplied by 100) among their occupants.

served distance variables. This indicates that there is only one set of structurally equivalent experts present. Indicator experts for each jointly occupied position are marked with a dagger in the cluster analyses.[13] Presented below each cluster analysis are densities among the experts jointly occupying positions. Densities are based on the normalized path distances used to compute distances for the cluster analyses, the z_{jik}, so N represents the complete lack of a direct or indirect connection from the row to the column category.

The intranetwork stratification in Figures 3.3 and 3.4 suggest three broad groups of elite experts within the college—a social psychology group, a statistics and mobility group, and a mathematical sociology group. By way of linking these substantive areas to specific network positions for the reader, I asked eight indicator experts for permission to use their names in the discussion. At the time, these eight experts were indicators of network positions and/or statuses that had a primary form. In other words, they were, and still are, highly prominent men whose work is likely to be known to the reader and accordingly likely to give the reader an added feel for the content of stratification in the college. I shall discuss all other indicator experts in terms of the general area to which each has made extensive contributions.

Social Psychology

Two statuses were occupied by experts specializing in social psychology as a general substantive area, S_1 and S_5. Distance to status S_1 was indicated by distance to James Davis (expert 6) and distance to Samuel Leinhardt (expert 23). The third expert occupying S_1, specialized, as did Mr. Davis and Mr. Leinhardt, in the analysis of triadic network structure. Accordingly, the status is discussed here as the position of a "triads elite" within the college. Distance to status S_5 was indicated by two experts referenced here by their principal contributions as Mr. Philosophy (expert 12) and Mr. Beliefs (expert 27). Of the experts occupying S_5 who claimed a substantive expertise (15 of the 18 occupants), 47% explicitly claimed the general area of social psychology, and another 40% claimed closely related areas such as education, marriage, and the family, religion, etc. Accordingly, the status is discussed here as the position of a general "social psychology elite" within the college.

A comparison of the columns in Figures 3.1, 3.3, and 3.4 shows that the

---

[13]Indicator experts have been selected on the basis of a principal component analysis of the covariance matrix among distances to their jointly occupied position. Basic results are given elsewhere (Burt 1978a:144–145). The average principal component ratio (Eq. [2.31]) for the four positions in the substantive network is .94 and that for the seven positions in the methodology network is .91 where the lowest ratio in either network is .84. Comparing these ratios to those in the second row of Table 3.4 (an average of .82) shows that intranetwork structural equivalence is much more clearly defined than is the structural equivalence of status occupants. Indicator experts for a position are the two experts with the highest weights on the first principal component.

social psychologists who occupied statuses S_1 and S_5 in Figure 3.1 occupied positions one, three, and four in the substantive network (Figure 3.4) and occupied positions three, four, and five in the methodology network (Figure 3.3). Some occupants of S_5 scattered to other positions; however, the bulk of social psychologists occupied the above six. As can be seen from the densities in Figure 3.3, occupants of all three social psychology positions relied on the first ($z_{31} = .67$, $z_{41} = .63$, $z_{51} = .36$) and seventh ($z_{37} = .26$, $z_{47} = .30$, $z_{57} = .57$) positions for methodological comments. Among themselves, they relied extensively on the occupants of the fourth position for such comments ($z_{34} = .70$, $z_{44} = .72$, $z_{54} = .19$). Although occupants of the third position had no direct or indirect methodology relations with one another, occupants of the fifth position did seek one another out for methodological comments ($z_{33} = N$, $z_{55} = .63$).[14] Of the three positions, then, the fourth appears to have been jointly occupied by methodology leaders in social psychology. Occupants of this position were the object of methodology relations from the social psychologists occupying other positions as well as one another. However, occupants of the fourth position had no direct nor indirect methodology relations to social psychologists occupying the other two positions ($z_{43} = z_{45} = N$). This conclusion regarding leadership in social psychology is corroborated by the relative extent to which the three positions were defined by relational patterns with primary form.[15] Only distance to the fourth position is negatively correlated with the measure of primary form ($r = -.39$; cf. Table 3.5). Further corroboration is obtained by considering experts occupying position four. All of the triads elite occupied the position (note Mr. Davis, 6, and Mr. Leinhardt, 23). Also occupying this position were social psychologists concerned with the general area of social psychology and who had accumulated credentials as leaders in methodology. Note David Heise (expert 9), who, along with Mr. Davis, was an indicator expert for position four. Also present in the position was George Bohrnstedt (expert 21) whose substantive concerns were more general than the study of triads and who accordingly occupied a position with Mr. Heise in the network of substantive relations (third position in Figure 3.4). Looking at the substantive network in Figure 3.4, the divergent substantive interests of methodology leaders in social psychology resulted in their dividing into two structurally nonequivalent positions. The triads elite occupied the first position. The other leaders occupied the third position. Since most experts specializing in social psychology here had substantive relations with a wide range of persons outside the college of elite

[14]Occupants of position five specialized in philosophy of science and theory construction issues so they probably relied on one another for methodological comments on these specialized issues.

[15]Distances to the two indicator experts for each position were averaged and correlated with the formal measure of primary form based only on methodology relations (prom_{jk} self_{jk} correlated with d_{j4k} for position four, cf. Eq. [2.19] and Table 3.5). The correlations were .75, $-.39$, and .67, respectively for the third, fourth, and fifth positions. Thus, experts with the relational pattern defining the fourth position had high primary form and those involved in relational patterns similar to the patterns defining the third and fifth positions had low primary form.

sociological methodology, most fell into the isolate position (fourth position in Figure 3.4).[16]

As an overview of the social psychologists, the two statuses they occupied were based on more subtle features of social differentiation. Methodology leaders for this group broke into two structurally nonequivalent positions owing to their divergent substantive interests. One position was occupied by experts pursuing the study of triads and defined status S_1 in the college. The other position was occupied by experts pursuing the general study of social psychology and was absorbed in status S_5, although its occupants were quite peripheral in the status (note the low indicator coefficients for experts 7, 9, and 21 under S_5 in Table 3.4). The remaining social psychologists (both those who depended on the leaders for advice on technical matters as well as those who were either self-reliant or pursuing nontechnical methodologies) occupied an isolate position within the substantive network. Many of these remaining social psychologists occupied status S_5 in the college.

Statistics and Mobility

Two statuses were occupied by experts who specialized in statistical methods and/or the substantive area of stratification and mobility. This group largely centered around the tradition (established in sociology by Blau and Duncan [1967]) of clearly defined parameters in statistical models in conjunction with reliable samples of data so as to rigorously assess hypotheses. The substantive work here followed directly from Blau and Duncan's study; however, the exemplar quality of the statistical analyses had resulted in close ties with individuals quite expert in statistics. Distance to status S_3 was indicated by distance to Robert Hauser (expert 13) and distance to Leo Goodman (expert 3). The other two experts occupying S_3 were also well known for their statistical competence, so the status is referenced here as the position of a "social statistics elite" in the college. Distance to status S_2 was indicated by distance to two experts referenced here according to their principal contributions as Mr. Mobility (expert 20) and Mr. Achievement (expert 44). The experts occupying this status who claimed an area of substantive expertise (5 of the 6 occupants) tended to claim stratification and mobility as that area (4 of the 5). Accordingly, status S_2 is referenced here as the position of a "mobility elite" within the college.

Recall from the analysis of role-set form and multiplexity that status S_2 had a secondary form while status S_3 was the only status with a primary form, the former having been a satellite to the latter. Occupants of these two statuses sought one another out for substantive comments but relied on the occupants of

---

[16]Occupants of the fourth position in the substantive network made an average of one citation per expert to persons outside the college (14 citations from 15 experts) and made no substantive citations to experts within the college.

S_3 for methodological comments. A deeper understanding of the connection between statuses S_2 and S_3 is obtained by considering the intranetwork positions of their occupants. The social statistics elite jointly occupied the most prominent position in the methodology network, the first position. The correlation between distance to this position and the measure of primary form is the highest negative correlation obtained for all seven positions in the network ($r = -.91$) and is higher than the corresponding correlations for statuses in Table 3.5. In the network of substantive relations, the social statistics elite and the mobility elite jointly occupied the second position (cf. the columns of Figures 3.1 and 3.4). In the network of influence relations, however, the mobility elite were scattered across several nonequivalent positions.

This suggests an almost symbiotic linkage between the social statistics elite and the mobility elite. The principal feature of the role-set defining the mobility elite was their common dependence on the social statistics elite. The largest element in row and column two of Table 3.6 is from the occupants of S_2 to occupants of S_3 ($a_{23} = .42$). Since the mobility elite did not have extensive direct interaction with one another ($a_{22} = .18$) and that interaction tended to be uniplex substantive relations ($a_{221}/a_{222} = .18$ in Table 3.7), it seems plausible to say that these experts jointly occupied a status in the college as a result of their common orientation to the social statistics elite. At the same time, it seems plausible to say that the social statistics elite jointly occupied a status in the college as a result of their asymmetric relations with the mobility elite and their own interest in mobility.[17] While the social statistics elite did interact extensively with one another for methodological reasons and were the object of extensive methodological relations from other experts, they acknowledged substantive comments from different members of the mobility elite and from different residual experts. In the same manner that methodology leaders in social psychology jointly occupied a prominent position in the methodology network (position four) but did not jointly occupy a single status in the college, the social statistics elite need not have defined a single status just because of their prominence in the methodology network (position one). The dense methodology and substantive relations in the mobility role-set (S_2) were by definition a major component in the social statistics role-set (S_3), elements z_{23} and z_{32} appearing in both role-sets. Structurally speaking, the mobility elite and social statistics elite served to define one another as statuses in the college of elite experts.

Mathematical Sociology

The third group of experts illustrates the potential consequences of failure to coordinate methodological expertise with some shared substantive interest.

[17]Two of the four social statistics elite claimed stratification and mobility as an area of special competence. The other two occupants of S_3 were principally concerned with statistical issues.

Elite experts specializing in mathematical sociology jointly occupied the seventh position in the methodology network. Distance to their position was indicated by distance to James Coleman (expert 2) and distance to Seymour Spilerman (expert 24). Of the experts occupying position seven, 78% claimed mathematical sociology as an area of special competence, so they are collectively referenced here as a "mathematical sociology elite" within the college.

There is no mixture of relational contents in the role-set defining the mathematical sociology elite since these elite did not define a status in the college. They did define a prominent position in the methodology network. Distance to their position (measured as an average distance to Mr. Coleman and Mr. Spilerman) has a strong negative correlation with the measure of primary form ($r = -.68$); experts close to the position were involved in relational patterns with high primary form. However, the divergent substantive interests of the mathematical sociology elite led them to be scattered across nonequivalent positions in the network of substantive relations (cf. the columns of Figures 3.3 and 3.4). This in turn resulted in their being scattered across nonequivalent statuses. In the cluster analysis in Figure 3.1, the mathematical sociology elite are scattered across the diagram (cf. columns of Figures 3.1 and 3.4). Three of its members occupied status S_5 and the remaining occupied no status. Were it not for the prominence of their jointly occupied position in the methodology network, these elites would have been invisible as a group within the overall stratification of the college. As it was, they could only have been visible as a group in the eyes of insiders familiar with both networks in the college (or an outsider armed with network data on the college).

3.4 CONCLUSIONS

I have sought to characterize and interpret the social topology of elite sociological methodology as it existed in 1975 defining the social context in which experts operated. The densities in Table 3.7 characterize relational patterns among status occupants and those in Figures 3.3 and 3.4 characterize intranetwork relational patterns. But these characterizations treat jointly occupied positions as places in the college's social topology. In fact, they are merely points of reference in the topology. Figure 3.5 offers a metric preserving, spatial characterization of the college's topology. The diagram is based on an eigenvalue decomposition of distances among 25 experts: the 4 social statistics elite marked SSE in the diagram), the 9 mathematical sociology elite (marked MSE in the diagram), the 6 methodology leaders in social psychology (marked SPL in the diagram), and 6 experts indicating statuses S_2, S_4, and S_5 who were less prominent members of the college.[18] The vertical axis corre-

---

[18]A (25,25) matrix, D, was constructed from the distances used to cluster experts in Figure 3.1 where rows/columns corresponded to the 25 experts in Figure 3.5. Crossproducts were then computed as $D'D$, and the eigenvalues for the matrix were found. The first four eigenvalues

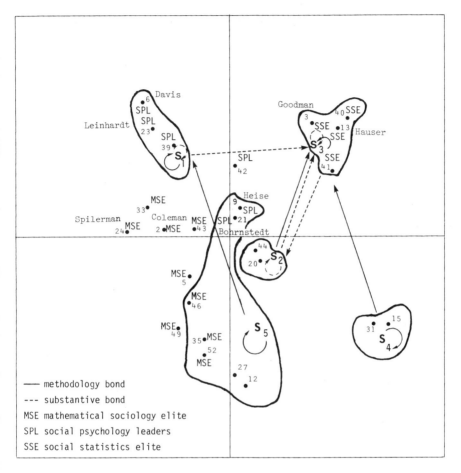

Figure 3.5. A two dimensional representation of the form and content of the college's social topology (status/role-sets indicated by enclosed spaces).

sponds to two dominant eigenvalues (43.54% of the sum of all eigenvalues), and the horizontal axis corresponds to two smaller, but still prominent, eigenvalues (26.25% of the sum of all eigenvalues). The center of the space is the intersection of all dimensions at their mean values. Sociogram-type arrows refer to bonds in the blockmodel coded from Table 3.7; solid lines indicate methodo-

accounted for 70% of the sum of all eigenvalues. The first axis in Figure 3.5 is a composite of the eigenvectors corresponding to the first two eigenvalues, and the horizontal axis is a composite of the eigenvectors corresponding to the third and fourth eigenvalues. Where two eigenvectors to be combined are orthogonal to one another, the composite is the line (positively correlated with both eigenvectors) that runs through their mean values with a 45 degree angle to each. Section 2.9 provides a detailed discussion of the crossproducts of distances to statuses as a measure of the similarity of their role-sets.

logy bonds and dashed lines indicate substantive bonds. For example, S_4 is tied to S_3 by an unreciprocated methodology bond.

Figure 3.5 is little more than a caricature of the college's social topology since it only distinguishes two dimensions.[19] However, it does summarize structural features emphasized in the preceding analysis. There were five jointly occupied statuses across which the experts were stratified. These statuses differed considerably in the form and content of their respective role-sets. The only status that can be termed prestigious in the sense of having a primary relational form was occupied by a social statistics elite (S_3) to whom a mobility elite were attached as a satellite status (S_2). While the occupants of both statuses acknowledged influential substantive comments from one another, all relied on the social statistics elite for influential methodological comments. Methodology leaders in social psychology jointly occupied a prominent position in the methodology network but split within the college to occupy a triads elite status (S_1) and a social psychology elite status (S_5). The latter was occupied under a very weak criterion of equivalence by many of the nonleaders in social psychology (note the large area in Figure 3.5 corresponding to status S_5). The social psychologists tended to rely on one another for methodological comments, but there was a higher tendency for the occupants of S_5 to seek such comments from the triads elite (S_1) than vice versa. Finally, a group of experts specializing in mathematical sociology jointly occupied a prominant position in the methodology network but jointly occupied no status in the college. Note in Figure 3.5 that the mathematical sociology elite are scattered through the left-hand side of the diagram, some in status S_5 with social psychologists, the remainder falling into a residual category.

Although the bulk of relations in the college involved occupants of the first three statuses, the typical elite expert was unlikely to occupy one of these statuses. This involvement in relations is the principal axis in terms of which the college was stratified. The vertical axis in Figure 3.5 is based on dominant eigenvalues and clearly stratifies the statuses; a higher density of relations occurs at the top of the diagram, but a higher density of experts occurs at the bottom.[20] However, the college was far from unidimensional, and involvement should not be confused with prestige. Only the social statistics elite were structurally prestigious within the college. Nonmembers of this group, connected to S_3 as a source of influential comments, were structurally distant from S_3 as indicated by their spatial separation from the status in Figure 3.5.[21]

---

[19]Figure 3.5 only considers 25 experts, fewer than half of the college's members, yet 22 dimensions are required to reconstruct the crossproducts of distances among these 25 (as many eigenvalues were nonzero in the matrix $D'D$ in footnote 18).

[20]Recall that statuses S_4 and S_5 were occupied by a total of 28 experts while the first three statuses were occupied by 13 (see Table 3.4).

[21]This contrast between relations and distances is a major issue in the treatment of social norms in Chapters 5 and 6. If relations are the basis for social norms, then the close tie between the social statistics and mobility elite should make them very similar. If distances are the basis, however, then

This points to an interesting feature of the connection between multiplex relations among the experts and their prominence within the college. The denser the substantive relations within a group of experts already tied by methodology relations, the more prominent the group was within the college.[22] The social statistics elite occupied the most prominent status in the system and developed an entire satellite status occupied by a mobility elite. The divergence of substantive relations among the methodology leaders in social psychology resulted in their occupying two statuses, neither of which was as prominent as that occupied by the social statistics elite. Finally, the lack of similar substantive relations among the mathematical sociology elite had the result that their prominent position within the methodology network was split into many nonequivalent positions within overall college stratification. Failure to coordinate their substantive work rendered these elite experts invisible as a group even though they were prominent as individuals.[23]

But why should a group of experts closely tied by personally communicated methodological comments come to rely upon one another for substantive comments? If the similarity in their substantive relations can be explained, then their prominence within the college itself is in part explained.

---

the social statistics elite could be very different from the mobility elite since they occupy clearly nonequivalent statuses within the college.

[22]Related to this point is Gaston's (1973) analysis of the prominence of different speciality groups within British high energy physics. The most prominent group, the "phenomenologists," are persons who are competent in both theoretical and experimental physics in the same sense of being able to communicate the results of one area into the terminology of the other area (Gaston 1973:170–172). While the bridging of methodologial and substantive concerns by phenomenologists in physics is not the same as the merger of such concerns by the social statistics elite, both situations demonstrate a close linkage between prominence and the integration of substance with methodology.

[23]The difference between individual and group prominence is an important one. Certainly the two experts indicating the position of elite mathematical sociology in the methodology network, Mr. Coleman and Mr. Spilerman, were prominent in the discipline at the time—as were other occupants of their position. Indeed, Coleman and Spilerman were ideal typical occupants in the sense that they pursued a great variety of substantive interests with a great variety of colleagues. But they were not part of a group of experts with similar methodological skills attacking a common substantive problem with a common set of colleagues in the sense that the social statistics elite dominated the study of occupational mobility and achievement. One might argue that the many uses to which mathematics can be put makes it impossible for there ever to be a prominent subfield called mathematical sociology (e.g., Leik & Meeker 1975:19); however, this is beside the point. There are a great many uses to which statistics can be put, yet the only prestigious status in the college was occupied by a social statistics elite. Not all experts with statistical skills occupied this status. It was only occupied by those experts who, in addition to being highly skilled in statistics, worked in close communication with a satellite status of persons analyzing mobility and achievement. Were mathematical sociology ever to define a prestigious status in the college, it would not be a status to which anyone could gain entry by acquiring mathematical skills. It would be a status occupied by experts who, in addition to being highly skilled mathematically, were also a principal source of influential methodological and substantive comments for a group of persons analyzing a substantive area opened up for exploration by the application of mathematics to important problems within the area. In this case, the prestigious status would not define mathematical sociology per se within the college. It would define the prestigious position of that aspect of mathematical sociology that had turned out to be substantively powerful in providing explanations and socially powerful in restructuring experts within the invisible college.

TABLE 3.9
Aggregate Attributes of Three Groups of Elite Expert Leaders

	Social statistics elite	Methodology leaders in social psychology	Mathematical sociology elite
Structural attributes			
Nonequivalent positions occupied in the college	1	3	7
95% interval estimate of mean primary form in group pattern	.25–.33	.08–.18	.13–.21
Substantive specialities			
Proportion claiming no substantive speciality	0.25	0.50	0.56
Maximum proportion claiming same substantive speciality	0.50	0.33	0.00
Institutional affiliations			
Proportion of pairs ever employed at the same institution at the same time	0.33	0.05	0.09
Proportion of pairs obtaining their Ph.D. from the same institution	0.17	0.05	0.05
Proportion of potential teacher–student relations observed	0.33	0.29	0.19
95% interval estimate of mean data of Ph.D.	1956 ± 12	1963 ± 5	1968 ± 17

[a]The number of nonequivalent positions occupied in the college refers to the cluster analysis in Figure 3.1. The social statistics elite occupied a single status, leaders in social psychology occupied two statuses (S_4, S_5) and a position in the residual category, and the mathematical sociology elite occupied S_5 as well as six positions in the residual category. Primary form in a group's relational pattern is given by Eq. (2.19) as in Table 3.5. Claims of substantive specialities are taken from the 1975–1976 ASA *Directory of Members*. For a position having N occupants, there are $N(N-1)/2$ pairs of occupants. Ratios here are the number of pairs sharing a characteristic. Data are taken from *American Men and Women of Science, Social and Behavioral Sciences*. A potential teacher–student relation existed between any pair that obtained their Ph.D.'s at different times. A potential teacher employed at the university where a potential student obtained his Ph.D. at the time that the student obtained his Ph.D. was coded as an observed teacher. Teacher–student relations are thus possibly overestimated.

Table 3.9 presents aggregate attributes of the three prominent positions in the methodology network: the social statistics elite (position one), methodology leaders in social psychology (position four), and the mathematical sociology elite (position seven). The first two rows of the table establish the rank order prominence of these three groups within the college as a whole. One way in which a group can be prominent is through the extent to which it occupies a single status so as to be visible as a group. The social statistics elite occupied one status while the mathematical sociology elite occupied seven nonequivalent positions. Intermediate between these two are the social psychology leaders who occupied three nonequivalent positions. Similarly, the relational patterns in which the social statistics elite were involved had a much higher primary form than did the patterns in which the other two groups were involved. What is required in order to explain the relative prominence of these three groups then is an attribute that reproduces the ranking, SSE, SPL, MSE.

This order is reproduced by the similarity of substantive concerns expressed by experts in each group. In row three of the table, only 25% of the social statistics elite claimed no substantive speciality while 56% of the mathematical sociology elite had no substantive speciality. Of the experts in each group who did claim a substantive speciality, 50% of the social statistics elite shared the same speciality while none of the mathematical sociology elite shared the same speciality. Under both measures, the methods leaders in social psychology fall in between the social statistics and mathematical sociology elite.

Mullins (1973) suggests that the prominence of a group of scientists is a function of the colleague and and teacher–student ties among scientists in the group. Groups are prominent to the extent that they have dense colleague relations and to the extent that "founding fathers" in a group prolifically generate graduate students to continue their work. The bottom four rows of Table 3.9 present alternative institutional affiliations that might account for the relative prominence of the elite experts. The data present plausible, if not overwhelming, support for Mullins' (1973) interpretation of speciality prominence.

Row six presents the density of colleague relations among experts in each group. The social statistics elite did have the highest tendency to have been employed together at one university. However, the other two groups had approximately equal, low, tendencies for such colleague relations.

Experts who obtained their doctorate from the same university might be expected to have developed similar substantive interests. Row seven shows that this explanation is about as adequate as the colleague explanation. The social statistics elite had the highest tendency to have received doctorates at the same university. Again, the other two groups had equal, low, tendencies for having the same doctorate source.

A better explanation is obtained when possible teacher–student relations are considered (row eight). A third of the possible teacher–student relations among the social statistics elite could have occurred. Among methods leaders in social psychology, this tendency is lower (.29). Among the mathematical sociology elite, the tendency is lower still (.19). In other words, the density of student–teacher relations rank orders the three groups of experts in the same manner as the prominence and shared substantive interests of the groups.

Yet another explanation of the relative similarity of substantive interests of the three groups involves the notion of cohorts. It seems reasonable to say that those experts with similar methodological expertise who have been trained at the same time could have developed similar substantive interests. This explanation is corroborated by the mean years in which the three groups obtained their doctorates. The bottom row of Table 3.9 shows that the social statistics elite had the oldest doctorates (mean of 1956). The methods leaders in social psychology had somewhat younger doctorates (mean of 1963). The mathematical sociology elite had the youngest docotrates (mean of 1968). The 95% confidence intervals around these mean dates overlap to such a high extent, however, that it is difficult to reliably distinguish among the three groups as separate cohorts.

The net inference I make is that the rank order of the three groups of elite expert leaders in terms of their similarity of substantive interests stems from the similarity of their academic training. To be sure, the inference is far from reliable since the data are approximations to colleague and teacher–student relations. Nevertheless, the inference is in accord with Mullins' (1973) fairly well supported interpretation. It is also in accord with commonsense. The social statistics elite had the highest density of possible teacher–student relations and so should have had the highest level of agreement on how to pursue their substantive concerns. At the other extreme, the mathematical sociology elite had the lowest density of such relations and so should have had the lowest tendency to agree on what are "the" important substantive questions to address with their methods.

The implication of the analysis is, to my mind, unpleasant. If the level of homogeneity of substantive concerns among a group of experts in some methodology is a function of their shared academic training, and homogeneity of substantive concerns in turn determines the prominence of the group, then academic training determines the group's prominence. Since academic training is a constant once an individual becomes established, the rank order of prominence for the three groups of elite experts in 1975 could be stable into the future. The mathematical sociology elite could continue to pursue myriad different substantive interests, generate new experts within each of these interests, and remain an invisible group: a group better known for its label than for its accomplishments and members. The social statistics elite could continue to coordinate their substantive efforts with the mobility elite and therefore remain the most prominent group.

The occurrence that would most obviously break this stability would be a major development in a substantive area that makes coordinated use of the statistical and mathematical skills of the elite experts. For the social statistics elite, this is what occurred with the Blau and Duncan study of occupational mobility. Although there has been no study with comparable impact since the Blau and Duncan monograph, there is always the possibility of one. A cohort or two of graduate students later, one could expect significant changes in the stratification of the college.

Of course, there is always the eroding force of time itself. Students previously drawn to the growth and prominence of statistical achievement models might become increasingly difficult to recruit as they search for areas less thoroughly explored. As of this writing, five years after the network data were obtained, there are signs of discontent with a continued dominance of mobility and achievement by statistical issues. However, the above conclusions regarding stratification in the elite college of sociological methodology by and large still hold. For the typical elite expert in 1975 and all persons aspiring at the time to membership in the college, most certainly, the existing stratification must have appeared an enduring definition of the social context within which methodological work was to be pursued. Accurate or not, it would be this perception that would make the context a significant feature in each expert's evaluations of alternatives. This is a topic to which I return in Chapter 6 after the network model of perception is introduced in Chapter 5.

4

STRATIFICATION IN AMERICAN
MANUFACTURING*

As in the preceding chapter, models of network structure are used here to describe stratification within a system of actors. However, I here describe the relational patterns in which organizations, instead of people, are involved and make inferences from relational data on a very small sample of actors in a system instead of using data on most actors in the system. The American economy is treated as a social topology in which economic sectors correspond to jointly occupied network positions. Corporate boards of directors, or more succinctly, directorates, are described as a medium through which establishments in separate sectors can be coordinated so as to circumvent market constraint on profits. My purpose in this chapter is to describe the manner in which manufacturing establishments were connected in 1967 through directorates to diverse economic sectors. I begin with a brief review of research on directorates as a cooptive device.

4.1 BASIC EVIDENCE ON DIRECTORATES AS COOPTIVE DEVICES

Stemming from seminal work by Adolf Berle, Gardiner Means, and Philip Selznick, there are political, empirical, and theoretical reasons for focusing on

*Portions of this chapter are drawn from an article reprinted with the permission of the *Administrative Science Quarterly* (Burt 1980e).

corporate directorates as a cooptive device. Describing corporate ownership, Berle and Means (1932) highlighted the importance of corporate boards of directors as the center of control in American corporations. If not the ultimate source of control (as discussed below), the directorate is a politically important center for the exercise of corporate control. With this in mind, Means's subsequent work directing the National Resources Committee in describing controls among American corporations (Means 1939) set the stage for later empirical work by introducing the concept of interlocking directorates (two firms are interlocked when one or more persons sit on the boards of both firms)—one method by which ostensibly competitive firms might avoid the market constraints on their profits that open competition ensures. Readily available data on directorate membership for American corporations make the directorate a convenient basis for empirical research on corporate control. As centers of corporate decision-making, finally, directorates constitute a theoretically interesting focus for describing corporate cooptation. Struck with the manner in which the Tennessee Valley Authority avoided conflicts with local voluntary organizations by appointing representatives of the organizations to positions in the TVA decision-making structure, Selznick (1949) proposed the now well-known concept of cooptation:

> coöptation is the process of absorbing new elements into the leadership or policy-determining structure of an organization as a means of averting threats to its stability or existence [p. 13].

In other words, if the interlocked directorates of separate firms allow them to coopt one another as ostensibly competitive participants in sales and purchase transactions, then extensive interlocking in the American economy might be evidence of an integrated economic elite.

Suspecting that such a condition exists in the United States, social scientists have devoted extensive research to describing interlocks among American corporations. This research can be brought together in an empirical generalization: There is extensive interlocking in the United States (especially in urban centers for corporate headquarters such as New York, Chicago, and Los Angeles), and those firms most likely to be involved in interlocking are large firms operating in capital-intensive industries where the firm is controlled by diffuse interest groups. Putting to one side the overall tendency for interlocks to occur, there are three principal findings to this empirical generalization. Each can be interpreted in terms of cooptation.[1]

Large firms tend to extensively interlock with other firms. Measuring firm size in terms of dollars of assets or annual sales, a ubiquitous finding in directorate research is the positive correlation between firm size and the number

[1] I am only concerned here with very basic features of directorate research. For discussion of this research in the more general context of how organizations cope with their environment, see Aldrich and Pfeffer (1976), Pfeffer and Salancik (1978), Aldrich (1979), Aldrich and Whetten (1981); especially the last work with its focus on network concepts.

of different corporations represented on the firm's board (e.g., Warner & Unwalla 1967; Dooley 1969; Pfeffer 1972a; Allen 1974, Pennings 1980). This finding can be interpreted in terms of cooptation. The larger a firm is, the more impact its actions have on other organizations, and accordingly, the more the firm needs representatives who can integrate and legitimate the firm in its external environment (cf. Dooley 1969:316; Pfeffer 1972a:223; Allen 1974:395).

Firms operating in capital-intensive industries extensively interlock with other firms. This phenomenon occurs in two ways. The most extensively interlocked of all firms are those operating in finance, particularly banks. Among the many firms represented on the typical directorate, there is usually a representative from a major bank, usually a bank in the same geographical region as the firm itself (e.g., Warner & Unwalla 1967; Dooley 1969; Levine 1972; Pfeffer 1972a; Allen 1974, 1978; Bearden, Atwood, Freitage, Hendricks, Mintz, and Schwartz 1975; Mariolis 1975; Sonquist & Koenig 1975; Pennings 1980). Arguing for a cooptive interpretation of interlocking, Allen (1974) suggests that extensive financial interlocking is to be expected since capital is a "very generalized resource with a very dispersed demand from such economic organizations as corporations [p. 395]." An implication of this line of reasoning is that firms with high capital requirements should have disproportionate representation on their boards from other firms. Measuring capital requirements as a firm's ratio of debt to equity, Pfeffer (1972a:224) and Pennings (1980:115) report the expected positive correlation. However, Pennings (1980:115) also reports a slight negative correlation between this measure of capital requirements and the number of interlocks in which firms are involved. Using the ratio of assets to employees as a measure of a firm's capital intensiveness, Allen (1974:400) reports a low negative correlation with financial interlocking.[2] Similarly, Pennings reports a negative correlation between a firm's debt to equity ratio and its interlocks with financial institutions.

Finally, firms controlled by diffuse interest groups tend to interlock extensively. This finding is supported in research addressing the question of corporate control. The "management control" thesis advanced by Berle and Means (1932) and supported by subsequent research (Larner 1970; Allen 1976) is that the corporate officers as "management" have come to power as a result of the diffusion of shares among so many owners that individual owners no longer exercise control over the corporate use of capital. While Berle and Means (1932:196) refer to management as "a board of directors and the senior officers of the corporation," the term is more often reserved for officers—few or many of whom can also be directors. In contrast to this management control thesis, there is a "family control" thesis; extensive stock ownership by members of a family

---

[2]Both Allen and Pennings present correlations that control for the size of the firm involved in interlocking. Pennings (1980:115) also measures capital intensiveness as the ratio of assets to employees. Unlike Allen however, Pennings holds the number of employees constant before presenting correlations so that the low correlations he reports between this measure of capital intensiveness and interlocking are difficult to interpret or compare to Allen's.

enables a kinship group to be the ultimate source of corporate control (e.g., Burch 1972; Zeitlin 1974, 1976).[3] Research on these two theses has produced a basic result: Concentration of corporate control in either a kinship group or a firm's management is associated with infrequent interlocking. Measuring management control as the percentage of directors who are also officers in a corporation, Dooley (1969) and Pfeffer (1972a) report a negative correlation between management control and number of interlocks. Pennings (1980:90) reports a negative correlation between interlocking and the proportion of the board drawn from within the firm. Identifying family-controlled firms as those in which a kinship group holds more than 10% of available stock, Allen (1976) finds fewer interlocks in family-owned firms than in other firms. This negative correlation between concentration of corporate control and interlocking can be interpreted in terms of cooptation. The more concentrated corporate control is in a single group, the greater the loss of control incurred with the addition of a single outside group on the directorate. Selznick's analysis of the TVA demonstrates that cooptive efforts can backfire. When the TVA brought representatives of local organizations into its own decision-making structure, it was forced into some actions more beneficial to the local organizations than to the TVA (see Selznick 1949:113–114, 145–153, 205–213, 217, 259–261). But where control of a corporation is already dispersed such that each individual interest group sharing control has little control over eventual decisions, the addition of yet another voice on the directorate entails little loss of control for each person already on it. Therefore, dominant kinship or management groups on a directorate would be expected to oppose extensive interlocking with other firms in order to maintain a decision-making capacity unimpaired by their corporate environment. (cf. Dooley 1969:322; Pfeffer 1972a:224). In Zald's (1969) terms, concentration of corporate control in a single interest group, a kinship interest group, or management as an interest group, results in the directorate serving an "internal control" function rather than an "external representation" function.

Because of its political importance as the center for corporate control, the ease with which data can be obtained on it, and the fact that it is readily interpreted as a cooptive device, the corporate directorate has been a focus of interorganizational research. Characteristics of the firms most involved in representing other firms on their directorates can be interpreted as evidence

---

[3]A third thesis of corporate control has been discussed at length by Kotz (1978) as financial control. In the same research style as that of Larner and Burch, Kotz shows that many large American firms can be viewed as operating under the full or partial control of financial institutions. Kotz's study raises the question of how differences in financial control over a firm are associated with corporate interlocking. Pennings (1980:107–134) provides a detailed report on financial interlocking; however, financial interlocking is only vaguely related to financial control since it need not imply that the financial firm(s) represented on a directorate have any influence over it. The association between financial control and patterns of directorate ties has yet to be systematically described as of this writing.

supporting the idea that directorates are a cooptive device. The firms most involved in interlocking have been large, capital-intensive firms controlled by dispersed interests.

4.2 ECONOMIC SECTORS AS THE SOCIAL CONTEXT FOR DIRECTORATES

Directorate research typically focuses on the extent to which other corporations are represented on a firm's board of directors. How many of the firm's directors sit on other boards? How many of its directors sit on the board of financial institutions? The composition of a firm's board is analyzed in terms of the variety of firms represented on it, and the specific composition for a given firm is expected to be a function of the market constraints confronting the firm. For example, mixed evidence notwithstanding, capital-intensive firms are expected to have high representation on the boards from financial institutions.

It is useful here to take a closer look at the structure of the economy as the social context in which directorates operate. The economy can be discussed as a network of sales and purchase transactions among organizations. Division of labor ensures considerable redundancy in such a network. Those organizations engaged in the production of similar commodities will have similar relations from other organizations (i.e., will require similar proportions of commodities as inputs from suppliers), and to other organizations (i.e., will offer similar types of commodities as outputs to consumers). In other words, organizations producing the same type of commodity could be expected to occupy economic network positions defined by the same pattern of purchase and sales transactions with other organizations as suppliers and consumers. Such organizations are structurally equivalent as described in Chapter 2. Those organizations producing some commodity j jointly occupy position j in the economy as a network; they have typical purchase transactions from each other jointly occupied position and typical sales transactions to each other jointly occupied position (as characterized in Figure 2.4). The M jointly occupied positions in Figure 2.4 correspond to "sectors" of the economy in an input–output table representation where z_{ji} is the total dollars of sales by organizations in sector j to those in sector i (e.g., Leontief 1968). As the total flow of dollars from organizations in sector j to those in sector i, z_{ji} corresponds to the density of relations from position j to position i before it is normalized by the number of actors in the two positions (see Eq. [2.16]). In short, the input–output tables representing the American economy in terms of aggregate market transactions between organizations in sectors of the economy (e.g., U.S. Department of Commerce 1974) can be interpreted as unnormalized density tables of interorganizational transactions between jointly occupied network positions in the economy. An (M, M) table of aggregate transactions among organizations in M

economic sectors models the social topology of the American economy thereby describing the social context in which corporate directorates operate. The organizations competing with one another in the production of commodity j jointly occupy sector j. Their supplier organizations are indicated by large z_{ij} to be occupants of sector i. Their consumer organizations are indicated by large z_{jk} to be occupants of sector k. In other words, these aggregate interorganizational transactions indicate competitors, suppliers, and consumers within the economy. Chapter 8 contains a description of how these transactions actually translate into market constraints on corporate profits.

The more immediate problem is the fact that the organizational units involved in these sales and purchase transactions need not be incorporated firms. Refer to a corporation's holdings within a single economic sector as an establishment. Following Department of Commerce terminology, an economic sector consists of all establishments engaged in the production of the same commodity. If a corporation owns two factories, one manufacturing bread and the other cigars, then it owns two establishments, one in the food sector and the other in the tobacco sector. If it owns two factories at separate locations but both engaged in the production of bread, then it owns a single establishment in the food sector.[4] In other words, market constraints stemming from sales and purchase transactions exist among establishments operating within economic sectors.

This creates an obvious problem for those who wish to do research on directorates as cooptive devices since most firms operate in more than one sector. The typical firm owns multiple establishments. Since each of a firm's establishments can be subject to different market constraints, the firm spanning several economic sectors is subject to a complex mixture of market constraints. As a social entity created to coordinate the activities of establishments, the firm is less an economic unit of cooptation than it is a means to cooptation. Since it is at the establishment level rather than the firm level that market constraints exist to be coopted, analysis of directorates as a cooptive device is obliged to focus on the establishment level.

Therefore, I diverge slightly from the traditional methodology for analyzing the corporate directorate as a cooptive device. Rather than analyze a corporate board in terms of the diversity of *firms* represented on it, I shall analyze the diversity of *establishments* represented on it. More specifically, I wish to know how directorates provide cooptive ties among establishments as competitors, suppliers, and consumers. To be sure, when a representative from another firm sits on a corporate board, he represents the other firm. More important to an analysis of coopting market constraints, however, he represents the establish-

---

[4]This usage of the term establishment is slightly different from that employed by the Department of Commerce. The Department of Commerce refers to each separate factory in a sector as a separate establishment whether or not multiple factories are owned by a single corporation. Since establishment-level data are not available for a national sample of firms and since my concern here is with the coordination of establishments in separate sectors through directorate ties, two or more Department of Commerce establishments that are owned by a single corporation within a single sector are treated as a single establishment.

ments of the other firm. It is access to those represented establishments that would allow the corporation's own establishments to coopt sources of market constraint.

4.3 DIRECTORATE TIES BETWEEN ESTABLISHMENTS

Given establishments as competitors, suppliers, and consumers within the economy, the set of establishments represented on a directorate, and accordingly coordinated through the directorate, is less obvious than might appear to be the case by casual inspection. Under different strategies of cooptation, different sets of establishments can be represented on a single corporate board.

Ownership Ties

The most direct strategy for coopting an organization constraining one or more of a firm's establishments is to purchase it outright or to create the firm's own establishment within the organization's sector. Since the previously owned establishments and the newly purchased/created establishment are controlled through the same directorate, they are very closely interlocked through it. Thus, the most obvious set of establishments represented by a corporate board consists of those directly owned and operated by the board. From the perspective of establishments, the most obvious, and intimate, interestablishment directorate tie is this ownership tie between them through their joint control by a single directorate.

There are several advantages to conducting market transactions of sales and purchases within the domain of a single corporation rather than conducting them between separate firms. A comprehensive discussion of these advantages is given by Williamson (1975).[5] He summarizes his discussion in terms of six advantages to conducting market transactions within a single corporate hierarchy (Williamson 1975:257–258). I have put the original terms in parentheses. A corporate hierarchy of establishments has the advantage of improving communication since each establishment can specialize in making internal decisions without having to glean information on its environment (bounded rationality), and establishments have perfect audit information on other establishments in the hierarchy (information impactedness). Further, the corporate hierarchy provides security from the environment by allowing a less Machiavellian exchange process than typifies the market (atmosphere), preventing dishonesty (small numbers and opportunism), and permitting adaptation to environmental contingencies by means of coordination among its constituent establish-

---

[5] In Williamson's terms (1975:151–154), the discussion here of establishments versus corporations would translate into a discussion of U-form (unitary) versus M-form (multidivisional) organizations, respectively.

ments (uncertainty). It is not surprising to find that establishments represented on a single corporate board are drawn from interdependent sectors of the economy. In his analysis of merger rates across industries, for example, Pfeffer (1972b; Pfeffer & Salancik 1978:114ff) reports a strong positive association between the extent of merger activity between establishments in two economic sectors and the extent to which the two sectors are connected by sales and purchase transactions. A similar association can be found between intersector market transactions and the extent to which establishments in separate sectors are formally tied in joint venture organizations spanning the separate sectors (Pfeffer & Nowak 1976; Pfeffer & Salancik 1978:152ff).

In order to make ownership directorate ties empirically more explicit, consider the position of Mr. W. H. Vaughn, president of Firestone Steel Products in 1967. This establishment was a division of Firestone Tire and Rubber, its establishment in the transportation equipment sector. The establishment manufactured wheels, a task nicely dovetailing with Firestone's general production of tires. Dividing the American economy into sectors according to two-digit Standard Industrial Classification (SIC) industries from the Department of Commerce, more specifically; the establishment Mr. Vaughn ran was connected to establishments in seven other manufacturing industries through the directorate of Firestone Tire and Rubber. (As a point of reference here, my focus will be on those economic sectors engaged in manufacturing so that in order to avoid writing manufacturing sector each time that I refer to one, I shall refer to such sectors as industries and reserve the term sector to refer to sectors generally—manufacturing as well as nonmanufacturing.) Figure 4.1 presents these establishments by SIC industry with bold lines to Firestone Tire and Rubber indicating ownership. These establishments do not appear to have been drawn at random; they were, to varying extents, located in interdependent industries, judging from aggregate data on transactions among sectors of the American economy in 1967.[6] The largest proportion of supplies for the textile industry, for example, was purchased from establishments in the chemical industry so that it would have been to the advantage of Firestone's textile establishment to conduct its transactions with Firestone's chemical establishment rather than being forced to deal on the open market. Similarly, the largest portion of supplies for the rubber industry was purchased from the chemical industry so that, again, the ownership tie between Firestone's establishments in the rubber and chemical industries could have enabled them to conduct this needed transaction without resorting to the open market. Returning to Mr. Vaughn, the two industries most responsible for supplying the transportation equipment industry (excluding the industry itself) were the two metals industries. Here again, Firestone owned establishments in both the primary and fabricated metals industries. In contrast, the economic sectors most responsible

[6]Transaction data for the American economy are taken from the 1967 Input–Output Study (U.S. Department of Commerce 1974). The aggregate transaction data are reported for 85 categories and are analyzed here in terms of 45 sectors as explained below (see footnote 8).

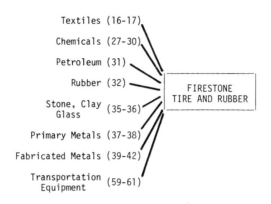

Figure 4.1. Establishments represented on the directorate of Firestone Tire and Rubber in 1967. (Numbers in parentheses are input-output sectors aggregated to two-digit SIC industries.)

for consuming transportation equipment output were not represented on Firestone's directorate through ownership. Other relations were needed to reach these sectors.

Direct Interlock Ties

The advantages of hierarchy notwithstanding, economies of scale and federal regulations make it impossible for a firm to own all of its establishments' competitors, suppliers, and consumers. As a convenient surrogate for actually owning an establishment in an important sector, the firm can create a tie between itself and some other firm that owns an establishment in the sector. While offering less control than the internal connection provided by direct ownership, a second type of interestablishment directorate tie occurs when two establishments are owned by separate firms that share one or more directors, that is, by separate firms with interlocked directorates. I shall refer to this type of directorate tie as a direct interlock tie.

Strategic recruitment of directors from other firms can be advantageous. Mace (1971) provides a particularly useful discussion of such directors based on field work he conducted during the 1960s; the field work consisted of participation on directorates and interviews with other directors. These directors are typically selected by a firm's chief executive; typically they do not interfere with the firm's management or attack proposals put forth by its management during board meetings, but they do play three important roles within the firm:

1. Within their respective areas of expertise, outside directors offer advice and counsel to the management.
2. They constitute a corporate superego in the sense that, in order to avoid

embarassing questions during board meetings, the management takes particular care in preparing proposals before bringing them to the board for approval. As one president put it (Mace 1971), "the mere existence of outside directors makes us think a little bit harder, makes us organize our thoughts. It sharpens up the whole organization [p.24]."

3. Finally, they offer the firm stability by being collectively empowered to replace the firm's chief executive in the event of his death or incompetence. Since they have been appointed by the same office, however, the latter event is most likely to result in their resignations from the board or their collective request for an evaluation of the current management's performance by an outside consulting firm—a subtle hint to the reigning chief.

There are exceptions to these typical roles; however, the roles as general patterns of behavior are quite in keeping with the kinds of people one would expect to fill them: bright, successful individuals who are absorbed in their own activities, so that they have little time to get involved in another firm's problems.

The advice and counsel role of the outside director most clearly animates the cooptive potential of a direct interlock tie. Given some important sector for a firm's establishments, it could be extremely useful to have a direct channel of personal communication with a firm operating its own establishment in the sector; the channel increases the possibility of learning about developments being undertaken within the sector as well as probable sector response to developments being considered within the firm. One of Mace's (1971) respondents put the matter in the following way:

> The board of directors serves as a sounding board—a wall to bounce the ball against. It is a kind of screen on major moves, whether it be acquisitions, or whether it be major shifts of policy or product line—the broad directions of the business. Board members serve as sources of information. . . . The decision is not made by the board, but the directors are a checkpoint for the management in adding their experience and knowledge to the program [p.13].

Of course, the flow of information can be symmetric; the outside director can advise the corporate president as well as carry his observations during the board meeting back to his own firm. There are two considerations that account for the willingness of individuals to serve as directors in other firms: the first is the opportunity to learn about corporate practices in the other firm's industry; the second is the other firm's prestige (Mace 1971:101–106).

In short, the direct interlock tie informs decision-making within the establishments it connects. Direct interlock ties improve the accuracy of an establishment's information on trade partners available in other sectors in which it is interested. With respect to sectors containing an establishment's competitors, suppliers, or consumers, this increased accuracy of information has the potential to lower uncertainty in the establishment's ability to obtain profits by increasing its ability to predict future developments in the sector and increasing its ability to determine the capacity and abilities of potential trade partners in the sector. For example, Firestone Tire and Rubber interlocked with Western Airlines in 1967. Western Airlines owned an establishment in the transportation and warehousing sector, a sector which is the the second largest consumer of output from the transportation equipment industry (aside from the industry itself). Firestone's transportation equipment establishment, run by Mr. Vaughn at the time, had the good fortune of having Leonard K. Firestone as the man interlocking Firestone with Western. As a member of the board of Firestone Tire and Rubber Company and president of Firestone Tire and Rubber of California (a division of the parent company), he was an eminently prestigious and partisan spokesman for Firestone products when Western planned its purchases of transportation equipment. Of the $7,175 million in manufactured commodities purchased by establishments in the transportation and warehousing sector, $4,847 million were purchased from industries in which Firestone owned an establishment in 1967. In other words, Mr. Firestone provided a personal communication channel between Western Airlines and Firestone's establishments operating in industries providing 53% of the supplies for the sector in which Western operated. At the same time that Mr. Firestone provided a communication channel to an important consumer sector for his company, his position with the company gave him the opportunity to make accurate inferences about developments in the transportation/warehousing sector based on his participation in Western's directorate, which he was able to report to Firestone Tire and Rubber.

Indirect Interlock Ties Through Financial Institutions

Another outside director on Firestone's directorate illustrates the ubiquitous financial interlock: Firestone was interlocked with the Cleveland Trust Company. George F. Karch, the President of Cleveland Trust, sat on Firestone's directorate. As the president of Cleveland Trust, Mr. Karch could have provided Firestone's establishments with the often mentioned corporate need for financial advice. Still, this need for financial counsel must be weighed against the obligations of having a financial firm represented on the board. This obligation is most obvious in the case of investment banks. In a response nicely illustrating the creation of favored trade partners through interlocking, one of Mace's (1971) respondents made the following comment:

> If you've got an investment banker on your board, you're sort of a little bit tied in with him, and I prefer not to have one on our board. An investment banker on the board restricts one's freedom of action—I mean you might or might not want to use his firm in some transaction, and *if he is on the board he thinks he is entitled to that business* [p.146; italics added].

Here again, however, there is a symmetry to the interlock tie that can work to the nonfinancial firm's advantage. Restrictions firm A faces as a result of its interlock with a financial institution can also be imposed on other firms interlocked with it—imposed in a manner advantageous to firm A. A banker-director represents more than his financial establishment on the board. He represents all of the sectors in which his firm controls establishments as well as those in which his firm has expert knowledge. Looking beyond direct interlocks with financial institutions, a third type of interestablishment tie occurs when two establishments owned by separate firms are connected indirectly through a financial institution interlocked with them both. In the language of graph theory, the two firms are connected by a two-step path distance through the financial institution (Eqs. [2.3, 2.4]). I shall refer to this type of directorate tie as an indirect interlock tie.

In one sense, these indirect interlock ties provide a market advantage similar to that provided by direct interlock ties. They channel the flow of information among establishments. However, they do so more efficiently, if possibly less accurately. Routine errors in transmission would suggest that the accuracy of information transmitted across multiple interlock ties would decline with the number of different ties over which the information has passed. Ceteris paribus, information communicated over indirect interlock ties should be less accurate than information communicated directly between directorates. But the banker-director as an indirect connection to many sectors is efficient since information on all sectors is probably not needed at any one time, and he only takes a single seat on a directorate as opposed to the many seats required to directly represent the sectors he indirectly represents. In the interest of maintaining some privacy in board meetings and maintaining a balance of voting power on the board, the efficiency of an indirect interlock tie would seem to outweigh the possibile distortion of information indirectly obtained through it. Once aware of an idea, a firm's management could always pursue it outside of the board meeting in order to obtain more accurate information on it. As an information source, financial interlocks seem to function in this manner. Summarizing his observations with respect to investment bankers in particular, Mace (1971) felt that these bankers

> through exposure to many different companies in many different industries and regions, bring to company presidents and company boards of directors what one president described as "a treasury of information." Bankers, as they practice their profession, are collectors of information—they hear the problems faced and approaches followed by presidents of a substantial number of other companies. Thus investment bankers as directors were described as "great pollenizers"—they lift ideas from one company and deposit them in other companies [p. 200].

In a second sense, indirect financial interlocks could be stronger than direct interlocks between nonfinancial firms and so offer a market advantage similar to ownership ties. With the growth of pension funds and insurance premium capital during the post–World War II period, stock ownership in American firms has become increasingly concentrated in banks and insurance companies (Kotz 1978:60–71; Metcalf 1978). In the same sense that a firm's establishments obtain advantages in conducting their market transactions with one another, it is in a financial firm's interest to maintain profit margins in its diverse holdings since those profits directly and indirectly translate into its own profits. This is the reason typically given to suggest that financial control is a threat to competition—the coordinating financial institution managing wasteful rivalry between members of its community of interest. Although there seems to be little or no systematic evidence on this point, occasional illustrations can be found.[7] Beyond the information he brings to the directorate, in short, the director from a financial firm brings preferential trade partners in diverse sectors to the extent of his firm's influence over potential trade partners.

It is interesting to reconsider the directorate of Firestone Tire and Rubber in the light of indirect interlock ties. Looking past the direct interlock between Firestone and Cleveland Trust in 1967, note that Cleveland Trust itself interlocked with American Airlines and Pan American Airlines. Each of these corporations owned an establishment in the transportation and warehousing sector in 1967. It could be coincidence, but by interlocking with Cleveland Trust, Firestone tripled the number of establishments with which it had an interlock tie in the transportation–warehousing sector, a sector for which 53% of the total manufacturing purchases were provided by industries in which Firestone owned an establishment.

4.4 DIRECTORATE TIES AS COOPTIVE RELATIONS

The cooptive potential of the three types of directorate ties follows immediately from the preceding description of them. All three absorb new elements into the management of a firm (the weakest being direct interlocks between nonfinancial firms). However, even the outside director with no power in a firm provides advice and counsel to the firm's management on the board. More importantly, I believe, all three types of directorate ties offer a means of averting threats to the stability and existence of establishments by providing them with an avenue for circumventing market constraints on their profits.

Market constraints among establishments as one another's competitors, suppliers, and consumers can be circumvented through directorate ties by

---

[7]Kotz (1978) describes and provides references for examples that have occurred over the history of the American economy. A succinct example is cited in Representative Patman's (1968) report on commercial banks, which drew from an earlier study of the General Motors Corporation:

> Several of the witnesses claimed that General Motors obtained business because directors of various transit companies were bankers who were anxious to obtain General Motors' banking business, and therefore urged their managers to purchase General Motors buses. These witnesses claimed that the managers of certain transit companies, although well satisfied with non-General Motors products which they had used for many years, switched to General Motors at the urging of their directors [p.25].

means of the creation of favored trade partners. The word circumvented is important here. Market constraints are not eliminated by directorate ties; they are avoided. An establishment in the apparel industry must purchase supplies from the textile industry; an establishment in the transportation equipment industry must purchase supplies from the primary metals industry, and so on. These sales and purchase transactions are a necessary part of manufacturing technology. However, there is a choice of supplier establishments within a supplier sector. Directorate ties make some establishments more attractive trade partners than other establishments. Ownership ties create the many advantages of conducting market transactions in the nonmarket context of a corporate hierarchy wherein buying and selling can be conducted more efficiently than it can on the open market, efficiency translating into increased profits for buyer and seller establishments especially in the context of severe competition on the open market. Direct interlock ties channel the flow of adverse and favorable information regarding trade partners available in other sectors so as to make specific establishments more attractive than others as suppliers and/or consumers. This same function is fulfilled by indirect interlock ties through financial institutions, with greater efficiency if lower accuracy, banker-directors in particular being a source of information on operations in many sectors. Moreover, the representative from a financial institution brings to the board the influence his firm can exercise over potential trade partners. Together, the three types of directorate ties create favored trade partners as establishments with which buying and selling can be conducted with lower uncertainty because of more accurate information and a third party authority over the transactions—the higher, joint authority of a shared board of directors and/or the brokered authority of an intermediary financial institution. The more that all three types of directorate ties connect competitor, supplier, or consumer establishments, the lower the proportion of buying and selling that must be transacted on the open market. In this sense of defining trade partners with which necessary buying and selling can be conducted in a nonmarket context, directorate ties have the potential to be cooptive interorganizational relations to sources of market constraint.

4.5 ANALYZING COOPTIVE DIRECTORATE TIES IN AMERICAN MANUFACTURING

I want to describe the manner in which manufacturing establishments were connected by ownership, direct interlock, and indirect interlock ties to competitor, supplier, and consumer establishments within the 1967 American economy. It would be impossible to analyze data on all ties among all establishments; there were simply too many firms owning to many establishments. Thus is raised the problem of how to draw sample information. There is also the problem of organizing the sample data in some meaningful way in order to provide an analytical description. I shall first address the sampling problem, then the analytical one.

Sampling

Firms are typically sampled for directorate research by size, large firms having extensive assets and/or extensive annual sales. For example, the pace setting study by the National Resources Committee (Means 1939) describes interlocks among the 200 largest nonfinancial corporations and the 50 largest financial institutions. Dooley (1969) and Allen (1974) describe identical samples for later points in time (1964 and 1970, respectively). In a similar vein, Representative Patman's Subcommittee on Domestic Finance (Patman 1968) analyzes the 500 largest industrial corporations and the 200 largest nonindustrial firms in the 1966 *Fortune* listing together with 49 large banks in urban centers. Mariolis (1975) and Pennings (1980) analyze the 500 largest manufacturing firms and the 247 largest nonmanufacturing firms, drawing principally from the 1970 *Fortune* listing. Bearden *et al.* (1975) analyze the 1131 largest American firms, drawing principally from *Fortune* listings between 1963 and 1974.

This sampling on a size criterion is justified by Berle and Means's (1932) finding that the top 200 nonbanking firms in 1929 controlled between 45 and 53% of all assets in nonbanking firms. Given this concentration of assets in the largest corporations, there is little need to analyze more than the largest firms if analysis is intended to make inferences about corporate assets in the economy as a whole.

Nevertheless, an innovative twist on this size criterion is proposed by Warner and Unwalla (1967). Defining a population of 20,989 firms listed in the 1961 *Fortune* compilation of the 750 largest American firms and the 1961 *Million Dollar Directory* from Dun and Bradstreet (a listing of firms with a million dollars or more of annual sales), a stratified random sample of 500 firms was drawn with the aid of *Moody's Industrial Manual*. The sample was stratified into 11 SIC categories, and the number of sampled firms within each category approximated the proportion of total net worth of firms in the population that was accounted for by the net worth of firms in the category (Warner & Unwalla 1967:24,124).

My purpose here requires a slight variation on the usual size criterion in directorate research, a variation anticipated by Warner and Unwalla. I am not concerned with describing either the control of assets in the overall economy or interlocking among firms generally. Instead, I wish to describe the manner in which establishments jointly occupying manufacturing industries as network positions are connected by directorate ties to establishments in sectors generally. A two-stage sampling procedure seems appropriate. The first stage yields a positional sample representative of manufacturing industries, and the second stage snowballs that sample into nonmanufacturing sectors.

The purpose of the positional sample is to ensure that directorates operating in each manufacturing industry, and likely to be responsible for directorate ties, are represented in the analysis. Since interlocking is more typical of large firms than small firms, the largest firms owning establishments in an industry are most likely to be responsible for any directorate ties linking establishments in the industry to sectors generally. Beginning with the 1968 *Fortune* listing of the 500 largest American manufacturing firms in 1967, the 4 largest firms owning an establishment in any one of the two-digit SIC manufacturing industries have been located using the SIC listings for each firm in the 1968 *Poor's Directory of Corporations, Directors and Executives.* The resulting 42 firms represent large American firms engaged in manufacturing. Since a single firm could have been the largest firm owning an establishment in more than a single industry, the sample does not contain 4 unique firms from each industry. Among the 42 sampled firms are the 4 largest owning an establishment in any one of the two-digit manufacturing industries. Although not the 42 largest manufacturing firms, the sampled firms are quite large. Liggett and Myers Tobacco is the smallest firm in the sample with its sales rank of 220, yet it sold an impressive $384,801,000 worth of products in 1967.

The purpose of the snowball sample is to locate large nonmanufacturing firms that the sampled manufacturing firms represented on their directorates. Directors in the largest 250 nonindustrials in the 1968 *Fortune* listing have been coded from *Poor's* and compared to the boards of the sampled manufacturing firms. Any nonmanufacturing firm that was interlocked with one or more of the sampled manufacturing firms was added to the sample. In effect, directors of the sampled manufacturing firms have been used as sociometric citations to nonmanufacturing firms in which they are also directors so as to snowball the initial sample into nonmanufacturing sectors. Of the 250 nonindustrials listed in *Fortune*, 110 were interlocked with one or more of the sampled manufacturing firms. These 110 nonmanufacturing firms added to the sample consisted of 32 banks, 22 insurance firms, 21 transportation firms, 20 utilities (including 2 communications firms and 4 holding companies), and 15 merchandising firms.

I have distinguished 45 economic sectors in which these sampled firms might have owned an establishment—21 manufacturing industries and 24 nonmanufacturing sectors. The manufacturing industries correspond to two-digit SIC categories. The nonmanufacturing sectors correspond to aggregate categories in the 1967 Input–Output Study (U.S. Department of Commerce 1974). Of the 85 input–output categories, 52 were aggregated into the two-digit SIC manufacturing industries, 24 correspond exactly to the nonmanufacturing sectors considered here, and the remaining 9 were deleted because they did not correspond to SIC categories and accordingly would not be listed in *Poor's* as sectors in which the sampled firms could have owned establishments.[8] If *Poor's* listed a firm, or one of a firm's subsidiaries or divisions, as operating within a SIC category corresponding to one of these sectors, the firm was coded as owning an establishment in the sector.

In total, the 152 firms owned 414 establishments, 260 of which were owned by the sampled manufacturing firms. This sample is designed to allow inferences to be made regarding the manner in which establishments in American manufacturing industries were connected in 1967 through corporate directorates to establishments more generally as their competitors, suppliers, and consumers. The corporate directorates through which these connections are to be described are the directorates of the 42 firms representative of large American firms engaged in manufacturing. Each of the sampled establishments is represented on the board of one or more of these 42 firms by one or more of the three types of directorate relations discussed previously. The sample provides a basis for describing the directorate ties among establishments and the types of firms most responsible for those ties.

Replicating Past Research

Given the small size of the sample and the fact that it is designed specifically to describe directorate ties through large firms involved, directly or indirectly, in manufacturing, it is important to know if these data replicate past research findings. If they do, then subsequent analysis of them can add to those findings.

Table 4.1 shows that characteristics of the sampled firms do conform to past research findings. Firms with extensive assets tended to have a large number of interlocks and a large per capita number of interlocks; the average number of interlocks per director in a large firm is higher than it is in a small firm. Of the mean 11 interlocks per manufacturing firm, 5.4 are with financial firms and 6.1 are with nonfinancial firms. Standardizing by the relative number of financial ($N = 54$) versus nonfinancial ($N = 98$) firms, the typical manufacturing firm had a .06 tendency to interlock with each nonfinancial firm and a .10 tendency to interlock with each of the financial firms. A higher tendency to interlock with financial firms is typical of past research findings. Capital intensiveness, however, is negatively correlated with interlocking. In keeping with the Allen (1974) and Pennings (1980) results, captial-intensive manufacturing firms tended to have fewer interlocks than did non–capital-intensive firms with other

---

[8]The 76 input–output categories corresponding in some way to SIC categories were sectors in which the sampled firms could have owned establishments using the SIC listings in *Poor's* to locate sectors in which each firm owned establishments. The 9 deleted sectors not corresponding to SIC categories were "special" industries (government industry, rest-of-the-world industry, household industry), "dummy" industries (office supplies, business travel–entertainment–gifts, scrap), imports, and government enterprises (federal, state, and local).

TABLE 4.1
Moments for Corporation Variables and Interlocking[a]

	Mean	S.D.	Assets	Capital output ratio	Management control	Family control
				Corporate variables		
Assets	3191.45	3269.21	1.00			
Capital output ratio	.95	.42	.32	1.00		
Management control	39.39	15.83	.09	.05	1.00	
Family control	1.79	.78	− .05	− .06	.29	1.00
Number of interlocks with financial firms	5.40	3.54	.21	− .23	− .38	− .17
Number of interlocks with nonfinancial firms	6.07	5.13	.30	− .18	− .35	− .29
Total number of interlocks	11.48	8.15	.28	− .21	− .39	− .26
Per capita number of interlocks with financial firms	.35	.24	.14	− .13	− .36	− .20
Per capita number of interlocks with nonfinancial firms	.38	.30	.23	− .10	− .38	− .30
Per capita number of total interlocks	.73	.51	.20	− .12	− .40	− .28

[a]Moments are computed across the 42 manufacturing firms, and a correlation greater in absolute magnitude than .25 is significant at the .05 level of confidence. Millions of dollars of assets (assets) and dollar assets divided by dollar sales (capital output ratio) are coded from the 1968 *Fortune* listings. Management control is the percentage of directors who are also officers in the firm according to the 1968 *Poor's*, and family control is a three point scale discussed in the text measuring the extent to which a kinship group controls the firm through stock ownership. Per capita interlocks are numbers of interlocks divided by number of directors.

firms generally, financial as well as nonfinancial. Family control of a firm is negatively correlated with interlocking where control is measured on a three point scale: A score of 3 is given if a single kinship group owned more than 10% of the firm's stock. A score of 2 is given if such a group owned less than 10% but more than 2% of the firm's stock. A score of 1 is given if the firm is probably not dominated by any one kinship group. Classifications by Larner (1970:70–117) and Burch (1972:36067) were used as data.[9] Measuring the probable percen-

[9]Larner's study allowed me to classify the 42 manufacturing firms as controlled by management or an external minority (any kinship group holding 10% or more of a firm's stock). Burch's more detailed data on stock holdings grouped the firms into three categories: probably family controlled, possibly family controlled, and probably not family controlled. All of the firms Burch classified as

tage of stock held by a single kinship group yields correlations nearly identical to those Table 4.1 contains.[10] The correlations among the corporation variables also replicate previous research findings. Management control is uncorrelated with firm size (cf. Dooley 1969:317). As argued by Zeitlin (1976), contradicting Allen (1976), family control is also uncorrelated with firm size. Since firms controlled by dispersed interests are low on both the management-control and family-control variables, there is a positive correlation between these two control variables (cf. Allen 1976:887), although management control has a stronger negative association with interlocking than does family control.

Cooptive Corporate Actor Networks

I shall describe the directorate tie data in terms of a type of ego-network in which a manufacturing firm is ego and the establishments represented on its

---

possibly family controlled or probably not family controlled, Larner classified as nonminority controlled. Of the 15 firms classified as probably family controlled by Burch, however, Larner only classified 5 as controlled by an external minority. Of the 10 disputed firms, Burch reported that single kinship groups controlled more than 10% of the stock in 4 firms (Ling-Temco-Vought; R.J. Reynolds Tobacco; U.S. Plywood-Champion Papers; and Uniroyal, previously known as U.S. Rubber). Given the greater detail of, and support for, Burch's figures, these 4 firms were assumed to actually be minority controlled firms. The remaining 6 of the disputed firms involved indirect control by a family or control by a family holding less than 10% of the firm's stock. These 6 firms were therefore classified as possibly family controlled. Of the 42 sampled manufacturing firms, 9 were classified as probably family controlled, 15 as possibly family controlled, and 18 as probably not family controlled.

[10]The three levels of family control (1, 2, 3) reflect quite unequal differences in percentages of stock ownership. Using the data in Burch's study, an average of 26.3% of the stock is owned by a family in the 9 firms classified here as probably family controlled. For the firms classified as possibly under family control, the average ownership by a family drops to 5.9% of the firm's stock. Further, the minimum percentage control in the probable family control category is 14% while the maximum in the possibly family control category is 8%. No data are presented for firms Burch classifies as probably not under family control. Some inferences can be made about the concentration of stock ownership in firms in all three categories, however, using data from a recent report on stock ownership (Metcalf 1978). Of the 42 manufacturing firms in the three categories of family control, 3, 2, 1, the sample of firms in Metcalf's report included 4, 8, and 10, respectively. The mean percentages of stock in these firms that was controlled by the five largest investors were 27.3, 6.7, and 8.4%, respectively. In other words, using Burch's or Metcalf's data, the category of probable family control represents a quantum leap in concentrated stock ownership over the other two categories. In order to see if the unequal differences in stock ownership between categories translate into significantly unequal differences in family control, a continuous variable of family control was constructed. Each firm's score on the variable was the percentage of its stock that was held by a family group according to Burch's study. Where specific figures were not given for a firm, the firm was assigned the mean level of stock ownership for its category. For example, Reynolds, Grey, and others controlling the R. J. Reynolds Tobacco Company were assumed to own 26.3% of the stock in the firm since Burch gives no specific data on how much they do own, and 26.3 is the average percentage of stock ownership held by a family in the other firms classified as family controlled. Firms in the category of probably not family controlled were assigned scores of zero. The ordinal and continuous measures of family control are highly correlated ($r = .89$). Since the continuous variable yields correlations almost identical to those obtained using the simple three point ordinal scale, and since the exact estimates of stock ownership involve guesswork anyway, the less complex ordinal scale has been retained in the analysis.

board by ownership and interlocking are the actors with whom ego has relations. As described in Section 2.3, ego-networks have been developed principally in anthropology but have proven useful in sociology as well. My conclusion in Chapter 2 was that models of ego-networks were nicely suited to describing the typical relations in which actors within a system are involved. That is my purpose here: to describe the manner in which directorate ties connected establishments in manufacturing industries to establishments in the 1967 American economy more generally. I shall analyze cooptive corporate actor networks, one network being the total set of establishments represented on a firm's board of directors by ownership, direct interlocking, or indirect interlocking through financial institutions. This ego-network centered on a corporate actor is a representation of the manner in which the firm is responsible for directorate ties among establishments in diverse sectors of the economy.[11]

The cooptive network of Firestone Tire and Rubber in 1967 has been described as an illustration of the three types of directorate ties. It is presented in Figure 4.2 as a sociogram type of diagram of ownership ties (bold lines) and interlocking directorates (light lines) among establishments (input–output numbers in parentheses) and firms (in boxes). The diagram makes immediately obvious the ownership ties among eight manufacturing establishments provided by Firestone's directorate, the direct interlock ties between these establishments and the transportation and warehousing sector created by the interlocked directorates of Firestone and Western Airlines, and the indirect interlock ties to the same sector created by the financial interlock between Firestone and Cleveland Trust, which in turn interlocks with Pan American airlines and American Airlines.

The analytical utility of the sociogram type of diagram of a firm's cooptive network lies in its ability to make features of the network explicitly obvious. If such a diagram were constructed for each of the 42 manufacturing firms, the diagrams could be compared visually in order to detect systematic patterns of directorate ties and characteristics of firms that seem to explain the different patterns for which they were responsible.

This visual strategy might be a useful first step in analysis or a helpful heuristic device for illustrating types of directorate ties, but it loses its utility when complex cooptive networks are to be described. Firestone's cooptive network was relatively simple in 1967. That is why I used it for illustration. The cooptive networks of the other manufacturing firms tended to be much more complex.

---

[11]The corporate actor network concept is similar to Evan's (1966, 1972) concept of an organization-set in the sense that a "focal organization" is taken as an anchoring point, and the organizations connected to this focal organization constitute notes in its network. In contrast to the organization-set, however, there is no distinction here between input and output organizations. The concern is with symmetric cooptive relations rather than with asymmetric flows of commodities. Further the organizations constituting nodes here are establishments rather than corporations. Instead of tampering with Evan's concept of organization-set, I have chosen to import the actor network concept from anthropology.

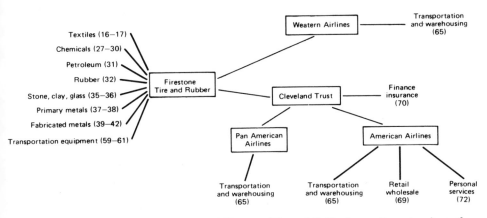

Figure 4.2. A sociogram-type diagram of Firestone Tire and Rubber's cooptive network as of 1967. (Ownership relations given by heavy lines, interlock relations by light lines, corporations in boxes, and input-output sectors of establishments by numbers in parentheses, cf. Table 4.2.)

Table 4.2 presents a representation of cooptive networks that has more general analytical utility. The 45 sectors in which establishments could have been owned are distinguished by rows in the table, and the three ways in which an establishment could have been represented on a directorate are distinguished by columns.

A comparison of Figure 4.2 with the first three columns in Table 4.2 should help in interpreting the data to be analyzed. Firestone owned 8 establishments in Figure 4.2, and these are given in Table 4.2 as 1's in the ownership column under Firestone (see column labeled "O"). Let o_{kj} equal 0, unless firm k has been coded as owning an establishment in sector j, whereupon o_{kj} equals 1. The ownership columns of Table 4.2 contain these o_{kj}. The two establishments represented on Firestone's board through direct interlocking, Western Airlines's establishment in transportation–warehousing (sector 65) and Cleveland Trust's establishment in finance (sector 70), are given in Table 4.2 as 1's in the direct interlock column (labeled "D"). More generally, the number of establishments in sector j represented on the board of firm k by direct interlocking, d_{kj}, is given as

$$d_{kj} = \sum_q b_{kq} o_{qj}, \tag{4.1}$$

where summation is across all 152 firms Q in the sample, and b_{kq} is an interlock variable equal to 0, unless the 1968 *Poor's* listed a director in firm k as a director in firm q as well, whereupon $b_{kq} = b_{qk} = 1$. In order to exclude direct interlock ties' being counted among the establishments firm k actually owns, b_{kk} is set equal to 0. Finally, the five establishments represented on Firestone's board by indirect interlocks through Cleveland Trust as a financial institution are given in the appropriate rows of the indirect interlock column of Table 4.2 (labeled "I"); two establishments in transportation–warehousing (sector 65),

TABLE 4.2
Cooptive Networks of Firestone and General Motors in 1967[a]

Sectors containing establishments	Firestone Tire and Rubber			General Motors		
	O	D	I	O	D	I
Livestock (1)	0	0	0	0	0	0
Other agriculture (2)	0	0	0	0	0	0
Forestry–fishery (3)	0	0	0	0	1	1
Agribusiness services (4)	0	0	0	0	0	0
Iron mining (5)	0	0	0	0	0	1
Nonferrous metal mining (6)	0	0	0	0	0	1
Coal mining (7)	0	0	0	0	3	4
Petroleum/gas (8)	0	0	0	0	5	8
Stone–clay mining (9)	0	0	0	0	0	0
Chemicals mining (10)	0	0	0	0	0	0
New construction (11)	0	0	0	0	1	3
Maintenance–repair (12)	0	0	0	0	1	3
Manufacturing industries						
Ordnance (13)	0	0	0	0	1	4
Food (14)	0	0	0	0	2	7
Tobacco	0	0	0	0	0	0
Textiles (16–17)	1	0	0	0	1	3
Apparel (18–19)	0	0	0	0	1	2
Lumber (20–21)	0	0	0	0	1	2
Furniture (22–23)	0	0	0	0	0	2
Paper (24–25)	0	0	0	0	3	7
Printing (26)	0	0	0	1	1	2
Chemicals (27–30)	1	0	0	1	4	13
Petroleum (31)	1	0	0	0	4	5
Rubber (32)	1	0	0	1	1	6
Leather (33–34)	0	0	0	0	0	2
Stone, clay, glass (35–36)	1	0	0	1	1	6
Primary metals (37–38)	1	0	0	1	2	6
Fabricated metals (39–42)	1	0	0	1	2	8
Mechanical machines (43–52)	0	0	0	1	3	12
Electrical machines (53–58)	0	0	0	1	1	10
Transportation equipment (59–61)	1	0	0	1	1	6
Instruments (62–63)	0	0	0	0	0	6
Miscellaneous manufacturing (64)	0	0	0	1	1	3
Transport–warehousing (65)	0	1	2	0	3	11
Communications (66)	0	0	0	0	1	3
Radio–television (67)	0	0	0	0	0	0
Utilities (68)	0	0	0	0	6	11
Wholesale/retail (69)	0	0	1	1	4	12
Finance–insurance (70)	0	1	1	0	10	25
Real estate (71)	0	0	0	0	1	2
Personal services (72)	0	0	1	0	0	2
Business services (73)	0	0	0	0	1	6

Continued

TABLE 4.2 *(continued)*

	Firestone Tire and Rubber			General Motors		
Sectors containing establishments	O	D	I	O	D	I
Automobile services (75)	0	0	0	0	0	1
Amusements (76)	0	0	0	0	0	0
Medical–educational services (77)	0	0	0	0	0	0
Total establishments	8	2	5	11	67	206

[a]Entries are the number of establishments represented on a corporate board by ownership (O), direct interlocking (D), or indirect interlocking through financial firms (I) as described in the text. Establishments are defined by input–output categories except that manufacturing industries have been aggregated to two-digit SIC industries (see footnote 8).

and one establishment in each of sectors 69, 70, and 72. More generally, the number of establishments in sector j represented on the board of firm k through indirect interlocking by means of financial institutions, i_{kj}, is given as

$$i_{kj} = \sum_q b_{kq}^* o_{qj}, \tag{4.2}$$

where summation is again across all 152 firms Q in the sample and b_{kq}^* is an indirect interlock variable equal to 0, unless the 1968 *Poor's* listed a director in firm k and a director in firm q as directors in one or more of the same financial institutions in the sample, whereupon $b_{kq}^* = b_{qk}^* = 1$.[12] Here again, b_{kk}^* is set equal to 0 in order to exclude indirect financial interlocks between firm k and its own establishments.

   Table 4.2 also presents the cooptive network for General Motors as of 1967—one of the more complex of those observed among the sampled manufacturing firms. In contrast to Firestone's 15 connections to establishments (8 through ownership, 2 through direct interlocking, 5 through indirect interlocking), General Motors had 284 connections (11, 67, and 206, respectively). In manufacturing, General Motors owned establishments in 10 industries and had direct interlock relations with establishments in all but 3

---

[12]The b_{kq}^* have been computed as two-step path distances between firms based on the direct interlocks b_{kq}. Firm k had an indirect interlock with firm q through a financial institution c if the product $b_{kc}b_{cq}$ is 1. The product is 0 otherwise. This does not preclude a direct interlock between firms k and q (i.e., b_{kq} could equal 1 at the same time that the product $b_{kc}b_{cq}$ is 1). The number of indirect connections between firms k and q by means of financial institutions in the sample is given as the sum

$$\sum_c b_{kc}b_{cq},$$

where c is any bank or insurance firm in the sample. The indirect financial interlock variable b_{kq}^* equals 0 unless this sum is nonzero and $k \neq q$ whereupon $b_{kq}^* = b_{qk}^* = 1$.

industries. The only manufacturing industry it could not reach by indirect interlocking through financial institutions was tobacco. Clearly, in order to analyze cooptive networks of this complexity, even when stated compactly as in Table 4.2, the relational data must be condensed in terms of basic structural concepts.

4.6 RANGE

Perhaps the least pretentious structural concept in network analysis is ego-network range. As discussed in Section 2.3, an ego-network has range to the extent that it includes a large number of different types of actors. In the organizational setting, a cooptive corporate actor network would have range to the extent that it encompassed a diversity of establishments—many establishments in many different sectors of the economy. To the extent that competitor, supplier, and consumer establishments in diverse sectors of the 1967 American economy were connected by cooptive directorate ties, the cooptive networks of large firms would have had extensive range.

Table 4.3 presents moments for network range variables. Network range is measured in two ways: the total number of establishments represented on a corporate board (column totals in Table 4.2) and the number of different sectors from which these establishments were drawn (number of nonzero entries in columns of Table 4.2). In the case of ownership, these two measures are identical since all of a firm's holdings in a single sector have been grouped together as a single establishment. In the case of interlocking, the two measures can differ. For example, Firestone represented five establishments on its board by means of indirect interlocking through financial firms, but these establishments were drawn from four different sectors.

I draw two conclusions from these results. Overall, network range was least extensive in the case of representation through ownership, intermediate in the case of direct interlocking, and most extensive in the case of indirect interlocking. Secondly, this relative range of directorate ties differed across firms. If similar relative ranges had existed for each firm, then the network range variables would be highly correlated, each firm's network through ownership consistently being the least extensive and its network through indirect interlocking being the most extensive. In fact, the variables are not perfectly correlated. Direct and indirect interlock range are strongly correlated to the point where it seems reasonable to infer that the relative range of directorate ties they provided had a consistent rank order, range by direct interlock ties being less than that by indirect interlock ties. However, range in terms of ownership ties is uncorrelated with the interlock range measures. As is illustrated by Firestone in Figure 4.2 and Table 4.2, there were some firms responsible for a more extensive range of directorate ties through ownership than the range of ties they provided through interlocking directorates. This is to be expected of

TABLE 4.3
Correlations among Network Range Variables[a]

	O	D	I	Mean	S.D.
Number of establishments represented on corporate board					
Through ownership (O)	1.00	.12	.02	6.19	3.84
Through direct interlocks (D)	.16	1.00	.79	24.00	17.42
Through indirect interlocks (I)	.03	.80	1.00	111.60	67.75
Number of sectors represented on corporate board					
Through ownership (O)	1.00	.09	−.03	6.19	3.84
Through direct interlocks (D)	.17	1.00	.65	13.36	8.09
Through indirect interlocks (I)	−.02	.70	1.00	28.55	9.03

[a]Correlations are computed across the 42 manufacturing firms, and a correlation greater in absolute magnitude than .25 is significant at the .05 level of confidence. Coefficients above the diagonal are product-moment correlations and those below are rank-order correlations (Kendall's tau).

Firestone since it was a family controlled firm, and such firms tend to avoid extensive interlocking with other firms. It seems likely that differences between types of firms would covary with differences in the range of directorate ties for which they were responsible. To be specific, those firms which would most benefit from coopting their environment should have been the firms most responsible for directorate ties by the extensive range of their cooptive networks. According to past research, these firms would have been large firms controlled by dispersed interest groups.

This appears to have been true. Table 4.4 presents correlations between network range and corporation variables corresponding in part to the correlations Table 4.1 contains. Two sets of network range variables are presented, one using establishments as nodes and the other using sectors as nodes. Summary canonical variables for each of the two sets of measures are also given. This summary canonical variable is that weighted combination of its three network range indicators which is maximally correlated with the corporate variables.

As might be expected from Table 4.3, overall network range was least indicated by ownership ties. The best indicator was the range of direct interlock ties. In other words, network range through direct interlocking (of the three cooptive strategies considered here) had the strongest association with the corporation variables and network range through the other two types of directorate ties.

Using either set of network range measures, number of establishments or number of sectors, the greatest network range tended to occur in large firms not dominated by management or a kinship group. Firms with extensive assets tended to have a large number of establishments represented on their boards

TABLE 4.4
Correlations between Corporate and Network Range Variables[a]

Network range variables	Corporate variables					
	Assets	Capital output ratio	Management control	Family control	R_1	R_2
Number of establishments represented on corporate board						
Through ownership (O)	−.02	−.01	−.27	−.02	.16	.21
Through direct interlocks (D)	.39	−.07	−.29	−.37	.91	.89
Through indirect interlocks (I)	.38	−.19	−.28	−.35	.97	.82
Summary canonical index (R_1)	.40	−.15	−.32	−.37	1.00	.90
Number of sectors represented on corporate board						
Through ownership (O)	−.02	−.01	−.27	−.02	.16	.21
Through direct interlocks (D)	.42	.01	−.30	−.29	.84	.95
Through indirect interlocks (I)	.31	−.16	−.24	−.23	.79	.82
Summary canonical index (R_2)	.41	−.06	−.34	−.29	.90	1.00

[a]Correlations are computed across the 42 manufacturing firms, and a correlation greater in absolute magnitude than .25 is significant at the .05 level of confidence. The summary canonical correlation indices are taken from a canonical correlation relating network range to the four corporate variables— a different model for each set of range variables. Second canonical correlations are negligible at even the .10 level of confidence. R_1 is completely determined by the number of establishment variables. R_2 is completely determined by the number of sectors variables.

($r = .40$) and a large number of sectors represented on their boards ($r = .41$). Once again, there is a low negative association between a firm's capital intensity and its involvement in directorate ties. Firms controlled by dispersed interests tended to be involved in such ties. Those dominated by management or a kinship group tended to have few establishments represented on their board ($r = −.32$ and $−.37$, respectively) and tended to have few sectors represented on their board ($r = −.34$ and $−.29$, respectively). Ownership ties are an exception here. Although firms dominated by management tended to own few establishments, the number of establishments a firm owned is not correlated with its size, capital intensity, or the extent to which it was controlled by a kinship group.

These results take sectors of the economy as given and describe the extent to which a firm's board was responsible for directorate ties among establishments in the sectors. Alternatively, the firm's cooptive network can be taken as given so as to describe the extent to which establishments in different sectors were represented on it. Table 4.5 presents data on the absolute and relative numbers of establishments represented on boards by means of direct interlocking. I have selected direct interlocking here since it is the best indicator of network range according to the results in Table 4.4. Three classes of establishments are distinguished: finance, manufacturing, and others. The same pattern of correlations given in Table 4.5 is obtained if manufacturing establishments are separated into durable versus nondurable manufacturing or if the "other" establishments are separated into six one-digit SIC categories (agribusiness, mining, construction, transportation–utilities, wholesale–retail, and services).

Looking at the absolute number of establishments represented on a firm's board, you can see from Table 4.5 that the mean 24 establishments in Table 4.3 were, on average, 5 financial establishments, 13 manufacturing establishments, and 6 establishments in other sectors. The representation of all three classes of

TABLE 4.5
Absolute and Proportionate Representation by Means of Direct Interlocking[a]

| Network range variables | Corporate variables | | | | | |
	Assets	Capital output ratio	Management control	Family control	Mean	S.D.
Number of establishments represented on corporate board from						
Finance	.18	−.21	−.34	−.39	5.00	2.99
Manufacturing	.43	.05	−.20	−.32	12.60	10.96
Other	.27	−.20	−.32	−.31	6.29	5.35
Proportion of establishments on corporate board that is drawn from						
Finance	−.31	−.16	.11	.33	29.59	20.53
Manufacturing	.49	.24	−.11	−.18	42.35	23.82
Other	−.24	−.23	−.12	−.01	26.68	15.10

[a]Correlations are computed across the 42 manufacturing firms, and a correlation greater in absolute magnitude than .25 is significant at a .05 level of confidence. Number of establishments in each class is computed by summing across sectors within each class. The proportion of establishments in each class is then determined by dividing the number of establishments in the class by the total number of establishments represented on the firm's board by direct interlocking.

establishments is similarly determined by attributes of the firm representing them. Firms with extensive assets tended to have high numbers of finance, manufacturing, and other types of establishments represented on their boards. Firms dominated by management or a kinship group tended to represent few establishments from any sector on their boards.

This consistency across the three classes dissolves when proportionate representation is considered. Considering the percentage of a network drawn from the three classes suggests that representation of financial firms on a corporate board was ubiquitous, but not without its limits. On the average, about 30% of the establishments represented on a firm's board were financial, 42% were in manufacturing, and 27% were in other sectors. For large, capital-intensive firms, however, the proportionate representation of manufacturing establishments was higher. After an initial representation of financial establishments on its board, a firm appears not to have continued to augment such representation in proportion to growth in its size. This could be explained by the fact that it is predominantly with other manufacturing establishments that any one manufacturing establishment had transactions. It is market constraints in these transactions that are supposedly coopted by directorate ties. Ceteris paribus, growth of a manufacturing firm in terms of assets should have been accompanied by growing representation on its board of manufacturing establishments. As given in Table 4.5, assets are positively correlated with percentage representation of manufacturing establishments and negatively correlated with percentage representation of financial establishments and establishments in other sectors. The same process of differential expansion into the three classes of economic sectors ensured a different pattern of correlations for firms dominated by a single interest group. Since few establishments in any economic sectors were represented on the boards of such corporations, the ubiquitous representation of financial establishments in their case should have constituted a high proportion of all establishments represented on their boards. This means that there should be a positive correlation between percentage representation of financial establishments on a firm's board and the extent to which it was dominated by a single interest group. Table 4.5 shows that this correlation exists if the dominant group is management ($r = .11$) and is significant if the dominant group is a family ($r = .33$).[13]

[13]This finding sparks the intriguing notion, fostered by some sociologists (e.g., Zeitlin 1974, 1976), that families use financial institutions to reach establishments in the sectors constraining their corporate interests, thereby avoiding the direct representation that would impair the family's voting control over the board. This interpretation of Table 4.5 is rejected in part by the positive association between assets and percentage representation of manufacturing establishments by the 18 firms classified as probably not under family control ($r = .29$) as well as the 9 classified as probably under family control ($r = .63$). These correlations are comparable to those in the fifth row of Table 4.5. There is additional evidence. If family controlled firms used financial institutions to coopt market constraints, assets should have been positively correlated for such firms with network range in terms of indirect interlocking but uncorrelated with network range in terms of direct interlocking. This would be expected since family controlled firms would have represented establishments on their board indirectly through their financial agents and restricted direct

These results on cooptive network range concern structural form—the extent to which establishments in many sectors were connected by each type of directorate tie. Looking more closely now at the content of directorate ties, I shall describe the manner in which the three types of ties were coordinated with one another.

4.7 MULTIPLEXITY

The coordination of relations with different contents is captured by the concept of multiplexity. As discussed in Section 2.3, an ego-network has multiplexity to the extent that ego has multiple types of relations to each actor in his network (Eq. [2.7]). In the organizational setting, a cooptive corporate actor network would have multiplexity to the extent that it creates multiple types of directorate ties between competitors, suppliers, and consumers. Establishments are defined as competitors, suppliers, and consumers according to the sectors of the economy they occupy. To the extent that separate sectors of establishments in these roles within the 1967 American economy were connected simultaneously by ownership ties, direct interlock ties, and indirect interlock ties through financial institutions, the cooptive networks of large firms would have been highly multiplex.

There are, however, many different ways in which a cooptive network could have exhibited multiplexity. Figure 4.3 presents Venn diagrams of three types of cooptive networks in terms of which multiplexity could be analyzed. The area of a circle indicates network range defined by the number of sectors in which establishments were represented on a corporate board. Their relative areas correspond to the mean number of sectors in which establishments were reached using ownership versus direct interlocking versus indirect interlocking through financial institutions (cf. Table 4.3). Circles overlap to the extent that each type of cooptive relation reached establishments in the same sectors.

If the three types of cooptive relations were used as alternative methods of reaching establishments, then cooptive networks should have been patterned as

---

representation on the board to the financial agents themselves. I discussed the greater efficiency of indirect financial interlock ties over direct interlock ties in Section 4.3. In fact, the 9 family controlled firms behaved just like the 18 nonfamily controlled firms. The number of establishments versus sectors represented on a family controlled firm's board increased with the firm's assets ($r = .66$ versus .71, respectively for representation through direct interlocking and $r = .42$ versus .48, respectively for indirect interlocking), and the number of establishments versus sectors represented on a corporate board probably not controlled by a family increased with the firm's assets ($r = .47$ versus .51, respectively for representation through direct interlocking and $r = .37$ versus .28, respectively for indirect interlocking). Further, the number of establishments by which network range in terms of indirect interlocking exceeded network range in terms of direct interlocking was positively associated with assets for both family and nonfamily controlled firms ($r = .21$ and .30, respectively). In short, family controlled firms do not seem to have been using financial instititutions as intermediaries to coopt establishments in preference to directly interlocking with the establishments.

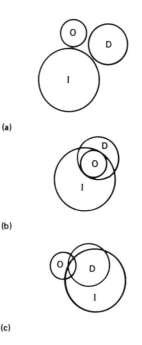

Figure 4.3. Ideal types of cooptive corporate actor networks where circles refer to the number of sectors represented on a corporate board via ownership (O), direct interlocking (D), or indirect interlocking through financial institutions (I).

illustrated in Figure 4.3a. In this diagram, the circles do not overlap, indicating that establishments in some sectors (say, manufacturing) were represented on a corporate board through ownership, while establishments in other sectors (say finance and manufacturing sectors not represented by ownership) were represented through direct interlocking, and establishments in still other sectors (say all nonmanufacturing sectors) were represented through indirect interlocking via financial institutions. Since each type of cooptive relation was directed at establishments in a unique group of sectors, there is no network multiplexity.

But there is reason to expect cooptive networks to be multiplex. In comparison to a single type of cooptive relation, multiple types directed at a single sector are more likely to endure in the sense that at least one cooptive relation to the sector will survive market changes which dissolve others. Moreover, there are the different ways in which the different types of directorate ties have cooptive potential as discussed in Sections 4.3 and 4.4 above. Multiplex directorate ties would provide the cooptive potential of all three types of relations as complementary cooptive relations rather than alternatives.

Figures 4.3b and 4.3c illustrate two types of networks that could result from firms deliberately creating multiplex directorate ties.

If directorate ties were coordinated solely in order to manage competition with the establishments a firm owned, then cooptive networks would have been structured as illustrated in Figure 4.3b. In this network, establishments in each sector containing one of the firm's own establishments are linked to the firm by means of interlock relations. Since interlocks with other firms, particularly interlocks through financial firms, can result in a firm being able to reach establishments in sectors in which it has no interest, the firm's cooptive network could extend beyond the sectors in which it owns establishments. The distinctive feature of this network aimed at managing competition is that all sectors in which a firm owned an establishment are represented on its board by direct and indirect interlocking.

Figure 4.3c illustrates a network aimed at managing competition with a firm's own establishments as well as managing constraint from other sectors containing their suppliers and consumers. In this network, some sectors in which the firm owns an establishment are linked to the firm by all three types of cooptive relations. In addition, however, there is a significant tendency for both direct and indirect interlocking to reach the same sectors beyond those in which the firm owns an establishment. It is this significant multiplexity in directorate ties to sectors in which the firm owns no establishments that is the distinctive feature here.

Table 4.6 presents moments for measures of multiplexity. A cooptive relation linking a firm to establishments in a sector is coded as multiplex if one or more of the establishments in the sector were represented on the firm's board by different types of ties, O–D–I referring to a sector in which the firm owned an establishment, had one or more direct interlock ties to establishments, and had one or more indirect financial interlocks to establishments. If the firm only owned an establishment in the sector and had direct interlock ties to one or more establishments there, then it had an O–D multiplex tie to the sector. Other possible multiplex ties would be ownership and indirect interlocking (O–I multiplexity) and the two types of interlocking (D–I multiplexity).[14] For

---

[14]These codings correspond to types of multiplexity referenced collectively by $z_{ji(m)}$ in Eq. (2.7). The multiplexity measure in Eq. (2.7) is the same as the "percentage of all sectors represented on corporate board that are represented by multiplex relations" measures in Table 4.6. It is worth noting here that these are not measures of the contingency between types of directorate ties. They are measures of the coordination of directorate ties. To a considerable extent in sparce networks, contingency between relations is a result of the simultaneous absence of relations. Consider an isolated person. This person has no friendship relations with others, no advice relations with others, and so on. He has null relations of many contents with others. Such a person is not usually discussed as having coordinated his relations with others so as to have achieved multiplexity. Multiplexity is concerned with the simultaneous presence of different types of relations between actors and not at all concerned with the simultaneous absence of different types of relations between them.

TABLE 4.6
Means and Standard Deviations in Multiplexity[a]

	Mean	S.D.	t-test (41 dfs.)
Number of sectors represented on corporate board by multiplex relations			
O–D–I	2.60	2.55	6.67
O–D	2.60	2.55	6.67
O–I	4.95	3.37	9.52
D–I	13.10	8.10	10.48
Percentage of sectors in which firm owns an establishment that are also represented on corporate board by interlocking			
O–D–I	41.42	37.16	7.24
O–D	41.52	37.16	7.24
O–I	78.44	28.93	12.10
Percentage of all sectors represented on corporate board that are represented by multiplex relations			
O–D–I	8.26	8.21	6.52
O–D	12.44	11.01	7.32
O–I	16.52	11.63	9.21
D–I	71.29	61.27	7.54

[a]Moments are computed across the 42 manufacturing firms, and a t-test of 3.55 indicates a mean significantly greater than zero at the .001 level of confidence. O–D–I refers to a sector represented on a board through ownership (O), direct interlocking (D), and indirect interlocking (I) simultaneously. The first set of percentages are computed by dividing the number of multiplex relations of some type in a network by the network range through ownership. The second set of percentages are computed by dividing the number of multiplex relations of some type in a network by the number of sectors in the network reached by the relevant relations (e.g., for Firestone in Table 4.2, O–D–I is 0/12, O–D is 0/10, O–I is 0/12, and D–I is 2/4).

illustration, consider the relational data in Table 4.2. The two multiplex relations in Firestone's network were D–I multiplex relations to the transportation–warehousing and finance sectors. These sectors were represented on Firestone's board by direct interlocking and indirect interlocking through financial firms. Establishments in no sector were represented on the board by ownership and interlocking simultaneously. On the General Motors board, in contrast, all three types of cooptive relations reach each of eleven sectors.

Table 4.6 presents t-tests of the significance of mean levels of multiplexity for each type of multiplexity. Multiplexity will be 0 if firms directed each type of cooptive relation to separate sectors. If this were true of the firms generally, then all t-tests in Table 4.6 would be insignificant. They would also be insignificant if multiplexity varied so much across firms that the mean level of multiplexity was, in comparison to its variance, indistinguishable from the total absence of multiplexity.

The *t*-tests show that neither of these possibilities occurred. The test statistics are all significant at beyond the .001 level of confidence. High multiplexity occurred in terms of the absolute number of multiplex relations, the percentage of ownership relations coordinated with interlock relations, and the percentage of sectors represented on a board that are represented by multiplex relations.[15]

The mean levels of multiplexity in Table 4.6 indicate that the network structure characterized by Figure 4.3c was most typical of the cooptive networks. Multiplex relations were coordinated as if they were intended to coopt sources of competition with a firm's own establishments and to coopt supplier and consumer establishments in sectors where the firm owned no establishments. The segregated network in Figure 4.3a is rejected. The three types of cooptive relations were not used as alternatives to one another since there was high multiplexity of all kinds. Neither were they coordinated so as to generate the network structure characterized by Figure 4.3b. In support of that structure, many sectors in which a firm owned an establishment were also represented on the firm's board by interlock relations. As expected under the structure in Figure 4.3c, however, there was high multiplexity to the interlock relations themselves. Both types of interlock relations appear to have been directed at the same sectors beyond those in which a firm actually owned an establishment. Of all sectors represented on a firm's board through interlocking, 71% were represented by both direct and indirect interlocking simultaneously. Of the sectors represented on a firm's board through direct interlocking, 95% were also represented on the board through indirect financial interlocking (which is quite different from 0 with its *t*-test of 37.3).

Although the network structure illustrated by Figure 4.3c seems most typical of the cooptive networks, deviations from that typical structure could have resulted from differences across types of firms. Recall from Table 4.5 that corporate growth in terms of assets seems to have been accompanied by increasing representation of establishments in manufacturing industries once an initial representation from financial institutions was created. Assuming that this spread into industries was an attempt to coopt sources of market constraint, the relations linking the firm to new industries should have been multiplex. Since these firms already owned establishments in manufacturing industries, it would have been the cooptive networks of firms already beginning to interlock extensively in manufacturing that would have been the most multiplex. Since it was firms with extensive assets controlled by dispersed interest groups that had networks interlocking extensively in manufacturing (see Table 4.5), these are

[15]An important consideration here is network range. Since there are only 45 sectors distinguished in this analysis, a firm with extensive network in terms of each cooptive relation considered separately is likely to have high multiplexity. However, significant multiplexity is also observed if 405 economic sectors are distinguished instead of the 45 considered here (Burt 1983: Table 3.6), so the limited number of sectors distinguished here is not a problem.

TABLE 4.7

Correlations between Corporate and Network Multiplexity Variables [a]

	Corporate variables			
Variables	Assets	Capital output ratio	Management control	Family control
Number of sectors represented on corporate board by all three types of cooptive relations	.44	.11	−.38	−.22
Percentage of sectors in which firm owns an establishment that are also represented on corporate board by interlocking	.36	.00	−.34	−.22
Percentage of all sectors represented on corporate board that are represented by means of all three types of cooptive relations	.36	.21	−.34	−.16
Percentage of sectors represented by means of direct interlocking that are also represented through indirect interlocking	.30	.15	−.29	−.24

[a]Correlations are computed across the 42 manufacturing firms, and a correlation greater in absolute magnitude than .25 is significant at the .05 level of confidence. The first multiplexity variable is the absolute number of O–D–I multiplex relations in a firm's network. The second is the ratio of these relations over the number of sectors in which the firm owns an establishment. The third is the ratio of these relations over the number of sectors to which the firm has any of the three types of relations. Thus, the third measure corresponds to the multiplexity measure in Eq. (2.7). The fourth multiplexity measure is the ratio of D–I multiplex relations in a firm's network over the number of sectors represented on its board through direct interlocking.

the firms that should have had the most multiplex networks. The results in Table 4.7 support such a conclusion.[16]

Four multiplexity variables in Table 4.7 are used to support the conclusion that the network structure illustrated by Figure 4.3c was most closely approximated by large firms not dominated by management or a kinship group. Firms with extensive assets tended to have large numbers of sectors represented on their board by means of all three types of cooptive relations ($r = .44$), tended to have a high proportion of the industries in which they owned establishments

[16]The number of sectors problem raised in footnote 15 is again an issue here. Controlling for the number of different sectors represented on a firm's board, however, does not eliminate the positive correlations between the number of sectors represented on the board by means of all three types of relations simultaneously (O–D–I multiplexity) and assets (partial $r = .38$, $p = .01$). Neither does a control for network rank eliminate the negative correlation with the percentage of directors who are officers (partial $r = −.32$; $p = .02$), although it does reduce the already weak negative correlation with the extent to which a kinship group controlled the firm (partial $r = −.15$). Finally, an analysis of ties to 405 economic sectors instead of the 45 distinguished here yields the same conclusions (Burt 1983: Table 3.7)

be represented on the board by means of interlocking ($r = .36$), and tended to have a high proportion of all sectors represented on their boards be represented by all three types of cooptive relations simultaneously ($r = .36$). Conversely, firms dominated by management or a kinship group tended to have a low proportion of all sectors represented on their board be represented by all three types of cooptive relations simultaneously ($r = -.34$ and $-.16$, respectively). Further, the distinctive coordination of direct and indirect interlocking illustrated in Figure 4.3c is associated with firm size and dispersed control. The proportion of sectors represented on a corporate board through direct interlocking also represented by indirect financial interlocking is positively correlated with assets ($r = .30$). The proportion is negatively correlated with the percentage of directors who were officers in the firm ($r = -.29$) and negatively correlated, weakly, with the level of family control over the firm ($r = -.24$). As in previous tables, there is no significant association with the capital intensity of a firm.

These multiplex directorate ties connected establishments across sectors of the economy. Since the firms most responsible for coordinating directorate ties as multiplex relations were the most prominent firms in the sense of holding extensive assets, and, by extension, the most prominent of the American manufacturing industries at the time would have been those in which these firms operated, it follows that establishments in prominent industries at the time should have had multiplex directorate ties to their competitors, suppliers, and consumers in diverse sectors of the economy generally. In other words, prominent industries should have had extensive, multiplex directorate ties to

TABLE 4.8
Directorate Ties Involving Core Versus Peripheral Industries[a]

	Prominence		Correlation with prominence	Correlation with mean assets of manufacturing firms in industry
	Core ($N = 14$)	Peripheral ($N = 6$)		
Number of sampled manufacturing establishments in industry	12	5	.63	.44
Mean assets of manufacturing firms owning the sampled establishments	$3,128	$1,502	.53	1.00
Number of sectors not reachable by O–D–I multiplex relations	19	27	−.42	−.38
Number of sectors not reachable by D–I multiplex relations	14	18	−.27	−.40

[a]Two-digit manufacturing industries have been classified as core or peripheral as discussed in the text. Assets are measured in millions of dollars as of 1967.

economic sectors generally just as prominent firms were responsible for creating extensive, multiplex directorate ties.

Table 4.8 presents evidence supporting this conclusion. Twenty two-digit SIC manufacturing industries have been separated into those that were "core" industries within the American economy versus those that were "peripheral." This dichotomy between core and peripheral industries is taken from an analysis by Tolbert, Horan, and Beck (1980) purporting to measure the extent to which sectors of the American economy in the late 1960s and early 1970s conformed to the idea of a dual economy in which prominent sectors represented the economy's core while the remaining sectors represented less integral features of the economy. They cite the colorful characterization provided by Bluestone, Murphy, and Stevenson (1973): "The core economy includes those industries that comprise the muscle of American economic and political power [p.28]," and empirically identify core economic sectors as those in which there were a small number of large corporate competitors, a high median annual income for workers, a high proportion of supervisory or nonproduction personnel, a full work week, and a high mean number of workers per establishment in the sector.[17] Large firms did tend to operate in the prominent core industries rather than the peripheral industries. More of the sampled manufacturing firms, themselves representative of large American firms involved in manufacturing, owned establishments in core industries than in peripheral industries—an average 12 establishments in core industries versus an average 5 in the peripheral ones. Further, the average size of the firms owning these establishments was larger in the core industries by a factor of two. The average assets held by a firm owning an establishment in a core industry was $3,128 million while the same average in a peripheral industry was $1,502 million. As expected, these differences translated into different patterns of cooptive directorate ties, core industries typically having more extensive multiplex directorate

[17] These variables have the highest unique contributions to the factor index Tolbert et al. (1980:1106) present where uniqueness is given by their "scoring weights." Of course, these variables have high correlations with the factor they estimate. These variables are X_3, X_6, X_9, X_{15}, and X_{17} in their factor analysis. There is a very large gap between two-digit core and peripheral industry index scores, the highest for a peripheral industry being the −.28 for textile mill products and the lowest for a core industry being the .26 for rubber and miscellaneous plastics (Tolbert et al 1980:1109). However, their classification of industries is not completely determined by these scores. The only industry affected here is SIC category 39, miscellaneous manufacturing, which they classify as peripheral because of wages/profits in the industry. The two-digit industries I have classified as peripheral industries based on their classification are apparel (SIC category 23), lumber (24), furniture (25) miscellaneous manufacturing (39), textiles (22) and leather (31). The last two industries receive mixed classification by Tolbert and his colleagues. Tolbert et al. (1980:1110) distinguish three leather industries, of which one, "footwear except rubber" is classified as a core industry. Since I required a single class for the two-digit leather industry, and since the Annual Survey of Manufactures (U.S. Department of Commerce 1973) lists establishments in "footwear except rubber" as accounting for 50% of leather assets in 1970, I have classified the leather industry as peripheral in keeping with the other two leather subindustries. Similarly, Tolbert et al. (1980:1110) classifiy two out of five textile subindustries as core industries. The Annual Survey of Manufactures lists establishments in these two subindustries as accounting for 26% of textile assets in 1970. I have classified textile as a peripheral industry.

ties than peripheral industries. Given the sampled establishments, the typical core manufacturing industry did not have simultaneous ownership ties, direct interlock ties, and indirect financial interlock ties to 19 of the 45 economic sectors distinguished. In comparison to this lack of multiplex access to 42% of the sectors, the typical peripheral industry did not have multiplex ties to 27, or 60%, of the economic sectors distinguished. The expected negative correlation between an industry's type of prominence (peripheral versus core) and the number of sectors not connected to it by an O–D–I multiplex relation ($r = -.42$) is significant at the .05 level of confidence. In contrast, there is no significant difference in the sectors beyond the reach of a core versus a peripheral industry's D–I multiplex relations, although peripheral industries on average were denied access to four more sectors than the average core industry using these ties.

4.8 CONCLUSIONS

My purpose in this chapter has been to describe the manner in which manufacturing establishments were connected in 1967 through corporate boards of directors to establishments in diverse sectors of the American economy. In contrast to the previous chapter, I have used relational data on a very small sample of actors within the system to be described instead of using data on most actors in it. For a system as large as the American economy, the typical relational data on all actors would be impossible to collect and, even if available, impossible to analyze with traditional sociometric methods. Fortunately, the sampled firms correspond to past research findings so that the generalizability of this description of them seems to me no more problematic than earlier analyses of much larger samples. The sampled firms were selected within the framework of known economic sectors as jointly occupied network positions in the economy. Data on the interestablishment directorate ties they provided in 1967 have been described in terms of cooptive corporate actor networks, an adaptation of the ego-network concept discussed earlier. Not only do I see no inherent antagonism between models of ego-networks and models of a system's social topology, they seem to me to be quite complementary, as I stressed in the conclusion to Chapter 2 and as my analysis here bears witness. Taking an input–output table representation of the economy as a type of density table describing aggregate transactions between sectors as network positions jointly occupied by business establishments, I have used the ego-network perspective to guide my description of cooptive directorate ties among the establishments.

Evidence can be mustered to support an interpretation of directorate ties as cooptive relations. All three types of these ties between establishments— ownership ties, direct interlock ties, and indirect interlock ties through financial institutions—have the cooptive potential of creating preferred trade partners among establishments. As conduits for information, advice, and influence, all three create nonmarket contexts in which essential buying and selling can be transacted between establishments in the absence of the market constraints characterizing those same transactions when conducted on the open market.

Therefore, it is not surprising to find that manufacturing establishments in the 1967 American economy were connected by directorate ties to other establishments as their competitors, suppliers, and consumers in diverse sectors of the economy. On average, many more establishments were connected by interlock ties than by ownership ties, the latter having a less extensive range. While this relative range was not maintained by all firms responsible for creating directorate ties (e.g., Firestone in Figure 4.2), it was typical of the firms. More interesting than the results documenting the range of directorate ties, which have been acknowledged by observers of the American economy for some time, was the documented coordination of different types of ties. The three types of directorate ties were not used as alternatives in the sense of one type being used to reach specific sectors while another type was used to reach other sectors (as illustrated by Figure 4.3a). Rather, there was significant multiplexity in these cooptive relations. Sectors represented on a corporate board through ownership tended also to be represented on the board through direct interlocking and indirect interlocking through financial institutions. This multiplexity in cooptive relations is to be expected since multiplex relations should provide better protection from market fluctuations, and their component types of directorate ties would complement one another with their different potentials to provide a nonmarket context in which market constraints can be circumvented. There was a clear tendency for competitors to be connected by directorate ties—manufacturing industries being increasingly represented on directorates of manufacturing firms in categories of increasing assets and sectors in which a firm owned an establishment tending to be represented on its board by direct interlocking as well as indirect financial interlocking. But there was more to the structure of directorate ties than would be expected if they were only intended to connect competitors, a structure illustrated by Figure 4.3b. The significant multiplexity of cooptive relations directed at sectors in which firms owned no establishments (as illustrated by Figure 4.3c) suggests that firms were striving to manage constraint from sectors external to them. Recall from Figure 4.2 that Firestone directly interlocked with Western Airlines and indirectly interlocked, through Cleveland Trust as a financial institution, with two additional transportation firms, American Airlines and Pan American Airlines. In this example, Firestone created a multiplex interlock tie to a sector in which it owned no establishment, but a sector that consumed output from each industry in which it did.

Beyond the observed structure typical of directorate ties at the time, there were significant differences in the extent to which different types of firms were responsible for directorate ties. The firms most responsible were the firms most likely to benefit from cooptive relations: large firms controlled by dispersed interest groups, which is to say, large firms dominated by neither their own management nor a kinship group. These firms tended to be responsible for an extensive range of all three types of directorate ties, representing many establishments from many different sectors on their boards. They also tended to have developed the most multiplex directorate ties, representing diverse economic sectors on their boards simultaneously by ownership, direct interlocking, as well as indirect interlocking through financial firms. Since large firms were typically found operating within the prominent, core manufacturing industries of the American economy, their greater responsibility for multiplex directorate ties resulted in core industries tending to have multiplex directorate ties to diverse sectors of the economy. In short, the economy was stratified in terms of multiplex directorate ties among differentially prominent firms operating within differentially prominent industries.

Of course, a firm's cooptive network could be extended to include other types of potentially cooptive interorganizational relations such as mergers (Pfeffer 1972b), personnel flows (Baty, Evan, and Rothermel 1971; Pfeffer & Leblebici 1973), joint ventures (Pfeffer & Nowak 1976), or information and social support more generally (Galaskiewicz & Marsden 1978; Galaskiewicz 1979). Further, relations within the network could be analyzed in terms of their formality as institutionalized ties (Litwak & Rothman 1970). Berkowitz, Carrington, Kotowitz and Waverman (1979), for example, report that the structure of direct interlock ties is much clearer when analyzed in conjunction with stock ownership ties as ties between establishments within a common enterprise. They interpret the combination of stock ownership and interlocking to be a more formal interorganizational relation than is either kind of tie by itself. Different types of relations will probably have distinct global structures within a system of firms (e.g., Berkowitz et al., 1979; Galaskiewicz 1979:71–73), however, I should not expect analyses of them to invalidate the results reported here. In other words, a firm is likely to have multiple cooptive relations, formalized to the extent possible for each type of relation, with establishments in sectors posing the most severe market constraint for its own establishments. Moreover, I should expect the stratification found here to be preserved in the sense that the firms most extensively involved in cooptive relations would be the firms most responsible for the multiplex directorate ties described here—large firms controlled by dispersed interest groups—and that such firms would be found in the prominent, core sectors of the economy.[18]

The issue of market constraint raises a final point. In one very important regard, my analysis has been quite in keeping with traditional directorate

---

[18.]This assumes that types of cooptive relations would be analyzed as potentially multiplex relations. A large firm wishing to coopt some sector that is a potential constraint on its establishments has a great diversity of interorganizational relations to choose from in order to realize its goal. To say that I expect such a firm to have developed a multiplex cooptive relation to such a sector is not to say that it would have developed every possible type of cooptive relation to the sector.

research. I have only described patterns of directorate ties and interpreted them as cooptive relations. I have made inferences about market constraints among establishments as competitors, suppliers, and consumers, but I have nowhere explained how such constraints might have operated nor how they might have explicitly encouraged the development of cooptive relations between specific sectors of the economy. That task is one I defer until Chapter 8, pending the introduction in Chapter 7 of a network model of constraint.

SECOND COMPONENT:
ACTOR INTEREST

5

Interest: The Perception of Utility*

An actor is assumed to have an interest in taking an action because he perceives some advantage in that action relative to its alternatives. My purpose in this chapter is to propose a model of the way in which his perception of advantage is contingent on the social context in which he makes the perception. I begin by distinguishing two aspects of actor interests—subjective evaluation of concrete stimuli versus social context—and discuss algebraic representations of these aspects. The two are then brought together in a structural model of perception. Under the proposed model, actor interests are patterned by the positions of actors in social structure. The model is illustrated with data on two hypothetical systems then used to derive sufficient conditions for social norms in a system and a functional form for relative deprivation effects. The derived conditions are in accord with, yet generalize, classic empirical studies of social norms and relative deprivation. Moving to a less general level of abstraction, one with clearer empirical implications, I show how the derived social norms and deprivation effects can be used to clarify some conceptual ambiguities in diffusion research while simultaneously extending that research to include new substantive results.

*Portions of this chapter are drawn from articles reprinted with the permission of *Sociological Inquiry* and *Social Networks* (Burt 1980b, 1980f).

5.1 ACTOR INTEREST AS A STRUCTURAL CONCEPT

In the Introduction, I distinguished four elements of action within a "postulate of purposive action:" (a) a person or group as an actor; (b) in control of some commodities as resources; (c) motivated to use those resources to increase his personal well-being, or utility; and (d) selecting that action from its alternatives which yields him the greatest utility. The last two elements can be combined in what Coleman (1966, 1972, 1973) terms actor interests. Given a concrete event presenting an actor with two or more alternative actions, the actor is interested in the event to the extent that the utility to him of taking the alternative actions differs across the alternatives and he is interested in taking that action yielding him the highest utility. For example, consider the academician who has just finished a paper and is deciding whether to publish it in a specific journal. He is interested in sending the paper to the journal to the extent that its appearance there will greatly increase the utility he would otherwise have if it did not appear there. His utility is some composite of all those things determining his personal well-being; the recognition he receives for his work, the discretion he is allowed by his place of employment to pursue his own work, his ability to meet his own financial obligations, his ability to support students, and so on. In short, an actor's interest in taking one of a set of alternative actions rests on his perception of the utility offered by the alternatives. That perception has two analytically distinct features: There is some process by which the concrete, unambiguous features of alternative actions are translated into subjective evaluations independent of the social context in which evaluations are made. There is also some process by which social context affects subjective evaluations, even of unambiguous stimuli. Both processes operate in terms of the "postulate of marginal evaluation" discussed in the Introduction. Subjective evaluations are not made in some absolute sense but rather are made in reference to some criterion.

Subjective Evaluations of Objective Stimuli

Imagine the situation of an individual all by himself presented with some objective stimulus at a level τ^*. There is considerable evidence that his subjective evaluation of that stimulus, his perception of the level τ^*, follows a power function often discussed as Stevens' law (e.g., Stevens 1957, 1962; Thurstone 1959 and Stevens 1971 for detailed attention to measurement):

$$u = \mu(\tau^* - \tau_0^*)^\nu = \mu\tau^\nu, \tag{5.1}$$

where u is his subjective perception of the level of stimulus he is receiving, τ_0^* is a threshold level below which there is no response so that τ is the extent to which the actual level of stimulus exceeds the threshold, and μ is a constant determined by the units in which the stimulus is measured. The exponent v varies across types of stimuli ranging from about .33 for brightness to about 3.5 for electric shock (see Stevens [1968:125] for alternative values of v). In addition to physiological stimuli, there is extensive empirical support for Eq. (5.1) in regard to less easily measured responses such as the perception of prestige derived from levels of educational or economic achievement (Hamblin 1971, 1974; Hamblin, Hout, Miller, and Pitcher 1977). Equation (5.1) is an empirical generalization that I shall take as a baseline model of perception.

In the simplest case, actor interests are concerned with the following situation. Actor j derives a level of utility, u_j, from his control over a resource at level τ_j^*. This level is τ_j above a threshold below which he would perceive no utility in controlling the resource. This focus on one resource is not required in general (as I show at the end of this section), but is analytically useful for the moment.[1] I assume that control of the resource is measured on some ratio scale (e.g., dollars of assets). The actor is now confronted with an event offering him the option of taking an action that would increase his resource control. What is his subjective evaluation of the magnitude of that increase?

One criterion against which the increase could be judged is the actor's current resource control. A unit increase in resource control for a person currently controlling no resource is probably different from the same increase for a person currently controlling a high level of the resource. Assuming an isomorphism between j's perception of utility in increased resource control and his subjective evaluation of an objective stimulus, the rate of change in his utility resulting from a small increase in his resource control is given by the derivative of Eq. (5.1) with respect to his current level of control:

$$\partial u_j / \partial \tau_j = v u_j / \tau_j = \mu v \tau_j^v / \tau_j, \tag{5.2}$$

which, for $0 < v < 1$, states the standard assumption of marginal decreasing utility. A small unit increase in control $(\partial \tau_j)$ yields decreasing change in utility (∂u_j) as existing control increases (τ_j). For values of v greater than 1, actor j derives marginally increasing utility from increased resource control. Empirical research linking subjective evaluations of prestige to years of education, for example, shows that a year of college education yields much higher increases in prestige than the increases provided by a year of primary school education (Hamblin 1971). For all values of v, however, the criterion against which increased resource control is evaluated is an actor's current level of control—the denominator in Eq. (5.2). Other actors present during the evaluation are nowhere considered in the equation.

---

[1]This assumption frees the discussion from treating several issues tangential to the main argument. In particular, there is no need to treat the usual questions of budget constraints on purchasing, relative prices of, and substitutability of control over multiple resources. The issue of maximizing utility derived from multiple resources is addressed at the end of this section.

Social Context

However, we know that the presence of actors during the process of making subjective evaluations can affect the process. As discussed in the Introduction, an actor's evaluations are affected by others to the extent that he perceives them to be socially similar to himself.

Chapters 2, 3, and 4 provide detailed discussion of what it means for two actors to be socially similar within the context of a system of actors. Actors j and i are socially similar to the extent that they are structurally equivalent. In terms of the characterization in Figure 2.4, occupants of status S_j view their system from the same reference point. They have identical relations with others in their system and accordingly make evaluations within identical social contexts. More generally, they are socially similar to the extent that they occupy a single point in the social topology of their system.

As the spatial representation in Figure 3.5 of stratification in elite sociological methodology makes clear, however, structural equivalence is not an either/or phenomenon. It is a matter of degree. Mr. Hauser and Mr. Goodman are more structurally equivalent, for example, than are Mr. Spilerman and Mr. Coleman. The extent to which actor i occupies j's position in a system is given by the distance between them, d_{ji} in Eq. (2.14). This symmetric scalar varies from 0 (if the two actors are structurally equivalent) up to some finite positive value (for maximally dissimilar actors). It will be convenient to express similarity rather than dissimilarity between the two relational patterns in which actors i and j are involved. For actor j, let the maximum distance separating him from the position of any other actor in the system be $dmax_j$. This quantity minus his observed distance from actor i, $dmax_j - d_{ji}$, measures the similarity between j and i. The difference will be 0 if i is involved in the relational pattern most dissimilar to j's within the system and will be positive to the extent that i is structurally equivalent with j.

This structural similarity between the two actors is an objective condition that can be differentially perceived by separate actors. From actor j's perspective, his subjective similarity to actor i is given by Eq. (5.1) as

$$\mu(dmax_j - d_{ji})^\nu. \tag{5.3}$$

Since distances are meaningful only in comparison to other distances within a particular system, and since a system is being taken here as the social context for evaluations, actor j's perceptions can be normalized by the extent to which he sees himself as similar to all actors in the system:

$$\sum_{q=1}^{N} \mu(dmax_j - d_{jq})^\nu. \tag{5.4}$$

The ratio of these two quantities gives, without loss of generality in expressing structural equivalence to j, the extent to which actor j perceives actor i as socially similar to himself in comparison to all actors in the system:

$$l_{ij} = (\mathrm{dmax}_j - d_{ji})^v / [\sum_{q=1}^{N} (\mathrm{dmax}_j - d_{jq})^v]. \tag{5.5}$$

These structural proximity coefficients vary between 0 and 1. It sums across all actors i to equal 1. As actor j occupies a position increasingly distant from all other actors in a system, l_{ij} approaches 1. The extent to which i occupies j's position is captured by the extent to which l_{ij} is greater than 0.[2] The exponent allows one's position in social structure to have differential significance for different perceptions. Its magnitude determines the extent to which actors' distances from actor j are perceived to be socially similar; the higher v is, the less similar are distant actors. This means that the extent to which actor j perceives himself as structurally equivalent to i can vary as a function of the reason for making the perception. Under conditions of external threat to both actors, for example, their differences in relations might dissolve as negligible (low value of v). If the two actors are competing for the same job, on the other hand, minor differences in their relational patterns might be exaggerated in order to emphasize their respectively unique positions (high value of v).

Structural Interests

These results can be brought together in a concept of structural interests. Equation (5.2) says that actor j perceives utility (∂u_j) in the increased resource control offered by an action $(\partial \tau_j)$ with respect to his current level of control $(\tau_j,$

---

[2] This structural similarity, or proximity, measure can be affected by the size of a system since it is constrained to sum to 1 across the N actors in a system. In a system where every actor has the same relation to every other actor, for example, l_{ij} equals $1/N$, which will decrease as N increases. The measure need not decrease, however, with increases in system size. For example, consider the following binary matrix of relations:

$$\begin{bmatrix} 1 & 1 & 0 & 0 \\ 1 & 1 & 0 & 0 \\ 0 & 0 & 1 & 1 \\ 0 & 0 & 1 & 1 \end{bmatrix},$$

which gives distances (Eq. [2.14]) such that Eq. (5.5) gives the following proximities:

$$\begin{bmatrix} .5 & .5 & .0 & .0 \\ .5 & .5 & .0 & .0 \\ .0 & .0 & .5 & .5 \\ .0 & .0 & .5 & .5 \end{bmatrix};$$

an addition of a fifth actor will affect the proximities depending on the fifth actor's relations to the current four actors. If the new actor has relations with actors one and two but none with the others, the proximities for the system will be

$$\begin{bmatrix} .3 & .3 & .3 & .0 & .0 \\ .3 & .3 & .3 & .0 & .0 \\ .3 & .3 & .3 & .0 & .0 \\ .0 & .0 & .0 & .5 & .5 \end{bmatrix},$$

which has no affect on the proximities of actors four and five of the original system. The proximity measure's expected distribution with change in system size is a function of the structure of the system and the type of actors being added or subtracted in the system.

the denominator in the equation). In the context of a stratified system of actors, his evaluation is affected by other actors to the extent that he perceives them to be socially similar to himself. Equation (5.5) states that he perceives actor i to be socially similar to himself to the extent that i is involved in a relational pattern more similar to his own than any other pattern in the system as a social context. Taking these two results together, actor j's evaluation of an action's utility should occur interdependently with each other actor in a system to the extent that he perceives each other actor as jointly occupying his position. Instead of only evaluating the utility of an action with respect to his personal resource control, as in Eq. (5.2), he can be expected to consider the extent to which the action would improve his control with regard to levels exercised by persons he perceives to be in structural circumstances equivalent to his own. Beyond being concerned with himself, in other words, he is expected to be concerned with how the action might be perceived by persons in his social position, i.e., persons with whom he is structurally equivalent. He can be envisioned as symbolically taking on the role of persons with whom he is structurally equivalent so as to answer the question, Does this action improve my well-being as an occupant of my position in society?

This structural conception of evaluation can be expressed as a weighted linear composite. Actor j's perceived utility in the increased resource control offered by some action $(\partial \mathbf{u}_j/\partial \tau_j)$ is an evaluation made with respect to the level of control each actor i exercises (τ_i) weighted by the extent to which he is seen as structurally equivalent to j (l_{ij}):

$$\partial \mathbf{u}_j/\partial \tau_j = l_{1j}v u_j/\tau_1 + l_{2j}v u_j/\tau_2 + \cdots + l_{jj}v u_j/\tau_j + \cdots + l_{Nj}v u_j/\tau_N,$$

$$= \sum_{i=1}^{N} l_{ij}v\mu\tau_j^v/\tau_i. \tag{5.6}$$

In essence, Eq. (5.6) has actor j take each actor i as the criterion in terms of which he evaluates the utility of an action. In place of the one denominator in Eq. (5.2), actor j's own resource control τ_j, Eq. (5.6) considers each other actor's level of control as an alternative criterion against which j's utility can be compared. The relative importance of these comparisons for j's final evaluation of the action's utility is given by l_{ij}, the extent to which he perceives each actor as structurally equivalent to himself.[3]

---

[3]It might seem curious here to use an additive functional form across individuals after adopting the multiplicative form of Stevens' law for individual perceptions. Rewriting Eq. (5.6) in a multiplicative form yields the following:

$$\partial \mathbf{u}_j/\partial \tau_j = v\mu\tau_j^v(\prod_i^N 1/l_{ij})\,(\prod_i^N 1/\tau_i).$$

In this form, differences between separate actors' perceptions would be only a function of each actor's current level of control (τ_j) and the variability of distances between each actor's position and that of the other actors in a system $(\prod_i^N l_{ij}$, given $l_{ij} > 0)$. Since the parameters v, μ, and the product of inverse levels of resource control $(\prod_i^N 1/\tau_i)$ are constants across all actors, they will have no effect on interactor differences in evaluating the utility derived from an increase in resource control. This conclusion contradicts the argument that other actors affect actor j's evaluation to the extent that they are structurally equivalent to j, so the additive form has been proposed.

Although it is a modification of the derivative of Stevens' perceptual law, Eq. (5.6) is in complete accord with that law as a special case. In the laboratory setting, subjects are asked to independently make subjective evaluations of stimuli. This means that subject j is structurally unique within the laboratory setting so that all of the l_{ij} equal 0 with the exception of l_{jj} which equals 1. Under these conditions, Eq. (5.6) reduces to the derivative of Stevens' law given in Eq. (5.2).

The perceptual model from which Eq. (5.6) would have been derived can be obtained through integration. Assuming a constant structure of relations in the system and a fixed level of resource control for each other actor during actor j's evaluation of an action, the l_{ij} and τ_i will be constant during his deliberations (allowing τ_j to vary of course). Integration then yields:[4]

$$
\begin{aligned}
\mathbf{u}_j &= \int (\partial u_j / \partial \tau_j) \partial \tau_j, \\
&= \sum_{i=1}^{N} v\mu l_{ij} \int (\tau_j^v \tau_i^{-1}) \partial \tau_j, \\
&= v\mu l_{jj} \int (\tau_j^{v-1}) \partial \tau_j + \sum_{i=1}^{N} (v\mu l_{ij}/\tau_i) \int (\tau_j^v) \partial \tau_j, \qquad j \neq i \\
&= v\mu l_{jj}(\tau_j^v/v) + \sum_{i=1}^{N} (v\mu l_{ij}/\tau_i)(\tau_j^{v+1}/(v+1)), \qquad j \neq i \\
&= [l_{jj} + \sum_{i=1}^{N} v l_{ij}\tau_j/\tau_i (v+1)]\mu\tau_j^v, \qquad j \neq i. \qquad (5.7)
\end{aligned}
$$

Equation (5.7) is a structural law of perception obtained from Stevens' law by taking into consideration the relational patterns within which perception takes place. The bracketed term is the modification of Stevens' law. Note that when actor j is in a structurally unique position (e.g., alone), the social context of evaluation disappears since the bracketed term equals 1 ($l_{ij} = 0$ for $j \neq i$ and $l_{jj} = 1$). In such a situation, Eq. (5.6) reduces to Stevens' law in Eq. (5.1) as would be expected. When actor j occupies a position in a stratified system, however, his evaluations are interdependent with those of the other actors he perceives to be occupying his position.

Actor interests are determined by actor perceptions of utility, so they too are given by Eqs. (5.6) and (5.7). An actor is interested in taking a specific action to the extent that it offers him greater utility than its alternatives. For example, suppose that actor j is confronted with a single event offering him three alternative actions from which he would derive (according to Eq. [5.7]) three levels of utility: $\mathbf{u}_{j1}$, $\mathbf{u}_{j2}$, and $\mathbf{u}_{j3}$. An illustration would be an academician who has just received a "revise and resubmit" letter in regard to the paper he had submitted to a prestigious journal. There are at least three actions with which he could respond: (a) revise the paper as directed; (b) send the paper to a less prestigious journal; or (c) do nothing with the paper. His interest in the question of what to do with the paper is high to the extent that differences in the utility he would derive from these alternative actions is high. As actor j, his structural

---

[4]The integration constant has been deleted here since it has no effect on the propositions to be derived.

interest in the question of which action to take, x_j, could be given as the variance in utilities he would derive from the X alternative actions available:

$$x_j = \sum_{x=1}^{X} (\mathbf{u}_{jx} - \bar{\mathbf{u}}_j)^2/X, \qquad (5.8)$$

where $\bar{\mathbf{u}}_j$ is the mean utility he would derive from the alternative actions collectively, and X is the denominator, since this is not a sample estimate. To the extent that his structural interest is high, he can be expected to pursue that action yielding him the highest utility.[5] If he is under pressure from a promotion committee to publish in the prestigious journal, for example, the difference between $\mathbf{u}_{j1}$ versus $\mathbf{u}_{j2}$ or $\mathbf{u}_{j3}$ is likely to be considerable. In this circumstance, he can be expectd to revise the paper for resubmission.

It is in this sense of an actor taking that action yielding him maximum utility over its alternatives that I discuss actors pursuing their interests. Although empirical data on actor interests are likely to measure $\mathbf{x}_j$ in Eq. (5.8), the perception of utility in Eq. (5.7) determines those interests and is more easily analyzed directly in deriving propositions and hypotheses. Accordingly, my focus throughout this chapter is on the interest-generating utility $\mathbf{u}_j$ in Eq. (5.7).

In deciding how to act in accordance with his interests, however, an actor is typically assumed to pursue maximum overall utility from several actions affecting multiple resources. These resources can be exchanged with others in his efforts to maximize his overall utility. It is of some moment to know the conditions under which an actor's control of multiple resources maximizes his utility under the proposed structural model.

Consider the traditional situation of N actors in a system where actor j controls levels of G resources, $\tau_{j1}, \tau_{j2}, \ldots, \tau_{jg}$, each at a "price" for gaining a unit of control, $p_1, p_2, \ldots, p_g$. Let him derive an overall level of utility, $\mathbf{U}_j$, from his control over multiple resources as a general function of his perceived utility derived from control over each resource,

$$\mathbf{U}_j = f(\mathbf{u}_{j1}, \mathbf{u}_{j2}, \ldots, \mathbf{u}_{jg}),$$

where $\mathbf{u}_{jg}$ is his perception of the utility of controlling resource g at his current level of perceived control, τ_{jg}. Resource-specific utility $\mathbf{u}_{jg}$ is given by Eq. (5.7). Overall utility $\mathbf{U}_j$ is an undefined general function of resource specific utilities.[6]

---

[5]Coleman (e.g., 1973:71–72) discusses the difference between an actor's maximum and minimum utility (a two-action event) as his signed interest in the event. This idea of signed interest is convenient in analyses of events treated as binary, such as the passage of legislative bills (e.g., Coleman 1973:96–124) or the enactment of community policies (e.g., Marsden & Laumann 1977). Signed interests have not been used to capture the fact that bills or policies as events in general have many compromise outcomes between the extremes of success and failure.

[6]Michael and Becker (1973:134–135, 146–147) offer one argument for separating the function producing actor satisfaction with a commodity from the function generating overall utility from commodity-specific satisfaction. Alternative functional forms for obtaining $\mathbf{U}_j$ from resource-specific utilities cannot be reviewed here. Alternative forms have ranged from a single additive form (cf. Stigler 1950:97–102, Georgescu-Roegen 1968:239–242) to separable dimensions so as to define a utility structure or "tree" (cf. Leontief 1947; Strotz 1957; Georgescu-Roegen 1968:262–264; Burt, Wiley, and Minor 1978, 1979) up to the general functional form presented by Edgeworth (1881:20–56) and assumed here.

Actor j has a total "worth" in the system that is the weighted sum of his current level of resource control and the price of control over each resource:

$$w_j = \sum_{g=1}^{G} p_g \tau_{jg}. \tag{5.9}$$

Given their interests defined by their perceived utilities, actors can be expected to exchange control over the G resources such that each maximizes his own overall utility. In a perfect exchange market, each actor will be able to spend all, but no more than, his total worth in attempting to maximize utility. This "budget constraint" means that actor j's overall utility is at its maximum when the partial derivative of the following function with respect to control over each resource is equal to 0:

$$\mathbf{U}_j = f(\mathbf{u}_{j1}, \mathbf{u}_{j2}, \ldots, \mathbf{u}_{jg}) + \lambda(w_j - \sum_{g=1}^{G} p_g \tau_{jg}),$$

where λ is a Lagrangean multiplier linking the budget constraint to overall utility. For all combinations of resource control that exhaust j's total worth, overall utility is solely a function of his resource specific utilities. Differentiating $\mathbf{U}_j$ with respect to control of resource g and equating to 0 yields

$$\begin{aligned} 0 &= \partial \mathbf{U}_j / \partial \tau_{jg}, \\ &= \partial f(\mathbf{u}_{j1}, \mathbf{u}_{j2}, \ldots, \mathbf{u}_{jg}) / \partial \tau_{jg} - \lambda p_g, \\ &= MU_{jg} - \lambda p_g, \end{aligned} \tag{5.10}$$

where MU_{jg} is the marginal utility for actor j of acquiring control over another unit of resource g. Equation (5.10) yields the traditional representation of maximized utility when set equal to 0 across resources; namely, for all resources q and g, the marginal utility of controlling another unit of control over any resource divided by its price is the constant λ (e.g., Stigler 1950:91):

$$MU_{jg}/p_g = MU_{jq}/p_q = \lambda. \tag{5.11}$$

In other words, as long as the budget constraint is unaffected by the structural model (and there is no reason why it should be), maximum utility under the proposed structural model occurs under the traditional conditions defining the "general equilibrium" model in political economy. Unlike that model, however, the proposed structural model offers hypotheses regarding social norms and relative deprivation effects. It will be convenient to have numerical illustration as a reference during the discussion of those hypotheses.

5.2 NUMERICAL ILLUSTRATION

A hypothetical situation was presented above wherein an actor evaluates an action that would yield him an increase in control over a resource. In order to obtain numerical estimates of actor j's utility in this situation (i.e., $\mathbf{u}_j$ derived from τ_j), values of the τ_j, l_{ij}, μ and ν are needed for Eq. (5.7). Since units of resource measurement are secondary here, the constant μ can be deleted from consideration by setting it equal to 1. Merely for the sake of obtaining numerical results, let the resource specific parameter ν equal 2, its approximate value for subjective perceptions of the prestige a person obtains from a given number of years of education (Hamblin 1971:432).

As examples of social contexts for perceptions, Figure 5.1 presents two structured systems each composed of four actors and a single network. System A is composed of a transitive triad and one isolate where actors one and two have a mutual relation with one another. Actors one and two still have their mutual bond in system B. In addition, however, actor two has mutual bonds with actors three and four while actor one does not. Table 5.1 presents binary relations between the actors in Figure 5.1, distances computed by means of Eq. (2.14) from the binary relations, and levels of proximity to each actor's position computed with Eq. (5.5) from the distances. Note that actors one and two are structurally equivalent in system A since they have zero distance between them. Similarly, actors three and four are structurally equivalent in system B. An inspection of the relations from which distances are computed shows that actors one and two in system A and actors three and four in system B have equivalent relations with all actors in their respective systems.

If each actor but actor j possesses a single unit of resource control, how does j's perceived utility of control changes with increases in his own control? Figure 5.2 plots the values of $\mathbf{u}_j$ given by Eq. (5.7) for each actor in the two hypothetical systems where τ_j varies from 0 to 5, $\mu = 1$, $\nu = 2$, $\tau_i = 1$ for $j \neq i$, and the l_{ij} are given in Table 5.1. Actor one in system A, for example, derives utility from resource control according to the following equation:

$$\mathbf{u}_1 = .47(\tau_1^2) + .66(.47)\,(\tau_1^3) + .66(.06)\,(\tau_1^3),$$

while actor one in system B derives utility from identical resource control according to

$$\mathbf{u}_1 = .97(\tau_1^2) + .66(.03)\,(\tau_1^3).$$

Accordingly, actor one in system A has a level of utility equal to 55.48 if he controls five units of the resource, while actor one in system B has a level of utility equal to 26.73 if he controls five units. The bold line in each graph is

SYSTEM A   SYSTEM B

Figure 5.1. Two illustrative systems of actors.

TABLE 5.1
Relations, Distances, and Proximities in Two Hypothetical Systems of Actors[a]

Relations	Distances				Proximities			
1 1 1 0	.00	.00	1.7	2.7	.47	.47	.08	.00
1 1 1 0	.00	.00	1.7	2.7	.47	.47	.08	.00
0 0 1 0	1.7	1.7	.00	2.5	.06	.06	.84	.01
0 0 0 1	2.7	2.7	2.5	.00	.00	.00	.00	.99
1 1 0 0	.00	2.0	2.4	2.4	.97	.00	.00	.00
1 1 1 1	2.0	.00	1.4	1.4	.03	.84	.08	.08
0 1 1 1	2.4	1.4	.00	.00	.00	.08	.46	.46
0 1 1 1	2.4	1.4	.00	.00	.00	.08	.46	.46

[a]The systems are given in Figure 5.1; system A above and system B below. Relations are binary where z_{ji} is 0 unless actor j has a relation to i whereupon it equals 1. Distances are computed from the binary relations according to Eq. (2.14), and proximities are computed from the distances according to Eq. (5.5) where the exponent ν is set equal to 2.

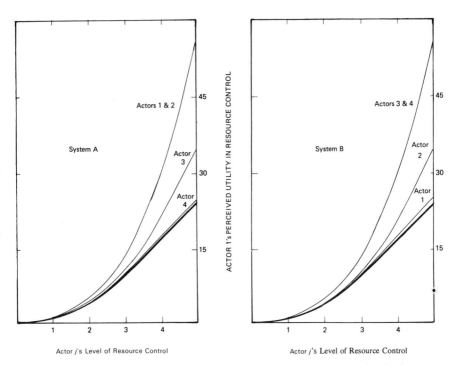

Figure 5.2. Levels of perceived utility in increasing levels of resource control while all other actors have a fixed level of control.

utility, assuming each actor makes his evaluations independently of other actors (u_j in Eq. [5.2]).

If each actor but actor two possesses three units of resource control, how does actor j's perceived utility of his own control change with increases in actor two's control? Figure 5.3 plots the values of $\mathbf{u}_j$ given by Eq. (5.7) for each actor in the two systems where τ_2 varies from 0 to 5, $\mu = 1$, $\nu = 2$, $\tau_1 = \tau_3 = \tau_4 = 3$, and the l_{ij} are given in Table 5.1. Actor one in system A, for example, derives utility from control of his three units of resource according to the following equation:

$$\mathbf{u}_1 = .47(3^2) + .66(.47)(3^3)/\tau_2 + .66(.06)(3^2),$$

while actor one in system B derives utility from three units of resource control according to

$$\mathbf{u}_1 = .97(3^2) + .66(.03)(3^3)/\tau_2.$$

If actor two controls five units of resource, actor one in system A derives 6.27 units of utility from his three units of control, while actor one in system B derives 8.84 units of utility from the same level of resource control. Again, the bold line in each graph is utility, assuming each actor makes his evaluations independently of other actors (u_j in Eq. [5.2]).

Figures 5.2 and 5.3 illustrate the hypotheses of social norms and relative deprivation implied by the structural model in Eq. (5.7). I shall refer back to them as hypotheses are introduced.

5.3 SOCIAL NORMS

In Chapter 2 the rights and obligations involved in performing the relations in a role-set were collectively referenced as a status. Individually, they can be referenced as social norms. For specific actions, including interactions, two or more persons share a social norm as a perception of an action's value in terms of its propriety. In the role-set defining the status of university professor, for example, close supportive relations with students are encouraged as long as they do not become too intimate, whereupon they run counter to our behavioral norms. Of course, a social norm is more than the mere equivalence of two actors' perceptions of an action's value. For example, imagine that professors in the English Department at some university were interviewed and most expressed a high valuation of familiarity with Dorothy Sayers' mystery novels. I should be more likely to view their shared perceptions as collective good taste than to interpret their shared perceptions as a social norm. However, if I subsequently learned that these professors met with one another on a regular basis to discuss literary issues and have come to perceive a knowledge of Sayers' work as an indicator of the literary cognoscente, then I would interpret their shared perception of Sayers' work as a social norm. More than a mere similarity of independently formulated interests, their shared perception has a

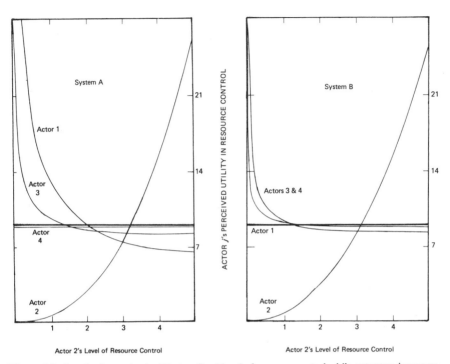

Figure 5.3. Levels of perceived utility in a fixed level of resource control while actor two increases his own level of control.

basis in, and in turn informs, their social ties with one another. In short, a social norm shared by two or more persons seems to have two components: the persons' shared perception of the value of an action, and a social basis for that shared perception.

Normative Perceptions of Empirically Grounded Actions

These two features are explicit in the proposed structural model. The model implies specific conditions as sufficient for two or more actors perceiving equivalent utility in an action. For any two actors j and k, $\mathbf{u}_j$ and $\mathbf{u}_k$ are given to be equal by Eq. (5.7) when the difference in Eq. (5.12) is 0 (where $j \neq i$ and $q \neq k$:

$$\mathbf{u}_j - \mathbf{u}_k = [l_{jj} + \sum_{i=1}^{N} l_{ij} v \tau_j / t_i (v + 1)] \mu \tau_j^v$$

$$- [l_{kk} + \sum_{q=1}^{N} l_{qk} v \tau_k / \tau_q (v + 1)] \mu \tau_k^v. \qquad (5.12)$$

If actors are assumed to evaluate utility independently, as is the case for Stevens' law in Eq. (5.1), then actors j and j's having equal resource control $(\tau_j = \tau_k = \tau)$ is a sufficient condition for them to perceive equal utility in an action (Eq. [5.2]). In fact, this is an explicit assumption in psychophysical research in the sense that the responses of persons to equal stimuli are averaged across persons to obtain an estimate of subject response minimizing individual differences (e.g., Stevens 1971). But the proposed structural model states that perceptions are affected by the social context in which they are made. Actors j and k need not perceive a stimulus equivalently if they are exposed to it in different social contexts. Equal resource control is not a sufficient condition to yield a zero difference in Eq. (5.12). Substituting τ for τ_j and τ_k in the equation yields a not necessarily zero result (where $i \neq j$ and $q \neq k$):

$$\mathbf{u}_j - \mathbf{u}_k = \mu\tau^\nu[(l_{jj} + \sum_{i=1}^{N} l_{ij}\nu\tau/\tau_i(\nu+1))$$
$$- (l_{kk} + \sum_{q=1}^{N} l_{qk}\nu\tau/\tau_q(\nu+1))],$$

which yields (for $i \neq j, k$):

$$\mathbf{u}_j - \mathbf{u}_k = \mu\tau^\nu[(l_{jj} - l_{kk}) + \nu(l_{kj} - l_{jk})/(\nu - 1)$$
$$+ \sum_{i=1}^{N} (l_{ij} - l_{ik})\nu\tau/\tau_i(\nu + 1)]. \tag{5.13}$$

Neither is structural equivalence a sufficient condition for equivalent perceptions. If actors j and k jointly occupy a single position so that d_{jk} equals 0, then $l_i = l_{ij} = l_{ik}$ for all actors i in the system and $l = l_{jj} = l_{kk} = l_{jk} = l_{kj}$. Substituting these equalities into Eq. (5.12) yields the not necessarily zero result (where $i \neq j$ and $q \neq k$):

$$\mathbf{u}_j - \mathbf{u}_k = [l + \sum_{i=1}^{N} l_i\nu\tau_j/\tau_i\,\nu+1)]\mu\tau_j^\nu - [l + \sum_{q=1}^{N} l_q\nu\tau_k/\tau_q(\nu+1)]\mu\tau_k^\nu,$$

which yields (for $i \neq j, k$):

$$\mathbf{u}_j - \mathbf{u}_k = l[(1 + \nu\tau_j/\tau_k(\nu + 1))\mu\tau_j^\nu - (1 + \nu\tau_k/\tau_j(\nu + 1))\mu\tau_k^\nu]$$
$$+ \mu\tau_j^\nu(\sum_{i=1}^{N} l_i\nu\tau_j/\tau_i(\nu + 1)) - \mu\tau_k^\nu(\sum_{i=1}^{N} l_i\nu\tau_k/\tau_i(\nu + 1)). \tag{5.14}$$

Taken together, however, structural equivalence and equal exposure to resource control as a stimulus are sufficient conditions for Eq. (5.12) to equal 0. Given equal resource control in Eq. (5.13), the additional assumption that actors j and k are structurally equivalent means that

$$(l_{jj} - l_{kk}) = (l_{kj} - l_{jk}) = (l_{ij} - l_{ik}) = 0,$$

so that Eq. (5.13) reduces to 0. Similarly, the assumption of equal exposure to resource control as a stimulus means that

$$\tau_j = \tau_k = \tau,$$

which when substituted into Eq. (5.14) reduces that equation too to zero. Neither equal resource control nor structural equivalence alone is sufficient for equal perceptions of utility in an action. However, both together are sufficient.[7]

This feature of the proposed structure model is illustrated in Figures 5.2 and 5.3. Note that the structurally equivalent actors in system B (actors 3 and 4) derive identical levels of utility from any given level of resource control. The structurally equivalent actors in system A (actors 1 and 2) derive identical levels of utility from any level of their own resource control as illustrated in Figure 5.2. When they have different levels of control as in Figure 5.3, however, they derive different levels of utility. In Figure 5.3, u_1 equals u_2 in system A only when the two actors have identical resource control ($\tau_1 = \tau_2 = 3$).

Normative Perceptions of Empirically Ambiguous Actions

There are a great variety of actions, however, that have such a vague linkage to resources as objective stimuli that they can be considered to be detached from empirical reality. Many of the perceptions studied by social scientists concern just such actions—perceptions such as attitudes, beliefs, rumors, and so on. A classic study of such perceptions is the study of student attitudes by Festinger, Schachter, and Back. They distinguish "facts" from "social attitudes" (Festinger *et al.* 1950):

> If a person driving a car down a street is told by his companion that the street ends in a dead end, this piece of information may be easily checked against physical "reality." He has only to drive on and soon he will find out whether or not the street really does end in this manner. . . . The situation with regard to social opinions and attitudes is quite different, however. Here there is no such "physical reality" against which to check. If one person offers the opinion to another that if the democratic candidate for president is

---

[7]Note that a single social topology is assumed here. Distance between actors j and k is given as a single scaler d_{jk} for all actors perceiving the distance. In fact, what appears to the outside observer as distances in a single topology defined by empirical relations among actors is seen by each actor within the system through his own psychological topology, as discussed by Lewin (1936). This poses no problems when structurally equivalent actors are compared since such actors should make similar perceptions, i.e. have similar psychological topology. To the extent that actors are separated by high distance within a system, however, it is possible that they perceive the system social topology differently. Consider the case of two positions, one subservient to the other. Formally, this is a primary position and a position secondary to it, as discussed in Chapters 2 and 3. There will be significant distance between these two positions since they are defined by different patterns of relations (occupants of the secondary position, e.g., statuses S_3 and S_2 in elite sociological methodology, Table 3.7). To the extent that individuals strive to maintain a positive self-image, it seems reasonable to expect the occupants of the secondary position to interpret their relations to the primary position so as to lessen in their own minds the fact that they are subservient (cf. Coser 1973). In such a situation, one could expect occupants of the secondary status to make perceptions *as if* they were structurally equivalent to the primary position. The argument here need not be modified since it gives correct conditions for similar perceptions; however, the necessity of the conditions is brought into question. It is possible for actors separated by distance to make similar perceptions by deliberately ignoring the distance. Accordingly, it is quite possible that there will be more homogeneity of perception in a system than would be expected by the argument here.

elected economic ruin may be expected, the second person may agree or not but he cannot definitely check this opinion against "reality." ... The "reality" which settles the question in the case of social attitudes and opinions is the degree to which others with whom one is in communication are believed to share these same attitudes and opinions [pp.168–169].

In other words, actions with an ambiguous link to empirical reality are evaluated on social grounds, what I have been discussing as the social context of evaluation. Festinger *et al.* (1950:Chap. 5) demonstrate that those sets of dwellings grouped together in a court so as to face one another and occupied by students who tend to choose one another as friends tend to have fewer individuals expressing attitudes different from the typical court attitude than do courts occupied by individuals with low levels of in-court friendship relations. In other words, they find a negative correlation between the density of in-court sociometric friendship citations and the frequency of deviance from court norms. This finding was in accord with their stated expectation (Festinger *et al.* 1950):

If residents had most of their friends within the court, the group was more attractive to them than if they had few friends within the court. The former situation will imply a more cohesive court which should be able to induce stronger forces on its members. This should result in greater homogeneity within the more cohesive court than within the less cohesive one [p. 91].

How does the proposed structural model account for these well-accepted results? In the case of perceptions ambiguously linked to resources as an empirical stimulus, all actors have equal control of resources relevant to the perception since no resource is the empirical basis for making the perception. In other words, the question begins with the difference in Eq. (5.13) where actors j and k are assumed to have equal resource control. I have demonstrated previously that the additional condition of structural equivalence between j and k is sufficient to expect them to perceive equal utility in an action, so actors j and k would be expected to perceive equal utility in an action ambiguously linked to resources as an empirical stimulus to the extent that they jointly occupy a single position, i.e., to the extent that they are structurally equivalent.

This result is in accord with the classic findings offered by Festinger *et al.* but extends their scope to include a wider range of empirical conditions. The Festinger *et al.* findings are based on cohesive subgroups within a system, which were discussed in Chapter 2 as network cliques. As reviewed there, a subgroup is ideal-typically cohesive if each member has exclusive, equal, and mutual maximum strength relations with other members, each actor relating to every other member as he relates to himself. Formally, this level of cohesion for a group G within a larger system of actors is given as $z_{ij} = z_{qk} =$ maximum for actors i, j, k, q members of G and $z_{jk} = 0$ for actor j member of G and k not a member. Such a group of actors defines a jointly occupied position in the larger system. The difference between corresponding relations to and from pairs of members is 0 so that the distance between each pair is 0 ($z_{jk} = z_{ik}$, and $z_{kj} = z_{ki}$ for i, j members of G and k any actor in the system, so $d_{ij} = 0$). Since the members are structurally equivalent to one another, they would be expected to have similar perceptions under the proposed structural model. The Festinger *et al.* findings are therefore to be expected as a special case of the proposed model.

But the proposed model extends and refines those classic results. It refines them by stating conditions under which two actors, connected by a strong, mutual, cohesive bond, need not have equal perceptions of an action ambiguously linked to empirical events. They need not if they are structurally nonequivalent. Note that in Figure 5.1 actors one and two are connected by a mutual bond in both systems. Although structurally equivalent in system A, they are not so in the second system (cf. distances in Table 5.1). As pointed out earlier, they derive equal utility from equal resource control in system A (their perceptions are identical), but they do not do so in system B (cf. Figure 5.2). Moreover, the proposed model extends the classic Festinger *et al.* results to nonclique groups. Actors jointly occupying a position yet having no relations with one another are still structurally equivalent and accordingly expected to share social norms under the proposed model. Ideal-typical secondary positions are one example of such a position. Actors occupying a secondary position direct relations at occupants of other positions rather than at one another (e.g., the hypothetical status S_1 in Table 2.2 or the third and sixth positions in the methodology network among elite experts in Figure 3.3).

Note that these results are obtained by a subtle conceptual change in the cohesion argument. Festinger *et al.* invoke socialization processes operating by means of the flow of information through cohesive relations as the causal force generating social norms. In this sense of relying on actual communication, their classic conception is behavioral. In comparison, the proposed structural model relies on symbolic processes. An actor makes an evaluation by putting himself in the position of others so as to imagine their evaluation. In much the same process that Mead describes for the individual conceptualizing normative behavior as a generalized other, an actor is here expected to generate a normative evaluation by carrying out this symbolic role-taking for each actor with whom he is structurally equivalent.[8] This mental activity does not require

---

[8]This is not to say that the proposed model is intended to capture Mead's concept of a generalized other. Mead (1934) defines the generalized other in terms of the individual's concept of self:

> The organized community or social group which gives to the individual his unity of self may be called 'the generalized other.' . . . If the given human individual is to develop a self in the fullest sense, . . . he must also, in the same way that he takes the attitudes of other individuals toward himself and toward one another, take their attitudes toward the various phases or aspects of the common social activity or set of social undertakings in which, as members of an organized society of social group, they are all engaged; and he must then, by generalizing these individual attitudes of that organized society or social group itself, as a whole, act toward different social projects which at any given time it is

(Continued on next page)

actual exchanges between actors so that the proposed model is able to anticipate norms shared among actors unconnected by direct relations. Although unconnected, occupants of a secondary position are capable of symbolically assuming one another's positions and thereby arriving at a common, or normative, perception without actually communicating that perception to one another. If they are not aware of one another's existence, of course, then the argument breaks down, since they would not be capable of imagining themselves occupying positions of which they are not aware.

This does not reject the socializing potential of communication. To the contrary, one could argue that structurally equivalent actors engage in similar relations with other actors in a system and are therefore similarly socialized (e.g., Burt 1978b). I suspect that, ceteris paribus, actors jointly occupying a position and connected by cohesive relations will adhere more closely to shared norms than will actors occupying a secondary position. Actors i and j are expected to use one another as a reference in making evaluations to the extent that they are structurally equivalent (i.e., to the extent that d_{ij} is 0 so that l_{ij} and l_{ji} are much greater than 0). Where relations are measured so as to allow self relations (z_{ii} and z_{jj} greater than 0), then d_{ij} is likely to be lower for occupants of a cohesive position than for occupants of a secondary position, since the following difference terms in Eq. (2.14) are more likely to be 0: $(z_{jj}-z_{ji})$, $(z_{jj}-z_{ij})$, $(z_{ii}-z_{ji})$, and $(z_{ii}-z_{ij})$. Although occupants of a cohesive position can be structurally equivalent, under a strong criterion, for example, occupants of a secondary position where z_{ji} is given as the normalized path distance in Eq. (2.5) can never be structurally equivalent under a criterion distance less than 2.0 according to Eq. (2.14), since the above difference terms are each 0-1 or vice versa. The key point here is that the cohesion argument typified by Festinger *et al.* has not been rejected so much as its conceptual emphasis on actual behavior (interpersonal communication) has been shifted to a concern with symbolic behavior more generally (intrapersonal role-taking).

In short, the proposed structural model predicts the empirical results obtained by Festinger and his colleagues in their classic study but goes further by stating conditions under which subsequent findings might contradict those results

---

(Continued from previous page)
        carrying out, or toward the various larger phases of the general social process which
        constitutes its life and of which these projects are specific manifestations [pp. 154–155].
The proposed structural model differs from this concept in two important ways. (*a*) Mead proposes that the individual take on the attitudes of all others in the individual's experience while the proposed model focuses on others in structural circumstances equivalent to the individual's. (*b*) Mead proposes that the individual take on the attitudes of others while the proposed model only suggests that the individual take on the objective features of others (τ_i). I find the proposed model to be more plausible than Mead's conception since the actor making an evaluation is not assumed to use all other actors as an alter-ego in making his evaluation (e.g., the professor need not use the janitor as an alter-ego), and he is not assumed to be able to discern the internal states of others (i.e., he need not know the attitudes others take toward an action when using them as a reference in evaluating the action for himself).

(structurally nonequivalent actors connected by a close bond) and by stating more general conditions under which the same results might be expected (social norms among structurally equivalent actors unconnected by relations). I return to this theme in Chapter 6 to determine the structural conditions under which the elite experts share normative perceptions of journal significance.

5.4 RELATIVE DEPRIVATION

In their classic study of American soldiers during World War II, Stouffer, Suchman, De Vinney, Star, and Williams (1949) observed that "becoming a soldier meant to many men a very real deprivation. But the felt sacrifice was greater for some than for others, *depending on their standards of comparison* [p. 125]." The persuasiveness of this observation in the study led Merton and Rossi (1950) to outline a body of theory well known by name if not by content: "reference group theory aims to systematize the determinants and consequences of those processes of evaluation and self-appraisal in which the individual takes the values or standards of other individuals and groups as a comparative frame of reference [p. 288]."

This is exactly the task addressed by the proposed model of interests; actors make evaluations in a social context by using other actors in the context as reference criteria. The advantage offered by the model over available alternatives is the precision with which it implies substantive hypotheses.[9] As was the case in deriving social norms, note here that the model in Eqs. (5.1) and (5.2), assuming actors make evaluations independent of one another, offers no basis for relative deprivation since it does not take other actors into consideration during j's evaluation of utility. For the proposed model in Eqs. (5.6) and (5.7), relative deprivation poses the following question: Given a pair of actors j and i, under what conditions will an action taken by i result in a decline in j's satisfaction with (i.e., his perceived utility in) his existing resource control?

Relative Deprivation from Changed Resource Control

One result of i's action could be an increase in his level of resource control. Actor j will perceive a decline in the utility of his own resource control as a result of this action to the extent that (*a*) he perceives i to be structurally

---

[9]Davis (1959) alludes to the ambiguity of available alternatives in his effort to use reference group theory in empirical research on students: "Rereading these two works left us short of our goal. While *The American Soldier* (Stouffer *et al.*) text was highly informal and the theory was uncodified . . . , the Merton and Kitt (Merton & Rossi) theory is devoid of substantive propositions about relative deprivation [p. 280; parentheses added]." Davis then outlines a method of expecting proportions of persons in a system to experience relative deprivation and relative advantage given a division of the system into deprived versus nondeprived groups.

equivalent with himself such that l_{ij} is greater than 0, and (b) he controlled more of the resource than did i prior to actor i's action such that τ_i^2 was less than τ_j^{v+1} This proposition expresses in words the partial derivative of the structural law of perception in Eq. (5.7) with respect to actor i's increased resource control:

$$\partial \mathbf{u}_j/\partial \tau_i = -l_{ij}(\tau_j^{v+1}/\tau_i^2)\,[\mu v/(v+1)]. \qquad (5.15)$$

The magnitude of this relative deprivation effect decreases for a small increase in actor i's resource control to the extent that (a) actor j perceives i to be structurally equivalent to himself such that l_{ij} is greater than 0, and (b) actor i controlled less of the resource prior to taking his action than did actor j such that τ_i^3 was less than τ_j^{v+1}. This proposition expresses in words the second-order partial derivative, the positive sign of which indicates the decreasing negative effect in Eq. (5.15):

$$\partial^2 \mathbf{u}_j/\partial \tau_i^2 = l_{ij}(\tau_j^{v+1}/\tau_i^3)[2\mu v/(v+1)]. \qquad (5.16)$$

The maximum relative deprivation effect occurs therefore when an actor structurally equivalent to j takes an action that increases his own resource control from a level less than j's to a level higher than j's (specifically, when τ_i increases from τ_i^2 less than τ_j^{v+1} to τ_i^2 greater than τ_j^{v+1}).

This expectation conforms to commonsense notions of what sociologists mean by relative deprivation. For example, consider twin children playing in their family living room where one child is in possession of the toy with which both wish to play. Here are two structurally equivalent actors, j and i, where actor j, controlling the toy, has higher resource control than does actor i. The child in possession of the toy no doubt enjoys his triumph over his twin brother. But suppose that their father arrives with a new toy, clearly superior to the one under debate, and gives it to the child currently without a toy. I should expect the child playing with the old toy to be less satisfied with it than he was before, to suffer feelings of relative deprivation, to take the new toy away from his brother. In terms of Eq. (5.15), the father's gift has increased actors i's resource control from a level lower than j's (i having no toy) to a level higher than j's (i having a better toy) to the short-term detriment of j's satisfaction.

For specific numerical illustration of the propositions, consider the results in Section 5.2. Figure 5.3 plots actor utility for different levels of resource control by actor two given three units of control exercised by each other actor. To the extent that the other actors (1, 3, and 4) suffer a decline in their utility as a result of actor two's increasing resource control, the most dramatic declines occur as actor two increases his control from zero to three units. Thereafter, the other actors suffer little decline. This illustrates the positive relation between the rate of decline in actor j's utility ($\partial \mathbf{u}_j/\partial \tau_i$) and the ratio of his prior resource control to the level exercised by i (τ_j^{v+1}/τ_i^2), the sharpest declines occurring when he previously controlled much more of the resource than did actor i. It also illustrates Eq. (5.16): the rate at which actor j experiences relative deprivation declines as the ratio of resource control by j versus i decreases (τ_{j}^{v+1}/τ_i^3). Further, the sharpest declines in utility are suffered by those actors with the least distance to actor two. This illustrates the positive relation between rate of declining utility for actor j and his perception of the structural equivalence between himself and actor i (l_{ij}). In system A, actor four is isolated from actor two ($l_{24} = 0$ in Table 5.1) so that actor two's increasing resource control has no effect on four's perception of utility. As is the case under the assumption of independent evaluation (the bold line in Figure 5.3), u_4 is a horizontal line in system A in Figure 5.3. In contrast, actor one is structurally equivalent to actor two in system A and suffers the most severe decline in his utility with two's increased resource control. Figure 5.2 illustrates a relative advantage effect. Those actors closest to being isolates derive the least utility from high levels of resource control. Actor four in system A is a nearly perfect isolate ($l_{44} = .99$ in Table 5.1) and derives utility almost identical to that expected under the assumption that actors evaluate utility independently (bold line in Figure 5.2). In contrast, the structurally equivalent actors in each system (actors one and two in system A and actors three and four in system B) derive the most utility from high levels of resource control. This increased well-being occurs because they have increased their control beyond that exercised by the actor structurally equivalent to each (τ_j^y / τ_i is greater than 1, cf. Eq. [5.6]).

Relative Deprivation from Structural Change

The above results assume that actor i has taken some action increasing his resource control which affects actor j's satisfaction with his own level of control. This assumes a static social structure as the social context for j's evaluation. However, change in the social structure itself can also affect j's evaluation by changing the social context in which he makes his evaluation.

Unfortunately, relative deprivation due to structural change is not as easily interpreted as is deprivation due to change in resource control. Unlike resource control, levels of structural equivalence with actor j are interdependent when normalized by means of Eq. (5.5) to obtain the proximity coefficients l_{ij}. Since l_{ij} measures the extent to which actor j perceives actor i to be involved in a relational pattern more similar to his own than are other actors in the system, an increase in l_{ij} must be compensated for by a decrease in one or more l_{kj} to other actors. In other words, if j perceives i as more structurally equivalent to himself in comparison to others then there must be one or more others he now perceives to be less structurally equivalent to himself.

An analysis of relative deprivation based on structural change therefore requires a consideration of at least three actors j, i, and k. An increase in l_{ij} is offset by a decrease in l_{kj}. In actuality there can be many l_{kj} and l_{ij}; a change in one position within a system entails subtle changes in the distribution of distances among all actors. In order to derive relative deprivation effects, however, it is sufficient to focus on a triad of actors.

Given the triad of actors j, i and k, if actor i takes actions changing his relational pattern so that his distance from j decreases and the distance between j and k increases (where the increase in l_{ij} equals the decrease in l_{kj}), actor j will suffer a decline in satisfaction with his own resource control to the extent that his level of control is higher relative to actor k than it is relative to actor i such that τ_j^{y+1}/τ_i is less than τ_j^{y+1}/τ_k. This proposition expresses in words the total derivative of the structural law in Eq. (5.7) with respect to actor j's perception of his structural equivalence to some other actor i (l_{ij}):[10]

$$du_j/dl_{ij} = (\tau_j^{y+1}/\tau_i - \tau_j^{y+1}/\tau_k)\mu v/(v + 1). \qquad (5.17)$$

Recall that the relative deprivation effect of i's increasing his resource control (Eq. 5.15) has a decreasing rate of change to the extent that actors i and j have equal resource control (Eq. [5.16]). In contrast, the magnitude of the above deprivation effect resulting from structural change is constant no matter what the original proximity of i to j. This proposition expresses in words the fact that the second-order partial derivatives of the structural law in Eq. (5.7) with respect to l_{ij} or l_{kj} are zero.

The relative deprivation effect in Eq. (5.17) is closely related to the better known effect in Eq. (5.15). Instead of suffering deprivation as a result of the fact that some actor structurally equivalent to him increases his resource control as in (5.15), actor j in (5.17) suffers deprivation by having his position change from one occupied by persons with lower resource control than his own to one occupied by persons with higher resource control than his own. An example would be a ghetto student in a classroom recently filled with children bused in from a more affluent area whose schooling has been superior. The ghetto student's classroom performance, which might have been excellent in the class previously composed of other ghetto students, now appears inferior in comparison to the performance level of his new classmates. A similar case is a top student in an average undergraduate college who is admitted to a top graduate institution. The student's academic ability, adequate relative to the other

---

[10]The total derivative in Eq. (5.17) expresses both the direct change in actor j's utility resulting from an increase in l_{ij} as well as the indirect change resulting from l_{kj}'s changing so as to compensate for the increase in l_{ij}. The partial derivatives of Eq. (5.7) with respect to l_{ij} and l_{kj}, given the constraint $\Sigma_i^N l_{ij} = 1$, are given as

$$\partial u_j/\partial l_{ij} = f_i = v\mu\tau_j^{y+1}/\tau_i(v+1) - \lambda,$$
$$\partial u_j/\partial l_{kj} = f_k = v\mu\tau_j^{y+1}/\tau_k(v+1) - \lambda,$$

where λ is a Lagrangean multiplier. The change in actor j's utility, du_j, resulting from changes in the proximity of actors i and k to his position $(dl_{ij}$ and dl_{kj}, respectively) is given by the total differential

$$du_j = f_i dl_{ij} + f_k dl_{kj}.$$

The rate of change in actor j's utility with increases in actor i's proximity to j is then given by dividing the total differential by change in l_{ij} to obtain the total derivative given in Eq. (5.17) since $dl_{kj}/dl_{ij} = -1$.

students in his undergraduate classes, is far less adequate when considered relative to the students in his graduate cohort, most of whom were top students themselves in undergraduate classes. In both cases, the distribution of ability among students has not changed but the classroom context in which that ability is demonstrated has—to the detriment of those students accustomed to less able competition.

Observed Relative Deprivation

In fact, relative deprivation effects are to be expected as a combined result of changes in resource control and structural change where both types of changes occur continuously over time. The effects can be illustrated in terms of empirical examples drawn from the Stouffer *et al.* study of soldiers in the context of social structure in World War II America. Their examples, when expressed in the terms used here, demonstrate that either of two soldiers perceiving themselves as jointly occupying a status will suffer a decline in satisfaction to the extent that he perceives the other occupant to have higher resource control than his own. While I see no advantage in reinterpreting each example of relative deprivation given by Stouffer and his colleagues, an interpretation of two well-known examples in terms of the above propositions would be illustrative.

Of those soldiers stationed in the United States, black soldiers stationed in Southern camps were more dissatisfied with Army life than White soldiers in the same camps. Black soldiers who originally lived in the South, however, had consistently better attitudes toward Army life than did black soldiers originally living in the North. This consistency was a result of the North and the South as different social contexts for evaluation (Stouffer *et al.* 1949):

> Relative to most Negro civilians whom he saw in Southern towns, the Negro soldier had a position of comparative wealth and dignity. . . . Putting it simply, the psychological values of Army life to the Negro soldier in the South *relative to the Southern Negro civilian* greatly exceeded the psychological values of Army life to the Negro soldier in the North *relative to the Northern Negro civilian* [pp. 563–564].

To reinterpret, Southern blacks occupied a nonequivalent position in the social structure of World War II America to that occupied by Northern blacks. Kinship and friendship relations linked the soldiers to different regions. Further, there were differences in their probable positions in the occupational structure, since the North was more urbanized than the South. With each position there were considerably different levels of respect in the sense that the Southern black was more exposed to racial segregation (and accordingly less respect) than the Northern black. Being drafted into the army and stationed in the South affected Southern versus Northern blacks differently. The army's attempt to treat individuals equally was an increase in respect for the Southern black relative to other occupants of his status. For the Northern black, exposure to the segregation policies of the South was a decrease in respect relative to the other occupants of his status.

Both experiences illustrate the propositions in Eqs. (5.15) and (5.17). The increased respect given the Southern black in comparison to that accorded others he perceived to be occupying his civilian status in the South created a feeling of relative advantage as expressed by Eq. (5.15). Similarly, the decreased respect given the Northern black in comparison to that accorded others he perceived to be occupying his civilian status in the North created a feeling of relative deprivation as expressed by Eq. (5.15). Alternatively, these experiences can be viewed as a result of structural change. The Southern black with a perception of self-worth based on the segregation policies in the South, when drafted by the army and particularly when stationed in the North, was accorded greater respect than his previous experience had led him to expect. A shift in his position from civilian black to army personnel increased his perception of self-worth by shifting the social context in which that perception was made. This is the gist of Eq. (5.17). A similar interpretation of the Northern black's experience can be offered in terms of Eq. (5.17): His structural transfer from the status of Northern civilian black to Southern Army black changed the social context in which he evaluated self-worth from one in which his race was an indicator of membership in a racial group to a social context in which his race was an indicator of inferiority. Clearly, the effects of resource change (Eq. [5.15]) and structural change (Eq. [5.17]) are intricately entwined in empirical events.

Not surprisingly, Stouffer and his colleagues found that soldiers with more education tended to be promoted more often than those with less. Counter to intuition, it was those soldiers with better education who tended to be most critical of promotion opportunities. Here again, there is a question of social context as a frame of reference for evaluation (Stouffer *et al.* 1949):

> But relative rate of advancement can be based on different standards by different classes of the Army population. For example, a grade school man who became a corporal after a year of service would have had a more rapid rate of promotion compared with most of his friends at the same educational level than would a college man who rose to the same grade in a year. Hence we would expect, at a given rank and a given longevity, that the better educated would be more likely than others to complain of the slowness of promotion. The facts, as we shall see, tend to bear this out [p. 250].

To reinterpret, position in the United States social structure (then as well as now) was largely determined by educational achievement or determinants of such achievement so that individuals with similar levels of educational achievement would occupy similar positions, at least in regard to position prestige. To the extent that position occupants in the civilian labor force had high opportunities for promotion, army personnel with equivalent education would be subject to declines in the perceived utility of their army rank. This works for intra-army comparisons as well. Every time someone in an Army position is promoted, the others occupying that position might be expected to suffer a drop in satisfaction with their own rank. The least satisfied individuals should, therefore, occupy the positions with the highest levels of promotion. Since those individuals with better education were more often promoted, complaints about the Army promotion opportunities should increase with educational level as observed. This same interpretation explains why Air Force personnel had lower opinions of their promotion opportunities than the Military Police did of their own promotion opportunities (Stouffer *et al.* 1949:251). Since the Air Force personnel were more often promoted, those not promoted more often suffered a decline in satisfaction with their own rank and accordingly were more critical of their promotion opportunities.

Here again, the propositions in Eqs. (5.15) and (5.17) are mixed together in empirical events. Within the formal structure of the Army, ranks are a good indication of the occupants' quality of life; higher ranks control greater resources than low ranks, and patterns of relations among Army personnel are defined by their ranks, structurally equivalent persons jointly occupying a rank in the chain of command. Therefore, each time a person of a given rank is given a promotion, the remaining occupants of the rank can be expected to suffer a decline in their satisfaction with their own rank, since a person previously structurally equivalent to themselves has increased his resource control. This feeling would be particularly strong (according to Eq. [5.15]) if persons occupying low ranks were promoted several steps at once to high ranks, since all of the occupants of skipped ranks would now perceive a person with less resource control than their own increasing his control to a level higher than their own. Accordingly, the lowest feelings of satisfaction should be expressed by personnel occupying positions with the highest rates of promotion. In some respects, the findings regarding education can be interpreted as a consequence of deprivation by structural change. The Army employee with a given level of education and time on the job, perceiving himself to be structurally equivalent to a civilian employee with similar education and longevity, suffered relative deprivation as a result of structural change. As expressed in Eq. (5.17), the Army changed his position from one in which his resources offered him high potential for improving his quality of life to one in which those same resources held less value. The opportunities for him to improve his position in the civilian labor force, given his educational achievement, were higher than those available to him in his current position as an Army employee.

Of course, there are a great many models that can be used to interpret empirical findings in *The American Soldier* (e.g., Merton & Rossi 1950:286; Davis 1959). I am not suggesting that the proposed structural model is more accurate than its alternatives in describing those findings. In fact, the proposed model is so much more precise than the findings themselves that using it to describe them amounts to a type of mathematical overkill. But if the phenomenon of relative deprivation is to be analyzed empirically with greater precision than that achieved in its discovery by Stouffer and his colleagues, then the proposed model is quite useful. My purpose in discussing the above examples is to show that classic empirical results make sense in terms of the proposed model. What the model offers beyond those empirical results is a precise functional form (Eqs. [5.15, 5.16, 5.17]) for relative deprivation effects so that the effects can be studied substantively in greater detail. Moreover, since the propositions offered here are themselves derived from a general perceptual model also describing the conditions under which social norms should be shared by two or more actors within a system, the proposed model ties relative deprivation effects in with other related phenomena. In this sense of refining the substantive meaning of relative deprivation and putting it in a more general theoretical context, I believe the proposed structural model extends classic empirical findings on the phenomenon.

5.5 INNOVATION ADOPTION

The uncertainty of the advantages to be obtained from adopting an innovation makes the study of innovation adoption nicely suited to gaining an understanding of the connections between social structure and perception. Social scientists have not been remiss in capitalizing on this opportunity, and there has developed an extensive literature on the influence of social structure on innovation. This literature is discussed later in terms of two propositions that predict innovation from a potential adopter's social integration. Unfortunately, the use of social integration in diffusion research does not lend itself to the precision of expression demanded by the concept of network position as a potential adopter's social context. Three ambiguities ensuing from attempts to do so are discussed below.

My purpose in this section is to use the proposed structural model of actor perceptions to describe the conditions under which an actor would be interested in adopting a specific innovation. I derive two propositions from the model: one concerned with the above treatment of social norms and the other with the above treatment of relative deprivation. As in the two previous sections, these propositions are able to replicate existing empirical results in diffusion research, but refine it to avoid conceptual ambiguities in that research and extend it to include new substantive results.[11]

Social Integration and Innovation: Past Research

The ambiguity of advantages to be obtained from adopting an innovation means that an actor's perception of advantages have a basis not only in the

---

[11]I have elsewhere described statistical tests for hypotheses derived from the innovation propositions discussed here (Burt 1980f). The tests are specifically stated for a reanalysis of the Coleman et al. classic, *Medical Innovation*, in regard to the relative importance of personal attributes versus network position for a doctor's adoption and the manner in which structural equivalence has its effect on adoption over time.

concrete, material aspects of the innovation, but a basis in social structure as well. It is from his position in that structure that the actor evaluates the concrete advantages of adoption. Agencies advocating adoption are likely to design media for communicating the concrete advantages of adoption.[12] In a system of actors equally able to adopt, however, each potential adopter relies on others similarly located in a social structure. Before prescribing a new drug, for example, a doctor must weigh the demonstrated benefit of the drug against its less tangible qualities. How serious and how likely to occur are the side effects of use of the drug? To what extent can other drugs, more thoroughly understood drugs, accomplish similar curative effects? In their arrant study of social structure and medical innovation, Coleman and his colleagues (1966) note

> the extensive trials and tests by manufacturer, medical schools, and teaching hospitals—tests that a new drug must pass before it is released—are not enough for the average doctor. He hesitates to make extensive use of a new drug until it has been proven either by his own tentative trials or by the experiences of other practicing physicians. Apparently, testing at the expert level cannot substitute for the doctor's own testing of the new drug; but testing through the everyday experiences of colleagues on the doctor's own level can substitute, at least in part [p. 32].

The influence of social structure on a potential adopter's perception of an innovation has been researched in terms of social integration. Two propositions are usually supported in that research.

One proposition concerns the time of adoption: Research has shown that social integration is associated with early adoption of normative innovations. To the extent that a person's pattern of relations with others in a system integrates him into the system, the person has a maximum exposure to others who might have experience with an innovation and accordingly becomes an "opinion leader" within the system. Such opinion leaders will be among the first to adopt an innovation consistent with the prevailing norms in the system. When an innovation runs counter to system norms, those persons highly integrated into the system will be least likely to be early adopters.[13]

Social integration has been operationalized in terms of two types of network variables; centrality and prestige (see Rogers & Shoemaker 1971:188–189,

[12]Lin and Burt (1975) describe these specially developed media as local media: "those communication media which, while able to reach a large audience, are capable of customizing messages for different groups or geographical areas which would be undifferentiated by the mass media [p. 258]." For example, farmers tend to discover new corn grains from salesmen (Ryan & Gross 1943). Doctors tend to discover new antibiotics from representatives of drug companies, detail men (Coleman et al. 1966). Housewives in rural villages tend to discover available health innovations from government-sponsored announcers sent to specific villages (Lin 1971; Lin & Burt 1975).

[13]Of course, this association between prominence within a system and innovation adoption need not be perfectly linear. For example, Cancian (1967) argues that it is nonlinear: positive for highly prominent and peripheral persons but zero for persons who are neither high nor low in prominence. He interprets this nonlinearity in terms of differential resource control and demonstrates its presence in earlier studies of agricultural innovations.

215–223 for a literature review). For example, housewives in rural El Salvador who are *central* in their village friendship networks (in the sense that they have direct or short indirect sociometric connections with many other housewives) tend to be most aware of health and family planning ideas as well as most likely to adopt these ideas as medical innovations (Burt 1973; Lin & Burt 1975). Doctors who have *extensive connections* with other doctors (in the sense that they have hospital affiliations, participate in professional associations, tend to choose other doctors as friends, etc.) tend to be more aware of medical innovations and more likely to prescribe new drugs as they become available (Coleman *et al.* 1966). Doctors who have high *prestige* in their local medical community (in the sense that they are often cited by other doctors in the community as sources of medical advice) are likely to prescribe new drugs as they become available (Coleman *et al.* 1966). In a related approach, Becker (1970) compared the tendency for health administrators to adopt two types of health programs as innovations. Measles immunization was chosen as a "high adaptive potential" (HAP) program since it conflicted with the interests of few groups typically supportive of health administrators. Diabetes screening was chosen as a "low adaptive potential" (LAP) program since it did conflict, according to judges' ratings, with the community medical and economic interests typically supportive of health administrators. State health administrators who received numerous citations from fellow health officials as sources of advice on health programs tended to be early in implementing measles immunization programs. In contrast, administrators who received very few citations were the first to implement diabetes screening programs. Becker (1970) concludes:

> Pioneer adopters of the low adoptive potential innovation were identified as marginals, while earliest adopters of the high adoptive potential innovation were found to be individuals with high relative centrality (sic). . . . LAP innovation pioneers innovate to obtain prestige in their communities, while HAP innovation pioneers adopt earliest to gain the admiration of their professional peers [p. 281].

A second proposition gives the pattern of adoption: Just as social integration forces prominent persons to adopt innovations consistent with system norms, research has shown that it imposes innovation homogeneity within subgroups. This proposition is built on the empirical results Festinger and his colleagues obtained (discussed in Section 5.3). Dense communication relations among friends in a group reinforces a common group attitude on issues relevant to the group, in this case the adoption of an innovation. In their study of doctors prescribing a new antibiotic, Coleman *et al.* (1966:113–132) extended this line of reasoning to the dyad as a group. They found that a pair of doctors connected by an advice relation (one citing the other as a source of medical advice) tended to begin prescribing the new antibiotic at about the same time. After the drug had been available for several months, those doctors who had not yet prescribed the drug and were connected by friendship relations (one citing the other as someone he often saw socially) tended to prescribe the antibiotic at about the same time. As did Festinger *et al.* before them (cf. their remarks quoted on pp. 187–188), Coleman and his colleagues (1966) argue:

> Confronted with the need to make a decision in an ambiguous situation—in a situation that does not speak for itself—people turn to each other for cues as to the structure of the situation. When a new drug appears, doctors who are in close interaction with their colleagues will similarly interpret for one another the new stimulus that has presented itself, and will arrive at some shared way of looking at it [pp. 118–119].

To summarize an already brief review, a potential adopter who is socially integrated into a system of other potential adopters is (*a*) likely to adopt a normative innovation early; and (*b*) likely to adopt the innovation at a time when persons directly connected to him by innovation-relevant relations are adopting the innovation. Those who are on the periphery of the system are (*a*) likely to adopt a normative innovation late, while adopting nonnormative innovations early; and (*b*) likely to adopt innovations at a time predicted by their personal preferences rather than by their relations with other potential adopters.

Abstracting still further, this understanding of the connection between social structure and innovation is based on a center-periphery conception of social structure. Opinion leaders at the center of social structure are normatively innovative and learn of innovations by means of relations with others integrated into the social structure such that diffusion occurs as a contagion process.[14] Marginal persons at the periphery of social structure are nonnormatively innovative and tend to discover innovations on their own.

Network Position and Social Integration: Ambiguities

This center-periphery conception of social structure is quite in keeping with the way in which social networks were analyzed at the time that much of the basic diffusion research was being conducted. Building on the development of sociometry, a social psychological approach to analyzing network data, those working with network analysis during the 1950s and 1960s were principally concerned with locating primary groups as network cliques—sets of persons connected by intense relations at the center of the clique with a possible decline in intensity at the clique's periphery (see Section 2.5 for review). The single most important point that distinguishes this approach from the models built from

---

[14]This contagion process is assumed to underly the often noted exponential curve in which the proportion of a population adopting an innovation is low at the beginning and end of the diffusion process but very rapid in the middle of the process (e.g., Hamblin, Jacobsen, and Miller 1973; Leik & Meeker 1975:128–138; Hamblin, Miller, and Saxton 1979). In contrast to this macrolevel of analysis, my concern here is with the structural process by which individuals adopt an innovation which in turn generates an ostensible contagion effect in diffusion among many individuals (see Rogers 1976 for a succinct review of issues within this concern).

a system's social topology is the emphasis on relational pattern rather than relation per se. This point is developed in Chapter 2 as a difference between a relational and a positional approach to network analysis (cf. Table 2.1). As characterized in Figure 2.4, the positional approach abstracts social structure in a patchwork rather than center-periphery image. Instead of a center of intense interaction that decreases toward the periphery of social structure, occupants of positions determined to be statuses are differentially connected by role relations to occupants of other statuses such that their system is stratified in terms of possibly multiple centers each with its contingent of secondary statuses. The implication for diffusion research of this shift from a relational to a positional perspective is a need to rethink the meaning of social integration as a structural concept. Three problems ensue from such a reconsideration.

The most immediate problem is determining a potential adopter's social integration. What is it about his relational pattern that defines integration and accordingly leads to innovation adoption? The problem here is a cavalier distinction between the concepts of centrality and prestige in much diffusion research. As reviewed in Section 2.4, centrality refers to the extent that an actor is involved in all relations among actors in the system, and prestige refers to the extent that he is the object of intense relations from actors who are themselves the object of intense relations. Becker's (1970) analysis provides an obvious mixture of these concepts since integration is measured as prestige (choice status) and discussed as centrality (see p. 200).

It should be stressed that the concepts of prestige and centrality are very similar in a center-periphery conception of social structure. Persons at the center of the system are most prestigious in the system. This might have obviated a distinction between centrality and prestige as social integration in past diffusion research. There remains the current problem of how to translate network position into integration for future research.

Moreover, past research suggests neither that centrality be ignored in favor of prestige, nor that prestige be ignored in favor of centrality. While Coleman *et al.* (1966) measure social integration as connectedness and prestige, they are careful to distinguish the effects of the two concepts on innovation. They document the tendency for prestigious doctors to prescribe a new antibiotic earlier than doctors with low prestige. They stress, however, that prestige alone cannot account for the apparent contagion process by which the innovation spread among doctors by means of their interpersonal relations; this contagion process operated most visibly for centrally located doctors (Coleman *et al.* 1966:111–112).

A second problem lies in determining what aspects of a potential adopter's relational pattern do not define his social integration. There is an infinite variety of variables that can be computed from the pattern of relations defining an actor's network position (*passim,* Moreno 1960). Which of the possible network variables are to be excluded as irrelevant? The easiest strategy here is to rely on empirical results. The features of a pattern of relations significant for social integration's effect on innovation will be those features captured by variables strongly correlated with innovation variables. For example, Burt (1973) presents six network variables (culled from an earlier list of twelve) that measure various aspects of a potential adopter's social integration. Variables having different correlations with measures of innovation and several demographic variables were argued to be measuring different aspects of social integration. The results suggested separating a dimension of integration in terms of ability to communicate with other potential adopters from a dimension of integration in terms of influence over other potential adopters. The absence of theoretical guidance notwithstanding, results such as these are to be taken with a grain of salt. Inevitably, there are other network variables not considered in such analyses. Among the unconsidered variables could be the one aspect of network position most important for predicting innovation in the circumstances being studied. Further, inference is limited to the observations analyzed. Burt (1973) analyzes the diffusion of innoculations among housewives in rural El Salvador during the Fall of 1969. The connection between social structure and innovation observed there need not recur in a study of the diffusion of a new antibiotic among doctors, nor indeed need it ever recur.

A third problem, associated with the first two, lies in the contextual importance of network position. The problem here is that the importance of a potential adopter's relational pattern in part derives from the social structure in which it occurs. As a relatively unsophisticated example, consider the following variable: the number of sociometric choices of some type that a potential adopter receives from other potential adopters. Past research demonstrates that this variable is often correlated with innovation; early adopters of normative innovations tend to receive many choices. The correlation, however, is contingent on the social structure of potential adopters. In a pluralistic system composed of persons each receiving an equal number of citations, there will be no correlation since there is no variability in the network variable. The highest correlation would be expected in an elitist system where a set of persons at the center of the social structure receive all choices from persons at the system's periphery. Systems intermediate between these two ideal types would be expected to yield correlations of intermediate magnitude. In fact, the literature review by Rogers and Shoemaker (1971:368–369, 357–360, 379) finds erratic empirical support for the correlation between early adoption and various measures of social prestige.

There is more of a problem here than merely controlling for contextual effects in an analysis of covariance. We have no a priori knowledge of the basis for the contextual importance of network position in a specific system. Just as network variables can be generated ad nausem from the pattern of relations defining a potential adopter's position, so there are many ways in which the potential adopter can be structurally distinct from other potential adopters. In one system, a person might adopt an innovation early as a result of the disproportionate number of persons who routinely ask for advice on such innovations. In another system, a person might adopt early as a result of being the only individual with relations to leaders of rival factions in dispute over the innovation. Both of these early adopters are integrated into their systems, but for different reasons, as a function of the social structure of their systems.

In short, social integration as it is used in diffusion research will not easily translate into a structural concept defined in terms of a potential adopter's network position. There are different aspects of the pattern of relations defining a position that have been shown to be important in predicting innovation as a consequence of social integration. There is no clear boundary for the diversity of possible network variables that could be generated as measures of social integration. There is no obvious way in which the contextual importance of network position can be determined from the concept of social integration. Of course, these problems only concern zero-order associations between social integration and innovation. Higher order coefficients in structural equation models controlling for personality and demographic differences in potential adopters would be more seriously distorted by failure to correctly specify social integration.

Innovation Adoption as a Structural Interest

Given the difficulty of translating social integration as it is used in diffusion research into a structural concept defined in terms of network position, a more direct connection between network position and innovation is needed. The fundamental issue in linking social structure with innovation lies in determining how a potential adopter's evaluation of the intangible advantages of adoption is affected by his network position.

This is precisely the issue addressed by the proposed structural model in Eqs. (5.6) and (5.7). Let the resources actor j would acquire by adopting an innovation be referenced as t_j. Further, let each potential adopter receive a similar level for his adoption (e.g., t_j is the same as t_k). This means that adoption is a dichotomy rather than a continuous, quantitative variable measuring level of adoption.[15] By replacing resource control in Eq. (5.7) with adoption (i.e., replacing τ_i and τ_j with t_i and t_j), the proposed structural model gives actor j's perception of his adoption utility—the level of utility he would experience if he had adopted the innovation (where $j \neq i$):

$$\mathbf{u}_j = [l_{jj} + \sum_{i=1}^{N} v l_{ij} t_j / t_i (v+1)] \mu t_j^v, \tag{5.18}$$

[15]A level of adoption variable could be used, but use of a dichotomy here means that I can ignore the problem of thresholds for individual perceptions. Adoption for each actor means the same performance of some action, e.g., beginning to prescribe a new drug, beginning a new health practice, first wearing a new clothing fashion.

where μ and ν are innovation specific constants, the former defined by the metric in which adoption is measured and the latter defined by the rate at which distance between actor j and some actor i makes i's adoption unimportant for j's evaluation of the utility he would derive from his own adoption (Eq. [5.5]). Numerical illustration will help explain the advantages and limitations of this formulation.

Figure 5.4 presents four hypothetical systems of potential adopters. There is only one network defining each system, and relations are reduced to binary ties. In the Z matrix next to each diagram, z_{ji} is 0 unless actor j has a relation to actor i, whereupon it equals 1. There are seven actors in each system. Table 5.2 presents distances and proximities computed from the binary relations. For this illustration, ν is set equal to 1 so as to emphasize the possible effects of social context on the perception of adoption utility.

One implication of Eq. (5.18) is similar to the above discussion of social norms. Actor j's perceived utility in adoption is the sum of two components: his personal perception of adoption's utility ($l_{jj}\mu t_j^{\nu}$) and his perception based on the extent to which others have adopted so as to present him with a social norm of adoption ($\Sigma_i \, \nu l_{ij} \, t_j^{(\nu+1)}/t_i(\nu+1)$, where $j \neq i$). To the extent that his relational pattern is unique within his system, l_{ij} will approach 0 and l_{jj} will approach 1. This means that his adoption utility will be based solely on his personal criteria rather than the extent to which his structurally equivalent peers have already adopted. As a first proposition, in other words: An actor will adopt an innovation as a function of his personal preferences to the extent that he perceives himself to be structurally unique within a system of potential adopters ($l_{jj} = 1.00$ for him as actor j).

This proposition is in accord with the earlier mentioned finding that potential adopters not well integrated into a system, isolates, seem to adopt innovations on an individual basis rather than adopting as part of a contagion process. Coleman et al. (1966:79–99) vividly document this when they show that diffusion of a new drug among isolated doctors occurs as if diffusion were a result of random connections among doctors. Within system A of Figure 5.4, person one is an isolate. Table 5.2 shows that his adoption utility is based solely on his personal preferences since l_{11} equals 1; all other l_{i1} equalling 0.

This proposition extends beyond isolates. There are many ways in which an actor can be structurally unique, only one of which is isolation. In system B of Figure 5.4, for example, actor one is a liaison between two cliques. He is the only channel of communication between the two cliques and is accordingly unique within the system. Looking down column one of the proximities for system B in Table 5.2, l_{11} is .78; the only actors whose adoption would influence his perception of adoption utility are his contacts in the two cliques, actor two ($l_{21} = .11$) and actor five ($l_{51} = .11$). The predominant determinant of the liaison's adoption, in other words, will be his personal preferences. System C is more hierarchical. Actors three through seven constitute a gaggle of

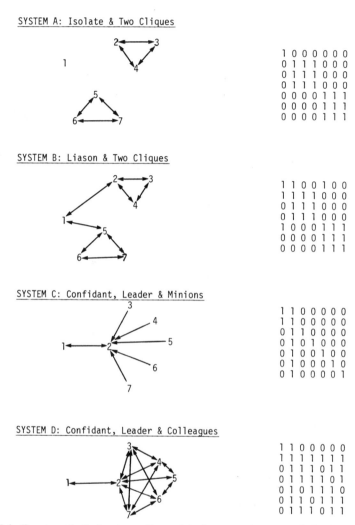

Figure 5.4. Four hypothetical systems of potential adopters each composed of a single network of binary relations.

minions in the system who have no relations with one another and whose relations to a leader (actor two) are not reciprocated. Actor one is a confidant to the leader. As the only person cited by the leader, he is unique in the system. Looking down column one of the proximities for system C in Table 5.2, the only element greater than 0 is l_{11}. The leader's confidant will adopt an innovation as the result of his personal preferences. This situation changes in system D. Actor one is still a confidant to actor two as a leader; however, actors three through seven are colleagues rather than minions. Their relations to actor two as a leader are reciprocated, and they have some relations with one another. As a

TABLE 5.2
Distances and Proximities among Hypothetical Adopters

Distances	Proximities

```
            Distances                              Proximities

         0.0 2.8 2.8 2.8 2.8 2.8 2.8        1.0 .07 .07 .07 .07 .07 .07
             0.0 0.0 0.0 3.5 3.5 3.5        .00 .31 .31 .31 .00 .00 .00
                 0.0 0.0 3.5 3.5 3.5        .00 .31 .31 .31 .00 .00 .00
                     0.0 3.5 3.5 3.5        .00 .31 .31 .31 .00 .00 .00
                         0.0 0.0 0.0        .00 .00 .00 .00 .31 .31 .31
System A                     0.0 0.0        .00 .00 .00 .00 .31 .31 .31
                                 0.0        .00 .00 .00 .00 .31 .31 .31


         0.0 2.4 2.8 2.8 2.4 2.8 2.8        .78 .13 .07 .07 .13 .07 .07
             0.0 1.4 1.4 3.5 3.7 3.7        .11 .38 .21 .21 .03 .00 .00
                 0.0 0.0 3.7 3.5 3.5        .00 .23 .34 .34 .00 .02 .02
                     0.0 3.7 3.5 3.5        .00 .23 .34 .34 .00 .02 .02
                         0.0 1.4 1.4        .11 .03 .00 .00 .38 .21 .21
System B                     0.0 0.0        .00 .00 .02 .02 .23 .34 .34
                                 0.0        .00 .00 .02 .02 .23 .34 .34


         0.0 2.2 2.2 2.2 2.2 2.2 2.2        1.0 .18 .09 .09 .09 .09 .09
             0.0 2.8 2.8 2.8 2.8 2.8        .00 .82 .00 .00 .00 .00 .00
                 0.0 2.0 2.0 2.0 2.0        .00 .00 .43 .12 .12 .12 .12
                     0.0 2.0 2.0 2.0        .00 .00 .12 .43 .12 .12 .12
                         0.0 2.0 2.0        .00 .00 .12 .12 .43 .12 .12
System C                     0.0 2.0        .00 .00 .12 .12 .12 .43 .12
                                 0.0        .00 .00 .12 .12 .12 .12 .43


         0.0 3.2 3.2 3.2 2.8 3.2 3.2        .89 .00 .00 .00 .00 .00 .00
             0.0 2.0 2.0 2.4 2.0 2.0        .00 .36 .11 .14 .08 .14 .11
                 0.0 2.0 2.4 2.0 0.0        .00 .14 .30 .14 .08 .14 .30
                     0.0 2.4 2.0 2.0        .00 .14 .11 .36 .08 .14 .11
                         0.0 2.4 2.4        .11 .08 .07 .08 .60 .08 .07
System D                     0.0 2.0        .00 .14 .11 .14 .08 .36 .11
                                 0.0        .00 .14 .30 .14 .08 .14 .30
```

[a]Distances (d_{ji} in Eq. [2.14]) and proximities (l_{ij} in Eq. [5.5] where $v = 1$) have been computed from the binary data in Figure 5.4.

result, actor one is unique as an outsider rather than a confidant. Actor two occupies a position in System D that is more similar to those of his colleagues than to that occupied by his confidant. The proximities for system D in Table 5.2 reflect these structural changes. Actor one is nearly unique as an outsider within the system ($l_{11} = .89$) while actor two, nearly unique in system C as a leader ($l_{22} = .82$), is nonunique in system D as one of a group of colleagues ($l_{22} = .36$ for system D).

In short, actors at the center or the periphery of a social system could adopt an innovation for personal, rather than social, reasons to the extent that they are structurally unique within the system. This has bearing on the often noted

TABLE 5.3
Adoption Utilities for Some Hypothetical Adopters[a]

Adoptions	System A		System B		System C		System D	
	u_7	u_1	u_7	u_1	u_7	u_1	u_7	u_1
No adoption	2.0	2.0	2.0	2.0	2.0	2.0	2.0	2.0
#2 adopts	2.0	2.0	2.0	1.9	2.0	2.0	1.9	2.0
#3 adopts	2.0	2.0	2.0	1.9	1.9	2.0	1.6	2.0
#4 adopts	2.0	2.0	2.0	1.9	1.8	2.0	1.5	2.0
#5 adopts	1.7	2.0	1.8	1.8	1.6	2.0	1.4	1.9
#6 adopts	1.4	2.0	1.4	1.8	1.5	2.0	1.3	1.9
#7 adopts	—	2.0	—	1.8	—	2.0	—	1.9
#1 adopts	—	—	—	—	—	—	—	—

[a]Utilities have been computed from Eq. (5.18) using an arbitrarily chosen metric. Everyone is given one unit of the resource obtained through adoption and adoption itself increases this to two units (t_j is 1 if actor j has not adopted and is 2 when he adopts). The innovation specific constant μ is used to eliminate the metric of adoption by setting it equal to $t_j - 1$. If actor j does not adopt the innovation, $t_j = 1$ so $\mu = 0$, and he derives zero utility from his own control. Adoption raises t_j to 2 so that $\mu = 1$, and actor j derives nonzero utility from adoption. Also for the sake of illustration the innovation specific constant ν is set equal to 1 as it was in Table 5.2. Substituting these measures and parameters into Eq. (5.18) yields $\mathbf{u}_j = 2(l_{jj} + \Sigma_i^N l_{ij}/t_i)$, for $j \neq i$. Consider actor seven in system A (first column above). Before any actors have adopted the innovation, his adoption utility is 2 (2(.07/1 + .31/1 + .31/1 + .31)). Proximities are taken from Table 5.2. After actors two, three, four, five, and six have adopted the innovation, seven's subsequent adoption will have the utility of 1.38 (2(.07/1 + .31/2 + .31/2 + .31)).

correlation between social integration and time of adoption. The proposed structural model does not state when adoption will occur so much as it states what should be responsible for time of adoption. Adoption will not be caused by structural factors to the extent that an actor is structurally unique. It will be caused by his personal attributes, such as exposure to communication media outside the system of potential adopters, age, personality, etc. A positive correlation between social integration and early adoption is spurious for structurally unique actors. Controlling for differences in the personal attributes of potential adopters, there should be no association between the social integration of structurally unique actors and the time of adoption.

Structurally nonunique actors are another matter. A second implication of Eq. (5.18) is similar to the above discussion of relative deprivation. The model implies an ostensible contagion effect. I say "ostensible" because the implied process does not require interaction between actors transmitting the innovation. To the extent that a potential adopter's relational pattern is similar to one or more of the patterns in which other potential adopters are involved, l_{ij} will be greater than 0 and l_{jj} will approach 0. According to Eq. (5.18), such an actor would perceive utility in adopting an innovation as a function (in part) of the extent to which others have adopted.

The nature of the contingency between perceptions of potential adopters as a result of their proximate positions in social structure can be illustrated with a simple example. Table 5.3 presents changes in adoption utilities for actors one and seven in Figure 5.4 as an innovation spreads through their systems. Arbitrary values have been given for adoption resource (the dichotomy, t_i) and the innovation–specific constants μ and ν. When no one has adopted the innovation, all potential adopters derive equal utility from adoption. The arbitrary scales and parameters place this utility at 2.0. To the extent that a potential adopter is structurally unique within his system, the level of utility never declines despite the diffusion an innovation has taken. In systems A and C, actor one is structurally unique, and Table 5.3 shows no change in his adoption utility as the innovation diffuses through his system. However, to the extent that a potential adopter is structurally equivalent with other potential adopters, his adoption utility declines as actors jointly occupying his network position adopt. For actor seven in system A, his adoption utility remains stable across adoption by actors two, three, and four. These are members of the clique separate from his own. But when comembers of his own clique adopt the innovation (actors five and six), his adoption utility declines. In system D, actor seven is a member of a group composed of everyone but actor one. With the sequential adoption by each of his colleagues—first actor two, then actor three, then actor four, and so on—his utility adoption steadily declines.

These examples illustrate the way in which the proposed model induces contingency between the utilities two potential adopters perceive in adoption as a result of their proximate network positions. Contingency results from relative deprivation. Adoption of a normative innovation is desirable. To the extent that others occupying one's status have adopted the innovation, however, the innovation is no longer an innovation per se. It is an expected action, a social norm. The greatest utility to be obtained from adopting an innovation, qua innovation, is therefore available before others structurally equivalent to one's self have adopted it. This relative deprivation effect probably varies across innovations according to the extent to which an innovation is purely social, fashions being most subject to such an effect and technological changes being least subject to such an effect. In other words, the innovations most subject to the social factors in Eq. (5.18) are those whose advantages have the weakest basis in empirical reality—the type of stimulus discussed as an object for social norms in Section 5.3. The empirical question of its scope notwithstanding, the following proposition is a general implication of the proposed model: An actor will quickly adopt an innovation after actors he perceives to be structurally equivalent to him have adopted it ($l_{ij} \gg 0$ for him as actor j).[16]

---

[16]How quickly this relative deprivation effect operates is an unresolved question. The relative deprivation effect illustrated in Table 5.2 is given by the partial derivative in Eq. (5.15). For the adoption model in Eq. (5.18), this effect is given as

$$\partial \mathbf{u}_j / \partial t_i = -l_{ij}(t_j^{\nu+1}/t_i^2)[\mu\nu/(\nu+1)].$$

Since t_j is dichotomous, this effect on actor j occurs only once with each actor i's adoption. The

(Continued on next page)

This proposition is consistent with evidence supporting the idea that an innovation spreads through a system of interconnected actors because of a contagion process. Actors with the least unique work positions in a system of potential adopters will adopt an innovation in what appears to be a contagion process—the innovation spreading rapidly to all but the structurally unique. This also offers one explanation of the problem posed by Coleman *et al.* (1966:112) regarding social integration measured as prestige versus connectivity, prestige being correlated with early adoption but incapable of accounting for the seeming contagion process by which an innovation spreads among interconnected persons. To the extent that a prestigious opinion leader is structurally unique in his system (note that the leader in system C of Figure 5.4, actor two, is unique within his system, $l_{22} = .82$ in Table 5.2), he can be expected to adopt early as a result of his cosmopolitan perspective rather than as a result of the relational pattern linking him to other adopters within the system. This is the first proposition derived from Eq. (5.18). On the other hand, the observed contagion process is to be expected among the structurally equivalent, that is, actors involved in similar relational patterns. This is the second of the two propositions derived from Eq. (5.18). In system D of Figure 5.4, for example, actor two's colleagues have relations with one another so as to form a clique, and they are expected to follow one another's adoption quickly or suffer the rapid decline in adoption utility reserved for the last to adopt (actor seven in Table 5.3).

As a further point of agreement between the formulation here and past research, two structurally equivalent actors will adopt an innovation at approximately the same time since adoption by either will be quickly followed by the other's adoption. Coleman and his colleagues (1966:113–130) showed that doctors connected by friendship, advising, or discussion relations tended initially to prescribe a new antibiotic at approximately the same time (although their similarity varied over time). To the extent that two persons connected by a close relation have similar relations with others—my friend's friends are my friends, her colleagues are my colleagues—the two persons are structurally equivalent and should adopt an innovation at approximately the same time according to the proposition illustrated by Table 5.3.[17]

(Continued from previous page)

overall deprivation effect on actor j at one point in time therefore comes from the number of actors i occupying his network position who adopt at that time. The more of his cooccupants who adopt, the more severe his feelings of deprivation. The next problem is to determine if actor j's adoption is a result of the gradual cumulation of these effects over time until they reach some threshold resulting in his adoption or if his adoption is precipitated by the sudden adoption of many actors jointly occupying his network position. I have discussed this issue elsewhere with statistical tests for both time effects in regard to the Coleman *et al.* study, *Medical Innovation* (Burt 1980f).

[17]This could account for their observation (Coleman *et al.* 1966:117) that the similarity of adoption time for doctors connected by sociometric choices was no more than was to be expected from random chance when all doctors were combined across different times of adoption. According to the above proposition, such a result could occur if structurally equivalent and nonequivalent doctors are confused. If two doctors connected by a close relation have similar relations with other

But this second proposition extends beyond potential adopters tied by intense relations. Structurally equivalent actors neet not be connected by any relations. In system C of Figure 5.4, for example, the five minions of actor two (actors three, four, five, six, and seven) affect one another's perception of adoption utility even though they have no direct relations with one another. Table 5.3 shows that actor seven in this system suffers a decline in his perceived adoption utility each time one of the other minions adopts. In short, two or more structurally equivalent actors are expected to adopt an innovation at about the same time even if they do not have direct relations with one another.

In closing, note that by using the formulation in Eq. (5.18) one can avoid the issues plaguing social integration as the concept of social structure used to explain innovation adoption. Since distances between actors are computed in terms of each corresponding relation defining their respective network positions, and proximities are merely transformations of those distances, there is no need to determine what aspects of relational pattern are important for predicting innovation. All aspects have been considered. Moreover, the contextual importance of a potential adopter's relational pattern has been captured. The extent to which actor j's relational pattern is different from those defining the positions of other potential adopters is given by the extent to which l_{jj} approaches 1. In short, and as was discussed at length in Chapter 2, all abstract representations of social structure purporting to describe relational patterns among actors in a system are quantitatively contained in the system's social topology. Equation (5.18), based on the proposed structural model in Eqs. (5.6) and (5.7), a model itself based on the social topology of a system, captures a potential adopter's social context in a very general manner.

5.6 CONCLUSIONS

My purpose in this chapter has been to propose a model of the manner in which an actor's evaluation of the utility in alternative actions is affected by his or her network position in social structure. The gist of my proposal is as follows: The actor evaluates an action by taking on the positions of others to see what the action might look like to them. Given the resource(s) to be gained by taking the action, what is the utility to others of taking the action? The specific others whose positions he temporarily assumes are actors in the same social circumstances he is in himself. Those others are persons with whom he is structurally equivalent. Speaking more formally, the extent to which actor j perceives actor i to be in the same social circumstances as himself is given by the proximity coefficient l_{ij} in Eq. (5.5). The coefficient is close to 1 to the extent that the

---

doctors, then they should adopt at the same time. If they have different relations with others (e.g., actors one and two in system B of Figure 5.1), they are not structurally equivalent and need not adopt at the same time.

distance between actors i and j within a social topology (d_{ji} in Eq. [2.14]) is close to 0. Stevens's work in psychophysics is then the basis for proposing a structural model of the change in actor j's utility ($\partial \mathbf{u}_j$) that would result from the increased resource an action offers him ($\partial \tau_j$). This basic result is given in Eq. (5.6) as the partial derivative:

$$\partial \mathbf{u}_j / \partial \tau_j = [l_{jj} \nu \mu \tau_j^{\nu} / \tau_j] + [\sum_i^N l_{ij} \nu \mu \tau_j^{\nu} / \tau_i],$$

where $j \neq i$. Integration then yields a model of structural perception in which actor j's perceived utility, $\mathbf{u}_j$ in Eq. (5.7), is given as a function of the extent to which his resources are high relative to those controlled by others occupying his position. His structural interests are determined in turn by differences in the utility he perceives in alternative actions (Eq. [5.8]).

Perhaps the single most important conclusion I can draw from the chapter is that the proposed model is in accord with significant empirical results, but extends them in a substantively meaningful way.

1. It is consistent with results in psychophysics supporting Stevens's well-known law of perception. When an actor is alone, no other actors define his social context so that l_{jj} equals 1 and all other l_{ij} for actor j equal 0. In this case, the second of the above two bracketed terms equals 0, and the equation reduces to Stevens's psychological model (Eq. [5.2]). In addition, however, the proposed model identifies social contexts in which an actor should make evaluations as if he were alone. The second of the above two bracketed terms will equal 0 (and therefore reduce to Stevens's model) whenever actor j is involved in a unique relational pattern (i.e., a pattern unlike others observed in a system, such as a leader, a liaison between two polarized factions, a confidant to a leader; see Figure 5.4 and Table 5.2). In other words, an actor can be extensively involved in relations with others, but the pattern of those relations can be sufficiently unique to make him perceive actions as if he were all alone. To the extent that other actors occupy j's network position, however, the second bracketed term is nonzero, and his perceptions are accordingly affected.

2. This enables the proposed model to be used to define conditions under which homogeneous perceptions as social norms can be expected. Actions ambiguously linked to empirical reality should be similarly perceived by structurally equivalent actors. The proposed model replicates the empirical results obtained in the classic analysis of group standards by Festinger *et al.*, but goes further by stating conditions under which subsequent findings might contradict those results (structurally nonequivalent actors not sharing a norm despite their connection by a close bond) and by stating more general conditions under which the same results might be expected (structurally equivalent actors sharing a norm despite the absence of direct relations among them).

3. The proposed model also offers an explicit functional form for actors feeling relative deprivation (or advantage) as a result of changes in the

distribution of resources within a system or structural change in the system. Classic empirical results reported by Stouffer *et al.* in their study of American soldiers make sense in terms of the proposed model. Beyond those classic results, the proposed model offers a more precise statement of relative deprivation effects so that such effects can be studied substantively in greater detail. Moreover, since the relative deprivation effects are derived from a general perceptual model also describing social norms, the proposed model ties the concept of relative deprivation in with other related phenomena. In this sense of refining the substantive meaning of relative deprivation and putting it in a more general theoretical context, I believe the proposed structural model extends classic empirical findings on the phenomenon.

4. Finally, these implications of the proposed model are used to describe the manner in which social context affects an individual's decision to adopt an innovation. Here again, the proposed model replicates empirical generalizations on innovation adoption (isolates adopting late and members of a clique adopting quickly after one another in a contagion process), but goes on to predict new results (structurally unique persons adopting for purely personal reasons, even if they are at the center of a system, and structurally equivalent persons adopting in an ostensible contagion process despite the absence of relations among them). Moreover, ambiguities created in describing the adoption decision in terms of an actor's "social integration" are avoided under the proposed structural model.

At this point, the proposed model of structural interests could be used to explore a concept of structural action. Figure 1.1 shows that the premise underlying a structural theory of action has actor interests patterned by social structure and action patterned by those interests. In the same manner that political economists have followed out the implications of an atomistic concept of action based on individuals pursuing independently maintained interests, or preferences, I could now follow out the implications of a structural concept of action based on individuals pursuing interests defined by the proposed structural model. This is one way in which atomistic, normative, and structural action models are compared in Chapter 9.

Although this is a potentially rewarding direction for work in pure theory, it is substantively unrealistic. As presented in Figure 1.1, there are two causal processes by which social structure affects action. It has one effect on action by patterning the interests that actors pursue. Interest formation is a distinctly intraactor process that is affected by the actor's position in social structure. One actor's interests are not affected directly by another's interests, even though they are affected by another's resources (there is no u_i in the definition of actor j's utility u_j in Eq. [5.7]). Interest formation is an interactor process according to the traditional concept of social norms, in which members of a clique share similar perceptions of some object as a result of their constant socializing communications with one another. The concept of structural interests proposed here, however, involves a far more symbolic process in which an individual takes on the positions of others as alter-egos. The entire process is conducted internally. That is not to say that communication has no effect on interest formation; rather communication is not necessary to the definition of interest formation given here. In contrast, action is the intersection of the interests of separate actors, each pursuing his or her own interests. Unlike the effect of social structure on interest formation, action is a distinctly interactor phenomenon capturing the differential ability of actors to pursue and realize interests. An actor's behaviors are open to the scrutiny of others, and so his pursuit of interests must take into account the nature of his pattern of relations with others who might oppose his interests. This is the direct effect of social structure on action given in Figure 1.1. Capturing that direct effect is the task I have set for Chapter 7.

6

Conformity and Deviance with Respect to Journal Norms in Elite Sociological Methodology*

The single most controversial implication of the proposed structural interest model is the idea that normative perceptions are determined by the similarity in two actor's relational patterns rather than the strength of their interaction with one another. In order to test the substantive adequacy of the proposed model, I use it in this chapter to describe the interests of elite experts in journals recognized as publishing the most significant work in sociological methodology. The proposed model is not only more adequate than the relational model in sociometry, it reveals systematic errors inherent in that model.

6.1 THE SUBSTANTIVE PROBLEM POSED BY SCIENTIST INTEREST IN JOURNALS

Sociologists of science have repeatedly demonstrated the existence and importance of invisible colleges among scientists active in research and publication (e.g., Price 1963; Price & Beaver 1966; Griffith & Miller 1970; Griffith & Mullins 1972; Crane 1972; Mullins 1973; Gaston 1973; Mulkay, Gilbert, and Woolgar 1975). This social context exists for the individual scientist as a set of colleagues working on similar problems, colleagues with

*Portions of this chapter are drawn from an article reprinted with the permission of *Social Networks* (Burt 1978a) and from a paper I wrote with Patrick Doreian (Burt & Doreian 1980).

whom he or she is in close personal communication through leaders in the college. Whereas the important coordinating function served by leaders within an invisible college has been recognized (e.g., see Mullins 1973 for several examples in sociology and Mulkay 1976 for a more general discussion), the developments in network analysis operationalizing the status/role-set in terms of structural equivalence have given that recognition renewed emphasis in descriptions of invisible colleges as stratified systems in which individual scientists occupy positions in the social structure of the college (Breiger 1976; Mullins *et al.* 1977; Lenoir 1979; Hargens *et al.* 1980, and, of course, the extended description in Chapter 3 of elite sociological methodology). A scientist occupies a prominent position in a college to the extent that he is acknowledged as a source of ideas and advice within the college, which is in turn a function of his publications in reputable journals.[1] This observation corresponds to other lines of research showing that a scientist's publications in reputable journals affect personal income (Tuckman & Leahey 1975), research funding (Liebert 1976), and overall scholarly prominence in a cumulative process over the course of his career (Merton 1968; Cole & Cole 1973:237–247; Allison & Stewart 1974; Reskin 1977; Gaston 1978:Chaps. 7, 8). These results add detail to the widely held view of reputable journals as the fundamental institution in science (e.g., Hagstrom 1965:Chap. 1; Ziman 1968:Chap. 6; Zuckerman & Merton 1971); other institutions with which the scientist is involved (such as funding agencies, universities, or corporate employers more generally) are tolerated as a means necessary to the individual's intellectual pursuits (e.g., Ziman 1968:Chap. 7; Ben-David 1971:Chap. 8). In short, it seems clear that scientists are organized in terms of stratified invisible colleges and that their respective positions in that stratification are strongly determined by their publications in reputable journals.

A journal's reputation, in turn, is determined by the interest in it maintained by a scientific community. A scientist can be expected to be interested in a particular journal as a source of ideas and an outlet for his own work to the extent that he perceives the journal to be publishing more significant work than that published in other journals purporting to publish the same type of work. He will allocate some proportion of his interest in journals to each of the journals publishing within an area, some journals being perceived as publishing the most significant work and others being perceived as comparatively trivial. Commenting on his life as a physicist, John Ziman (1968) refers to this as a "sort of law of specialization":

> There are good journals and bad ones, so that we only keep in touch with those likely to contain good papers by reputable authors. There is a sort of law of specialization that

---

[1] This is not to say that occupying a prominent position cannot have its own effect on successful publication activities subsequent to achieving the position (Hargens, Mullins, and Hecht 1980:65–67). However, available evidence stresses the importance of publications in reputable journals for achieving a prominent position in the first place.

ensures that the number of journals containing significant papers on one particular subject does not increase; one simply narrows one's field of vision to keep the influx constant [p. 119].

The more that scientists within an invisible college are interested in a particular journal, the more "reputable" will it be and the more will publications in it contribute to the prominence of the positions occupied by its contributors within the college.

But significance is a very ambiguous quality to perceive in an argument. There is nothing inherent in a journal's articles that guarantees them significance that will stimulate scientist interest. Significance is judged by individuals in terms of consensual standards. Like most such standards, those defining significance have a taken-for-granted nature. They are known, but difficult to articulate. In discussing the ambiguity of excellence, certainly a component of significance, Merton (1960) notes that "many of us are persuaded that we know what we mean by excellence and would prefer not to be asked to explain [p. 422]." This ambiguity is not confined to the social sciences. Commenting on inference and research, the biologist Peter Medawar (1969) humorously notes the typical scientist's inability to articulate standards by which research is to be conducted:

Ask a scientist what he conceives the scientific method to be, and he will adopt an expression that is at once solemn and shifty-eyed: solemn, because he feels he ought to declare an opinion; shifty-eyed, because he is wondering how to conceal the fact that he has no opinion to declare [p.11].

The empirical ambiguity of significance criteria support the intuitive idea that individual scientists do not judge significance in some manner apart from their colleagues. When evaluating an article, the individual assesses its significance in terms of his colleagues as a reference group. As emphasized in Ziman's (1968) essay; "he does not say, 'Can I believe this?' but rather, 'Would *they* be convinced by this evidence?' Far from being *im*personal he tries to be *omni*personal in his judgement [p.79]." In the process of making such evaluations and being exposed to evaluations made by his colleagues under similarly ambiguous conditions, the scientist comes to be interested in specific journals as the most probable outlets for significant work on a given subject.

Knowledge of the social mechanism by which this interest is created and maintained within an invisible college is crucial to an understanding of stratification in science. It is crucial because journal reputation is not an exogenous variable in the stratification process. We know that scientists active in research and publication are organized in terms of stratified invisible colleges. We know that the positions they occupy within those invisible colleges are determined in large part by their publications in reputable journals. However, journal reputations are consensual standards maintained through some social mechanism by the very people they help stratify. What we do not know is how positions in invisible colleges pattern scientist interest in journals so as to make some journals more reputable than others. What is yet to be systematically researched, in short, is one side of the reciprocally causal connection between the stratification of scientists and the stratification of journals.

The proposed model of structural interests provides one social mechanism by which scientist interest in a journal could be maintained as a journal norm—a level of interest to be expected of a scientist because of his network position in the social structure of an invisible college. Assessing its plausibility as such a mechanism is my purpose in this chapter. Note that as a level of interest expected of network position occupants, a journal norm can vary across positions within an invisible college in the sense that different scientists in the college can adhere to different norms. Further, this idea of a journal norm does not require a description of the actual significance criteria used to justify a norm. In contrast to discussions building on Merton's (1942) description of universalism, communism, disinterestedness, and organized skepticism as evaluative norms in science generally, I am concerned here with the social psychological problem of how any norm might be maintained within a scientific community.

6.2 JOURNAL NORMS IN AN INVISIBLE COLLEGE

The level of interest a particular scientist expresses in a particular journal is to be accounted for as a social norm. More specifically, following Ziman's metaphorical law of specialization, I wish to account for the extent to which a particular scientist is only interested in a particular journal. Let x_{jk} be a proportion expressing the extent to which scientist j is only interested in journal k as an outlet for work on some subject. In keeping with the idea of structural interest in Eq. (5.8), this proportion will be greater than 0, close to 1, to the extent that scientist j has evaluated the significance of work appearing in all journals publishing work on the subject and has concluded that the only significant work appears in journal k. She reaches this evaluation through some omnipersonal social process in which her colleagues are combined to define a generalized other in her own perception of significance, thereby ensuring her conformity to consensual standards of significance. The evaluation she could expect from her colleagues as a generalized other, a collegial alter to her ego, then constitutes a journal norm. A model of the social mechanism she uses to construct such an alter defines the journal norm as x_{jk}^{*}: the level of interest in journal k to be expected from scientist j as a reflection of the alter she should have constructed from her colleagues as a reference group. To the extent that scientist interest in journals is a result of the modeled social mechanism, expressed interest in a journal (x_{jk}) should be very similar to normative interest in the journal (x_{jk}^{*}).

Traditional sociometry suggests a relational model of the social mechanism responsible for an individual's selecting particular others as alters. By communicating their uncertainties to one another regarding some empirically ambiguous object, people socialize one another so as to arrive at a consensual evaluation of the object. The study of student attitudes as consensual group standards by Festinger *et al.* (1950) is a classic analysis, which sets the tone for subsequent research within this perspective. As I discussed in Section 5.3, they show that those sets of student dwellings grouped together in a court so as to face one another and occupied by students who tended to chose one another as friends tended to have fewer individuals expressing attitudes deviant from the typical court attitude than did courts occupied by individuals with low levels of in-court friendship citations. In short, they find a negative correlation between the density of in-court sociometric friendship citations and the frequency of deviance from court norms. This finding is consistent with their discussion of attitudes as consensual answers to questions about empirically ambiguous objects (Festinger *et al.* 1950):

> The 'reality' which settles the question in the case of social attitudes and opinions is the degree to which others with whom one is in communication are believed to share these same attitudes and opinions [p.169].

This emphasis on dyadic communication as the basis for homophily is repeated in two subsequent studies which have become widely cited. I have already discussed the diffusion classic, *Medical Innovation*, in Section 5.5. Among other results, Coleman *et al.* (1966) use an "index of simultaneity" to show that doctors begin prescribing a new antibiotic at about the same time as those doctors they cite as sources of medical advice. This index is much higher than would be expected by chance (showing high simultaneity of adoption) in the first months of the drug's diffusion. Building quite explicitly on the Festinger *et al.* study, Coleman and his colleagues (1966) reason that

> when a new drug appears, doctors who are in close interaction with their colleagues will similarly interpret for one another the new stimulus that has presented itself, and will arrive at some shared way of looking at it [p. 119].

This is precisely the reasoning behind Blau's (1974) use of Coleman's index in her study of communication patterns among theoretical high energy physicists (THEPs). Given a sociometric citation from one THEP to another as someone with whom he often exchanges research information, Blau (1974:396, 402) finds that the two THEPs tend to share the same country of employment, country of citizenship, research area speciality, professional age, and status as a research leader. A very different method of researching this idea of pair homophily has been used in the study of occupational and educational aspirations. Haller & Butterworth (1960) argued that the social context in which such aspirations were made affected them so that aspirations expressed by a student's peers were likely to be reflected in his own aspirations. Pursuing this idea, Duncan, Haller, and Portes (1968) compare a high school student's aspirations to those expressed by the student he cites as his best friend. They use a simultaneous equation model to hold constant socioeconomic background differences in students while estimating the magnitude of the association between a high school student's aspirations and those expressed by his avowed best friend. They find significant, positive effects: students with high occupational and education aspirations have best friends who express high aspirations.

In short, a relational model of the social mechanism responsible for journal norms would construct a scientist's collegial alter from those of his colleagues within an invisible college who are likely to personally communicate comments to him, comments which influence his work within the college. It is relational in the sense that all one needs in order to predict homophily between two scientists is a knowledge of their relations with one another. Their overall patterns of relations with other colleagues in the invisible college are not necessary to the prediction. Let z_{ji} be scientist j's tendency to have his work within an invisible college be influenced by personally communicated comments from scientist i, also a member of the college. Under a relational model, j would be expected to construct an alter from those of his colleagues i for whom z_{ji} is strong. More specifically following the models utilized by Coleman, Duncan, and their colleagues, the interest one scientist expresses in a journal should be very similar to someone else's interest in the journal to the extent that that someone else is a source of influential comments on the scientist's work (i.e., $\mathbf{x}_{jk}$ should equal $\mathbf{x}_{ik}$ to the extent that z_{ji} is strong). The interest to be expected of scientist j in regard to journal k based on his relations to these alters ($\mathbf{x}_{jkr}^{*}$) therefore can be expressed as the sum of interest in the journal expressed by each of his colleagues i ($\mathbf{x}_{ik}$) weighted by the extent to which each of them is j's only source of influential comments:

$$\mathbf{x}_{jkr}^{*} = \sum_{i}^{N} \mathbf{x}_{ik}(z_{ji}/(\sum_{i}^{N} z_{ji})), \qquad (6.1)$$

where N is the number of scientists within the invisible college being considered and scientist j himself is excluded from his collegial alter (i.e., $j \neq i$). As a journal norm, $\mathbf{x}_{jkr}^{*}$ is the interest to be expected of scientist j in journal k as a result of his relations to sources of comments influencing his work within the invisible college. The "r" subscript indicates that this is a relational model of a journal norm.[2]

---

[2]The weighted linear composite of colleagues as a generalized collegial alter in Eq. (6.1) is repeated for the proposed model of structural interests in Eq. (6.4) and has been discussed in the statistics literature in terms of spatial effects models (e.g., see Doreian 1980, 1981). There are other methods for constructing an alter for ego—the selection of specific persons as the most likely actors to be an alter for ego (e.g., the dyadic analyses of Coleman, Duncan, and their colleagues) as well as the assignment of egos to network subgroups group alters (e.g., the contextual effects models often

A relational model provides a useful benchmark against which alternative network models can be compared. There are several reasons for this. Relational models have been fruitful in past substantive research; people who communicate with one another do often share the same attitudes toward empirically ambiguous objects as the previously cited studies, among others, demonstrate. Relational models have a high face validity stemming from their consistency with classic concepts of communication in face-to-face primary groups as the socializing unit in society. Such primary groups, lastly, have been captured in a proliferation of network models of cliques as a set of actors connected by strong relations, the justification for these models being that members of a clique socialize one another by means of these strong relations so that members of the same clique can be expected to have similar attitudes and beliefs as evaluations of empirically ambiguous objects (see Section 2.5 for review of network clique models). Having made inroads into the substantive research, theory, and methodology of an era, relational models are a force to be reckoned with. Ideally, an alternative model should not only offer adequate description of empirical data, it should be more accurate than a relational model, the benchmark level of adequacy. Moreover, the alternative should clarify systematic errors made by a relational model. Such an alternative exists in the proposed model of structural interests.

The model of structural interests in Chapter 5 defines a positional, as opposed to relational, social mechanism responsible for individual scientists' selecting particular colleagues to form an alter underlying journal norms. The model takes networks of relations among all actors in a system as input and predicts the extent to which each pair of actors should have similar attitudes. That is, two scientists should have similar interest in a journal to the extent that they perceive one another as occupying the same position within an invisible college producing work for the journal. The homogeneity arises because each of the two persons puts himself in the position of the other and symbolically evaluates the journal as if he were the other. Communication between the two may or may not be a part of the process. Interest in a journal is a special case of the model; the model is stated for the general process of an individual evaluating the utility to him of control over a resource. However, a modicum of algebra and the temporary assumption that journal significance can be measured in terms of empirical criteria can clarify the social mechanism by which journal norms are maintained as a structural interest under the model.

For a moment, imagine that a scientist evaluates journal significance impersonally in some asocial process independent of his colleagues and that signifi-

---

used in sociology). The decision to use one of these alter models is a methodological decision discussed in some detail elsewhere (Burt & Minor 1982:Chap. 17). When available data and computer algorithms make it possible to use the generalized alter model in Eqs. (6.1) and (6.4), as is the case in this analysis of journal norms in elite sociological methodology, the model's generality over actor alter or subgroup alter models makes it the most satisfactory method to use in constructing an alter for each respondent as an ego.

cance can be measured empirically. Let τ_{jk}^* be the significance of work in journal k to which scientist j is actually exposed. Of course, τ_{jk}^* could not actually be measured as such an intensity variable since it is empirically ambiguous. But it is convenient to assume, for the moment, that it could be so measured. Assuming that he reads journals in order to obtain significant knowledge and publishes in them in order to disseminate significant work, the scientist should derive high utility from a journal to the extent that he perceives it to be publishing significant work. Let u_{jk} be the utility, scientist j's perception of the utility to him of journal k as an outlet for significant work. In other words, u_{jk} is his subjective perception of the hypothetical concrete stimulus τ_{jk}^*. This suggests that Stevens's law of perception in Eq. (5.1) offers an empirical generalization stating u_{jk} as a power function of τ_{jk}^*, namely,

$$u_{jk} = \mu(\tau_{jk}^* - \tau_0^*)^\nu = \mu(\tau_{jk})^\nu,$$

where τ_0^* is a threshold level of significance below which significance cannot be perceived so that τ_{jk} is the extent to which the actual level of stimulus exceeds the threshold.

The increase in utility that scientist j would perceive in journal k as a result of a small increase in the concrete significance of the journal to which he is being exposed is given by the partial derivative of the above equation with respect to τ_{jk}—assuming that he makes this evaluation independent of colleagues (cf. Eq. [5.2]):

$$\partial u_{jk}/\partial \tau_{jk} = \nu u_{jk}/\tau_{jk}.$$

It is the evaluative process implied by this equation that I wish to emphasize here. For all values of the exponent ν, the criterion against which increased exposure to significant work is evaluated is his own current level of exposure, the denominator in the equation. Colleagues do not appear in this equation.

Given the importance of evaluations of journal significance and their ambiguity, however, it seems eminently reasonable for a scientist to ask those of his colleagues who influence his work within an invisible college for their opinions regarding the significance of a journal or specific article in it. This would lead to a relational model of scientist interest in a journal. His communication with some colleague i would have the result that j's evaluation of journal k is based on the significant work to which he has been exposed (τ_{jk}) as well as that to which his colleague i has been exposed (τ_{ik}) to the extent that z_{ji} is strong. It seems likely that such a process would occur from time to time within an invisible college.

Such a process could not be responsible for evaluations of journal significance generally, however, because of limitations on legitimate opportunities for communicating evaluations. For one thing, there is a limited amount of time for communication. Time is a precious commodity among active scientists, and there is little of it in their schedule for negotiating consensual standards of excellence with colleagues. Therefore, members of an invisible college can be expected to refrain from badgering one another with questions regarding an idea's significance every time such a question arises. Each member is aware of the limited number of such questions he can legitimately ask a colleague to respond to, not to mention the limited number his colleague will tolerate. In addition to limited opportunities, there are often prohibitions against communicating significance evaluations until they are complete. The idealized referee process contains one or more reviewers within an invisible college who render an impersonal evaluation of the significance of a paper being considered for research funding or publication. In making this evaluation, the reviewer is explicitly prohibited from discussing the evaluation with colleagues either because they are closely associated with the paper's author or they too are being asked to provide an impartial evaluation of its significance.

In the face of constraints on actual communication during a scientist's evaluation of significance, the ambiguity of significance itself calls for some form of symbolic communication between the scientist and his colleagues. He can put himself in the position of a colleague and ask how he would evaluate an object's significance if he were his colleague. Without physically communicating with his colleagues he can make an evaluation as if he were communicating with them, the entire conversation occurring symbolically within him. To repeat Ziman's (1968) remark on scientific evaluation, "he does not say, 'Can I believe this?' but rather, 'Would they be convinced by this evidence [p. 79]?'" Questions and answers here flow between the scientist and himself. This symbolic role-taking between members of an invisible college allows a scientist to take the position of any other member as an alter in terms of whom he might evaluate significance by pretending that he was the person for a moment during the evaluation. Once the scientist is free from physically communicating with his alters, he is free to treat anyone as an alter. But this role-taking occurs in the context of a stratified invisible college. Members of the college are not equal; some are more prominent as college leaders than are others; some are key bridges between factions within the college whereas others are faction members. When scientist j evaluates the significance of a piece of work, whose positions will he symbolically adopt during the evaluation? Under the model of structural interests in Chapter 5, he will adopt the positions of scientists socially similar to him within the college. Specifically, he will make a significance evaluation as an occupant of his position in the network of influence relations among members of the invisible college. He will construct or will have constructed an image of the flow of interpersonal influence within the college and will locate himself within it. When evaluating significance, he will select some other member as an alter to the extent that he perceives that member to be equivalent to himself within the college. To paraphrase Ziman's remark, he would not ask himself if any member of the college would be convinced by the evidence under evaluation, he would ask if a person of his standing within the college ought to be convinced by the evidence. As a person occupying my position in the college, how significant is this idea, this analysis, this journal?

The actual extent to which two scientists within an invisible college are involved in different patterns of influence relations within the college is given by the distance between them in the overall network within the college. Given influence relations as the z_{ji}, the distance between two scientists j and i in terms of differences in their influence relations with all N scientists in an invisible college is given by Eq. (2.14) as

$$d_{ij} = \left(\sum_q^N (z_{jq} - z_{iq})^2 + \sum_q^N (z_{qj} - z_{qi})^2 \right)^{1/2},$$

and the extent to which scientist j perceives scientist i as the only person structurally equivalent to himself within the college is given by Eq. (5.5) as the structural proximity coefficient l_{ij} ranging from 0 to 1 and summing across all persons i to equal 1:

$$l_{ij} = (\mathrm{dmax}_j - d_{ij})^v / \left(\sum_q^N (\mathrm{dmax}_j - d_{qj})^v \right) . \qquad (6.2)$$

The extent to which scientist i is perceived by j as similarly involved in influence relations within the college is given by the extent to which the proximity coefficient l_{ij} is greater than 0. The exponent v allows perceived similarity to vary for different kinds of evaluations, as described in Section 4.1. Under a threat from outside the invisible college, for example, minor differences in the relations involving i and j might dissolve as negligible so that a low value of v would be appropriate in perceiving social similarity. If the two scientists were competing for the same university chair, on the other hand, minor differences in their relational patterns might be exaggerated in order to emphasize their respectively unique positions in the college, whereupon a high value of v would be appropriate.

The proposed model of structural interests brings these ideas together. The partial derivative $\partial u_{jk}/\partial \tau_{jk}$ states that scientist j perceives increased utility in journal k with increased exposure to significant work in the journal as a function of his existing exposure to significant work in the journal (τ_{jk}, the denominator in the derivative vu_{jk}/τ_{jk}). In the social context of a stratified invisible college, this evaluation is affected by those of his colleagues whom he perceives to be structurally equivalent to himself in the sense that they are similarly involved in the flow of interpersonal influence within the college. This perception is given by the proximity coefficients l_{ij}. As an extension of the impersonal evaluation implied by the partial derivative $\partial u_{jk}/\partial \tau_{jk}$, the following linear composite states that scientist j will evaluate significance as if he were each other member i in an invisible college to the extent that he perceives himself to be structurally equivalent to i in terms of influence relations within the college:

$$\partial u_{jk}/\partial \tau_{jk} = l_{1j} vu_{jk}/\tau_{1k} + \cdots + l_{jj} vu_{jk}/\tau_{jk} + \cdots + l_{Nj} vu_{jk}/\tau_{Nk}.$$

This linear composite corresponds to Eq. (5.6) and has scientist j take each member i of an invisible college as an alter in terms of whom he might evaluate significance. In place of the one denominator in the impersonal evaluation implied by $\partial u_{jk}/\partial \tau_{jk}$, this equation has him consider the exposure each other member of the college is experiencing, τ_{ik}. The relative importance of scientist i's exposure to j's final evaluation is given by l_{ij}, the extent to which j perceives i to be his structural peer within the college. If scientist j is structurally unique (e.g., alone), then l_{jj} equals 1.0 so that the only term remaining in the above equation is the impersonal evaluation, vu_{jk}/τ_{jk}. The network model of perception from which the above equation would have been derived is given by integration to yield the following version of Eq. (5.7):

$$\mathbf{u}_{jk} = \left(l_{jj} + \sum_q^N v l_{qj} \tau_{jk}/\tau_{qk}(v+1) \right) \mu \tau_{jk}^v, \qquad q \neq j. \qquad (6.3)$$

When scientist j occupies a position in a stratified invisible college, his evaluations are interdependent with those of the other members he perceives to be structurally equivalent to him in terms of interpersonal influence within the college. More specifically, scientists i and j will have identical evaluations of a journal's utility to them as an outlet for significant work under whatever conditions result in $\mathbf{u}_{jk}$ being equal to $\mathbf{u}_{ik}$.

Section 5.3 demonstrates that this equality only occurs if the two scientists are structurally equivalent and currently experiencing identical levels of exposure to significant work in the journal (Eqs. [5.12, 5.13, 5.14]). But exposure to significant work in a journal is a hypothetical measure introduced in order to highlight the role-taking behavior implied by the model. In the case of a stimulus which has no clear empirical reality in terms of which it can be measured, all persons have equal exposure to the ambiguous stimulus.[3] In this case, also as described in Section 5.3 under empirically ambiguous stimuli, the critical condition for scientists i and j to perceive equal utility in a journal is the extent to which they perceive one another as structurally equivalent. When i and j are

---

[3]It is interesting, however, to consider the implications of concrete significance criteria. For example, a prima donna model of scientist interest in a journal could have τ_{jk} equal the personal involvement of scientist j in journal k, personal involvement consisting of the extent to which he edits the journal and/or publishes his work there. According to the impersonal evaluation process implied by the model $u_{jk} = \mu \tau_{jk}^v$, a journal would have utility to a scientist to the extent that he was responsible for its content, utility being the perception of significant work in the journal. According to Eq. (6.3), the journal would have utility to him to the extent that he is more responsible for its content than are scientists with whom he is structurally equivalent in the intracollege flow of interpersonal influence. Under such a model, a scientist could be expected to experience relative deprivation as a decrease in the utility a journal offers him whenever one of his structural peers publishes a paper in the journal. The exact function form for such feelings of relative deprivation is given by the partial derivative of $\mathbf{u}_{jk}$ with respect to τ_{ik}, the extent to which some other scientist i is personally responsible for the content of journal k. Section 5.4 provides a detailed discussion of such effects (the partial derivative itself is given in Eq. [5.15]). Whereas such a prima donna model would not apply to scientists generally, it would be interesting to assess its ability to account for the occasional rivalries that do occur between individuals and their attendant faithful.

structurally equivalent, $\mathbf{u}_{jk}$ will equal $\mathbf{u}_{ik}$ for all journals k publishing work pertinent to their invisible college. Accordingly, they should be similarly interested in any one journal k as the journal publishing the most significant work in the college. In other words, $\mathbf{x}_{jk}$ will equal $\mathbf{x}_{ik}$ as a function of $\mathbf{u}_{jk}$'s being equal to $\mathbf{u}_{ik}$, which is in turn determined by scientists i and j's perceiving one another as structurally equivalent within their invisible college (i.e., $l = l_{ij} = l_{ji} = l_{ii} = l_{jj}$).

As a social mechanism responsible for journal norms, the proposed model states that a scientist constructs a collegial alter from those of his colleagues within an invisible college whom he perceives to be his structural peers in the flow of interpersonal influence within the college. In contrast to a relational model which would expect j to construct an alter from those of his colleagues i for whom z_{ji} is high because i communicates influential comments to j, the proposed model expects him to construct an alter from those of his colleagues i for whom l_{ij} is high because j symbolically takes the position of his structural peers within the college during his own evaluations of significance. The interest to be expected of scientist j in regard to journal k based on his structural peers ($\mathbf{x}^*_{jkp}$), therefore, can be expressed as the sum of interest in the journal expressed by each of his colleagues i ($\mathbf{x}_{ik}$) weighted by the extent to which each of them is the only person j perceives as structurally equivalent to him within the flow of intracollege interpersonal influence:

$$\mathbf{x}^*_{jkp} = \sum_{i}^{N} \mathbf{x}_{ik}(l_{ij}/(1-l_{jj})), \qquad (6.4)$$

where N is the number of scientists in the invisible college and scientist j himself is excluded from his collegial alter (i.e., $j \neq i$). Since j's own expressed interests are not used to generate his expected interests, the l_{ij} in Eq. (6.4) sum across the other N-1 scientists to $(1-l_{jj})$ rather than 1 so that the denominator in the parenthetical term is required.[4] As a journal norm, $\mathbf{x}^*_{jkp}$ is the interest to be expected of scientist j in journal k as a result of his position in the network of influence relations within an invisible college. The "p" subscript indicates that this is a positional model of a journal norm. The model is positional in the sense that in order to predict homophily between two scientists, one needs to know the entire pattern of influential communication relations connecting them with each member of an invisible college. Predictions cannot be made if one only knows the relations between the two scientists.

These positional and relational models are at once related but distinct, as I

---

[4]This assumes that no scientist is structurally unique within the college since $1 - l_{jj}$ would then equal 0 and $\mathbf{x}^*_{jkp}$ would be undefined (e.g., person one in systems A and C of Table 5.2). None of the elite experts in sociological methodology was structurally unique to this extreme as of 1975. As can be seen in Figure 3.3, the structure of methodology relations in the college was quite complex. In the context of this complexity, no expert was involved in a relational pattern completely dissimilar to all others. The maximum l_{jj} is .363, and its mean value across all 52 respondents is .169.

have discussed in Section 5.3 with regard to social norms. Their different empirical predictions can be illustrated by a simple example.

Consider an invisible college composed of six key members and a variety of other persons randomly attached to these six. Two of the six are intellectual prima donnas responsible for initial advances in the subject addressed in the invisible college. These two scientists hold positions in the same university department. They trained the remaining four key members who have since taken key positions at separate universities. In response to a sociometric question asking each key member to name those persons with whom he has personal communication whose comments have the highest influence on his work in the college, the two senior figures each say that no such person exists, and each of the four other members claims such a relation to the two senior figures. The resulting sociogram of the college appears in Figure 6.1. If relations are treated as binary, the z_{ji} are given in the adjacency matrix presented in the figure. Distances between members and structural proximity coefficients can then be computed from these relations. The d_{ij} and l_{ij} are also presented in Figure 6.1 where ν, for the purpose of this illustration, has been set equal to 1. How would interest in a journal be distributed in such an invisible college?

Under the relational model, $\mathbf{x}_{jk}$ would equal $\mathbf{x}_{ik}$ to the extent that z_{ji} is strong. In other words, the four erstwhile students would be expected to be influenced by their communication with the two senior figures and so reflect similar interest in a journal as an outlet for significant work in the college. This is a center-periphery model of journal norms in the sense that significance evaluations by the two leading figures at the structural center of the college determine interest in journals as journal norms for the whole college. If this model is an accurate representation of the social mechanism maintaining journal norms in an invisible college, then the people responsible for the stratification of journals (some journals being the object of extensive interest while others languish) are the people who have succeeded in reaching the most prominent positions in a stratified invisible college.

Under the positional model, $\mathbf{x}_{jk}$ would equal $\mathbf{x}_{ik}$ to the extent that l_{ij} is greater than 0. The results in Figure 6.1 show that the two leading figures are structurally equivalent to one another ($d_{12} = 0$; $l_{11} = l_{22} = l_{12} = l_{21} = .5$), and the four erstwhile students are structurally equivalent to one another (again, they are separated by zero distance and have equal proximity coefficients among themselves). In other words, the two leaders would be expected to use one another as an alter in making significance evaluations. Even though their rival leadership prevents them from communicating with one another, they constitute a reference group for one another as leading figures in the invisible college. Similarly, the four second-generation members would be expected to use one another as alters since they too occupy the same position within the college. Each would not be expected to ask himself, How would this evidence appear to the two leading figures in the college? but rather, How should this evidence appear to a second-generation member of the college such as myself?

In short, the positional model predicts that the two leaders will adhere to one set of journal norms, and their four erstwhile students will adhere to their own set of journal norms. This may or may not be the same set of norms. Similarity in the interests of the leaders and the remaining four members is merely an empirical question under the positional model. In contrast to the relational model, the positional model does not imply a center-periphery model of journal norms for this hypothetical college. It is quite possible for each jointly occupied position in the social structure of the college to maintain its own stratification of journals, some journals being more reputable in the eyes of one position's occupants than they are in the eyes of scientists occupying a different position in the same college.

This focuses attention on the problem of obtaining evidence on the comparative adequacy of the two models. If all six scientists in Figure 6.1 expressed identical interest in a journal, then both the relational and positional models would be adequate. However, if the leaders expressed widely different interests, and/or the four second-generation members expressed grossly divergent interests, then the positional model would be wrong. If the leaders expressed similar interests and those interests were very different from the interests shared by the second-generation members, on the other hand, then the relational model would be wrong.

6.3 EXPERT INTEREST IN CORE SOCIOLOGICAL METHODOLOGY JOURNALS

The social structure of elite sociological methodology has been described in Chapter 3 as an invisible college. Data were obtained from the 52 respondents within the college regarding their interests in specific journals that they perceived to be publishing the most significant work in sociological methodology.

Measuring Expert Interest

A three-step process has been used to measure an expert's interest in a journal as an outlet for significant work in sociological methodology. In keeping with Eq. (5.8) and the preceding discussion, expert j's interest in journal k, x_{jk}, is a proportion greater than 0 to the extent that he only perceived utility in having his work appear in journal k as an outlet for significant work in sociological methodology.

First, respondents were asked to name those journals "which you believe publish the articles having the most significance for sociologists working in the area of _____." The blank was filled in by methods and statistics or mathematical sociology or both depending on the respondent's special areas of

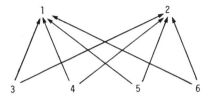

$$
\begin{array}{cccccc}
0 & 0 & 0 & 0 & 0 & 0 \\
0 & 0 & 0 & 0 & 0 & 0 \\
1 & 1 & 0 & 0 & 0 & 0 \\
1 & 1 & 0 & 0 & 0 & 0 \\
1 & 1 & 0 & 0 & 0 & 0 \\
1 & 1 & 0 & 0 & 0 & 0
\end{array} = \{z_{ji}\}
$$

$$
\begin{array}{cccccc}
0.0 & 0.0 & 2.4 & 2.4 & 2.4 & 2.4 \\
0.0 & 0.0 & 2.4 & 2.4 & 2.4 & 2.4 \\
2.4 & 2.4 & 0.0 & 0.0 & 0.0 & 0.0 \\
2.4 & 2.4 & 0.0 & 0.0 & 0.0 & 0.0 \\
2.4 & 2.4 & 0.0 & 0.0 & 0.0 & 0.0 \\
2.4 & 2.4 & 0.0 & 0.0 & 0.0 & 0.0
\end{array} = \{d_{ij}\}
$$

$$
\begin{array}{cccccc}
.50 & .50 & .00 & .00 & .00 & .00 \\
.50 & .50 & .00 & .00 & .00 & .00 \\
.00 & .00 & .25 & .25 & .25 & .25 \\
.00 & .00 & .25 & .25 & .25 & .25 \\
.00 & .00 & .25 & .25 & .25 & .25 \\
.00 & .00 & .25 & .25 & .25 & .25
\end{array} = \{\ell_{ij}\}
$$

Figure 6.1. Stratification among the six key members of a hypothetical invisible college.

competence listed in the 1973 American Sociological Association's *Directory of Members*. If he or she claimed expertise in both, then journals publishing in both areas were elicited. This established the domain of journals the respondent perceived to be publishing significant work in sociological methodology.

Second, respondents were asked to indicate, for each of the journals he or she named as publishing significant work, "the level of your interest in publishing articles concerning the area in each journal." Level was evaluated in reference to one journal as a numeraire following the procedure outlined by Glenn (1971). The instructions read as follows:

Use articles in the *American Sociological Review* as a reference point. Let your interest in publishing an article in ASR equal 10. A level of interest of 5 for a journal below indicates that you are half as interested in publishing in that journal as you are in ASR concerning the subject matter. A level of 20 for a journal indicates that you are twice as interested in publishing in that journal as you are in ASR concerning the subject matter.[5]

These raw ratings indicated the relative extent to which a respondent was interested in the journals he named as publishing significant work in sociological methodology.

Third, each respondent's raw ratings were normalized by the range of his or her perceived domain of significant journals. Not only were separate journals of differential interest relative to ASR, experts differed in the number of journals they perceived to be publishing significant work. Consider the expert j who named ASR and the *American Journal of Sociology* as the only significant outlets for his work versus expert i who named many journals in addition to these two. Even if the two experts gave equal ratings to the two journals, they did not have equal interest in them as outlets for significant work. Expert j allocated a higher proportion of his total interest to the *American Journal of Sociology* than did expert i owing to the larger domain of of journals that expert i perceived to be publishing significant work. To borrow Ziman's pithy phrase, j would have been operating under a more restrictive "law of specialization" than expert i. In order to hold these interexpert differences constant, I have measured interest x_{jk} as the proportion of expert j's total interest in journals publishing significant sociological methodology that he allocated to journal k in particular:

$$\mathbf{x}_{jk} = x_{jk}/(x_{j1} + x_{j2} + \cdots x_{jk*}), \qquad (6.5)$$

where x_{jk} is expert j's raw rating of his interest in journal k relative to ASR and $k*$ is the number of journals he named as publishing significant work in sociological methodology.

Core Journals in Sociological Methodology

Across the 52 respondents, 31 journals were named as publishing significant work in sociological methodology of which 23 were named by two or more experts. Table 6.1 presents three statistics on each of these 23 journals: (*a*) the percentage of the respondents naming it as a forum for significant methodological work (nonzero x_{jk} in Eq. [6.5]). (*b*) the mean interest in it expressed by all respondents (the average x_{jk} across all respondents j); (*c*) a *t*-test for the hypothesis that the respondents as a whole had no interest in it (the average x_{jk} is 0). The journals are listed in Table 6.1 by the extent to which this null hypothesis of no interest can be rejected, the hypothesis being most easily rejected for the *American Sociological Review* (*t*-test of 10.3) and least rejected for *Multivariate Behavioral Research* (*t*-test of 1.3).

---

[5]Three statisticians in the sample had no interest in ASR and complained that it was therefore a meaningless reference point. They were sent a second questionnaire using the *Journal of the American Statistical Association* as a reference point. Most respondents who had low interest in ASR, however, indicated their perceptions by giving three-digit ratings to other journals.

TABLE 6.1
Expert Interest in Sociological Methodology Journals[a]

Journals	$\%x_{jk} > 0$	$100\bar{x}_k$	t-test
Core Journals			
American Sociological Review	90.4	21.6	10.3
American Journal of Sociology	71.2	14.2	8.9
Sociological Methodology	55.8	11.8	7.1
Journal of the American Statistical Association	59.6	15.9	6.1
Sociological Methods & Research	40.4	4.7	5.0
Journal of Mathematical Sociology	32.7	4.9	4.6
Social Science Research	25.0	3.4	3.8
Social Forces	23.1	3.7	3.7
Noncore Journals			
Psychometrika	13.5	2.2	2.5
Journal of the Royal Statistical Society (both series)	9.6	2.0	2.3
Demography	7.7	1.6	2.2
Quality and Quantity	5.8	1.2	2.0
Psychological Bulletin	9.6	2.2	2.0
Public Opinion Quarterly	7.7	1.3	1.9
Econometrica	7.7	1.3	1.9
Annals of Mathematical Statistics	7.7	1.2	1.8
Biometrika	5.8	1.6	1.8
American Statistician	5.8	.4	1.8
Biometrics	5.8	1.1	1.7
Social Psychology Quarterly (Sociometry)	5.8	.7	1.5
Technometrics	3.8	.4	1.4
Journal of Econometrics	3.8	.8	1.4
Multivariate Behavioral Research	3.8	.5	1.3

[a] Expressed interests are measured as given by Eq. (6.5). The first column is the proportion of the 52 respondents giving a journal some interest. The next column is the mean interest all respondents gave the journal multiplied by 100. The last column is the t-test for the hypothesis that the mean interest is zero. Distributed with 51 degrees of freedom, the hypothesis is rejected with a value of 3.5 at beyond the .001 level of confidence.

There are no journals in which every expert was interested; however, all three statistics in Table 6.1 show that there was a clear concentration of expert interest in 8 "core" journals: the official journal of the American Sociological Association—the *American Sociological Review* (ASR), the *American Journal of Sociology* (AJS), the annual methodology volume sponsored by the American Sociological Association—*Sociological Methodology* (SM), the *Journal of the American Statistical Association* (JASA), *Sociological Methods & Research (SMR), the Journal of Mathematical Sociology* (JMS), *Social Science Research* (SSR), and *Social Forces* (SF). All three statistics show a clear break in Table 6.1 between these 8 core journals and the remaining 15 noncore journals . More experts tended to be interested in these journals. An average of 50% of the respondents expressed some interest in each core journal whereas an average of only 7% expressed an interest in each noncore journal.

The lowest mean interest in any core journal $\bar{x}$ is .037 for *Social Forces*) is one and a half times the highest mean interest in any noncore journal ($\bar{x}$ is .022 for *Psychometrika*) and three times the mean interest the listed noncore journals ($\bar{x}$ is .012). Finally the hypothesis of no college interest in a journal can only be rejected beyond the .001 level of confidence (*t*-test > 3.5) for the 8 core journals.

These core journals reflect the typical interests of elite experts in sociological methodology as of 1975. With the exception of the three general sociology journals—ASR, AJS, and SF—the eight core journals tended to publish technical articles not easily accessible to the typical sociologist. Moreover, many of the articles appearing in the three general journals from elite experts were too technical for this typical sociologist to assimilate. The prominence of the official journal of the American Statistical Association, JASA, among these core journals in sociological methodology attests to the prominence of statistical issues in the college at the time.

As would be expected from available research, an expert's prominence was closely tied to his publications in these core journals. Based on the description of stratification in elite sociological methodology (Chapter 3) and the idea of measuring an actor's prestige in terms of his distance from a prestigious status (Eq. [2.21]), an expert occupied a prestigious position in sociological methodology as of 1975 to the extent that he had low distance from the status jointly occupied by the social statistics elite (S_3 in Figure 3.5, for example). Expert *j*'s prestige has been computed from Eq. (2.21) as negative one times the average of his distances to Mr. Hauser and Mr. Goodman as indicator actors for status S_3 (the distribution of scores is given in Figure 4 of Burt [1978a]). In order to measure the relative extent to which each expert had published in each core journal as of 1975, the number of manuscripts he had authored or coauthored since the beginning of the rapid rise of the invisible college around 1969 up through the middle of 1976 (so as to include manuscripts in press in the middle of 1975) was obtained by coding past issues of the eight core journals.[6] This coding provided eight publishing scores for each expert as the number of articles he had published in a core journal between the beginning of 1969 and the middle of 1975. Table 6.2 demonstrates the positive association between an expert's prominence in elite sociological methodology and his publications in the core journals. Publications in the core journals are positively correlated with an expert's prestige and the logarithm of the number of citations his work received from other elite experts in 1975 according to the *Social Science Citation Index*. Interexpert differences in prestige are most closely associated with differences in the number of articles each had published in the *American Journal of*

---

[6]Book reviews were ignored since they are not usually refereed and since some of the journals do not publish book reviews. Articles have been coded in all issues of the ASR from February 1969 to June 1976, the AJS from January 1969 to May 1976, SM from 1969 to 1976, the JASA from March 1969 to June 1976, SMR from August 1972 to May 1976, the JMS from 1971 to 1974 (the 1974 issues appearing in 1976), SSR from April 1972 to March 1976, and SF from March 1969 to June 1976.

TABLE 6.2
Expert Prominence and Publications in Core Journals

Core Journals	Correlations		Betas	t-tests
	Prestige	Log expert citations		
American Sociological Review	.43	.26	.02	0.1
American Journal of Sociology	.61	.38	.39	3.0
Sociological Methodology	.24	.24	.10	0.9
Journal of the American Statistical Association	.44	.32	.43	3.9
Sociological Methods & Research	.21	.13	.12	1.0
Journal of Mathematical Sociology	.36	.35	.08	0.7
Social Science Research	.43	.59	.31	2.7
Social Forces	.01	.03	.10	1.0

[a] As explained in the text, publications have been coded from 1969 to 1976; prestige refers to an expert's prominence in the invisible college of elite experts; citations refer to the citations his work received in 1975 from other elite experts; and the regression betas have been obtained by regressing an expert's prestige over his publications in the eight core journals. The squared multiple correlation for this prediction is .641, and standardized betas are presented here (the metric coefficients are given in Burt 1978a:137).

Sociology, the *Journal of the American Statistical Association*, and *Social Science Research*, publications in these journals having a significant, positive association with prestige in the regression results given in Table 6.2 (the journals having respective t-tests of 3.0, 3.9, and 2.7). Taken together, publications in the eight core journals can predict 64% of the variance in expert prestige within the college.

At the risk of redundancy, let me stress that these were the core journals in sociological methodology as of 1975—reputable outlets for work in mathematical and quantitative sociology. When questioned about their substantive interests, the experts named a great many more journals and particularly increased the prominence of *Demography* and the *Social Psychology Quarterly*.[7] My purpose here, however, is to explain the interest experts expressed in those journals reputed to be publishing the most significant work in sociological methodology. It is those journals, the core sociological methodology journals,

[7] A table on expert interests in journals regarding methodological and substantive work is given elsewhere (Burt 1978a:149–150). Even extending expert interests to include their substantive concerns, however, does not change the conclusion that the eight journals identified above are core journals for elite experts. With substantive interests considered, these eight journals are still the only journals for which the hypothesis of no interest can be rejected at beyond the .001 level of confidence, and the same pattern of concentrated interest in the core rather than noncore journals is observed.

which I believe are the most likely to be the object of normative perceptions by the elite experts.

Measuring Normative Interest

Given the expressed interests of each expert in the core journals (the x_{jk} in Eq. [6.5]) and given the influence relations among experts with regard to their work in sociological methodology (the methodology z_{ji} in Chapter 3), the normative interests to be expected of each expert can be computed for the relational model (x^*_{jkr} in Eq. [6.1]) and for the positional model (x^*_{jkp} in Eq. [6.4]).

The exponent v used to convert objective distances into subjective perceptions of distance in Eq. (6.2) for the positional model is 6. Values lower than this yield weaker correlations between expressed interests and normative interests (x_{jk} with x^*_{jkp}) while an exponent of 7 yields slightly weaker or no higher magnitudes. The correlation between x_{jk} and x^*_{jkp} does not change at the same rate nor in the same direction for each core journal across different values of v; however, it does change in a very similar manner. When v is set equal to 1, .11 is the mean correlation between x_{jk} and x^*_{jkp} across the eight core journals K. This mean correlation increases to .21, .28, .31, .32, and .33 for v equal to 2, 3, 4, 5, and 6, respectively. It falls back to .32 when v is set equal to 7, so the value of 6 is used to determine normative interests.[8]

6.4 EXPERT INTEREST CONFORMING TO JOURNAL NORMS

To the extent that either of the two network models is empirically adequate, expressed interest should reflect normative interest. Of course, individuals differ in their conformity to a social norm without violating it, and there were differences among the elite experts that could have biased their perceptions of journals without violating journals norms. An expert with a healthy view of himself can be expected to perceive significance in the work of a journal that publishes his own work. Similarly, he can be expected to perceive significance in a journal over which he exercised editorial control, since he was responsible for the work appearing in the journal. Each expert's publication record with the eight core journals has been obtained as has been described. In order to measure the relative extent to which each expert had editorial control over sociological

---

[8]Thinking that relations might also have a power function effect, the normative interests in Eq. (6.1) were recomputed with powered weights (z^2_{ji} instead of z_{ji} in the equation); however, the normative interests generated by these powered weights yield the same mean correlation ($r = .22$) as that obtained in the unpowered model. Moreover, operationalizing z_{ji} as the original binary sociometric choices lowered the correlation for all journals except SF and JMS. The adequacy of the z_{ji} as operationalized here could result from their already being path distances normalized as perceived relations (Eq. [2.5]).

methodology articles appearing in a core journal as of 1975, respondents to the question eliciting names of journals publishing significant work were also asked to "indicate the number of papers you have been sent for review during the past two years for each journal." These data were used to compute eight scores for each expert as the proportion of sociological methodology manuscripts refereed by elite experts for a core journal that the expert himself refereed.[9]

The following equation is therefore a basic population model in which the interest expert j expressed in journal k (x_{jk}) results from journal norms as his collegial alter's interest in the journal (x_{jk}^* representing either x_{jkp}^* or x_{jkr}^*), from his personal editorial control over the journal (ED_{jk}), or from his own work's being published in the journal (PUB_{jk}):

$$x_{jk} = \beta + \beta_{nk}(x_{jk}^*) + \beta_{ek}(\mathrm{ED}_{jk}) + \beta_{pk}(\mathrm{PUB}_{jk}) + \eta_{jk}, \qquad (6.6)$$

where β is an intercept term and η_{jk} is a random error in measuring expert j's interest in journal k. The normative effect for journal k (β_{nk}) should be positive to the extent that the network model generating the journal norm x_{jk}^* correctly captures the social mechanism maintaining journal norms. If the social mechanism maintaining journal norms is actual communication between experts, then x_{jk} should reflect x_{jkr}^* as predicted by the relational model. In this case, β_{nk} would be most strongly positive when x_{jkr}^* is substituted for x_{jk}^* in Eq. (6.6). On the other hand, if the social mechanism maintaining journal norms is symbolic role-taking among experts as implied by the proposed model of structural interests, then x_{jk} should reflect x_{jkp}^* as predicted by the positional model so that a strong, positive value of β_{nk} should be obtained when x_{jkp}^* is substituted for x_{jk}^* in Eq. (6.6)[10] The effects of an expert's personal involvement

[9]This measure of editing assumes that an expert who does not feel that a journal is publishing significant work in sociological methodology will exercise negligible editorial control over the journal. This need not be true; however, the assumption was forced on the analysis since core journals were not known prior to mailing questionnaires. The seven experts who did not return questionnaires present a problem here since they too exercised editorial control over the core journals. Measures of editorial control exercised by the respondents could be biased by a failure to consider the levels exercised by missing experts. In order to avoid this bias, the numbers of manuscripts refereed by respondents were used to estimate the average number of methodological/mathematical manuscripts an expert reviewed per year for each of the core journals according to the type of editorial position he held with each journal—reader, associate editor, or head editor. Means for these positions in each core journal are given elsewhere (Burt 1978a:152). Since the editorial positions of the missing experts between 1973 and 1975 are published in each journal, these results make it possible to estimate the probable number of methodological/mathematical manuscripts each missing expert refereed for each core journal as a function of the editorial positions he occupied between 1973 and 1975. Where e_{jk} is the estimated number of sociological methodology manuscripts expert j refereed for journal k between 1973 and 1975, the proportion of such manuscripts refereed by all elite experts for which j was personally responsible is given as $\mathrm{ED}_{jk} = e_{jk}/(\Sigma_i e_{ik})$, where summation is across all 59 elite experts i; the 52 respondents as well as the 7 experts not responding to the questionnaire.

[10]A center-periphery pattern of interests might be expected as a static third option. The center-periphery conception of norms is critically described by Shils (1961). Persons most prominent in the college would embody its journal norms while persons at its periphery would be most likely to deviate from these norms. This idea does not work well in describing the data on elite experts in

(Continued on next page)

with a journal on his interest in the journal (β_{ek} for editorial involvement and β_{pk} for publishing involvement) should be positive or negligible. Without rejecting a journal prescribed by his collegial alter as an outlet for significant work in sociological methodology, expert j could have a stronger interest in the journal than that expected by his collegial alter to the extent that he edits the journal or publishes his own work there.

Maximum likelihood estimates of the effect parameters in Eq. (6.6) are presented in Table 6.3, first for the relational model and then for the positional model. Note that expressed interests appear on both sides of Eq. (6.6), x_{jk} on the left and x_{ik} pooled as a journal norm x_{jk}^* on the right. This explicit interdependency among responses by separate observations invalidates the general use of ordinary least squares to estimate the betas in models such as Eq. (6.6). A detailed discussion of the special problems posed by regressing x_{jk} over x_{jk}^* and numerically obtaining maximum likelihood estimates of parameters is provided by Doreian (1980, 1981). The estimates given in Table 6.3 were graciously provided by Patrick Doreian for use here. I draw two conclusions from the results.

First, personal involvement with a journal had more effect on an expert's interest in the less prominent of the core journals. As expected, personal involvement had a positive or negligible effect on expert interest; $\hat{\beta}_{ek}$ and $\hat{\beta}_{pk}$ are nonnegative for all core journals. However, the journals for which these effects are strongest are JMS, SSR, and SF. A quick look at Table 6.1 shows that the null hypothesis of no interest is least strongly rejected for these three journals of all the eight core journals. Editorial control over SM did have some unique association with expert interest in it ($\hat{\beta}_{ek} = .49$ for the relational model, .55 for the positional); however, this effect is only significant at the .10 level of confidence. By and large, the effects of editing a journal or being published in it are the same if normative interest is defined by the relational or the positional models. With the exception that editing has a lower effect on interest in SF under the relational model in comparison to its effect under the positional

---

(Continued from previous page)

sociological methodology. Four experts received an unusually high number of citations as sources of influential comments on methodological work. They each received an average of eight citations while the next highest recipient received five. The average interest of these four leaders was treated as a journal norm to which the "center" of the college adhered. The absolute value of the difference between this interest and that expressed by an individual expert in the college was taken as the expert's deviation from normative interest in the journal. For each of the core journals, an expert's deviation from normative interest was correlated with his choice status, the proportion of the college citing him as a source of influential methodology comments. With one exception, the correlations were not significant even at the .10 level of significance. The one exception, SMR, generated a correlation significant at the .01 level. Interest in this journal was low among the four leaders so the observed negative correlation ($r = -.35$) shows that experts at the center of the college were less likely to be interested in SMR than those at its periphery. Across the eight core journals, however, the center-periphery conception of norms was not accurate. It assumes too simplistic a picture of stratification within the college. Instead of one center, there were multiple centers, each with its constituent leaders and followers as described in Chapter 3.

TABLE 6.3
Conformity to Journal Norms Holding Publication and Editing Constant[a]

	Relational model			Positional model		
Core Journals	β_{nk}	β_{ek}	β_{pk}	β_{nk}	β_{ek}	β_{pk}
American Sociological Review	.16	.21	.01	.26*	.31	.01
	(1.1)	(0.4)	(0.8)	(1.4)	(0.5)	(0.9)
American Journal of Sociology	.09	.65	.02	.21	.59	.01
	(0.6)	(1.2)	(1.0)	(1.1)	(1.1)	(1.1)
Sociological Methodology	.27**	.49*	.01	.25*	.55*	.02
	(1.9)	(1.3)	(1.0)	(1.4)	(1.4)	(1.0)
Journal of the American Statistical Association	.15	.39	.01	.45**	.31	.00
	(0.9)	(0.8)	(0.6)	(3.0)	(0.7)	(0.1)
Sociological Methods & Research	.36**	.50*	.01	.29**	.46*	.01
	(2.6)	(1.6)	(0.5)	(1.7)	(1.4)	(0.7)
Journal of Mathematical Sociology	.31**	.69**	.05**	.31**	.74**	.05**
	(2.6)	(2.7)	(2.6)	(2.1)	(2.8)	(2.7)
Social Science Research	.06	.27**	.03**	.26*	.27**	.03**
	(0.4)	(3.0)	(3.2)	(1.5)	(3.0)	(3.3)
Social Forces	.42**	.10	.03**	.54**	.27*	.04**
	(3.0)	(0.5)	(2.2)	(4.5)	(1.5)	(2.9)

[a]These results were obtained by Patrick Doreian at the University of Pittsburgh, who graciously provided them for use here. The relational model estimates were obtained for Eq. (6.6) when x^*_{jkr} was substituted for x^*_{jk}, and the positional model estimates were obtained when x^*_{jkp} was substituted for x^*_{jk}. Parentheses contain t-tests for parameters, and effects significantly greater than zero are marked with asterisks (* for the .10 level, ** for the .05 level).

model, very similar t-tests for editing and being published are obtained under the two models in predicting interest in each journal.

Second, the positional model seems to be slightly better than the relational model in capturing the social mechanism maintaining journal norms. This conclusion is based on a comparison of corresponding estimates of the normative effect, β_{nk}, under the two models. As expected, all normative effects are positive; x_{jk} increases across experts in proportion to x^*_{jk}. For SMR, JMS, and SF, the normative effect is significant for the relational and positional models at beyond the .05 level of confidence. Interest in SM is slightly better predicted by the relational model than the positional model ($\hat{\beta}_{nk} = .27$ versus .25, respectively); however, interest in JASA is much better predicted by the positional model than it is by the relational model ($\hat{\beta}_{nk} = .45$ versus .15, respectively). Only the normative effect estimated under the positional model is significant for JASA. At a lower level of contrast, the normative effect on interest in ASR and SSR is only significant when estimated under the positional model (however, significance in these examples is only at the .10 level of confidence). Summarizing the slight advantage to be gained by using the positional model rather than the relational model in capturing journal norms, I find the mean value of the normative effect for the eight core journals under the relational model to be .23 ($.23 = \Sigma_k \hat{\beta}_{nk}/8$), whereas the higher value of .32 is obtained for the same mean normative effect using the positional model.

These results on expert conformity to journal norms offer some support for the positional model in preference to the relational model; however, they are inconclusive. A closer look at the data is required in order to better understand the conditions under which the two models seem to be in error.

6.5 DEVIANT EXPERT INTEREST

In theory, an expert should have expressed interest in a journal in proportion to that expressed by his collegial alter, thereby ensuring a strong positive association between $\mathbf{x}_{jk}$ and $\mathbf{x}_{jk}^*$. Empirical reality allows for much more flexibility than this. In the same sense that role relations can vary when performed by actors jointly occupying a status (and so mandating a weak criterion of structural equivalence in network analyses as discussed in Section 2.6), normative interests can vary when actually expressed by individuals. In other words, it seems likely that expressed interests ($\mathbf{x}_{jk}$) will differ even if they reflect the same journal norm ($\mathbf{x}_{jk}^*$). But how different can the expressed interests of two experts be before they must be treated as qualitatively different? This seems to me to be an intractable question for the general case.

Festinger, Schachter, and Back (1950) adopted an empirically useful strategy for circumventing this question. Instead of analyzing the extent to which people conform to a group normative standard, they analyze the extent to which people strongly deviate from it. Empirically, it is usually clearer when someone is deviating from a social norm than when he or she is conforming to it. Moreover, an analysis of deviance from a norm introduces the methodological possibility of describing the *manner* in which deviance does occur, as opposed to an analysis of conformity which focuses on the *extent* to which deviance does not occur. This turns out to be a crucial consideration in understanding journal norms among the elite experts. I first distinguish two ways in which experts might be considered deviant with respect to journal norms, then describe the prevalence of each type of deviance among the elite experts, and finally describe the conditions under which experts tended to deviate from journal norms.

Types of Deviant Experts

Table 6.4 offers a typology of expert responses to a journal norm. The three columns distinguish an expert exposed to a norm not prescribing a journal as an outlet for significant work in sociological methodology (an expert j for whom $\mathbf{x}_{jk}^*$ lies in the lowest 25% of all $\mathbf{x}_{jk}^*$ in the college for journal k) from one exposed to a norm prescribing some, but not high interest in the journal (an expert j for whom x_{jk}^* lies within the interquartile range of x_{jk}^* in the college) and from one exposed to a norm actually prescribing the journal as an outlet for the most significant work in the sociological methodology (an expert j for whom x_{jk}^* lies in the top 25% of all x_{jk}^* in the college). Although arbitrary, the choice of 25% as a criterion level of normative interest is useful. It distinguishes those members of the college exposed to very high versus very low normative interest in a journal while ensuring a sufficient number of observations in each category to allow comparisons between experts in each category. The three rows of Table 6.4 distinguish levels of expressed interest: an expert who did not recognize the journal under consideration as an outlet for significant work in sociological methodology ($x_{jk} = 0$), an expert who recognized the journal's significance within the college but did not express a high interest in having his own work appear there ($x_{jk} > 0$, but not in the top 25% of all x_{jk} for the college), and an expert who expressed the highest interest in the journal (x_{jk} lies in the top 25% of all x_{jk} for the journal in the college). The nine cells created by the cross-classification of these levels of expressed versus normative interest define qualitatively different types of responses by experts to journal norms.

Five of the nine cells in Table 6.4 refer to moderates—experts who themselves or whose collegial alters expressed some interest in a journal without expressing extreme interest. Moderates neither violated nor endorsed an explicit journal norm. Although important in a quantitative comparison of expressed and normative interest such as that in Table 6.3, these experts are of secondary interest in an analysis of deviance.

If an expert was exposed to high normative interest in a journal, then his significant others can be viewed as precribing the journal to him as an outlet for important work within the college. The third column of Table 6.4 distinguishes three ways in which he could have responded to such a prescription. He could have mirrored the journal norm by expressing high interest in the journal (and so been a conservative) or he could have acknowledged the significance of the journal without committing himself to especially high interest in it (and so been a moderate). Either of these responses represents conformity to the journal norm in the sense of not signalling its violation.

But if the expert responded by completely ignoring the prescribed journal as an outlet for significant work, he could be viewed as explicitly violating a journal norm. More than merely expressing interest in the journal that deviated from normative interest, the expert would be deviating from normative interest in a particularly egregious way. His failure to recognize the prescribed journal contradicts the perception by his significant others as a collegial alter that work typically published in the journal bears the seal of scientific authority within the college. He would be, in effect if not in behavior, "rebelling" against normative interest in the journal as a bastion of reputable knowledge within the college. For his own preservation as an occupant of his position in the college, such a person would be expected either to keep his opinions to himself or to have his

TABLE 6.4
Types of Expert Response to Journal Norms

	Normative interest		
Expressed interest	Journal is not prescribed (lowest 25%)	Journal has some interest	Journal is prescribed (highest 25%)
Journal is ignored (zero interest)	Conservatives (conformers)	Moderates (conformers)	Rebels (deviants)
Journal is given some interest	Moderates (conformers)	Moderates (conformers)	Moderates (conformers)
Journal is important (highest 25%)	Eccentrics (deviants)	Moderates (conformers)	Conservatives (conformers)

[a]Normative interest for expert j is either x_{jkr}^* or x_{jkp}^* as given by Eqs. (6.1) and (6.4), respectively. His expressed interest is x_{jk} as given by Eq. (6.5).

evaluation of the journal changed under the tutoring of his surprised significant others seeking to outdo one another in demonstrating to the heretic his misperception of significant work in the journal. Whether by direct communication from his significant others, or by his own perception of his stuctural peers publishing work in the journal and/or citing papers appearing in the journal, no expert would be expected to ignore a journal in which his significant others were highly interested. In short, an adequate network model of the social mechanism maintaining journal norms would result in few experts falling into the cell of Table 6.4 labeled "rebels."

The first column in Table 6.4 distinguishes three ways in which an expert could have responded to low normative interest in a journal. He could have idealized this interest by not even acknowledging the journal as an outlet for significant work in sociological methodology (and so been a conservative) or he could have expressed some interest in it without expressing particularly high interest (and so been a moderate). Again, these responses do not signal norm violation.

But if he had a strong interest in the journal despite its low normative interest, then he was not conforming to journal norms. His deviation, however, is more appropriately labeled as eccentric than rebellious. His strong interest does not imply that he was raising to special importance a journal proscribed by his significant others nor does it imply (in contrast to the rebel) that he was rejecting the significance of work published in a prescribed journal. He would be merely expressing unexpectedly high interest in a journal to which his significant others gave little or no credence. Nevertheless, his would have been a deviant interest within the college and so not expected to occur under a network model correctly defining journal norms; i.e., few experts should fall into the cell of Table 6.4 labeled "eccentrics."

Before returning to the data, let me stress that these labels, rebel versus eccentric, are not being proposed as generalizable to all forms of defiance. They seem to me to be slightly awkward here, but preferable to alternatives. As will become clear in the following, the distinction between these two types of deviant experts is a crucial one.

The Prevalence of Deviant Experts

Table 6.5 presents frequencies for Table 6.4 under the relational versus positional models of journal norms with respect to one of the core journals, *Sociological Methodology*. Those percentages most directly relevant to assessing the prevalence of deviance are enclosed in squares. For both of the two network models, the same percentage of the respondents express no interest in SM (23 experts, 44%), and the same percentage express high interest (14 experts, 27%). If deviance was a chance occurrence with respect to SM, then similar percentages should occur in each column of Table 6.5. Consider experts for whom SM is not a prescribed journal. Under the relational model, 13 experts had collegial alters expressing low interest in SM (column 1 of Table 6.5). Only one of these experts expressed high interest in SM, so the relational model defines journal norms such that 8% of the experts who could have been eccentric deviants (1 of 13) actually fall into the eccentric deviant cell of Table 6.4. The remaining 92% of the experts whose collegial alters expressed low interest in SM conformed to that journal norm of low interest. Under the positional model, 16 experts had collegial alters expressing low interest in SM (column 5 of Table 6.5). Of these, two expressed high interest in SM so that the positional model defines journal norms such that 13% of the experts who could have been eccentric deviants actually fall into the eccentric deviant cell of Table 6.4. In other words, both of the network models define journal norms such that experts are less likely to express high interest in SM when they have a journal norm of low interest than they are likely to express high interest in SM within the college as a whole. The relevant percentages here occur in boxes in the third row of Table 6.5 (8% and 13% versus 27% for the college as a whole). Consider experts for whom SM is a prescribed journal. Under the relational model, 18 experts had collegial alters expressing high interest in SM (column 3 of Table 6.5). Six of these experts did not mention SM as an outlet for significant work in sociological methodology, so this model defines journal norms such that 33% of the experts who could have been rebel deviants (1 of 3) actually fell into the rebel deviant cell of Table 6.4. Under the positional model, SM was a prescribed journal for 13 experts (column 7 of Table 6.5) of whom two did not mention it as an outlet for significant methodological work. The positional model defines journal norms such that 15% of the experts who could have been rebel deviants (1 of 7) actually fell into the rebel deviant cell of Table 6.4. Here again, both of the network models define journal norms such that experts are less likely to ignore SM when they have a journal norm of high interest than they are likely to ignore SM within the college as a whole. The

TABLE 6.5
Expressed Versus Normative Interest in *Sociological Methodology* under the Two Network Models

Expressed interest (x_{jk})	Normative interest under the relational model (x^*_{jkr})				Normative interest under the positional model (x^*_{jkp})			
	Low	Some	High	All norms	Low	Some	High	All norms
None	7 (54%)	10 (48%)	6 (33%)	23 (44%)	8 (50%)	13 (57%)	2 (15%)	23 (44%)
Some	5 (38%)	8 (38%)	2 (11%)	15 (29%)	6 (38%)	5 (22%)	4 (31%)	14 (29%)
High	1 (8%)	3 (14%)	10 (56%)	14 (27%)	2 (13%)	5 (22%)	7 (54%)	14 (27%)
All interests	13 (100)	21 (100)	18 (100)	52 (100)	16 (101)	23 (101)	13 (100)	52 (100)

[a]Cells of the table are explained in Table 5.4 where normative interest under the relational model is given in Eq. (6.1), and normative interest under the positional model is given in Eq. (6.4). The percentages in parentheses might not sum to 100 down a column because percentages have been rounded to the nearest percent.

relevant percentages here occur in boxes in the first row of Table 6.5 (33% and 15% versus 44% for the college as a whole).

Focusing on rebel deviance, Table 6.6 presents statistics on the prevalence of rebel deviants under the two network models with respect to each of the core journals. For each journal, three percentages are given: the percentage of the college failing to mention the journal as an outlet for significant methodological work, the percentage of experts having no interest in the journal when it was prescribed by their collegial alters under the relational model, and the same percentage when collegial alters are defined by the positional model. In other words, the percentages in Table 6.6 correspond to the boxed-in percentages in the first row of Table 6.5. Comparing the first row of Table 6.5 with the third row of Table 6.6, note that 44.2% of the experts generally did not mention SM as an outlet for significant methodological work, 33.3% of the experts whose collegial alters prescribed SM under the relational model ignored the journal, and 15.4% of those whose collegial alters prescribed SM under the positional model ignored the journal. In order to interpret these percentages, unit test statistics are presented in parentheses. A strong, negative test statistic indicates that a percentage is statistically much less than would be expected by chance given the distribution of interest in the overall college.[11]

Overall, fewer experts fall into the rebel deviant category when journal norms are defined by the positional model rather than the relational model. There are differences in the extent to which experts expressed no interest in the core journals: ASR, AJS, SM, and JASA were much less likely to be ignored than were SMR, JMS, SSR, or SF. For each journal individually, however, less deviance occurred under the positional model than the relational model. For example, one in ten experts had no interest in ASR (9.6%). For those experts whose collegial alter under the relational model prescribed ASR as an outlet for significant methodological work, the ratio drops to slightly less than one in ten (7.7%). Under the positional model, however, the ratio drops to 0. As described

---

[11] These test statistics are taken from a log-linear model of frequencies in Table 6.4 for a network model. Since parameters in the model do not add substantively to the discussion of simple percentages, I have not discussed the log-linear model in the text. However, knowledge of the model is useful in understanding the test statistics. Let f_{ij} be the frequency with which experts fall into cell (i,j) of Table 6.4 under one of the two network models. This frequency can be expressed in terms of four parameters in a log-linear model:

$$\log f_{ij} = \lambda + \lambda_i + \lambda_j + \lambda_{ij},$$

where λ is an overall mean adjustment, λ_i and λ_j are adjustments for the extent to which experts in the college as a whole express interest in the journal at level i (row i in Table 6.4) and experts in the college as a whole have a journal norm of interest at level j (column j in Table 6.4), and λ_{ij} is an adjustment for the extent to which experts fall into cell (i,j) with a frequency greater than would be expected by the marginal frequencies for row i and column j. Table 6.6 presents test statistics for the significance of λ_{13}, the extent to which the frequency of rebel deviants is different from the frequency to be expected as a result of marginal distributions of interest in the college as a whole, and Table 6.7 presents test statistics for the significance of λ_{31}, the extent to which the frequency of eccentric deviants is unexpectedly high or low. The unit normal test statistics themselves are the value of the log-linear coefficient λ_{ij} divided by its standard error and have an approximately normal distribution (e.g., see Goodman 1970:229).

in Table 6.5, four in ten experts were not interested in SM (44.2%), which drops to a ratio of three in ten under the relational model (33.3%), but drops still further to a ratio of two in ten under the positional model (15.4%). The unit test statistics show that only under the positional model are rebel deviants with respect to SM significantly unlikely at the .05 level of confidence. This pattern is repeated across the eight core journals to varying extents. With the exceptions of JASA and SMR, journals for which rebel deviants are significantly unlikely under both network models, rebel deviants are less likely to be created by the positional model than they are by the relational model. For SM, SF, and JMS, this difference is statistically significant. Further, the relational model actually creates *more* rebel deviants than would be expected by random chance for AJS and SSR. Of all respondents, 28.8% expressed no interest in AJS, but 33% of those who collegial alter prescribed the journal under the relational model expressed no interest in it. Similarly, 78.6% of those whose collegial alter prescribed SSR under the relational model expressed no interest in the journal while 75% of the respondents generally expressed no interest in the journal. As a heuristic summary, the mean unit normal test statistic for the prevalence of rebel deviants when journal norms are defined by the relational model is -0.4, while the same mean decreased to -1.6 when journal norms are defined by the positional model.

Table 6.7 presents the same data on eccentrics that Table 6.6 contains on rebels: the percentage of the college expressing high interest in a journal, the percentage of experts exposed to low normative interest in the journal according to the relational model who nevertheless expressed high interest in it, and the percentage of experts expressing high interest in the journal despite the low normative interest given it by their collegial alters. Unit normal test statistics indicate the extent to which deviants occurred less often than might be expected by chance.

The general conclusion I draw from Table 6.7 is that eccentric deviants tended to occur by and large by chance. With two exceptions, the test statistics in Table 6.7 are negative, showing that eccentrics occurred less often than might be expected from the distribution of high interest in the college. Percentages in columns two and three of Table 6.7 tend to be lower than corresponding percentages in column one. However, the differences are negligible. As a heuristic summary, the mean unit normal test statistic for the prevalence of eccentric deviants when journal norms are defined under the relational model is -0.1, and the same near zero mean is obtained when journal norms are defined by the positional model. Eccentrics do tend to be absent under the relational model with respect to JMS at the .05 level of confidence, but finding one percentage of sixteen to be significant at this level of confidence is almost itself attributable to chance.

The lack of significant results in Table 6.7 and the significant results in Table 6.6 is not overly surprising given the substantive meaning of eccentrics versus rebels as deviants within an invisible college. The latter is a more serious threat

TABLE 6.6
The Prevalence of Rebel Deviants

	Percentage not citing journal as significant		
Core Journals	Whole college	Prescribed by relational model	Prescribed by positional model
American Sociological Review	9.6	7.7 (0.0)	0.0 (−0.7)
American Journal of Sociology	28.8	33.3 (0.7)	21.4 (−0.7)
Sociological Methodology	44.2	33.3 (−.09)	15.4** (−2.2)
Journal of the American Statistical Association	40.4	15.4** (−2.0)	21.4** (−1.7)
Sociological Methods & Research	59.6	31.3** (−2.7)	36.8** (−2.3)
Journal of Mathematical Sociology	67.3	61.5 (0.1)	28.6** (−2.4)
Social Science Research	75.0	78.6 (1.2)	55.6 (−.09)
Social Forces	76.9	68.8 (0.2)	46.2** (−1.7)

*a*Rebel deviants are defined in Table 6.4, and unit normal test statistics are given in parentheses (see footnote 11 for explanation of statistics). The significance of differences between percentages and their expected values is marked by asterisks (* for the .10 level, ** for the .05 level).

to consensual perceptions of significant knowledge in the college, so it seems appropriate that they should be rare in fact and not often created by a network model that correctly captures the social mechanism maintaining journal norms. In support of the proposed model of structural interests, there are never more deviant experts under the positional model than would be expected from the distribution of interests in the overall college, and rebel deviants have a statistically significant tendency to be absent. More experts tend to fall into the deviant categories under the relational model and in some cases with a frequency greater than would be expected from the distribution of interests in the overall college. This evidence supporting the positional model over the relational model is strengthened by taking a closer look at the conditions under which experts fall into the deviant categories.

Relational Pattern as a Condition for Deviance

As discussed earlier in regard to Figure 6.1 as illustration, the relational and positional models differ in a way that suggests that some deviance could be

TABLE 6.7
The Prevalence of Eccentric Deviants

	Percentage giving journal high significance		
Core journals	Whole college	Ignored under relational model	Ignored under positional model
American Sociological Review	28.8	14.3* (−1.3)	25.0* (−1.5)
American Journal of Sociology	25.0	13.3 (−1.2)	23.1 (−0.2)
Sociological Methodology	26.9	7.7* (−1.5)	12.5* (−1.6)
Journal of the American Statisticsl Association	25.0	21.4 (−.04)	21.4 (−.03)
Sociological Methods & Research	25.0	15.4 (−.07)	7.7* (−1.3)
Journal of Mathematical Sociology	25.0	7.1** (−1.8)	21.4 (0.0)
Social Science Research	25.0	29.2 (0.5)	20.0 (−0.2)
Social Forces	23.1	12.9 (−0.7)	0.0* (−1.6)

[a]Eccentric deviants are defined in Table 6.4, and unit normal test statistics are given in parentheses (see footnote 11 for explanation of statistics). The significance of differences between percentages and their expected values is marked by asterisks (* for the .10 level, ** for the .05 level).

attributable to the relational pattern defining an expert's position in the network of methodology influence relations. Under the positional model, structurally equivalent followers in the college could have journal norms different from those to which their leaders subscribed. Leaders would be expected to have similarly perceived significance to the extent that they were structurally equivalent with one another. Since leaders would not be structurally equivalent with their followers, the latter having a relational pattern different from the former, there is no prediction that leaders and their followers should have had similar journal interests. In contrast, the relational model predicts that the influential comments from leaders to their followers will result in the followers' sharing the same interests with their leaders. In short, the crucial difference between the two network models in predicting journal interests in elite sociological methodology concerns those experts who relied on persons structurally nonequivalent to themselves for influential methodological comments.

Table 6.8 continues the illustration in Figure 6.1 of this point, but uses actual data on the elite experts to label deviants. Weights are presented which describe the extent to which each expert relied on the others as significant others. The

TABLE 6.8
Illustrating the Leader–Follower Dichotomy with Six Experts[a]

Parameters and data	Experts in sociological methodology					
	1	2	3	4	5	6
Weights for relational model	—	.50	.50	.00	.00	.00
$[z_{ji}/(\Sigma_i z_{ji})]$	.50	—	.50	.00	.00	.00
	.50	.50	—	.00	.00	.00
	.20	.40	.40	—	.00	.00
	.13	.13	.38	.38	—	.00
	.11	.22	.22	.44	.00	—
Weights for positional model	—	.69	.31	.00	.00	.00
$[l_{ij}/(1-l_{jj})]$	.56	—	.43	.00	.00	.00
	.38	.60	—	.01	.00	.00
	.00	.02	.12	—	.01	.85
	.00	.00	.06	.83	—	.11
	.00	.00	.00	.99	.01	—
Expressed and normative interests in JASA						
x_{jk}	.55	.99	.25	.00	.00	.12
	(H)	(H)	(S)	(N)	(N)	(S)
x_{jkr}	.62	.40	.77	.61*	.30*	.33
	(H)	(H)	(H)	(H)	(H)	(H)
x_{jkp}	.76	.42	.80	.15	.03	.00
	(H)	(H)	(H)	(S)	(L)	(L)

[a]Given the z_{ji} among these six experts, weights for the relational model are computed as given in Eq. (6.1) and from the z_{ji}, distances are computed as $d_{ji} = [\Sigma_q(z_{jq} - z_{iq})^2 + \Sigma_q(z_{qj} - z_{qi})^2 - z_{ji}^2 - z_{ij}^2]^{1/2}$, cf. footnote 6 in Chapter 3. The l_{ij} are computed from distances as $(dmax_j - d_{ji})^6 / [\Sigma_i(dmax_j - d_{ji})^6]$ from which weights for the positional model are computed as given in Eq. (6.4). Normative interest under the relational model is computed from Eq. (6.1), and the same interest under the positional model is computed from Eq. (6.4). Qualitative interest is given in parentheses as coded for Table 6.4 in the whole college. Asterisks mark rebel deviants.

first three experts were leaders (members of the social statistics elite discussed in Chapter 3) whereas the second three were followers in the sense that the first three were the object of unreciprocated relations from the last three and only acknowledged one another as sources of influential comments. Notice that the weights for the relational model show that the leaders took one another as equally significant others, but ignored follower perceptions (e.g., cells 1,2 and 1,3 equal .5 while cells 1,5 and 1,6 equal 0). The followers relied extensively on the leaders as significant others, by and large ignoring one another (reliance on expert four notwithstanding). This patterning of significant others in a collegial alter changes under the positional model. The weights for the positional model also show that the leaders took one another as significant others. The extent to which any leader served as a significant other for any other leader varies since their structural equivalence to one another varied. However, shared unreciprocated relations to the leaders now make the followers structurally equivalent (under a weak criterion) so that they would be expected to have taken one another as significant others. Expert four would have perceived expert six as his strongest structural peer (cell 4,6 equals .83) while experts five and six would have both relied on expert four as their structural peer (cell 6,4 equals .99 and cell 5,4 equals .83).

The bottom three rows of Table 6.8 present each expert's expressed interest in JASA (x_{jk}) and his normative interest under the two network models (x^*_{jkr} and x^*_{jkp}). The qualitative interest implied by each quantitative interest is given in parentheses according to the codes in Table 6.4, which distinguish types of responses to journal norms. For example, the second expert allocated .99 of his interest to being published in JASA (which put him in the top 25% of the college so that his qualitative interest in the journal was high, "H").

The first three columns of quantitative and qualitative interests refer to the leaders. Since they had strong ties with one another and are structurally equivalent with one another, the relational and positional models make similar predictions. All three leaders would be expected to share the journal norm of high interest in JASA. There were no deviant experts among the leaders.

The last three columns refer to the followers. Experts four and five did not perceive JASA as a significant outlet for work in the college, but the relational model predicts that they should have subscribed to their leaders's journal norm of high interest in the journal. Both experts are rebel deviants under the relational model. Since the positional model does not predict high interest in JASA among the followers, none were deviants under that model.

This pattern of erroneously created rebel deviants is typical of the relational model when it is used to define journal norms for the experts more generally. Table 6.9 presents a cross-classification of rebel and eccentric deviants by the relational pattern defining an expert's network position. Distinguished by column are "nonfollowers" and "followers." These two categories of relational patterns were clearly distinguished in the college by a gap in the distribution of the continuous variable used to measure the extent to which an expert relied on others structurally nonequivalent to himself for influential comments on his methodological work.[12] Followers were those experts who relied on persons structurally nonequivalent to themselves. Nonfollowers were those whose only sources of influential comments were structurally equivalent to themselves.

---

[12]To the extent that expert j only acknowledged influential comments from experts structurally equivalent to himself, the following index will be close to 1: $(\Sigma_i(1 - z_{ji}d_{ji})/(\Sigma_i d_{ij})$. This is the "self$_{jk}$" index in Chapter 2 (see Eq. [2.17]). For the experts in the follower category of Table 6.9, this index varies without discernable gaps between .65 and .85. For nonfollowers, it ranges from .94 to a perfect score of 1 without missing any two-digit decimals in between these extremes. Thus, the two groups are clearly distinguished.

TABLE 6.9
Relational Pattern and Deviance

	Network position	
Deviance across all core journals	Nonfollowers N (%)	Followers N (%)
Under the relational model		
Never deviant	5 (25.0)	4 (12.5)
Rebel	4 (20.0)	21 (65.6)
Eccentric	6 (30.0)	2 (6.3)
Rebel eccentric	5 (25.0)	5 (15.6)
Under the positional model		
Never deviant	9 (45.0)	10 (31.3)
Rebel	6 (30.0)	11 (34.4)
Eccentric	2 (10.0)	6 (18.8)
Rebel eccentric	3 (15.0)	5 (15.6)

Among the nonfollowers were cliques of leaders and isolated cliques composed of a few experts who relied on one another for comments. Pooling the extent to which an expert deviated from normative interest in all eight journals under one of the network models, four categories of experts are distinguished by rows in Table 6.9; those who never deviated from normative interests ("never"), those who were rebels in regard to one or more journals but never eccentrics ("rebels"), those who were eccentrics in regard to one or more journals but never rebels ("eccentrics"), and those who were rebels in regard to some journal(s) as well as eccentrics in regard to some journal(s).[13]

Deviance and relational pattern are closely associated for the relational model but not for the positional model. Twenty experts had sources of influential comments structurally equivalent to themselves. Under both network models, about half of these experts were rebel deviants in regard to at least one of the core journals (9 out of 20 experts, or 45%). As observed for the first 3 experts in Table 6.8, the similar results are to be expected for the two models since each expert's source of influential comments is also his structural peer within the college. This is not true of followers in the college. Under the positional model, the same rate of deviance is observed among followers and nonfollowers: half of the followers were rebel deviants in regard to at least one core journal (16 of 32, or 50%). Since 45% of the nonfollowers were also rebels, it is not surprising to find no interaction between deviance under the

[13]Tabulations of the number of journals in regard to which an expert was deviant (as opposed to whether he was deviant) yield the same inferences I obtained by analyzing the collapsed data in Table 6.9. Although one expert was a rebel deviant under the relational model with respect to five of the eight core journals, no expert was an eccentric in regard to more than two journals, and few were rebels in regard to more than two journals (one expert under the positional model and six under the relational model).

positional model versus the follower–nonfollower distinction. The chi-square statistic for the null hypothesis of no interaction is 1.16 with three degrees of freedom; there is no interaction. Under the relational model, in contrast, this chi-square increases to 11.44, which is significant at the .01 level of confidence. The rate of ostensible rebel deviance is much higher among followers than nonfollowers under the relational model. While 45% of the nonfollowers were rebel deviants under this model, 81.3% of the followers were labeled as rebel deviants. As illustrated in Table 6.8, experts who relied on persons structurally nonequivalent to themselves for influential comments had an increased tendency to be labelled rebel deviants under the relational model. Under the positional model, however, rebel deviance was independent of whether or not an expert was a follower.[14] This link with relational pattern was reversed for eccentric deviance. Followers had a lower tendency than nonfollowers to be eccentric deviants. While four of five followers were never eccentric deviants under the relational model, half of the nonfollowers fell into this category with respect to at least one core journal.

In short, followers did not perceive journal significance in emulation of leaders within the college. Rather, they shared the interests of their structurally equivalent peers—even if they did not use those peers as sources of influential methodological comments. More specifically, they tended not to be interested in journals most valued by their sources of influential comments (i.e., they tended to be rebel deviants under the relational model), although they did not have an extraordinary interest in the journals to which these same sources gave little interest (i.e., they tended not to be eccentrics under the relational model).

Personal Involvement as a Condition for Deviance

Beyond supporting the positional model over the relational model, Table 6.9 suggests that some experts were deviant for personal reasons. For one thing, there is no contingency between rebel deviance and eccentric deviance. The

[14]This statement is based on an analysis of a tabulation of rebel deviance under either the relational or positional model for followers versus nonfollowers. Of the 20 nonfollowers, 8 were never classified as a rebel deviant under the relational or positional model, 4 were only classified as a rebel under the relational model, 4 were only classifed as a rebel under the positional model, and 4 were classified at least once as a rebel under either model (3 experts were classified as a rebel in regard to one or more journals by both models simultaneously). Of the 32 followers, the corresponding frequencies were 2, 13, 3, and 14, where 12 experts were classified as a rebel in regard to one or more journals by both models simultaneously. Fitting a log-linear model to this three-way tabulation yields only one significant interaction effect. The tendency for followers to be labeled as rebel deviants under the relational model is significant at beyond the .001 level of confidence (unit normal test statistic of 3.01). There is no tendency for the relational and positional models to label the same experts as rebel deviants (unit normal test statistic of .27) nor is there a tendency for followers to be labelled rebel deviants under the positional model (unit normal test statistic of .86). In fact, the hypothesis of no interaction between rebel deviance under the positional model and whether or not an expert is a follower is not rejected by the data ($\chi^2 = 1.52$ with 3 degrees of freedom so the null hypothesis has better than a .50 probability of being true).

chi-square statistic for the null hypothesis of no interaction between being a rebel deviant in regard to one or more journals and being an eccentric deviant in regard to one or more journals is .68 for both network models. With two degrees of freedom, this is negligible, indicating that there was no class of experts who tended to be deviant in one way as well as the other. Further, most experts were deviant in regard to only one or two journals. If there were some experts whose relational patterns were consistently responsible for deviance, then there should have been some experts who were deviant in regard to many journals. Yet most experts were deviant in regard to few, if any, journals (see footnote 13).

If experts expressed deviant interest in a journal for personal reasons, perhaps the most likely explanation can be found in their publication or editorial activities in the journal, as discussed earlier. If an expert published in a journal or was editorially responsible for its content, then he might have been biased toward perceiving a deviantly high significance in it. The results in Table 6.3 show that experts had an increased interest in a journal in some cases to the extent that they were personally involved with it. Alternatively, an expert might be prone to ignore a journal prescribed by his collegial alter if he had no responsibility for its content and had not published any work there.

Personal involvement, however, was not responsible for deviant interests on the part of the experts. Consider the data on deviance under the positional model with respect to the *American Journal of Sociology*. Table 6.10 presents a three-way tabulation of expert deviance and involvement in AJS as of 1975. Involvement is operationalized by two dichotomous variables: whether an expert had published in AJS (0 versus any nonzero score on PUB in Eq. [6.6]) and whether he exercised editorial control over methodological work appearing in AJS (0 versus any nonzero score on ED in Eq. [6.6]). The high interest of eccentrics might have been a result of their editing articles or having them

TABLE 6.10
Personal Involvement in the *American Journal of Sociology* and Deviance under the Positional Model

	Published			
	No		Yes	
	Edited		Edited	
	No	Yes	No	Yes
Rebel	1	0	2	0
Conformer	15	5	11	15
Eccentric	0	1	1	1

[a]Publishing and editing variables are explained in the text, and deviance categories are taken from Table 6.4.

published in AJS. Table 6.10 shows that there was an eccentric who had edited articles for AJS and been published there. However, there was also an eccentric who had not published there as well as one who had not served the journal in any editorial capacity. The lack of interest expressed by rebel deviants might have been a result of their not being involved in the journal. Table 6.10 shows that the three rebel deviants were experts who had not participated in editing AJS. However, two of these experts had had work published in the journal. Overall, there does not seem to be much support for the idea that personal involvement in AJS was responsible for experts' expressing a deviant interest in the journal under the positional model. This conclusion is corroborated by the insignificant chi-square obtained for the null hypothesis of no interaction among the three variables in Table 6.10 ($\chi^2 = 3.87$ with 6 degrees of freedom).

Table 6.10 was constructed for each of the eight core journals under both the relational model and the positional model. With one exception, the chi-square statistic for the null hypothesis of no interaction in each of the resulting 16 tables is negligible.[15] The results are presented in Table 6.11. The one exception is SSR, for which there was significant interaction between deviance and involvement at the .01 level of confidence. However, holding involvement constant and reestimating the unit normal tests in Tables 6.6 and 6.7 does not change the inferences made there. The reestimated test statistics show rebel deviants occurring with a slightly more than expected frequency under the relational model (test statistic of 1.43 versus the 1.2 in Table 6.6) and slightly less than expected frequency under the positional model (test statistic of -1.00 versus the -0.9 in Table 6.6). These effects are stronger than those reported earlier for SSR, but they are still negligible at the .05 level of significance. Controlling for publication and/or editing has no effect on test statistics regarding the prevalence of eccentric deviance.

---

[15]I considered a third order hypothesis that might have been true despite the insignificance of personal involvement in direct association with interest. Personal involvement could have led to deviance to different extents for different experts. Those who jointly occupied a network position with other experts would have been less likely to be deviant than a structurally unique expert, since the latter had so little in the way of structural peers on which to base a journal norm. The strongest effect of personal involvement on interest, therefore, might be expected among structurally unique experts in the college. This same idea was discussed in Section 5.5 as a prediction that actors should adopt an innovation for personal (rather than social) reasons to the extent that they are structurally unique in a system of potential adopters. This idea was not true of experts deviating from journal norms. For each core journal, chi-square statistics were computed for the hypothesis of no interaction among three variables: an expert who was structurally unique relative to other experts (a dichotomy constructed from the l_{jj}—low l_{jj} for nonunique experts high l_{jj} for structurally unique experts), his involvement in the journal (a dichotomy between those who had never published or edited the journal versus those who had done either), and his deviance in regard to the journal (eccentric, rebel, nondeviant). The results in Table 6.11 are by and large replicated, so I have not presented them. Of course, none of the elite experts was structurally unique in the network of methodology influence relations to any extreme extent (see footnote 4), so it is possible that more extreme differences in the l_{jj} between unique and nonunique experts could have resulted in significant interaction between deviance, involvement and being structurally unique within the college.

TABLE 6.11
The Lack of Interaction Between Deviance and Personal Involvement in Core Journals[a]

| | Test for lack of contingency between being published/editing and deviance | | | |
| | Relational Model | | Positional model | |
Core journals	χ^2	p	χ^2	p
American Sociological Review	2.62	>.5	.50	>.5
American Journal of Sociology	1.81	>.5	3.87	>.5
Sociological Methodology	5.93	~.43	4.11	>.5
Journal of the American Statistical Association	1.55	>.5	1.13	>.5
Sociological Methods & Research	3.35	>.5	2.33	>.5
Journal of Mathematical Sociology	2.21	>.5	4.93	>.5
Social Science Research	17.17	~.01	8.92	~.18
Social Forces	9.09	~.17	4.03	>.5

[a]Chi-square statistics are distributed with six degrees of freedom for the three-way tabulation in Table 6.10.

Although an expert's personal involvement can increase his interest in a journal above that expressed by his collegial alter, it does not explain extreme deviance from collegial alters. Whatever the reasons for experts' expressing deviant interest in one or two of the core journals, it is not their differential tendencies to edit articles or have them published in those few journals.

6.6 CONCLUSIONS

In short, the expressed interests of the elite experts in journals as outlets for significant work in sociological methodology could be viewed as reflections of journal norms systematically maintained by the network of interpersonal influences among the experts. There was a tendency for an expert's personal involvement with a journal, his level of being published in and/or editing the journal, to increase his interest in it above that expressed by his significant others as a collegial alter. However, this tendency was most pronounced for the less prominent of the core journals, only occurred in conjunction with a significant normative effect on expressed interest, and did not account for experts' occasionally expressing deviant interest in a journal.[16]

As a representation of the social mechanism responsible for journal norms in elite sociological methodology, the proposed model of structural interests seems to be superior to the more traditional relation model. The relational model states that an expert should have expressed interests similar to those expressed by persons from whom he acknowledged influential comments on his methodological work. This model builds on the classic argument that was presented by Festinger *et al.* (1950) and subsequently developed with more statistical sophistication by Coleman *et al.* (1966) and Duncan *et al.* (1968). The relational model offers two basic predictions in this context: experts connected by strong relations in what is commonly termed a clique should have shared journal interests, and followers tied to those experts as sources of influential comments should have emulated the interests of those experts as leaders. This second prediction was quite in error for the invisible college of elite sociological methodology. Followers tended not to be interested in the journals highly valued by their leaders (yet they showed no tendency to be highly interested in the journals to which their leaders gave low credence). Although the predicted homophily between leaders and followers is clearly implied in the network models utilized by Coleman *et al.* (1966) and Duncan *et.al.* (1968) since they make no effort to exclude follower to leader relations, it is not a feature of the original empirical analysis by Festinger and his colleagues. The original analysis simply shows that the prevalence of deviant group members declines with the density of strong relations among members of the group. One might argue that the relational model in Eq. (6.1) should be restricted to the original argument. For example, z_{ji} and z_{ij} might be forced to equal zero if either is 0. However, adopting this is proposal requires that the relational model be viewed almost as a special case of the structural interest model proposed in Chapter 5. The proposed model predicts homophilous interests among structurally equivalent experts jointly occupying the same position in the network of methodology influence relations. This homophily is expected as a result of each expert's symbolically role-playing the position of his structural peers in the college when he evaluates the significance of a journal article. Freed of the requirement that expert interests be determined only by actual communication between experts, the resulting positional model in Eq. (6.4) predicts that structurally equivalent experts would have shared the same interests as a journal norm whether or not they actually communicated with one another, i.e. whether they were followers

---

[16]These points have been discussed in the analysis; however, the contingency of a personal involvement effect on a normative effect is only true when the journal norms are defined by the positional model. Table 6.3 shows that for each journal asterisked, personal involvement effects only occur with an asterisked normative effect—except for SSR when journal norms are defined by the relational model. I have ignored this exception in my concluding remarks since I conclude that the relational model is inferior to the positional model as a representation of the social mechanism responsible for journal norms. Oddities occurring under the relational model are therefore of secondary importance.

or nonfollowers. This prediction seems to be true. Not only does the positional model do as well as the relational model in predicting the absence of deviant experts among nonfollowers (i.e., among members of a clique), it goes on to predict equally well the absence of deviant experts among followers—experts who had no direct relations with one another but whose unreciprocated relations to the same other experts within the college made them structurally equivalent to one another. In short, they key issues indicating the superiority of the positional model are accuracy and scope. The positional model was more accurate in predicting conformity to journal norms and more accurate in predicting the absence of deviance; in particular, the systematic error of the relational model's, predicting homophily between structurally nonequivalent experts tied by strong influence relations was avoided. If the relational model is restricted to its prediction of intraclique homophily, the two network models have equal accuracy. However, this means that the positional model has greater scope than the relational model, since the positional model explains the interests of experts within cliques as well as those of experts unconnected to one another who have in common their unreciprocated relations to others.

A second general conclusion concerns the substance of conformity and deviance in a network analysis of journal norms. Nonconformity with norms of journal significance does not in and of itself constitute deviance from those norms. Experts who did not acknowledge the significance of a prescribed journal have been distinguished in Table 6.4 as "rebel" deviants whereas those who were highly interested in journals to which their significant others gave little attention were discussed as "eccentric" deviants. On a surface level, these two types of deviation from a journal norm differ merely in the direction of quantitative difference between expressed interest and normative interest, eccentrics overestimating normative interest and rebels underestimating that interest. This interpretation is implicit in a regression model using normative interests to predict expressed interests. Such a model is the basis for the analysis of conformity in terms of Eq. (6.6). But there is more here than variation in conformity to journal norms. Rebels were actually rejecting the significance of a normatively prescribed journal. A comparable deviance would be overestimation of journal significance by an expert who perceived high significance in a normatively proscribed journal, a journal whose articles are stigmata on their authors in the eyes of their significant others. In practice, such journals rarely exist. Rather, there are journals that an academic and his or her significant others prescribe for one another. Nonprescribed journals are merely unimportant. An article in a nonprescribed journal is not a stigma on its author (unless he or she makes a practice of publishing there) but it does not contribute to the author's prominence in the eyes of his or her significant others. Accordingly, and as was stressed in discussing Table 6.4, the eccentric expert did not constitute a threat to consensual knowledge published in prescribed journals. This interpretation is reinforced by the analysis of deviant interests. An expert who was a rebel deviant had no significant tendency to be an eccentric deviant.

In other words, eccentrics were not experts who had rejected prescribed journals in favor of nonprescribed journals. They were merely experts who had an unexpected interest in a journal, an interest that was not based on their editing articles or having them published in the journal and that was not shared by their significant others. In contrast to the rebel's violation of journal norms, the eccentric was merely incongruent with those norms. The methodological point to this is that testing network models of social norms should distinguish between a simple lack of conformity to norms and their actual violation. It is the prevalence of the latter that best tests a model's adequacy. Note the relative clarity of substantive findings here concerning rebel versus eccentric deviants. Rebels occurred less often than would be expected by chance under the positional model and systematically occurred more often than would be expected by chance among followers under the relational model. Rebel deviants nicely distinguish the adequacy of the two network models. Eccentric deviants, in contrast, occurred with a frequency to be expected by chance. Their comparatively innocuous nonconformity to journal norms does not distinguish the two network models at all well.

These conclusions inform the original substantive problem with which I began the chapter, the problem of disentangling the reciprocally causal connection between the stratification of scientists within an invisible college and the stratification of journals in which their work receives the imprimatur of scientific knowledge. Members of the invisible college of elite sociological methodology conformed to past research in two senses. They perceived a stratification of reputable journals in which some core sociological methodology journals were the object of strong interest from many experts whereas less reputable journals did not receive widespread interest. Second, differences in the extent to which experts had published in the core sociological methodology journals accounted for differences in their prominence within the stratification of experts. The analysis here has shown that the relational patterns defining expert positions in that stratification in turn accounted for expert interest in specific journals. The model of structural interests in Chapter 5 describes the social mechanism responsible for expert journal interests as of 1975; experts symbolically occupied the positions of their structurally equivalent peers within the college when they made significance evaluations. As a result, structurally equivalent experts jointly occupying a position in the network of interpersonal influence relations among experts had similar interests in a journal as an outlet for significant work in sociological methodology. These similar interests occurred even if the structurally equivalent experts had no direct, influential communication with one another. With journal norms defined on the basis of jointly occupied positions in the invisible college, a general acceptance of an expert's occasional high interest in a journal ignored by his structural peers (eccentrics being accepted as legitimate deviants from journal norms), and social pressure against experts failing to maintain interest in a journal prescribed by their structural peers (rebels being converted or ostracized as threatening deviants from journal norms), some interesting inferences can be drawn regarding journal norms and the stability of stratification in elite sociological methodology.

A positive association could be expected between the prominence of a research group within the college and the clarity of their journal norms. In Chapter 3, I found that groups of elite experts varied in their prominence within the invisible college as a function of their successful merger of a methodological approach with a substantive area. The social statistics elite were most prominent and had renovated stratification research with structural equation models. The methodology leaders in social psychology were less prominent, and they split into two groups with different substantive concerns, one concerned with balance and transitivity in triads and the other concerned with general social psychology questions. Finally, the mathematical sociology elite were all but invisible as a status within the college, and they pursued a great diversity of substantive questions with an equally diverse array of methodological approaches. A group that had reached some consensus on how a substantive area should be researched could be expected to agree on specific journals as the best outlets for work in the area. The colleagues each member of the group used as alters in making significance evaluations should have agreed on certain journals as the best outlets for their work. Exposed to collegial alters expressing the same normative interests, members of a prominent group could have been expected to have comparatively homophilous journal norms; they would exhibit high consensus on journal norms. A group with low concensus on journal norms would be one whose members found their collegial alters expressing different journal interests, some members being exposed to one set of journal norms while others were exposed to different journal norms. Obviously, low concensus could be expected in a group whose members pursued diverse substantive and methodological questions. Moreover, the different journal norms to which they subscribed would facilitate their continued pursuit in those diverse directions since there would be no consensual pressure for their work to reflect developments previously appearing in a set of prescribed journals. In other words, journal norm concensus within a research group should not only result from the conditions making the group prominent as a status within an invisible college, it should contribute to that prominence by integrating the research efforts of group members in terms of their shared interests in the same prescribed journals.

Therefore, the stratification of elite sociological methodology in 1975 was reinforced by journal norms—and so likely to endure—to the extent that the rank order of journal norm concensus for the three groups of leaders in the college corresponds to their rank order prominence as described in Chapter 3 (especially Table 3.9). The social statistics elite should show the greatest concensus in journal norms. The methodology leaders in social psychology should show consensus, but at a lower level than that found among the social statistics elite. The mathematical sociology elite should show much less consensus than that exhibited by either of the other two groups.

Table 6.12 shows that this is precisely what is observed. Across the three groups of methodology leaders, Table 6.12 presents the percentage of leaders within a group sharing the modal journal norm for the group (high interest, some interest, low interest, as these three categories of normative interest were defined in Table 6.4), the specific journals which were the object of normative interest from the group, and the mean expressed interest for the group. The journal norm for a group was selected as the modal interest for the group, the category of normative interest (high, some, low values of x^*_{jkp}) containing the greatest number of group members. For example, the only journal prescribed for the social statistics elite (i.e., the only journal for which the modal normative interest was "high") was JASA. All of the social statistics elite had significant others who expressed high interest in JASA; 100% of these experts had the same journal norm. The average interest a member of the social statistics elite actually expressed in JASA was .51—a high level of interest relative to the mean of .16 for the whole college (see Table 6.1). About half of the interest a member of the social statistics elite gave to journals was given to JASA. Table 6.12 also presents information on journal norms of "some" interest. For example, three of the four of the social statistics elite had significant others who were interested in JMA and SSR, not at a high level, but within the interquartile

TABLE 6.12
Journal Norm Consensus in Three Groups of Elite Expert Leaders

	Social statistics elite	Methodology leaders in social psychology	Mathematical sociology elite
Prescribed journals			
Mean percentage with modal norm	100%	81%	58%
Journals $(\bar{x}_{jk})$	JASA (.51)	ASR (.30) SM (.17) JMS (.11)	ASR (.24) AJS (.15) JMS (.11)
Journals given moderate interest			
Mean percentage with modal norm	75%	71%	56%
Journals $(\bar{x}_{jk})$	JMS (.03) SSR (.02)	JASA (.12) AJS (.09) SMR (.05) SF (.02)	JASA (.14) SM (.14) SSR (.03)

range of normative interest for the college as a whole (see Table 6.4 on the category of "some" normative interest). Table 6.12 shows that the mean percentage of social statistics elite falling into the modal "some" normative interest category is 75% across these two journals. The interest they actually expressed in the journals is a little less, on average, than the mean interest expressed in them by the college as a whole (.03 versus a college mean of .05 for JMS and .02 versus a college mean of .03 for SSR; see Table 6.1).

A comparison across the three groups of leaders in Table 6.12 reveals that the highest norm concensus occurred among the social statistics elite; a lower level occurred among the methodology leaders in social psychology; and a much lower level occurred among the mathematical sociology elite. All of the social statistics elite (100%) had a journal norm of high interest in JASA. Of the six methodology leaders in social psychology, a mean of 81% had journal norms of high interest in ASR, SM, and JMS. Of the nine of the mathematical sociology elite, a mean of 58% had journal norms of high interest in ASR, AJS, and JMS. There is lower journal norm concensus regarding norms of some, rather than high, interest; however, the same relative levels of consensus are observed across the three groups of methodology leaders. The social statistics elite were most likely to share the same journal norm of some interest (75%); the methodology leaders were less likely (71%); and the mathematical sociology elite were comparatively much less likely (56%). In short, the rank order of consensus on journal norms among the three groups of methodology leaders is inversely linked to group prominence. The less prominent the group, the more likely that they pursued diverse intellectual questions legitimated by diverse journal norms. Members of the least prominent group, the mathematical sociology elite, were most likely to have different journal norms while members of the most prominent group, the social statistics elite, were least likely to disagree on journal norms.

My inference that stratification among the elite experts was reinforced by journal norms is strengthened by a consideration of journal norm consensus among experts jointly occupying secondary positions. These would be the followers within the college in the sense that they did not acknowledge one another as sources of influential comments, but had in common their influence relations to the same leaders.

Figure 3.3 shows that there were two such positions in the network of methodology influence relations. Occupants of position I_3 were the object of no influence relations and had in common their use of the social statistics elite and methodology leaders in social psychology as sources of influential comments on their methodological work. They also went to the mathematical sociology elite for such comments, but much less often. Occupants of position I_6 were also the object of no influence relations. They had in common their use of the social statistics elite and the mathematical sociology elite as sources of influential comments on their methodological work. They too went to methodology leaders in social psychology for such comments, but much less often.

TABLE 6.13
Journal Norm Consensus in Two Groups of Elite Experts Occupying Secondary Positions

	Position I_3	Position I_6
Prescribed journals		
Mean percentage with modal norm	75%	82%
Journals ($\bar{x}_{jk}$)	ASR (.22)	SM (.21)
	AJS (.17)	AJS (.18)
	SMR (.18)	SMR (.07)
		SSR (.06)
Journals given moderate interest		
Mean percentage with modal norm	75%	82%
Journals ($\bar{x}_{jk}$)	SM (.11)	ASR (.19)
	SF (.04)	JASA (.05)
	SSR (.02)	JMS (.04)
	JMS (.01)	SF (.02)

Table 6.13 presents the same information on journal norms among followers that Table 6.12 presented on leaders. I wish to emphasize two points.

First, there was considerable journal norm consensus among experts occupying secondary positions. Three out of four occupants of position I_3 fell into the modal category of normative interest in a journal when their collegial alters expressed high or some interest in the journal. This rate increases to four out of five for the experts occupying position I_6. This level of journal norm consensus is roughly equivalent to the level observed among the social statistics elite and methodology leaders in social psychology. It is much higher than the level of consensus observed among the mathematical sociology elite.

Second, this journal norm consensus included journals uniquely prescribed for experts occupying secondary positions. Table 6.13 shows that occupants of position I_3 had collegial alters expressing high normative interest in ASR, AJS, and SMR. Methodological work by experts occupying this position was most influenced by comments from the social statistics elite and methodology leaders in social psychology. AJS and SMR were not prescribed journals for either of these groups of leaders, although both journals had journal norms of some interest among the methodology leaders in social psychology. Occupants of position I_3 had collegial alters expressing high normative interest in SM, AJS, SMR, and SSR. Their methodological work was most influenced by comments from the social statistics elite and mathematical sociology elite. SM, SMR, and SSR were not prescribed journals for either of these groups of leaders, although SSR had a journal norm of some interest among both groups of leaders, and SM had the same journal norm among the mathematical sociology elite. SSR was also a prescribed journal among occupants of position I_2, a position whose occupant experts relied on the social statistics elite for influential methodology comments (see Figure 3.3). In other words, SMR and SSR were not prescribed journals among leaders in the college, but they were legitimated by journal norms of high interest for experts occupying secondary positions. Leader and follower norms suggest that the two journals would have differed in content, with SMR receiving more manuscripts on social psychology while SSR would have received more manuscripts on sophisticated mathematical and statistical models.

The above two points taken together suggest to me that journal norms can be viewed as stabilizing the existence of secondary positions in elite sociological methodology. The prescribed journals for the leading experts would be the outlets in which one could expect to see mathematical or statistical innovations that affected the practice of sociological methodology generally. But there is a great deal of methodological work that is not a major innovation so much as it is a necessary component in the continuing development of sociological methodology. In the words of Thomas Kuhn, there is some work that could be termed "revolutionary" methodology and other work that is better termed "normal" methodology in the sense that it does not attempt to replace old ways of thinking with new ones so much as it attempts to make more complete our understanding of existing methodology. The people most likely to be exclusively involved in producing normal methodology in this sense are the occupants of secondary positions. They can be viewed as brokers between the leading figures in sociological methodology and persons outside the invisible college, occupants of secondary positions producing methodological work frankly building on innovations sponsored by occupants of primary positions. This is not to say that methodology leaders would never build on one another's innovations, but rather methodology leaders are more likely than followers to be responsible for significant innovations in sociological methodology. There must be journals to serve as outlets for normal methodology if persons involved in such work are to continue with such work. Not only must there be journals available to publish papers on normal methodology, those journals must be legitimated as outlets for significant work. No one wants to be the author of papers on trivial methodological questions. Therefore, I perceive the high consensus on journal norms which uniquely prescribe some journals among experts occupying secondary positions as a reinforcement to the stability of those positions. These journal norms seem to me to have had the potential to legitimate normal methodology as significant work, thereby legitimating the probable research activities of experts occupying secondary positions in an invisible college composed of elite experts in sociological methodology.

The bottom line here is that the analysis of journal norms extends and solidifies the analysis in Chapter 3 of stratification alone. Beyond demonstrating the superiority of the proposed model of structural interests over the relational model in sociometry as its principal alternative, and beyond demonstrating the importance of analyzing deviance as well as conformity with respect to norms purportedly patterned by social networks, the analysis of journal norms corroborates my earlier conclusion regarding the stability of stratification among the elite experts. Not only does the social structure of the college appear to be stable in terms of the relational patterns in which experts were involved, as described in Chapter 3, but journal norms prescribing specific journals as outlets for significant work can be interpreted as reinforcing the stratification of experts as it existed in 1975.

THIRD COMPONENT: ACTION

7

Autonomy and Cooptation*

Our relational patterns in society bind us to one another through a division of labor ensuring our interdependency and stratification across multiple status/role-sets. But these patterns neither bind the occupants of different statuses in the same manner nor to the same extent. My purpose in this chapter is to propose a model of the manner in which the role-set defining a status determines its occupants' "structural autonomy" within their system—their ability to pursue and realize interests without constraint from other actors in the system.[1]

*Portions of this chapter are drawn with revisions from an article reprinted with the permission of the *American Journal of Sociology* (Burt 1980a).

[1] This phrase "without constraint from other actors in the system" is to be emphasized here. It explicitly excludes from the domain of autonomy those interests that involve deliberate opposition from other actors. In order to realize interests "despite constraint from other actors in the system" an actor needs to have high power within the system. A discussion of power in terms of network positions within a social topology is given elsewhere (Burt 1977a, 1979b). While a hermit can have autonomy, few would consider him powerful. Also, autonomy as it is discussed here does not consider behaviors that are performed after the original impetus for performance has disappeared. Such a view of autonomy is elaborated, for example, by Simmel (1917:41–43) as "the autonomization of contents," by Allport (1937, 1961:Chap. 10) as "functional autonomy," and by Kelman (1961) as "internalization." Piaget's (1932:Chap. 3) discussion of "moral autonomy" in terms of the internalization of rules and subsequent demand for justice in the establishment of rules mixes the treatment given here with the previously cited discussions of behavior without impetus.

I begin by distinguishing two aspects of autonomy, oligopoly in economics and conflicting group-affiliations in sociology. The two are captured algebraically in terms of network structure and brought together in a structural model of autonomy. The model indicates the relative autonomy of status occupants within a system and the extent to which occupants of any one status are constrained by their role relations with occupants of each other status. These constraints indicate the places in social structure where cooptive relations should appear as well as the places where they should not appear.

7.1 AUTONOMY AS A STRUCTURAL CONCEPT

Figure 2.4 presents a diagram of the social context in which occupants of status S_j evaluate and take actions. The model of structural interests in Chapter 5 implies that occupants of a status will have common interests to the extent that they equally control resources and will have common interests regardless of their resource control whenever those interests are ambiguously tied to empirical events. In pursuing those interests, however, the occupants of status S_j must contend with the occupants of other statuses also pursuing their own interests. To the extent that they can pursue their interests without constraint from occupants of other statuses, actors occupying status S_j collectively have high autonomy within their system. The question I wish to address here concerns the link between the relational pattern defining their status (the elements in row/column j of Figure 2.4) and their relative autonomy. Note that I am concerned with the autonomy of occupying a position (not with the autonomy of particular actors per se) and am concerned with the relative autonomy of occupying separate positions (not with an absolute level of autonomy per se).

There seem to me to be two basic aspects to the idea of being autonomous in the above sense. Political economists have developed the concept of oligopoly while sociologists have focused on the concept of conflicting group-affiliations.

Oligopoly

Developing Adam Smith's discussion in *The Wealth of Nations* (1776) political economists treat the concept of autonomy in terms of collusion resulting in oligopolistic statuses. As a consequence of competition among actors in a market system, "market prices" for any type of commodity (the prices for which the commodity is "sold") gravitate toward the "natural price" for the commodity (the price for which the commodity can be brought to market). Actors are equally constrained by the balancing of supply and demand through competition. The division of labor ensures that types of positions develop where each position is jointly occupied by actors who produce similar commodities, drawing supplies from the same types of other actors and making their sales to the same types of other actors. This means that interactor competition is sharpest between actors jointly occupying a status; each actor occupying the status is the structural equivalent of, and therefore substitutable for, other actors occupying the status.[2] To the extent that decision-making is centralized among structurally equivalent actors, the actors define an oligopoly able to eliminate competition within their position. They accordingly escape the constraints of supply and demand. The autonomy of actors in an oligopoly, with regard to the constraint of supply and demand, is illustrated by their ability to raise the market price for their "commodity" far above the natural price (cf. Stigler 1964; Shepherd 1970:11–47).[3]

Thus, one aspect of autonomy concerns the relations among actors jointly occupying a status in a system. This is element (j,j) in Figure 2.4. The actors jointly occupying position j will be able to escape the constraints of supply and demand imposed by actors in other positions (and accordingly will be autonomous within their system) to the extent that among persons[4] or corporate actors[5] occupying the position there exists an oligopoly (few competitive

---

[2]The idea that structurally equivalent actors are substitutable goods and have substitutable perceptions is elaborated elsewhere (Burt 1979b). The idea that intrastatus competition is particularly intense is implied by the structural model proposed in Chapter 5 in the sense that one actor's gain in resources is a perceived loss in utility for actors jointly occupying the status. In order to make up, and/or avoid, such losses, each occupant of a status can be expected to feel competition with cooccupants of the status (see Section 5.4 on relative deprivation and Section 5.5 on innovation adoption).

[3]A similar idea is mentioned in Weber's (1925) discussion of economic systems. He suggests the idea of "market power" as "the degree of autonomy enjoyed by the parties to market relationships in price determination and in competition [p.182]."

[4]In his discussion of the determinants of wages and the advantages of employers over laborers given by the greater ease with which the former are capable of organizing to collectively oppose the interests of the latter, for example, Smith (1776:66) states:

> It is not, however, difficult to foresee which of the two parties must, upon all ordinary occasions, have the advantage in the dispute, and force the other into a compliance with their terms. The masters, being fewer in number, can combine much more easily; and the law, besides, authorises, or at least does not prohibit their combinations, while it prohibits those of the workmen.

Locke (1689:Chap. 5) develops a similar theme in which individuals forced to sell their labor in order to survive are less able to compete in society than are individuals whose accumulated capital goods enable them to purchase the labor of others (cf. Macpherson's 1962:221–238 discussion of how Locke generalizes this argument from an exchange of property to a loss of natural rights).

[5]After making general remarks concerning the monopolistic purpose of corporations (Smith 1776:123–129), Smith considers some corporate actors in detail, e.g., the wool industry (pp. 612–619) and the trading companies with exclusive franchises in the colonies (pp. 557–606), as supporting evidence. Examples more meaningful in current industrial society are discussed by Bain (1959) and Kaysen and Turner (1959). Shepherd (1970:39–42) reviews characteristics of the presence of few independent firms within a sector of the economy as "internal market structure."

decision-makers) or in the extreme of centralization, a monopoly (a single decision-maker). Let y_{j1} be a measure of the extent to which decision-making within position j is centralized where $0 \leq y_{j1} \leq 1$. Alternative centrality models are reviewed in Chapter 2 (see Sections 2.4 and 2.8, particularly the latter). Whatever centrality model is chosen, its essential feature here is the extent to which all occupants of a position can act as a single actor in pursuing their collective interest(s).

Group Affiliation

What if collusion develops between actors in separate sectors of the market so that the entire market becomes what sociologists term an undifferentiated, cohesive system? Then actors in each sector are constrained by their lack of differentiated relations to other actors in the system. Durkheim's *The Division of Labor in Society* (1893) at a macrolevel and Simmel's *Web of Group-Affiliations* (1922) at a more microlevel contain discussions emphasizing the constraining effects of an absence of differentiation within a system of actors.

For both Durkheim and Simmel, differential freedom from constraint by society occurs as a result of differential complexity in an actor's relations to other actors.[6] Durkheim focuses on the balancing of forces between occupational groups as statuses created in a division of labor[7] and the moral authority

---

[6]I have deliberately replaced the term autonomy with freedom in this sentence because Durkheim and Simmel use the term autonomy differently even though they similarly emphasize what has been discussed here as a group-affiliation hypothesis. Simmel uses autonomy to refer to the content of relations that are continued to be performed after the original impetus for the relations is gone ("autonomization of contents," Simmel 1917:41–42). Durkheim uses "moral individualism" to refer to what is here discussed as autonomy. His (1925:95–126) discussion of autonomy is a mixture of what is here outlined as autonomy and Piaget's (1932) discussion of autonomy as morality based on an understanding of the rules by which action is guided as "fair" or "just" rules.

[7]To say that the division of labor creates a stratification of statuses at some point in time does not in itself add to the oligopoly hypothesis. Indeed, the assumption of fixed requirements in input–output analysis corresponds to just such a condition. Instead of freely choosing transactions for the exchange of property, actors freely choose to occupy positions, i.e., sectors, within the system, and the capacity of actors occupying a position to restrict free entry to their position can be treated under the oligopoly hypotheses (cf. Bain 1956). It is by a consideration of the form and content of the pattern of relations defining a position that the group-affiliation hypothesis as represented in Durkheim's discussion differs from the oligopoly hypothesis.

[8]Actors are occupants of professions, and these professions are constrained by the authority of the government. Durkheim (1893:131) views this liberation of the actor from the direct authority of either profession or government favorably:

> Even in the exercise of our occupation, we conform to usages, to practices which are common to our whole professional brotherhood. But, even in this instance, the yoke that we submit to is much less heavy than when society completely controls us, and it leaves

of government.[8] Simmel (1908) focuses on the competition among groups linked to an actor for his attention and conformity.[9] He emphasizes the potential oppression of relations with groups unchecked by competition from other relations:

> Almost all relations—of the state, the party, the family, of friendship or love—quite naturally, as it were, seem to be on an inclined plane: if they were left to themselves, they would extend their claims over the whole of man. . . . But it is not only through the extensity of claims that the egoism of every sociation threatens the freedom of the individuals engaged in it. It does so also through the relentlessness of the claim itself, which is one-tracked and monopolistic. Usually, each claim presses its rights in complete and pitiless indifference to other interests and duties, no matter whether they be in harmony or in utter incompatibility with it [p.121].

In other words, competitive claims by groups of actors can be balanced against one another to limit constraint from others. This principle works for those occupying positions of authority as well as for those occupying subordinate

---

much more place open for the free play of our initiative. Here, then, the individuality of all grows at the same time as that of its parts. Society becomes more capable of collective movement, at the same time that each of its elements has more freedom of movement.

He (Durkheim 1906:72) is more general at a later date in his response to a critic claiming that "civilization" is the continuing liberation of man from the material structure of society:

These rights and liberties are not things inherent in man as such. If you analyse man's constitution you will find no trace of this sacredness with which he is invested and which confers upon him these rights. This character has been added to him by society. Society has consecrated the individual and made him preeminently worthy of respect. His progressive emancipation does not imply a weakening but a transformation of the social bonds. The individual does not tear himself from society but is joined to it in a new manner, and this is because society sees him in a new manner and wishes this change to take place. The individual submits to society and this submission is the condition of his liberation.

[9]Giving attention to the pattern of multiple ties between an individual and multiple disparate groups in society, Simmel (1922) points out a cycle of causation between the individual's position as a set of ties to groups and actions undertaken by the individual:

The groups with which the individual is affiliated constitute a system of coordinates, as it were, such that each new group with which he becomes affiliated circumscribes him more exactly and more unambiguously. . . . As the person becomes affiliated with a social group, he surrenders himself to it. A synthesis of such subjective affiliations creates a group in an objective sense. But the person also regains his individuality, because his pattern of participation is unique; hence the fact of multiple group-participation creates in turn a new subjective element. *Causal determination of, and purposive actions by, the individual appear as two sides of the same coin* [pp.140–141, emphases added].

He (1922) concludes after reviewing issues in multiple group affiliation, "Thus one can say that society arises from the individual and that the individual arises out of association [p. 163]."

positions.[10] Autonomy is high for actors occupying a position with many conflicting group affiliations and low for those occupying a position affiliated with only one other position.

It is important to recall that the intent here is to describe the autonomy of a jointly occupied position rather than that of an actor per se. Under the idea of group affiliation, actors jointly occupying a position that forms an oligopoly are subject to the constraints of the oligopoly. These constraints, in contrast to autonomy by means of oligopoly relative to other positions, actually serve to limit the autonomy of the individual wishing to deviate from other actors occupying his position. Substantively, the constraint on individual actors of being too strongly integrated into a group of similar others is documented in a range of studies such as Festinger *et al.*'s (1950) description of the formation of social norms within cohesive groups of students at MIT, Riesman's (1950: Chap. 14) description of "enforced privatization" as the constraints one's peers enforce concerning appropriate behaviors for someone occupying their position in society, Bott's (1957) description of the formation of conjugal roles as a function of a husband and wife's being absorbed into separate cohesive groups, and Gans's (1962) description of the maintenance of social norms among Italian-Americans in Boston's West End through cohesive "peer" groups. In contrast to these studies, I am concerned with the relative autonomy of separate positions. My use of the term group affiliations accordingly refers to the affiliations of actors with occupants of other positions rather than to affiliations among structurally equivalent actors.

Thus, a second aspect of autonomy concerns the manner in which actors jointly occupying a status are related to actors occupying other statuses in their system. These are the elements of row and column j in Figure 2.4 excluding element (j,j). Actors jointly occupying position j will be able to balance demands on them from other actors (and accordingly will be "autonomous" within their system) to the extent that the pattern of relations defining position j ensures high competition among those actors who interact with the occupants of position j. Autonomy through group affiliation emphasizes two characteristics of the pattern of relations defining a position. First, actors occupying position j will have high autonomy to the extent that they have relations to many other statuses rather than only with one other. Second, actors occupying position j

---

[10]Simmel (1896) emphasizes the symbiotic constraints imposed on actors occupying positions of authority by actors occupying the positions over which authority is exercised and vice versa. Riesman (1950:Chaps. 13,14) provides illustrations relevant to our day-to-day experience in his elaboration of two impediments to an individual's having high autonomy; "false personalization" and "enforced privatization." The former refers to autonomy that is lowered because of an individual's absorption in artificial social relations arising from occupancy of a position rather than from relations necessary to the position (e.g., the need of a secretary, whose life outside the office is dull, for personalistic rather than universalistic relations with the employers [Riesman 1950:264–266]), and the latter refers to autonomy that is lowered when other occupants of the position place constraints on what is proper behavior for someone occupying their position.

will have high autonomy to the extent that the statuses of those occupants with whom they do have relations are not oligopolies. In other words, a measure of autonomy through group affiliation must be based on two things: the extent to which actors occupying a status have diversified relations with other statuses and the extent to which they have relations only with statuses that are themselves too poorly organized to make collective demands.

Simply stated, the extent to which these two characteristics are found in the relational pattern defining status S_j in Figure 2.4 is captured by the following group affiliation index (where $j \neq i$):

$$y_{j2} = [2 - \sum_{i=1}^{M} (a_{ji})]/2,$$

$$= [2 - \sum_{i=1}^{M} (y_{i1} \{z_{ij}/\sum_{q} z_{qj}\}^2 + y_{i1}\{z_{ji}/\sum_{q}^{M} z_{jq}\}^2)]/2, \qquad (7.1)$$

where z_{ji} is the typical relation from actors occupying status S_j to those occupying status S_i, y_{i1} is the above-mentioned centrality measure of oligopoly among the occupants of status S_i, and M is the number of statuses across which actors are stratified in the system. For each status S_i other than S_j, the component a_{ji} measures the extent to which the status is an oligopoly and all the relations involving occupants of S_j link them with the occupants of S_i. This component ranges from a value of 0 to its maximum of 2. It equals 2 when the occupants of S_j are only involved in relations with the occupants of S_i and that status is perfectly centralized ($y_{i1} = 1$). The component approaches 0 as occupants of S_i are completely decentralized ($y_{i1} = 0$) or have no relations with the occupants of S_j ($z_{ji} = z_{ij} = 0$). The sum of these a_{ji} across all statuses S_i (excluding S_j itself) varies from 0 to 2 as the extent to which the occupants of S_j have relations with a single, oligopolistic status. In other words, the sum of the a_{ji} in Eq. (7.1) measures the lack of conflicting affiliations in the role-set defining status S_j. This sum is therefore subtracted from its maximum and divided by its maximum in Eq. (7.1) to yield y_{j2}, a variable ranging from 0 to 1 as the extent to which the occupants of status S_j are not constrained in their relations with other statuses by a lack of conflicting group affiliations.

Structural Autonomy

Autonomy by means of oligopoly and autonomy by means of group affiliation seem to be complementary aspects of autonomy rather than alternative concepts. The separation of them in the past can be attributed, it seems to me, to disciplinary history rather than to substantive necessity. It seems reasonable, therefore, to propose a network concept of autonomy that is a simple combination of these two well-known aspects, oligopoly capturing the effect of relations among structurally equivalent actors occupying a status and group affiliation capturing the effect of relations linking those occupants to other statuses.

As a simple first approximation, status S_j can be said to offer its occupants high structural autonomy to the extent that its role set has three character-istics:

1. There is high centralization among occupants of the status such that they form an oligopoly. This would occur as a high value of y_{j1}.
2. Relations with other statuses are diversified and exist only with statuses that do not themselves constitute oligopolies. This would occur as a high value of y_{j2}.
3. The first two conditions occur simultaneously as an interaction effect; the autonomy increasing effect of centralization among status occupants is increased by the lack of organization among the actors with whom they have relations.

These three conditions together determine the structural autonomy a_j of occupying status S_j in the following equation:

$$a_j = b + b_o y_{j1} + b_g y_{j2} + b_x y_{j1} y_{j2},   \tag{7.2a}$$

where b_o, b_g, and b_x, respectively, weight the above three characteristics determining structural autonomy. The constant b is specified in the equation as no more than an arbitrary adjustment to the scale on which structural autonomy is measured. It does not affect the relative meaning of scores, and the scores do not have an absolute value as I stressed earlier. Structural autonomy is analyzed here as an interval, as opposed to a ratio, measure. This interval quality to the measure makes the following equation better suited to statistically testing the three effects on structural autonomy even though it defines values of a_j identical to those defined by Eq. (7.2a):[11]

---

[11] Parameters in Eq. (7.2) will be estimated as regression coefficients predicting some outcome measure of structural autonomy (e.g., see Eq. [8.2]). With the interaction term in the equation, the slopes b_o and b_g will increase as y_{j1} and y_{j2} increase (since the interaction effect b_x is expected to be positive). For example, when $y_{j2} = 0$, structural autonomy is defined as $a_j = b + b_o y_{j1}$. When $y_{j2} = 1$, it is defined as $a_j = b + b_g + (b_o + b_x) y_{j1}$. The slope of status structural autonomy A over status oligopoly Y_1 increases with decreasing oligopoly among those with whom the status occupants interact, i.e., increases with increases in Y_2. Conceptually, this is precisely how the model is intended to perform. Oligopoly within a status provides higher autonomy for status occupants when they interact with competitive others than when they are obliged to interact with oligopolistic others (this point is discussed in detail elsewhere in an application of the structural autonomy model, Burt 1983:Chap. 2). However, note that the slope b_o is the slope of structural autonomy over oligopoly only when $y_{j2} = 0$. The slope b_g is similarly the slope of structural autonomy over conflicting group affiliations only when $y_{j1} = 0$, ($a_j = b + b_g y_{j2}$ when $y_{j1} = 0$). But structural autonomy (as well as its component concepts of oligopoly and conflicting group affiliations) is an interval scale rather than a ratio scale. It does not have a meaningful zero point so

$$\mathbf{a}_j = \beta + \beta_o y_{j1} + \beta_g y_{j2} + \beta_x (y_{j1} - \bar{y}_1)(y_{j2} - \bar{y}_2). \qquad (7.2b)$$

The positive effect of oligopoly on structural autonomy is given by β_o, the positive effect of conflicting group affiliations is given by β_g, and their positive interaction effect is given by β_x. Empirical results in the next chapter suggest that the effects of oligopoly and group affiliations are equally significant and both approximately two and a half times the significance of their interaction effect.

Equation (7.2) can be summarized thus: The occupants of status $\mathbf{S}_j$ in Figure 2.4 enjoy high structural autonomy within their system to the extent that their relational patterns ensure low competition with one another while simultaneously ensuring high competition among the nonoccupant actors with whom they interact.

7.2 COOPTATION

Besides indicating the relative autonomy of status occupants across statuses in a system, Eq. (7.2) also indicates where cooptive relations should occur in the system. Cooptive relations have been discussed in Chapter 4; however, there is merit in restating Selznick's (1949) brief definition here: "Coöptation is the process of absorbing new elements into the leadership or policy determining structure of an organization as a means of averting threats to its stability or existence [p.13]."

Without doing violence to Selznick's analysis of corporate actors, I wish to extend this idea to actors in general, and I shall refer to a "cooptive" relation w_{ji} as an informal relation giving the actor(s) occupying position j some effect on decision(s) made by actor(s) occupying position i. By an informal relation, I refer to a relation that is relatively dependent on, or at the discretion of, the individuals performing the relation. This is in contrast to a formal relation such as a role or technical requirement that is imposed on the individuals performing

---

much as it has relative meaning in the sense of one status offering more autonomy than another. Accordingly, estimates of the parameters b_o and b_g in Eq. (7.2a) are difficult to interpret. They refer to the effects of oligopoly (Y_1) and conflicting group affiliations (Y_2) under substantively uninterpreted conditions. What I have done in Eq. (7.2b) is to specify these effects at the center of the data distributions for a system, i.e., at the mean values of Y_1 and Y_2 for a system. This seems to be a more substantively appropriate point at which to evaluate the effects in much the same way that a score on an interval variable has greater substantive meaning as a deviation from its mean rather than as a raw score. The slope β_o in Eq. (7.2b) is the slope of structural autonomy over oligopoly when y_{j2} equals the mean value of Y_2 within the system under study, and β_g is similarly the slope of structural autonomy over conflicting group affiliations when y_{j1} equals the mean value of Y_1 within the system. The oligopoly effect β_o is the direct effect of Y_1 on average across values of Y_2. The group affiliation effect β_g is the direct effect of Y_2 on average across values of Y_1. For details on the identical values of a_j generated by Eqs. (7.2a) and (7.2b) and the fact that they estimate identical interaction effects (i.e., $b_x = \beta_x$), see Allison (1977). Marsden (1981b) provides a useful discussion of interpreting effects in regression model containing interaction terms.

the relation.[12] Within a corporate bureaucracy, for example, lines of authority would be formal relations between actors as employees. Their friendship ties would be informal relations between actors as individuals. Authority relations would be formal in the sense that the people to whom one gives direction and from whom one takes direction are defined by one's "job." Friendship relations in this context would be informal in the sense that they could be created and destroyed at the discretion of the individuals engaged in them. Of course, a friendship need not be cooptive. But if a friendship relation in this context is used to affect another person's decisions, the friendship is a cooptive relation in the sense used here. Persons with a "friend" in the purchasing department, for example, seem to get their requests filled more quickly than do persons without such a friend.

Thinking back to the social context in which occupants of status S_j operate (Figure 2.4), a cooptive relation w_{ji} should appear wherever such a relation could increase the autonomy of S_j's occupants—assuming that cooptive relations were being used to eliminate constraints on the occupants.

The increased autonomy resulting from cooptive relations among the occupants of S_j is given by the partial derivative of Eq. (7.2) with respect to the level of oligopoly within the status. This assumes that cooptive relations among occupants increase their potential for collusion so that they can better act as an oligopoly. There should be significant cooptation among occupants of status S_j (i.e., $w_{jj} > 0$) as long as they are not more constrained by actors in the system than are status occupants on average, i.e., as long as they are not subject to high constraint from actors not occupying their status. This proposition expresses in words the partial derivative of a_j with respect to an increase in y_{j1} (assuming that the infinitesimal increase in y_{j1} would not affect the mean value across all statuses, $\bar{y}_1$):

$$\partial a_j / \partial y_{j1} = b_o + b_x y_{j2},$$
$$= (\beta_o + \beta_x \bar{y}_2) + \beta_x y_{j2},$$
$$= \beta_o - \beta_x (y_{j2} - \bar{y}_2). \qquad (7.3)$$

Since β_o and β_x are positive, this partial derivative is positive as long as the occupants of S_j have an above average lack of constraint from other statuses; otherwise the term $\beta_x(y_{j2} - \bar{y}_2)$ is negative. If constraint from other statuses is so high that this term exceeds β_o, then $\partial a_j / \partial y_{j1}$ will be negative, implying that occupants of S_j would not obtain an increase in their autonomy from a small increase in their centralization. In such a circumstance, a large increase in

---

[12]This formal–informal contrast is not to be confused with Granovetter's (1973) strong–weak contrast. Strong relations differ from weak relations in terms of the form of a relation; strong relations are far more intense than weak relations. In the formal–informal contrast, I wish merely to highlight two extremes in the content of relations, formal relations being far more subject than informal relations to social sanctions or technical requirements beyond the control of the individuals performing the relations.

centralization (y_{j1}) is needed, or more importantly, a change in their relations with other statuses is needed so that y_{j2} decreases.

In order to predict interstatus cooptive relations, Eq. (7.2) must be disaggregated. The additive form of the group affiliation index facilitates this disaggregation—under the bold assumption that the group affiliation and interaction effects are linear over each sector's contribution to the index y_{j2}. Stating the group affiliation index in terms of its component a_{ji}, Eq. (7.2) can be rewritten in terms of the contribution relations with each status $\mathbf{S}_i$ make to the structural autonomy of $\mathbf{S}_j$'s occupants:

$$\mathbf{a}_j = b + b_o y_{j1} + b_g(y_{j2}) + b_x y_{j1}(y_{j2}),$$

$$= b + b_o y_{j1} + b_g\left(1 - \sum_i^M .5a_{ji}\right) + b_x y_{j1}\left(1 - \sum_i^M .5a_{ji}\right), \qquad j \neq i$$

$$= b + b_g + (b_o + b_x)y_{j1} - \sum_i^M (b_g + b_x y_{j1}) .5a_{ji}, \qquad j \neq i$$

$$= b + b_g + \sum_i^M a_{ji}^*$$

where a_{jj}^* is the contribution of status oligopoly $(b_o + b_x)y_{j1}$, so that the extent to which relations between occupants of statuses of $\mathbf{S}_j$ and $\mathbf{S}_i$ contribute to the autonomy of occupying $\mathbf{S}_j$ can be written as the ratio

$$\mathbf{a}_{ji} = a_{ji}^*/\mathbf{a}_j. \qquad (7.4)$$

The raw contributions a_{ji}^* have been normalized by structural autonomy for status $\mathbf{S}_j$, $\mathbf{a}_j$, in order to facilitate comparisons of the $\mathbf{a}_{ji}$ across separate statuses $\mathbf{S}_j$. As defined by Eq. (7.4), $\mathbf{a}_{ji}$ is a marginal contribution to status structural autonomy. Consider intrastatus, then interstatus ties.

Centralization among occupants of status $\mathbf{S}_j$ will always make a nonnegative contribution to the structural autonomy of occupying the status. Given $\mathbf{a}_{jj}$ as $(b_o + b_x)y_{j1}/\mathbf{a}_j$, its definition in terms of the coefficients in Eq. (7.2b) is[13]

$$\mathbf{a}_{jj} = [\beta_o + \beta_x(1 - \bar{y}_2)]y_{j1}/\mathbf{a}_j.$$

Since β_o and β_x are positive and $\bar{y}_2$ must lie between 0 and 1, $\mathbf{a}_{jj}$ is positive. Note

---

[13]The connections between parameters in Eqs. (7.2a) and (7.2b) are easily demonstrated (see Allison 1977 for further discussion). Equation (7.2b) can be rewritten as

$$\mathbf{a}_j = (\beta + \beta_x \bar{y}_1 \bar{y}_2) + (\beta_o - \beta_x \bar{y}_2)y_{j1} + (\beta_g - \beta_x \bar{y}_1)y_{j2} + \beta_x y_{j1} y_{j2},$$

which defines the following equivalences when compared to Eq. (7.2a);

$$b = (\beta + \beta_x \bar{y}_1 \bar{y}_2), \qquad b_o = (\beta_o - \beta_x \bar{y}_2), \qquad b_g = (\beta_g - \beta_x \bar{y}_1),$$

and

$$b_x = \beta_x.$$

that the numerator in this expression is identical to the partial derivative in Eq. (7.3) with y_{j2} replaced by its maximum value of 1. In other words, the maximum increase in structural autonomy that would be expected to result from an infinitesimal increase in status oligopoly is given by the numerator in the above expression. If competition among other actors were a maximum so that y_{j2} were equal to 1, then the partial derivative of $\mathbf{a}_j$ with respect to y_{j1} would be defined by Eq. (7.3) as $[\beta_o + \beta_x(1 - \bar{y}_2)]$, so that the increase in structural autonomy expected from status centralization increasing from 0 to its existing level of y_{j1} would be the product of this partial derivative and y_{j1}; $d(\mathbf{a}_j) = [\partial \mathbf{a}_j/\partial y_{j1}]y_{j1} = [\beta_o + \beta_x(1 - \bar{y}_2)]y_{j1}$. This is the numerator in the above definition of $\mathbf{a}_{jj}$. As the ratio of this expected increase over existing structural autonomy, $\mathbf{a}_j$, in other words, the coefficient $\mathbf{a}_{jj}$ can be interpreted as the marginal contribution status oligopoly makes to status structural autonomy.

Relations between occupants of statuses $\mathbf{S}_j$ and $\mathbf{S}_i$ will typically make a nonpositive contribution to the structural autonomy of occupying $\mathbf{S}_j$. Given $\mathbf{a}_{ji}$ as $-.5(b_g + b_x y_{j1})a_{ji}/a_j$, its definition in terms of the coefficients in Eq. (7.2b) is

$$\mathbf{a}_{ji} = [\beta_x(\bar{y}_1 - y_{j1}) - \beta_g]\,[a_{ji}/2]/a_j.$$

Compare this to the partial derivative of Eq. (7.2) with respect to a_{ji}, the component in the group affiliation index measuring the constraint relations between occupants of $\mathbf{S}_j$ and $\mathbf{S}_i$ pose for occupants of $\mathbf{S}_j$:

$$\partial \mathbf{a}_j/\partial a_{ji} = -.5[(b_g) + b_x y_{j1}],$$
$$= -.5[(\beta_g - \beta_x \bar{y}_1) + \beta_x y_{j1}],$$
$$= [\beta_x(\bar{y}_1 - y_{j1}) - \beta_g]/2. \tag{7.5}$$

The structural constraint $\mathbf{a}_{ji}$ and the partial derivative in Eq. (7.5) are closely related. The increase in structural autonomy that occupants of $\mathbf{S}_j$ could expect if they were able to completely eliminate the constraint posed by $\mathbf{S}_i$ is given by the product of a_{ji} times the partial derivative in Eq. (7.5). When this product is divided by their existing structural autonomy, $\mathbf{a}_j$, the structural constraint $\mathbf{a}_{ji}$ is obtained;

$$\mathbf{a}_{ji} = [\partial \mathbf{a}_j/\partial a_{ji}]\,[a_{ji}]/a_j.$$

In other words, the structural constraint $\mathbf{a}_{ji}$ is the marginal increase in structural autonomy that the occupants of $\mathbf{S}_j$ could expect if they were able to completely eliminate the constraint posed by their relations with the occupants of status $\mathbf{S}_i$.

To the extent that the constraint $\mathbf{a}_{ji}$ is negative, occupants of $\mathbf{S}_j$ have an incentive to develop cooptive relations to occupants of $\mathbf{S}_i$ in order to bring that constraint under control. Since β_g and β_x are positive, $\mathbf{a}_{ji}$ will be negative for any status in which oligopoly is no more than a fraction below average. When occupants of S_j are highly disorganized in comparison to other statuses in their system, the term $(\bar{y}_1 - y_{j1})$ is positive. If y_{j1} falls below the mean $\bar{y}_1$ by more than the fraction β_g/β_x (the ratio of the direct effect over the interaction effect of conflicting group affiliations), the partial derivative $\partial a_j/\partial a_{ji}$ (and so the constraint a_{ji}) will be positive, implying that occupants of S_j would not obtain an increase in their structural autonomy by a small decrease in the constraint posed for them by actors occupying other statuses. In order to increase their autonomy, they would have to radically alter their relations with other statuses or organize themselves so that they can better act collectively as a centralized decision-making unit (i.e., dramatically increase y_{j2} or increase y_{j1}). However, the difference between y_{j1} and its mean can never exceed a value of 1 since Y_1 varies from 0 to 1. Therefore, a_{ji} will be nonpositive whenever the direct effect of conflicting group affiliations on structural autonomy (β_g) is greater than its interaction effect with status oligopoly (β_o). In this circumstance, as is the case in the next chapter applying the structural autonomy model, a_{ji} will be nonpositive for all statuses, implying that relations between occupants of statuses S_j and S_i have either no effect, or have a constraining effect, on the structural autonomy of S_j's occupants. Assuming that cooptive relations would give occupants of S_j an opportunity to affect decisions reached by S_i's occupants and that the occupants of S_j are purposive (in the general sense proposed in Chapter 1), the following proposition is implied: Cooptive relations could be expected from status S_j to each status S_i, constraining the structural autonomy of occupying S_j (i.e., $w_{ji} > 0$ when $a_{ji} < 0$) and could be expected not to be developed or maintained to each status S_i, having no effect on that autonomy (i.e., $w_{ji} \simeq 0$ when $a_{ji} = 0$).

In short, the proposed structural autonomy model uses the network of formal relations within a system (the z_{ji}) to define structural constraints (the a_{ji}), and these constraints indicate where informal relations (the w_{ji}) should occur (and should not occur) if they are intended to coopt sources of constraint.

A further implication of the model is that cooptive success can be analyzed as multiplex constraint and informal relations. Suppose that a description of the social topology of a system only considered formal relations. The structural autonomy of employees in a corporate bureaucracy, for example, could be computed using Eq. (7.2) from the network(s) of formal authority relations in the bureaucracy without considering the network of informal friendships among employees. This is illustrated in Section 7.3. The propositions given by the partial derivatives in Eqs. (7.3) and (7.5) concern the incentive actors have to establish informal, potentially cooptive relations with statuses constraining their structural autonomy. Not all actors, however, need to be equally successful in coopting the actors constraining them. Some will be able to eliminate all constraints on their autonomy while others might not be able to eliminate any.

This variability in successful cooptation would mean that structural autonomy stated in terms of formal relations alone would be erroneous in a predictable manner. Those statuses S_j jointly occupied by actors who have coopted occupants of statuses S_i detracting from their structural autonomy (i.e., statuses S_i for which a_{ji} is negative) should have higher than expected autonomy. Those statuses occupied by actors failing to coopt sources of constraint on them should have lower than expected autonomy.

The extent to which the autonomy of status S_j's occupants is increased by their efforts to coopt occupants of other statuses is given as the product of the partial derivative of structural autonomy with respect to constraint ($\partial a_j/\partial a_{ji}$ in Eq. [7.5]) and the level of constraint they have managed to coopt. Unfortunately, the proposed model offers no indication of how w_{ji} should compare to a_{ji} when occupants of status S_j have eliminated the constraint from S_i (a_{ji}) by establishing cooptive relations with its occupants (w_{ji}).[14] One answer here concerns the multiplexity of constraint and cooptation. When w_{ji} is nonzero, indicating the presence of potentially cooptive informal relations from S_j to S_i, and a_{ji} is negative, indicating a constraint on the autonomy of S_j's occupants from their formal relations with the occupants of S_i, the relation from S_j to S_i is a multiplex mixture of coopted constraints. The extent to which occupants of S_j have coopted sources of constraints they face might then be given as the sum of -1 times the a_{ji} weighted by w_{ji} across all statuses S_i ($j \neq i$):

$$d(a_{ji}) = \sum_{i=1}^{M} -a_{ji}w_{ji}, \qquad (7.6)$$

so that the increase in their structural autonomy resulting from their cooptive efforts would be given as ($j \neq i$):[15]

$$d(\mathbf{a}_j) = (\partial \mathbf{a}_j/\partial a_{ji})\,(d(a_{ji})),$$

$$= (\partial \mathbf{a}_j/\partial a_{ji})\,(\sum_{i}^{M} -a_{ji}w_{ji}), \qquad (7.7)$$

where the cooptive relation w_{ji} varies from 0 to 1 so that no more than the observed level of constraint on S_j is measured as coopted. This index will be high when the occupants of status S_j are constrained by their formal relations with occupants of many other statuses and cooptive relations have been established with each of the statuses constraining S_j.

The true extent to which actors occupying S_j can pursue their interests

[14]This lack of information makes it impossible to state a priori the functional form of an association between constraint (the a_{ji}) and cooptation (based on the w_{ji}). Empirically, however, the issue can be addressed. The results in Chapter 8 suggest a simple functional form; w_{ji} increases exponentially with increases a_{jj} up to a limit after which it decreases exponentially with continuing increases in a_{jj}, and w_{ji} increases linearly with increasing constraint from status S_i (i.e., with increasingly negative a_{ji}).

[15]More generally, the increase in structural autonomy resulting from overall cooptation would include the success of intrastatus cooptation. Equation (7.7) is only concerned with the elimination of interstatus constraints.

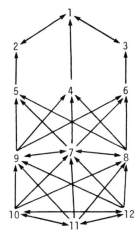

Figure 7.1. Sociogram of work relations among employees in a hypothetical bureaucracy.

without constraint from other actors in their system is then given by their structural autonomy defined by formal relations (a_j) in combination with the added freedom they have obtained by successfully coopting constraints on them ($d(a_j)$). To the extent that they have been cooptively successful (i.e., $d(a_j) \gg 0$), their structural autonomy in Eq. (7.2) understates their actual ability to pursue their interests without constraint.

7.3 NUMERICAL ILLUSTRATION

These implications of the proposed structural model can be made clearer with a simple numerical illustration. Figure 7.1 presents a sociogram of choices among 12 persons working in a bureaucracy. The choice data were obtained from the sociometric question, To whom do you go for information on your work? Choices here indicate the flow of job-related directions, so I shall treat them as formal relations. Table 7.1 presents the adjacency matrix for Figure 7.1 and choice densities among structurally equivalent persons in the bureaucracy. Employees are distributed across four jointly occupied positions ($M = 4$). These positions are statuses within the bureaucracy since there is only one network.

The densities describe typical relations among occupants of the four statuses. Occupants of status S_1 only seek job-related information from one another. Occupants of S_2 have no relations with one another, but each seek information from an occupant of S_1 and are themselves the source of information for employees occupying status S_3. Occupants of S_3 and S_4 seek information from cooccupants of their respective statuses. In addition, occupants of S_4 go to employees occupying S_3 for information.

TABLE 7.1
Sociometric Choices and Choice Densities[a]

		Statuses											
		S_1			S_2			S_3			S_4		
	1	0	1	1	0	0	0	0	0	0	0	0	0
	2	1	0	0	0	0	0	0	0	0	0	0	0
	3	1	0	0	0	0	0	0	0	0	0	0	0
	4	1	0	0	0	0	0	0	0	0	0	0	0
	5	0	1	0	0	0	0	0	0	0	0	0	0
Binary	6	0	0	1	0	0	0	0	0	0	0	0	0
choices	7	0	0	0	1	1	1	0	1	1	0	0	0
	8	0	0	0	1	1	1	1	0	0	0	0	0
	9	0	0	0	1	1	1	1	0	0	0	0	0
	10	0	0	0	0	0	0	1	1	1	0	1	1
	11	0	0	0	0	0	0	1	1	1	1	0	1
	12	0	0	0	0	0	0	1	1	1	1	1	0
	S_1	.7			.0			.0			.0		
	S_2	.3			.0			.0			.0		
Densities	S_3	.0			1.0			.7			.0		
	S_4	.0			.0			1.0			1.0		

[a]Densities have been computed from the binary choices as the ratio of observed choices over possible choices (Eq. [2.16]). The four statuses have been located in Figure 7.1, as described in Chapter 3. As a check on the clustering, there is a single dimension of distance to each set of status occupants. The ratio of predicted to observed variance in distance to actors occupying each status under a single principal component is, respectively, .87, .57, .85, and .97 (ratio in Eq. [2.31]).

Table 7.2 presents the structural autonomy of these four statuses within the bureaucracy. The binary relations in Table 7.1 show that the statuses are differentially centralized. I shall treat status centralization as the extent to which any one occupant can be an intermediary between occupants of his status.[16] Statuses S_1 and S_3 are perfectly centralized since a single occupant of each is involved in all relations among occupants of his status (person one in S_1 and person seven in S_3, so $y_{11} = y_{31} = 1$). The occupants of S_4 have relations with one another, but the relations are not centralized in one occupant. Nevertheless, they have the capacity for collusion since they rely on one another for job information. Of the two connections between any two of the

[16]This is related to the idea of centrality discussed by Freeman (1977) and reviewed in Section 2.8. As I mentioned earlier (see footnote 35 of Chapter 2), the inequality model of stratification (Eq. [2.24]) is inappropriate here since it would treat as equally decentralized and incapable of collusion a status occupied by completely unconnected actors (e.g., S_2) and one occupied by completely connected actors (e.g., S_4).

TABLE 7.2
Centralization, Group-Affiliation, and Structural Autonomy[a]

	Statuses			
	S_1	S_2	S_3	S_4
Centralization (y_{j1})	1.00	.00	1.00	.50
Group-affiliation (y_{j2})	1.00	.00	.91	.88
Interaction ($y_{j1}y_{j2}$)	1.00	.00	.91	.44
Structural autonomy ($\mathbf{a}_j$)	2.87	1.00	2.77	2.20

[a]These results have been computed from the binary relations and densities in Table 7.1; centralization is explained in the text, Eq. (7.1) gives the group-affiliation index, and structural autonomy is computed from Eq. (7.2) where arbitrary values have been used for the three weights based on the t-tests for four-digit manufacturing industries in the next chapter (Table 8.1). The oligopoly and group affiliation effects are about equal and larger than their interaction effect by about five to two, so the weights here were chosen to be $\beta_0 = 1$, $\beta_g = 1$, and $.4 = \beta_x$. which means that $b_0 = .721, b_g = .750$, and $.4 = b_x$ (see footnote 13). The arbitrary constant b has been set equal to 1. This avoids the problem of normalizing constraints by 0 in Eq. (7.4) since $\mathbf{a}_j$ would be 0 for status S_2 if b were 0.

occupants (one direct and one indirect through the third occupant), each occupant is involved as an intermediary in one so that y_{41} is given in Table 7.2 as .5. Finally, the occupants of S_2 are completely decentralized since they have no relations with one another ($y_{21} = 0$). Based on the densities in Table 7.1, the group-affiliation index in Table 7.2 shows that occupants of S_1 suffer no constraint from the other statuses ($y_{12} = 1$), the occupants of S_2 suffer a maximum constraint ($y_{22} = 0$), while occupants of the remaining two statuses are subject to low constraint ($y_{32} = .91$, $y_{42} = .88$). These computed values of y_{j1} and y_{j2} are then used to generate relative levels of structural autonomy for each status, $\mathbf{a}_j$, using weights suggested by the discussion of Eq. (7.2) and the analysis in the next chapter. As with the group-affiliation index, status S_1 offers its occupants the highest structural autonomy, and S_2 offers the lowest while the remaining two statuses offer an intermediate level.

The relational patterns in Table 7.1 explain these scores. Status S_1 offers its occupants freedom from constraint since their only relations with persons outside their own status are with the occupants of S_2, a status completely decentralized so that its occupants cannot collectively impose demands on occupants of S_1. Given this lack of constraint from other statuses and their own high centralization, the occupants of S_1 enjoy the highest structural autonomy within the bureaucracy ($\mathbf{a}_1 = 2.87$). The employees occupying status S_3 are centralized to the same extent as those occupying S_1. Although status S_1 is a source of job information for occupants of S_2 wherein there are no relations, status S_3 is a source of job information for status S_4, a status jointly occupied by employees who rely extensively on one another for job information and thus are better able than occupants of S_2 to collectively make demands. Because of the greater cohesion among their assistants, in other words, the occupants of status

TABLE 7.3
Structural Constraints, Partial Derivatives, and Predicted Cooptive Relations[a]

	Statuses			
	S_1	S_2	S_3	S_4
Structural constraints (a_{ji})	.39	.00	.00	.00
	−.38	.00	−.38	.00
	.00	.00	.40	−.04
	.00	.00	−.05	.25
Intrastatus cooptation				
$\partial a_j / \partial y_{j1}$	1.1	.7	1.1	1.1
Cooptive relations (w_{jj})	yes	yes	yes	yes
Interstatus cooptation				
$\partial a_j / \partial a_{ji}$	−.6	−.4	−.6	−.5
Cooptive relations (w_{ji})	—	no	no	no
	yes	—	yes	no
	no	no	—	yes
	no	no	yes	—

[a]Structural constraints have been computed from Eq. (7.4); the partial derivatives have been computed from Eqs. (7.3) and (7.5); and a cooptive relation w_{ji} appears where predicted by a negative a_{ji}.

S_3 have less structural autonomy within the bureaucracy than the occupants of S_1 ($a_3 = 2.77$). The unfortunate employees occupying status S_2 have all their relations with statuses S_1 and S_3, both of which are completely centralized. Completely decentralized themselves and facing maximum constraint from outside their status, occupants of S_2 have the lowest level of autonomy in the bureaucracy ($a_2 = 1.00$). Even though the employees occupying S_2 serve as brokers between the prestigious status S_1 and the less "influential" statuses S_3 and S_4, and even though the role of broker is traditionally thought of as an autonomous role optimum for the profit-seeking entrepreneur, the fact that S_2 deals exclusively with two oligopolistic statuses (S_1 and S_3) reduces its occupants to a minimum level of structural autonomy—a level even lower than the most humble assistants in the bureaucracy ($a_4 = 2.20$).

Table 7.3 presents information concerning constraint and cooptation within the bureaucracy. Constraints have been computed from Eq. (7.4). The only positive contributions to autonomy come from collusion among occupants of three statuses (a_{11}, a_{33}, and $a_{44} > 0$). The exception is status S_2 within which there is no centralization ($a_{22} = 0$). Since the partial derivative given in Eq. (7.3) is positive for all four statuses, occupants of each status could improve their structural autonomy by establishing cooptive relations with their co-occupants. Accordingly, Table 6.3 indicates that intrastatus cooptive relations (w_{jj}) are expected in each status. Further, the partial derivative in Eq. (7.5) is negative for each status so there should be cooptive relations superimposed on interstatus constraints. Accordingly, Table 7.3 indicates interstatus cooptive relations (w_{ji}) wherever a negative a_{ji} is observed. The four negative a_{ji} are not surprising in light of the above discussion. Occupants of status S_2 confront high constraint from statuses S_1 and S_3, so cooptive relations linking them to the occupants of S_1 and S_3 are expected ($-.38 = a_{21} = a_{23}$). Similarly, occupants of statuses S_3 and S_4 constrain one another ($a_{34} = -.04$; $a_{43} = -.05$) so that cooptive relations are expected between occupants of these two statuses. As a result of the lack of constraint imposed on their status, employees occupying status S_1 are expected not to establish cooptive relations with occupants of other statuses ($a_{12} = a_{13} = a_{14} = 0$).

Suppose that after obtaining the above sociometric data in interviews with the employees, an observer was placed in the bureaucracy to obtain richer relational data. His observation was that employees occupying each of the statuses developed social relations with one another as a result of their work-related activities, but the occupants of status S_2 were particularly social. In the course of serving their intermediary role between status S_1 and the less prestigious statuses, S_3 and S_4, occupants of S_2 developed friendships with occupants of all statuses in the bureaucracy. The image matrix of social bonds among status occupants appears as follows after coding the direct observation records:

$$\begin{bmatrix} 1 & 0 & 0 & 0 \\ 1 & 1 & 1 & 1 \\ 0 & 0 & 1 & 0 \\ 0 & 0 & 0 & 1 \end{bmatrix}$$

These relations would offer mixed evidence regarding social bonds as cooptive ties within the bureaucracy. As expected from Table 7.3, intrastatus social bonds have developed in each status (all w_{jj} equal 1). Only two of the expected interstatus bonds have developed ($w_{21} = w_{23} = 1$). The expected ties between employees occupying statuses S_3 and S_4 were not observed. Nevertheless, only one social tie occurs in the absence of constraint (all but one w_{ji} equals 0 when $a_{ji} = 0$).

If social bonds can function as cooptive relations, demands being easier to make on mere employees than on one's friends, then it is the occupants of status S_2 who have been most successful in coopting sources of constraint they face. The observed interstatus social bonds are superimposed on constraints suffered by the occupants of S_2 (a_{21} and a_{23} are negative in Table 7.3). Therefore, the level of demands imposed on S_2's occupants might be lower than expected from the analysis of purely work-related relations in Tables 7.2 and 7.3. Specifically, social bonds offer a .28 increase in the structural autonomy of S_2's occupants ($.28 = d(a_2)$ in Eq. [7.7]). This added discretionary ability, in conjunction with the fact that no other status occupants have coopted constraints, makes the occupants of S_2 appear far less oppressed within the bureaucracy. Their status still offers the lowest structural autonomy within the bureaucracy; however, it is no longer subject to unchecked constraint.

7.4 CONCLUSIONS

My purpose in this chapter has been to propose a model of structural autonomy that describes the manner in which the relational pattern defining a status "frees" its occupants from demands by occupants of other statuses in a system. The model brings together two well-known concepts—oligopoly in economics and group affiliation in sociology. In reference to the diagrammed social context in Figure 2.4, the structural autonomy offered by status $\mathbf{S}_j$, $\mathbf{a}_j$ in Eq. (7.2), is determined by two features of the relational pattern defining the status: (a) Oligopoly (relations among occupants of status $\mathbf{S}_j$, cell j,j in Figure 2.4). Status occupants have structural autonomy to the extent that they are centralized so as to act as an oligopoly, coordinating their actions in pursuit of the common interests expected as structurally equivalent actors. (b) Conflicting group affiliations (relations with occupants of other statuses, cells j,i and i,j in figure 2.4 where $j \neq i$). Occupants of status $\mathbf{S}_j$ have structural autonomy to the extent that they have conflicting group affiliations in the sense of having relations with occupants of many different statuses, none of which constitutes an oligopoly. The occupants of status $\mathbf{S}_i$ constitute a threat to the structural autonomy of status $\mathbf{S}_j$ to the extent that they are centralized so as to act as an oligopoly against $\mathbf{S}_j$ and all the relations in which the occupants of $\mathbf{S}_j$ are involved tie them to status $\mathbf{S}_i$. This condition is measured by the a_{ji} in Eq. (7.1):

$$a_{ji} = y_{i1} \left[(z_{ij} / \sum_q^M z_{qj})^2 + (z_{ji} / \sum_q^M z_{jq})^2 \right],$$

where z_{ji} is the formal, obligatory relation from occupants of status $\mathbf{S}_j$ to those occupying status $\mathbf{S}_i$, and y_{i1} is the centralization of $\mathbf{S}_i$'s occupants (ranging from 0 to 1). Occupants of status $\mathbf{S}_j$ have high structural autonomy (i.e., are able to realize interests without constraint from others) to the extent that they are at once centralized ($y_{j1} = 1$) and they are not subject to constraint from the other $M - 1$ statuses ($\mathbf{a}_{ji} = 0$ for all statuses $j \neq i$). The specific level of constraint they confront from status $\mathbf{S}_i$ is given in Eq. (7.4) as the marginal increase in structural autonomy that they could expect if they could eliminate the constraint posed for them by their formal relations with occupants of $\mathbf{S}_i$:

$$\mathbf{a}_{ji} = [-(b_g + b_x y_{j1})/2] a_{ji} / \mathbf{a}_j = [\partial \mathbf{a}_j / \partial a_{ji}] a_{ji} / \mathbf{a}_j.$$

In order to coopt the constraints they face, occupants of status $\mathbf{S}_j$ are expected to develop informal, discretionary relations with the occupants of $\mathbf{S}_i$ to the extent that $\mathbf{a}_{ji}$ is negative and cooptation holds the promise of lowering constraint (Eq. [7.5]). In the process of developing these cooptive relations, actors modify their relational patterns and by so doing have the potential to change their structural autonomy as given by $d(\mathbf{a}_j)$ in Eq. (7.7).

Although the proposed model does capture one direct effect from social structure on action as diagrammed in Figure 1.1, it is conceptually rudimentary. It is far less general than the interest model proposed and explored in Chapter 5. That model was defined in terms of well-established empirical research on subjective perceptions and in terms of distances on a social topology, a very general representation of empirical and abstract social structure in a system. In contrast, the structural autonomy model opens empirically unresearched issues and makes four seriously restrictive conceptual assumptions. These assumptions call for tests of the model's empirical adequacy before casting the model in a more sophisticated form mathematically.

1. The model assumes that structural autonomy is defined by a single idealized relational pattern for all systems. In the same sense that there are alternative relational patterns that might capture social integration (Section 5.5), there are alternative patterns that might capture the ability to realize interests without constraint. For example, using structural autonomy as an explanation for differential profits in manufacturing industries quickly revealed that relations *from* actors jointly occupying a position did not affect their structural autonomy in the same manner as relations directed *to* them. The group affiliation index in Eq. (7.1) had to be disaggregated into two components—one capturing the extent to which occupants of positon j were the object of relations from many different positions and the other capturing the extent to which they directed relations to occupants of nonoligopolistic positions (Burt 1979a, 1983:Chap. 2). I have not modified the structural autonomy model to take these results into account because, as I stressed in Chapter 1, I do not wish to propose a model that is so good a description of one system that it is an accordingly poor description of systems generally. I have no doubt that other specifications of structural autonomy are plausible in different systems, even if structural autonomy is consistently given by $\mathbf{a}_j$ in Eq. (7.2) as a baseline model.

2. The proposed model assumes unambiguous status boundaries; each actor in a system explicitly occupies a single status. Empirically, this is rarely the case; structural equivalence under a weak criterion is the rule rather than the exception, as discussed in Section 2.6 and illustrated in Chapter 3. Because it requires each actor in a system to be unambiguously assigned to one status (and this is often an empirically based, arbitrary decision) the proposed model is not in a general form. The general case would relax the assumption of perfect status boundaries by somehow capturing the centralization of actors in a status field within a social topology and defining structural autonomy as a consequence of actor distance from, and formal relations with, occupants of the status fields within the actor's system.

3. The proposed model assumes an unambiguous distinction between formal relations (the z_{ji}) and informal relations (the w_{ji}). The former are immutable relations that status occupants are obliged to perform. The pattern of these relations defines the differential structural autonomy of status occupants. Informal relations are performed at the discretion of all parties involved in them and can serve as a method of coopting constraints created by formal relations. But this distinction between formal and informal relations is more a matter of degree than an absolute difference in content. In the invisible college of elite experts in sociological methodology, for example, influence relations between experts in regard to methodological work are more formal than substantive exchange relations. It takes more training to acquire methodological expertise than is required to gain a familiarity with a specific substantive area. However, no member of the college is obliged to go to a specific status for methodological advice. If one source of advice becomes too arrogant, one can always rely on other sources. In the sense that methodological influence relations are somewhat discretionary, if not as discretionary as substantive exchange relations, they do not conform perfectly to what I have discussed as formal relations. Unfortunately, until the content of relations is better understood, action models that distinguish two or more types of relations will be less than general models.

4. The proposed model assumes that interests pursued by occupants of different statuses are not complementary, the interests pursued by occupants of status S_j being different from those pursued by occupants of status S_i. In this circumstance, a negative a_{ji} means that occupants of status S_j could be diverted from pursuit of their own interests in favor of interests being pursued by the occupants of S_i. In other words, the proposed model assumes that all possible constraints (the a_{ji}) will be utilized by actors in the pursuit of their interests. But what if the interests of actors occupying statuses S_j and S_i coincide? For example, a decision favorable to the occupants of S_j might also be favorable to the occupants of S_i. In this circumstance, a negative a_{ji} represents a potential constraint rather than a constraint in fact since occupants of both statuses will pursue identical interests. Accordingly, occupants of status S_j would be less constrained in fact than the negative a_{ji} predicted by the proposed model would suggest. A model more general than that proposed would take into account the actual interests of status occupants so as to more accurately locate the constraints imposed on occupants of each individual status.[17]

[17]Although not discussed in detail here, one such extension could be made by modifying the group affiliation index in Eq. (7.1). Let x_{ji} vary from 1 to -1 as the extent to which the interests of actors occupying statuses S_i and S_j are identical; x_{ji} equals -1 if their interests are identical, 0 if their interests are independent and occupants of neither status can help occupants of the other in their pursuits, and 1 if their interests are antagonistic. For example, one measure of x_{ji} would be -1 times the correlation between levels of utility (Eq. [5.7]) occupants of S_i would obtain by taking each of several actions ($u_{i1}, u_{i2}, \ldots$) and levels of utility occupants of S_j would obtain by taking each of the actions ($u_{j1}, u_{j2}, \ldots$). The correlation r_{ji} would be positive when occupants of S_i and S_j obtained high utility by taking the same actions whereupon $x_{ji} = -r_{ji}$ would be strongly

In no sense then does the proposed structural autonomy model capture all nuances of the ideas commonly refered to as oligopoly and conflicting group affiliation. It is not proposed as a general representation of structural autonomy. In contrast to the general simplicity of the perceptual model in Chapter 5, the structural autonomy model is arbitrarily simplified. It is an initial, plausible, baseline model of what oligopoly and group affiliation mean in terms of status/role-sets and the manner in which these ideas come together to define the structural autonomy of status occupants within a stratified system.

Nevertheless, when a substantive area conforms to the model's limitations, I believe that the model can be a rewarding guide for empirical research. Within a corporate bureaucracy, for example, structural autonomy predicts the relative discretion that is allowed to executives occupying positions in the corporation and predicts that informal friendships will develop when constraint on each position is high. Jointly occupied positions (jobs) are clearly defined by formal, authority relations within the bureaucracy, and there is a clear distinction between job-defining authority relations and discretionary friendships. Yet another substantive area aptly suited to the proposed model is the study of corporations and markets. Demonstrating that fact is my next task.

---

negative. Now let a_{ji} in Eq. (7.1) be respecified as follows:

$$\alpha_{ji} = [(z_{ij}/ \sum_{q}^{M} z_{qj})^2 + (z_{ji}/ \sum_{q}^{M} z_{jq})^2]y_{i1}x_{ji} = a_{ji}x_{ji}.$$

This coefficient will range from -2 to 2 as the extent to which the occupants of status S_i pose a constraint on the structural autonomy of actors occupying status S_j. The coefficient a_{ji} ranges from 0 to a maximum of 2; equalling its maximum when the occupants of status S_i are perfectly centralized and the only actors with whom occupants of S_j have relations. When multiplied by x_{ji} to yield α_{ji}, the coefficient equals 2 when the occupants of status S_i are perfectly centralized and the only actors with whom S_j's occupants have relations, and the interests of S_i's occupants are antagonistic toward those of S_j's occupants. The coefficient α_{ji} equals -2 if the same structural conditions exist but the occupants of S_i have interests identical to the occupants of S_j. This coefficient, when substituted for a_{ji} in Eq. (7.4), offers a more precise measure of the constraint S_j's occupants experience from actors occupying S_i:

$$\alpha_{ji} = [-(b_g + b_x y_{j1})\alpha_{ji}/2]/a_j,$$

which will be negative to the extent that status S_i has the potential to constrain occupants of S_j *and* occupants of S_i are pursuing interests that are antagonistic to those pursued by S_j's occupants. It will be positive to the extent that status S_i has the potential to constrain occupants of S_j *but* occupants of S_i are pursuing interests that will simultaneously realize the interests of S_j's occupants. In other words, the α_{ji} more directly capture the idea of conflicting group affiliations than do the a_{ji}. Unfortunately, they also require data on the interests actors would pursue if they were free to do so, and such data are difficult to obtain (see Section 8.2). Alternatively, the proposed model of structural perception in Chapter 5 could be drawn on to estimate x_{ji} as -1 times the correlation between distances to statuses S_j and S_i within the social topology of their system (e.g., $-\phi_{ij}$ in Eq. [2.33]). To the extent that occupants of statuses S_j and S_i are involved in similar role sets, and therefore have similar interests according to the structural model in Chapter 5, ϕ_{ij} will be positive so that $x_{ji} = -\phi_{ji}$ will be strongly negative. Here again there is a drawback, however. While structurally equivalent actors (i.e., statuses S_j and S_i for which ϕ_{ji} is positive) are expected to have similar interests, structurally nonequivalent actors (i.e., statuses S_j and S_i for which ϕ_{ji} is negative) need not have dissimilar interests (e.g., footnote 7 in Chapter 5).

8

Market Constraints and Directorate Ties with Respect to American Manufacturing Industries*

In order to test the substantive adequacy of the proposed structural autonomy model, I use it in this chapter to describe constraint and cooptation within a system ideally suited to testing the model. I return to the sampled establishments in sectors of the 1967 American economy which were discussed in Chapter 4. The relational pattern defining one of the manufacturing industries jointly occupied by these establishments is taken as its typical pattern of sales and purchase transactions with supplier and consumer sectors of the economy. The form of this pattern defined market constraints on profits in the industry as an indicator of industry structural autonomy. Directorate ties are then shown to be cooptive relations in the sense that they were strongly patterned by the estimated market constraints.

8.1 THE SUBSTANTIVE PROBLEM POSED BY COOPTIVE DIRECTORATE TIES

Are corporate boards of directors used as a cooptive device for circumventing market constraint so as to control uncertainty in corporate profits? I suspect that

*Portions of this chapter are drawn from articles reprinted with the permission of *Social Networks,* the *American Journal of Sociology, Social Science Research,* and the *American Sociological Review* (Burt 1979c, 1980a, 1980d, Burt, Christman, and Kilburn 1980). The issues addressed in this chapter are addressed in greater detail with more extensive data in a book devoted to them (Burt, 1983).

the answer is yes because it seems to me to be a very rational course of action. Moreover, the evidence reviewed and presented in Chapter 4 lends itself to interpretations of the corporate directorate as a cooptive device. The firms most likely to benefit from cooptive relations have tended to be most responsible for directorate ties—large firms controlled by dispersed interest groups. In the 1967 American economy, these types of firms were most likely to be responsible for systematically coordinating different types of directorate ties as multiplex relations between manufacturing industries and economic sectors generally. However, these descriptive results neither confirm nor allay my suspicions. Although they describe the existence of directorate ties, these results do not link such interorganizational relations to interorganizational competition as competition constrains profits.

It might seem intuitively obvious that directorate ties enable organizations to coopt one another. Indeed, such ties would not be analyzed as a threat to perfect competition unless they were potentially cooptive. As described in Section 4.4, directorate ties have the cooptive potential of creating preferred trade partners among establishments. As conduits for information, advice, and influence, they create nonmarket contexts in which essential buying and selling can be transacted between establishments in the absence of the market constraints characterizing those same transactions when conducted on the open market.

By itself, however, interpreting directorate ties as cooptive relations does not advance our understanding of such interorganizational relations so much as it provides a sociological label for them. Like instinct theories of action in which a person's behaviors are explained by attributing to the person an instinct for those behaviors, cooptation is a rationalization for action without a specification of parameters for action. In other words, there is no criterion under which a directorate tie between two organizations is not cooptive. Accordingly, there is no method of rejecting an argument interpreting directorate ties as cooptive. What is known is that some types of firms use their directorates in what can be interpreted as a cooptive manner. What is not known is whether these ostensibly cooptive uses of directorates are patterned by market constraint on profits so as to reduce competition between firms or whether there are merely some types of firms which engage in representing their organizational environment on their boards.

In short, the key to answering the question with which I began lies in the concept of market constraint—as I see the matter. A model of market constraints on corporate profits is needed. If corporate boards are being used to control uncertainty in corporate profits, then directorate ties should occur as a function of, and can be assessed as successful cooptive relations in terms of, market constraints on corporate profits.

8.2 MARKET CONSTRAINTS ON CORPORATE PROFITS

The network model of structural autonomy is nicely suited to this task. Two immediate reasons for this concern the ready availability of appropriate data.

Market Structure

As discussed in Section 4.2, there is a ready-made density table of sales and purchase transactions within the American economy. Compiled by the U. S. Department of Commerce, this density table is distributed as an input–output table representation of market structure in the American economy where z_{ji} is an unnormalized density, the total dollars of sales by establishments jointly occupying sector j as a network position in the economy to establishments similarly occupying sector i. I have constructed a (51,51) table of dollar transactions between 51 sectors of the 1967 American economy from the 1967 Input–Output Study (U. S. Department of Commerce 1974). The first 45 of these sectors correspond to Standard Industrial Classification (SIC) categories and are the sectors distinguished in Chapter 4 (see Table 4.2). The remaining 6 sectors do not correspond to SIC categories but are active in the economy: government enterprises, imports, and three "dummy" industries representing secondary production activities.[1] I shall continue the convention adopted in Chapter 4 of referring to those sectors involved in manufacturing as industries while referring to sectors more generally merely as sectors. For reasons that will become obvious shortly, it is market constraints on manufacturing industries that are the focus of my attention here. Among the 51 sectors, 20 correspond to two-digit SIC manufacturing industries and will be analyzed here as the object of market constraint.[2] In short, each of these 20 manufacturing industries was jointly occupied by establishments in 1967 and characterized by a typical pattern of sales and purchase transactions with establishments in each of 51 sectors of the American economy; the sales transactions are given in a row of the (51,51) input–output table, and the purchase transactions are given in the corresponding column of the table. This relational pattern defined the industry as a network position within the economy.

Following the lead of economic research on oligopoly within manufacturing industries, the level of oligopoly within a manufacturing industry has been measured in terms of four-firm concentration ratios—the ratio of the combined sales of the four largest establishments in the industry over the combined sales of all establishments in the industry where, as introduced in Section 4.2, an establishment refers to all of a single corporation's holdings within an economic sector. To the extent that there were only four competitors within an industry, the industry concentration ratio is one. Concentration ratios for four-digit SIC categories are given in the 1967 *Census of Manufactures* (U.S. Department of Commerce 1971), and pooled ratios allowing high concentration within sub-

---

[1] The input–output sectors not corresponding to SIC categories are listed in footnote 8 of Chapter 4.

[2] SIC category 23, apparel, includes some portions of SIC category 22, textiles. The 1967 input–output apparel sector contains establishments falling within four-digit SIC industries 2251, 2252, 2253, 2254, 2256, and 2259, although these are SIC textile establishments. I have therefore corrected the price–cost margins and concentration ratios introduced below to take into account the changes in these two industries as aggregate input–output sectors.

sectors of each industry have been computed for the two-digit industries from the four-digit data.[3] These concentration ratios provide a measure of the lack of competition within industry j, y_{j1} in Chapter 7, that varies between 0 and 1 as the extent to which establishments in the industry are able to act collectively. Since four-digit SIC industries are much more narrowly defined than two-digit industries, it would be easier for four establishments to dominate a four-digit industry, thereby ensuring higher concentration ratios on average in four-digit industries. For 335 four-digit manufacturing industries corresponding to unique sectors of the input–output table, an average 40% of industry output in 1967 was accounted for by the four largest establishments. Among the 20 two-digit industries, this average drops to a somewhat smaller 36% (i.e., $\bar{y}_1 = .36$). Even in the highly aggregated two-digit industries, however, concentration varied from a minimum in the lumber industry ($y_{j1} = .16$) to a maximum in the tobacco industry ($y_{j1} = .74$).

Given the relations defining each manufacturing industry as a network position and concentration ratios as a measure of oligopoly, values of the group-affiliation index have been computed using Eq. (7.1).[4] Establishments in industry j faced a maximum level of constraint when they relied upon a single sector to supply their inputs, a single sector to consume their outputs, and there were four or fewer competitors within either sector. Under these conditions, y_{j2} in Eq. (7.1) would equal 0. The establishments were subject to a minimum level of constraint when they had market transactions with many economic sectors as suppliers and consumers, and each of those sectors contained many more than

---

[3]These concentration ratios have been computed as the weighted sum of four-digit concentration ratios subsumed by each two-digit industry;

$$y_{j1} = \sum_k (VS_k y_{k1})/VS_j,$$

where k is a four-digit SIC category within two-digit category j. Value of shipments, VS_k, and concentration, y_{k1}, for four-digit category k are taken from the 1967 *Census of Manufactures*, Table 8 of the special report series. Concentration ratios for nonmanufacturing sectors are approximations based on a variety of census data presented for the 484 sector input–output table in my unpublished doctoral dissertation in sociology, University of Chicago, *Actors in Structures: Empirical Statics* (Table 79).

[4]Intraindustry transactions have been excluded from the total volume of sales and purchased made by establishments in an industry. The two-digit industries are so highly aggregated that a considerable portion of interindustry buying and selling at the four-digit level is intraindustry buying and selling at the two-digit level. In order to more clearly capture constraint from other sectors on two-digit industries, therefore, I have deleted z_{qq} from the row and column sums in Eq. (7.1). This means that the proportion of transactions an industry had with some sector, e.g., proportion of sales to the sector, is the proportion of transactions with other sectors that occurred with the specific sector. In other words, the group-affiliation index measures the extent to which an industry's transactions with *other* sectors occurred with oligopolistic sectors. Although true to the condition intended to be captured by the index, this deletion of z_{qq} in Eq. (7.1) is a slight divergence from the specification in Chapter 7 and is accordingly noted. Given the much more narrow set of manufacturing activities encompassed by four-digit industries and the many more potential consumer/supplier sectors, intraindustry transactions are included in the group-affiliation index scores for these industries.

four competitors. Under those conditions, y_{j2} would be close to 1. By and large, the manufacturing industries were subject to low constraint as captured by the group-affiliation index. The average value of y_{j2} was .97 across the two-digit industries. For comparative purposes, the index was also computed for those input–output sectors corresponding to unique four-digit SIC codes. Instead of being based on an industry's transactions with 50 other sectors, these four-digit scores were computed from transactions with 492 other sectors. Here again, the average index value was high, indicating low overall constraint; $\bar{y}_2 = .96$. Among the two-digit industries, constraint from other sectors was most severe for the apparel industry ($y_{j2} = .89$) and least severe for the tobacco industry ($y_{j2} = 1.00$).

Given aggregate data on market transactions as the z_{ji} in a dollar flow input–output table and concentration ratios as measures of oligopoly within each sector (y_{j1}) from which scores on the group-affiliation index can be computed (y_{j2}), it is possible to compute the structural autonomy of industries as jointly occupied network positions and to estimate the extent to which the industry's transactions with any one sector of the economy constrained the structural autonomy of its constituent establishments. Such a procedure was illustrated in Section 7.3 and could be replicated with any system of actors for which z_{ji} and y_{j1} are available.

But this presupposes information on the manner in which oligopoly and conflicting group affiliations combine to define structural autonomy. In order to estimate the oligopoly effect represented by β_o, the effect of conflicting group affiliations represented by β_g, and their interaction effect represented by β_x, some criterion variable is required that can be regressed over structural autonomy in Eq. (7.2b). This requirement means that not all systems of actors are equally suited to empirically testing the proposed model.

Profits as a Reflection of Structural Autonomy

A second reason why the structural autonomy is nicely suited to an analysis of market constraint is the availability of data on an indicator of relative autonomy—profits. In order to appreciate the indicator problem, consider the idea of testing the proposed model on some randomly selected system. Given data on relations among actors in the system and oligopoly within the system's jointly occupied statuses, the subsequent problem is to select an indicator of autonomy to regress over the terms in Eq. (7.2).

It could be argued, for example, that the methodology relations among the elite experts are formal; an expert had a position in the college as a function of his technical expertise and that expertise would not have been obtained easily. Substantive relations could be interpreted as more informal than formal in the sense that experts were free to select substantive areas in which to apply their technical expertise. When tired of one substantive area, an expert was free to move on to another. It would have been much less easy to acquire a new technical expertise that would have been recognized in the college. Experts tended, and tend, to be known for specific areas of expertise. Given the patterns of methodology relations among structurally equivalent experts in Figure 3.3 and the original relations among occupants of each network position, the structural autonomy of each position could have been computed as illustrated in Chapter 7 for the hypothetical system in Figure 7.1. The constraints imposed on each jointly occupied position could then have been located, and the pattern of substantive relations could have been analyzed as potentially cooptive relations for circumventing constraints. For example, was the substantive interest of the mobility elite in occupational achievement their response to a methodological dependence on the social statistics elite who themselves were interested in that substantive area? Given a dependence on some other group for technical advice, say in regard to structural equation models, could that dependence have been offset by gaining a thorough knowledge of the substantive area in which that group wanted to apply the models? It is often the case that peculiarities of a substantive area call for special technical treatment. A person interested in the area and himself having extensive technical training can usually benefit from interaction with a person extremely familiar with substantive issues in the area. It is not impossible, in other words, to envision a mutually advantageous exchange of substantive and methodological comments between the social statistics elite and their satellite mobility elite within the college.[5] But what would be an indicator of autonomy for such a system so that values of the coefficients in Eq. (7.2) could be estimated?

The indicator problem stems from the lack of specific behaviors unambiguously reflecting autonomy. The act of adopting an innovative idea or mode of dress, for example, would be a reflection of autonomy in some circumstances. The adoption would demonstrate freedom from constraint by the traditional ideas or mode of dress endorsed by social norms. Where most actors are a priori favorably disposed toward the innovation, however, adoption could instead be a reflection of constraint by social norms rather than freedom from them. Similarly, early use of path analysis diagrams of structural equation models by a member of the mobility elite in sociological methodology might be taken as an indicator of the expert's freedom to choose new methods of representing conceptual schemes. But it might also be taken to be a dictum imposed on him by his sources of influential methodological comments—the social statistics elite. In general, autonomy is not a prediction of behavior, it is a prediction of freedom of choice of behavior.[6]

---

[5]This idea of substantive competence being exchanged for methodological competence within the college is explored elsewhere (Burt 1979b). It is rejected for the college as a whole. This does not rule out the possibility of such an exchange within limited sectors of the college, such as statuses S_2 and S_3—the social statistics and mobility elite.

[6]This point is emphasized by Riesman (1961:xvff) in his complaint that readers have tended to equate the concept of autonomy with his idea of "inner-directed" man, an equivalence that reduces autonomy to a type of behavior rather than keeping it as an ability to freely choose behaviors.

It is only when an actor's interests and behaviors are known to an observer that the two can be compared by the observer so as to determine whether observed behaviors are a result of the actor's own interests rather than the interests of others. As a practical research problem, unfortunately, determining all of the interests of all actors in a system is a formidable task; certainly a task beyond the capabilities of easily available research methodologies.

Another strategy is to look for a system composed of actors pursuing one nonzero-sum interest. In such a system, each actor's manifest behavior would be oriented toward realizing a single interest for himself. Given the single interest pursued by all actors, manifest behavior could be analyzed in terms of its discrepancy from that interest. Discrepancy would indicate the extent to which each actor is subject to constraint from other actors in the system. Those actors subject to the least constraint would evidence behaviors most directly realizing the common interest for themselves.

This brings me back to the advantages of business establishments in manufacturing industries. These establishments can be assumed to have a common motivating interest. Over time, they can be expected to seek maximum, stable profits (in addition, of course, to a range of goals specific to more narrowly defined classes of organizations). In seeking profits, an establishment does not commit the whole economy to some course of action (a type of interest the realization of which would require corporate power[7]). The level of profit obtained by an establishment thus provides a clue to the lack of market constraint it experiences. Those establishments obtaining the highest profits should be the establishments with the highest structural autonomy in the market.

Fortunately, data on profits need not be obtained for individual establishments nor obtained on an absolute scale. Since the proposed model only purports to capture the relative levels of autonomy provided by different positions in a system, profits need only be measured so as to capture the relative ability of establishments in separate industries to make profits.

Inferential measures of profits are available for whole manufacturing industries. As introduced by Collins and Preston (1968:13–17, 54–57; 1969), the

---

[7]Again, the close linkage between power and autonomy should be emphasized. Powerful corporations will be able to derive high profits for their investors. There can be corporate actors that are autonomous yet not powerful, however, and these corporate actors will also be able to derive high profits according to the proposed autonomy model. It could be said that a powerful corporate actor is a firm that controls highly valuable resources and has exchange relations with others controlling resources, such as labor unions, government agencies, other business firms, and so on. This concept of power is discussed elsewhere in terms of community elites (Burt 1977c). According to the proposed autonomy model, however, all that a corporate actor needs in order to derive high profits is to have low competition with other firms operating in its industries and extensive transactions with establishments in economic sectors within which there is high competition. Of course, that is not to say that power in combination with autonomy would not result in increased profits over time. As pointed out by an anonymous reviewer for the *American Journal of Sociology*, autonomy could be a sufficient condition for obtaining profits in the short run, but power is required in order to ensure the continued ability to obtain high profits. Strategically created directorate ties to constraint sectors might be sufficient to ensure long-term autonomy, and therefore profits, but unfortunately, the issues arising from a consideration of profit and autonomy time series are well beyond the scope of this discussion.

relative level of profit obtained by firms in separate industries can be compared in terms of "price–cost margins" for the industries. The price–cost margin for industry j, PCM_j, is given as the ratio of dollars of net income over dollars of sales;

$$PCM_j = (VA_j - L_j)/VS_j,$$

where VS_j is the total dollars of sales by establishments in industry j (value of shipments), L_j is the gross annual earnings of employees on the payroll of firms in industry j, and VA_j is the value added by industry j as the difference between VS_j and direct costs (including materials, supplies, fuel, electric energy, cost of resales, and contract work done by others). Since the difference between VA and L does not take into account the cost to different industries of purchasing capital commodities for production, price–cost margins have been corrected for interindustry differences in capital requirements (CR_j) in order to estimate the profit margin in industry as follows:

$$y_{j0} = PCM_j - b(CR_j - \overline{CR}), \tag{8.1}$$

where $\overline{CR}$ is the mean capital output ratio for industries generally, and the profit margin y_{j0} is intended only to measure the average ability of establishments in industry j to obtain profits relative to the ability of those in other industries.

Industry profit margins have been computed using Eq. (8.1) for the 335 four-digit industries discussed above as well as the 20 highly aggregated two-digit industries.[8] If y_{j0} is high relative to other industries, then establishments in industry j were able to 1967 to obtain profits further in excess of direct costs than would be expected as a result of the industry's capital requirements. On average, industries had a 26% profit margin in 1967 as profits are measured here; $\overline{y}_0$ is .26 for the four-digit and two-digit industries.[9] Profit margins were not

[8]Data used to compute price-cost margins are taken from the 1967 *Census of Manufactures* (U.S. Department of Commerce 1971). The lack of coresponding data on nonmanufacturing sectors restricts my analysis here to manufacturing industries as the object of market constraint. Capital requirements are computed as the gross book value of depreciable assets for industry j divided by the value of shipments for the industry;

$$CR_j = ASSETS_j/VS_j,$$

both of which are taken from the 1970 *Annual Survey of Manufactures* (U.S. Department of Commerce 1973). For the four-digit industries, the raw value of b is .077 and it is .064 for the two-digit industries. Although previous studies have controlled for interindustry differences in capital requirements by specifying CR as an additional variable in regression equations predicting profit margins (e.g., Collins & Preston 1969; Rhoades 1963, 1974; Khalilzadeh-Shirazi 1974; Lustgarten 1975), I have taken the more conservative position of completely removing the effect from price-cost margins. The difference is nominal (raw and corrected price-cost margins are correlated .98 for the two-digit industries, .97 for the four-digit) and I do not wish to carry CR as a variable throughout the analysis.

[9]The income reported as profit to the Internal Revenue Service is much lower than these numbers suggest. Using the tax return data compiled in the *Statistics of Income, Corporation Income Tax Returns* for firms showing a profit during 1967, the mean ratio of income after taxes (profit) over total receipts (total sales) is only .048 for two-digit industries in constrast to the .258 reported in Table 8.1 (Internal Revenue Service 1971). Nevertheless, the census and tax return measures of

TABLE 8.1
Structural Autonomy Effects on Profit Margins[a]

	Two digit industries ($N=20$)		Four digit industries ($N=325$)	
	Raw	standardized	Raw	standardized
Multiple correlation	.493		.403	
Oligopoly effect (β_0)	0.027	.062	0.102	.272
	(0.2)		(5.4)	
Group-affiliation effect (β_g)	1.089	.482	0.488	.291
	(1.8)		(5.6)	
Interaction effect (β_x)	4.726	.299	0.529	.037
	(1.1)		(1.7)	

[a]Least-squares regression coefficients are presented with t-tests given in parentheses. Coefficients are taken from Eq. (8.2).

constant across industries. They were lowest in the apparel industry ($y_{j0} = .17$) and highest in the chemical industry ($y_{j0} = .39$). Structural autonomy should have been similarly high for the chemical industry and low for the apparel industry.

Results

It was. Table 8.1 presents least-squares estimates for the three autonomy effects in Eq. (7.2b) that were obtained by regressing industry profits (y_{j0}) over industry concentration (y_{j1}), freedom from external constraint (y_{j2}), and the interaction of these two variables in the following equation:

---

profit margin are strongly correlated ($r = .80$), the industries showing a high profit margin in their tax returns also having high price–cost margins. However, the tax return data are less adequate to the task of analyzing market constraints than are the census data on price–cost margins: (a) Whole corporations are assigned to a single industry in the tax return data. The 1120 tax return form includes a list of economic sectors distinguished by the Standard Enterprise Classification system. The 20 broadly defined two-digit SIC industries correspond to aggregate SEC categories. The person filling out a corporation's tax return is asked to indicate which industry group provided the "largest percentage of total receipts" for the firm's activities during the year. Since large firms typically own establishments in multiple economic sectors, this self-assignment to a single sector is increasingly likely to be unreliable as economic sectors are increasingly narrowly defined. Large firms cut across even the two-digit industries as described in Chapter 4, not to mention the much more narrowly defined four-digit industries. (b) In addition to the problem of corporate self-assignment to a single sector, the tax return data are not census compilations. The 1967 data are tabulated from returns for almost all firms owning assets of over 10 million dollars; however, smaller firms are sampled, and the sample tabulations are then used to project population totals (Internal Revenue Service 1971:145–146). For reasons of reliability and accuracy, therefore, the census data used to compute price–cost margins seem preferable to tax return data. Still, it is worth noting that y_{j0} probably overstates the actual profit margin in industry j even though it is strongly correlated with that margin.

$$y_{j0} = [\mathbf{a}_j] + \eta_j,$$
$$= [\beta + \beta_o y_{j1} + \beta_g y_{j2} + \beta_x (y_{j1} - \bar{y}_1)(y_{j2} - \bar{y}_2)] + \eta_j, \quad (8.2)$$

where the bracketed term is industry j's structural autonomy measured as its profit margin predicted by the proposed model in Eq. (7.2b). Industries with high structural autonomy tended to have high profit margins. The multiple correlation between profit margin and structural autonomy is a little over .4 in Table 8.1. The three autonomy effects are weaker for the 20 two-digit industries than they are for the 335 four-digit industries; however, all effects are in the expected direction, and the results for the four-digit industries strongly support the proposed model.

Intraindustry oligopoly, measured by industry concentration, had a positive effect on industry profits. Profits and concentration have a positive correlation (.28 and .24, respectively, for two-digit and four-digit industries). The oligopoly effect captured by β_0 is .1, which is identical to the estimated regression of price–cost margins over concentration found by economists for earlier time periods (e.g., Collins & Preston 1969; Lustgarten 1975). This effect is robust over a wide variety of control variables. In an equation containing many more structural indicators of competition among industry suppliers and consumers, this oligopoly effect is still .1 (Burt 1979a, 1983:Chap. 2).

The strongest determinant of industry profits was the lack of external constraint; high profits were associated with low constraint from other sectors. The correlation between profits and the group-affiliation index is .38 for the two-digit industries and .29 for the four-digit industries. Standardized estimates of the group-affiliation effect captured by β_g are .48 and .29, respectively, for the two-digit and four-digit industries. Above and beyond its direct effect on profits, competition among an industry's suppliers and consumers had a moderate effect on profits in interaction with industry oligopoly. Standardized estimates of the interaction effect captured by β_x are .30 and .09, respectively, for the two-digit and four-digit industries. The zero-order correlation between industry profits and the product of industry concentration with the group-affiliation index, $y_{j1}y_{j2}$, is .34 and .28 for the two-digit and four-digit industries.

In short, the observed association between industry profit margins and market structure in the 1967 American economy conforms to the predictions of the structural autonomy model.[10] Using Eq. (7.4) and the parameter estimates in

---

[10]I have elsewhere described the association between profit margins market structure in much greater detail (Burt 1979a, 1983:Chap. 2). The results suggest a refinement to the structural autonomy model in order to improve its ability to predict industry profits. Market transactions with suppliers affected profits in a manner different from that in which transactions with consumers affected profits. Only one type of product flows from an industry to its consumers, who have no trouble seeing the value of collusion despite the multiple sectors in which their products are sold, but products from different sectors can flow to the industry without creating the competition among suppliers that prompts collusion. The result was that the group-affiliation index in Eq. (7.1) had to be separated into two indices; an index of the extent to which an industry had many different supplier sectors, and an index directly corresponding to Eq. (7.1) of the extent to which the industry had few oligopolistic consumer sectors. In short, oligopoly within supplier sectors matters less than

Table 8.1, market constraints from specific sectors on each industry can be computed, a_{ji} being the extent to which the profit margin in industry j can be traced to market transactions between establishments in sector i and those in the industry. More specifically, a_{ji} is the increased profit margin in industry j to be expected if market constraint from sector i is completely eliminated. This means that a_{ji} is negative to the extent that it would have been profitable for establishments in industry j to develop cooptive relations with establishments in sector i.[11] For the purposes here, I describe market constraints confronting the two-digit industries in 1967.[12]

The textiles industry provides a helpful illustration of the connection between market constraint and profits under the structural autonomy model, helpful in the sense of being heuristically simple. The industry was SIC category 22, which consisted of several (14) four-digit categories in 1967 ranging from cotton weaving mills (SIC category 2211), synthetics weaving mills (SIC category 2221), cotton finishing plants (SIC category 2261), synthetics finishing plants (SIC category 2262), carpets and rugs (SIC category 227), thread mills (SIC category 2284), padding and upholstery filling (SIC category 2293), and tire cord and fabric (SIC category 2296), to cordage and twine (SIC category 2298). The two-digit industry was an amalgam of establishments involved in diverse manufacturing activities producing textiles.

Textile establishments did not enjoy high profit margins as an industry in

---

having many different supplier sectors. Obviously, this is quite in keeping with the idea of conflicting group affiliations and merely constitutes an empirical refinement for the system under consideration. I have not incorporated these results into this analysis because a thorough analysis of market constraint is tangential to my purpose here of assessing the structural autonomy model; the proposed general model is empirically adequate as it stands; and finally, I wish to emphasize simple general models in this book rather than complex, slightly more accurate models.

[11]The mathematical niceties on this point are given with the partial derivative in Eq. (7.5) in Chapter 7. I should stress, however, that this is a theoretical, not an empirical estimate of the contribution to industry profits made by market transactions between industry and sector. The market constraint a_{ji} has been estimated by assuming that the total effect on profits in industry j from its transactions with other sectors is an additive linear composite of subeffects proportional to the extent to which the industry's transactions with sector i contribute to its group-affiliation-index score; i.e., that the group-affiliation effect $(\beta_g \Sigma_i a_{ji}, j \neq i)$ equals the sum of effect from each sector $(\Sigma_i \beta_g a_{ji}, j \neq i)$. This is an algebraically correct disaggregation of effects in the proposed model: however, a_{ji} has not been estimated directly by gathering data on profits obtained in actual market transactions between establishments. Accordingly, analyzing the a_{ji} involves a risk of making ecological errors, i.e., making erroneous inferences about individuals $(\beta_g a_{ji})$ from data on aggregates $(\beta_g \Sigma_i a_{ji}, j \neq i)$. Unfortunately, there are no data available on the extent to which transactions between each pair of sectors in the economy are profitable to the parties involved in them. Indeed, one advantage that the structural autonomy model has to offer is the estimate of a_{ji} as a theoretical guess at the extent to which transactions between industry j and sector i are profitable, on average, for establishments in the industry.

[12]I introduced four-digit industries here both because two-digit concentration ratios and profit-margins have been constructed from four-digit data and because the much larger number of four-digit industries provides a stronger test of the autonomy effects in Eq. (7.2). A detailed description of the connection between four-digit market constraints and directorate ties is beyond the scope of this single chapter. I provide such a description elsewhere (Burt 1983), and the results obtained there merely corroborate in detail the conclusions I reach here.

1967. The industry's corrected price–cost margin indicates that 19¢ out of each dollar of product sold was profit above and beyond direct manufacturing costs ($y_{j0} = .188$). This was among the lowest margins obtained in the two-digit industries. It was well below the 26¢ on the dollar profit margin obtained on average across all 20 of the two-digit industries in 1967.

This low profit margin indicates that the pattern of market transactions defining the industry's network position in the economy contained severe market constraints for establishments within the industry. Competition within the industry was about average so that it contributed little to this low profit margin ($y_{j1} = .38$, a z-score of .14). However, severe market constraint confronted the industry from it suppliers and consumers ($y_{j2} = .918$, a z-score of -1.67). Only the apparel industry faced markedly more severe constraint.

This high constraint from other sectors can be understood very quickly by considering the pattern of market transactions between textiles establishments and other sectors. Table 8.2 lists three items on each economic sector with respect to the textiles industry: the percentage of all buying and selling with other sectors that textile establishments transacted with the sector, concentration in the sector (y_{i1}), and the intensity of market constraint posed for the textiles industry by the sector (a_{ji}). One number stands out in column one of the table. Far and away the most typical transactions in which textile establishments were involved were transactions with the apparel industry. Of all the buying and selling that textile establishments transacted with other sectors, 44% was transacted with apparel establishments. Looking down column one of Table 8.2 shows that the next highest percentage was the 15% transacted with establishments in the chemicals industry. Lower than that were the 7% and 6% transacted with establishments in the other agriculture and rubber sectors, respectively. Unfortunately for the textile establishments, the two sectors on which it most depended were not the most competitive. The average level of concentration in the 51 sectors is .234. The apparel industry was slightly below this average ($y_{i1} = .201$), but well above the most highly competitive sectors. The chemicals industry was well above this average ($y_{i1} = .417$). In short, the textiles industry was in the unpleasant position of relying heavily on two other sectors for the bulk of its buying and selling where one of those sectors was a comparative oligopoly.

These features of the industry's market transactions determine the structural autonomy of textile establishments in 1967. Drawing on the results in Table 8.1 to compute structural autonomy from Eqs. (7.2b) or (8.2) yields a value of .195 for a_j. This is the profit margin expected in the textiles industry given the constraints implied by its pattern of market transactions: a mean profit margin expected for industries generally ($\bar{y}_0 = \bar{a} = .258$), plus a minor adjustment for the slightly above average concentration within the industry (.001), minus a rather large adjustment for the severe constraint facing the industry from other sectors (a direct effect, $-.055$, and an indirect effect in interaction with industry oligopoly, $-.009$, for a total of $-.064$) so that $a_j = .258 + .001 -$

TABLE 8.2
Market Structure for the Textiles Industry in 1967

Supplier/consumer sectors	Percentage of nonapparel buying and selling that is done with sector	y_{i1}	Market constraint a_{ji}
Livestock	2	.000	.000
Other agriculture	7	.000	.000
Forestry–fishery	0	.000	.000
Agribusiness services	0	.000	.000
Iron mining	0	.435	.000
Nonferrous metal mining	0	.302	.000
Coal mining	0	.025	.000
Petroleum–gas	0	.028	.000
Stone–clay mining	0	.116	.000
Chemicals mining	0	.290	.000
New construction	1	.032	.000
Maintenance–repair	0	.033	.000
Ordnance	0	.083	.000
Food	0	.323	.000
Tobacco	0	.736	.000
Textiles (intraindustry)	—	.380	.356
Apparel	44	.201	−.621
Lumber	0	.163	.000
Furniture	3	.185	−.002
Paper	2	.311	−.001
Printing	1	.189	.000
Chemicals	15	.417	−.356
Petroleum	0	.329	.000
Rubber	6	.313	−.010
Leather	1	.251	−.001
Stone–clay–glass	1	.373	−.001
Primary metals	0	.451	.000
Fabricated metals	0	.283	.000
Mechanical machines	1	.365	−.001
Electrical machines	0	.462	.000
Transportation equipment	1	.670	−.002
Instruments	1	.494	.000
Miscellaneous manufacturing	1	.276	−.001
Transport–warehousing	2	.254	−.004
Communications	0	.060	.000
Radio–television	0	.060	.000
Utilities	1	.999	−.005
Wholesale–retail	4	.001	.000
Finance–insurance	0	.014	.000
Real estate	1	.000	.000
Personal services	0	.002	.000
Business services	1	.002	.000

Continued

TABLE 8.2   *(Continued from previous page)*

Supplier/consumer sectors	Percentage of nonapparel buying and selling that is done with sector	y_{i1}	Market constraint a_{ji}
Automobile services	0	.001	.000
Amusements	0	.004	.000
Medical–educational services	0	.000	.000
Federal government	0	.999	.000
State–local government	0	.999	.000
Gross imports	3	.000	.000
Expense accounts	0	.000	.000
Office supplies	0	.000	.000
Scrap	1	.000	.000

.064 = .195. A profit margin of 20¢ on the dollar would be expected in the industry based on its pattern of market transactions and a margin of 19¢ was actually observed.[13]

A quick look down column three of Table 8.2, the column containing market constraints on the textiles industry, shows that this low expected profit can be traced principally to market transactions with the apparel industry (for which $a_{ji} = -.621$) and, to a lesser extent, market transactions with the chemicals industry (for which $a_{ji} = -.356$). The remaining market constraints on the industry were comparatively negligible. The next most severe constraint originated from the rubber industry (a negligible a_{ji} of $-.010$). The apparel industry posed a constraint because textile establishments conducted such a large proportion of their buying and selling there. The chemicals industry posed a constraint because it was somewhat oligopolistic, and textile establishments conducted a significant proportion of their buying and selling there.[14] The textile

[13]Not all predictions are this accurate. Figure 8.4 at the end of this chapter shows that profits in the textiles industry were more accurately predicted by the structural autonomy model than were profits generally. The multiple correlations in Table 8.1 show that only a fifth of the variation in industry profit margins is described by industry structural autonomy. This proportion increases to about a third of the variation, however, for a slightly more complex specification of structural autonomy (multiple correlations of .592 and .546 are reported for two-digit and four-digit industries respectively in a detailed analysis given elsewhere, Burt 1983: Table 2.6).

[14]These market constraint relations are deceptively simple. They can mask fundamentally different processes by which a sector constrains an industry as its supplier as opposed to the constraint it poses as one of the industry's principal consumers. This point is discussed elsewhere in detail with the apparel industry for illustration (Burt 1983:Chap. 2), but it is relevant to the constraints on textile establishments described here. The percentages in Table 8.2 suggest that the apparel industry was a much more typical source of market constraint for textile establishments than the chemicals industry. With respect to textile sales, this was true. The $60 million of textile goods sold to the chemicals industry in 1967 represented less than 1% of sales to nontextile establishments. The $7,924 million worth sold to the apparel industry represented 73%. With respect to purchases by textile establishments, the situation is completely reversed. Textile establishments purchased $2,764 million worth of goods from the chemicals industry in 1967. This represented

establishments had strong market incentives in 1967 to develop cooptive relations with establishments in the apparel industry and the chemicals industry, but little incentive to develop such relations with nontextile establishments in any other sectors of the economy. If directorate ties were being used to coopt sources of market constraint in 1967, they should have occurred where the a_{ji} indicate profit incentives for cooptive relations to be developed.

8.3 COOPTIVE DIRECTORATE TIES

A third feature of corporate establishments that makes them an area of research nicely suited to the structural autonomy model is the sharp distinction between market transactions as formal relations and a host of comparatively informal corporate relations such as directorate ties. Relations in the input–output table constitute "formal" relations in the sense that an establishment choosing to manufacture a type of commodity must adopt the relational pattern characterizing the commodity as specific proportions of inputs from supplier sectors and outputs to consumer sectors. For example, an establishment in the food industry can expect to purchase the bulk of its supplies from establishments in the livestock and other agriculture sectors as well as from other establishments in the food industry itself. The establishment perhaps has discretion in selecting others as suppliers within these sectors, but the production of food products requires some input from at least one establishment in these sectors. In contrast, there are many interestablishment relations that can be interpreted as "informal" in the sense that they are performed at the discretion of the parties involved. It is this discretionary nature that makes a class of relations informal as discussed in Section 7.2. Consider the merger between two establishments which would create an ownership tie between them. There are no establishments with which any one must merge. To be sure, when two establishments merge, the resulting connection is less fragile than a friendship tie between erstwhile colleagues. But informal here refers to discretion, not fragility.[15] An establishment's decision to merge with another is reached at the establishment's

---

37% of all supplies they purchased outside the textiles industry. The $206 million in apparel products purchased by textile establishments represented less than 3%. Different organizational units within a textile establishment, in short, could be expected to have different perceptions of the most serious market constraints confronting the establishment. The sales department would have been very interested in developing cooptive relations with apparel establishments since that would be where profits in sales were most constrained. The production department would have been interested in developing cooptive relations with chemicals establishments since that would be where savings in production were most constrained.

[15]Accordingly, the formal/informal distinction between relational contents should not be confused with Litwak and Rothman's (1970) discussion of formality in interorganizational relations. They refer to the formality of a relation as its noncasual, institutionalized character. Like the distinction Granovetter makes between strong and weak relations (see footnote 12 in Chapter 7), Litwak and Rothman refer to relational form (strength) with their concept rather than the relational contents I am distinguishing with the formal/informal dichotomy.

discretion—perhaps related to, but definitely not a technical requirement of, the establishment's production of output. As such, the merger is an informal relation potentially useful as a means of circumventing market constraints generated by market transactions as formal relations. In short, the three types of directorate ties discussed in Chapter 4, ownership ties, direct interlock ties, and indirect interlock ties through financial institutions, fall into the category of relations discussed as informal in Chapter 7.

Four different measures of the cooptive relation between industry j and sector i, w_{ji}, have been computed from the data generated by Eqs. (4.1) and (4.2) in Chapter 4. The ownership estimate of w_{ji} equals the number of establishments in sector i that were owned by one of the 42 manufacturing firms also owning an establishment in industry j. For example, there is one ownership tie between the primary metals industry and transportation equipment industry in Figures 4.1 and 4.2. The binary variable o_{kj} is zero unless firm k owned an establishment in sector j, whereupon o_{kj} is one. Across all 42 manufacturing firms k, the following sum equals the frequency of directorate ties through ownership between establishments in industry j and sector i:

$$w_{ji(o)} = \sum_k o_{kj} o_{ki}. \tag{8.3}$$

The direct interlock estimate of w_{ji} equals the number of establishments in sector i that were owned by any one of the other 151 sampled firms that was interlocked with one of the 42 manufacturing firms owning an establishment in industry j. For example, there is one direct interlock tie between the transportation equipment industry and the finance sector in Figure 4.2. As given in Eq. (4.1), d_{kj} is the number of establishments in sector j that are represented on the board of firm k through direct interlocking. Across all 42 manufacturing firms k, the following sum equals the number of establishments in sector i connected by direct interlock ties to manufacturing establishments in industry j:

$$w_{ji(d)} = \sum_k o_{kj} d_{kj}. \tag{8.4}$$

The indirect financial interlock estimate of w_{ji} equals the number of establishments in sector i that were owned by any one of the other 151 firms that was in turn interlocked with a bank or insurance company in turn interlocked with one of the 42 manufacturing firms owning an establishment in industry j. For example, there are two indirect financial interlock ties between the transportation equipment industry and the transportation–warehousing sector in Figure 4.2. As given in Eq. (4.2), i_{kj} is the number of establishments in sector j that were represented on the board of firm k through indirect financial interlocking. Across all 42 manufacturing firms k, the following sum equals the number of establishments in sector i connected indirectly through financial institutions to manufacturing establishments in industry j:

$$w_{ji(i)} = \sum_k o_{kj} i_{ki}. \tag{8.5}$$

Finally, the O–D–I multiplex estimate of w_{ji} equals the number of establishments in industry j that simultaneously had an ownership, direct interlock, and indirect financial interlock tie to establishments in sector i. There are no such ties in Figure 4.2. These multiplex ties were characteristic of corporate directorate ties to other sectors, as is discussed in Chapter 4, but they were less prevalent in the economy than were the directorate ties considered individually. This is to be expected since an O–D–I multiplex tie is the intersection of all three of the other ties considered individually. It is the overlapping area of all three circles illustrating cooptive networks in Figure 4.3. Let $m_{ki} = 0$ unless three things happen simultaneously: firm k owns an establishment in sector i ($o_{ki} = 1$), firm k has a direct interlock tie to some other firm which owns an establishment in sector i ($d_{ki} > 0$), and firm k has an indirect financial interlock tie to some other firm which owns an establishment in sector i ($i_{ki} > 0$). When these three conditions occur at the same time, firm k has an O–D–I multiplex tie to sector i and $m_{ki} = 1$. Across all 42 manufacturing firms k, the following sum equals the number of establishments in industry j with O–D–I multiplex directorate ties to establishments in sector i:

$$w_{ji(m)} = \sum_k o_{kj} m_{ki}. \tag{8.6}$$

For each of the 45 $\mathbf{a}_{ji}$ estimated as market constraints on profits in industry j the preceding equations provide four w_{ji} estimates as directorate ties involving the industry with sectors generally. The 45 sectors are the first 45 rows in Table 4.2. They correspond in some manner to SIC categories so that it was possible to locate establishments owned in these sectors by the sampled firms.

Figure 8.1 presents box-and-whisker plots of uniplex directorate tie frequencies for three types of sectors that they would reach: intraindustry ties, extraindustry ties to sectors other than finance, and extraindustry ties to the finance sector. These data plots quickly communicate the overall distribution of the tie frequencies. The "box" of a distribution extends from the score representing the point below which 25% of the distribution falls up to the score representing the point below which 75% of the distribution falls. A horizontal line within the box marks the median of the distribution. A "whisker" extends from the top of the box to the maximum score in the distribution and from the bottom of the box to the minimum score. For example, consider the distribution of direct interlock ties between the industries and other, nonfinancial, sectors—$w_{ji(d)}$ in Eq. (8.4) where $j \neq i$ and sector i is not the finance sector. There are 860 relations of this type. The median number of direct interlock ties was 2 with 50% of all $w_{ji(d)}$ falling between 0 and 6. The maximum number of such ties connecting an industry with any nonfinancial sector was 35.

The first point made clear by Figure 8.1 is the relative ranges of the three types of directorate ties. As would be expected from the analysis in Chapter 4,

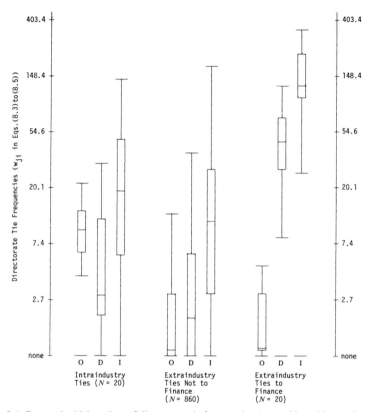

Figure 8.1. Box-and-whisker plots of directorate tie frequencies (natural logarithm scale, the log of a null frequency is set equal to a zero, O refers to ownership ties, D to direct interlock ties, and I to direct interlock ties through financial institutions).

ownership ties were the least frequent, direct interlock ties more frequent, and indirect financial interlock ties the most frequent. With the exception of intraindustry direct interlock ties, which are less frequent than the number of establishments operating in the industry, all features of $w_{ji(i)}$ tend to exceed corresponding features of $w_{ji(d)}$, which exceed corresponding features of $w_{ji(o)}$, maximum scores, minimum scores, median scores, and so on.

The second point illustrated by Figure 8.1 is the disproportionate extent to which finance establishments were involved in directorate ties. On almost all corresponding features of their distributions, extraindustry ties to sectors generally were lower than ties to finance in particular. For example, the median number of direct interlock ties to some other sector was 2, but this increased to 43 if the sector was finance; the maximum number of such ties to another sector was 35, but this increased to 108 if the sector was finance; the median number of indirect financial interlock ties to some other sectors was 11, which increased to 120 if the sector was finance, and so on. These extraordinary frequencies of directorate ties require some special treatment in a comparison of market constraint and directorate ties. This is all the more true given the market constraint posed by the finance sector on the manufacturing industries in 1967—none. Each of the manufacturing industries faced near zero a_{ji} from the finance sector. There are two very possible explanations of this low market constraint from the finance sector and extraordinary interlocking. It is quite possible that the finance sector exercises its constraint through some process other than the sales and purchase transactions on which the a_{ji} are based. The estimated a_{ji} only indicate that finance was a negligible source of market constraint in terms of its buying and selling transactions with manufacturing industries in 1967. Alternatively, the finance sector could merely be a broker between firms in other sectors so that the high directorate tie frequencies associated with the sector would be the result of the sector's being a channel through which other sectors are reached rather than an object of cooptive relations. This is the justification discussed in Section 4.3 for analyzing indirect interlock ties through financial establishments as a separate type of cooptive directorate tie. In light of that discussion and the availability of data on indirect financial interlock ties, I shall set aside the 20 industry to finance sector relations in favor of analyzing the role of the finance sector in terms of the indirect interlock ties it generated

As also would be expected from the analysis in Chapter 4, the three types of directorate ties occurred between the same industries and sectors. Table 8.3 presents correlations among the frequencies with which the three types of directorate ties occurred: those that occurred within the 20 industries (above diagonal) and those that occurred between those industries and other sectors (below diagonal). The 860 extraindustry relations exclude those reaching the finance sector. Frequencies of intraindustry ties are more strongly correlated across types of ties than are extraindustry ties; however, correlations in both cases are quite strong. Among the extraindustry correlations, the lowest is between the number of establishments in sector i connected by direct interlock ties to industry j and the number of establishments in the sector owned by firms

TABLE 8.3
Correlations and Means for Directorate Tie Frequencies

	$w_{ji(o)}$	$w_{ji(d)}$	$w_{ji(i)}$	$w_{ji(m)}$	Means
$w_{ji(o)}$	1.00	.96	.90	.89	10.00
$w_{ji(d)}$	.57	1.00	.97	.95	6.70
$w_{ji(i)}$	.67	.94	1.00	.95	35.93
$w_{ji(m)}$	.81	.66	.73	1.00	4.15
Means	1.64	4.27	21.17	.59	

[a]Moments above the diagonal are computed from data on the 20 intraindustry relations, and those below the diagonal have been computed from the 860 extraindustry relations to nonfinancial sectors.

in the industry. However, this is a strong correlation; $w_{ji(o)}$ has a .57 correlation with $w_{ji(d)}$.

These high correlations suggest that very similar patterns of market constraint effects on directorate tie frequencies can be expected for the different types of directorate ties. The question now is how ties were distributed with respect to market incentives for them to be created. I first describe ties among establishments within an industry and then ties between establishments in separate industries.

Intraindustry Results

At the outset, intraindustry ownership ties much be distinguished from interlock ties. Ownership ties within an industry are different in meaning from intraindustry interlocks. Between industry j and sector i, $w_{ji(o)}$ is the number of ownership ties between industry and sector. A comparable intraindustry figure would be the number of separate establishments within the industry that were owned by the same firm or perhaps the frequency of intraindustry mergers. However, $w_{jj(o)}$ is the number of large firms operating in the industry, not the number of competitors per se, but rather the number of sampled firms (representing large manufacturing firms) attracted to the industry. Intraindustry interlock ties, in contrast, conform to the discussion in Chapter 4, $w_{jj(d)}$ being the number of intraindustry direct interlock ties between establishments and $w_{jj(i)}$ being the number of intraindustry indirect financial interlock ties.

As a network position in the economy, an industry could be attractive to large firms and encourage intraindustry interlock ties for at least two reasons. First, a negative value of the partial derivative $\partial a_j / \partial y_{j1}$ in Eq. (7.3) would indicate that industry j was repressed by dependence on a single oligopolistic supplier or consumer sector to the point that establishments within the industry had no market incentive to develop cooptive relations with one another. A positive value of this derivative would indicate that industry j was free of such constraint and accordingly an attractive product market. Second, the coefficient a_{jj} indicates the extent to which the structural autonomy of industry j, which is to say its predicted profit margin, was a result of a lack of competition within the industry as measured by industry concentration. Specifically, a_{jj} is a marginal contribution from industry concentration to the industry profit margin predicted by market structure. To the extent that a_{jj} is positive, industry j was an attractive product market to large firms since the low competition within it would ensure comparatively stable profits—assuming that the large, dominant firms within the industry allowed competitors to enter the market.

Up to a certain limit, this reasoning seems adequate. Table 8.4 presents correlations between the w_{jj} and a_{jj}. Results are presented for all industries and then presented for repressed ($\partial a_j / \partial y_{j1} < 0$) versus unrepressed ($\partial a_j / \partial y_{j1} \geq 0$) industries separately. There is evidence of association between w_{jj} and a_{jj};

TABLE 8.4
Intraindustry Correlations; a_{jj} with w_{jj}

	Raw scores	Log scores
All industries ($N = 20$)		
Owned establishments	.34	.49
Direct interlock ties	.25	.36
Indirect financial interlock		
ties	.35	.45
O–D–I multiplex ties ($w_{jj(m)}$)	.34	.38
Repressed industries ($N = 4$)		
Owned establishments	.06	.33
Direct interlock ties	−.02	.34
Indirect financial interlock		
ties	−.06	.39
O–D–I multiplex ties	.10	.45
Unrepressed industries ($N = 16$)		
Owned establishments	.40	.52
Direct interlock ties	.28	.36
Indirect financial interlock		
ties	.40	.47
O–D–I multiplex ties	.38	.38

[a]Repressed industries are those confronted with severe market constraint as discussed in the text, and log scores refer to the natural logarithms of raw scores. Since some industries contained no interlock ties, the observed interlock tie frequencies have been increased by one before taking logs.

however, the association is exponential rather than linear. Correlations between raw scores are lower than corresponding correlations between natural logarithms of scores. Further, there is little evidence that the lack of competition within repressed industries is less attractive to firms than the lack of competition within unrepressed industries. Correlations between log scores do not vary enormously between repressed and unrepressed industries in Table 8.4.

That is not to say that there is a monotonoic association between a_{jj} and w_{jj}. Figure 8.2 illustrates the nonmonotonic association with a graph of direct interlock tie frequencies, $w_{jj(d)}$, against the marginal contribution industry concentration made to predicted industry profits, a_{jj}. Very similar graphs are obtained using any one type of directorate tie frequency, so I have only produced a single graph of the frequencies clearly referring to connections between separate establishments and highly correlated with the other types of directorate ties (see upper diagonal of Table 8.3).[16] Repressed industries are

[16]Graphs of the ownerships, direct interlock ties, and indirect financial interlock ties are presented in an early analysis (Burt 1980d: Figure 3). I have analyzed these directorate tie data in two other contexts, each with a different autonomy model. In the above cited analysis, I used an initial specification of the model (Burt 1980a) similar to the one used here except that the metric of the a_{jj} is different, and the model used here is algebraically clearer. The shape of the data distributions in Burt (1980d:Figure 3) and those described here are nearly identical (ignoring the

(Continued on next page)

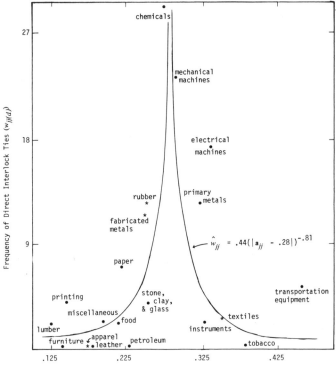

Figure 8.2. Intraindustry direct interlock ties (repressed industries are represented in the graph by asterisks).

represented in Figure 8.2 by asterisks. These asterisks do not systematically stand apart from the dots representing unrepressed industries.

The distribution in Figure 8.2 illustrates a kinked association between a_{jj} and w_{jj}. It suggests a criterion level of a_{jj} past which increasing values of a_{jj} were associated with exponentially decreasing—rather than increasing—frequencies of directorate ties. All four graphs of w_{jj} against a_{jj} show a sharp peak in the distribution before and after which tie frequency decreases rapidly. Refer to this criterion as **a**, the level of a_{jj} that tended to have the highest frequency of

(Continued from previous page)

obvious difference in the metric of the horizonal axis). In a much more detailed analysis of market structure and directorate ties at the two-digit and four-digit industry levels (Burt 1983), an empirically refined autonomy model is used which produces a_{ji} substantively different from those used here, although the results are very similar. In the initial analysis of the two-digit data (Burt 1980d), the tobacco and transportation equipment industries were set aside as outliers, and a monotonic function was used to describe the data. The higher levels of concentration in the four-digit data emphasized that the kinked function in Eq. (8.7) was a better description of the data (Burt 1983:Chap. 4), so I have adopted it here even though there are many fewer two-digit industries to the right of the criterion **a**.

TABLE 8.5
Predicting intraindustry ties from a lack of intraindustry market constraint

w_{jj}	α	β	t-test	Correlation
Owned establishments	2.71	−.42	4.3	−.71
Direct interlock ties	.44	−.81	3.8	−.66
Indirect financial interlock ties	.53	−1.18	3.6	−.65
O–D–I multiplex ties	.68	−.59	3.1	−.60

[a]Parameters are specified in Eq. (8.7), the criterion **a** is .28 for all four equations, and the regression line of predicted direct interlock ties is given as a bold line in Figure 8.2. In order to compute logs of the interlock tie frequencies, all frequencies have been increased by one before taking logs.

directorate ties. For the two-digit data, **a** appears to be about .28. In other words, the frequency of establishments in an industry and intraindustry directorate ties increased exponentially with increasing contributions from industry concentration to industry profits up to this criterion ratio **a**. Past that criterion level, increasing contributions from industry concentration were associated with exponentially decreasing tie frequencies. This kinked exponential association can be captured by the following equation predicting w_{jj} from $\mathbf{a}_{jj}$:

$$\begin{aligned} w_{jj} &= \alpha \left(\mid \mathbf{a}_{jj} - \mathbf{a} \mid \right)^{\beta} \eta_j, \\ &= (\hat{w}_{jj}) e_j, \end{aligned} \tag{8.7}$$

where e_j is a residual term, **a** is the criterion level of $\mathbf{a}_{jj}$, and estimation can be accomplished by taking the natural logarithms of both sides of the equation to obtain the following estimation equation:

$$\ln w_{jj} = \ln \alpha + \beta \ln(\mid \mathbf{a}_{jj} - \mathbf{a} \mid) + \ln \eta_j.$$

The term in parentheses is high when $\mathbf{a}_{jj}$ is far above or below the criterion level **a** so that β should be significantly negative, the highest frequencies occuring at the criterion **a**.

Table 8.5 presents estimates of the parameters in Eq. (8.7). The correlations for the kinked regression line in Eq. (8.7) are all stronger than corresponding correlations in Table 8.4 for monotonic functions. Moreover, the association between $\mathbf{a}_{jj}$ and each type of directorate tie is statistically significant; β is significantly less than 0 for ownership of establishments, direct interlock ties, indirect financial interlock ties, as well as mixed ties. Showing the form of the function, the direct interlock tie frequency $w_{jj(d)}$ that is predicted by $\mathbf{a}_{jj}$ (i.e., $\hat{w}_{jj}$ in Eq. [8.7]) is presented in Figure 8.2 as a bold line.[17]

---

[17]The regression line in Figure 8.2 does not correspond exactly to what would be predicted by substituting coefficients in Table 8.5 into Eq. (8.7). Since observed interlock frequencies were increased by 1 in order to compute logs, I have subtracted 1 from the frequencies predicted, i.e., $\hat{w}_{jj(d)}$ in Figure 8.2 is 1 less than the number predicted by the estimates Table 8.5 presents for direct interlock ties.

The specific industries labeled in Figure 8.2 can be used to interpret the association between $\mathbf{a}_{jj}$ and w_{jj}. Industry concentration is the principal determinant of where an industry appears in the graph. At the left where $\mathbf{a}_{jj}$ is very low, one finds the highly competitive industries that have low concentration ratios: lumber, apparel, furniture, printing, and so on. At the extreme right where $\mathbf{a}_{jj}$ is very high, one finds two industries dominated by a small number of firms: the tobacco industry and the transportation equipment industry. At this extreme level of concentration, firms had no need for directorate ties with one another in order to coordinate their actions. They were so few in number that they could easily anticipate one another's behavior.[18] This implicit coordination of action by dominant firms in an industry presents a formidable barrier to entry for other firms so that the small number of firms operating within the industry ensures a low frequency of interlock ties. Industry concentration is not solely responsible for intraindustry ties. Note that the textile industry appears to the right in Figure 8.2 with a value of $\mathbf{a}_{jj}$ well past the criterion $\mathbf{a}$. The textile industry had a slightly above average level of concentration ($y_{j1} = .38$, which is .14 standard deviations above the mean), but it experiences severe market constraint from other sectors so that the positive contribution of industry concentration to textile profits is comparatively high relative to the profit margin expected from market structure generally ($\hat{\mathbf{a}}_{jj} = .36$, which is 1.16 standard deviations above the mean).

The bottom line here is that intraindustry directorate ties were patterned by intraindustry market constraint, but by a nonmonotonic function. Across industries, as the contribution to industry profits from industry concentration increased up to a criterion level, large firms were attracted to the industry, and interlock ties among establishments in the industry occurred with an exponentially increasing frequency. Past that criterion, the association is reversed. As large firms within an industry became increasingly dominant so as to lower intraindustry competition, increase industry concentration, and accordingly lower the uncertainty of market constraint within the industry, they had less need for interlock ties with one another in order to coordinate their actions. Past the criterion $\mathbf{a}$, large firms operated in an industry and interlock ties occurred

---

[18]That there is a small number of competitors able to coordinate their actions in the absence of interorganizational ties with one another is well recognized (e.g., Phillips 1960; Galbraith 1973; Pfeffer & Salancik 1978). For example, Galbraith (1973) refers to firms capable of dominating their industry as part of the "planning" system in the American economy. He stresses that for these firms, the firms responsible for high concentration within their industries,

> the prices that serve the growth of one firm will, generally speaking, serve the growth of others. One firm, accordingly, can set prices knowing that others will find them broadly acceptable. And, the number of firms in the industry being small, the pacesetting firm can know or judge what will be acceptable to the other firms and be so guided. The others will then conform [p.126].

among establishments in the industry with an exponentially decreasing frequency.[19,20]

[19]This negative association contradicts the monotonically positive association Pennings (1980: 94ff) reports in his analysis of interlocks among large American firms in 1969, intraindustry interlocking being high in the most concentrated industries. A close look at his measures reveals the reason for this contradiction. Pennings assigns each of 386 large firms to a two-digit industry and then correlates the concentration in a firm's industry with the firm's involvement in interlocking (Pennings 1980:101). The positive correlation he reports between concentration and intraindustry (horizontal) interlocking can be traced to two features of his operationalization—two-digit concentration ratios and firms as units of analysis. The two-digit industries aggregate four-digit industries so that many of the highly concentrated industries disappear. In fact, there are only two two-digit industries that stand out as highly concentrated—tobacco and transportation equipment. In an analysis of two-digit directorate ties, I found that there were few intraindustry directorate ties in these two industries as of 1967. I decided to put them aside as outliers, as I have explained with data distributions elsewhere (Burt 1980d:156–161). With these two industries put to one side, I found a monotonic association between concentration (in terms of $\mathbf{a}_{jj}$ based on an initial autonomy model) and intraindustry directorate ties, high levels of concentration being associated with more frequent directorate ties. An analysis of the four-digit data quickly revealed, however, that the tobacco and transportation equipment industries were not outliers so much as they were examples of high concentration industries (Burt 1983:Chap. 4). By taking firms as his units of analysis, Pennings deemphasizes the tobacco and transportation equipment industries in his correlations; few firms operated in these industries so the bulk of his observations (firms) operated in other two-digit industries. In these other industries, I too found a positive, monotonic association between concentration and directorate ties. The four-digit data make it clear that this monotonic association, based on a plausible analysis of the two-digit data, is quite wrong as a general understanding. There is a systematic tendency for intraindustry interlocking to decrease past a criterion level of increasing industry concentration. This tendency is also empirically adequate in the two-digit data as Table 8.5 makes very clear, but it is even more explicit in the four-digit data.

[20]At this point it is convenient to note the similarity between Eq. (8.7) and an equation estimated by Pfeffer and Salancik (1978:156). In terms of the symbols used here, Pfeffer and Salancik specify the following equation in which the number of interorganizational ties within industry j, w_{jj}, is predicted by the level of concentration within the industry, y_{j1}:

$$\ln w_{jj} = \ln \alpha + b_1 \ln(y_{j1}) + b_2(\ln | y_{j1} - y |) + \ln e_j$$

where y is the median value of y_{j1} for all industries. Putting aside the difference between industry concentration (y_{j1}) and a measure of its marginal importance to industry profits ($\mathbf{a}_{jj}$) since the latter is an intrinsic part of the structural autonomy model, a model not available for previous analyses, there are two differences between the above equation and Eq. (8.7) that might call for a respecification of Eq. (8.7): use of the median y as the criterion $\mathbf{a}$ and introduction of the linear effect b_1. Pfeffer and Salancik select median industry concentration as the point at which competitive uncertainty within an industry is at a maximum, and accordingly, the point at which intraindustry cooptive ties should be most frequent. Although arbitrary, this selection is based on a visual inspection of a graph of merger rates in two-digit industries against levels of industry concentration. Moreover it is empirically adequate in the sense that Pfeffer and Salancik (1978:156,166) report significantly negative estimates of b_2 for frequencies of joint ventures and aggregate direct interlock ties. I have similarly chosen the criterion $\mathbf{a}$ from a visual inspection of graphs. My choice is also arbitrary, although it comes more directly from the observed data on directorate tie frequencies. In the absence of theory explaining why intraindustry ties should be most frequent at a specific level of industry concentration or a specific level of $\mathbf{a}_{jj}$, the value of the criterion $\mathbf{a}$ remains an essentially empirical question. Ideally, $\mathbf{a}$ would be estimated simultaneously with α and β as an unknown parameter in Eq. (8.7). There remains the question of adding a linear effect to Eq. (8.7). Pfeffer and Salancik (1978) specify this linear term for interlocks and joint ventures because "as the number of firms in the organizational field to be coordinated increases, the probability of developing an

(Continued on next page)

Extraindustry Results

The coefficient a_{ji} measures the extent to which the profit margin in industry j as of 1967 could be traced to market transactions between the industry and sector i. To the extent that the sector was the industry's principal supplier, principal consumer, and itself oligopolistic, a_{ji} is negative indicating that the sector was a source of market constraint on industry profits. Since all establishments could have expected an increased industry profit margin by coopting sources of market constraint ($\partial a_j/\partial a_{ji}$ being negative for all industries, see Eq. [7.5]), directorate ties should have existed in 1967 between each industry and those sectors constraining industry profits—assuming that such ties were being used to coopt sources of market constraint.

In fact, with a minor qualification, directorate tie frequency is linearly proportional to market constraint intensity. Table 8.6 presents correlations between raw and log scores for three different sets of relations to nonfinancial sectors: those from industries generally, those from industries repressed by severe constraint from other sector(s), and those from unrepressed industries. The minor qualification here is that the proportionality of directorate tie frequency to market constraint intensity is affected by the overall level of constraint that confronted an industry.

Although each industry could have benefited from cooptive relations to sources of market constraint on it (in the sense that $\partial a_j/\partial a_{ji}$ is negative for all of them), they were not equally successful in developing directorate ties with sectors in proportion to the intensity of constraint posed by other sectors. In Table 8.6, the linear association between w_{ji} and a_{ji} is consistently stronger than that between log scores; however, the strength of the linear association across industries generally is not particularly strong.[21] The strongest association is

---

(Continued from previous page)

interorganizational structure through informal or semiformal linkages decreases [p.153]." In other words, b_1 should be positive, as they report it is. To some extent, this effect is captured by Eq. (8.7), infrequent directorate ties being expected in industries in which there are many competitors ($a_{jj} \ll a$) as well as those in which there are only a few ($a_{jj} \gg a$). Nevertheless, I reestimated Eq. (8.7) with a linear term, $b_1(\ln a_{jj})$. In this equation, β is still significantly negative for all four types of directorate ties. In keeping with the two-digit results Pfeffer and Salancik report, b_1 is consistently positive with values of .42, .50, 1.24, and .54, respectively, for ownerships, direct interlock ties, indirect financial interlock ties, and multiplex ties (t-tests of 1.9, .9, 1.5, and 1.1). Note that only ownerships significantly show the expected linear effect. Moreover, the results at the four-digit level are consistently negligible. Therefore, there seems to be little reason to complicate Eq. (8.7) with a monotonic effect.

[21]Manipulation of an arbitrary constant necessary to compute log scores here can affect the log correlations significantly. Since the a_{ji} are typically negative fractions, they must be converted to positive values before taking logs. I have added a_{ji} to 1 before taking logs in order to maintain the relative values of the a_{ji}, particularly with respect to zero values. There were several sectors i posing zero constraint for industry j where sector and industry were connected by no directorate ties. When a_{ji} is converted to a positive fraction before taking logs, the constant arbitrarily assigned to zero takes on great importance because of these null observations. If a_{ji} is converted by multiplying it times -1 and adding a small, arbitrary constant to change zero values to some nonzero value, the strength of the correlation between the log scores will depend on the constant chosen; the smaller

TABLE 8.6
Extraindustry Correlations; a_{ji} with $w_{ji}{}^a$

	Raw scores	Log scores
All industries (N = 860)		
Ownership ties	−.36	−.24
Direct interlock ties	−.15	−.13
Indirect financial interlock ties	−.19	−.12
O–D–I multiplex ties ($w_{jj(m)}$)	−.35	−.23
Repressed industries ($N = 172$)		
Ownership ties	−.33	−.24
Direct interlock ties	−.10	−.08
Indirect financial interlock ties	−.11	−.08
O–D–I multiplex ties	−.26	−.18
Unrepressed industries (N = 688)		
Ownership ties	−.52	−.38
Direct interlock ties	−.25	−.25
Indirect financial interlock ties	−.33	−.25
O–D–I multiplex ties	−.55	−.45

[a]Repressed industries are those confronted with severe market constraint as discussed in the text, and log scores refer to the natural logarithms of raw scores. Since some industries had no directorate ties to some sectors, all frequencies have been increased by one before taking logs. Also in order to compute logs, the typically negative a_{ji} have been added to one before taking logs so that they were all positive fractions.

between $w_{ji(o)}$ and a_{ji} with its correlation of −.36; sectors severely constraining an industry tending to be connected to the industry by ownership ties. When repressed industries are separated from unrepressed industries, the association is clearer. Recall that the repressed industries are those confronted with high constraint (i.e., a low value of the group-affiliation index y_{j2}) to the point where

---

the constant, the stronger the correlation. If a_{ji} is transformed to $(-1)(a_{ji}) + .001$ before taking logs, for example, then the following correlations are obtained for ownership, direct interlock, indirect financial interlocking, and multiplex ties, respectively, .54, .38, .39, and .42. There are positive since a_{ji} is being measured by magnitude rather than direction. These correlations are much stronger than the log correlations given in the first row of Table 8.6 (−.24, −.13, −.12, and −.23, respectively). Decreasing constants yield increasing correlations. A much smaller constant, say .00001, yields much stronger correlations; .64, .48, .53, and .55, respectively. Moreover, the stength of these correlations is unaffected by distinctions between levels of overall constraint on an industry; for example, repressed versus unrepressed industries. The coincidence of zero constraint and zero ties is being pushed further and further away from the bulk of the observations by increasingly small constants; the natural log of .001 is −6.9 and that of .00001 is −11.5. This in turn makes the association between a_{ji} and w_{ji} appear stronger because values far removed from their means occur simultaneously (i.e., values of a_{ji} and w_{ji} equal to 0 are increasingly distant from their respective means). By adding a_{ji} to 1 before taking logs, this arbitrary inflation of correlations is avoided because a_{ji} equal to 0 maintains an appropriate proximity to the nearest nonzero value of a_{ji}.

the partial derivative $\partial a_j/\partial y_{j1}$ is negative. These four industries, textiles, apparel, rubber, and fabricated metals, were less successful than industries generally in developing directorate ties with some other sector at a frequency proportional to the constraint posed by the sector. They were particularly unsuccessful in comparison to industries not repressed by severe external constraint. The association between ownership ties and market constraint in Table 8.6 is $-.33$ for repressed industries but $-.52$ for unrepressed industries, $-.10$ versus $-.25$ in regard to direct interlock ties, $-.11$ versus $-.33$ in regard to indirect financial interlock ties, and $-.26$ versus $-.55$ in regard to O–D–I multiplex ties.[22]

The graph in Figure 8.3 illustrates the stronger association between directorate tie frequency and market constraint intensity for industries unrepressed by severe external constraint. Multiplex tie frequencies, $w_{ji(m)}$, are graphed against market constraints, a_{ji}. These data are used to compute the correlations at the top of Table 8.6. Relations a_{ji} for repressed industries j are indicated in the graph by asterisks where possible. Similar distributions are obtained with uniplex ties, but the multiplex ties most clearly represent strong ties since they require the coordination of three different kinds of ties between establishments in separate sectors as discussed in Chapter 4.[23]

Note the four particularly severe constraints to the left of the graph in Figure 8.3. From left to right in the graph they are the constraint posed by apparel for the textiles industry, the constraint posed by primary metals for the fabricated

[22]For the purposes of this analysis, I am using the partial derivative $\partial a_j/\partial y_{j1}$ to distinguish two classes of industries, repressed and unrepressed. In fact, the partial derivative is a continuous variable and need not suggest the repressed versus unrepressed dichotomy. The four repressed industries did not confront equally severe constraint from other sectors. The partial derivative $\partial a_j/\partial y_{j1}$ is much less negative for the rubber industry $(-.035)$ than it is on average for the remaining three repressed industries $(-.234)$. Further, there are two industries for which the partial derivative is only barely positive—the mechanical machines industry (for which the partial derivative is .003) and the primary metals industry (for which it is .005). The partial derivative is, on average, considerably higher for the remaining 14 industries (.097). This suggests that there were three groups of industries rather than two; textiles, apparel, and fabricated metals being repressed industries; rubber, mechanical machines, and primary metals being neither repressed nor unrepressed, and the remaining industries being unrepressed. Recomputing the correlations in Table 8.6 for this trichotomy, I do not find it advisable to substitute it for the repressed versus unrepressed dichotomy. Correlations between a_{ji} and w_{ji} for the rubber mechanical machines and primary metals industries are very similar to those obtained for unrepressed industries generally and much higher than those obtained for the three very repressed industries—textiles, apparel and fabricated metals. However, the results obtained for the three very repressed industries are not much different from those obtained for all four repressed industries in Table 8.6, and a negative value of the partial derivative $\partial a_j/\partial y_{j1}$ does, in theory, indicate what I denominate as a repressed industry. Therefore I have ignored differences in the extent to which industries were repressed.

[23]Graphs of ownership, direct interlocking, and indirect financial interlocking against the most severe market constraints are given elsewhere for an earlier specification of the structural autonomy model (Burt 1980d: Figure 4). The most noticeable difference between those graphs and Figure 8.3 is the prevalence in them of uniplex directorate ties to sectors not constraining an industry (i.e., the data distributions are denser up against the far right-hand side of the graphs). A more detailed analysis of constraint and directorate ties at the four-digit industry level strengthens the decision here to focus on the one best-fitting linear association (Burt 1983:Chap. 4).

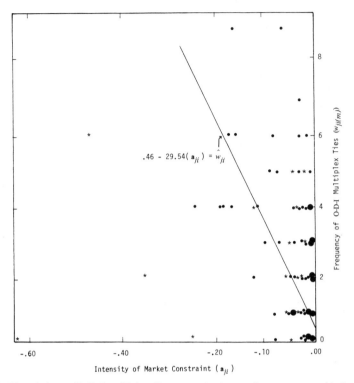

Figure 8.3. Extraindustry O–D–I multiplex directorate ties (constraints on repressed industries are represented in the graph by asterisks and large dots represent more than three constraints which could be confronting repressed or unrepressed industries).

metals industry, and constraint posed by chemicals for the textiles industry, and the constraint posed by textiles for the apparel industry. All four confronted repressed industries (they are indicated by asterisks in the graph). This suggests that firms operating in repressed industries might have been able to develop ties with other sectors in proportion to moderate constraint, but could not or did not develop them in proportion to these especially severe constraints. If this were true, then the correlation between w_{ji} and $\mathbf{a}_{ji}$ for repressed and unrepressed industries j should be identical when the four especially severe constraints are excluded from the computations. Computing correlations from the 168 moderate and negligible constraints on repressed industries yields coefficients of $-.41$, $-.24$, $-.27$, and $-.31$ for ownership, direct interlock, indirect financial interlock, and O–D–I multiplex ties, respectively. Log score correlations are lower ($-.25$, $-.20$, $-.18$, $-.27$, respectively). These results are stronger than those reported for repressed industries in Table 8.6, but consistently lower than those reported for unrepressed industries. In other words, the low association between w_{ji} and $\mathbf{a}_{ji}$ for repressed industries is not merely a result of the four

TABLE 8.7
Predicting Extraindustry Ties from Market Constraint Intensity

	α	β	t-test	Correlation
Ownership ties	1.41	-51.85	16.7	$-.50$
Direct interlock ties	3.96	-74.05	7.6	$-.25$
Indirect financial interlock ties	19.37	-425.66	9.8	$-.32$
O–D–I multiplex ties ($w_{jj(m)}$)	.46	-29.54	17.2	$-.51$

[a]Parameters are specified in Eq. (8.8), ordinary least-squares estimates have been computed for the 856 extraindustry relations excluding the four most severe market constraints, and the regression line of predicted multiplex frequencies is given as a bold line in Figure 8.3. The t-tests should be interpreted with caution (see footnote 25).

extraordinary constraints that they experienced; or if it is, then intense constraint lowered the ability of firms in repressed industries to develop directorate ties in general with other sectors.[24]

At the same time, the correlations are greatly strengthened if the four particularly severe constraints are put to one side. Moreover, the correlation between directorate tie frequency and market constraint intensity for industries generally is strengthened by setting those four relations aside as outliers. Table 8.7 contains the results of regressing w_{ji} over $\mathbf{a}_{ji}$ in the following equation when the four especially severe market constraints are excluded from the data:

$$w_{ji} = (\alpha + \beta\mathbf{a}_{ji}) + \eta_{ji},$$
$$= (\hat{w}_{ji}) + \eta_{ji}, \qquad (8.8)$$

where e_{ji} is a residual term and ordinary least-squares estimates are reported.[25] Illustrating the form of the function, the multiplex tie frequency $w_{ji(m)}$ predicted by market constraint intensity $\mathbf{a}_{ji}$ is presented in Figure 8.3 as a bold line. This is

[24]In fact, building on footnote 22, I find that the association between $\mathbf{a}_{ji}$ and w_{ji} for industry j declines rather systematically as the severity of market constraint on the industry from other sectors of the economy intensifies. This point is discussed in detail elsewhere for four-digit industry data (Burt 1983:Chap. 4).

[25]Statistical interpretations of the regression coefficient in this equation assume each of the w_{ji} to be observed independent of the other w_{ji}. As with much of network analysis, the correct number of independent observations is difficult to determine here. Directorate ties have been computed from 152 separate firms for which 2903 persons served as directors in the operation of 414 of what I refer to here as establishments. Any one, or some mixture, of these numbers could be the correct number of independent observations. Nor is it clear how a matrix of interdependent errors in the w_{ji} could be specified in a spatial autocorrelation model such as those discussed by Doreian (1980). Interdependence could be a function of firms or directors coordinating establishments, and both are intrinsic features of the directorate ties being predicted so it would be inappropriate to completely control all variance traceable to these sources. In the absence of a more appropriate treatment, I have reported routine t-tests in table 8.7 (cf. Fienberg and Wasserman, 1981:158; Holland and Leinhardt, 1981:36, for very similar working assumptions in their applications of log-linear models to network dat). These statistics probably overstate the significance of the beta in Eq. (8.8) since there are fewer organizations used to compute the w_{ji} than there are w_{ji} used to compute regression coefficients.

$\hat{w}_{ji}$ in Eq. (8.8). The results in Table 8.7 show a strong, monotonic association between tie frequency and constraint intensity. The correlations here are nearly equal to those reported in Table 8.6 for unrepressed industries alone.

In short, all three types of directorate ties occurred between industries and sectors with a frequency linearly proportional to the market constraint a sector posed for profits in the industry. As might be expected from the analysis in Chapter 4, the different types of ties were coordinated as multiplex ties. A source of market constraint was simultaneously the object of ownership ties, direct interlock ties, as well as indirect interlock ties through financial institutions. It was the object of these coordinated ties from some industry in proportion to the constraint it posed on profits in the industry. But the strength of this association varied with the overall level of constraint an industry experienced, decreasing as the intensity of overall constraint increased. This interindustry variation in the association between constraint intensity and tie frequency raises the possibility that industries varied in the success with which they coopted sources of market constraint.

8.4 SUCCESSFUL COOPTATION

At this point, it seems clear that the three types of directorate ties were patterned in 1967 as if they were intended to coopt sources of market constraint. This does not mean that establishments in every industry were equally successful in coopting sources of market constraint. To the extent that those in some industries were more successful than establishments in other industries, "successful" cooptation should have translated into unusually high industry profits.

The structural autonomy of industry j defined by Eq. (8.2) is the profit margin expected in the industry as a result of the pattern of market transactions defining its position in the economy. The patterns of directorate ties among economic sectors at the time have not been included in the computation of autonomy. But where establishments in the industry managed to circumvent market constraint on the industry—circumvent it in the sense of having directorate ties with the sources of constraint—the level of constraint *actually* confronting the industry in 1967 has been overestimated. Computing structural autonomy from transactions in an input–output table, I assume that all transactions were conducted on the open market in which case a_{ji} represents the *potential* constraint supplier/consumer sector i could have posed for industry j. By moving some or all of their market transactions with sector i off the market and into the nonmarket context created by directorate ties, establishments in industry j need not have been subject to all of the potential market constraint on their industry. In other words, where establishments in industry j were able to develop cooptive directorate ties as of 1967 with sectors constraining profits in the industry, a_j is a conservatively biased prediction of the industry profit margin. The profit margin should have been higher than $\mathbf{a}_j$ since ostensible market constraints considered in computing $\mathbf{a}_j$ had been circumvented. In this situation, the residual term in the prediction of profit margins from structural autonomy should have been positive, that is, $y_{j0} > \mathbf{a}_j$, showing that the industry had a higher profit margin than would have been expected from the pattern of market transactions defining its network position in the economy.

As discussed in Chapter 7, the increased structural autonomy, which in this case is the increased industry profit margin, to be expected by coopting sector i as a source of constraint is given by $d(\mathbf{a}_j)$ in Eq. (7.7). This index is the sum of the levels of constraint coopted sectors could have posed weighted by the rate of change at which an industy's profit margin would have increased by coopting sources of constraint. Under the assumption that the presence of ownership ties, direct indirect ties, and interlock financial interlock ties between industry j and sector i provided sufficient cooptive relations for establishments in the industry to circumvent market constraint from the sector, let w_{ji} be a crude measure of the extent to which constraint from the sector could have been circumvented by establishments in the industry where w_{ji} is 0 if $w_{ji(m)}$ is 0 and 1 if $w_{ji(m)}$ is nonzero. Values of w_{ji} have been substituted into Eq. (7.7) to obtain values of $d(\mathbf{a}_j)$. This index of successful cooptation will be high to the extent that establishments in industry j were subject to strong potential market constraint but had successfully developed ownership ties, direct interlock ties, and indirect financial interlock ties with those sectors that were the sources of constraint.

This index should be correlated positively with the errors made in predicting industry profit margins. The error η_j in Eq. (8.2) is high when the profit margin in industry j was higher than would have been expected from the potential market constraint confronting it. The index $d(\mathbf{a}_j)$ is high when establishments in industry could have circumvented strong potential market constraint through directorate ties with the sources of that constraint. Accordingly, a high value of $d(\mathbf{a}_j)$ should have resulted in a high value of η_j.

It did not. Table 8.8 shows that there is a negligible positive correlation between the extent to which the observed profit margin in an industry exceeded its expected margin and successful cooptation. When multiplex ties are used to measure w_{ji} as a dichotomous variable as described in the preceding, the resulting values of $d(\mathbf{a}_j)$ are correlated .098 with errors in predicting profit margins $(\eta_j = y_{j0} - \mathbf{a}_j)$. Table 8.8 shows that even lower correlations are obtained if ownership ties, direct interlock ties, or indirect financial interlock ties are dichotomized as w_{ji} and used to compute values of $d(\mathbf{a}_j)$.

Figure 8.4 illustrates the weak association between successful cooptation as captured by $d(\mathbf{a}_j)$ and profitability. Values of $d(\mathbf{a}_j)$ multiplied by 1000 are presented in the graph where industry j is located according to its observed profit margin (y_{j0} on the vertical axis) versus its structural autonomy as its expected profit margin ($\mathbf{a}_j$ on the horizontal axis). The error made in predicting profits from market structure can be discerned from an industry's position above or below the regression line in the graph. An industry high above the line (e.g.,

TABLE 8.8
Indications of Successful Cooptation by Means of Directorate Ties[a]

		Correlations with profit indicators	
Type of directorate ties used to compute increased profit $d(\mathbf{a}_j)$	Mean profit margin increase expected $E[d(\mathbf{a}_j)]$	Extent by which observed margin exceeded expected $(y_{jo} - \mathbf{a}_j)$	Expected profit margin $\mathbf{a}_j$
Ownership ties	.031	.013	−.573
Direct interlock ties	.031	.019	−.594
Indirect financial interlock ties	.031	−.001	−.589
O–D–I multiplex ties	.024	.098	−.355

[a]Correlations are computed across the 20 two-digit industries, and the directorate tie frequencies, the w_{ji}, have been dichotomized as zero versus nonzero before computing $d(\mathbf{a}_j)$, using Eq. (7.7).

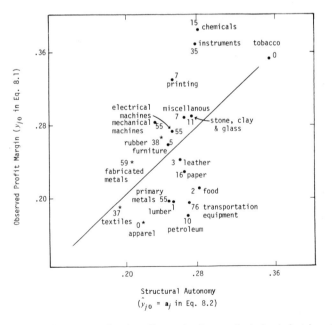

Figure 8.4. Observed versus predicted profit margins in manufacturing industries with success of cooptive O–D–I multiplex directorate ties as $d(\mathbf{a}_j)$ multiplied by 1,000 given in the graph (repressed industries are represented by asterisks).

the chemical industry) had a profit margin much higher than would have been expected from its structural autonomy. An industry far below the line (e.g., the petroleum industry) had one much less than would have been expected. To the extent that successful cooptation through directorate ties explains why some industries had higher than expected profit margins, high values of $d(\mathbf{a}_j)$ should occur above the regression line and low values should occur below it. There are some industries that conform to the expected pattern. For example, the profit margin in the instruments industry was 33% higher than the margin expected from market structure ($.091/.277 = (y_{j0} - \mathbf{a}_j)/\mathbf{a}_j$), and at the same time, the industry was connected by ownership ties, direct interlock ties, and indirect financial interlock ties to sectors posing market constraints on it so that it should have obtained a profit margin that was 13% higher than the margin predicted as its structural autonomy ($.035/.277 = d(\mathbf{a}_j)/\mathbf{a}_j$). On the other hand, there are many industries that do not conform to the expected pattern. The profit margin in the insportation equipment industry, for example, was less than would have been expected from market structure ($y_{j0} - \mathbf{a}_j = -.070$), yet a well above average level of market constraint confronted the industry from sectors with which the industry had all three types of directorate ties ($d(\mathbf{a}_j) = .076$).

This lack of association between successful cooptation and unexpected profits results from the strong association between directorate ties and market constraints. In order for strategically created directorate ties to be responsible for some industries' having higher profits than would have been expected from market structure, some industries must be unsuccessful in creating directorate ties with sectors constraining industry profits. There must be variability in successfully matching market constraints with directorate ties. But there is little or no variability. Each industry tended to have all three types of directorate ties with sectors constraining profits in the industry. Since directorate ties were strongly determined by market constraints, a knowledge of the pattern of directorate ties linking an industry to its supplier and consumer sectors adds nothing to the prediction of industry profits by market structure alone. The differential $d(\mathbf{a}_j)$ does vary across industries, but only as a function of the extent to which each industry was faced with market constraint from other sectors. Table 8.8 shows that this differential is strongly correlated negatively with industry structural autonomy, $\mathbf{a}_j$, the extent to which industry establishments were free from market constraint. The differential is similarly correlated with the group affiliation index, y_{j2} (correlations not presented). In other words, the more constraint that an industry faced from other sectors, the more constraint establishments in the industry could have coopted and did coopt through directorate ties to the sectors. This same conclusion is reached if successful cooptation, $d(\mathbf{a}_j)$, is measured in terms of each type of directorate tie individually, or is measured in terms of mergers (Burt 1980a), or if the much more narrowly defined four-digit industries are analyzed as the object of market constraint (Burt 1983:Chap.4).

8.5 CONCLUSIONS

As a representation of market constraints on corporate profits, the proposed model of structural autonomy does well. The model predicts that the profit margin typical of establishments in an industry will be high to the extent that the industry provides high structural autonomy. That is to say, high profit margins should have been observed in an industry to the extent that there was low competition among its constituent establishments and high competition among establishments in its supplier and consumer sectors. In 1967, profit margins were high in American manufacturing industries to the extent that they were structurally autonomous. Industry profits were positively associated with a lack of competition within the industry (the oligopoly effect, $\beta_o > 0$) but more strongly associated with the extent to which the industry was free from constraint by its supplier and consumer sectors (the group-affiliation effect, $\beta_g > 0$). Further, the model's definition of the extent to which an industry was constrained by each sector of the economy proved accurate in predicting directorate ties as cooptive relations. This was true of all three types of directorate ties considered together as multiplex ties or considered individually as ownership ties, direct interlock ties, or indirect financial interlock ties. Within industries, directorate ties occurred with a frequency predicted by a kinked function. Comparing separate industries, as the contribution to industry profits from a lack of competition within the industry increased up to a criterion level, I find that large firms were attracted to the industry and interlock ties among establishments in it occurred with an exponentially increasing frequency. Past that criterion, the association is reversed. As large firms within an industry became increasingly dominant so as to lower intraindustry competition and accordingly lower the uncertainty of market constraint within the industry, they had less need for interlock ties with one another in order to coordinate their actions. Past the criterion lack of intraindustry competition, large firms operated in an industry and interlock ties occurred among establishments in the industry with an exponentially decreasing frequency. Extraindustry directorate ties, ties between an industry and establishments in other sectors of the economy, occurred with a frequency in proportion to the constraint a sector posed on industry profits. The more severe the constraint posed by a sector on profits in an industry, the more frequent were ownership, direct interlock, and indirect financial interlock ties between industry and sector. This proportionality was not equally strong across all industries. To the extent that an industry experienced massive constraint from its suppliers and consumers, it was less characterized by directorate ties with other sectors in proportion to the constraint posed by any one sector for profits in the industry. However, all industries tended to have all three types of directorate ties connecting them to any sector posing a severe market constraint on industry profits. This omnipresence of ties to sources of market constraint made an analysis of industry success in developing cooptive directorate ties to such sources uninformative; no industries were especially unsuccessful in this way.

In short, directorate ties were patterned in the 1967 American economy as if they were intended to control uncertainty in industry profits. They appeared between industry and sector to the extent that the sector posed a market constraint could have been a necessary precursor to corporate survival rather and those sectors constraining industry profits, however, no industry gained singular advantage from them in the sense of obtaining unusual profits. Interindustry differences in successful cooptation do not add to the prediction of industry profit margins by market structure alone. This does not rule out the possibility that directorate ties changed the nature of competition in the economy, but it does show that the mere strategic placement of such ties did not distinguish unusually profitable manufacturing industries from those in which low profits were typically obtained.

In fact, strategically created directorate ties could significantly change the nature of economic competition without explaining interindustry differences in profit margins. By creating a nonmarket context in which necessary buying and selling can be transacted, and by occurring wherever especially competitive market transactions must be carried out, directorate ties could ensure that little of the most competitive buying and selling actually will occur on the open market. Rather, such transactions would have been conducted between favored trade partners detected by means of directorate ties as described in Chapter 4. Establishments without directorate ties to constraint sectors would have been forced to conduct their buying and selling on the open market—a business context fraught with the constraints on profits described by the structural autonomy model. In other words, strategic cooptation of sources of market constraint could have been a necessary precursor to corporate survival rather than an opportunity for obtaining unusual profits.

If this is the case, then a whole new class of unanticipated corporate constraints in a structural mirror of the economic market must be recognized as a second market, the economic market consisting of buying and selling commodities, the social market consisting of interorganizational directorate ties. The necessary involvement of establishments in this social market could raise or lower their efficiency and so raise or lower the efficiency of the economy as a whole.

One could argue that such a social market of directorate ties would increase the efficiency of production by facilitating the flow of information regarding the economic market. From this perspective, the close association between market constraints and directorate ties that I have found merely indicates that corporations had improved the efficiency of the economic market thereby lowering the price of commodities eventually consumed as final demand—that final demand consisting of the dollars we spend as individual consumers and those the government spends as our proxy in making particularly large purchases.

One could also argue for a far less benevolent perspective on the social market of directorate ties. They could decrease the efficiency of the economic market by selectively facilitating the flow of information in determining favored trade partners so as to suppress innovation while ensuring markets for overpriced commodities. From this perspective, the close association between market constraints and directorate ties that I have found indicates that corporations had arrived at a point where they controlled the market in a manner enabling them to raise, rather than lower, the price of commodities eventually consumed as final demand.

My inference is that a social market of directorate ties, a market patterned by economic market constraints on profits, would increase the efficiency of the economic market but not by as much as it could. Ceteris paribus, it seems likely that the economic market would be significantly less efficient without directorate ties than it is with them. It would be too difficult for the management of an establishment to keep informed about the activities of significant actors in all sectors affecting their profits. This problem is alleviated by the advice, counsel and influence function of directorate ties. At the same time, directorate ties do selectively facilitate the flow of information in creating favored trade partners. Where they facilitate transactions between specific establishments, they must at the same time inhibit transactions between those establishments and other establishments generally.[26] Moreover, ties need not bring together establish-

---

[26]In this sense, directorate ties bear a striking resemblance to the ceremonial necklaces and bracelets, *vaygu'a*, exchanged among natives in the primative barter economy of the Trobriand Archipelago. Describing these ornaments as part of the ceremonial Kula exchange, Malinowski (1922) describes something very similar to seats on a prestigious directorate in the sense that the ornaments

> are neither used nor regarded as money or currency, and they resemble these economic instruments very little, if indeed there is any resemblance at all, except that both money and *vaygu'a* represent condensed wealth. *Vaygu'a* is never used as a medium of exchange or as a measure of value, which are the two most important functions of currency or money. Each piece of *vaygu'a* of the Kula type has one main object throughout its existence—to be possessed and exchanged . . . circulate round the Kula ring, to be owned and displayed in a certain manner. . . . And the exchange which each piece of *vaygu'a* constantly undergoes is of a very special kind; limited in the geographical direction in which it can take place, narrowly circumscribed in the social circle of men between whom it may be done, it is subject to all sorts of strict rules and regulations; it can neither be described as barter, nor as simply giving and receiving of presents, nor in any sense is it a play at exchange [pp.510–511].

Only Kula partners may exchange *vaygu'a*, and these partnerships ensure relations between inhabitants of separate islands—partnerships that affect economic trade. As Malinowski (1922) points out:

> The ceremonial exchange of the two articles (necklaces and bracelets) is the main, the fundamental aspect of the Kula. But associated with it, and done under its cover, we find a great number of secondary activities and features. Thus, side by side with the ritual

(Continued on next page)

ments in maximizing the efficiency of their transactions so much as they stablize those transactions and make them profitable.

This is, of course, no more than an inference from the conclusions I reached in this analysis. The analysis rests on the premises that (*a*) the network model of structural autonomy could define market constraints on corporate profits; and (*b*) directorate ties would occur as a function of those constraints if such ties were intended to coopt sources of market constraint. It did and they did in the 1967 American economy. More extensive data analysis corroborates this conclusion (Burt, 1983). These results certainly augment the description of multiplex directorate ties in Chapter 4 as cooptive relations. Not only can such ties be interpreted plausibly as cooptive relations, they tended to occur in precisely those locations in the economy where they would do the most good as cooptive relations.

The immediate problem posed for directorate research is the discovery of processes by which directorate ties are created to circumvent constraint. Ties of diversification and interlocking directorates were patterned in 1967 so as to facilitate necessary buying and selling within the economy but had no direct effect on differences in industry profit margins above and beyond the effect of market structure alone. Where is the incentive to maintain the directorate tie market as a structural mirror of economic market constraints on corporate profits? In contrast to my analysis of the 1967 American economy, an analysis motivated by a curiosity about the extent to which directorate ties might be cooptive relations patterned by market constraints on corporate profits, subsequent analyses can focus on processes responsible for the observed association between directorate ties and market constraints. For example, the economic market does not create directorate ties. It only encourages them by providing a profit incentive for developing them in particular structural locations in the economy. The actual decision-making actor that creates directorate ties is the firm. Given the significance of differences between types of firms in Chapter 4, it seems reasonable to ask how different types of firms might be differentially responsible for a social market of directorate ties—different firms adopting

---

(Continued from previous page)
> exchange of arm-shells and necklaces, the natives carry on ordinary trade, bartering from one island to another a great number of utilities, often unprocurable in the district to which they are imported, and indispensible there [p.83; parentheses added].

The analogy to directorate ties is clear even if the context seems far removed from the typical board meeting. Substitute establishments for natives, seats on prestigious directorates for *vaygu'a*, and contracts for barter. The Kula exchange created social ties between potential trade partners, which facilitated necessary economic exchanges between islands. Similarly, directorate ties create favored trade partners, which facilitates necessary market transactions between sectors of the economy. In these two very different contexts, a social market of ties (Kula/directorate) between actors in an economic market facilitates transactions between specific actors, which lowers the likelihood of those transactions occurring between actors not connected by the relevant ties. By so doing, the social market integrates the economic. The idea of a social market of ties integrating an economic market of transactions is neither new nor unique to corporate economies.

different strategies for coopting sources of market constraint. Further, there are the differences between individual directors as people. There are many different types of people serving as directors of large American firms; they are different in their social backgrounds, their histories as corporate leaders, and the cluster of corporate boards they individually represent (e.g., see Useem 1980 for review and references). How do these differences underly processes by which specific persons constitute the interlock ties between establishments posing the most severe market constraint for one another's profits? In the currency of interlocking directorates, firms and directors are merely opposite sides of the same coin. For the purposes of this analysis, I have ignored differences among firms and differences among directors. For purposes of better understanding how directorate ties operate as cooptive relations, these differences should be explicitly connected with the extent to which types of firms and types of directors are responsible for directorate ties reaching sources of market constraint.[27]

---

[27]I have elsewhere described models and research focusing on individual firms and individual directors as differentially autonomous actors responsible for a social market of directorate ties (Burt 1983:Chaps. 8,9).

9

Toward a Structural Theory of Action*

I have worked toward a structural theory of action by focusing on its internal features in order to demonstrate that such a theory is plausible at a high level of conceptual rigor while maintaining considerable substantive promise. Shorn of details, the logical structure of this enterprise has been very simple: state the premise, identify the most basic issues contained in the premise, and present empirically acceptable, mathematically simple models providing some resolution to these issues.

I began with two postulates and the belief that their intersection was the premise for a structural theory of action. A postulate of purposive action defined motivated actors. People, or groups of people, are expected to use their resources to realize their interests. An action has utility to an actor to the extent that he perceives it as improving his well-being. He is interested in it to the extent that it would more seriously affect his well-being than would alternative actions. A postulate of marginal evaluation emphasized the context in which utility is perceived. Actors evaluate an action's utility in terms of the marginal increase it would provide in reference to some criterion. These evaluations are made, and interests pursued, in the context of social structure generated by the division of labor. Thus the premise for a structural theory of action: actors are

*Portions of this chapter are drawn from an article reprinted with the permission of *Sociological Inquiry* (Burt 1980b).

purposive under social structural constraint. In the preceding chapters, I have been once around the causal cycle (diagrammed in Figure 1.1) of basic issues spanned by a structural theory of action, capturing social context, capturing its effects on actor interests, and capturing its constraints on the ability of actors to pursue their interests, one of which is to modify the social context so as to avoid constraint.

I first reviewed the many alternative network models developed to represent social differentiation within a system of actors (Chapter 2). My conclusion was that those built from the social topology of a system best captured the social context in which actors made perceptions and took actions. The basis for my analysis then became actors jointly occupying network positions in social structure.

The subsequent problem was to represent the manner in which this social context would pattern actor perceptions so as to determine their interests (Chapter 5). Actors jointly occupying a network position symbolically role-play one another's positions in making evaluations of an action's utility, an action thereby having utility to the extent that it improves an actor's well-being as an occupant of his position within a system of actors. Social norms and feelings of relative deprivation are to be expected from this process among actors jointly occupying a position.

Finally, I described one way in which social context would differentially constrain occupants of different positions in terms of their ability to pursue interests (Chapter 7). Actors jointly occupying a position and therefore pursuing similar structural interests will have the structural autonomy to realize their common interests to the extent that their relational patterns ensure low competition with one another while simultaneously ensuring high competition among the nonoccupant actors with whom they interact. In order to alleviate the constraints they face from the occupants of other network positions, actors would be expected to develop cooptive relations with those occupants thereby modifying the original social context.

I have been careful to stress that these conceptual developments, while basic to a structural theory of action, do not of themselves constitute such a theory. They dovetail with one another as components in such a theory; each model builds on the others in a complementary fashion. Were the construction of a structural theory of action an architectural endeavor, I would say that my purpose here had been to lay cornerstones with no intention of presenting blueprints for the final edifice.

Similarly, I have only slipped my foot in the door with the empirical applications presented. The analyses in Chapters 3, 4, 6, and 8 lead me to believe that the status/role-set, structural interest, and structural autonomy models are pregnant with the potential to be substantively accurate as well as revealing. But I am an easy convert here, and these are personal conclusions each person must draw individually. The net conclusion I draw from these applications at this point is that the models are substantively acceptable. As stated in Chapter 1, the purpose in presenting these applications was not to prove that the proposed models were correct so much as to give them empirical meaning and make sure that they were not wrong in describing two systems of actors well suited to assessing them. They have not been rejected by the empirical tests to which I have put them. Their substantive adequacy more generally is an empirical question for subsequent research.

In short, the preceding chapters document the internal adequacy of the status/role-set, structural interest, and structural autonomy models as a plausible start toward a structural theory of action. I have addressed questions regarding their conceptual and substantive adequacy in summarizing conclusions to each chapter. I do not propose to repeat those results here. In presenting those results, the proposed models have been compared to popular alternative models, but I have nowhere systematically discussed the external adequacy of the structural approach they develop. In conclusion to this monograph, some comment on external adequacy is in order. Beyond the internal adequacy of the proposed models as a start toward a structural theory of action, the structural approach they illustrate avoids what seems to me to be very fundamental problems with the two alternative approaches to action theory—the atomistic and the normative. This too, in its own way, contributes toward a structural theory of action.

9.1 ATOMISTIC, STRUCTURAL, AND NORMATIVE APPROACHES TO ACTION

As discussed in Chapter 1, different approaches to action theory can be distinguished by the criterion each assumes to underlie marginal evaluations. More specifically, approaches differ in the extent to which other actors constitute a criterion in any one actor's evaluation of marginal utility. Under the postulate of purposive action, these alternative models of evaluation imply alternative microanalytical models of action by defining ideal types of actors.

As an individual, or social atom, an actor exists today in reference to his previous conditions and evaluates alternative future actions in reference to his current conditions. An atomistic perspective assumes that alternative actions are evaluated independently by separate actors so that evaluations are made without reference to other actors. An atomistic approach to action theory has been defined by separate actors having exogenously formed interests, one actor's interests or preferences being analytically independent of another's. *Atomistic action* would then refer to behaviors performed according to this model of exogenous interests. Motivated by analytically independent interests, actors use their resources to realize their interests.

Extensive evidence shows that actors do not exist as social atoms. As a member of society, an actor exists within a system of actors and evaluates alternative actions within that context. A normative perspective assumes that actions are evaluated interdependently by separate actors as a function of socializing processes that integrate them within a system of actors. A normative approach to action theory has been defined by separate actors within a system having interdependent interests as social norms generated by actors socializing one another. *Normative action* would then refer to behaviors performed according to this model of endogenous interests. Motivated by values and beliefs acquired through socialization, actors within a system use their resources to realize their interests.

These two modal approaches to action theory are the basis for two conflicting traditions of work: atomistic action underlying the deductively powerful theory in political economy and normative action underlying the substantively rich research in anthropology, political science, and sociology (see Chapter 1 for references). Of course, these are idealized constructs. In characterizing these alternative approaches, I am not suggesting that an intelligent person working within either one could not adapt the approach to explain any given empirical phenomenon, but rather that, in comparison to the structural approach, these alternatives lend themselves less easily to the task of stating general action theory capable of directing substantive research. Without attempting to synthesize a third perspective from the atomistic and normative extremes, I have argued for a structural approach which seems to bridge their extremes. Role-playing among the structurally equivalent occupants of a status generates interdependent interests among them. *Structural action* then refers to behaviors performed in the pursuit of structural interests. Motivated by their interests as occupants of their positions in social structure, actors use their resources to realize their interests.

Unfortunately, the analytical distinctions between atomistic, structural, and normative action become muddled in empirical behaviors. While interests are internal to the actor, his behavior is subject to the behavior of others. In other words, all three action models imply interdependent action no matter what process of interest formation is assumed. This is clearest in the case of atomistic action. While two actor's interests are assumed to be independent, their actions are not; for example, one actor may be interested in an exchange with another but unable to perform the exchange because he controls no resource of interest to the other actor. Observed behaviors in a system are the result of juxtapositioning actor interests. Behaviors are interdependent among actors even if their interests are independent. But if behaviors are inherently interdependent no matter what approach is assumed, then what does structural action offer beyond its atomistic and normative alternatives? It is above all a bridge between these two antagonistic alternatives, but a bridge that avoids some fundamental problems inherent in the alternatives themselves. At the heart of this matter are the alternative conceptions of social structure as a consequence of a division of labor.

9.2 SOCIAL STRUCTURE AND THE DIVISION OF LABOR

The alternative approaches to action theory can be distinguished on two dimensions with respect to their treatment of social structure and its underlying division of labor, the causes of a division of labor giving rise to social structure and the level of abstraction at which the resultant social structure exists. Explaining these dimensions sets the stage for comparing structural action to its atomistic and normative alternatives.

The Division of Labor Underlying Social Structure

In section 2.6, I described three ways in which a division of labor would create status/role-sets within a system of actors; specialization, aggregation, and in the discussion of prestige, resource concentration. Not discussed there were the causal processes that might be responsible for these phenomena. Atomistic and normative action differ from structural action in their treatment of those causes. These alternatives can be compared in terms of two classic accounts: Adam Smith's (1776:Chaps. 1–3) description of the division of labor from an atomistic perspective and Émile Durkheim's (1893:Book 2) argument against this view in support of a normative perspective.

Although Durkheim expresses divergence from the atomistic approach represented by Smith, he and Smith have similar opinions on the macrolevel causes of a division of labor—communication density within a system and markets for the goods and labor of its constituent actors. Discussing the degree to which the division of labor is a function of the "extent of the market," Smith emphasizes the importance of consumers for the goods and labor of actors in a system[1] and subsequently emphasizes the degree to which improved communication (as reflected by improved sea trade) involving actors in the system determines the potential division of labor within it.[2] Using different terms but similar concepts,

---

[1]Smith (1776) observes that

> when the market is very small, no person can have any encouragement to dedicate himself entirely to one employment, for want of the power to exchange all that surplus part of the produce of his own labour, which is over and above his own consumption, for such parts of the produce of other men's labour as he has occasion for [p.17].

[2]As the most advanced form of communication and transportation at the time, sea trade was a crucial determinant of the division of labor for Smith (1776):

> As by means of water-carriage a more extensive market is opened to every sort of industry than what land-carriage alone can afford it, so it is upon the sea-coast, and along the banks of navigable rivers, that industry of every kind naturally begins to subdivide and improve itself, and it is frequently not till a long time after that those improvements extend themselves to the inland parts of the country [p.18].

Durkheim emphasizes the degree to which improved communication involving actors within a system as "density" or "condensation" determines the system division of labor[3] simultaneously with the population size available for exchange of property as "social volume" or "growth."[4]

This macrolevel similarity between the two approaches dissolves at the microlevel when explanations are provided for why individuals act so as to generate a division of labor. Smith (1776:13–15), dismissing its origins as exogenously determined, claims that the division of labor proceeds under the above conditions as an inherent propensity for humans

> to truck, barter, and exchange one thing for another. . . . man has almost constant occasion for the help of his brethren, and it is in vain for him to expect it from their benevolence only. . . . It is not from the benevolence of the butcher, the brewer, or the baker, that we expect our dinner, but from their regard to their own interest. We address ourselves, not to their humanity but to their self-love, and never talk to them of our own necessities but of their advantages. . . . As it is by treaty, by barter, and by purchase, that we obtain from one another the greater part of those mutual good offices which we stand in need of, so it is this same trucking disposition which originally gives occasion to the division of labor.

In other words, the division of labor proceeds because atomistic actors engage in mutually rewarding exchanges of property up to the extent of markets for their goods and labor. Their interest in this behavior is exogenously determined as an inherent propensity intended to improve their well-being. For Smith, the division of labor is a phenomenon emergent from atomistic action. In contrast to this perspective in which the division of labor "is made to depend upon individual aspirations toward well-being and happiness, which can be satisfied so much better as societies are more extensive and more condensed," Durkheim (1893) views the determination of the division of labor by density of communi-

---

[3] As Durkheim (1893) states it,

> The division of labor develops, therefore, as there are more individuals sufficiently in contact to be able to act and react upon one another. If we agree to call this relation and the active commerce resulting from it dynamic or moral density, we can say that the progress of the division of labor is in direct ratio to the moral or dynamic density of society [p.257].

[4] Density leads to the division of labor through increased communication involving actors within the system, Durkheim (1893) continues,

> But these will be still more numerous, if, in addition, the total number of members of society becomes more considerable. If it comprises more individuals at the same time as they are more intimately in contact, the effect will necessarily be re-enforced. Social volume, then, has the same influence as density upon the division of labor [p.260].

cation (condensation) and available markets (growth) as a supraindividual phenomenon:

> We say, not that the growth and condensation of societies permit, but that they necessitate a greater division of labor. It is not an instrument by which the latter is realized; it is its determining cause [p.262].

Durkheim uses two arguments to support his proposed normative revision of Smith's atomistic approach—the inadequacy of increasing individual well-being as the cause of the division of labor and the necessity of shared norms between persons forced into a competitive situation if they are to exchange property in a division of labor rather than fight for control over it. Neither argument, upon close inspection, need reject the conception of a division of labor as a emergent phenomenon.

Durkheim's (1893:Book 2, Chap. 1) first argument uses the findings of Weber and Fechner in psychophysics (the basis for Stevens's subsequent empirical generalization in Eq. [5.1]) to emphasize that there are limits to the levels of well-being or happiness that individuals can effectively evaluate. If individual well-being were the motivating force for a division of labor, Durkheim (1893) concludes that the phenomenon would reach an upper limit and stop:

> If, then, the division of labor had really advanced only to increase our happiness, it would have arrived at its extreme limit a long time ago, as well as the civilization resulting from it, and both would have stopped [p.237].

Since civilization has not stopped, individual well-being cannot be the motivating force for a division of labor, nor can related atomistic emotions such as boredom or a desire for variety; "other considerations lead to the same conclusion."

This argument rests on a fundamental misunderstanding of atomistic action. Instead of treating separate actions performed by separate actors as separate units of analysis, Durkheim treats the history of action by a system of actors as a unit. Atomistic action, however, only claims that an individual will perform that action, of alternatives, which he perceives as promising the greatest reward. History is then a series of such evaluations at successive points in time. At each point in time, that action, among alternatives, which is perceived as promising the greatest reward to an individual will be the action he performs. There is no assumption that the desire to increase well-being within a system as a whole is the cause of a division of labor. In fact, Smith's (1776) discussion of the causes of a division of labor opens with the often quoted statement that the division of labor "is not originally the effect of any human wisdom, which foresees and intends that general opulence to which it gives occasion [p.13]." To reject the hypothesis that the division of labor occurs as a result of actors seeking to achieve increasing collective well-being over time is to reject a hypothesis never proposed.

Durkheim's second argument not only fails to discredit the atomistic approach, it places that approach on more solid footing than did Smith. Drawing on Spencer's notions of societal evolution, Durkheim (1893:262–275) proposes that in the same manner that species differentiate within an ecological niche so as to coexist, actors within a system are increasingly thrust into situations of competition with one another as social density and volume increase so that they distinguish the types of goods each produces within the system in order to survive. In his opinion,

> If work becomes divided more as societies become more voluminous and denser, it is . . . because struggle for existence is more acute. . . . Animals, themselves, prosper more when they differ more. . . . Men submit to the same law. In the same city, different occupations can co-exist without being obliged mutually to destroy one another, for they pursue different objects. The soldier seeks military glory, the priest moral authority, the statesman power, the business man riches, the scholar scientific renown. Each of them can attain his end without preventing the others from attaining theirs [pp. 266–267].

Why do individuals cooperate in this division of labor? Again erroneously attributing purposive action by a system of actors as a whole over time to the atomistic perspective, Durkheim (1893) indicates that increasing societal happiness is not the answer: "With all these changes, is there an increase in average happiness? There is no reason for so believing [p.270]." He makes his preferred answer clear:

> What bring men together are mechanical causes and impulsive forces, such as affinity of blood, attachment to the same soil, ancestral worship, community of habits, etc. It is only when the group has been formed on these bases that co-operation is organized there [p.278].

In other words, the division of labor can only occur among "members of an already constituted society."[5] A second reason for rejecting the atomistic approach therefore is that it fails to account for the fact that individuals will fight rather than cooperate as is required for a division of labor. Need this be the case? I think not, although common ancestry certainly could facilitate the division of labor. The atomistic approach can equally well account for the division of labor within an evolutionary perspective. In fact, the evolutionary adaptation argument seems a much stronger rationale for the division of labor than does Smith's claim of an innate human "propensity to truck, barter and exchange." The atomistic argument could be stated as follows. If an actor were faced with two alternatives—either to compete with other actors in the production

---

[5]This quote represents Durkheim's (1893:275) corollary to his second argument for a normative approach to the division of labor.

of commodities for which they are better suited or to begin producing a different type of goods for which he is more adequately suited—he would be expected to perform the latter action to the extent that there is a market for the type of goods he would produce. In Smith's (1776) words:

> In a tribe of hunters or shepherds a particular person makes bows and arrows, for example, with more readiness and dexterity than any other. He frequently exchanges them for cattle or for venison with his companions; and he finds at last that he can in this manner get more cattle and venison, than if he himself went to the field to catch them. From a regard to his own interest, therefore, the making of bows and arrows grows to be his chief business, and he becomes a sort of armourer [p.15].

In other words, competition is the mainspring—not a threat—to the division of labor. With increasing density of communication involving actors in a system and available markets for their goods and/or labor, there would be increasing competition among them and a resulting incentive for actors to differentiate the commodities they produce such that there would emerge a division of labor creating status/role-sets within the system. Actors freely choose to expand, contract, or compete within the existing division of labor as a function of the potential rewards to be obtained by these alternative courses of action. The phenomenon to be understood is the growth, decline, or stability of a division of labor within an already differentiated system rather than the etiology of a division of labor within an undifferentiated system.[6]

Despite the empirical complexity of the processes by which a division of labor actually generates social differentiation, eventually status/role-sets, the preceding with its simplified examples emphasizes one point. The divergence between atomistic and normative perspectives on the motivating force for a division of labor reduces to a claim within the latter perspective that shared social norms are necessary within a system in order for a division of labor to proceed. Moreover, this claim is not at all as obvious as proponents of the normative perspective, most notably Durkheim, would claim. Of course, to say that shared values and beliefs as social norms are not necessary to a division of labor is not to say that they have no effect on it. A central weakness in the atomistic approach, discussed in the following, is its failure to recognize the causal force of the relational patterns ensured by it through a division of labor.

The Resultant Social Structure

These different perspectives on the division of labor are carried over into differences in representing social structure. It is convenient at this point to

---

[6]This point is reflected in Kemper's (1972) rejection of what is here presented as Durkheim's second argument for the reason that shared norms are not a component in the etiology of a division of labor. Kemper relies on the inherent interdependence of humans so that "the division of labor could have existed all along [p. 741]."

distinguish by name three levels of social structure distinguished in the preceding chapters. Although all three levels are contained within the social topology of a system as described in Chapter 2, they are analytically distinct. Empirically, social structure exists as the N relational patterns defining each actor's network position within a system of actors. Through the three processes of differentiation described in Chapter 2 (specialization, aggregation, and resource concentration), status/role-sets exist at a higher level of abstraction as relational patterns with a special significance within the system. The relational patterns defining the M statuses in a system have a special significance within that system at the time it was observed. Social structure stated in terms of the M status/role-sets in a system can be termed ideographic—relational patterns with a form and content of special significance within a particular system at a particular point in time. Just as an ideograph refers to a graphic symbol in toto as a thing without indicating a word for it, ideographic structure refers to relational patterns significant in a given system without indicating its significance over time or across systems. This does not, of course, mean that ideographic structures cannot occur repeatedly over time or in separate systems. Where (N,N) matrices of relations z or interactor distances d characterize the empirical structure of a system, (M,M) density tables or interstatus distances characterize the ideographic structure of the system. At a still higher level of abstraction, nomothetic features of the system's social structure are given as relational patterns with form of special significance within multiple systems of actors over time. Examples of particularly significant forms here are position prestige and centrality as discussed in Chapter 2, the measures of a relational pattern's primary versus secondary form, also discussed there, and the measure of the structural autonomy a position's relational pattern ensures its occupants, as discussed in Chapter 7. Where ideographic structure corresponds to an ideograph as a description of a significant relational pattern without indicating a word for the pattern, nomothetic structure corresponds to the word generalizing the meaning of the ideograph.[7] Atomistic and normative action attend to different levels of abstract social structure.

With its emphasis on the independent exhanges among separate actors, atomistic action describes empirical social structure. In order to deal with the complexity of describing empirical structure, ideographic structure is often used. This perspective reaches an extreme in economics where the most serious attention given to relational patterns within a system of actors is found in input–output analysis. Here, as described in Chapters 4 and 8, sectors of an economy correspond to statuses in a system more generally. These sectors are not given by the structural equivalence of actors within a sector (although they can be interpreted that way) as much as by computational restrictions. The

---

[7]The difference between ideographic and nomothetic structure is clearly one of degree rather than an absolute difference. This point is emphasized in Nadel's (1957:Chap. 5) discussion of abstraction in social structure and will be raised below.

emphasis on numerical over conceptual issues in defining the aggregation of actors is highlighted by Leontief (1951) himself:

> It is true, of course, that the individual transactions, like individual atoms and molecules, are far too numerous for observation and description in detail. But it is possible, as with physical particles, to reduce them to some kind of order by classifying and aggregating them into groups. This is the procedure employed in input–output analysis in improving the grasp of economic theory upon the facts with which it is concerned in every real situation.... Such a table (of market transactions) may of course be developed in as fine or as coarse detail as the available data permit and the purpose requires [p.15; parentheses added].

This perspective is not confined to economics, although it is less extreme in other disciplines. Radcliffe-Brown (1940) similarly defines the empirical positions of actors as the condition to be explained:

> direct observation does reveal to us that these human beings are connected by a complex network of social relations. I use the term "social structure" to denote this network of actually existing relations.... So atomic physics deals with the structure of atoms, chemistry with the structure of molecules, crystallography and colloidal chemistry with the structure of crystals and colloids, and anatomy and physiology with the structure of organisms. There is, therefore, I suggest, place for a branch of natural science which will have for its task the discovery of the general characteristics of those social structures of which the component units are human beings [p. 190].

Beyond a computational convenience, however, ideographic structure is viewed by Radcliffe-Brown (1940) as necessary to the generalization of social structural explanations:

> In the first place, I regard as a part of the social structure all social relations of person to person.... Secondly, I include under social structure the differentiation of individuals and of classes by their social role. The differential social positions of men and women, of chiefs and commoners, of employers and employees, are just as much determinants of social relations as belonging to different clans or different nations. In the study of social structure the concrete reality with which we are concerned is the set of actually existing relations, at a given moment of time, which link together certain human beings. It is on this that we can make direct observations. But it is not this that we attempt to describe in its particularity. Science (as distinguished from history or biography) is not concerned with the particular, the unique, but only with the general, with kinds, with events which recur [pp. 191–192].

Whether stated at the empirical or ideographic level, social structure under the atomistic approach is principally an interpersonal, interactor phenomenon, and these interactions between actors are eminently negotiable as might be expected from a conception of the division of labor as a phenomenon emergent from ongoing negotiations between actors. This is nicely illustrated in the interesting advances made by Thibaut and Kelley (1959), Homans (1961), and Blau (1964) in using atomistic action to describe social interaction. Ekeh (1974:22–24, 79–187, 194–217) provides a succinct review of these advances. Within this atomistic approach to interaction, Blau makes the most deliberate effort to incorporate normative action into his considerations in his emphasis on the emergent character of exchange relations and his distinction between the contractual obligations created by exchanges as purchases of commodities (termed economic exchange) and the moral obligations created by exchanges as offers of social bonds (termed social exchange).[8] Nevertheless, in his later review of interaction as social exchange, a review that reiterates these earlier distinctions, Blau (1968) is able to state that

> The very term "social exchange" is designed to indicate that social interaction outside the economic sphere has important similarities with economic transactions. Above all, the expectation that benefits rendered will yield returns characterizes not only economic transactions but also social ones in which gifts and services appear to be freely bestowed. Moreover, the economic principle of eventually declining marginal utility applies to social exchange as well. Advice from an expert colleague is worth much to a

----

[8]For example, Blau (1964) makes it clear that he is attempting to address the emergent characteristics of systems of actors rather than the features of individuals per se:

> It is this fundamental concern with utilizing the analysis of simpler processes for clarifying complex structures that distinguishes the approach here from that of other recent students of interpersonal processes, notably George C. Homans and John W. Thibaut and Harold H. Kelley [p.2].

However even Homans, whose atomistic assumptions are clear from his attempted merger of behavioral psychology and utility theory as a basis for exchange, incorporates normative considerations into his theory through the concept of distributive justice. An actor evaluates a just return on his efforts in comparison to those made by others; Homans (1961) summarizes:

> A man in an exchange relation with another will expect that the rewards of each man be proportional to his costs—the greater the rewards, the greater the costs—and that the net rewards, or profits, of each man be proportional to his investments—the greater the investments, the greater the profits. ... Finally, when each man is being rewarded by some third party, he will expect the third party, in the distribution of rewards, to maintain this relation between the two of them [p.232].

Further, the relative status (used by Homans to indicate the prestige one actor gives to another, see Homans 1961:149) of an individual is determined by discrepancies in justice. For example, Homans (1961) states:

> Thinking now of status rather than of justice, we shall say that a condition of *status congruence* is realized when all of the stimuli a man presents rank better or higher than the corresponding stimuli presented by another man—or when, of course, all of the stimuli presented by the two men rank as equal [p.248].

These relational indicators of status according to exchange asymmetry can be cast in more network type terms (e.g., Emerson 1972; Cook & Emerson 1978), and Blau extends to many more traditionally normative issues this explanation of behavior in terms of atomistic action. Despite these advances, however, social structure is a phenomenon emergent from negotiations among its constituent actors as individuals. As Ekeh (1974) describes at length, the normative approach emphasizes the collective nature of some types of relations. In economic terms, the price of some commodities, social commodities, is not determined by supply and demand so much as it is determined by social norms maintained through socialization.

man who needs help with a problem, but once the problem has been clarified, additional
counsel is no longer valuable [p.454].

Within the limits to which he pushes his analysis, this analogy between market
and nonmarket relations seems to me to be elegantly true.[9] Still, with the
differentiation of actors by a division of labor, the emergence of status/role-sets
introduces a distinct feature to exchange beyond a mere transfer of property or
labor such as counsel. Actors come to depend on specific types of other actors
for continued exchange. At the simple level of economic exchange, the baker
depends on the flour mill, the flour mill on the farmer, the farmer on the baker.
At the more complex level of social exchange, the professor depends on bright
students, such students on educated parents, and such parents on their own
professors. These patterns of exchange relations need not be ignored in social
theory assuming atomistic action as is illustrated in the extreme example of
Leontief's input–output analysis; however, the dependency and obligation
involved in these relations is most directly addressed in social theory assuming
normative action. Actors perform as bearers of shared social norms, and the
appropriate basis for social theory is the ideographic or nomothetic structure of a
system. This is a small analytical increase in abstraction, but a major shift in
perspective.

Actors do not simultaneously determine prices for goods through market
mechanisms but rather through ongoing socialization processes among themselves that determine norms prohibiting and mandating particular exchanges.
That is not to say that shared social norms are necessary to a division of labor
but rather that such norms form around the relational patterns generated by a
division of labor and that those norms guide the ongoing division of labor.
Taking society as a system of actors, this perspective is classically represented
by Durkheim's analysis (1893, especially the preface to the second edition in
1902) of the transformation of the collective conscience underlying individual
actions from the oppressive homogeneity of mechanical solidarity to the moral
individualism of organic solidarity, the latter being created by the division of
labor and the increasing structural autonomy it ensures (see footnotes 6, 7, and
8 in Chapter 7). A second classic in this societal level tradition, of course, is
provided by Weber's (1904) analysis of the Calvinist norms legitimating the
exchange of goods for a profit as a moral activity for man, thereby laying the
foundation for the capitalist system of exchange relations so freely assumed
under atomistic action.

---

[9]However, the description this approach provides does not explain the existence of relations so
much as it takes some relations for granted and explains empirical fluctuations in them with changes
in other variables. This point is illustrated in my discussion of Becker's (1974) theory of social
interaction in the next section.

It is in social anthropology, however, that the structural basis for normative action in property exchanges is made most vivid. Beyond the notion of obligation incurred by exchanges, a notion inherent in this line of work and capable of being addressed within the atomistic approach,[10] the idea of what might be termed normative prices in exchange is developed in the work of Malinowski, Mauss, and Levi-Strauss—normative prices in the sense that the incentive for performing a behavior is not a negotiable price in the market sense so much as a social norm making it obligatory. Malinowski (1922) illustrates normative prices and patterns of exchange in his discussion of the Kula exchange of necklaces and bracelets among the Trobriand Islanders (see footnote 26 to Chapter 8). The Kula ensured economic exchange between people on separate islands, necessary economic exchanges, but the social exchange of Kula was not to be confused with the economic exchange they ensured. As Malinowski (1922) put it, the necklaces and bracelets (*vaygu'a*) circulated were transferred from person to person in exchanges of a very special kind,

> limited in the geographical direction in which it can take place, narrowly circumscribed in the social circle of men between whom it may be done, it is subject to all sorts of strict rules and regulations; it can neither be described as barter, nor as simply giving and receiving of presents, nor in any sense is it a play at exchange. . . . The acts of exchange of the valuables have to conform to a definite code. The main tenet of this declares that the transaction is not a bargain. The equivalence of the values exchanged is essential, but it must be the result of the repayer's own sense of what is due to custom and to his own dignity. The ceremonial attached to the act of giving, the manner of carrying and handling the *vaygu'a* shows distinctly that this is regarded as something else than mere merchandise [p.511].

Moreover, participation in these exchange relations are tied to an individual's status on his island, a circumstance conveniently tied to the individual's responsibility for the commodities exchanged once Kula ties have been established.[11] Mauss's (1925) more comprehensive consideration of separate systems similarly documents the existence of obligatory normative exchange, varying in degree to the near pathalogical frenzy reached in the ostentatious exchanges among Indians in the Northwest United States as described by Mauss's concept of "potlatch." Here too, normative exchange occurs not between individuals so much as between types of individuals—actors occupying

---

[10]For example, Blau's (1964:14–18, 91–106) discussion of reciprocity in social exchange relations recaptures, for the dyad, Mauss's (1925) succinct statement of the obligations incurred by gifts: "The gift not yet repaid debases the man who accepted it, particularly if he did so without thought of return [p.63]."

[11]As Malinowski (1922) points out, "A commoner in the Trobriands would have a few partners only, whereas a chief would number hundreds of them [p.91]."

statuses defined by role relations.[12] It remained for Levi-Strauss (1949) to generalize exchange relations in terms of interstatus normative patterns. This he accomplishes through the concepts of "generalized exchange" and "univocal reciprocity."[13] Feeling the inadequacy of dyadic exchange relations in his analysis of kinship structures, Levi-Strauss introduces the concept of generalized exchange to account for interconnecting patterns of exchange relations; actor j gives to actor i who gives to actor n who in turn gives to actor j.[14] Univocal reciprocity is the pattern of obligations generated by these patterns of exchange relations; actor n is obliged to give to actor j even though it is actor i who gave to n. The kinship structures discussed by Levi-Strauss require an elaboration of this simple notion of exchange among chains of status occupants (an elaboration eventually leading to the blockmodel role structures proposed by Boorman and White [1976] as discussed in Section 2.8); however, the point emphasized for the present purposes by generalized exchange and univocal reciprocity is the importance of credit in exchange since these patterns of exchange relations need not occur simultaneously. As Levi-Strauss (1949) points out in his description of the circulation of brides:

> generalized exchange always contains an element of trust (more especially when the cycle requires more intermediaries, and when secondary cycles are added to the principal cycle). There must be the confidence that the cycle will close again, and that after a period of time a woman will eventually be received in compensation for the

---

[12]Mauss (1925) emphasizes this in his discussion of the general context for his monograph:
In the systems of the past we do not find simple exchange of goods, wealth and produce through markets established among individuals. For it is groups, and not individuals, which carry on exchange, make contracts, and are bound by obligations; the persons represented in the contracts are moral persons—clans, tribes and families; the groups, or the chiefs as intermediaries for the groups, confront and oppose each other [p.3].

[13]Of course, building on the tradition established by Malinowski and Mauss, Levi-Strauss similarly emphasizes the normative aspect of prices. His thoughts on this are illustrated in his rejection of Frazer's (1919) atomistic and economic interpretation of the process by which brides are exchanged (Levi-Strauss 1949:134–142).

[14]Levi-Strauss (1949) defines generalized exchange in comparison to restricted exchange:
Systems exhibiting this characteristic . . . are called *systems of restricted exchange*, meaning that the systems can operate mechanisms of reciprocity only between two partners or between partners in multiples of two. . . . But there is a second possibility . . . expressed by the formula: if an A man marries a B woman, a B man marries a C woman. Here the link between the classes is expressed simultaneously by marriage and descent. We propose to call the systems using this formula, *systems of generalized exchange*, indicating thereby that they can establish reciprocal relationships between any number of partners. These relationships, moreover, are *directional relationships*. For example, if a B man depends for his marriage upon class C, placed after his own, a B woman depends upon class A, placed before [p.178].

woman initially surrendered. The belief is the basis of trust, and confidence opens up credit. In the final analysis, the whole system exists only because the group adopting it is prepared, in the broadest meaning of the term, *to speculate* [p.265].

With the introduction of flows of credit, relations are no longer to be analyzed in terms of interpersonal exchanges, nor even dyadic interstatus exchanges, but rather in terms of the interlocking role-sets defining a system's statuses generally.

This leads Levi-Strauss to a very abstract level of social structure—to the level I have described as nomothetic structure. He strongly differs from Radcliffe-Brown in his (1953) argument that[15]

the term "social structure" has nothing to do with empirical reality but with models which are built up after it. This should help one to clarify the difference between two concepts which are so close to each other that they have often been confused, namely, those of *social structure* and *social relations*. It will be enough to state at this time that social relations consist of the raw materials out of which the models making up the social structure are built, while social structure can, by no means, be reduced to the ensemble of the social relations to be described in a given society [p.525].

These models built up after the observed relations defining empirical structure can be either "mechanical" or "statistical" where this distinction by Levi-Strauss (1953:528–531) corresponds to the distinction I have made between ideographic and nomothetic structure. I have avoided these labels because of the obvious confusion they would create in sociologists; the former because of Durkheim's concept of mechanical solidarity and the latter because of the common understanding of statistics to mean things numerical. In Levi-Strauss's terms, mechanical models of social structure are on the same scale as the phenomenon they describe, that is, are groupings of individuals into patterns of relations actually observed in a given system of actors. Statistical models are on a different scale than the phenomena they describe in the sense that they are interconnected relational patterns that tend to occur, to varying extents, in

[15]This statement is later elaborated in a contrast between his perspective and that he attributes to Radcliffe-Brown (Levi-Strauss 1953):

it is obvious that, in many respects, Radcliffe-Brown's conception of social structure differs from the postulates which were set up at the outset of the present paper. . . . In the first place, Radcliffe-Brown's empirical approach makes him very reluctant to distinguish between *social structure* and *social relations*. As a matter of fact, social structure appears in his work to be nothing else than the whole network of social relations. . . . In the second place, this merging of social structure and social relations induces him to break down the former into the simplest forms of the latter, that is, relations between two persons. . . . It may be questioned whether such dyadic relations are the materials out of which social structure is built, or whether they do not themselves result from a pre-existing structure which should be defined in more complex terms [p.541–542].

multiple systems of actors. As with nomothetic versus ideographic structure, statistical models are reflected in particular systems of actors as mechanical models.

Although there is a qualitative difference in the perspectives atomistic versus normative action bring to social structure and exchange relations, their images of social structure are not as remote from each other as they might seem. Since ideographic structure (a mechanical model) is merely an abstraction of empirical structure (where the epistemic connection between the two is clear since all positions within the social topology of a system are of finite distance from one another as discussed in Section 2.8), it is clear that the extreme proposed by Levi-Strauss does not contradict the perspective advanced by Leontief or Radcliffe-Brown as much as reorient it in a direction he believes to be more fruitful conceptually. That direction is not qualitatively separated from empirical structure since nomothetic structure too is contained within the social topology of a system.

Nadel's (1957) succinct treatment of social structure is especially clear in emphasizing the continuous nature of the epistemic linkage between levels of social structure. Drawing on Parsons, Nadel (1957) first separates the empirical from abstract structure generally:

> We arrive at the structure of a society through abstracting from the concrete population and its behavior the pattern or network (or "system") of relationships obtaining between actors in their capacity of playing roles relative to one another [p. 12].

This abstracting actually separates structure at three levels as is later emphasized in his discussion of abstraction:

> To reduce qualitative features and to disregard the characteristics of particular cases is to apply some method of *abstraction*. This, we might note, is our third level of abstraction. We began by disregarding the varying concrete instances of behaviour between people in order to define the constant linkages, the relationships between them. Again, we abstracted these from the concrete living beings performing them, thus proceeding from individuals and populations to actors in roles and relationships. We must now drive abstraction a stage further, beyond the qualitative character of the roles and actor relationships [p.106].

This further abstraction can proceed to the extent that relations are completely emptied of their content, to the point where relational form is all that remains of observed interaction:

> Thus we must continue to speak, very broadly, of relationships, noting only their greater or less abstractness or "formal" character. At the same time we have an appropriate choice of terms for roles which are similarly emptied of qualitative content; for here we may say that in this process roles (or "statuses") turn into mere *positions*.... In this sense we can say of our third level of abstraction that it is one at which relationships mean relative position and little else [p.108].

Nadel's analysis is obviously concerned with the abstract structure of a system. He emphasizes the fact that abstraction "enhances" comparisons of structure across systems (e.g., p. 125) and adds to this point by noting (p. 147) the similarity between his concept of social structure and Levi-Strauss's concept of a statistical model, what I have described as nomothetic structure. However, Nadel reaches a conclusion regarding the connection between empirical and abstract structure that is quite different from Levi-Strauss's despite their similar sense of abstract structure:

> Now I am not prepared to dismiss empirical reality so completely from the positional picture we call a social structure. Its statistical nature apart, it has some remoteness from "real conditions"—the remoteness that goes with progressive abstraction and as-if assumptions. But these are still methods whereby we attempt to catch reality as best we can. . . . I consider social structure, of whatever degree of refinement, to be still the social reality itself, or an aspect of it, not the logic behind it [p.150].

In short, Nadel's analysis of social structure leads him to focus on a level of abstraction somewhere between the extremes of those adopted by, say, Leontief and Levi-Strauss. I understand his adopted level to be the ideographic, and I can appreciate his argument—that is the level at which the structural approach developed in the preceding chapters is proposed.

Structural action is similar to atomistic and normative action in emphasizing a particular level of abstraction but different in the level emphasized. Within the proposed structural approach, evaluations by separate actors are interdependent to the extent that they are structurally equivalent occupants of a network position. Theory is constructed at the level of ideographic social structure. While avoiding the conceptual insignificance of the relational patterns defining the positions of specific actors in empirical structure, status/role-sets as ideographic structure are clearly linked to empirical structure by finite distances; empirical relational patterns are the data on status defining role-sets. Although less susceptible to the disciplinary whims of individual theorists than is nomothetic structure (see Leach's [1974:Chap. 6] comments on Levi-Strauss's work on kinship structures), the relational patterns defining positions in ideographic structure are clearly linked to abstract nomothetic relational forms such as prestige, centrality, and so on; nomothetic structure is the conceptual framework in terms of which status defining role-sets are interpreted. In short, structural action bridges the diverse levels of abstraction because of its basis in the continuous distance social topology of a system, using empirical structure as data to analyze status/role-sets as ideographic structure interpreted in terms of nomothetic structure as a conceptual reference. In Leontief's terms, structural action implies an emphasis on interconnected sectors of a system analyzed in terms of the relational patterns defining different sectors (e.g., the industry patterns of market transactions analyzed in Chapter 8). In Levi-Strauss's terms, it implies an emphasis on mechanical models analyzed in terms of statistical models as an interpretive frame of reference (e.g., the analysis in

Chapter 8 of transaction patterns in terms of their similarity to an idealized relational form defining maximum structural autonomy). In Nadel's terms, it implies an emphasis on the "second" level of abstraction—the interconnected role-sets defining statuses within a system of actors. With these ideas in mind, structural action can be succinctly compared to its atomistic and normative alternatives.

9.3 COMPARING ATOMISTIC ACTION WITH STRUCTURAL ACTION

Within the atomistic approach as I have characterized it here the social differentiation generated by a division of labor is an emergent phenomenon; it is emergent from the simultaneous behaviors of many actors each pursuing his own interests. It is also to be understood at this actor level of empirical structure. Relations between actors are at all times negotiable in the sense that ongoing exchange between two actors will cease if they find exchanges of the same commodities with other actors to be more rewarding. Of course, there have been many developments within the atomistic approach since Adam Smith first sketched its principal themes. These developments have been particularly rapid since those themes were given a mathematical basis in classical and neoclassical economics toward the end of the nineteenth century. These developments, however, have not changed the understanding articulated by Smith that relations between actors, as one type of behavior in which they are involved, are negotiable consequences of individuals making behavioral choices according to their exogenously determined interests. It is possible to introduce exogenous status constraints as well as exogenously determined interests; however, this does not improve the generality of the atomistic approach. To some extent, the recent developments by Thibaut and Kelley (1959), Homans (1961), and Blau (1964) illustrate this in their efforts to explain social interaction within an atomistic framework. However, it is clearer when a dyed in the wool economist attempts the same task, so I shall describe a recent economic example—a substantively and intellectually powerful example. Gary Becker has developed a diversity of explanations for social behavior from atomistic action, behaviors including altruism, interaction and discrimination, marriage and the family, criminal justice, and so on. MacRae (1978) provides a sociological exegesis of those gathered together in a recent collection (Becker 1976).

Becker himself is concerned with the problem in atomistic action of assuming actor interests to be exogenously fixed so as to be independent across actors when each makes behavioral choices. In a reconsideration of consumer behavior, R. Michael and he (1973) state that

> For economists to rest a large part of their theory of choice on differences in tastes is disturbing since they admittedly have no useful theory of the formation of tastes, nor can

they rely on a well-developed theory of tastes from any other discipline in the social
sciences, since none exists. Put differently, the theory which the empirical researcher
utilizes is unable to assist him in choosing the appropriate taste proxies on a priori
grounds or in formulating predictions about the effects of these variables on behavior.
The weakness in the received theory of choice, then, is the extent to which it relies on
differences in tastes to "explain" behavior when it can neither explain how tastes are
formed nor predict their effects [p.133].

Still, he believes in the general applicability of the approach for deriving
hypotheses about human action. The stated theme of his collection is that
(Becker 1976) "all human behavior can be viewed as involving participants who
maximize their utility from a stable set of preferences and accumulate an
optimal amount of information and other inputs in a variety of markets [p.14]."
This statement implies that a very general theory of action has been invoked.

In order to illustrate what I see as the lack of generality in atomistic action, I
shall consider Becker's (1974) theory of social interaction. Actor j's utility, u_j,
is a function of his control over a commodity as a resource at level x and some
characteristic of other actors at level R;

$$u_j = f(x, R),$$

where R is the sum of j's control over a characteristic of others as a result of his
own efforts (call this control level "h") and control provided to him by his
"social environment" (call this level "D_j"). R can be stated as

$$R = D_j + h.$$

Actor j's monetary income, I_j, is then the sum of his control over these two
resources weighted by their respective prices:

$$I_j = p_x x + p_r h,$$

and substituting $R - D_j$ for h in this income equation then yields a budget
constraint for actor j's "social income" which is spent on his "own" goods, x,
and on the characteristic of others, R:

$$S_j = I_j + p_r D_j,$$
$$= p_x x + p_r R.$$

In the same manner demonstrated earlier in Eq. (5.11), equilibrium occurs
when each actor has spent his social income such that the marginal utility of a
good divided by its price is a constant:

$$MU_{jx}/p_x = MU_{jr}/p_r.$$

To the extent that the well-being of others—as the term R—enters into actor j's
utility, one can expect j to behave so as to increase the well-being of others.
Becker (1974:260–264) describes the consequences of changes in actor j's
income, I_j, and the price of the characteristic of others, p_r (i.e., how much does it
"cost" to increase the well-being of others). Using his analysis, Becker

describes the way in which an actor would increase his support of members of his family as his monetary income increased since he would derive utility from the well-being of other family members. Also with increases in income, an actor could be expected to have an increasing tendency to make charitable donations since he would derive utility from the well-being of the recipients. An actor would be expected to refrain from personal assault on others as his monetary income increased to the extent that the monetary income of others did not change and the actor derives utility from the well-being of others.

Becker's analysis of social interaction, in other words, consists of an analysis of the effects on social interaction of changes in income and the cost of interaction—given the initial assumption that actors have an exogenously determined interest in, or preference for, the well-being of the people who would be the object of interaction. The contribution here lies not in explaining social interaction per se. An interest in such a commodity has merely been incorporated into the initial assumptions of the analysis. Rather, the contribution Becker makes is to explain how changes in social interaction would result from changes in monetary income and the cost of interaction. In keeping with the theme of his collection and his self-professed inability to account for actor preferences, Becker is not attempting to explain actor preferences for specific interactions; he merely atempts to account for patterns of behavior given actor preferences to particular behaviors.[16]

I agree with the general applicability of Becker's strategy for explaining human action—if one first agrees that actor preferences as interests must be given exogenously. If interests are indeed stable, exogenously fixed attributes of actors, then one would do well not to rely on them in explaining human behavior. One is otherwise led to an instinct brand of theory wherein actor differences in behavior are merely labeled with appropriate differences in instinctual preferences, or one is forced to be content with empirical generalizations stating covariation between differences in behavior and differences in actor attributes. Either path is unsatisfactory if one's purpose is to construct a general theory of action.

But my argument in putting forth the structural approach is that one need not

---

[16]Winship (1977b) elegantly summarizes this point in concluding his analysis of the time actors spend with one another, an analysis closely related to Becker's work and, of course, proposed within what I have discussed as the atomistic approach:

> Perhaps the major difference between the present model and the usual network model is this: Whereas the usual network model seeks to explain why people like each other (in terms of some pattern of relationships), the present model takes people's preferences for others as given. There are both good and bad aspects of this characteristic. On the bad side, the model is weaker because it does not explain this aspect of relations. On the good side, taking people's preferences as given has allowed us to look at the relationship between people's preferences (likes) and the actual behavior that exists between them (the amount of time they spend together)[pp. 93–94].

assume interests to be exogenous to one's analysis. Rather, interests are patterned by actor position in social structure. Further, the division of labor ensures that particular patterns of relations will acquire a special significance so as to define statuses within a stratified system thereby patterning actor interests and behaviors within the system. This division of labor is to be expected even if individuals are assumed to behave according to atomistic action, as I have explained in the above comparison of Smith and Durkheim. But even though these status defining relational patterns are a logical implication of atomistic action, through a division of labor, atomistic action fails to take them into account. Becker's work is the most sophisticated attempt to account for social phenomena within an atomistic action framework. Yet even here one finds that relations as interactions are free to occur or not as a function of an actor's personal utility in the interaction—even when an interest in the interaction is built into initial assumptions. This is not characteristic of many relations in terms of which the social sphere is stratified; role relations defining statuses tend not to be negotiable as are market transactions, and even market transactions develop into behavior constraining relational patterns through the division of labor, as I have demonstrated in Chapter 8. Not only is atomistic action unnecessarily restrictive in forcing actor interests to be exogenously determined, but in short, the approach itself contains a logical and empirical flaw responsible for this restriction, atomistic action logically implies the known to be substantively important status defining relational patterns created in a division of labor but fails to take them into account when hypotheses are derived.

In contrast, structural action explicitly takes into account the social structure providing a frame of reference for an actor's perception of utility in behavioral choices. *Structural action is atomistic action occurring in the stratified system of actors created by a division of labor implied by atomistic action. As such, structural action is a logical implication of atomistic action.* Although it does not affect the relation between marginal utility and price at equilibrium under the atomistic model in political economy (Eq. [5.11]), structural action introduces into atomistic action the status/role-sets in terms of which actor interests are patterned and well-being is maximized. In essence, the proposed structural approach offers a handle on the constraints patterning actor interests and the manner in which they limit an actor's ability to realize his interests. Further, since it is such a sensitive issue in social theory assuming atomistic action (e.g., Stigler 1950:117–135; Georgescu-Roegen 1968:259–262), I should stress that this introduction of status/role-sets into the atomistic model does not involve comparisons of utility across individuals (although such comparisons are typically made in empirical research on well-being within the normative approach, e.g., see Burt, Wiley, and Minor 1978 and Burt, Fischer, and Christman 1979 for discussion and references). Rather, actors make evaluations based on the current conditions of other actors perceived to be socially similar to themselves. There is no implication in Eq. (5.7) that actors make evaluations based on their perception of evaluations made by other actors.

As a cost, structural action is less parsimonious than atomistic action. Structural action requires information on the network(s) of relations among actors whereas atomistic action ignores such information. This complication is a manageable one, fortunately, since the status defining role-sets described in Chapter 2 have a general algebraic and empirical meaning.

9.4 COMPARING NORMATIVE ACTION WITH STRUCTURAL ACTION

Within the normative approach as I have characterized it here, the social differentiation generated by a division of labor is laced with a web of values and beliefs as social norms. Social structure is to be understood in the abstract as patterns of role relations among occupants of statuses; actors obliged to perform the role relations defining their statuses.

It seems obvious to me that values and beliefs are created through socialization processes guiding human action. I agree with the ideals of normative action. I find it commonsensical that empirical research within the normative approach tends to be substantively richer than that within the atomistic approach.

Although rich in conceptual schemes sensitizing research to substantively important items, the normative approach is notoriously bankrupt with respect to general deductive theory stating hypotheses based on the socialization processes by which values are formed and guide behavior. The problem is not a lack of explanations. It is a plethora of unintegrated explanations. Perhaps the most explicit definitions are the clique and dyadic models intended to capture primary group socialization processes. But these are very ambiguous definitions, as I have discussed in Chapter 2, and can be empirically misleading, as I have discussed in Chapter 6. If atomistic action dismisses the problem of actor interests by treating them as exogenously determined, normative action comes close to doing the same thing by legitimating myriad processes by which socialization could occur so as to guide behavior.

In contrast, structural action serves to place explicit restrictions on the manner in which interdependency arises among actor interests. At the same time it maintains the implications of social norms and relative deprivation; two phenomena that make normative action, relative to atomistic action, a superior approach for empirical research on human action. In fact, the propositions concerning social norms and relative deprivation go beyond consistency with significant empirical findings in past research. As I have described in Chapter 5, they extend those findings in a substantively meaningful way. *The central point here is that structural action describes a logical subset of behavioral choices potentially described by normative action, namely, that subset composed of empirical conditions recognized as support for normative action.* Structural action explicitly rejects interdependent interests between actors separated by extensive distance within a system.[17] By imposing this restriction, it is a more powerful approach than the normative.

Statuses in social structure have been recognized in empirical research within the normative approach for a long time; however, structural action is built on an especially clear theoretical definition of the role-sets underlying statuses as network positions. The expected interdependency of interests among actors jointly occupying a status/role-set can be defined rigorously in terms of their structural equivalence rather than in terms of the structurally ambiguous colloquial labels used to denote status/role-sets by the general public. The ambiguity of these labels as the basis for empirical research is well known. Even Linton's (1936) early analysis contains a caution against the premature analysis of status labels without careful specification of the role relations in terms of which the statuses are defined for a particular system:

> Since patterns find expression only through the medium of the individuals who occupy the statuses which they establish, it is the statuses which are first brought to the attention of the investigator. . . . As a result, most investigators have shown a tendency to treat statuses as though they were fixed points between which various behavioral relation-

---

[17]Of course, this does not exclude the possibility that actors in distant positions will have empirically similar interests (see footnote 7 in Chapter 5) nor does it preclude the possibility of actors' being evaluated with regard to actors in distant positions. Consider the "like-me" versus the "prestige" hypotheses of interaction advanced by Laumann (1966) and Laumann and Senter (1976); the former claiming that actors seek interaction with others having the same level of prestige (structurally equivalent peers) and the latter claiming that actors seek to interact with others of higher prestige. With its emphasis on structurally equivalent peers, the model of structural interests might be taken to imply the like-me hypothesis and accordingly might be taken to be in contradiction to Laumann's results supporting the prestige hypothesis as well. However, either hypothesis could be true as a structural interest. If the like-me hypothesis is true, the model states that actors evaluate the utility of increased interaction with others of similar prestige in comparison to the existing tendency for other actors occupying their position to perform such interaction. If the prestige hypothesis is true, the model states that actors evaluate the utility of increased interaction with others of higher prestige in comparison to the tendency for others occupying their position to perform such interaction. Similarly, the use of individuals outside one's own status as reference points as reported in *The American Soldier* does not contradict the model of structural interests since there, as in the like-me and prestige hypotheses, actors can be seen as evaluating the conditions of these external statuses vis-à-vis their own in terms of the other actors occupying their own status. For example Merton and Rossi (1950) described the tendency of enlisted men to be more critical of officers in combat situations than when officers and enlisted men were behind the lines. In the combat situation, both officers and enlisted men are structurally equivalent in the sense of occupying a position most clearly defined by killing relations to the enemy yet instead of being given the same rights and obligations, officers were to be given deference by the enlisted man. Behind the lines, officers and enlisted men were defined by different relational patterns so that the differences in their rights and obligations were legitimately associated with different statuses. I conclude that a distinction exists between the criterion in terms of which evaluations are made under the postulate of marginality (structural action assuming it to be the resources of one's structurally equivalent peers) and the objects of evaluation.

ships might develop. . . . The fallacy of regarding statuses in this way comes out very clearly when we try to apply our own status terminology to the statuses in other social systems. Thus we have a single term, *uncle*, which we apply indiscriminantly to the brothers of both parents and the husbands of both parents' sisters. This usage reflects that fact that in our particular system there is a single pattern for the child's relation with these four male relatives. In other systems the same four groups of relatives . . . may be sharply distinguished, with a different pattern for the child's relation with each group. Moreover, none of the four patterns will agree in all respects with our own uncle-child pattern. To lump these four statuses together under our own term *uncle* is to completely misrepresent the situation [pp.257–258].

Structural action goes past colloquial labels directly to the relational patterns constituting status defining role-sets. Its predictions of social norms and relative deprivation are based on those bedrock conditions and accordingly avoid much of the ambiguity inherent in making predictions from colloquial labels. The usefulness of structural action from a theory construction point of view lies in its use of jointly occupied network positions as a replacement for colloquial labels vaguely defining norms and statuses. Although it is difficult to specify values and beliefs as behavior guiding norms in a general algebraic form, there is no such problem with specifying status/role-sets as network positions underlying social norms as structural interests, a point demonstrated in Chapters 2 and 5.[18] Moreover, structural action accomplishes this specificity without requiring an a priori assumption that a system of actors exists as a cohesive society into which actors have been socialized.

Using the idea that actors in a system are integrated into the system by common values generated by socialization processes has been a very convenient way to address the problem of system stability in the face of changes in the system's environment. It is, of course, a fundamental point throughout Parsons's (e.g., 1951, 1961) normative approach to social systems generally and especially in his treatment of pattern-maintenance and integration as necessary system functions. Without necessarily implying it, this assumption of system cohesion lends itself to the inference that status/role-sets stratifying a system of actors today serve some function under a "postulate of indispensability" and so will stratify the system for a long period of time. This stability need not be true at all, as shown by Merton's (1949) careful wading through the assumptions of early functionalist thought, since alternative relational patterns might also serve the function—to the extent that a function actually existed in the system. Nevertheless, the ease with which the stability conclusion can be reached, given the assumption of a cohesive system, has resulted in status/role-sets being

---

[18]Parsons's (1937:77–84) attempt to specify parameters of different action theories and Hayes's (1980) sophisticated representation of Parson's normative action perspective in the AGIL and pattern-variable schemes illustrate the difficulty of rigorously specifying cultural values and social norms in general terms. Hayes provides an interesting framework for pursuing questions raised by Parsons' action perspective; however, he is careful to note that he has made no more than a beginning—a representation of concepts rather than a derivation of empirical hypotheses.

traditionally viewed as "relatively invariant features of social situations" and traditionally discussed in terms of labels "suggestive of, and suitable for, static states, as *if* the positions were fixed and timeless, and the relationships simply continuous." These remarks on tradition are taken from Nadel (1957:125, 128). Further, this stability bias narrows the way in which structural change is analyzed. If the status/role-sets stratifying a system are stable, then structural change is a very empirical phenomenon. The relational patterns of individuals might change as they moved from one status to another (the son becoming a father, the daughter becoming a business executive, and so on), but the role-sets defining the statuses they move among would endure. Thus, structural change reduces to mobility. This stability of abstract structure could be justifed by distinguishing long- versus short-term stability (e.g., Levi-Strauss 1953; Nadel 1957: Chap. 6) or by distinguishing a changeable component to structure such as Firth's (1951:39–40) discussion of social organization as the relations among individuals capable of change over time and social structure as the enduring features of those relations. But these are merely conceptual patches on a theoretical failure to address change in status/role-sets. Through the three processes of differentiation in a division of labor, there can be changes in empirical structure which affect the ideographic structure of a system. If there is a profit to be had in performing activities that define a new relational pattern within the system, actors will be drawn to perform those activities thereby eventually creating a new status/role-set when occupants of the new position are recognized by the system. Similarly, when a particular relational pattern defines a no longer profitable activity within the system, the position will disappear, its former occupants dying off or moving to new, profitable activities. These changes in ideographic structure can have variable consequences for nomothetic structure as a function of the form of the relational patterns defining the emerging and disappearing positions. In a system where nomothetic structure consists of one primary position and several other positions secondary to it, the emergence of a status/role-set with primary form entails greater change than does the emergence of yet another secondary position. The former change would introduce a new set of leaders within the system whereas the latter would merely extend the existing domain of the existing leaders. For want of a better term, this change in the abstract structure of a system can be termed transformation. A major problem with the assumption of a cohesive system in the normative approach is the ease with which it lends itself to the inference that status defining role-sets are stable so that the analysis of transformation is supplanted by the analysis of mobility.[19]

---

[19]Interesting examples here are provided by Ellis's (1971) discussion of the emergence of order exchange and Clark's (1972) discussion of the institutionalization of exchange. Both Ellis and Clark feel that the normative perspective Parsons developed deemphasizes the manner in which structure arises in favor of the manner in which actors operate within existing structure. These are interesting treatments of the bias in a normative perspective toward mobility as structural change to the exclusion of what I have discussed as transformation.

Structural action is not encumbered with this bias toward stability, this emphasis on mobility over transformation, since it carries no implication that a system is cohesive. A system of actors is the frame of reference within which each actor forms his or her interests and pursues them. Actor interests and behaviors are defined in terms of the relational patterns defining the statuses they occupy in a given system at a given time. Whereas the colloquial labels for those statuses might last through time unchanged, the relational patterns defining them need not, and if they do, then the bedrock features of them that affect interests and behavior are indeed stable. At once a strength and a weakness, this basis in ideographic structure simply acknowledges the stability of status/role-sets over time to be an empirical question. My substantive applications in Chapters 3, 4, 6, and 8 make no pretentions to be generalizable over time; each is presented in the past tense in keeping with my conclusions in Chapter 2 regarding the temporal specificity of status/role-sets. Mobility and transformation are modes of structural change that can occur at any time as a function of actors' ability to act and their structural interests. In response to the existing distribution of resources and actors across statuses in a system, patterns of mobility can occur. The observation that the same flows between statuses occur at separate points in time (e.g., Hauser, Koffel, Travis, and Dickinson 1975) is an empirical generalization contingent on those resources and interests. Changes in either could change the mobility patterns (cf. Boudon 1973). Changes in the role-sets defining statuses, i.e., changes in ideographic structure itself, could change the mobility patterns. This is not to say that structural action reduces social structure to the epiphenomenon it becomes under atomistic action. Transformation of the status/role-sets in a system is possible under structural action; however, it will occur as a consequence of the interests and abilities of actors as occupants of statuses in the system as it exists. In other words, structural action accounts for continuing social order in a system by incorporating current social order into actor evaluations of the utility to be obtained by alternative adaptations to a changing environment. As Parsons (1966) cogently observed, "At the most general theoretical levels, there is no difference between processes which serve to maintain a system and those which serve to change it [p.21]."

9.5 CONCLUDING COMMENTS

I view the structural approach to action as a most promising bridge between the atomistic and normative approaches that have divided social scientists. Structural action is a logical implication of atomistic action, and it describes a logical subset of behaviors legitimate under normative action. Structural action yields the classic features of a general equilibrium so fruitfully explored under atomistic action in political economy while describing empirical findings on social norms and relative deprivation which have supported the use of normative action in empirical research within anthropology, political science, and sociology.

My purpose in this monograph has been to translate into concrete terms some of the promise I see in a structural theory of action. As I stated at the beginning of the chapter, I have only scratched the surface. Representing status/role-sets and structural interests within the social topology of a system as described in Chapters 2 and 5 provides rather general models within a structural theory of action. My preceding remarks focus on these models. The structural autonomy model is not at all in the same class of generality. As I stressed in the conclusion to Chapter 7, the model is an arbitrary simplification, a plausible baseline model for empirical research that describes how relational patterns constrain the ability to act. Not only are there many directions in which this model could be generalized, there is the concept of structural power to be considered, namely, the ability to act despite constraint (as opposed to structural autonomy, which is the ability to act without constraint).[20] Power and autonomy together would underlie transformational changes in social structure as described in the preceding. Clearly, there is much to be done.

[20]More specific comments on a concept of power within the framework proposed here are given in footnote 13 in Chapter 1.

References

Abbott, W. F. 1973. Prestige mobility of university sociology departments in the United States: 1964–1969. *American Sociologist 8*:38–41.

Alba, R. D. 1973. A graph-theoretic definition of a sociometric clique. *Journal of Mathematical Sociology 3*:113–126.

Alba, R. D., Kadushin, C. 1976. The intersection of social circles: a new measure of social proximity in networks. *Sociological Methods & Research 5*:77–102.

Alba, R. D., Moore, G. 1978. Elite social circles. *Sociological Methods & Research 7*:167–188.

Aldrich, H. E. 1979. *Organizations and Environments.* Englewood Cliffs: Printice-Hall.

Aldrich, H. E., Pfeffer, J. 1976. Environments of organizations. *Annual Review of Sociology 2*:79–105.

Aldrich, H. E., Whetten, D. A. 1981. Organization-sets, action-sets, and networks: making the most of simplicity. In *Handbook of Organizational Design: Adapting Organizations to Their Environments*, eds. P. C. Nystrom, W. H. Starbuck. New York: Oxford University Press.

Allen, M. P. 1974. The structure of interorganizational elite cooptation: interlocking corporate directorates. *American Sociological Review 39*:393–406.

Allen, M. P. 1976. Management control in the large corporation: comment on Zeitlin. *American Journal of Sociology 81*:885–894.

Allen, M. P. 1978. Economic interest groups and the corporate elite. *Social Science Quarterly 58*:597–615.

Allison, P. D. 1977. Testing for interaction in multiple regression. *American Journal of Sociology 83*:144–153.

Allison, P. D. 1978. Measures of inequality. *American Sociological Review 43*:865–880.

Allison, P. D., Stewart, J. A. 1974. Productivity differences among scientists: evidence for accumulative advantage. *American Sociological Review 39:*596–606.

Allport, G. 1937. The functional autonomy of motives. *American Journal of Psychology 50:*141–156.

Allport, G. 1961. *Pattern and Growth in Personality.* New York: Rinehart & Winston.

Arabie, P. 1977. Clustering representations of group overlap. *Journal of Mathematical Sociology 5:*113–128.

Arabie, P., Boorman, S. A., Levitt, P. R. 1978. Constructing blockmodels: how and why. *Journal of Mathematical Psychology 17:*21–63.

Arney, W. R. 1973. A refined status index for sociometric data. *Sociological Methods & Research 1:*329–353.

Asch, S. E. 1951. Effects of group pressure upon the modification and distortion of judgements. In *Groups, Leadership and Men,* ed. H. Guetzkow. Pittsburgh: Carnegie Press.

Bain, J. 1956. *Barriers to New Competition.* Cambridge: Harvard University Press.

Bain, J. 1959. *Industrial Organization.* New York: John Wiley.

Baker, F. B., Hubert, L. J. 1976. A graph-theoretic approach to goodness-of-fit in complete-link hierarchical clustering. *Journal of the American Statistical Association 71:*870–878.

Barnes, J. A. 1969. Networks and political processes. In *Social Networks in Urban Situations,* ed. J. C. Mitchell. Manchester: Manchester University Press.

Barnes, J. A. 1972. Social Networks. *Addison-Wesley Modular Publ. 26:*1–29.

Barry, B. M. 1970. *Sociologists, Economists, and Democracy.* London: Collier-Macmillan.

Baty, G. B., Evan, W. M., Rothermel, T. W. 1971. Personnel flows as interorganizational relations. *Admistrative Science Quarterly 16:*430–443.

Bavelas, A. 1948. A mathematical model for group structures. *Human Organization 7:*16–30.

Bavelas, A. 1950. Communication patterns in task oriented groups. *Journal of the Acoustical Society of America 22:*271–282.

Bearden, J., Atwood, W., Freitage, P., Hendricks, C., Mintz, B., Schwartz, M. 1975. The nature and extent of bank centrality in corporate networks. Paper presented at the annual meetings of the American Sociological Association.

Beauchamp, M. A. 1965. An improved index of centrality. *Behavioral Science 10:*161–163.

Becker, G. S. (1974) 1976. A theory of social interactions. In *The Economic Approach to Human Behavior,* ed. G. S. Becker. Chicago: University of Chicago Press.

Becker, G. S. 1976. *The Economic Approach to Human Behavior.* Chicago: University of Chicago Press.

Becker, M. 1970. Sociometric location and innovativeness: reformulation and extension of the diffusion model. *American Sociological Review 35:*267–282.

Ben-David, J. 1971. *The Scientist's Role in Society.* Englewood Cliffs: Prentice Hall.

Beniger, J. R. 1976. Sampling social networks: the subgroup approach. Proceedings of the Business and Economic Statistics Section, American Statistical Association, pp. 226–231.

Berkowitz, S. D., Carrington, P. J., Kotowitz, Y., Waverman, L. 1979. The determination of enterprise groupings through combined ownership and directorship ties. *Social Networks 1:*391–413.

Berle, A. A., Means, G. C. (1932) 1968. *The Modern Corporation and Private Property.* New York: Harcourt, Brace & World.

Bernard, H. R., Killworth, P. D. 1973. On the social structure of an ocean-going research vessel and other important things. *Social Science Research 2:*145–184.

Bernard, H. R., Killworth, P. D. 1977. Informant accuracy in social network data II. *Human Communication Research 4:*3–18.

Bielby, W. T., Hauser, R. M. 1977. Structural equation models. *Annual Review of Sociology 3:* 137–161.

Blau, J. R. 1974. Patterns of communication among theoretical high energy physicists. *Sociometry 37:*391–406.

Blau, P. M. 1964. *Exchange and Power in Social Life.* New York: John Wiley.

Blau, P. M. 1968. Interaction: social exchange. In *The International Encylopedia of the Social Sciences.* New York: Free Press and Macmillan.

Blau, P. M. 1974. Parameters of social structure. *American Sociological Review 39:*615–635.

Blau, P. M. 1977. A macrosociological theory of social structure. *American Journal of Sociology 83:*26–54.

Blau, P. M., Duncan, O. D. 1967. *The American Occupational Structure.* New York: John Wiley.

Bluestone, B., Murphy, W. M., Stevenson, M. 1973. *Low Wages and the Working Poor.* Ann Arbor: Institute of Labor and Industrial Relations, University of Michigan.

Bock, R. D., Husain, S. Z. 1950. An adaptation of Holzinger's *B*-coefficients for the analysis of sociometric data. *Sociometry 13:*146–153.

Bogardus, E. S. 1925. Measuring social distances. *Journal of Applied Sociology 9:*216–226.

Boissevain, J. 1974. *Friends of Friends: Networks, Manipulators, and Coalitions.* New York: St. Martin's Press.

Boissevain, J., Mitchell, J. C., eds., 1973. *Network Analysis: Studies in Human Interaction.* Paris: Mouton.

Bonacich, P. 1972a. Factoring and weighting approaches to status scores and clique identification. *Journal of Mathematical Sociology 2:*113–120.

Bonacich, P. 1972b. Technique for analyzing overlapping memberships. In *Sociological Methodology 1972,* ed. H. L. Costner. San Francisco: Jossey-Bass.

Bonacich, P. 1977. Using Boolean algebra to analyze overlapping memberships. In *Sociological Methodology 1978,* ed. K. F. Schuessler. San Francisco: Jossey-Bass.

Bonacich, P. 1980. The "common structure semigroup," a replacement for the Boorman and White "joint reduction." *American Journal of Sociology 86:*159–166.

Bonacich, P., McConaghy, M. J. 1979. The algebra of blockmodeling. In *Sociological Methodology 1980,* ed. K. F. Schuessler. San Francisco: Jossey-Bass.

Boorman, S. A. 1975. A combinatorial optimization model for transmission of job information through contact networks. *Bell Journal of Economics 6:*216–249.

Boorman, S. A., Arabie, P. 1980. Algebraic approaches to the comparison of concrete social structures represented as networks: reply to Bonacich. *American Journal of Sociology 86:*166–174.

Boorman, S. A., White, H. C. 1976. Social structure from multiple networks, II. role structures. *American Journal of Sociology 81:*1384–1446.

Bott, E. 1957. *Family and Social Network.* New York: Free Press.

Bott, E. 1971. Reconsiderations. In *Family and Social Network,* 1971 ed. New York: Free Press.

Boudon, R. 1973. *Education, Opportunity and Social Inequality.* New York: Wiley-Interscience.

Boyd, J. P. 1969. The algebra of group kinship. *Journal of Mathematical Psychology 6:*139–167.

Boyd, J. P. 1980. The universal semigroup of relations. *Social Networks 2:*91–118.

Boyd, J. P., Haehl, J., Sailer, L. 1972. Kinship systems and inverse semigroups. *Journal of Mathematical Sociology 2:*37–61.

Boyle, R. P. 1969. Algebraic systems for normal and hierarchical sociograms. *Sociometry 32:*99–119.

Breiger, R. L. 1974. The duality of persons and groups. *Social Forces 53:*181–190.

Breiger, R. L. 1976. Career attributes and network structures: a blockmodel study of a biomedical research speciality. *American Sociological Review 41:*117–135.

Breiger, R. L. 1979. Toward an operational theory of community elite structures. *Quality and Quantity 13:*21–57.

Breiger, R. L., Boorman, S. A., Arabie, P. 1975. An algorithm for clustering relational data with application to social network analysis and comparison with multidimensional scaling. *Journal of Mathematical Psychology 12:*328–383.

Breiger, R. L., Pattison, P. E. 1978. The joint role structure of two communities' elites.

Sociological Methods & Research 7:213–226.

Buchanon, J. M., Tullock, G. 1962. *The Calculus of Consent.* Ann Arbor: University of Michigan Press.

Burch, P. H. Jr. 1972. *The Managerial Revolution Reassessed.* Lexington, MA: D. C. Heath.

Burt, R. S. 1973. The differential impact of social integration on participation in the diffusion of innovations. *Social Science Research* 2:125–144.

Burt, R. S. 1975. Corporate society: a time series analysis of network structure. *Social Science Research* 4:271–328.

Burt, R. S. 1976a. Interpretational confounding of unobserved variables in structural equation models. *Sociological Methods & Research* 5:3–52.

Burt, R. S. 1976b. Positions in networks. *Social Forces* 55:93–122.

Burt, R. S. 1977a. Power in a social topology. *Social Science Research* 6:1–83.

Burt, R. S. 1977b. Positions in multiple network systems, part one: a general conception of stratification and prestige in a system of actors cast as a social topology. *Social Forces* 56:106–131.

Burt, R. S. 1977c. Positions in multiple network systems, part two: stratification and prestige among elite decision-makers in the community of Altneustadt. *Social Forces* 56:551–575.

Burt, R. S. 1978a. Stratification and prestige among elite experts in methodological and mathematical sociology circa 1975. *Social Networks* 1:105–158.

Burt, R. S. 1978b. Cohesion versus structural equivalence as a basis for network subgroups. *Sociological Methods & Research* 7:189–212.

Burt, R. S. 1979a. Disaggregating the effect on profits in manufacturing industries of having imperfectly competitive consumers and suppliers. *Social Science Research* 8:120–143.

Burt, R. S. 1979b. Relational equilibrium in a social topology. *Journal of Mathematical Sociology* 6:211–252.

Burt, R. S. 1979c. A structural theory of interlocking corporate directorates. *Social Networks* 1:415–435.

Burt, R. S. 1980a. Autonomy in a social topology. *American Journal of Sociology* 85:892–925.

Burt, R. S. 1980b. Actor interests in a social topology: foundatioin for a structural theory of action. *Sociological Inquiry* 50:107–132.

Burt, R. S. 1980c. Models of network structure. *Annual Review of Sociology* 6:79–141.

Burt, R. S. 1980d. On the functional form of corporate cooptation: empirical findings linking the intensity of market constraint with the frequency of directorate ties. *Social Science Research* 9:146–177.

Burt, R. S. 1980e. Cooptive corporate actor networks: a reconsideration of interlocking directorates involving American manufacturing. *Administrative Science Quarterly* 25:557–582.

Burt, R. S. 1980f. Innovation as a structural interest: rethinking the impact of network position on innovation adoption. *Social Networks* 2:327–355.

Burt, R. S. 1981a. Studying status/role-sets as ersatz network positions in mass surveys. *Sociological Methods & Research* 9:313–337.

Burt, R. S. 1981b. Comparative power structures in American communities. *Social Science Research* 10:115–176.

Burt, R. S. 1982a. Disentangling relational contents. In *Applied Network Analysis: Structural Methodology for Empirical Social Research,* eds. R. S. Burt, M. J. Minor. Beverly Hills: Sage Publications.

Burt, R. S. 1982b. Range: reachability and structural autonomy. In *Applied network analysis: Structural methodology for empirical social research,* eds. R. S. Burt, M. J. Minor. Beverly Hills: Sage Publications.

Burt, R. S. 1983. *Corporate Profits and Cooptation: Networks of Market Constraints and Directorate Ties in the American Economy.* New York: Academic Press.

Burt, R. S., Christman, K. P., Kilburn, H. C. 1980. Testing a structural theory of corporate cooptation: interorganizational directorate ties as a strategy for avoiding market constraints on profits. *American Sociological Review* 45:821–841.

Burt, R. S., Doreian, P. 1980. Testing a structural theory of perception: conformity and deviance with respect to journal norms in elite sociological methodology. Unpublished manuscript, University of Pittsburgh.

Burt, R. S., Fischer, M. G., Christman, K. P. 1979. Structures of well-being: sufficient conditions for identification as restricted covariance structures. *Sociological Methods & Research* 8:111–20.

Burt, R. S., Leiben, K. L., Fischer, M. G. 1980. Network power structures from informant perceptions. *Human Organization* 39:121–133.

Burt, R. S., Lin, N. 1977. Network time series from archival records. In *Sociological Methodology 1977*, ed. D. R. Heise. San Francisco: Jossey-Bass.

Burt, R. S., Minor, M. J. eds. 1982. *Applied Network Analysis: Structural Methodology for Empirical Social Research.* Beverly Hills: Sage Publications.

Burt, R. S., Wiley, J. A., Minor, M. J. 1978. Structure of well-being: form, content and stability over time. *Sociological Methods & Research* 6:365–407.

Cancian, F. 1967. Stratification and risk-taking: a theory tested on agricultural innovation. *American Sociological Review* 33:921–927.

Carrington, P. J., Heil, G. H. 1979. A method for finding blockmodels of networks. Paper presented at the annual meetings of the American Sociological Association.

Cartwright, D. 1968. The nature of group cohesiveness. In *Group Dynamics,* eds. D. Cartwright, A. Zander. New York: Harper & Row.

Cartwright, D., Harary, F. 1956. Structural balance: a generalization of Heider's theory. *Psychological Review* 63:277–293.

Cartwright, D., Harary, F. 1977. A graph-theoretic approach to the investigation of system-environment relationships. *Journal of Mathematical Sociology* 5:87–111.

Cartwright, D., Zander, A. eds., 1968. *Group Dynamics.* New York: Harper & Row.

Catton, W. R. Jr. 1964. The development of sociological thought. In *Handbook of Modern Sociology,* ed. R. E. L. Faris. New York: Rand McNally.

Clark, T. N. 1972. Structural functionalism, exchange theory, and the new political economy: institutionalization as a theoretical linkage. *Sociological Inquiry* 42:275–298.

Clark, T. N. 1975. Community Power. *Annual Review of Sociology* 1:271–295.

Clemente, F., Sturgis, R. B. 1974. Quality of department of doctoral training and research productivity. *Sociology of Education* 47:287–299.

Cole, J. R., Cole, S. 1973. *Social Stratification in Science.* Chicago: University of Chicago Press.

Coleman, J. S. 1958. Relational analysis: the study of social organization with survey methods. *Human Organization* 16:28–36.

Coleman, J. S. 1961. *The Adolescent Society.* New York: Free Press.

Coleman, J. S. 1964. *Introduction to Mathematical Sociology.* New York: Free Press.

Coleman, J. S. 1966. Foundations for a theory of collective decisions. *American Journal of Sociology* 71:615–627.

Coleman, J. S. 1970. Clustering in N dimensions by use of a system of forces. *Journal of Mathematical Sociology* 1:1–47.

Coleman, J. S. 1972. Systems of social exchange. *Journal of Mathematical Sociology* 2:145–163.

Coleman, J. S. 1973. *The Mathematics of Collective Action.* Chicago: Aldine.

Coleman, J. S., Katz, E., Menzel, H. 1966. *Medical Innovation: A Diffusion Study.* New York: Bobbs-Merrill.

Collins, B. E., Raven, B. H. 1968. Group structure: attraction, coalitions, communications, and power. In *Handbook of Social Psychology,* eds. G. Lindzey, E. Aronson. Reading, MA: Addison-Wesley.

Collins, N. R., Preston, L. E. 1968. *Concentration and Price-Cost Margins in Manufacturing Industries.* Berkeley: University of California Press.

Collins, N. R., Preston, L. E. 1969. Price-cost margins and industry structure. *Review of Economics and Statistics 51:*271–286.

Cook, K. S. 1982. Network structures from an exchange perspective. In *Social Structure and Network Analysis,* eds. P. V. Marsden, N. Lin. Beverly Hills: Sage Publications.

Cook, K. S., Emerson, R. M. 1978. Power, equity, and commitment in exchange networks. *American Sociological Review 43:*721–739.

Cooley, C. H. (1909) 1962. *Social Organization.* New York: Schocken.

Coser, L. A. 1973. Servants: the obsolescence of an occupational role. *Social Forces 52:*31–40.

Coser, L. A. 1974. *Greedy Institutions.* New York: Free Press.

Coser, L. A. 1975. Presidential address: two methods in search of a substance. *American Sociological Review 40:*691–700.

Crane, D. 1972. *Invisible Colleges.* Chicago: University of Chicago Press.

Cronbach, B. E., Gleser, G. C. 1953. Assessing similarity between profiles. *Psychological Bulletin 50:*456–473.

Davis, J. A. 1959. A formal interpretation of the theory of relative deprivation. *Sociometry 22:*280–296.

Davis, J. A. 1967. Clustering and balance in graphs. *Human Relations 20:*181–187.

Davis, J. A. 1970. Clustering and hierarchy in interpersonal relations: testing two graph theoretical models on 742 sociograms. *American Sociological Review 35:*843–852.

Davis, J. A., Leinhardt, S. 1972. The structure of positive interpersonal relations in small groups. In *Sociological Theories in Progress*, eds. J. Berger, M. Zelditch Jr., B. Anderson. New York: Houghton-Mifflin.

Denzin, N. K. 1969. Symbolic interaction and ethnomethodology: a proposed synthesis. *American Sociological Review 34:*922–934.

De Sola Pool, I., Kochen, M. 1978. Contacts and influence. *Social Networks 1:*5–51.

Deutsch, M., Gerard, H. B. 1955. A study of normative and informational social influences upon individual judgement. *Journal of Abnormal and Social Psychology 51:*629–636.

Domhoff, G. W. 1970. *The Higher Circles: The Governing Class in America.* New York: Random House.

Dooley, P. D. 1969. The interlocking directorate. *American Economic Review 59:*314–323.

Doreian, P. 1969. A note on the detection of cliques in valued graphs. *Sociometry 32:*237–242.

Doreian, P. 1970. *Mathematics and the Study of Social Relations.* London: Weidenfeld & Nicolson.

Doreian, P. 1974. On the connectivity of social networks. *Journal of Mathematical Sociology 3:*245–258.

Doreian, P. 1980. Linear models with spatially distributed data: spatial disturbances or spatial effects? *Sociological Methods & Research 9:*29–60.

Doreian, P. 1981. On the estimation of linear models with spatially distributed data. In *Sociological Methodology 1981*, ed. S. Leinhardt. San Francisco: Jossey-Bass.

Downs, A. 1957. *An Economic Theory of Democracy.* New York: Harper & Row.

Dumont, R. G., Wilson, W. J. 1967. Aspects of concept formation, explication, and theory construction in sociology. *American Sociological Review 29:*985–995.

Duncan, O. D. 1975. *Introduction to Structural Equation Models.* New York: Academic.

Duncan, O. D., Haller, A. O., Portes, A. (1968) 1971. Peer influences on aspirations: a reinterpretation. In *Causal Models in the Social Sciences,* ed. H. M. Blalock. Chicago: Aldine.

Durkheim, É. (1893) 1933. *The Division of Labor in Society*, trans. G. Shimpson. New York: Free Press.

Durkheim, É. (1906) 1974. Philosophy and moral facts. In *Sociology and Philosophy*, trans. D. F. Pocock. New York: Free Press.

Durkheim, É. (1925) 1961. *Moral Education*, trans. E. K. Wilson and H. Schunurer. New York: Free Press.

Edgeworth, F. Y. 1881. *Mathematical Psychics*. London: Paul.

Ekeh, P. P. 1974. *Social Exchange Theory*. Cambridge: Harvard University Press.

Ellis, D. P. 1971. The Hobbesian problem of order: a critical appraisal of the normative solution. *American Sociological Review 36:*692–703.

Emerson, R. M. 1972. Exchange theory, part II: exchange relations and networks. In *Sociological Theories in Progress*, eds. J. Berger, M. Zelditch Jr., B. Anderson. Boston: Houghton-Mifflin.

Erickson, B. H. 1978. Some problems of inference from chain data. In *Sociological Methodology 1979*, ed. K. F. Schuessler. San Francisco: Jossey-Bass.

Erickson, B. H., Kringas, P. R. 1975. The small world of politics. *Canadian Review of Sociology and Anthropology 12:*585–593.

Evan, W. M. 1966. The organization-set: toward a theory of interorganizational relations. In *Approaches to Organizational Design*, ed. J. D. Thompson. Pittsburgh: University of Pittsburgh Press.

Evan, W. M. 1972. An organization-set model of interorganizational relations. In *Interorganizational Decision-Making*, eds. M. F. Tuite, M. Radnor, R. R. Chisholm. Chicago: Aldine.

Fararo, T. J. 1973. *Mathematical Sociology*. New York: Wiley-Interscience.

Festinger, L. 1949. The analysis of sociograms using matrix algebra. *Human Relations 2:*153–158.

Festinger, L., Schachter, S., Back, K. W. 1950. *Social Pressures in Informal Groups*. Stanford: Stanford University Press.

Fienberg, S. E., Wasserman, S. S. 1981. Categorical data analysis of single sociometric relations. In *Sociological Methodology 1981*, ed. S. Leinhardt. San Francisco: Jossey-Bass.

Firth, R. (1951) 1963. *Elements of Social Organization*. Boston: Beacon Press.

Fischer, C. S., Jackson, R. M., Stueve, C. A., Gerson, K., Jones, I. M., Baldassare, M. 1977. *Networks and Places: Social Relations in the Urban Setting*. New York: Free Press.

Flament, C. 1963. *Applications of Graph Theory to Group Structure*. Englewood Cliffs: Prentice-Hall.

Foster, C. C., Hovarth W. J. 1971. A study of a large sociogram III. reciprocal choice probabilities as a measure of social distance. *Behavioral Science 16:*429–435.

Frank, O. 1978. Sampling and estimation in large social networks. *Social Networks 1:*91–101.

Frank, O. 1979. Estimation of population totals by use of snowball samples. In *Perspectives on Social Network Research*, eds. P. W. Holland, S. Leinhardt. New York: Academic.

Frazer, J. G. 1919. *Folklore in the Old Testament* (3 Vols.). London: Macmillan.

Freeman, L. C. 1968. *Patterns of Local Community Leadership*. New York: Bobbs-Merrill.

Freeman, L. C. 1977. A set of measures of centrality based on betweenness. *Sociometry 40:*35–41.

Freeman L. C. 1979. Centrality in social networks: conceptual clarification. *Social Networks 1:*215–239.

Freeman, L. C., Roeder, D., Mulholland, R. R. 1980. Centrality in social networks: II. experimental results. *Social Networks 2:*119–141.

Friedell, M. F. 1967. Organizations as semilattices. *American Sociological Review 32:*46–54.

Galaskiewicz, J. 1979. *Social Networks and Community Politics*. Beverly Hills: Sage.

Galaskiewicz, J., Marsden, P. V. 1978. Interorganizational resource networks: formal patterns of overlap. *Social Science Research 7:*89–107.

Galaskiewicz, J., Wasserman, S. 1979. A study of change in a regional corporate network. Paper presented at the annual meetings of the American Sociological Association.

Galbraith, J. K. 1973. *Economics and the Public Purpose*. New York: Houghton Mifflin.

Gans, H. J. 1962. *The Urban Villagers*. New York: Free Press.

Garfinkel, H. 1967. *Studies in Ethnomethodology*. Englewood Cliffs: Prentice Hall.

Gaston, J. 1973. *Originality and Competition in Science*. Chicago: University of Chicago Press.

Gaston, J. 1978. *The Reward System in British and American Science*. New York: Wiley-Interscience.

Georgescu-Roegen, N. 1968. Utility. In *The International Encyclopedia of the Social Sciences*. New York: Free Press and Macmillan.

Gibbs, J. P., Martin, W. T. 1962. Urbanization, technology and the division of labor: international patterns. *American Sociological Review 27:*667–677.

Gibbs, J. P., Poston, D. L. 1975. The division of labor: conceptualization and related measures. *Social Forces 53:*468–476.

Ginsberg, M. 1934. *Sociology*. London: Butterworth.

Glanzer, M., Glaser, R. 1959. Techniques for the study of group structure and behavior: analysis of structure. *Psychological Bulletin 56:*317–332.

Glanzer, M., Glaser, R. 1961. Techniques for the study of group structure and behavior: empirical studies of the effects of structure in small groups. *Psychological Bulletin 58:*1–27.

Glenn, N. D. 1971. American sociologist's evaluations of sixty-three journals. *American Sociologist 6:*298–303.

Goodman, L. A. 1961. Snowball sampling. *Annals of Mathematical Statistics 32:*148–170.

Goodman, L. A. 1970. The multivariate analysis of qualitative data: interactions among multiple classifications. *Journal of the American Statistical Association 65:*226–256.

Granovetter, M. 1973. The strength of weak ties. *American Journal of Sociology 78:*1360–1380.

Granovetter, M. 1974. *Getting a Job: A Study of Contacts and Careers*. Cambridge: Harvard University Press.

Granovetter, M. 1976. Network sampling: some first steps. *American Journal of Sociology 81:*1287–1303.

Griffith, B., Miller, A. J. 1970. Networks of informal communication among scientifically productive scientists. In *Communication among Scientists and Engineers*, eds. C. E. Nelson, D. K. Pollock. Lexington, MA: Heath Lexington.

Griffith, B., Mullins, N. C. 1972. Coherent social groups in scientific change: "invisible colleges" may be consistent throughout science. *Science 177:*959–964.

Haber, R. N., ed., 1968. *Contemporary Theory and Research in Visual Perception*. New York: Hold, Rinehardt & Winston.

Hagstrom, W. O. 1965. *The Scientific Community*. New York: Basic.

Hall, E. T. 1959. *The Silent Language*. Garden City: Doubleday.

Haller, A. O., Butterworth, C. E. 1960. Peer influences on levels of occupational and educational aspiration. *Social Forces 38:*289–295.

Hallinan, M. T. 1974a. *The Structure of Positive Sentiment*. New York: Elsevier.

Hallinan, M. T. 1974b. A structural model of sentiment relations. *American Journal of Sociology 80:*364–378.

Hallinan, M. T. 1978. The process of friendship formation. *Social Networks 1:*193–210.

Hallinan, M. T., Felmlee, D. 1975. An analysis of intransitivity in sociometric data. *Sociometry 38:*195–212.

Hallinan, M. T., Hutchins, E. E. 1979. Structural effects on dyadic change. Paper presented at the annual meetings of the American Sociological Association.

Hallinan, M. T., McFarland, D. D. 1975. Higher order stability conditions in mathematical models of sociometric or cognitive structure. *Journal of Mathematical Sociology 4:*131–148.

Hamblin, R. L. 1971. Mathematical experimentation and sociological theory: a critical analysis. *Sociometry 34:*423–452.

Hamblin, R. L. 1974. Social attitudes: magnitude measurement and theory. In *Measurement in the Social Sciences*, ed. H. M. Blalock. Chicago: Aldine.

Hamblin, R. L., Hout, M., Miller, J. L., Pitcher, B. L. 1977. Arms races: a test of two models. *American Sociological Review 42:*338–354.

Hamblin, R. L., Jacobsen, R. B., Miller, J. L. 1973. *A Mathematical Theory of Social Change*. New York: Wiley-Interscience.

Hamblin, R. L., Miller, J. L., Saxton, D. E. 1979. Modeling use diffusion. *Social Forces 57:*799–811.

Harary, F. 1969. *Graph Theory*. Reading, MA: Addison-Wesley.

Harary, F., Norman, R. Z., Cartwright, D. 1965. *Structural Models: An Introduction to the Theory of Directed Graphs*. New York: John Wiley.

Hargens, L. L., Mullins, N. C., Hecht, P. K. 1980. Research areas and stratification processes in science. *Social Studies of Science 10:*55–74.

Hauser, R. M., Goldberger, A. S. 1971. The treatment of unobserved variables in path analysis. In *Sociological Methodology 1971,* ed. H. Costner. San Francisco: Jossey-Bass.

Hauser, R. M., Koffel, J. N., Travis, H. P., Dickinson, P. J. 1975. Temporal change in occupational mobility: evidence for men in the United States. *American Sociological Review 40:*270–297.

Hayes, A. C. 1980. A semi-formal explication of Talcott Parsons's theory of action. *Sociological Inquiry 50:*39–56.

Heider, F. 1958. *The Psychology of Interpersonal Relations*. New York: John Wiley.

Hempel, C. G. (1942) 1965. The function of general laws in history. In *Aspects of Scientific Explanation,* ed. C. G. Hempel. New York: Free Press.

Hobbs, T. (1651) 1968. *Leviathan*. New York: Penguin.

Holland, P. W., Leinhardt, S. 1970. A method for detecting structure in sociometric data. *American Journal of Sociology 70:*492–513.

Holland, P. W., Leinhardt, S. 1971. Transitivity in structural models of small groups. *Comparative Group Studies 2:*107–124.

Holland, P. W., Leinhardt, S. 1973. The structural implications of measurement error in sociometry. *Journal of Mathematical Sociology 3:*85–111.

Holland, P. W., Leinhardt, S. 1975. Local structure in social networks. In *Sociological Methodology 1976,* ed. D. R. Heise. San Francisco: Jossey-Bass.

Holland, P. W., Leinhardt, S. 1976. Conditions for eliminating intransitivities in binary digraphs. *Journal of Mathematical Sociology 4:*315–318.

Holland, P. W., Leinhardt, S. 1977. A dynamic model for social networks. *Journal of Mathematical Sociology 5:*5–20.

Holland, P. W., Leinhardt, S. 1978. An omnibus test for social structure using triads. *Sociological Methods & Research 7:*227–256.

Holland, P. W., Leinhardt, S. 1981. An exponential family of probability distributions for directed graphs. *Journal of the American Statistical Association 76:*33–50.

Homans, G. C. 1950. *The Human Group*. New York: Harcourt, Brace & World.

Homans, G. C. 1961. *Social Behavior: Its Elementary Forsm*. New Work: Harcourt, Brace & World.

Homans, G. C. 1968. The study of groups. In *The International Encyclopedia of the Social Sciences*. New York: Free Press and Macmillan.

Horan, P. M. 1975. Information-theoretic measures and the analysis of social structures. *Sociological Methods & Research 3:*321–340.

Hubbell, C. H. 1965. An input–output approach to clique identification. *Sociometry 28:*377–399.

Hubert, L. J. 1974. Some applications of graph theory to clustering. *Psychometrika 39:*283–309.

Hubert, L. J., Baker, F. B. 1978. Evaluating the conformity of sociometric measurements. *Psychometrika 43:*31–41.

Hunter, F. 1953. *Community Power Structure*. Chapel Hill: University of North Carolina Press.

Internal Revenue Service. 1971. *Statistics of Income: Corporate Income Tax Returns*. Washington, DC: Government Printing Office.

Jedlicka, D. 1979. Opportunities, information networks and international migration streams. *Social Networks 1:*277–284.

Johnson, S. C. 1967. Hierarchical clustering schemes. *Psychometrika 32:* 241–254.

Jöreskog, K. G. 1969. A general approach to confirmatory maximum likelihood factor analysis. *Psychometrica 34:*183–202.

Jöreskog, K. G., Sörbom, D. 1979. *Advances in Factor Analysis and Structural Equation Models*. Cambridge, MA: Abt Books.

Kadushin, C. 1966. The friends and supporters of psychotherapy: on social circles in urban life. *American Sociological Review 31*:786–802.

Kadushin, C. 1968. Power, influence and social circles: a new methodology for studying opinion makers. *American Sociological Review 33*:685–698.

Kadushin, C. 1974. *The American Intellectual Elite*. Boston: Little, Brown.

Kapferer, B. 1969. Norms and the manipulation of relationships in a work context. In *Social Networks in Urban Situations,* ed. J. C. Mitchell. Manchester: Manchester University Press.

Kapferer, B. 1973. Social network and conjugal role in urban Zambia: towards a reformulation of the Bott hypothesis. In *Network Analysis: Studies in Human Interaction*, eds. J. Boissevain, J. C. Mitchell. Paris: Mouton.

Katz, F. E. 1958. Occupational contact networks. *Social Forces 37*:252–258.

Katz, L. 1947. On the matrix analysis of sociometric data. *Sociometry 10*:233–241.

Katz, L. 1953. A new status index derived from sociometric analysis. *Psychometrika 18*:39–43.

Katz, L., Powell, J. H. 1953. A proposed index of the conformity of one sociometric measurement to another. *Psychometrika 18*:249–256.

Kaysen, C., Turner, D. F. 1959. *Antitrust Policy*. Cambridge: Harvard University Press.

Kelley, J. L. 1955. *General Topology*. New York: Springer-Verlag.

Kelman, H. C. 1961. Processes of opinion change. *Public Opinion Quarterly 25*:57–78.

Kemper, T. D. 1972. The division of labor: a post-Durkheimian analytical view. *American Sociological Review 37*:739–753.

Kephart, W. M. 1950. A quantitative analysis of intergroup relationships. *American Journal of Sociology 55*:544–549.

Khalilzadeh-Shirazi, J. 1974. Market structure and price-cost margins in the United Kingdom manufacturing industries. *Review of Economics and Statistics 56*:67–76.

Killworth, P. D. 1974. Intransitivity in the structure of small closed groups. *Social Science Research 3*:1–23.

Killworth, P. D., Bernard, H. R. 1974. Catij: a new sociometric and its application to a prison living unit. *Human Organization 33*:335–350.

Killworth, P. D., Bernard, H. R. 1976. A model of human group dynamics. *Social Science Research 5*:173–224.

Killworth, P. D., Bernard, H. R. 1978. The reverse small-world experiment. *Social Networks 1*:159–192.

Klovdahl, A. S., Dhofier, Z., Oddy, G., O'Hara, J., Stoutjesdijk, S. Whish, A. 1977. Social networks in an urban area. *Australian and New Zealand Journal of Sociology 13*:169–175.

Kotz, D. M. 1978. *Bank Control of Large Corporations in the United States*. Berkeley: University of California Press.

Lankford, P. M. 1974. Comparative analysis of clique identification methods. *Sociometry 37*:287–305.

Larner, R. J. 1970. *Management Control and the Large Corporation*. Cambridge, MA: Dunellen.

Laumann, E. O. 1966. *Prestige and Association in an Urban Community: An Analysis of an Urban Stratification System*. New York: Bobbs-Merrill.

Laumann, E. O. 1973. *Bonds of Pluralism: The Form and Substance of Urban Social Networks*. New York: Wiley-Interscience.

Laumann, E. O., Galaskiewicz, J., Marsden, P. V. 1978. Community structure as interorganizational linkages. *Annual Review of Sociology 4*:455–484.

Laumann, E. O., Marsden, P. V. 1979. The analysis of oppositional structures in political elites: identifying collective actors. *American Sociological Review 44*:713–732.

Laumann, E. O., Marsden, P. V., Galaskiewicz, J. 1977. Community influence structures: extension of a network approach. *American Journal of Sociology 83*:594–631

Laumann, E. O., Marsden, P. V., Prensky, D. 1982. The boundary specification problem in network analysis. In *Applied Network Analysis: Structural Methodology for Empirical Social Research*, eds. R. S. Burt, M. J. Minor. Beverly Hills: Sage Publications.

Laumann, E. O., Pappi, F. U. 1976. *Networks of Collective Action: A Perspective on Community Influence Systems.* New York: Academic.

Laumann, E. O., Senter, R. 1976. Subjective social distance, occupational stratification, and forms of status and class consciousness: a cross-national replication and extension. *American Journal of Sociology 81:*1304–1338.

Laumann, E. O., Verbrugge, L. M., Pappi, F. V. (1974) 1976. A causal modelling approach to the study of a community elite's influence structure. In *Networks of Collective Action: A Perspective on Community Influence Systems*, E. O. Laumann, F. U. Pappi. New York: Academic.

Lawley, D. N., Maxwell, A. E. 1971. *Factor Analysis as a Statistical Method.* New York: American Elsevier.

Lazarsfeld, P. F. 1959. Problems in methodology. In *Sociology Today*, eds. R. K. Merton, L. Broom, L. S. Cottrell Jr. New York: Harper & Row.

Leach, E. 1974. *Claude Levi-Strauss.* New York: Viking.

Leavitt, H. J. 1951. Some effects of communication patterns on group performances. *Journal of Abnormal and Social Psychology 46:*38–50.

Lee, N. H. 1969. *The Search for an Abortionist.* Chicago: University of Chicago Press.

Leik, R. K., Meeker, B. F. 1975. *Mathematical Sociology.* Englewood Cliffs: Prentice-Hall.

Leinhardt, S. 1972. Developmental change in the sentiment structure of children's groups. *American Sociological Review 37:*202–212.

Leinhardt, S., ed. 1977. *Social Networks: A Developing Paradigm.* New York: Academic.

Lenoir, T. 1979. Quantitative foundations for the sociology of science: on linking blockmodeling with co-citation analysis. *Social Studies of Science 9:*455–480.

Leontief, W. 1947. Introduction to the theory of the internal structure of functional relationships. *Econometrica 15:*361–373.

Leontief, W. (1951) 1966. Input–output economics. In *Input–Output Economics,* W. Leontief. New York: Oxford University Press.

Leontief, W. 1968. Input–output analysis. In *The Encyclopedia of the Social Sciences.* New York: Free Press and Macmillan.

Levi-Strauss, C. (1949) 1969. *The Elementary Structures of Kinship*, trans. J. H. Bell, J. R. von Sturmer, R. Needham. Boston: Beacon Press.

Levi-Struss, C. 1953. Social structure. In *Anthropology Today*, eds. A. L. Kroeber *et al.* Chicago: University of Chicago Press.

Levine, J. 1972. The sphere of influence. *American Sociological Review 37:*14–27.

Lewin, K. 1936. *Principles of Topological Psychology,* trans. F. Heider, G. Heider. New York: McGraw-Hill.

Liebert, R. J. 1976. Productivity, favor, and grants among scholars. *American Journal of Sociology 82:*664–673.

Lin, N. 1971. Information flow, influence flow, and the decision-making process. *Journalism Quarterly 48:*33–40.

Lin, N. 1976. *Foundations of Social Research.* New York: McGraw-Hill.

Lin, N., Burt, R. S. 1975. Differential effects of information channels in the process of innovation diffusion. *Social Forces 54:*256–274.

Lin, N., Dayton, P. W., Greenwald, P. 1978. Analyzing the instrumental use of relations in the context of social structure. *Sociological Methods & Research 7:*149–166.

Lincoln, J. R., Miller, J. 1979. Work and friendship ties in organizations: a comparative analysis of relational networks. *Administrative Science Quarterly 24:*181–199.

Lindzey, G., Byrne, D. 1968. Measurement of social choice and interpersonal attractiveness. In *Handbook of Social Psychology*, eds. G. Lindzey, E. Aronson. Reading, MA: Addison-Wesley.

Linton, R. 1936. *The Study of Man.* New York: D. Appleton-Century.

Litwak, E., Rothman, J. 1970. Towards the theory and practice of coordination between formal organizations. In *Organizations and Clients,* ed. W. Rosengren, M. Lefton. New York: Charles Merrill.

Locke, J. (1689) 1955. *Of Civil Government.* Chicago: Henry Regnery.

Lorrain, F. P., White, H. C. 1971. Structural equivalence of individuals in social networks. *Journal of Mathematical Sociology 1:*49–80.

Lott, A. J., Lott, B. E. 1965. Group cohesiveness as interpersonal attraction: a review of relationships with antecedent and consequent variables. *Psychological Bulletin 64:*259–309.

Luce, R. D. 1950. Connectivity and generalized cliques in sociometric group structure. *Psychometrika 15:*169–190.

Luce, R. D., Perry, A. D. 1949. A method of matrix analysis of group structure. *Psychometrika 14:* 95–116.

Lustgarten, S. H. 1975. The impact of buyer concentration in manufacturing industries. *Review of Economics and Statistics 57:*125–132.

Mace, M. L. 1971. *Directors: Myth and Reality.* Boston: Graduate School of Business Administration, Harvard University.

Macpherson, C. B. 1962. *The Political Theory of Possessive Individualism.* New York: Oxford University Press.

MacRae, D. Jr. 1960. Direct factor analysis of sociometric data. *Sociometry 23:*360–371.

MacRae, D. Jr. 1978. The sociological economics of Gary S. Becker. *American Journal of Sociology 83:*1244–1258.

Malinowski, B. 1922. *Argonauts of the Western Pacific.* New York: E. P. Dutton.

Mandel, M., Winship, C. 1979. Roles, positions and networks. Paper presented at annual meetings of the American Sociological Association.

Mariolis, P. 1975. Interlocking directorates and control of corporations: the theory of bank control. *Social Science Quarterly 56:*425–439.

Marsden, P. V. 1981a. Introducing influence processes into a system of collective decisions. *American Journal of Sociology 86:*1203–1235.

Marsden, P. V. 1981b. Conditional effects in regression models. In *Linear Models in Social Research,* ed. P. V. Marsden, Beverly Hills: Sage.

Marsden, P. V. 1982a. Brokerage behavior in restricted exchange networks. In *Social Structure and Network Analysis,* eds. P. V. Marsden, N. Lin. Beverly Hills: Sage Publications.

Marsden, P. V. 1982b. Methods for the characterization of role structure. In *Research Methods for Social Network Analysis,* eds. L. C. Freeman, A. K. Romney, D. R. White. Unpublished Collection.

Marsden, P. V., Laumann, E. O. 1977. Collective action in a community elite: exchange, influence resources, and issue resolution. In *Power, Paradigms, and Community Research,* eds. R. J. Liebert, A. W. Imersheim. London: Sage.

Mauss, M. (1925) 1967. *The Gift,* trans. I. Cunnison. New York: W. W. Norton.

Mayer, A. C. 1966. The significance of quasi-groups in the study of complex societies. In *The Social Anthropology of Complex Societies,* ed. M. Banton. London: Tavistock.

Mayhew, B. H., Levinger, R. L. 1976. Size and the density of interaction in human aggregates. *American Journal of Sociology 82:*86–110.

McCallister, L., Fischer, C. S. 1978. A procedure for surveying personal networks. *Sociological Methods & Research 7:*131–148.

McConaghy, M. J. 1981. The common role structure: improved blockmodelling method applied to two community elites. *Sociological Methods & Research 9:*267–285.

McFarland, D. D. 1969. Measuring the permeability of occupational structures: an information-theoretic approach. *American Journal of Sociology 75:*41–61.

McFarland, D. D., Brown, D. J. 1973. Social distance as a metric: a systematic introduction to smallest space analysis. In *Bonds of Pluralism: The Form and Substance of Urban Social Networks,* E. O. Laumann. New York: Wiley-Interscience.

McGuire, W. J. 1969. The nature of attitudes and attitude change. In *Handbook of Social Psychology*, eds. G. Lindzey, E. Aronson. Reading, MA: Addison-Wesley.

Mead, G. H. 1934. *Mind, Self and Society.* Chicago: University of Chicago Press.

Means, G. C. (Chairman) 1939. *The Structure of the American Economy: Basic Characteristics.* Washington, DC: Government Printing Office.

Medawar, P. B. 1969. *Induction and Intuition in Scientific Thought.* Philadelphia: American Philosophical Society.

Merton, R. K. (1942) 1973. The normative structure of science. In *The Sociology of Science*, ed. N. W. Storer. Chicago: University of Chicago Press.

Merton, R. K. (1949) 1968. Manifest and latent functions. In *Social Theory and Social Structure*, R. K. Merton. New York: Free Press.

Merton, R. K. 1957a. The role-set: problems in sociological theory. *British Journal of Sociology* 8:106–120.

Merton, R. K. (1957b) 1968. Continuities in the theory of reference groups and social structure. In *Social Theory and Social Structure*, R. K. Merton. New York: Free Press.

Merton, R. K. (1960) 1973. "Recognition" and "excellence:" instructive ambiguities. In *The Sociology of Science,* ed. N. W. Storer. Chicago: University of Chicago Press.

Merton, R. K. (1968) 1973. The Mathew effect in science. In *The Sociology of Science,* ed. N. W. Storer. Chicago: University of Chicago Press.

Merton, R. K., Rossi, A. S. (1950) 1968. Contributions to the theory of reference group behavior. In *Social Theory and Social Structure*, R. K. Merton. New York: Free Press.

Metcalf, L. (Chairman) 1978. *Voting Rights in Major Corporations.* Washington, DC: Government Printing Office.

Michael, R. T., Becker, G. S. (1973) 1976. On the new theory of consumer behavior. In *The Economic Approach to Human Behavior,* G. S. Becker. Chicago: University of Chicago Press.

Mills, J. S. (1881) 1950. *Philosophy of Scientific Method.* New York: Hafner.

Mitchell, J. C. 1969. The concept and use of social networks. In *Social Networks in Urban Situations*, ed. J. C. Mitchell. Manchester: Manchester University Press.

Mitchell, J. C. 1974. Social networks. *Annual Review of Anthropology. 3:*279–299.

Mokken, R. J. 1979. Cliques, clubs and clans. *Quality and Quantity 13:*161–173.

Moreno, J. L. 1934. *Who Will Survive?* Washington, DC: Nervous and Mental Disease Publishing.

Moreno, J. L., ed., 1960. *The Sociometry Reader.* New York: Free Press.

Morgan, D. L., Rytina, S. 1977. Comment on "Network sampling: some first steps" by Mark Granovetter. *American Journal of Sociology 83:*722–727.

Morrison, D. F. 1976. *Multivariate Statistical Methods.* New York: McGraw-Hill.

Moxley, R. L., Moxley, N. F. 1974. Determining point-centrality in uncontrived social networks. *Sociometry 37:*122–130.

Mulaik, S. A. 1972. *The Foundations of Factor Analysis.* New York: McGraw-Hill.

Mulkay, M. J. 1976. The mediating role of the scientific elite. *Social Studies of Science 6:*445–470.

Mulkay, M. J., Gilbert, G. N., Woolgar, S. W. 1975. Problem areas and research networks in science. *Sociology 9:*187–203.

Mullins, N. C. 1973. *Theories and Theory Groups in Contemporary American Sociology.* New York: Harper & Row.

Mullins, N. C., Hargens, L. L., Hecht, P. K., Kick, E. L. 1977. The group structure of cocitation clusters: a comparative analysis. *American Sociological Review 42:*552–562.

Nadel, S. F. 1957. *The Theory of Social Structure.* London: Cohen & West.

Nieminen, J. 1973. On the centrality in a directed graph. *Social Science Research 2:*371–378.

Nieminen, J. 1974. On centrality in a graph. *Scandinavian Journal of Psychology 15:*322–336.

Olson, M. 1965. *The Logic of Collective Action*. Cambridge: Harvard University Press.

Parsons, T. 1937. *The Structure of Social Action* (2 Vols.). New York: Free Press.

Parsons, T. 1951. *The Social System*. New York: Free Press.

Parsons, T. 1961. An outline of the social system. In *Theories of Society*, eds. T. Parsons, E. Shils, K. D. Naegele, J. R. Pitts. New York: Free Press.

Parsons, T. 1966. *Societies: Evolutionary and Comparative Perspectives*. Englewood Cliffs: Prentice-Hall.

Parsons, T., Shils, E. A., eds. 1951. *Toward a General Theory of Action*. New York: Harper & Row.

Patman, W. (Chairman) 1968. *Commercial Banks and Their Trust Activities: Emerging Influences on the American Economy*. Washington, DC: Government Printing Office.

Pattison, P. E. 1981. Equating the "joint reduction" with blockmodel common role structure: a reply to McConaghy. *Sociological Methods & Research 9*:286–302.

Peay, E. R. 1974. Hierarchical clique structures. *Sociometry 37*:54–65.

Peay, E. R. 1976. A note concerning the connectivity of social networks. *Journal of Mathematical Sociology 4*:319–321.

Pennings, J. M. 1980. *Interlocking Directorates: Origins and Consequences of Connections among Organizations' Boards of Directors*. San Francisco: Jossey-Bass.

Perrucci, R., Pilisuk, M. 1970. Leaders and ruling elites: the interorganizational basis of community power. *American Sociological Review 35*:1040–1057.

Pfeffer, J. 1972a. Size and composition of corporate boards of directors. *Administrative Science Quarterly 17*:218–228.

Pfeffer, J. 1972b. Merger as a response to organizational interdependency. *Administrative Science Quarterly 17*:382–394.

Pfeffer, J., Leblebici, H. 1973. Executive recruitment and the development of interfirm organizations. *Administrative Science Quarterly 18*:449–461.

Pfeffer, J., Nowak, P. 1976. Joint ventures and interorganizational interdependence. *Administrative Science Quarterly 21*:398–418.

Pfeffer, J., Salancik, G. 1978. *The External Control of Organizations: A Resource Dependence Perspective*. New York: Harper & Row.

Phillips, A. 1960. A theory of interfirm organization. *Quarterly Journal of Economics 74*:602–613.

Piaget, J. (1932) 1965. *The Moral Judgment of the Child*, trans. M. Gabin, New York: Free Press.

Pitts, F. R. 1979. The medieval river trade network of Russia revisited. *Social Networks 1*:285–292.

Price, D. J. de S. 1963. *Little Science, Big Science*. New York: Columbia University Press.

Price, D. J. de S., Beaver, D. de B. 1966. Collaboration in an invisible college. *American Psychologist 21*:1011–1017.

Proctor, C. H. 1967. The variance of an estimate of linkage density from a simple random sample of graph nodes. Proceedings of the Social Statistics Section, American Statistical Association.

Project in Structural Analysis. 1981. STRUCTURE: a computer program providing basic data for the analysis of empirical positions in a system of actors. Computer Program 1, Survey Research Center, University of California at Berkeley.

Radcliffe-Brown, A. R. 1940. On social structure. *Journal of the Royal Anthropological Society of Great Britain and Ireland 70*:1–12.

Ramsay, J. O. 1978. Confidence intervals for multidimensional scaling analysis. *Psychometrika 43*:145–160.

Rapoport, A. 1957. Contribution to the theory of random and biased nets. *Bulletin of Mathematical Biophysics. 19*:257–277.

Rapoport, A. 1979. A probabilistic approach to networks. *Social Networks 2*:1–18.

Rapoport, A., Hovarth, W. J. 1961. A study of a large sociogram. *Behavioral Science 6*:279–291.

Reskin, B. F. 1977. Scientific productivity and the reward structure of science. *American Sociological Review 42:*491–504.

Rhoades, S. A. 1973. The effect of diversification on industry profit performance in 241 manufacturing industries: 1963. *Review of Economics and Statistics 55:*146–155.

Rhoades, S. A. 1974. A further evaluation of the effect of diversification on industry profit performance. *Review of Economics and Statistics 56:*557–559.

Riesman, D. (1950) 1961. *The Lonely Crowd.* New Haven: Yale University Press.

Riesman, D. 1961. Preface. In *The Lonely Crowd,* D. Riesman. New Haven: Yale University Press.

Riker, W. H., Ordeshook, P. C. 1973. *An Introduction to Positive Political Theory.* Englewood Cliffs: Prentice-Hall.

Rogers, E. M. 1976. New product adoption and diffusion. *Journal of Consumer Research 2:*290–301.

Rogers, E. M., Shoemaker F. F. 1971. *Communication of Innovations.* New York: Free Press.

Ryan, B., Gross, N. 1943. The diffusion of hybrid seed corn in two Iowa communities. *Rural Sociology 8:*15–24.

Sailer, L. D. 1978. Structural equivalence: meaning and definition, computation and application. *Social Networks 1:*73–90.

Sarbin, T. R. 1954. Role theory. In *Handbook of Social Psychology,* ed. G. Lindzey. Cambridge, MA: Addison-Wesley.

Sarbin, T. R., Allen, V. L. 1968. Role theory. In *Handbook of Social Psychology,* eds. G. Lindzey, E. Aronson. Reading, MA: Addison-Wesley.

Schmidt, S. W., Scott, J. C., Landé, C., Guasti, L. 1977. *Friends, Followers and Factions.* Berkeley: University of California Press.

Schwartz, J. E. 1977. An examination of CONCOR and related methods for blocking sociometric data. In *Sociological Methodology 1977,* ed. D. R. Heise. San Francisco: Jossey-Bass.

Seidman, S. B., Foster, B. L. 1978. A graph-theoretic generalization of the clique concept. *Journal of Mathematical Sociology 6:*139–154.

Selznick, P. 1949. *TVA and the Grass Roots: A Study in the Sociology of Formal Organization.* New York: Harper & Row.

Shepherd, W. G. 1970. *Market Power and Economic Welfare.* New York: Random House.

Sherif, M. 1935. A study of some factors in perception. *Archives of Psychology* No. 187.

Shils, E. 1961. Centre and periphery. In *The Logic of Personal Knowledge.* London: Routledge & Kegan Paul.

Simmel, G. 1896. Superiority and subordination as subject matters of sociology, trans. A. Small. *American Journal of Sociology 2:*167–189, 392–415.

Simmel, G. (1908) 1950. Sociology: studies in the form of socialization. In *The Sociology of Georg Simmel,* trans. and ed. K. H. Wolff. New York: Free Press.

Simmel, G. (1917) 1950. Individual and society. In *The Sociology of Georg Simmel,* trans. and ed. K. H. Wolff. New York: Free Press.

Simmel, G. (1922) 1955. *Conflict and the Web of Group-Affiliations,* trans. K. H. Wolff, R. Bendix. New York: Free Press.

Simon, H. A. 1974. How big is a chunk? *Science 183:*482–488.

Smith, A. (1776) 1937. *An Inquiry into the Nature and Causes of the Wealth of Nations.* New York: Random House.

Snyder, D., Kick, E. L. 1979. Structural position in the world system and economic growth, 1955–1970: a multiple network analysis of transnational interactions. *American Journal of Sociology 84:*1096–1126.

Sonquist, J. A., Koenig, T. 1975. Interlocking directorates in the top U.S. corporations: a graph theory approach. *The Insurgent Sociologist 5:*196–229.

Sørenson, A. B., Hallinan, M. T. 1976. A stochastic model for change in group structure. *Social Science Research 5:*43–61.

Sorokin, P. A. (1927) 1959. *Social and Cultural Mobility*. New York: Free Press.

Spilerman, S. 1966. Structural analysis and the generation of sociograms. *Behavioral Science* *11*:312–318.

Stein, A. A. 1976. Conflict and cohesion: a review of the literature. *Journal of Conflict Resolution* *20*:143–172.

Stevens, J. C. 1968. Psychophysics. In *The International Encyclopedia of the Social Sciences*. New York: Free Press and Macmillan.

Stevens, S. S. 1957. On the psychophysical law. *The Psychological Review 64*:153–181.

Stevens, S. S. 1962. The surprising simplicity of sensory metrics. *American Psychologist 17*:29–39.

Stevens, S. S. 1971. Issues in psychophysical measurement. *Psychological Review 78*:426–450.

Stigler, G. J. (1950) 1965. The development of utility theory. In *Essays in the History of Economics*, ed. G. J. Stigler. Chicago: University of Chicago Press.

Stigler, G. J. 1964. A theory of oligopoly. *Journal of Political Economy 72*:44–61.

Stouffer, S. A., Suchman, E. A., DeVinney, L. C., Star, S. A., Williams, R. M. 1949. *The American Soldier, Adjustment During Army Life*. Princeton: Princeton University Press.

Strotz, R. H. 1957. The empirical implications of a utility tree. *Econometrica 25*:269–280.

Swanson, G. E. 1971. Framework for comparative research: structural anthropology and the theory of action. In *Comparative Methods in Sociology*, ed. I. Vallier. Berkeley: University of California Press.

Tajfel, H. 1969. Social and cultural factors in perception. In *Handbook of Social Psychology,* eds. G. Lindzey, E. Aronson, Reading, MA: Addison-Wesley.

Taylor, D. G., Coleman, J. S. 1979. Equilibrating processes in social networks: a model for conceptualization and analysis. In *Perspectives on Social Network Research*, eds. P. W. Holland, S. Leinhardt. New York: Academic Press.

Taylor, M. 1969. Influence structures. *Sociometry 32:*490–502.

Theil, H. 1967. *Economics and Information Theory*. Chicago: Rand McNally.

Thibaut, J. W., Kelley, H. H. 1959. *The Social Psychology of Groups*. New York: John Wiley.

Thoden van Velzen, H. U. E. 1973. Coalitions and network analysis. In *Network Analysis: Studies in Human Interaction,* eds. J. Boissevain, J. C. Mitchell. Paris: Mouton.

Thomas, I. W., Znaniecki, F. 1918. *The Polish Peasant in Europe and America,* Vol. 1. Chicago: University of Chicago Press.

Thurstone, L. L. 1959. *The Measurement of Values*. Chicago: University of Chicago Press.

Tolbert, C., Horan, P. M., Beck, E. M. 1980. The structure of economic segmentation: a dual economy approach. *American Journal of Sociology 85:*1095–1116.

Travers, J., Milgram, S. 1969. An experimental study of the small world problem. *Sociometry 32:* 425–443.

Tuckman, H. P., Leahey, J. 1975. What is an article worth? *Journal of Political Economy 83:*951–967.

Turbayne, C. M., ed. 1963. *Berkeley: Works on Vision*. New York: Bobbs Merrill.

U. S. Department of Commerce. 1971. *1967 Census of Manufactures, Concentration Ratios in Manufacturing*. Washington, DC: Government Printing Office.

U. S. Department of Commerce. 1973. *Annual Survey of Manufactures, 1970–1971*. Washington, DC: Government Printing Office.

U. S. Department of Commerce. 1974. Input–output structure of the U. S. economy: 1967. *Survey of Current Business* 54:24–55.

Useem, M. 1980. Corporations and the corporate elite. *Annual Review of Sociology 6*:41–77.

Verbrugge, L. M. 1977. The structure of adult friendship choices. *Social Forces 56*:576–597.

Verbrugge, L. M. 1979. Multiplexity in adult friendships. *Social Forces 57*:1286–1309.

Warner, W. L., Unwalla, D. B. 1967. The system of interlocking directorates. In *The Emergent American Society: Large Scale Organizations,* ed. W. L. Warner, D. B. Unwalla, J. H. Trimm. New Haven: Yale University Press.

Wasserman, S. 1977. Random directed graph distributions and the triad census in social networks. *Journal of Mathematical Sociology 5:*61–86.

Wasserman, S. 1978. Models for binary directed graphs and their applications. *Advances in Applied Probability 10:*803–818.

Weber, M. (1904) 1958. *The Protestant Ethic and the Spirit of Capitalism,* trans. T. Parsons. New York: Free Press.

Weber, M. (1925) 1947. *Social and Economic Organization,* trans. A. M. Henderson, T. Parsons. New York: Free Press.

Weil, A. (1949) 1969. On the algebraic study of certain types of marriage laws (Murngin system). In *The Elementary Structures of Kinship,* Levi-Strauss, trans. J. H. Bell, J. R. von Sturmer, R. Needham. Boston: Beacon Press.

Wellman, B. 1979. The community question: the intimate networks of East Yorkers. *American Journal of Sociology 84:*1201–1231.

White, D. R. 1982. Structural equivalence in social networks: concepts and measurement of role structures. In *Research Methods in Social Network Analysis,* eds. L. C. Freeman, A. K. Romney, D. R. White. Unpublished Collection.

White, H. C. 1963. *An Anatomy of Kinship.* Englewood Cliffs: Prentice-Hall.

White, H. C. 1977. Probabilities of homorphic mappings from multiple graphs. *Journal of Mathematical Psychology 16:*121–134.

White, H. C., Boorman, S. A., Breiger, R. L. 1976. Social structure from multiple networks. I. blockmodels of roles and positions. *American Journal of Sociology 81:*730–780.

White, H. C., Breiger, R. L. 1975. Pattern across networks. *Society 12:*68–73.

Whitten, N., Wolfe, A. 1973. Network analysis. In *Handbook of Social and Cultural Anthropology,* ed. J. J. Honigmann. Chicago: Rand McNally.

Williamson, O. E. 1975. *Markets and Hierarchies: Analysis and Antitrust Implications.* New York: Free Press.

Winship, C. 1977a. A distance model for sociometric structure. *Journal of Mathematical Sociology 5:*21–39.

Winship, C. 1977b. The allocation of time among individuals. In *Sociological Methodology 1978,* ed. K. F. Schuessler. San Francisco: Jossey-Bass.

Wolfe, A. 1970. On structural comparisons of networks. *Canadian Review of Sociology and Anthropology 7:*226–244.

Wright, B., Evitts, M. S. 1961. Direct factor analysis in sociometry. *Sociometry 24:*82–98.

Zald, M. N. 1969. The power and function of boards of directors: a theoretical synthesis. *American Journal of Sociology 75:*97–111.

Zeitlin, M. 1974. Corporate ownership and control: the large corporation and the capitalist class. *American Journal of Sociology 79:*1073–1119.

Zeitlin, M. 1976. On class theory of the large corporation: response to Allen. *American Journal of Sociology 81:*894–903.

Zelditch, M. Jr. 1971. Intelligible comparisons. In *Comparative Methods in Sociology,* ed. I. Vallier. Berkeley: University of California Press.

Ziman, J. 1968. *Public Knowledge.* Cambridge: Cambridge University Press.

Zuckerman, H., Merton, R. K. (1971) 1973. Patterns of evaluation in science: institutionalization, structure and the functions of the referee system. In *The Sociology of Science,* ed. N. W. Storer. Chicago: University of Chicago Press.

Subject Index

QUANTITATIVE STUDIES IN SOCIAL RELATIONS
(Continued from page ii)